Introducing the New Sexuality Studies

Introducing the New Sexuality Studies is an innovative, reader-friendly anthology of original essays and interviews that introduces the field of sexuality studies to undergraduate students. Examining the social, cultural, and historical dimensions of sexualities, this anthology is designed to serve as a comprehensive textbook for sexualities and gender-related courses at the undergraduate level.

The book's contributors include both well-established scholars, including Patricia Hill Collins, Jeffrey Weeks, Deborah L. Tolman, and C.J. Pascoe, as well as emerging voices in sexuality studies. This collection will provide students of sociology, gender, and sexuality with a challenging and broad introduction to the social study of sexuality that they will find accessible and engaging.

Nancy L. Fischer is an Associate Professor of Sociology and Director of Urban Studies at Augsburg College in Minneapolis, Minnesota, USA. In 2009, she chaired the American Sociological Association's Section on Sexualities. In 2013, she edited a special section of *The Sociological Quarterly* on Critical Heterosexuality Studies. Besides sexuality, her research interests include a project on the US secondhand and vintage clothing industry.

Steven Seidman is a Professor of Sociology at the University at Albany (SUNY), USA, and world renowned in the field of sexuality studies. He has authored many books, including *Romantic Longings* (Routledge), *Embattled Eros* (Routledge), *Beyond the Closet* (Routledge), *The Social Construction of Sexuality* (Norton), and, recently, *Intimacies* (Routledge).

Introducing the New Sexuality Studies

Third edition

Nancy L. Fischer and Steven Seidman

Routledge
Taylor & Francis Group

LONDON AND NEW YORK

First published 2016
by Routledge
2 Park Square, Milton Park, Abingdon, Oxon OX14 4RN

and by Routledge
711 Third Avenue, New York, NY 10017

Routledge is an imprint of the Taylor & Francis Group, an informa business

British Library Cataloguing in Publication Data
A catalogue record for this book is available from the British Library

Library of Congress Cataloging in Publication Data
Names: Fischer, Nancy, editor. | Seidman, Steven, editor.
Title: Introducing the new sexuality studies: 3rd edition / edited by Nancy Fischer and Steven Seidman.
Other titles: Handbook of the new sexuality studies
Description: 3rd edition. | New York: Routledge, 2016. | Revised edition of Introducing the new sexuality studies, 2011.
Identifiers: LCCN 2015043514| ISBN 9781138902930 (hardback) | ISBN 9781138902947 (pbk.) | ISBN 9781315697215 (ebook)
Subjects: LCSH: Sex. | Sex–Social aspects. | Sexual orientation. | Sex and law. | Sexology.
Classification: LCC HQ21.I685 2016 | DDC 306.7–dc23
LC record available at http://lccn.loc.gov/2015043514

ISBN: 978-1-138-90293-0 (hbk)
ISBN: 978-1-138-90294-7 (pbk)
ISBN: 978-1-315-69721-5 (ebk)

Typeset in Scala Sans
by Sunrise Setting Ltd, Brixham, UK

Printed and bound in Great Britain by
TJ International Ltd, Padstow, Cornwall

Contents

Part 5
Intimacies   261

Illustrations

Figures

Tables

Acknowledgments

We would like to thank all of the authors who have contributed to this volume over the years. It has been deeply satisfying for us to work with authors who wrote thoughtful, very smart, yet highly readable essays. Thank you to Gerhard Boomgaarden, Alyson Claffey and Lindsey Hall at Routledge. Thanks also to student editor Devin Wiggs, who read all of the new essays and offered thoughtful feedback and discussion questions for the accompanying website. And last but not least, a warm thank you to the wonderfully diverse students of Augsburg College, who come from nearly every income level, racial and ethnic group, and gender and sexual identity category. Their willingness to thoughtfully share their knowledge, experiences and opinions has been key to shaping this book.

General introduction

In the last few decades, there has been a revolution in the study of sexuality. Sex is today understood as fundamentally social. The aspects of sex that scholars – and ordinary folks – are most interested in, such as issues of desire, pleasure, identity, norms of sexual behavior, and intimate arrangements, are today recognized by the leading scholars in the field as social phenomena. This deep sociology of sexualities is what we call the new sexuality studies.

It wasn't too long ago that most Americans and Europeans viewed sexuality as natural. In America and Europe, scientists such as sexologists, psychologists, demographers, and medical researchers believed that sex was built into the body, into human genetics, hormones, into the very physiology of individuals. Humans were, it was assumed, born sexual. Just as nature programs humans to eat and sleep, humans were wired for sex. Humans were thought to be driven by a sexual instinct, a procreative gene, or a maternal drive to reproduce and rear children. While many of us still believe this to be true, the new social studies of sexuality have challenged the idea of sex as natural.

Initially, this new social perspective on sexuality was advanced by social activists. Feminists challenged a conventional wisdom that assumed a natural division between men and women that extended into their sexualities. It was widely assumed that men's sexuality is naturally genital-centered, pleasure-oriented, and aggressive in ways that express a masculine gender identity. By contrast, women's sexuality was said to be oriented to intimacy and relationship-building, diffusely erotic, and passive or other-directed in a way that reflected a feminine gender identity.

Against this naturalistic view of gender and sexuality, feminists argued that society, not nature, creates gender and sexual differences. In particular, feminists argued that women's sexuality is socially shaped in ways that sustain men's social and political dominance. For example, the view of women's sexuality as being oriented to pleasing men or driven by a maternal instinct reinforced the idea that women's appropriate social role should be that of wife and mother. In fact, as women have gained social and economic independence in the decades after the 1960s, they have also claimed control over their own bodies and sexualities. Today, as women have more choices, their sexualities are more openly varied. Some women still approach sexuality as a means to reproduction or as a way to gain intimacy, but other women look to sex for sensual pleasure, or want intimacy but not marriage or children. In short, women's sexuality, like men's, is not fixed by nature but shaped by social forces and circumstances, by factors such as economic independence, social values, peers, or family culture.

Alongside the women's movement, there developed a lesbian and gay movement. Lesbian and gay activists challenged a society that declared heterosexuality and heterosexuals to be natural and normal while homosexuality and homosexuals were stigmatized as unnatural and abnormal. This belief has had powerful social consequences. It contributed to making heterosexuality into a social norm and ideal, while often criminalizing and polluting homosexuality. Individuals, who were labeled homosexual, were subject to discrimination, punishment, harassment, and sometimes violence and imprisonment.

Gay and lesbian activists not only protested against laws and practices of discrimination, but challenged the idea that nature produces two distinct human types or social identities: heterosexuals and homosexuals. Some activists argued that it is society that creates the idea of sexual identities or roles. Why? By stigmatizing and criminalizing homosexuality, heterosexuality is made into the only right way to be sexual and to organize families. Furthermore, some activists argued that a norm of heterosexuality reinforces a gender order that not only emphasizes gender difference but privileges men.

Historians and other scholars have since documented that, while there has always been heterosexual and homosexual behavior, there has not always been "heterosexuals" and "homosexuals" as human types or sexual identities. For example, in nineteenth-century America, homosexuality was viewed as a behavior, typically a criminal behavior punishable as an act of "sodomy." But sodomy included not only homosexual acts but a wide range of non-procreative, non-marital sexual acts such as fornication, oral genital sex, and bestiality. It was only in twentieth-century America that homosexuality was understood as indicating a social and sexual identity. It was, of course, initially constructed as a dangerous and abnormal identity, in contrast to a normal heterosexual identity. The point we want to underscore is this: it was only in the early decades of the twentieth-century in America that sexuality became the basis of a social identity. This fact underscores the historical and social character of sexuality.

Feminists and gay and lesbian activists developed the beginnings of a social view of sexuality as part of their politics. But the activists were soon followed by the scholars. By the 1970s, sociologists were also beginning to view sex as social. Sociological researchers were studying the social patterns of heterosexuality, marriage, reproduction, and dating. Researchers highlighted the role of social forces such as gender, religion, occupation, and the role of peers in shaping variations in patterns of sexual behavior. And, some sociologists were fashioning labeling perspectives on homosexuality.

However, both activists and sociologists of the 1960s and 1970s had a limited view of the social character of sexuality. While they spotlighted the role of social forces in shaping patterns of sexual behavior and norms, their sociological analysis did not extend into the social making of sexual bodies, desires, acts, pleasures, and identities. These social researchers assumed an already sexualized body, assumed a natural landscape of sexual acts and pleasures.

The new sexuality studies raise questions that were not addressed, or even posed, earlier. For example, how is it that certain body parts become sexualized? In this regard, what social forces explain why the clitoris was not viewed as a sexual organ until the 1960s, at least in the United States and in many European societies? Or, what social changes help to explain the recent emergence of "anal sex" as a legitimate erotic pleasure? The new sexuality studies understand sexual identities as historically emergent. Homosexuality, as we've seen, was not always a sexual identity, and, even in societies where it serves as an identity, its meaning can vary and change. For example, "lesbian" may indicate a sexual orientation or identity, or a political standpoint against male dominance. Today, in the United States and the United Kingdom, "gay" may signal a master identity or a secondary identity or, as in many European nations, a behavior but not an identity. And new sexual identities may emerge, such as a bisexual or an S/M identity.

The new sexuality studies perspective does not deny the biological aspects of sexuality. There would be no sexuality without bodies. However, it is social forces which determine which organs and orifices become "sexual," how such organs and orifices may be used or expressed, their social and moral meaning, which desires and acts become the basis of identities, and what social norms regulate behavior and intimacies. It is this deep view of sex as social that we hope to convey in this volume.

PART 1

Laying the foundations

Introduction

At the foundation of current views of the new sociology of sexualities is the notion of the social construction of sexuality (as Christiansen and Fischer illustrate). However much biology is part of the story of sexuality, it is chiefly social factors that shape the way we experience sexuality by establishing its meaning and organization. Let's try to illustrate this notion.

Consider the following statements. "There have always been homosexuals." "Just as nature produces heterosexuals, so it produces homosexuals." And "homosexuals are different from heterosexuals – sexually, psychologically and socially." In other words, heterosexuals and homosexuals are two different human or social types. *These statements are widely believed by many people across the globe.*

However, scholars have questioned these beliefs. True enough, there have always been individuals who desire individuals of the same gender. In many societies, there are individuals conventionally defined as men who sexually prefer others of the same gender; the same is true for individuals considered to be women. But these individuals may experience their sexuality very differently depending on the *meaning* and social *organization* of same-gender sexuality. If homosexuality is understood as a personal and social identity, especially a stigmatized identity, it will be experienced very differently than if it is understood as just a desire or behavior, especially if it's also normalized. If stigmatized, the individual may be viewed as a danger to society. This person might be driven to the margins of society or even forced to exit society. If homosexuality is viewed as type criminal behavior, the specific action, not the individual, will be punished. Homosexual behavior will be treated like any other legal violation such as drinking under age, adultery or prostitution. In nineteenth-century America, same-gender behavior was often treated the same as fornication, adultery or bestiality – as a minor criminal violation.

In fact, we now know that the idea of a homosexual identity only appeared late in history, and only in some societies. Even today, as the chapters on same-gender experience in Beirut and the Netherlands show, being gay or lesbian is not an identity in those nations like it is in the US or the UK. Moreover, as Westbrook illustrates, the very meanings of sex and gender are in flux, with new categories forming that imply new types of sexual identities.

One of the pioneers of a social perspective on sexuality and homosexuality is the British sociologist Jeffrey Weeks. His research suggests that it was in the late nineteenth century in the US and Europe that the idea of homosexuality as an identity initially emerged. It was in no small measure a creation of a new science of sexuality forged by sexologists and psychologists who classified sexual behaviors into sexual types or identities. While Weeks' research is historical, other sociologists have used interviews or surveys to examine the social patterns of sexuality. In one of the largest national surveys ever done in the United States, Edward Laumann and his colleagues charted the changing sexual habits of Americans. One of the more interesting findings was how little change occurred in the last few decades. For example, "sexual dysfunction" continues to preoccupy Americans while finding intimate happiness in marriage remains a compelling ideal. Yet there is a new frankness about sexual talk, especially about sexual troubles, and these researchers discovered a big divide between younger and older generations in terms of their sexual attitudes and behaviors. This generational divide suggests potentially significant change in the future.

Although sociologists have been innovators in the new sexuality studies, other social approaches have been equally important. For example, Marxists have underscored the role of the economy and class differences in shaping sexual desires, identities, and patterns of behavior. Similarly, feminists have pointed to gender dynamics. They force us to consider the ways men and women differ in their sexual values, behaviors, and approaches to intimacy. Moreover, sexual pleasure for women carries unique dangers associated with pregnancy and violence. And, as the interview with Patricia Hill Collins makes clear, gender identities and sexualities are complicated by our class and racial statuses. Historically, for example, Black women have validated kin, even gender conventional families, as a refuge from racism. There are also perspectives that focus on the role of scientific knowledges, medical experts, and popular culture in shaping sexual meanings, norms and behaviors. For example, in order for homosexuality or heterosexuality to become a publicly known social identity, these social constructs had to circulate throughout society by means of popular and scientific-medical culture.

In this section, you'll be introduced to different social perspectives on sexuality. These should not be seen as mutually exclusive; rather, they are conceptual resources that can help you to understand the complexities of sexual meanings and practices.

chapter 1

Working in the (social) construction zone

Lars D. Christiansen and Nancy L. Fischer

Imagine a scientist sitting at home, looking through old family photos of her extended family – parents, siblings, aunts and uncles, cousins, grandparents, great grandparents. Suddenly she thinks she sees a pattern. In all the photos of couples that have been together longest, both members appear to have attached or "adherent" earlobes (meaning their earlobes don't really dangle below where the ear and side of the face come together). This is true regardless of the individuals' sexual identities. Likewise, she notices that her family photos of couples whose relationships failed were ones in which the individuals had unattached or "free" earlobes (larger, more fleshy lobes that dangle slightly). "How strange," the scientist thinks, "there's no logical reason people would be attracted to others on the basis of their earlobes and it certainly wouldn't affect their relationship success." But the pattern bothers her over the next couple of weeks. She asks her friends for their extended family photos and finds the same pattern – that lasting couples are by and large composed of people with attached earlobes.

The scientist shares her observation with other scientists. She's wondering if they should empirically test her hypothesis that lasting couples are composed of people who have adherent earlobes. While some colleagues greet her hypothesis with ridicule, they now have a nascent awareness of potential "earlobe preference" among couples; soon they start noticing the pattern among their own families and friends. They eventually return to tell their colleague, "You might be onto something here." They decide to launch a quantitative study using a representative sample of couples to see if there is a statistically significant relationship between earlobe form and relationship success. The study, published as "Free vs Adherent Earlobes as Predictor of Relationship Longevity," found that couples where both members possess adherent earlobes have relationships that last longer than those of mixed couples and much longer than couples where members both have free earlobes, regardless of individuals' sexual identities.

After this quantitative study, they also conduct a small qualitative study, interviewing couples with different earlobe patterns to learn what sorts of meanings couples attach to earlobes and relationship longevity. Interestingly, the findings of the qualitative study are inconclusive – the couples interviewed were simply confused about being asked about the significance of their earlobes in their relationships. They reported earlobes had nothing to do with how they chose their partner – they weren't even aware of their partner's earlobe style. In other words, earlobe choice as a relationship factor was not legible to them.

The published quantitative study meets deep skepticism by the larger scientific community. However, soon the media begins doing stories on the studies with headlines like "Attached Earlobes Produce Greater Attachment" and "Do Free Earlobes Mean Free Love?" The media attention coaxes research agencies like the National Science Foundation to fund quantitative studies conducted with larger, more diverse samples of couples; these studies also find that couples with attached earlobes have greater relationship longevity. Social scientists work to develop an Earlobe Theory of Attraction to explain why this pattern persists that relates sexual health, earlobes and evolution.

At this point, the binary of earlobe types is an underlying, unquestioned assumption. In the 1930s, scientists did in fact believe there were these simple, binary earlobe types. There are two things happening in this hypothetical example: The establishment of the earlobe binary, and the hypothesis that this binary is related to romantic attraction and relationship stability.

As the attached earlobe hypothesis becomes common knowledge, on-line dating profiles change, always including a sexy photo with a clear view of earlobes. Ear jewelry (which doesn't hide the earlobe) becomes outrageously popular. Some states pass laws to list earlobe type on government forms like birth certificates and photo I.D.s. Politicians running for office prominently feature photos of their earlobes in campaign materials, believing their adherent ears demonstrate their trustworthiness. Movies and television begin to portray free earlobe people as villains, promiscuous lovers and as losers, while celebrities with attached lobes usually save the day.

As the notion of earlobe types and how it relates to romantic relationships gains publicity, over time, people with free, dangling earlobes find themselves facing discrimination in employment and the dating market. Some even have surgery to make their earlobes appear attached.

Eventually, groups of free earlobe people begin to politically organize and challenge the negative labeling, claiming "Free Lobe Pride!" They hold rallies and protests, demanding that earlobes be dropped from government documentation. Some form counter-narratives about the superiority of Free Lobes as creative, free-spirited individuals who offer alternative lifestyles to those of boring, confining Attached Lobe people.

In the middle of the earlobe debate are those who possess ambiguous earlobes that don't quite dangle or adhere. They struggle to have their earlobes recognized as attached or else they too face discrimination, as most people interpret their in-between status as "creepy" and regard them suspiciously. In-Betweens also protest the earlobe

Lars D. Christiansen and Nancy L. Fischer

status hierarchy and use their in-between status to challenge the very idea of an earlobe binary. They document how attached and free lobes are actually two sides of an earlobe continuum with a great deal of variation in between – earlobes are not binary. At first In-Betweens are scoffed at, but eventually the scientific community begins to explore earlobe variation. Scientists – after systematic study of human ears – eventually conclude that earlobe types are not binary, but exist on a continuum. However, the social practices and stereotypes attached to both sides of the earlobe binary persist. It takes decades for government forms to change and for media to represent "both" types fairly.

Construction, literally

A *social construct* refers to a phenomenon or category created and developed by society through its cultural and social practices. The fictional earlobe scenario above demonstrates the processes of *social construction*, ongoing practices of the building of a concept (earlobe binary), a theory (binary theory of attraction), through collective actions of groups (like the scientists or the Free Lobe activists), organizations (like the funding agencies of the earlobe research) and institutions (such as the media). The fact that many people participate in a construction process means that what is built is a social act. This is why constructions are usually called *social constructions* (though that phrase contains a redundancy, as nearly all things and concepts that are built require interactions and transactions between persons).

The idea that even concepts and ideas are constructions, rather than notions that exist regardless of human activity – ethereal (beyond human hands and minds) and universal (true for all at all times) – is difficult for some people to grasp for at least two reasons: First is that we are taught otherwise by people and institutions throughout much of our lives; and second is that the idea of construction applied to seemingly universal concepts (gravity; the sex binary) is arrogantly anthropocentric. How dare we humans claim to have made gravity!

The word "construction," taken in isolation, might conjure images of people wearing hard hats, driving nails, carrying sheetrock, using cranes to hoist steel beams, erecting a building using countless other materials and tools. For understanding how *concepts* are made, buildings and other sites where construction (as we usually think of it) is happening is a useful metaphor. Indeed, we recommend that every time you run into difficulty conceptualizing the construction of a concept (like the earlobe binary, or the sex binary) as ideas that are made, think about buildings and all of the concepts and tools that are required to make those buildings.

If you walk by a construction site in its early stages, you'll notice workers with machines, pounding large steel pillars into the ground that support a building. The foundation is laid with these pillars, and with thick cinder block walls. Eventually the foundation and steel pillars are hidden from view, as workers cover them with sheetrock and build exterior and interior walls, add windows, a brick facade, and paint. After all of this collective effort, the construction workers (heavy equipment operators, carpenters, plumbers, electricians, etc.) leave the site, their work complete. Residents move into the building. They don't think about it, yet their lives are shaped by the building's structure – where bedrooms, kitchens, bathrooms are placed, how many elevators versus stairwells are allotted to a floor, whether there is a gym – all of these aspects of the building's original design and construction impact residents' daily habits and routines, the people they are likely to run into, and even how often they go outside the building. The original design and construction process is now taken for granted, and people simply adapt to the built structure in which they live.

It is no different with ideas, concepts, and categories. Some people lay the initial foundation for an idea, as the scientific, media and government workers did in the earlobe scenario above. In the realm of sexuality, religious scholars formed foundational ideas about western sexuality (for example that sex should only occur between married persons) and religious knowledge was regarded as the ultimate Truth. Since the twentieth century, knowledge workers like scientists (including anthropologists, biologists, geneticists, psychiatrists, psychologists, sociologists) have been particularly productive at laying the foundations of accepted sexual knowledge. Today in the west, scientists have the authority to claim that science has the ability, through systematic research, to reveal the Truth – what Foucault (1990) referred to as "truth claims." For example, the sexual categories "heterosexual" and "homosexual" originally arose from clinical work and scientific studies on sexual perversions (Katz 2007).

After the initial foundations of a concept are laid, other knowledge workers can continue to build a broader knowledge base around the initial ideas. They conduct more studies on what people representing particular sexual categories are like, their preferences, their behaviors, their health, and so on. French sociologist Bruno Latour (1987) refers to this as a "fact-making process" where new scientific facts are built through scientists' discussions – scientific discourse. *Discourse* describes systems of thought that are composed of ideas, beliefs and practices that systematically construct the subject matter of which they speak (Foucault 1976). Sexual discourse, for example, expands its construction through the actions of reporters in the news media, bloggers, novelists, those posting their thoughts through social media, or people simply talking to friends about the sexual categories. For example, currently, sexual discourse on what it means to be asexual is expanding through accounts in the *New York Times* or *The Guardian*, posts on blogs, and through the studies published by social scientists studying those who identify as asexual, thus launching a fact-making process on asexuality.

The construction of discourse about sexuality, by all of the people referred to in the previous paragraphs, required techniques and tools that knowledge workers use to build particular claims. Some use scientific method as a technique, meaning that their knowledge claims must be based on systematic observations of measurable phenomenon. All use existing ideas (knowledge, concepts, objects, plans, computers, pens, paper, instruments of observation), means of communication (internet, journals), allies (peers, networks) and even energies (sugars, calories) that humans need to do the construction work. When we use the term construction in this paper, we mean it literally, not just metaphorically.

Nevertheless, the metaphor remains helpful for the point we are making. Just like residents who are housed in a building, individuals can find themselves housed within sexual categories, against their will or by their own desire. In the fictional earlobe scenario, Free Lobes were placed into a category in which they didn't want to be placed.

Lars D. Christiansen and Nancy L. Fischer

Likewise, people who are disabled or elderly might find themselves assumed to be asexual when in fact they actively desire, seek and find sexual connections with others. For some, the category asexual is chosen and experienced as liberating from society's sexual expectations. For others, it is an unwanted label that does not capture the identity they want to project to the world.

People can also ultimately refuse to live within the categories in which they are expected to place themselves (like the In-Betweens in the earlobe scenario). For example, some people find the gender categories woman and man too limiting and instead identify as genderqueer, which is an umbrella term that means one can identify as both a man or woman, neither a man or woman, gender fluid (moving between genders), or another non-western gender category (gender.wikia.com 2016). These important gender innovators (like the In-Betweens in the earlobe scenario above) pushed gender – and, by association, sexuality – discourse in new directions by arguing that the binary categories woman and man were not well constructed, or were harmful constructions that need to be challenged. The dominant binary gender categories are too limited to all who want to express gender identities in diverse ways. In essence, those who point out the flaws in the intellectual foundations of categories encourage us to build better ideas that better serve the needs of today's gender and sexual subjects.

When studying sexuality through a constructionist lens, we are led to many important and fascinating questions. What concepts, objects and means of communication, and allies, are marshaled to support one conception of sexuality over another? What actors (including non-human actors) are assembling tools in such a way as to make claims that, for example, sexual fluidity is innate, or a lifestyle choice? What are the tools of the construction or deconstruction of sexuality, gender and sex categories? What is being built as alternatives, and how is it being built? What resources are being marshaled to make the alternatives? What existing networks (social ties, associations) are involved in the process of maintaining or challenging gender and sex categories? Whose ideas are cited? What conferences witness the articulation of these ideas? Which organizations are holding the conferences? Who is supplying the funding for the research and assembly of scholars at conferences? What communications networks are utilized for the dissemination of ideas? Thus, inquiry about construction provides many points of entry.

In social scientific work on sexuality, researchers deploy different research methods – to gather empirical data – as part of their fact-making process. For example, Edward Laumann (interviewed in this volume) used large-scale surveys of the American population to gain knowledge about American sexual beliefs and practices. Sexuality researchers also often conduct interviews to learn how people interpret the meanings of their sexual lives (see the interview of Gloria González-López in this volume). Still other sexuality researchers engage in ethnographies where they participate in the communities they want to study and write about their observations as participants.

What is important as we think about categories, beliefs, ideas, etc. as socially constructed is thinking about how and how well they were constructed, as well as the consequences of those constructions. For example, when we evaluate the construction of sexual identity as dichotomous – the idea that one must be either straight or gay – what do we think of the construction techniques: Are they based on systematic observation? Did the research include the experiences of people from different class backgrounds, racial and ethnic groups? Did the research include different gender identities (gender fluid, men, transmen, transwomen, women)? Do the research methods fit the type of claims that the authors want to make? For example, if knowledge workers are making claims about all Americans, did they draw from a representative sample of Americans or just a college class? Remembering the construction metaphor helps us to evaluate the quality of an idea not just as a finished product, but in terms of how it was made in the first place.

Constructed or real? That is the (trick) question

Let's pretend that a large number of students reading this book are actually convinced by the earlobe scenario described earlier. They believe that ears can be divided dichotomously and that there is something to the notion that the stability of one's love life relates to earlobe type. In the next 20 years, the earlobe scenario plays out just as we have described above and our society develops an Earlobe Theory of Attraction, including earlobe status as significant to one's sexual identity. If the Earlobe Theory of Attraction became accepted common sense, then how would you answer this question: Is the Earlobe Theory of Attraction real or is it socially constructed?

If you answered that that the Earlobe Theory of Attraction is not real, it is socially constructed, then you are not alone. You are in the company of probably many of your peers, and perhaps your professors. If you answered that we have posed a trick question, then you are on to something important about social construction.

When we first learn about ways to categorize humans and human behaviors, we are encouraged to treat those categories as fixed, stable, and permanent. This is no surprise, as the very meaning of categorizing is the act of drawing a boundary between one thing and another. When we construct a category it is as if we were taking a pen and drawing a line, allotting some characteristics to one side, and other characteristics to the other (such as dividing sex into the dichotomous categories male/female even though actual bodies display more ambiguity). Categories are islands of meaning, determinations of difference that distinguish between *this* and *that* which serve as tools for understanding the world around us (Zerubavel 1993). Does this mean we should just give up on categorizing? According to scholars spanning wide-ranging disciplines, thinking categorically cannot be helped; categories are a necessity of human thought, reflection, and communication.

So, we cannot help but to think categorically. For some, this raises the question: Are there categories that just exist – that are natural? Are all categories just creations of the human mind? Whether we regard categories as natural or as human creations, it *seems* as if there is a difference between what we think and what is real – between the ideal and the material.

Consider the title of a popular and important documentary series on race: *Race: The Power of an Illusion*. The documentary shows how race has been constructed with some races believed to be biologically superior and others inferior. Racial categories were institutionalized through slavery and through policies like Jim Crow segregation

Lars D. Christiansen and Nancy L. Fischer

and anti-miscegenation laws, with deep and everlasting consequences for entire generations of humanity that remain today in persisting residential and educational segregation. Yet, at this point in time, race is increasingly considered a cultural fiction. Race is an illusion, a social construction.

The separation of constructed and real is also apparent in the way that many people make the distinction between "sex" and "gender." "Sex" is often presented in essential-ist terms as absolute, biologically based categories of "male" and "female," while "gen-der" refers to cultural constructions of "masculinity" and "femininity." Gender is more easily understood in terms of gradations and combinations of gender that are made clear in light of gender-variant practices like genderqueer or gender fluid identities. For many, however, sex is seen as a fixed category with two clear dimensions based on dis-tinctive, patterned characteristics. In terms of "sex," many people believe that "male" and "female" and even perhaps "intersex" are natural categories. This is unlike how race is often perceived today, where absolute categories are difficult to defend on any natural (biological) basis. What about sexuality? Sexuality categories seem to fall some-where in the middle of how race and sex are often discussed. There are those who see sexuality as "chosen," while others claim that sexuality preferences are something that one is born with – biological or "wired" – and is therefore not a choice or a lifestyle. A third position is that sexuality is performative (Butler 1993) in that one does not nec-essarily consciously choose to perform a heterosexual sexual identity, for example, but rather is subconsciously reflecting and imitating the idealized ways that heterosexuality is depicted in a heteronormative culture.

This brings us to the point that there is no need to draw a distinction between what is constructed and what is real. When we asked above whether the Earlobe Theory of Attraction was real or socially constructed, it was a trick question. If the idea gained consensus, instead we would say that the theory *is real because it is constructed*.

The impossibility of establishing the existence of any category outside of (prior to, disconnected from) human production (Hazelrigg 1995) seems to assert the notion as life as merely a state-of-mind, or an illusion, not real. However, this is mistaken. Constructionism is concerned with how everything – from concepts to objects – is real, not because things refer to some natural condition outside of human production, but *because* of that human production. Things (objects and events) and quasi-things (concepts) are real because they are made. Just as Patricia Hill Collins (1990) argues that both/and frames are more useful than either/or, we can say that race is *both* real *and* an illusion because of how realness and illusion are produced by humans utilizing conceptual tools. Both fictions and facts are realities of human production – a novel is as real as a documentary. The question is not *whether* some-thing is real or artificial, but how that realness or artificiality is suggested, asserted, and proven through the use of (material and immaterial) tools. Thus, the question is not whether sexuality is a lifestyle choice, innate, or performative, but rather how these truth claims are produced and reproduced, and what consequences flow from those claims. This is the task of the analyst, of the social scientist and the historian. So we instead can ask, "What are the means by which something is made real?" We can focus on how well an argument, category or idea is made, and the rules which guided its making.

Given our culture's entrapment in the dualism between real and artificial, the "realness" of the constructionist argument needs explanation. According to Bruno Latour (2005: 88–89) in *Reassembling the Social*:

> [T]o say that something is constructed means that it's not a mystery . . . popped out of nowhere. . . . (T)o say that something is constructed has always been associated with an appreciation of robustness, quality, style, durability, worth, etc. . . . (N)o one would bother to say that a skyscraper . . . or an automobile are 'constructed' . . . The great questions are rather: How well designed is it? How solidly constructed is it?

At this point it may be useful to look at the etymology of words like "artificial." The root of that word is "artifice," meaning handcrafted or made. Something artificial is made. Again, this does not necessarily mean that what is made is unreal or untrue. Indeed, to claim something humans have made is "unreal" is nonsensical. To make something can mean to objectify it, to materialize an idea or a notion. The question is not one of existence, but rather the qualities of construction and maintenance. So, for example, if the Earlobe Theory of Attraction became a matter of social consensus, then we would not question whether the theory exists, but instead evaluate the premises upon which it was made (that human ears fall into dichotomous types and that these types are the basis of attraction and ultimately relationship stability). Moreover, we would examine the different practices that maintain the Earlobe Theory's existence – the use of it in government I.D.s, the way stories are told about it in film, television, books and magazines, the way people use their earlobes to explain their identities, etc.

Conclusion

The works that make up this book can be read in a constructionist light as well – as constructs that make claims of knowledge about sexuality. A word of caution is warranted, and brings our chapter to a conclusion: It would be very easy to slip into the notion that a constructionist account means that the social scientist or historian is simply *reporting* on construction processes in all of their intricacies and dynamics. However, the acts of analyzing and writing are also constructions involving assemblages of actors and tools. The writer or scholar is never just a messenger or reporter, but is participating in the act of making the evidence, the argument, the story – they too are construction workers. Thus, they are implicated in *reconstructing* that which they are studying and reporting.

For example, when a sociologist studies a clinic that serves transgendered persons, that scholar is contributing to the associations and actions that they observe when they re-make the scenes they observed in their writings/descriptions. By writing about what they have observed, and analyzing those observations and drawing conclusions, they are breathing life into, upholding, and reproducing the persons, institutions, and situations they have observed. To write or study is not a neutral act, it is a decision to contribute to the ongoing realization of the object of inquiry. In other words, it is a decision to contribute to its ongoing construction. As Latour points out

Lars D. Christiansen and Nancy L. Fischer

in *Science in Action* (1987), the most profound way to destroy knowledge claims (especially young claims) is to *ignore them altogether*, to never read them nor ever cite them. To ignore an idea is ultimately to deconstruct it – never mentioning something, never thinking about something, contributes to the atrophy or decay of anything or quasi-thing. Erasure is best achieved by disappearance from discourse. In contrast, to reference an idea – as we did here by resurrecting the 1930s idea that earlobe type is dichotomous – is to remake. Moreover, to cite is to support (even as critique); to publish is to objectify, to fasten or stabilize, through a broader communication.

This book, for example, is constructed by all the authors, the publisher, the companies responsible for felling the trees that produced the paper on which this print is placed (as well as the print makers); all are collectively contributing to the making of the ideas expressed in this volume. It is up to you as reader to determine if the floor and foundation of this building is made well enough to stand upon, and possibly build upon these ideas.

References

Butler, Judith. 1993. "Imitation and Gender Insubordination." In *The Lesbian and Gay Studies Reader*, Henry Abelove, Michele Aina Barale and David Halperin, editors. New York: Routledge, pp. 307–320.

Foucault, Michel. 1976. *The Archeology of Knowledge*. New York: Harper & Row.

Foucault, Michel. 1990. *The History of Sexuality: An Introduction* (vol. 1). New York: Vintage Books.

Gender Wiki. 2016. "Gender Fluid." http://gender.wikia.com/wiki/Gender_Fluid. Accessed April 11, 2016.

Hazelrigg, Lawrence. 1995. *Cultures of Nature*. Tallahassee: University Presses of Florida.

Hill Collins, Patricia. 1990. *Black Feminist Thought: Knowledge, Consciousness, and the Politics of Empowerment*. New York: Routledge.

Katz, Jonathan Ned. 2007. *The Invention of Heterosexuality*. Chicago: University of Chicago Press.

Latour, Bruno. 1987. *Science in Action*. Cambridge: Harvard University Press.

Latour, Bruno. 2005. *Reassembling the Social*. Chicago: University of Chicago Press.

Zerubavel, Eviatar. 1993. *The Fine Line: Making Distinctions in Everyday Life*. Chicago: University of Chicago Press.

chapter 2

Theoretical perspectives

Steven Seidman

What is the relationship between sex and society? Beginning with sexologists who propose a view of sex as fundamentally biological, I review various social approaches to understanding sexuality. I take for granted the belief that there is a biological basis for human impulses, drives, and desires. However, it is social forces that fashion a biological reality into "sexuality." Individuals and groups give meaning to bodily sensations and feelings, make erotic acts into sexual identities, and create norms distinguishing between acceptable and unacceptable sexualities.

Sexology: a natural order of sexuality

Why do many of us in America and Europe view sexuality as natural? One reason is the development of a science of sexuality. In the late nineteenth and early twentieth centuries, there developed a science aimed at discovering the laws of sexuality. This science has come to be called sexology.

Who are the sexologists? Among the more famous are Richard von Krafft-Ebing, Havelock Ellis, and Magnus Hirschfeld. While few of us today have heard of these nineteenth-century pioneers of sexology, many of us have heard of Alfred Kinsey or of Masters and Johnson. Sexologists have produced a body of knowledge that has influenced the way many of us think about sex, in part because their ideas have been stamped with the imprimatur of science.

What are the key ideas of sexology? First, sexology claims that humans are born with a sexual nature, and that sexuality is part of the biological makeup of all individuals. Second, sexology views sexuality as being at the core of what it means to be human: our sexual drive is no less basic than our need to eat or sleep. Sexuality is said to be basic to who we are. Third, sexuality is viewed as a powerful and driving force in our behavior. It influences all aspects of our lives, from the physical to the psychological. It motivates much of human behavior. Fourth, sexology states that the sexual instinct is, by nature, heterosexual. There is said to be a natural attraction between men and women. While few sexologists today believe that the chief purpose of sexuality is to procreate, they continue to think that heterosexuality is the natural and normal form of sexuality.

Sexologists aim to discover the laws of sexuality. Just as physics and biology distrust inherited ideas and test them in experiments, sexology has championed a vigorously scientific approach. Facts, not beliefs, are to guide this science. The truth of sexuality is to be discovered by means of the "case study" method. Like physicians or psychiatrists, sexologists use intensive interviews and observation to uncover the true nature of sexuality. The details of human sexual desires, fantasies, and practices are recorded for the purpose of revealing the laws of the sexual instinct. Sexologists develop elaborate classifications of sexual types and detail the range of normal and abnormal forms of sexuality.

Sexology has always had a social purpose. In the nineteenth and early twentieth centuries, some sexologists sought to expand tolerance for different forms of human sexuality by emphasizing that sexuality is natural. Other sexologists saw their work as a way to contribute to creating a healthy, fit population. Often this meant that sexology was aligned to a belief in racial purity and improvement. Some sexologists even discouraged the sexual intermingling of races.

As racist ideas lost favor during the twentieth century, sexology has often been allied to a mission of strengthening the institutions of marriage and the family. Sexologists have argued that sex is at the core of love and marriage, and that a stable happy marriage requires a mutually satisfying sexual relationship. Individuals should not be burdened by guilt; they must be sexually knowledgeable and skilled. Sexology has aimed to make sexually enlightened and skillful citizens who would marry and stay married, in part because of a mutually satisfying sex life.

While their writings are sometimes technical and often tedious, sexologists have shaped Western sexual culture. Their ideas about the naturalness of sexuality have been popularized by an army of sex advice writers. Many of us believe in the idea of a natural sexuality because of the sexologists.

Freud: between biology and sociology

Alongside sexology, the discipline of psychology has been the source of many of our ideas about sex. In particular, Freud, the founder of psychoanalysis, has been probably the single most influential thinker in shaping Western sexual culture.

Freud aimed to uncover the roots of human psychology in our sex drives. Freud accepted many of the ideas of the sexologists. He believed in the biological basis of sexuality and insisted that sexuality is at the root of many of our feelings and actions. Freud also thought that there is a normal course of sexual development and there are abnormal or perverse forms of sexuality. The defining feature of sexual abnormality was deviation from genital-centered, intercourse-oriented heterosexuality based on love and monogamy.

But Freud also disagreed with the sexologists. Whereas sexologists defined the sexual instinct as reproductive and naturally heterosexual, Freud argued that the sexual instinct is oriented to pleasure. Moreover, humans get pleasure not only from sexual intercourse, but also from kissing, touching, caressing, looking, and sometimes dominating and being dominated. Freud argued that the body has many erotic areas and there are many ways of experiencing sexual satisfaction. Accordingly, he held that nongenital pleasures are not necessarily abnormal. It is normal, for example, to enjoy the range of pleasures that are today called foreplay.

Viewing the sexual instinct as a drive for pleasure blurs the line between normal and abnormal. To most sexologists, any sexual expression that deviated from a heterosexual reproductive aim was abnormal. However, Freud allows for a wide range of normal sexual expression beyond heterosexual reproduction. Pursuing nonprocreative pleasures is not in itself abnormal; sex drives become abnormal only when they are fixated on one specific sex act or pleasure. For example, it is normal for individuals to feel pleasure from looking at someone or from kissing and touching. It is abnormal, though, when these pleasures replace heterosexual intercourse.

Freud was convinced that sex is at the core of the self. It is, he thought, the drive for erotic pleasure that places the individual in conflict with social norms of respectability and self-control. Sexuality is then a major focus of psychological and social conflict. The psychological character of the individual rests on how the sex drive is managed. Too much sexual expression leads to psychological and social instability. Excessive social control results in psychosexual frustration that brings personal unhappiness.

Freud held to a much deeper social understanding of sexuality than the sexologists. If the sexual instinct is somewhat flexible in its purpose, it is society that shapes its form and meaning. In particular, the family is the formative social environment shaping our psyches and sexualities. Our psychological and sexual selves take shape as we struggle with the conflict between a drive for sexual pleasure and the social expectation to be productive, responsible citizens.

Marxism: the economics of sexuality

The ideas of the sexologists and psychologists have established important traditions in thinking about sex. However, they emphasize the natural, biological roots of sexuality. They have little to say about how social forces such as religion, the state, or the economy actually form biological impulses into sexual desires, create sexual identities, and establish rules and norms that regulate our sexual behavior.

In the twentieth century, *new social ways of thinking about sex* appeared. We will review some of the chief social theoretical perspectives that continue to influence the sociology of sexuality.

We begin with Karl Marx. Now, Marx himself had little to say about sex, but he was a great social thinker. One of his key insights was that human nature, including our sexuality, is shaped by society and changes historically.

Marxists argue that the economy is the most important social force shaping human behavior. Consider the way a capitalist economy shapes sexuality. Capitalism is oriented toward profit and economic growth. Marx believed that profit is based on exploiting labor, and growth occurs by reinvesting profits back into an enterprise. Marxists distinguish two phases of capitalist development in Europe and the United States. A market-based capitalism was dominant throughout the nineteenth century; since the early twentieth century, capitalism has been shaped by large corporations.

In the market phase, the chief challenge is to produce enough goods to meet the needs of the population. The answer: a disciplined labor force must be created. Individuals must adapt to the rhythms of a system of mass production that progressively strips work of individual imagination and skill. Ideally, capitalists would like to see laborers become machine-like. Anything that interferes with maximizing production, such as emotional or erotic feelings, is an impediment to efficient production. In other words, capitalists try to desexualize the work process and the body of laborers.

Business owners too must learn to avoid personal indulgence in order to remain competitive. While capitalists may flag their class status by acts of conspicuous consumption, their lives are fraught with anxiety. The market is unpredictable, and competitors threaten to take away their own and their family's livelihood. This drives capitalists to become economically and socially disciplined.

In a market economy, a repressed personality type is prominent. This kind of person is performance- and success-oriented and exercises tight internal controls over emotions and sensual desires. To this type of person, sexual impulses and desires are potentially disruptive of discipline; sexuality needs to be rigidly controlled. Accordingly, in market economies the pressures of industrial production and discipline shape a sexual culture that values self-control and the avoidance of sensual pleasure.

In the market economies of the nineteenth century, a sexual culture takes shape organized around procreation in marriage. Sex that is oriented to pleasure, sex outside marriage, autoerotic sex, sex in public, all nonheterosexual sex, and nongenital sex were viewed as deviant. These sexualities were at odds with capitalism's need for disciplined, productive workers.

In the twentieth century, the corporation replaced the small business as the major economic institution. This development brought about changes in modern sexual culture. New technologies and a scientific approach to the labor process created a new problem: how to ensure that the vast sea of goods being produced would be consumed?

Many corporations looked to expand the domestic market. They brought commerce into areas of daily life such as leisure, recreation, and entertainment. For example, every aspect of sports, from clothes and equipment to games, has gradually been commercialized. Capitalists also tried to convince individuals to consume more goods. But how does this shift to consumption affect sexuality?

Marxists argue that the new consumer economy weakens the Victorian culture and its emphasis on privacy, self-control, and the desexualization of the body and intimacy. In the process of creating higher levels of consumption, advertising gains a new importance. Sex is used to sell commodities; the public realm is now filled with images and talk of sex.

The commercialization of sex challenged Victorian culture in another way: capitalism places a new value on sex as a source of pleasure. As sex is used to sell goods and sex businesses flourish (porn, sex toys, phone sex), sex is no longer just a procreative or loving act, but a form of pleasure and self-expression. From a Marxist perspective, business owners want one thing: to make money by selling their goods. If sex can be marketed as pleasure or as an authentic form of self-expression or identity, then sex becomes a valuable marketing resource.

Corporate capitalism promotes a view of sex as a basis of self-fulfillment. To most Marxists, however, this pleasure-oriented sexual culture does not promote real sexual freedom. A culture that celebrates a superficial drive for pleasure leads to an aimless, unhappy search for gratification. Moreover, with its focus on sexual performance, sex has come to resemble work; accordingly, it has lost much of its tender, intimate, and caring qualities. Finally, Marxists argue that, as we search for personal happiness, the gross inequalities between rich and poor go unchallenged. There can be no real sexual freedom until there is real individual freedom, which is impossible under capitalism.

Feminism: the gender of sexuality

Feminism offers an equally forceful social view of sexuality. Feminists challenge Marxists. They point out that all of us step into the world as men or women, regardless of the economic system. Our gender identity is not a superficial part of our lives, but shapes the personal and social aspects of our lives in important ways. Feminists view gender as a social identity and a set of norms that guide behavior. We are not born men or women but acquire these gender identities through a social process of learning and sometimes coercion. Feminists believe that our sexual desires, feelings, and preferences are imprinted by gender.

Feminists say that individuals acquire a sexual nature as they develop a gender identity. What exactly is the relationship between gender and sexuality?

In *The Reproduction of Mothering*, Nancy Chodorow argues that when women do the chief parenting work, gender patterns of sexual and individual development are different. For both boys and girls, the mother is often the primary source of love. However, girls sustain an intimacy with their mothers throughout their maturation; boys separate from their mothers at an early age in order to learn to be men. This difference shapes the psychosexual character of girls and boys.

The extended and intense intimacy between mothers and daughters results in girls developing a psyche that is relationship-oriented. Accordingly, girls tend to connect sex with intimacy and as a means of caring. They often approach sex more as a means of communication and intimacy than as a vehicle of erotic pleasure. Because boys typically break sharply from their mothers at an early age, and identify with their achievement-oriented fathers, they are more performance- and goal-oriented. Boys' sexuality tends to be more performance- and body-oriented. Boys can be intimate, but they will likely express sexual love in terms of the giving and receiving of erotic pleasure.

Chodorow's perspective is important because she holds that the family plays a crucial role in the making of the sexual self. Also, she says that boys and girls develop different sexual values and orientations.

Adrienne Rich also believes that gender dynamics creates sexual differences between men and women. She emphasizes the social creation of heterosexual men and women. In "Compulsive Heterosexuality and Lesbian Existence" she argues that we are all taught and coerced into adopting conventional gender identities. Why? Gender difference, Rich says, reinforces a society organized around the norm of heterosexuality.

Steven Seidman

Shaping individuals into heterosexual men and women is a complex social process. Societies use positive inducements like economic rewards or a culture that romanticizes heterosexuality, but also resorts to ridicule, harassment, and violence to punish gender nonconformists and nonheterosexuals. The belief that heterosexuality is normal and natural plays a key role in creating heterosexual men and women. For example, many Europeans and Americans believe that there is a natural attraction between the sexes, that their bodies and minds "naturally" fit. Heterosexuality is then viewed as an extension of a natural order composed of two complementary sexes.

Catherine MacKinnon insists on the role of male dominance in shaping women's sexuality. She views sexuality as a product of men's power; sex is a means by which men control women. Indeed, it is the very basis of male domination. To the extent that men have the power to define what desires, feelings, and behaviors are sexual, they can define women's sexuality in a way that positions them as subordinate. For example, in male-dominated America, women's sexuality is supposed to be oriented to vaginal intercourse in marriage with the ultimate aim of procreation. This view defines women as heterosexual, or needing men, and as motivated to become wives and mothers, and therefore dependent on men.

Feminists like Rich and MacKinnon claim that the very essence of sexuality expresses men's wish for dominance. Every sexual desire and behavior in male-dominated societies is said to be related to gender dynamics, and either expresses men's dominance or women's resistance. From this perspective, feminists criticize the notion that women's sexual liberation is about claiming the right to pleasure or the freedom to do as one pleases, an approach that expresses men's view of sexual freedom. Instead, women's sexual liberation involves fashioning a sexual life that reflects their own needs, feelings, and desires. The point is not to liberate sexuality from social control, which could lead to more violence or unwanted pregnancy, but to claim the power to define one's own sexual desires and forge sexual-intimate lives.

Some feminists, like the anthropologist Gayle Rubin, have objected to the view that sexuality is a direct expression of gender politics. She argues that this perspective ignores considerable variation within women's and men's sexuality. Rubin believes that sexuality is connected to gender, yet also has its own dynamics.

In "Thinking Sex," Rubin makes the case that sex is fundamentally about erotic desires, fantasies, acts, identities, and politics – none of which are reducible to gender dynamics. She argues that all societies create sexual hierarchies that establish boundaries between good and bad or legitimate and illicit sexualities. Societies value specific desires, acts, and identities as normal, respectable, good, healthy, and moral; other forms of sexuality are classified as unhealthy, abnormal, sinful, and immoral. Society supports and privileges the "normal and good" forms of sexuality and aims to punish the "abnormal and bad" ones through law, violence, ridicule, or stigma. These sexual hierarchies create a series of outsider sexualites. This system of sexual regulation applies to both men and women. American society considers heterosexuality, monogamy, marriage, and reproductive sex to be considered good and normal; S/M (sadomasochism) and multiple-partner sex, commercial and public sex are defined and treated as bad. There are of course many sexualities that fall somewhere in between – for example, promiscuous heterosexuals or gays and lesbians in long-term monogamous relationships. It may be less socially acceptable for a woman to have multiple sex partners or to engage in S/M because of a gender order that associates femininity with purity and maternal feelings; still, these behaviors are disparaged by both men and women. Those who engage in such behaviors, regardless of gender, will be stigmatized and subject to a range of sanctions, from ridicule to criminalization. Rubin's point is simply that gender influences patterns of sexuality, but there is still a great deal about the organization and dynamics of sexuality that cannot be viewed solely through the lens of gender.

Sociology

Since the early decades of the twentieth century, sociologists have researched the role of religion, gender, class, race, and social values in shaping patterns of premarital, marital, and extramarital sex. In the 1960s and 1970s, Ira Reiss charted cultural and behavioral shifts among American youth as a sexual morality that associated sex exclusively with marriage transformed into one that permitted sex in a context of affection. Reiss believed that this cultural change was related to women's growing economic and social power. In this regard, he observed the decline of a double standard that permitted men to have sex outside of marriage, while labeling women who engaged in the same behavior as "bad girls."

Some sociologists urged a full-blown sociology of sexuality. John Gagnon and William Simon proposed a "script" theory of sexuality. Instead of understanding humans as born sexual, they argued that sexuality is socially learned. In the course of growing up, society teaches us what feelings and desires count as sexual and what the appropriate "scripts" for sexual behavior are. Sexual scripts tell us with whom we're supposed to have sex (based on age, race, or class), where, when, and what it means when we do. Gagnon and Simon were in effect saying that sexuality is not an inborn property, but a product of social labeling.

The British sociologist Ken Plummer developed a labeling perspective on sex. In *Sexual Stigma*, he argued that individuals aren't born homosexual, but learn to be homosexual. An individual may feel desire or attraction to people of the same sex, but he or she must learn that these feelings are sexual and that they indicate a homosexual identity. People learn this in the course of interacting with both the straight and gay world. For example, a high-school student hearing derogatory comments about "fags" and "dykes" begins to associate homosexuality with a stigmatized identity. This same individual may eventually be exposed to a gay subculture, which champions a view of homosexuality as natural and good.

One of the pioneers of a sociological approach to sexuality was the British sociologist Jeffrey Weeks. He introduced the ideas of essentialism and constructionism. Essentialism is the notion that sexuality is a basic and essential part of being human. Constructionism states that sexuality is a product of social forces. Weeks (1986: 18–19) proposed a strong view of the social character of sexuality:

> First, we can no longer set 'sex' against 'society' as if they were separate domains. Secondly, there is a widespread recognition of the social variability of sexual forms, beliefs, ideologies, and behavior. Sexuality has ... many histories. ...

Thirdly, we must learn to see that sexuality is something which society produces in complex ways. It is a result of diverse social practices that give meaning to human activities, to struggles between those who have power to define and regulate, and those who resist. Sexuality is not given, it is a product of negotiation, struggle.

Gay and lesbian studies

Paralleling the rise of a gay movement, many advocates argued that some people are just born homosexual. If homosexuals have always existed, it is a natural status and therefore they should not be punished.

However, this view has been challenged by the new gay/lesbian studies. These new scholars assume that homosexual behavior is a natural part of the human condition, but the appearance of a homosexual identity is a rare historical event. When and why did a homosexual identity emerge, and how has the meaning of homosexuality changed historically?

Jonathan Katz argued that, between colonial times and the 1970s, homosexuality in the US changed from indicating a behavior (sodomy), to an abnormal personality (the homosexual), and finally to an affirmative social identity (gay/lesbian). Carroll Smith-Rosenberg showed that Victorian women, whose lives were organized around domestic tasks, often formed close ties with each other that at times blurred the line between friendship and romance. These intimate bonds sometimes developed into romantic relationships that were celebrated as complementary to marriage. These "romantic friendships" were often life-time romantic bonds. Similarly, Lillian Faderman wrote the first history of lesbianism in the United States, in which she documents changes in the meaning of same-sex behavior and in the social organization of lesbianism. Both Smith-Rosenberg and Faderman make the provocative argument that tolerance for intimacy between women diminished in the first decades of the twentieth century. As women started to attend college, work outside the home, and demand equal rights, their close ties to one another were often viewed as threatening. These women were stigmatized as lesbians.

Building on this growing body of historical scholarship on sexuality, John D'Emilio offered the first detailed analysis of the rise of a homosexual identity and community in the United States. He analyzed the social forces that shaped homosexuality into an identity, community, and social movement. For example, D'Emilio argued that the Second World War played a key role in shaping an awareness of homosexuality and homosexual bonds. During the war, many soldiers were, for the first time, exposed to individuals who thought of themselves as homosexual. Moreover, the intense closeness among the men and women in the military encouraged homosexual experimentation. After the war, many of these men and women with homosexual feelings settled in New York, Chicago, San Francisco, and Los Angeles. It was in these cities that the first major gay and lesbian political organizations initially took shape in the 1950s.

Historians have continued to refine their conceptions of the sexual past. One significant revision is in George Chauncey's *Gay New York*. Whereas historians and sociologists had come to believe that the modern homosexual emerged in the early twentieth century and was immediately stuffed into the closet, Chauncey argues that, in working-class New York, individuals were not classified as either homosexual or heterosexual, but as either "normal men" or "fairies." The former were masculine men, while the latter were effeminate. In other words, the homosexual indicated a type of gender deviance. If you were a masculine man who had sex with effeminate men, you were not necessarily considered a homosexual. Gender expression, not sexual preference, defined being a homosexual. Moreover, rather than being isolated and closeted, an open public gay life flourished in bars, taverns, speakeasies, restaurants, ballrooms, and parks.

Queer studies

The new gay/lesbian studies proposes a deeply social view of homosexuality. It helped to give rise to so-called "Queer studies." A queer perspective advances two key ideas. First, the idea of a natural human sexuality is a belief or cultural notion, not a biological truth. Second, this idea divides sexual behaviors and identities into those that are normal and healthy, and those that are abnormal and sick. Queer studies shifts the focus from homosexuality to sexuality and broadens our view of sexuality to see it also as a type of social control.

The ideas of Michel Foucault are central. He challenged the idea that sex was biological and natural. He proposed that it was the very idea or, in his terms, the discourse of sexuality that created what we know as sex. We are not born sexual, but learn to be sexual beings; this occurs only in societies that have created the idea of "sexuality."

But when did this idea of sexuality originate, and why? The birth of the science of sexuality in the nineteenth century was crucial. Scientists aimed to discover the hidden truth of human nature by uncovering the secrets of the sexual instinct. Sexologists charted the physiology and behavior of sexual desire, psychiatrists listened to their clients confess to a shadowy world of sexual fantasies, and demographers surveyed human fertility. But these researchers did not discover an uncharted territory of sex; they fashioned human pleasures, excitations, and acts into a new object of knowledge and social regulation: human sexuality. Foucault is not saying that the feelings and behaviors associated with the body were created by these discourses. Rather, these discourses compelled us to view these bodily experiences as expressions of human sexuality. The science of sexuality conceptualized our diverse somatic experiences into a coherent, organized subject called sexuality.

Why did a discourse of sexuality appear and what was its social importance? Foucault thought that the modern state and other social institutions had good reasons to want to control people's sexuality. Between the seventeenth and nineteenth centuries in many European nations there were massive migrations to cities, a growing need for mass literacy and schooling, intense economic competition between nations, and the growing dependence of national power on economic prosperity. These developments created a strong political interest in gaining detailed and useful information about human bodies – how they reproduce, stay healthy, react to different external stimulation, and can be made more productive, efficient, and cooperative. For example, as cities became social and economic centers, governments and other institutions responsible for keeping order and for the care of the indigent sought information about migration patterns, fertility rates, nutrition, and health. This growing need to know and control bodies helped to create the idea of sexuality. To control sex is to exercise great control over the individual and whole populations. Sexuality is at the center of a modern system of social control.

Did Foucault give up the notion of sexual freedom? He wrote during a period of sexual rebellion. Sexual liberationists of all types declared that today we are more enlightened; the present is pregnant with possibilities for sexual freedom. Sexual liberation had two aspects. The first was a negative freedom – freedom from unnecessary control. Liberation also had a positive aspect – the right to express one's true sexual nature and identity.

Foucault agreed that expanding individual choice is a good thing. He supported the fight for gay rights. But gay rights is not liberation. It does relieve individuals of horrific stigma and social discrimination. Also, the gay rights movement has reinforced a system that forces individuals to declare themselves either straight or gay, and reinforces the deviant status of bisexuality and other nonconventional sexualities. Moreover, a gay movement has its own ideal of how a gay person is supposed to look and act. In other words, the gay movement exercises control over its members, pressuring them to identify exclusively as gay and to act in ways that are recognized as gay.

If sexuality is today a system of social control, then ironically sexual liberation might involve freeing ourselves from the idea of sexuality. This would mean approaching our erotic desires and acts not as expressions of sexuality but as simply feelings and acts that give pleasure, create social ties, or are a source of cultural creativity. Foucault advocates a politics against sexuality – against a society that sexualizes selves, identities, and acts. Why would this be a good thing? By not assigning a moral meaning (either normal or abnormal) to adult, consensual sexual desires and behaviors, individuals would be subject to less social regulation. For example, instead of reversing the stigma of homosexuality by championing a normal gay identity, we could approach homosexuality as a desire and as a source of pleasure, new relationships and cultural expressions. Or, instead of celebrating the sexualization of the human body and all of its feelings and sensations, perhaps it is more liberating to desexualize pleasures, focus on nonsexual pleasures, learn to enjoy a wide range of sensual pleasures, and be free of controls that rely on notions of normality.

Foucault emphasized the role of discourses or networks of ideas in producing and regulating human sexuality. The philosopher Judith Butler has drawn from Foucault in order to offer a new social point of view on gender and sexuality.

Butler thinks that societies that believe in a natural gender order are also organized around the norm of heterosexuality. Heterosexuality is the basis of a culture of romance, marriage, and the family, and is enforced by our laws, government, churches, schools, and military. Viewing men and women as naturally complementary makes heterosexuality seem like the natural, normal, and right way of living.

A system of compulsory heterosexuality may help to explain why societies divide individuals into two gender types, but it does not explain how gender – and sexual – identities are sustained daily. Butler's ideas about gender identity have been very influential in the sociology of sexual identity.

Growing up in a society that classifies feelings, behaviors, and social roles as appropriate either for men or for women, we learn how to act in gender-correct ways. By means of a system of rewards and sanctions, we learn to present ourselves as either men or women. We come to know, almost without thinking, what gestures, styles of dress and grooming, and ways of walking and talking are considered "normal" for men and women. If a male acts "masculine," if his posture, talk, friends, dating, and job conform to masculine norms, his gender identity as a man will be taken for granted. If a male acts "feminine," he may not be considered a "normal" man.

Furthermore, Butler argues that, as we conform to gender norms, others will likely interpret our behavior as expressing a core gender identity. For example, most of us would probably assume that a male who looks and acts like a man (e.g. is aggressive, competitive, or decisive) *is* a man, and this status is at the core of his identity. In other words, his masculine actions are understood as expressing a deeply rooted male gender identity. However, Butler suggests that there is no core gender identity that drives our behavior. Rather than viewing our gender performances as expressing an inner gender identity, she says that these behaviors are modeled after images of what it means to be a woman or man that we take over from our families and our culture. The illusion of core feminine and masculine gender identities conceals the social and political forces that shape humans into gendered selves. Similarly, the ideology of a natural gender order conceals the role of gender in the perpetuation of heterosexual dominance.

Butler's ideas encourage us to view sexual identity as a process. We project a sexual identity by our actions. Accordingly, researchers would analyze the micro-dynamics of identity formation. For example, we would try to explain which behaviors and things (clothes, cars, homes, furniture, eyeglasses) come to be signs of sexual identity, and why. How do individuals acquire the skills to read each other's behaviors in terms of sex identity categories? A performative approach does not claim that sex identities are not real because they are produced through a performance. They are quite real as we experience them and in terms of their personal and social consequences. And, while they may be performances, they are hardly chosen; a system of compulsory heterosexuality exerts enormous social pressure on each of us to "perform" the appropriate gender and sexual identities. Deviance from gender or sexual norms carries serious dangers, from being denied respect to being the target of harassment or violence.

To summarize this chapter, there has been a revolution in the way scholars think about sexuality. Until recently, scholars believed that humans were born with a sexual nature; the natural order created a series of sexual types: heterosexuals, homosexuals, masochists, pedophiles, and so on. A science of sexuality would reveal the nature of the sexual instinct. The idea of sexual normality would serve as the standard to judge and regulate sexual behavior.

Today, the leading edge of scholarship views sex as fundamentally social. We're born with bodies but it is society that determines which parts of the body and which pleasures and acts are sexual. And, the classification of sex acts into good and bad or acceptable and illicit is a product of social power; the dominant sexual norms express the dominant social groups. If we are supposed to grow up to be heterosexual, and if we are expected to link sex to love and marriage, this is because specific groups impose these social norms. Beliefs that there are natural and normal ways to be sexual are ideologies. How we come to have such beliefs, and their personal and social consequences, are important questions for the study of sexuality. Indeed, the question of who gets to define what is sexual and which institutions are responsible for regulating our sexualities are key sociological and political questions.

Bibliography

Judith Butler, *Gender Trouble: Feminism and the Subversion of Identity* (New York: Routledge, 1990).

George Chauncey, *Gay New York: Gender, Urban Culture, and the Making of the Gay Male World, 1890–1940* (New York: Basic Books, 1994).

Nancy Chodorow, *The Reproduction of Mothering: Psychoanalysis and the Sociology of Gender* (Berkeley: University of California Press, 1978).

John D'Emilio, *Sexual Politics, Sexual Communities: The Making of a Homosexual Minority in the United States, 1940–1970* (Chicago, IL: University of Chicago Press 1983).

Lillian Faderman, *Odd Girls and Twilight Lovers: A History of Lesbian Life in Twentieth-Century America* (New York: Columbia University Press, 1991).

Michel Foucault, *The History of Sexuality. Vol 1: An Introduction* (New York: Vintage, 1980).

John Gagnon and William Simon, *Sexual Conduct: The Social Sources of Human Sexuality* (Chicago, IL: Aldine, 1973).

Jonathan Ned Katz, *Gay American History* (New York: Crowell, 1976) and *Gay/Lesbian Almanac* (New York: Harper & Row, 1983).

Catherine MacKinnon, *Towards a Feminist Theory of the State* (Cambridge, MA: Harvard University Press, 1989).

Ken Plummer, *Sexual Stigma: An Interactionist Account* (London: Routledge & Kegan Paul, 1975).

Ira Reiss, *Premarital Sexual Standards in America* (Glencoe, IL: Free Press, 1960) and *The Social Context of Premarital Sexual Permissiveness* (New York: Holt, Rinehart & Winston, 1967).

Adrienne Rich, "Compulsory Heterosexuality and Lesbian Existence," *Signs* 5 (1980).

Gayle Rubin, "Thinking Sex: Notes for a Radical Theory of the Politics of Sexuality," in *Pleasure and Danger: Exploring Female Sexuality*, ed. Carole Vance (Boston, MA: Routledge & Kegan Paul, 1984).

Carroll Smith-Rosenberg, "The Female World of Love and Ritual," *Signs* 1 (1975).

Jeffrey Weeks, *Sexuality* (London: Tavistock, 1986), p. 26.

chapter 3

Black sexual politics revisited

Interview with Patricia Hill Collins

Patricia Hill Collins is a Distinguished University Professor at the University of Maryland. She is the author of many respected works including *Black Feminist Thought* (1990), *Black Sexual Politics* (2004) and *On Intellectual Activism* (2012).

How would you describe your intersectional approach to social analysis in Black Feminist Thought and Black Sexual Politics?

My scholarship on intersectionality is dedicated to social justice, a concept that characterizes domination and empowerment as intimately connected. People may be oppressed within race, class, gender, sexuality, age and ability as distinctive systems of oppression, yet they also resist their subordination in response to these same systems. One major insight of intersectionality has been to see these broader systems of oppression themselves as interconnected and mutually constructing. For example, racism draws meaning from sexism and vice versa – they make sense only in relation to one another. A similar intersectional lens can be applied to questions of political empowerment and resistance. Does it make sense to resist only one form of domination when multiple forms may be at work? In the academy, intersectionality is often used to describe the ways that domination operates. But for me, the question of bringing intersectional analyses to political projects for social justice has been paramount.

Conceptualizing intersectionality and figuring out how to do it are two different issues. For the past three decades, I have approached intersectionality by starting with the social issues or specific challenges facing particular populations such as African American women. I test and deepen my grasp of intersectionality through the lens of particular social justice projects. I have focused on African Americans not as a special or extreme case, but rather as a specific social location from which to see larger issues.

Because I consider my work to be intellectual activism, the corpus of my scholarship examines varying dimensions of intersectionality (Collins 2012). For example,

Black Feminist Thought (1990), my first book, analyzed how intersections of racism and sexism shaped Black women's experiences both with social injustice and what Black women did to empower themselves in the face of those injustices (Collins 2000). I recognized that class, sexuality and nation, for example, were important components of an intersectional analysis, primarily because Black feminists had already pointed this out. But because my project was simultaneously academic and political, I wrote *Black Feminist Thought* within a space that emphasized one intersection as primary and included intersections of class, sexuality and nation as secondary.

I saw the need for a book on *Black Sexual Politics* in the early 1990s even before I finished the first edition of *Black Feminist Thought*. During the 1990s, and certainly by the time the second edition was published in 2000, it was clear that African American politics needed a thoughtful analysis of sexuality that analyzed how depictions of black sexuality functioned to oppress both Black women and Black men. Many of the issues on the list of social problems that disproportionately impact African American communities – violence, educational equity, poverty and income inequality, health disparities, and the status of Black children and youth – are organized through ideas of gender and sexuality. What African Americans needed was an analysis of black sexual politics that saw how ideas about black sexuality could be used to oppress and/or liberate.

I knew that sexuality was important intellectually, but the question of when and how to develop an engaging, analytically solid analysis of black sexual politics faced four challenges: (1) it had to analyze the ways historic depictions of black sexuality as deviant, exotic and wild, e.g., non-normative, contributed to racial oppression; (2) it had to analyze the uncritical acceptance of conservative norms of gender and sexuality within African American communities that in turn shaped ideas about Black masculinity, Black femininity and black families; (3) it had to critique the moral discourse on black sexuality advanced by Black churches and black civil rights organizations alike without appearing to attack the very same organizations that had been at the forefront of anti-racist politics; and, most importantly, (4) it had to be written not just about African Americans, but for them. I was not going to write yet another book on African Americans that Black people could not read.

I delayed writing *Black Sexual Politics* until the early 2000s, primarily because the 1990s provided a narrow intellectual space for this particular project. In the early 1990s, queer theory emerged, contesting hegemonic understandings of sexuality as a biological entity or alternately through the lens of moral discourse of religion. I needed an analysis of sexuality for my own project, but was disappointed with what I found. Unfortunately, major figures in the field neither seemed to know much about racism nor emphasized the kinds of bread and butter social class issues within queer theory that had long preoccupied African American scholars. Queer theory at that time claimed intersectionality, but it was an intersectional framework that deemphasized race and class. Quite frankly, the new language of heteronormativity, non-normative sexuality, and the random appearance of brackets in the middle of words seemed like inside jokes that only the initiated could understand. Stated differently, queer theory felt mighty white and elite.

Things improved by the end of the 1990s. By then, individual scholars and nascent communities of progressive scholars found ways to analyze and critique how black sexual politics actually worked within African American communities and pointed out new ways of thinking about sexuality, gender and race (see., e.g., Battle, Cohen, Warren,

Fergerson, and Audam 2002; Boykin 1996; Carbado 1999; Cohen 1999; Douglas 1999). Innovative work on black sexuality as a source of pleasure reopened the closed door of black sexuality itself (Dent 1992). Queer theory provided important interpretive tools for this endeavor. For my project, African American scholars had developed important intersectional analyses of Black masculinity, in particular its reliance on hyper-heterosexuality.

Can you give an example of an intersectional approach from your Black Sexual Politics?

In *Black Sexual Politics*, I used intersectionality to make two main points. First, the sexual politics within African American communities could best be explained by intersecting oppressions of racism and sexism and heterosexism; and second, anything short of a comprehensive analysis of black sexual politics would be insufficient for social justice work. Black sexuality could no longer be the stepchild in the corner of African American politics or black intellectual production. That was the goal. The question was how to write the book.

Rather than beginning my analysis within social theories of race, gender, or sexuality, writing within some sort of abstract space of intersectionality, I began by asking, what actual social issues impacted Black people's lives?; and what kind of analysis was needed to address those issues? I had a long list to choose from. For example, sadly, no matter how much details change, the discussion of violence within *Black Sexual Politics* remains applicable today (see., e.g. Collins 2004, 48–49 and Collins 2012, 187–197). From Treyvon Martin to Michael Brown in Ferguson, current analyses of African Americans and violence continue to focus on the archetype of white men killing young Black men as the symbol of violence affecting African Americans. Of course this issue is extremely important. We know that. But Black women, Black children, Black lesbian, gay, bisexual, transgendered, and queer (LGBTQ) people and the Black elderly also encounter violence in myriad forms. How effective can an analysis of violence be, let alone political responses to it, that emphasizes only one segment of the African American population and neglects others? An intersectional analysis not only shows the parallel nature of violence within separate systems of oppression, but also how these forms of violence work to interconnect systems of oppression. Developing an intersectional analysis is hard enough. I also tried to keep the question of political agency in mind. How might African Americans develop adequate responses to the question of violence?

In Black Sexual Politics *you discuss the "new racism." Why did you decide to discuss black sexual politics in the context of racism?*

I made this choice for intellectual and strategic reasons (Collins 2012, 41–48). The task is not to hold racism steady in order to analyze black sexuality. That approach suggests that we *already* know what racism is and that we need to add in the missing ingredient of sexuality. This can be a starting point, but cannot be an end point in intersectional work. Instead, the goal was to analyze racism, sexism and heterosexism in such a way that they could not be unbundled. I aimed to make the case that the specific forms of oppression that affected African Americans could be addressed politically without an intersectional analysis of all three systems of power.

Strategically, I wanted to reach an African American audience. What I wrote had to ring true for them, and not just for scholarly colleagues. Because racism remains such a deep tap root for African American analysis and politics, many African Americans see intersectional frameworks or anything other than discussing race as potentially muddying the waters of fighting racism. I also explicitly focused on racism to counteract the tendency to move onto the next fashionable system of oppression, leaving the rest behind. Not only did I feel that analyses of racism and, by implication, anti-racism were and remain overly narrow, African Americans lacked exposure to analyses of racism that took sexism, class exploitation and heterosexism into account. Discussing racism in terms such as "old" and "new" was familiar terrain for my target audience. Discussions of sexism, capitalism and heterosexism were not. Rather than berate my audience for the critical education that they had been denied, I took on the much harder task of writing an intersectional analysis of racism that ironically did not privilege racism.

My goal in *Black Sexual Politics* was to write about racism in such as way that it would be virtually impossible to extricate analyses of sexism and heterosexism from it, or to assign these systems to second class status. My readers had to make the leap from seeing the world primarily through the lens of racial systems of oppression, to understanding the idea of gender oppression and sexual oppression, to the big theme of recognizing that racism as a system of oppression could not be adequately addressed without an analysis of sexism and heterosexism. Any good teacher knows that you build on the familiar, even if critiquing it, in order to make the unfamiliar make sense.

What issues would you say are at the forefront of sexual politics in the African American community today?

Sometimes it is important to pause and celebrate success. Stacey Patton's 2012 article titled "Who's Afraid of Black Sexuality?" does a masterful job of summarizing the trajectory of black sexuality studies during and after the period when I wrote *Black Sexual Politics* (Patton 2012). Had I waited a few more years, I would have had so much more excellent work to use. That said, several things stand out for me.

I am also encouraged by the much greater interpretive space that is now available to Black LGBTQ youth and their allies to raise issues of sexuality both within scholarship, popular culture, electoral politics and grassroots politics. For example, the award winning documentary *The New Black* that shows Black LGBTQ youth involved in electoral politics in Maryland would have been far more difficult to make and circulate in the late 1990s (Richen 2013). Similarly, the formation of National Black Justice Coalition to promote the civil rights of Black LGBTQ youth constitutes an important way that black sexuality has become more visible within African American politics. Popular culture, film, video, social media and dimensions of the mainstream press remain far more receptive to analyses of black sexuality – the fact that Patton's article was published in the *Chronicle of Higher Education* and that *The New Black* garnered awards both illustrate the receptivity within mainstream media for analyses of black sexuality. Entering this interpretative space and presenting alternatives, especially alternative explanations of black sexuality that link it to power relations and that validate the spectrum of sexual expression and identities that come with it, takes courage, but no longer garners the danger of prior periods. Artists, intellectuals and academics who work on black sexuality are increasingly visible, and effective.

At the same time, I remain amazed at how resilient the controlling images and sexual stereotypes that I detail in both *Black Feminist Thought* and *Black Sexual Politics* have turned out to be. Popular culture, especially visual media of television and film, has emerged as a major terrain of struggle and is likely to remain so for some time. In this regard, LGBTQ Black characters may be riding the wave of acceptability of LGBTQ white characters, at least in the fictional world of Netflix and cable television. We seem to be a point of moving beyond the early phase of inclusion, one that simply added a LGBTQ Black character for interest without fleshing out the meaning of the character. The Black heterosexual sidekick increasingly shows up as the Black or Latino gay sidekick, neighbor or co-worker, a facile substitution that suggests that a dose of colorful, sexual difference is just as good as another. That's what pop culture wants for its imagined general audience. As I discuss in "Somebody's Watching You: To Be Young, Sexy and Black," in chapter 4 of *Another Kind of Education*, popular culture is happy to continue to market and sell commodified images of Black people generally, and black sexuality in particular (Collins 2009, 135–174). But that is clearly not necessarily what Black artists, writers, directors and filmmakers want to do. When you look beyond the screaming girls on some of the reality tv shows, there is some real substance. *Orange Is the New Black*, for example, broke new ground in exploring the complexities of sexuality, gender, race and incarceration, all themes that are vitally important for black sexual politics.

Independent films and videos are also at the forefront of creating space for issues of black sexuality. The general public may have been enamored with *Precious*, the remaking of Sapphire's novel about the abuse of a Black girl – this trope is familiar – or yet another dose of the long-suffering, heroic, asexual domestic worker played by Viola Davis in *The Help*. Such films reinforce depictions of downtrodden, albeit heroic, Black women whose place at the bottom of society remains unquestioned. We know they are unloved and viewers are encouraged both to feel sorry for them and grateful that we are not them. But I was much more impressed by *Pariah*, a wonderful independent film that traced the humanity of a 17-year-old Black teenager who was coming of age as a lesbian (Rees 2011). It was refreshing to see a clear rejection of dominant tropes of the hyper-masculine, homophobic Black father who knows how to keep his children in a straight line, and the nurturing, all-suffering Black mother whose love for her child requires all-consuming maternal sacrifice. In *Pariah*, the father clearly loves his daughter, isn't quite sure what to make of her, but does not reject her. He supports her to the best of his ability. In contrast, her mother's religious beliefs do not allow her to get beyond her daughter's sexuality, eventually shaping her daughter's decision to leave home.

I really liked *Pariah*, but how many African Americans have access to independent art films that show at the Sundance film festival? As a medium, television comes closest to reaching a large population of African American viewers who can handle substantive analysis of black sexual politics such as those advanced by Black scholars or directors but who may not be able to pay for it. In this regard, Shonda Rhimes's work on *Grey's Anatomy* and *Scandal* shatters sexual taboos, troubles black sexual stereotypes and clears considerable conceptual space for analyses of sexual politics generally, and black sexual politics in particular. In *How to Get Away with Murder*, introduced in the 2014 television season on ABC, Rhimes elevates her own game in taking on the complexities of sexuality, race, class and gender. Rhimes knows how to provide good, marketable entertainment to a mass audience. But her real skill lies in engaging in a stealth analysis of black sexuality that is effective because it is both popular and substantive.

No matter how well-received ideas may seem in selected academic circles or how popular they may be in mass market venues, it would be naïve to assume that ideas directly influence behavior. Just because the Disney Channel is racially desegregated doesn't mean that US society is racially integrated. Macklemore's song "Same Love" may challenge homophobia in hip hop, but it will take more than one song to change the genre. Cultural production plays an important part in political struggle, but it is a starting place, not the finish line.

As gay and lesbian politics began to mainstream and organize around rights struggles in the 1980s and 1990s, two reactions stand out: the intersectional approach pioneered by women of color; and a queer politics fashioned primarily by white academics. Could you suggest an intersectional account of this division? Is there a productive dialogue to be had here?

I think I would begin this dialogue in an entirely different place. I do not see the intersectional approach pioneered by women of color as a reaction to gay and lesbian politics that mainstreamed and organized around rights in the 1980s and 1990s. I actually see closer ties between black feminism and gay and lesbian politics during the social movement era. Queer politics fashioned primarily by white academics constitutes a reaction against the identity politics advanced by black feminism (intersectional analysis) and social movements for gay and lesbian rights. Quite simply, if groups as sites of political advocacy and action disappear, then group-based politics become impossible.

Black feminism and gay and lesbian politics both relied upon a progressive group-based form of identity politics to advance social justice agendas. Identity politics were both individual and collective, the act of coming to understand the effects of racism, sexism, heterosexism and class exploitation in one's individual life and in the groups that carry those identities. Group-based identity politics organized for political change often learn from one another and grapple with the difficulties of political coalitions. Black sexuality stands at the crossroads of both movements. The movements may have started in different places, but eventually there might have been a rich intersectional site of engagement.

Queer theory in the 1990s seems to have created a space for itself in academia via opposition to group-based identity politics in the abstract. Queer theory may have invoked and mentioned this prior period of multicultural, multiclass, multi-sexual political activism, yet the agenda of queer theory was far more closely aligned with the intellectual and political requirements of the neoliberal academy than with social movements. Measured by the acceptance of queer theory and scholarship in the academy and by the increasingly positive public attitudes toward LGBTQ people as evidenced by support for same-sex marriage in the US, by the 1990s and into the

2000s, it seems that claiming respectability in the eyes of academics who matter and the public delivers results. But for who?

Certainly, as individuals, people of color benefit from the more welcoming intellectual and political space and growing acceptance of LGBTQ people. At the same time, the question of who benefits from this respectability and who remains punished is important. The convergence of whiteness and wealth that has worked to render LGBTQ identities acceptable if not chic draws upon longstanding practices of Othering marginalized groups for meaning. The non-normative sexual practices of Blacks and gays and lesbians mark that margin. The whiteness and elitism of queer theory, and the related discourse of individual solutions to collective social problems (homophobia) that it seems to suggest, leave queer theory ill equipped to address the issues that will continue to face African Americans.

What kind of influence, if any, did the turn to queer politics and theory in the last couple of decades have in African American thinking and politics?

Influence is a hard thing to measure, especially when one is discussing a power differential. That said, I think that poststructuralist social theory generally and queer theory in particular provide important theoretical tools for African American social and political thought. African American intellectuals whose class position provides them with high levels of literacy and access to technology have gained access to these tools and made productive use of them. I've already alluded to some limitations of queer theory, but there is also real potential here, especially concerning intersectional analysis. Let me illustrate through two examples.

The first concerns the specific example of violence that I discussed earlier. Police violence targeted at young Black men is currently a major social issue. Beyond the obvious elevation of one kind of victim over others as the privileged face of victimization – women, LGBTQ people and the elderly who also lose their lives to violence are counseled to wait their turns – the theme of violence *among* Black men remains ignored. Young Black men harm and kill one another at alarming rates, with unexamined assumptions about Black masculinity, manhood, respect and sexuality at the center of these behaviors. This is different than simply protecting other victims from young Black men – domestic violence and marital rape are very important issues, but that's not my concern here – we need to develop more sophisticated analyses of Black masculinity where young Black men can have true sexual freedom and not the illusion of it.

This example points to the unfinished, persisting and highly important intellectual and political project of reclaiming Black heterosexuality from a place of derogation. I argued in *Black Sexual Politics* that Black sexual stereotypes remain foundational to racism. Where is the attention within either queer theory and politics or African American theory and politics that directly engages these issues? Raising the profile of LGBTQ issues *within* African American communities and not just through abstractions is long overdue. Social media and the blogosphere are important here, but the question remains of how to link these venues to actual social institutions.

The second concerns the institution of marriage. Marriage has long been a major controversy for liberals and conservatives alike. While I am happy for and supportive of all the gay and lesbian couples who are finally allowed to marry – and there are a fair number of people of color in this population – the marriage equality victory does little to address longstanding efforts to promote marriage among African Americans. Many social scientists and pastors still think that Black people can marry themselves out of poverty – it's a values argument that claims that black values, especially the large number of single mothers and absent fathers, is the most important feature. Ironically, marriage equality and the victory of LGBTQ people in this arena does little to challenge the significance of marriage as an institution as a conduit for wealth and power in the US. This is notable, especially given the seeming swiftness of acceptance for LGBTQ issues that have been framed around the same heterosexual narrative of normal marriage and family (only with LGBTQ people in the center), which has long plagued African Americans. Neither queer theory nor African American social and political thought can grapple with these issues without a more comprehensive intersectional analysis.

As I said, influence is a hard thing to measure. In response to your question, I would pose a counter question – in what ways, if any, has African American social and political thought influenced queer theory and politics over the past several decades? Has it had the power to do so? Certainly queer theory appropriates the language of anti-racism, feminism and similar oppositional knowledge projects, often under the guise of intersectionality; yet what influence have these discourses had on the core questions and concerns of queer theory and queer politics? Stated differently, where can one find attention to the longstanding political agendas of African American politics for jobs and justice (the full title of the 1963 March on Washington that so energized a generation of civil rights activists) within queer theory and politics?

Sometimes advocates for racial justice and sexual justice compete by claiming their group oppression is more urgent and severe. How can an intersectional approach explain these tensions and suggest a way forward?

It's been clear for some time that competing in the Oppression Olympics constitutes a failing strategy for everyone save elites. Scholars and activists alike presented a compelling case that the relational thinking points toward new ways of engaging a changing world. Confronting power requires a sophisticated coalitional politics and intersectionality offers a theoretical base for thinking through such coalitions (Collins 2012, 230–243). The issue is less the integrity of intersectional argument than the more basic question of whether those who are in positions of power are listening.

I think that the way forward lies in committing to a specific population, understanding that the needs of that group can only be addressed adequately via coalition politics that are informed by intersectional analyses. The analysis that I have written about extensively elsewhere is not the issue. We have plenty of ideas. The issue is developing the political will and commitment to act. My choices have been clear. I have devoted my entire career focused on the question of educating a young Black public, recognizing that a social justice agenda for Black youth will remain inadequate without intersectional analyses and political coalitions that take on the hard work of making things happen. Black youth are at the front of the line of many important social issues, especially the shifting terrain of sexuality. Yet they are at the back of the line in receiving resources to grapple not only with their own sexual identifications, but also with the political implications of sexuality and inequality. It's time to turn that around.

Further reading

Battle, Juan, Cathy J. Cohen, Dorian Warren, Gerard Fergerson, and Suzette Audam. 2002. *Say It Loud, I'm Black and I'm Proud: Black Pride Survey 2000*. New York: The Policy Institute of the National Gay and Lesbian Task Force.

Boykin, Keith. 1996. *One More River to Cross: Black and Gay in America*. New York: Anchor Books.

Carbado, Devon W. 1999. "Introduction: Where and When Black Men Enter." Pp. 1–17 in *Black Men on Race, Gender, and Sexuality*, edited by D. W. Carbado. New York: New York University Press.

Cohen, Cathy J. 1999. *The Boundaries of Blackness: AIDS and the Breakdown of Black Politics*. Chicago: University of Chicago Press.

Collins, Patricia Hill. (1990) 2000. *Black Feminist Thought: Knowledge, Consciousness, and the Politics of Empowerment*. New York: Routledge.

—. 2004. *Black Sexual Politics: African Americans, Gender, and the New Racism*. New York: Routledge.

—. 2009. *Another Kind of Public Education: Race, Schools, the Media and Democratic Possibilities*. Boston: Beacon Press.

— . 2012. *On Intellectual Activism*. Philadelphia: Temple University Press.

Dent, Gina. 1992. "Black Pleasure, Black Joy: An Introduction." Pp. 1–19 in *Black Popular Culture*, edited by M. Wallace and G. Dent. Seattle: Bay Press.

Douglas, Kelly Brown. 1999. *Sexuality and the Black Church: A Womanist Perspective*. Maryknoll, N.Y.: Orbis.

Patton, Stacey. 2012. "Who's Afraid of Black Sexuality?" Pp. B6–9 in *Chronicle of Higher Education*, vol. 12/7/2012.

Rees, Dee. 2011. "Pariah." Focus Features.

Richen, Yoruba. 2013. "The New Black." California Newsreel.

chapter 4

Transforming the sex/gender/sexuality system

The construction of trans categories in the United States

Laurel Westbrook

In the last century, beliefs about sex, gender, and sexuality have changed dramatically. Part of these changes has been the increased knowledge and acceptance of practices that have been termed at various times *transsexual*, *transvestite*, *transgender*, *trans*, and *trans** (the asterisk a reference to a wildcard when searching digital archives). The construction of trans categories in the United States has the potential to trouble the assumed link between sex at birth and gender identity, expand the number of acceptable ways of doing gender, and denaturalize both sex and gender. Due to the intertwined nature of sex, gender, and sexuality, increased acceptance of trans people may also fundamentally alter understandings of sexuality.

Sex, gender, and sexuality are often conceived of as natural and biologically determined, but they are in fact socially constructed systems of classification, changing over time and varying across cultures. In its current conception in the United States, *sex* is the division of bodies into categories based on genitalia, hormones, and/or chromosomes. While bodies actually exist on a spectrum, only two categories are usually acknowledged (male and female). Those who are not easily classifiable as male or female are termed *intersex*, and doctors regularly encourage hormone treatments and surgeries to compel intersex bodies to fit into established binary sex categories

(Fausto-Sterling 2000). *Gender* refers to a set of behaviors and identities often assumed to be caused by, and to reflect, a person's sex (West and Zimmerman 1987). Males are expected to be masculine and identify as men, while females are supposed to be feminine and identify as women. Those who do not follow these norms are frequently met with social sanctions ranging from harassment and employment discrimination to sexual and physical assault (Harrison, Grant, and Herman 2012). Just as sex is believed to produce gender, gender presentation is thought to reflect sex. Those presenting as women are assumed to have vaginas and those presenting as men are expected to have penises. Finally, *sexuality* systems place people into status categories based on sexual desires, behaviors, and identity. These classification schemas can use a wide variety of criteria, ranging from the type of sexual acts in which one wants to engage (what Freud 1949/2000 termed *sexual aim*) to the type of person with whom you want to engage in them (aka *sexual object*). In the contemporary United States, sexual orientation is defined by sexual object, specifically the sex(es) a person is attracted to.

In current mainstream U.S. culture, sex, gender, and sexuality are mutually reinforcing. Each can be conceptualized as a social structure on its own, but they also work together as a larger system, as understandings of each are dependent on, and naturalized by, beliefs about the other two. Since "males" and "females" are thought to be biologically opposite (although they are actually much more similar than different), they are expected to behave in opposite ways (e.g. doing physical labor vs. care work) and are seen as natural sexual pairs. Similarly, understandings of sexuality are predicated on beliefs about sex and gender. If there were no sex categories, current understandings of sexual orientation would not exist, as the orientations heterosexual, homosexual, and bisexual are defined by one's own sex and the sex(es) of one's sexual partner(s). Gendered behaviors also support the existing sexuality system. While sexual orientation is defined by desire for certain sexed bodies, sex (genitals, hormones, and/or chromosomes) is not visible in everyday interactions. Instead, people signal membership in a sex category by *doing gender* (West and Zimmerman 1987). These gendered presentations of self thus indicate whom it is acceptable to sexually desire according to the expectations of one's sexual orientation; for example a heterosexual male desires people presenting as women, using their gender as a proxy for their femaleness.

The academic conception of sex, gender, and sexuality as *separate* systems is relatively new; in the past, they were seen as one and the same. Males were believed to be biologically programmed to behave in masculine ways and sexually desire women, while females were thought to be biologically programmed to behave in feminine ways and sexually desire men. Deviations from the norms of gender and sexuality were held to be caused by abnormalities of sex (Meyerowitz 2002). For example, homosexual desires were thought to be caused by a mismatch of sex and gender. Males who desired men were deemed to be gender "inverts"—male bodied people with the minds of women—since part of what is was to be a woman was to desire men. Similarly, females attracted to women were imagined to be men on the inside.

As medical practitioners studied so-called deviants, the belief that gender is determined by sex shifted. Doctors puzzling through how to categorize and "treat" intersex people in the 1950s began to use *gender* to describe a set of masculine and feminine *behaviors* that were separate from biological sex (Meyerowitz 2002). During this same time period, medical professionals who were working with those who came be to

　　　　　　　　　　　　　　　　　　　　　　　　　　Laurel Westbrook

known as *transsexuals* furthered the analytic distinction between sex and gender. The acknowledgement and acceptance of males who identified as women and females who identified as men encouraged a theorization that sex did not determine gender. This acknowledgement came at a price, however, as doctors medicalized this "mismatch" of sex and gender, diagnosing trans people as "sick" and in need of "treatment."

In their attempts at self-legitimization, those labeled as deviants also pushed for distinguishing between sex, gender, and sexuality, often with dire consequences for the more marginalized members of their communities. In an attempt to reduce the stigma around homosexuality, many gay and lesbian organizations and bars became hostile towards gender non-conforming people. As the gay and lesbian rights movement became more mainstream during the 1970s and 80s, feminine males and masculine females were pushed out of gay and lesbian communities (Denny 2006; Valentine 2007). Similarly, activists in transsexual communities worked to distance themselves from the stigma of homosexuality, frequently emphasizing their heterosexual identities (Meyerowitz 2002), and many cross-dressing organizations explicitly banned gay men from participating (Denny 2006). Combined with shifts in medical understandings, these practices of social distancing have unlinked gender and sexual nonconformity, constructed sex, gender, and sexuality as separate, and parsed out identities and practices that would all have previously been seen as forms of "gender inversion."

The understanding of sex, gender, and sexuality as three distinct systems is not universal, however, and many Americans still assume a biological and causal relationship between them. While it was once thought that biology made all females behave in feminine ways and desire males, many now believe, for example, that biology causes some females to identify as men and/or to desire females. Moreover, while there has been increased acceptance of trans people and of gay men and lesbians, most males are still assumed to be masculine and desire females, and most females are still expected to be feminine and partner with males. Vestiges of gender inversion theory remain, as people imagine that masculine women are lesbians and feminine men are gay. Thus, the academic distinctions detailed here have not been fully incorporated into the larger culture and sex, gender, and sexuality are still inextricably intertwined.

Transforming sex and gender categories

Mainstream culture in the United States has become gradually more supportive of trans people. In 2010 "actual or perceived gender identity" was added as a protected category in federal hate crime legislation, and in 2014 the Justice Department announced that trans people would be protected from workplace discrimination under Title VII of the federal Civil Rights Act. The 2010s have also seen a significant rise in trans characters on television and movies, as well as increased coverage of trans people in the news, including a *TIME* magazine cover article in 2014 featuring an interview with trans actress and activist Laverne Cox and headlined "The Transgender Tipping Point" and the 2015 *Vanity Fair* cover shoot, interview, and photo spread of Olympic gold medalist Caitlyn Jenner. As trans people publicly challenge some of the dominant understandings of sex and gender, this increased social acceptance is likely to alter the sex and gender systems.

Changing sex

Although people have always done gender in non-normative ways, trans categories have not always existed. Like all categories of thought, trans categories arose at particular cultural moments. The term *transsexual* did not come into use as meaning someone who identified as a sex other than that they were assigned at birth until 1949 and it did not widely enter the popular imagination until Christine Jorgensen's sex reassignment surgery in 1952. While Jorgensen was not the first person to undergo such surgeries, she was the first to become widely known in the United States. Meyerowitz (2002) attributes Jorgensen's fame to a number of factors, including being white, normatively attractive, and feminine and the fact that, at the time, the U.S. was particularly obsessed with the power of science and WWII-induced questions about the proper roles of men and women. This allowed for transsexuality to emerge in the larger cultural consciousness in a way that was not as possible earlier in the century. Jorgensen's fame then informed others of the social category and the possibility of body modifications and led to discussions about the relationship between sex, gender, and sexuality. Her case was contentious, as some celebrated, and others condemned, her. Much of the anxiety around her centered on sexuality, as she called into question the previously easy division of people in the category of heterosexual or homosexual.

While media coverage of Jorgensen made the general public aware of the possibility of being transsexual, access to body modification was tightly regulated by doctors. Hormone treatments and surgeries were usually only accessible through university clinics and to qualify for surgery, patients had to conform to dominant norms around gender and sexuality (Denny 2006). For example, after surgery, transsexual people were expected to be highly gender conforming and heterosexual; due to stigma around homosexual desires, transsexual patients were supposed to be non-sexual before surgery. Many clinics also required that transsexual patients not socialize with other transsexual men or women, hold a transsexual identity, or tell people about their transition. Doctors defined transsexual as a "liminal state" rather than an identity; it was what you were as you moved from one clear sex category to "the other."

Thus, while medical understandings of transsexuality shifted beliefs about sex and gender in some ways, others remained firmly in place. Doctors introduced the idea that people can, with the help of medical technology, change sex, and questioned the necessity that all people labeled male at birth identify as men and all people labeled female at birth identify as women. However, this change in understandings around the mutability of sex was accompanied by a belief that there were only two genders and only two sexes and that those who identified with a gender that did not "match" their sex should alter their bodies to conform to the expectation that gender reflects genitals. In subsequent years, some activists have rejected this medical model, and the term transsexual, as pathologizing.

Redoing gender

Early sex reassignment surgeries were often unsuccessful, extraordinarily painful, and damaged or destroyed sexual response. In the early 1980s, following academic publications arguing that sex reassignment operations were ineffective, university-funded clinics closed and for-profit facilities quickly took their place (Denny 2006). With the demise of the university-run gender clinics, denial of a trans identity and disassociation from other trans people were no longer prerequisites for access to medical technologies. Thus, trans community organizing became easier. Starting in the early 1990s, members of these communities coined a new term for themselves, and all others who did gender differently from the norm—the term *transgender* (Meyerowitz 2002).

The most accepted history of the term *transgender* is that Virginia Prince invented it as an alternative to the then-dominant terms *transsexual* and *transvestite*. It is said that she wanted *transgenderist* to describe someone who wanted to change gender but not have sex reassignment surgery. However, transgender was quickly adopted as an umbrella category that included transsexual, transvestite, transgenderist and other non-normative gender practices after Leslie Feinberg used it that way in *Transgender Liberation* (1992). This history is contested, however. Williams (2014) critiques what she terms the "Virginia Prince Fountainhead Narrative" and argues that many people before Prince used *transgenderism*, *transgendered*, and *transgender* to describe trans practices.

Regardless of who first used it, in the early 1990s in the United States trans people began using transgender as a way to unify a diverse population of people engaged in non-normative gender practices. Public knowledge of this new category *transgender* began to grow exponentially, aided by activist groups and the growing popularity of the internet (Whittle 1998). Part of this growth was trans people speaking publicly about themselves, including an increasingly vocal group of trans activists naming themselves, describing how they have been oppressed, and arguing for the value of trans people (Stryker 2008). Another part of this growth came from increased media attention to trans people, both in the news media and in fictional representations. By 1995, the use of transgender as an umbrella category for those who identified as a sex and/or gender other than the one they were assigned at birth was widespread.

Transgender as an umbrella category encompasses a wide variety of ways of doing gender. Unlike transsexual, a desire for body modification is not a prerequisite for category membership. Instead, transgender has been defined as "all persons who cross traditional gender boundaries" (e.g. Green 1994: 9). Since it is said to include all non-normative gender practices, transgender as a category is "almost infinitely elastic" (Valentine 2007: 39). Thus, the category includes a number of previously unnamed gender practices, making these ways of doing gender knowable and those who do them recognizable within the gender system (Westbrook 2010). This recognition moves them from what Judith Butler (1993) terms *abject* (not seen as human) into a realm of subjects eligible for social acknowledgement and rights.

As with all identity categories, trans categories have been intensely debated by those under their purview. Valentine (2007) has detailed how, in the struggle for the right to identify as transgender, many other identities are denied or ignored. Not everyone who identifies as a sex and/or gender other than what they were labeled at birth uses the term transgender or trans. In the 1990s, Valentine interviewed "male-bodied feminine people" who identified simultaneously as "gay," "women," and "femme queens." These people were often young, poor, urban, and of color (mainly black and/or Latino). For these individuals, gender and sexuality were not as separate as academics and transgender activists have posited. However, Valentine found that, while they did not identify as transgender, they were nevertheless named as such by leaders in the LGBT community and service providers. By arguing that people are transgender even when they do not identify as such, activists and academics treat transgender as a natural category (Westbrook 2010).

The usage of trans terms is constantly changing. Previous terms such as *transvestite*, *transgenderist*, *transgendered*, and *tranny*, which were used by academics and community members alike well into the 2000s, have fallen out of favor (GLAAD 2014); their use is now considered by some to be a sign of transphobia (disdain for trans people). Similarly, due to controversies over whether *transgender*, with its terminological focus on "gender," was inclusive enough, many people began to instead use *trans*. Some have taken this a step further, using *trans** as the umbrella term. These attempts at expanding the umbrella may actually reduce the legibility of trans ways of being gendered or sexed, as the terms themselves are difficult to search on the internet. While a search for "transgender" will immediately produce results on those whose sex and/or gender does not align with that assigned to them at birth, an internet search for "trans" or "trans*" will generate a much more diverse set of results, including translation websites, the homepage of Trans-Siberian Orchestra, and information on trans fats. As evidenced by the history detailed here, trans terms have changed over time and are likely to continue to change in the future.

The rise of the term transgender has spawned a new term—*cisgender*. *Cis* is the antonym of the Latin prefix *trans*, and *cisgender* refers to people who identify as the same sex and gender that they were assigned a birth. Before the advent of *cisgender*, the state of being not transgender was often left linguistically unmarked. Things that are unmarked are generally considered "normal," while those that are marked are seen as unusual. Having both trans and cis be marked with their own term challenges the assumed normalcy of one (cisgender) over the other (transgender).

Many activists and academics once thought that trans categories and practices would "undo" gender—i.e. dismantle or do away with the sex/gender/sexuality system—by highlighting the social, rather than biological, origins of gender norms and categories. However, rather than "undoing" gender, trans categories have, instead, "redone" it (West and Zimmerman 2009). This is not to argue that conceptions of *trans* or *transgender* do not challenge aspects of the current sex and gender systems. Trans categories have altered the sex and gender systems by introducing the ideas that sex and gender are changeable, gender identities and practices can be diverse and non-binary, and gender presentation and sexed embodiment do not have to "match." However, while they do challenge current ways of doing gender, they do not challenge the idea of *gender*—the belief that all people fit into a gender category and that behaviors reflect gender identity (Westbrook 2010). With transgender, *gender* is still posited as central to a person's identity and a vital part of social interactions. Indeed, with the promotion of preferred pronouns and diverse gender options on forms, gender may have become even more central to people's understandings of themselves and others.

Enduring inequality

Although trans people are increasingly acknowledged socially and legally, they still experience high levels of discrimination and violence. Much of this is linked to fears around sexuality. As Westbrook and Schilt (2014) demonstrate, at the national, state, and local levels, governments have been hesitant to extend antidiscrimination protections to trans people for fear that such legislation will allow trans women (whom legislators often conceive of as "really" male) access to "women's" only spaces such as restrooms and locker rooms. This fear comes from a belief that all male bodies are potentially inclined towards, and capable of, sexual assault of females and that all female bodies are vulnerable to such assaults when there are no males around to protect them. Although rooted in false assumptions that perpetuate gender inequality, such fears have been effective in preventing the inclusion of trans people in antidiscrimination legislation. Similarly, as Schilt and Westbrook (2009) show, much of the fatal violence experienced by trans people is also related to fears around sexuality. Most of the trans people killed in the U.S. are trans women and a majority of those are killed by cisgender men with whom they have had sexual relations. In these sexual interactions, it seems that the cisgender men either become aware of, or become uncomfortable with, the trans women's trans status and move from seeing the trans women as women to seeing them as "really" male. Thus, in their minds, the relationship moves from heterosexual to homosexual. Some of these men react with violence, as they fear being stigmatized as homosexual. Hence, the intertwined nature of sex, gender, and sexuality has resulted in discrimination and violence against trans people.

Transforming sexuality

Rising acceptance of trans people and categories and the related significant shifts in understandings of sex and gender may also produce changes in beliefs about sexuality, thereby reducing discrimination and violence. Thus far, the idea of trans people being sexually involved with anyone has not been accepted in mainstream culture. Like previous decades where gay or lesbian television and movie characters were not shown in sexual relationships, mainstream media has shied away from depicting trans people in romantic situations (Abbott 2013). This lack of cultural depiction is likely to perpetuate fears around what is now termed *transsexualities*, meaning trans people's sexual desires, behaviors, and identities. For a long time, academics did not focus on transsexualities, with the exception of studying sexually "risky" behavior (Pfeffer 2014a), such as sex work and sex with/by drug users. Doctors who worked with trans people assumed that they hated the body they were born with and, thus, were asexual unless they had surgically altered their genitals (Cromwell 2006). This silence around transsexualities is slowly changing, as evidenced by the *Journal of Homosexuality*'s 2014 special issue "Making Space for Trans Sexualities." In previous eras, shifting academic understandings, such as a move from seeing trans people as sick deviants to seeing trans as a legitimate gender identity, have resulted in changes in the larger culture. Extrapolating from this, there is potential for a number of possible changes in cultural understandings of sexuality.

As the number of acceptable ways of being sexed and gendered expand, so may the number of sexual orientation categories. Currently, there are no widely used terms for those who are attracted to trans people, except for the derogatory *tranny chaser* which stigmatizes such desire as a fetish (Tompkins 2014). Some have suggested *transamorous* or *transsensual* as terms that would legitimate and make legible such desires. We might also conceive of a system where people identify as *transsexual* (desiring trans people), *cis-sexual* (desiring cis people), or *pansexual* (desiring all genders). If such sexual orientation categories became more widespread, it would fundamentally alter dominant beliefs about sexuality.

In the current sexuality system, both trans people and their partners have often turned to *queer* as the label that best encapsulates their desires. In her interviews with cis women partners of trans men, Pfeffer (2014b) finds that, while these relationships are regularly "read" as straight, many identify as queer, in part because there is no other language to describe their identities and desires. Similarly, Kuper, Nussbaum, and Mustanski (2012) find that, in their sample of trans people, the most common gender identity was *genderqueer* and the two most common sexual orientations were *pansexual* and *queer*. This shift away from heterosexuality and homosexuality is the logical outcome of a genderqueer identity, since heterosexuality and homosexuality are dependent on "man" and "woman" as gender identities and cannot articulate desires by or for a genderqueer person. As the growing acceptance of trans categories and practices expands the possible ways of doing gender to include non-binary identities such as genderqueer, queer as a sexual identity category meaning attraction to multiple genders may become more widespread.

In addition to expanding the number of acceptable ways of doing gender and sexuality, trans categories also have the potential to unlink the assumed causal relationship between sex and gender. In everyday interactions, one's gender presentation is imagined to reflect one's genitals. The category *transsexual* calls into question the idea that sex at birth determines one's gender identity. However, the reverse relationship has remained unquestioned through the belief that all trans people desire surgeries to make their sex and gender "match." Currently, a fixed and knowable identity as either a man or a woman is needed for access to body modification. Those identified as cisgender women can access breast implants, vaginal tightening, and labia reductions with relative ease (Davis 2002), just as cisgender men can have surgery to reduce the size of their chests and increase the size of their testicles, as those surgeries assist in sex and gender conformity. Similarly, a clear identity as a trans *man* or trans *woman* facilitates access to body modification, as long as those modifications will increase their conformity to expectations of sex and gender. The shift towards embracing trans categories and identities may loosen the restrictions on access to body modifications for trans people, thus allowing for more "mixed" sexed embodiments. As more and more trans people decide whether to pursue surgical body modification at all or to engage in some available modifications but not others, the assumed link between sex and gender may change and a separate "sex identity" and "gender identity" may become acceptable, such that one could identify as both male and a woman. This would set the stage for a reconceptualization of attraction, distinguishing between attraction to gender presentation (desiring masculine people and/or feminine people and/or androgynous people, etc.), sex (desiring male bodies and/or female bodies and/or intersex bodies), and gender identity (being attracted to those who identify as men and/or women and/or trans and/or genderqueer). The unlinking of sex and gender would also fundamentally shift one of the premises on which the current sexuality system rests—that one can use gender presentation as a proxy for sexed embodiment.

Coming full circle, this may alter the current imperative within the gender system that one signals sex with gender, such that people may feel free to wear dresses because they enjoy them, rather than to indicate the presence of a vagina.

In Western thought, we tend to construct our classification systems as a set of binaries—you are either gay or straight, a man or a woman, or cisgender or transgender—rather than as a spectrum that, for example, acknowledges a diversity of sexual and gendered practices that may also change over the life course. As trans categories allow for more varied presentations of gendered and sexed selves, the assumption that sexuality is binary and fixed over the life course may change. The existence of trans people might problematize the belief that sexual orientation is stable over the life course, as a trans person's sexual orientation may change as their gender identity does. Similarly, the sex and/or gender transition of a romantic partner can significantly disrupt the understanding of sexual orientation as innate and fixed, as, if the relationship continues after the transition, the label put on the relationship would change from, for example, heterosexual to homosexual or queer (Sanger 2007).

Due to the intertwined nature of sex, gender, and sexuality, the transformation of one results in changes in the others. Just as trans categories have caused a redoing of understandings of sex and gender, over time they are likely to redo sexuality. As long as U.S. culture tends to emphasize sex, gender, and sexuality as central to the understanding of the self and vital to interactions with others, none of these systems will be "undone." But, as they move to accept those previously understood as "deviant," these systems will be transformed, possibly expanding sex categories beyond male and female, increasing gender identities beyond man and woman, and embracing sexual orientations beyond heterosexual and homosexual.

References

Abbott, Traci. 2013. "The Trans/Romance Dilemma in Transamerica and Other Films." *The Journal of American Culture* 36(1):32–41.

Butler, Judith. 1993. *Bodies That Matter: On the Discursive Limits of Sex*. New York: Routledge.

Cromwell, Jason. 2006. "Queering the Binaries: Transsituated Identities, Bodies, and Sexualities." In *The Transgender Studies Reader*, Susan Stryker and Stephen Whittle, eds. New York: Routledge.

Davis, Simone. 2002. "Loose Lips Sink Ships."*Feminist Studies* 28(1):7–35.

Denny, Dallas. 2006. "Transgender Communities of the United States in the Late Twentieth Century." In *Transgender Rights*, Paisley Currah, Richard Juang, and Shannon Minter, eds. Minneapolis: University of Minnesota Press.

Fausto-Sterling, Anne. 2000. *Sexing the Body: Gender Politics and the Construction of Sexuality*. New York: Basic Books.

Feinberg, Leslie. 1992. *Transgender Liberation: A Movement Whose Time Has Come*. New York: World View Forum.

Freud, Sigmund. 1949/2000. *Three Essays on the Theory of Sexuality*, translated by James Strachey. New York: Basic Books.

GLAAD. 2014. GLAAD Media Reference Guide—Transgender Issues. www.glaad.org/reference/transgender.

Green, James. 1994. "What is transgender?" *FTM Newsletter* July:9.

Harrison, Jack, Jaime Grant, and Jody L. Herman. 2012. "A Gender Not Listed Here: Gender-queers, Gender Rebels, and OtherWise in the National Transgender Discrimination Survey." *LGBTQ Public Policy Journal at the Harvard Kennedy School* 2(1):13–24.

Kuper, Laura, Robin Nussbaum, and Brian Mustanski. 2012. "Exploring the Diversity of Gender and Sexual Orientation Identities in an Online Sample of Transgender Individuals." *Journal of Sex Research* 49(2–3):244–54.

Meyerowitz, Joanne. 2002. *How Sex Changed: A History of Transsexuality in the United States.* Cambridge, MA: Harvard University Press.

Pfeffer, Carla. 2014a. "Making Space for Trans Sexualities." *Journal of Homosexuality* 61(5):597–604.

—. 2014b. "'I Don't Like Passing as a Straight Woman': Queer Negotiations of Identity and Social Group Membership." *American Journal of Sociology* 120(1):1–44.

Sanger, Tam. 2007. "Queer(y)ing Gender and Sexuality: Transpeople's Lived Experiences and Intimate Partnerships." In *Feeling Queer or Queer Feelings?: Radical Approaches to Counselling Sex, Sexualities and Genders*, Lyndsey Moon, ed. New York: Routledge.

Schilt, Kristen and Laurel Westbrook. 2009. "Doing Gender, Doing Heteronormativity: 'Gender Normals,' Transgender People, and the Social Maintenance of Heterosexuality." *Gender & Society* 23(4):440–64.

Stryker, Susan. 2008. *Transgender History.* Seattle: Seal Press.

Tompkins, Avery. 2014. "'There's No Chasing Involved': Cis/Trans Relationships, 'Tranny Chasers,' and the Future of a Sex-Positive Trans Politics." *Journal of Homosexuality* 61(5):766–80.

Valentine, David. 2007. *Imagining Transgender: An Ethnography of a Category.* Durham, NC: Duke University Press.

West, Candace and Don Zimmerman. 1987. "Doing Gender." *Gender & Society* 1(2):125–51.

—. 2009. "Accounting for Doing Gender." *Gender & Society* 23(1):112–22.

Westbrook, Laurel. 2010. "Becoming Knowably Gendered: The Production of Transgender Possibilities in the Mass and Alternative Press." In *Transgender Identities: Towards A Social Analysis Of Gender Diversity*, Sally Hines and Tam Sanger, eds. New York: Routledge.

Westbrook, Laurel and Kristen Schilt. 2014. "Doing Gender, Determining Gender Transgender People, Gender Panics, and the Maintenance of the Sex/Gender/Sexuality System." *Gender & Society* 28(1):32–57.

Whittle, Stephen. 1998. "The Trans-Cyberian Mail Way." *Social & Legal Studies* 7(3):389–408.

Williams, Cristan. 2014. "Transgender." *TSQ: Transgender Studies Quarterly* 1(1–2):232–34.

chapter 5

The social construction of sexuality

Interview with Jeffrey Weeks

Jeffrey Weeks is the author of numerous articles and some twenty books. These include *Coming Out* (1977), *Sex, Politics and Society* (1981), *Sexuality and its Discontents* (1985), *Sexuality* (1986/2003), *Between the Acts* (with Kevin Porter, 1990/1998), *Invented Moralities* (1995), *Making Sexual History* (2000), *Same Sex Intimacies* (with Brian Heaphy and Catherine Donovan, 2001), and *Sexualities and Society: A Reader* (edited with Janet Holland and Matthew Waites, 2003). He is Professor Emeritus at London's South Bank University, where he was executive dean of the Faculty of Arts and Human Sciences.

I understand that you were involved in the lesbian and gay movement in Britain in the 1970s. Could you talk about this?

I became involved in the Gay Liberation Front (GLF) in London in November 1970, soon after it had started. Its first base was at the London School of Economics (LSE), and it so happened that I had started work at the School the previous month, in my first academic job as a researcher. So from the beginning my political involvement in the movement and my career were inextricably intertwined – certainly to the detriment of what passed for my career at first.

I had in fact been out for the previous three or four years, had flirted with the London scene, and had accumulated a small, tightly knit group of gay friends. I was also vaguely on the political left, but somewhat detached from its mainstream activities largely because I felt unwelcome because of my sexuality. There seemed to be two separate worlds, that of my still largely secret personal hopes and desires, and the public worlds of ideology and great events. My involvement in gay liberation changed that. For the first time I began to see how the private and the public, the sexual and the political, the everyday and grand historic processes could be brought together. It literally changed my life: I met new friends, I became involved with my first long-term lover, and I went through an ideological revolution which has marked me to this day. I became heavily involved in gay politics for the rest of the 1970s, especially as an editor of *Gay Left* which, in the late 1970s, became for a while a leading forum for gay theory and analysis. Edmund White, at the end of *The Beautiful Room is Empty*, talks about how Stonewall was "Our Bastille Day . . . the turning point of our lives." That's what my immersion in gay liberation felt like to me.

How did your political involvement influence your academic work?

My involvement in the gay movement completely changed the direction of my academic work. When I got involved in GLF I had just moved to the LSE after a not very successful year teaching in a school. The school teaching in turn had been a hurried escape from my first attempt at postgraduate work, where I had felt lonely and isolated. I went to the LSE in the hope that I would resume my studies in a more congenial atmosphere (and I did in fact complete my master's dissertation whilst I was there – a study of early-twentieth-century socialist and pluralist thought, themes which in a strange, roundabout way came to influence my later writings on sexuality). I soon, however, became heavily involved in the theoretical issues thrown up by gay liberation, especially the question of what was homosexuality, why was it so oppressed, what sort of politics were necessary to transform the situation, and so on. As a trained historian I naturally began exploring the historical context, and as someone who had already researched into the political and moral debates of the late nineteenth century I became very interested in the links between early (homo-) sexual politics in Britain – especially the work of people like Edward Carpenter, John Addingtom Symonds and the pioneering sexologist, Havelock Ellis – and broader radical politics. My first book was written with Sheila Rowbotham, and called *Socialism and the New Life: The Personal and Sexual Politics of Edward Carpenter and Havelock Ellis* (1977) – and I wrote the section on Ellis, who has continued to fascinate me ever since. He says somewhere that his strategy was to write about the most outrageously (for the time) controversial issues around sexuality in a calm, rational, matter-of-fact style, as if everything was straightforward and perfectly normal. I have found this a very useful tactic myself over the past thirty years or so.

Anyway, this little book contains the germs of much of what I was to write on sexuality in *Coming Out, Sex, Politics and Society*, and *Sexuality and its Discontents* – what I later described as my "informal trilogy." The first traces the evolution of recognizably modern homosexual identities and ways of life from the nineteenth century; the second explores the wider social and political context of the regulation of sexuality in Britain; the third explores the ways in which sexuality became the object of would-be scientific attention, how sexology in particular can be said to have contributed to the "invention" of sexuality as a "continent of knowledge" – and how it was resisted through the emergence of grassroots knowledges.

In these brief descriptions you can see, I think, how my awareness of the significance of the new sexual movements (feminism as well as lesbian and gay politics) of the 1970s was influencing my thinking. My sense of the ways in which gay liberation had transformed the meanings of contemporary gay identities made me ask whether we could see similar shifts in meanings and identities in the past. My sense that you could not understand what was happening today with regard to homosexuality without putting it in the wider context of sexuality (and gender) led me to explore the changes over time. And my growing perception of the vital role of ideas and values pushed me into a study of the role of sexology as a science of desire.

Was it risky in the 1970s for an academic in Britain to study sexuality and homosexuality?

Writing about sex, Ken Plummer has written, makes you morally dubious, and it certainly felt like that for me in the 1970s and into the 1980s. I was gainfully employed at the LSE until 1977, but the job had nothing to do with sexuality – officially at least, though I had been able to do research on Havelock Ellis and for *Coming Out* during this period. Then I had a period of unemployment. This was followed by a year working with Ken Plummer and Mary McIntosh at the University of Essex, which had a liberal reputation, especially in the Sociology Department, which was at the cutting edge of radical theory. This was an immensely creative period, where we collectively refined our ideas of what became known as "social constructionism" – the main collective product was *The Making of the Modern Homosexual*, edited by Ken Plummer, and published in 1981. Unfortunately that intellectual idyll soon came to an end: when the Conservative Party came to power in 1979 they cut the funding of the Social Science Research Council, which in turn cut my funding, and I was unemployed again. So you could certainly say that my career was pretty rocky in the 1970s, and my writing about homosexuality certainly did not help. In fact I did not get a permanent and senior academic appointment until 1990, when I got the chair in social relations at the University of the West of England. Three things helped me then. First, by then I had a long list of publications, not all on sexuality, and was clearly qualified. Second, I had spent four years in academic administration and policy-making in an accreditation body, and was almost respectable. And finally, by a tragic irony, writing about sexuality was itself less morally dubious now because of the AIDS crisis. Indeed, I found myself in demand as an expert on sexuality and was again able to obtain funding from the same research council that had truncated my earlier career.

Your book, Coming Out, *was important in creating a new kind of history and sociology of homosexuality. Can you talk about how your view of homosexuality was different?*

When I first conceived of *Coming Out* in the early 1970s I wanted, in a sense, to find precursors for myself and my generation: I wanted to trace a history of oppression and resistance which would be *our* history. Unfortunately, once I began the research I found that the task was not that easy. First of all the existing literature assumed there was a continuity of experience and feeling – but a cursory look showed that homosexual life was immensely varied throughout history, and even across the 200 years or so that I was limiting myself to. Second, I looked for traces of a common identity through history – and couldn't find it. There were many different homosexualities, not a unitary homosexuality. Third, I was interested in how homosexuality was a female as well as male phenomenon – but women were largely absent from existing histories.

And fourth, I assumed that throughout history there would be a continuity of understandings of what homosexuality was – and there wasn't. On the contrary, the very idea of homosexuality as a distinct category did not exist until the late nineteenth century, and way into the twentieth century it was a very vague concept (alongside, it has to be said, the concept of heterosexuality). So I had to start again.

Luckily I had read Mary McIntosh's important essay on "The Homosexual Role," originally published in 1968, and this proved to be a revelation. She basically saw homosexuality as a social categorization that had a history worth exploring. She also demonstrated that this categorization was a specific historical pattern – based on the assumption that homosexuality was a characteristic of a certain type of person – that differed from other known patterns, where, for example, homosexuality might be seen as a gender inversion or as an aspect of the rites of passage of young boys. It wasn't even certain that the typical homosexual role that she described exhausted the ways we understood or lived homosexuality in our complex modern societies. Clearly the way we understood homosexuality – basically as the core of a particular type of identity that in the early 1970s was forcibly asserting itself through gay liberation – was a deeply historical phenomenon that had been, in a phrase that was subsequently to become notorious, "socially constructed." Here was a historical research agenda, and a theoretical debate, that I eagerly engaged with, and *Coming Out* was the first major product of my research.

Other people I got to know or know of at this time helped the evolution of my ideas: Ken Plummer, who was practically creating from scratch a sociology of sexuality in Britain by writing about sexual stigma; William Simon and John Gagnon, who talked about the need that must have existed at an unspecified period to "invent" sexuality, and explained the importance of sexual scripts; Randolph Trumbach, who was exploring homosexuality in eighteenth-century London; Jonathan Ned Katz, who was inventing gay American history single-handedly; Carroll Smith-Rosenberg, who was studying female friendship; Judith Walkowitz, who was exploring the categorization of the female prostitute in ways very similar to the way in which I was exploring the categorization of "the homosexual"; all these and others stimulated an intellectual excitement that I have rarely again encountered. And all this, I must note, came long before any of us encountered the work of Michel Foucault on sexuality. I had already completed *Coming Out* before I read the first volume of Foucault's *The History of Sexuality*. His work was certainly to influence mine, but my long-term preoccupations were already firmed up by the mid-1970s. And central to those preoccupations was, as I saw it, the need to develop a non-essentialist understanding of homosexuality (and indeed of sexuality generally), which tried to understand same-sex desires and practices in their real social and historical context; which saw all sexual identities (like indeed all identities) as historical contructs (even "fictions," as I subsequently argued); and which saw sexuality as a mobile field of power relation, shaped by a complex history and one in which we, the sexually marginalized, were increasingly becoming strategic actors. For the point of all this history, sociology, anthropology and theory was not simply to understand the world of sexuality, but to change it.

What do you mean by the idea that the homosexual came into existence some time in the late nineteenth century? And what social factors played a key role in creating this new sexual identity?

Mary McIntosh and Randolph Trumbach had argued that the early eighteenth century had been a key moment in the evolution of ideas of the homosexual as a distinct type of being. Whilst not disputing their evidence, I was more intrigued by what I saw happening in the late nineteenth century. This was the period when homosexually inclined writers like Ulrichs, Kertbeny (who invented the term homosexuality), Symonds, and Carpenter began to try to describe the "turning," "invert," "homosexual," as a person with feelings, sensitivities, hopes and desires – as a real, living, breathing, loving person, not a sinner or pervert; when the new breed of sexologists, such as Krafft-Ebing, Ellis, Hirschfeld and later Freud, tried to make sense of this phenomenon, and began to theorize (inconclusively, it goes beyond saying) the causes of same-sex attraction, and the social consequences of accepting them; when complex subcultures, of women as well as men, in London, Paris, Berlin, New York, began to emerge in the public eye (not least through scandals, of which the agonies of Oscar Wilde became the most notorious); and also the period which saw the first dawnings of homophile groupings seeking to change the law and create a more tolerant climate. The work of Magnus Hirschfeld in Germany was the most internationally famous of these groupings but there were smaller echoes elsewhere, including in Britain and the USA (as myself and Jonathan Katz respectively were able to demonstrate).

In other words, by the late nineteenth century there was a distinctive categorization, set of identities, ways of life, and political responses that certainly built on what had gone before, since at least the eighteenth century, but which had distinctive elements that were to come to full flowering only in the course of the next hundred years. I think in those early years I probably overemphasized the extent of the changes of the 1880s and 1890s. The process was uneven and complex, and was far from being universal. Recent studies have shown that into the 1950s and 1960s distinctive homosexual identities were by no means universally accepted (if indeed they are today). But the crucial point is that the late nineteenth century was when all this really got going.

Why? I am averse to monocausal explanations, such as "the triumph of capitalism" or whatever. But we can point to key aspects. Urbanization in the nineteenth century created new spaces of both anonymity and intimacy, where alternative ways of life away from the home and the closed communities of rural life could be explored, mainly by men in the first instance, but increasingly too by women. New forms of communication allowed an easier transmission of ideas, concepts, and identities. The writings of the early sexologists clearly show the ways in which homosexual meanings were constructed in dialogue between the new social actors and the self-styled experts – in the clinics, the prisons, but also in the new text books. Self-identified "third sexers" did not passively imbibe the sexologists' ideas. They often gave the new concepts to the specialists and then saw them circulated and re-circulated as scientific definitions for all to borrow and amend. Perhaps overarching all these developments was the sharper institutionalization of heterosexuality within the family and culture generally, which in a real sense required the creation of "the pervert" as the execrated Other, the measure against which normality could be judged. But this in turn provoked a sense of self assertion and identity amongst this new "species," as Foucault put it, that was now emerging. The invention of the homosexual was not a deliberate act; it was classically over-determined in that there were many potential factors leading to the rise of the modern homosexual. And as I have said already, to talk about such a being does not exhaust the homosexual experience, then or now. But that something new happened in the nineteenth century still seems to me undeniable; just as something new happened in same-sex life in the 1970s.

What are the key changes in the meaning of homosexuality since the nineteenth century?

Sometime it's easy to forget when faced by continuing bigotry (not least from religions and some state forms) and even violent hate how far we have come since the nineteenth century, and especially since the 1970s. We no longer have to assert a precarious identity; we have a proliferation of possible subject positions we can identify with, including identity positions – for example as "queer" – which happily negate the very value of identity. In most Western societies toleration and acceptance have become the norm, even as it is frequently breached. Civil rights and equality under the law are largely institutionalized. Most European countries, and a number of other states (Canada, Australia and New Zealand) have recognized same-sex partnerships and even marriage, and increasingly this includes equal parenting and adoption rights. In Britain, so long a laggard on these issues, civil partnerships came into force in 2005 that are little different from marriage, even if the word "marriage" is not used: the only difference is that, unlike marriage, same-sex unions do not require sexual consummation to make them legal. Even in the United States, where same-sex marriage is most divisive and contested, the heat of the battle obscures the steady progress towards equality and acceptance of lesbian and gay life choices in everyday life. On a global scale there are huge variations in attitudes, beliefs, and behaviours. But there are increasing commonalities. Every major city of the world now has elaborate subcultures and varied sexual identities. Even as HIV/AIDS threatened to wipe out the gains of the past couple of generations, there has been a new social recognition of the role of lesbians and gay men in contemporary societies – what Dennis Altman called "legitimization through disaster."

So what is homosexuality today: a perversion, an inversion, a sickness, a natural anomaly, an orientation, a preference, a lifestyle, a performance, a universal potentiality, a minority experience, a genetic variation, a product of a particular gay brain? It is all and none of these things in an ever-changing sexual world because someone, somewhere, believes in one or more of these descriptions, and sometimes tries to act on that basis. For me, homosexuality is a range of possibilities, shadowed by the heterosexual assumptions which still govern much of our thought and social organization, but offering, as Foucault once said, the opportunities for creative life. The great achievement of the past thirty-five years since Stonewall is that so many people have seized those opportunities to make meaningful lives for themselves.

Do you see any major differences between the US and Britain with regard to the meaning and social status of homosexuality?

The USA has always been a model for many of us in Europe as the pioneer of modern gay politics and culture. It has had a vibrancy and creativity that has been enormously encouraging and has shown us what can be achieved in a pluralist culture. But looking back over the past few decades, it is hard now not to think that more has been

Interview with Jeffrey Weeks

achieved in Europe in terms of formal recognition of equal citizenship than in the USA. Just take the question of same-sex partnership rights as an example. Since Denmark pioneered the process in 1989, most European countries have passed legislation with relatively little fuss. Here in Britain the legislation went through with the support even of the opposition Conservative Party, which less than twenty years earlier had banned the "promotion of homosexuality." And the reason for that difference is quite simple: lesbian and gay rights have not been trapped here in the culture wars, and have not become a symbolic totem for religious battles. What amazes even the most sympathetic British observer of the United States is the power of religion, especially religion of an absolutist, morally conservative tinge. Here in old Britain, and old Europe generally, religion no longer has that determining force, despite the best efforts of various forms of fundamentalism. We have become largely secular cultures. Responses to sexuality are largely pragmatic. Homosexuality now arouses less drama in Britain than in the USA. The massive energy of the American gay world still entices and excites, but by and large we have found we can do things OK in our own ways.

Your work is credited with establishing a social constructionist perspective on sexuality. Can you discuss what this means, and does this mean that nature or biology has no role in shaping sexuality?

The social constructionist approach, quite simply, is about understanding the historical context which shapes the sexual. The starting point is the assumption that sexuality, far from being a force of nature external to society, is in fact always inevitably central to the social and cultural, and malleable by them. Sexuality is a highly social phenomenon, and as society changes so must sexuality. Does that mean that nature has nothing to do with it? Not quite. Sexuality builds on biological potentials, and is subject to psychosocial organization, so both biology and psychology can no doubt help us understand individual sexual development. But we must also recognize that sexuality, like everything else, attains meaning only in culture. We just cannot understand the subtleties and complexities of the sexual world if we try to reduce everything to the imperatives of Nature, or a particular type of brain or a special gene for this or that behaviour. The genetic revolution has had one undesirable consequence in that it reinforces attempts to understand sexuality in terms of the transmissions of genes over unimaginable time scales. To my mind attempts to understand contemporary sexual forms in terms of what our pre-historic ancestors did 500,000 years ago is a complete mystification, and an abandonment of what we should be doing as historians, sociologists, and anthropologists, which is to understand specific cultural configurations.

Even if there were a gay gene it could not possibly explain the varied historical patterning of homosexuality over time, or even within a single culture. And in a sense it removes responsibility from us as humans. As humans we have a degree of choice. I am not suggesting that we can by act of will change our sexual make-up. I do believe that that is to a large degree organized quite early in our individual development. But what we make of it is more in our hands, shaped of course all the time by what is culturally possible for us to do. To take an obvious example: there may be a large number of people in a particular culture who have homosexual desires, whatever the reasons for this. But how we live out those desires must depend on what means of expression exist. Are there possible identities open to us? What is the degree of acceptance or rejection of those identities? Are there spaces where like-minded people can meet, interact, have sex, love each other? A whole series of limiting factors come into play: religion, family and peer pressures, differences of status, class, race and ethnicity, age, etc. Individual sexual identities are the result of a constant negotiation between human possibilities and social and cultural opportunities. Social constructionism, at its simplest, is an attempt to understand the processes through which social and individual meanings and practices of the erotic are shaped and reshaped in an ever-changing history.

I want to ask you what is perhaps an impossible question. What is sexuality, or at least what would you include if you were forced to define sexuality?

Freud commented on the great difficulty on agreeing on the sexual nature of a process. Gagnon and Simon talked about the need that must once have existed to invent the importance of sexuality. Plummer once wrote that nothing is sexual, but naming makes it so. Yet Foucault famously complained that sex has become "the truth of our being." As the question suggests, there is no simple definition of sexuality, or explanation of its undoubted power. What complicates the issue is that "sexuality" as a concept operates on two levels. It refers to the bundle of social phenomena that shape erotic life: laws, religion, norms and values, beliefs and ideologies, the social organization of reproduction, family life, identities, domestic arrangements, diseases, violence and love – everything we evoke when we speak of the sexuality of a culture. And it also refers to the level of the individual – to the pleasures and pains that can shape our lives for good or ill. The two constantly interact, as I have suggested, shaping and reshaping the other. I do not believe, as Krafft-Ebing suggested, that sex is an all-powerful volcanic force that demands satisfaction. But I do believe that the erotic potentialities of the human body are immense, and tutored by human interaction they can become the focus of the most intense pleasures and pains. Which is why our culture can't quite let it go. It still fuels the personal and societal imagination.

chapter 6

Surveying sex

Interview with Edward Laumann

Edward Laumann is the George Herbert Mead Distinguished Service Professor of Sociology at the University of Chicago. He is a co-author of *The Social Organization of Sexuality: Sexual Practices in the United States*. This volume is considered the most comprehensive survey of the sexual behavior of American adults since the work of Kinsey.

Much of your work as a sociologist has been in the area of urban and organizational studies. Why did you decide to study sexuality?

When I was serving as Dean of the Social Sciences Division at the University of Chicago in 1986, a medical faculty colleague, Dr. Mark Siegler, and I organized a joint Medical/ Social Science faculty, year-long seminar series devoted to "AIDS and Society." Based on what I learned in this seminar, I became convinced that a properly designed survey of the US population that asked about their sexual practices was critical if we were to develop appropriate public health interventions to change people's sexual behavior toward safer sexual practices that would protect them from acquiring AIDS. Since at the time there was little prospect of an effective medical intervention being developed in the short term, such as a vaccine to prevent infection by HIV, our only hope of forestalling a massive epidemic was to devise effective behavioral interventions against the transmission of the disease. Robert Michael, who is an economic demographer, was then the director of the NORC on campus, one of the largest academically oriented survey organizations in the country. He and I decided to respond to the National Institutes of Health's call for proposals to design a national sex survey. We recruited John Gagnon, an internationally noted sex researcher, to help us do the study. We won the design competition in 1987 and immediately began developing the survey. Unfortunately, conservative political figures strongly opposed the idea of a government-funded sex survey and successfully prevented funding of the study for several years.

You and your colleagues did one of the largest surveys of sexuality ever done. Who funded the survey, and why did they fund it?

We have the dubious distinction of having had an act of Congress, the Senate voting 66 to 35 in September 1991 to deny funding the survey in favor of a "say no to sex" campaign favored by Senator Jesse Helms, passed in an attempt to stop the study. We were able to secure funding from a consortium of eight private philanthropic foundations because we could now convince them that the Federal government was not going to fund the survey in a timely way. We fielded the survey in 1992, just four months after the Senate vote. Unfortunately we had to cut the sample to one-fifth of the size we had originally recommended as being necessary to provide the detailed information we needed.

Can you describe your general sociological approach to understanding sexuality? Many sociologists focus on gender, cultural representations, economics, or state and the law to understand sexuality. What social factors do you think are the most important in trying to understand patterns of sexual behavior and attitudes?

We combined elements of three theoretical traditions in devising a general framework: (a) script theory, originally proposed by John Gagnon and William Simon, that distinguishes among cultural sexual scripts, interpersonal scripts, and intrapsychic scripts; (b) social network theory, with special focus on the organization of the sexual dyad and the larger social networks in which the sexual partners are embedded (this gives a powerful purchase on the epidemiology of disease spread); and (c) choice theory, which foregrounds how people engage in sexual decision-making. More fundamentally, we stress those aspects of sociological theory that feature how master statuses (such as age, gender, marital status, socioeconomic status, ethnicity/race, and religious preference); and master relationships – that is, we focus on four types of sexual partnerships, including marriage, cohabitation, dating (not living together), and casual sex (one-night stands), and socially organize the differential distribution of sexual practices, behavior, and attitudes. My special interest, flowing out of my earlier work on friendship formation, class, and status groups, was in the application of network theory to issues related to the spread of disease, the formation of enduring or more ephemeral sexual partnerships, and partner choice. We found that only three master statuses, age, marital status, and gender, do the lion's share of the work in organizing sexuality socially.

Your survey asks very personal and intimate questions about individuals' sexual and intimate practices. Why do you think people agreed to be interviewed and why you think they gave truthful answers?

People agreed to be surveyed because we convinced them that the information we sought was critical for informing public health interventions in the battle against AIDS. We had an exceptionally high completion rate: about 80 percent of the persons we had identified to be in our target sample agreed to be interviewed. Contrary to many expectations, the public at large does not in fact experience many problems in discussing sexual matters if they have good reasons to do so and they are asked in an appropriate and respectful manner. In the book that we published based on the survey, *The Social Organization of Sexuality* (1994), we provide several lengthy chapters evaluating the extent and nature of systematic distortions in responses to sexual questions. In general, we provide, I think, convincing evidence that these distortions are quite modest in degree and can be effectively taken into account when interpreting the results. There certainly were certain questions (e.g., about masturbation and family income) where we knew people were likely to be exaggerating or underestimating the behaviors, but these were generally very modest distortions. In fact, if we take "refused to answer the question" as an indicator of the sensitivity of the question, nearly all the questions directly asking about sexual things had refusal rates around 1 or 2 percent. In contrast, we had a 12 percent refusal rate about family income – far and away the most sensitive item in the interview.

What do you see as the main advantage of researching sexuality through surveys?

The main advantage of survey research is the cost-efficient capacity to ask about a wide range of topics with varying levels of detail across a representative sample of the adult population, so that one can estimate with known precision the prevalence and distribution of risky sexual practices and thus pinpoint points of intervention in the subpopulations at greatest risk for adverse health outcomes. We acquired an enormous amount of information on such topics as sexual practices, including oral and anal sex, vaginal intercourse, masturbation, and same-gender sex, subjective sexual preferences for different practices, the social factors influencing sexual partner choice, circumcision status, sexual dysfunctions (including erectile and lubrication problems, premature ejaculation, and difficulty having orgasm), sexually transmitted infections, general health and specific health conditions, the influence of social network composition on sexual expression, sexual attitudes and beliefs about appropriate sexual behavior, and extensive demographic and social characteristics of the respondent and his/her partners. With such information we are in an excellent position to map the distribution of various sexual practices across various population subgroups and to determine whether subpopulations are subject to different levels of risk of disease, happiness, and sexual health.

To convey something of the richness of your research, I would like to ask you about your findings on oral sex. In general, which Americans are practicing oral sex the most? Are there noteworthy social patterns to this sexual practice?

Roughly 75 percent of the men and women in the United States have had oral sex at some time in their lives. But only 1 in 4 engage in oral sex as a current sexual practice. Oral sex, then, is a technique with which most people have at least some familiarity, but it has in no sense become a defining feature of sex between women and men (as vaginal intercourse or, perhaps, kissing is). Somewhat less than 50 percent of men report oral sex as subjectively "very appealing," while only about half that percentage of women find it "very appealing." This should obviously translate into a relative reluctance on the part of women to engage in oral sex (when compared to men), but even among the men there is less than a majority who especially favor the practice.

It is a practice that is likely to happen early on in a relationship, but does not remain a strong preference over the long haul of a relationship.

Did your survey find significant differences between men's and women's sexuality?

On practically every matter of sexual practice and preference, attitudes and beliefs, numbers of lifetime sex partners, reported levels of sexual fantasy and sexual interest and desire, there are marked differences in men's and women's modes of sexual expression. These gender differences are sometimes enhanced or moderated by marital status, educational level, socioeconomic status, religious group membership, or race/ethnicity. For example, there appears to be a greater gender gap between African-American men and women with respect to beliefs about appropriate sexual behavior than there is between white men and women. Men, in general, report a higher lifetime number of sexual partners (measured as a median) than do women. Older men (over 55) are substantially more likely to have an ongoing sexual partner than women will have. For example, 70 percent of women aged 70 will not have had a sex partner in the past year, compared to only 35 percent of men aged 70 who report that they lacked a partner in the past year. About 30 percent of women report that they lacked interest in sex for at least several months in the past year, when compared to only about 15 percent of the men.

Many Americans think of themselves as sexually enlightened and liberated. Does your survey support this view?

No, it most certainly does not. We asked a series of nine questions about people's beliefs about appropriate sexual behavior, including extramarital sex, abortion, homosexuality, the significance of religious beliefs in guiding sexual conduct, and premarital sex. There were huge differences of opinion on every one of these questions. We were able to group people on the basis of their shared beliefs into three broad categories that range from libertarian to "middle of the road" to conservative points of view. About 25 percent of the sample fell into a well-defined conservative camp and another 25 percent clustered around a strong pro-libertarian or "sexually liberated" point of view. The rest fell squarely in the middle, rejecting the more extreme views of either side. This split is not homogeneously distributed across the country but varies in important ways that greatly affect political debate in the various states. The east and west coasts tend to have more liberally oriented persons, while the south and midwest have substantially larger pluralities of sexually conservative believers. The correspondence with the "blue" and "red" voting patterns in the Presidential election 2004 is striking.

What was the most surprising finding in your research?

There is widespread evidence throughout the survey for the notion that persons who are involved in ongoing, mutually monogamous sexual partnerships report substantially higher levels of physical and emotional satisfaction with their sexual partnerships than those who report being in concurrent or overlapping sexual partnerships.

Sexual competition appears to interfere with the building of commitment and trust in the larger social relationship in which the sexual partnership is embedded, and this, in turn, seems to have consequences for the physical and emotional satisfaction with the partnership itself.

Based on your research, what are Americans' chief sexual frustrations and fears, and their chief sexual satisfactions?

Perhaps the most surprising finding of this research is the relatively high levels of sexual dysfunction being reported by both men and women at all phases of the life course. About 43 percent of the women and 31 percent of the men reported at least one episode of sexual dysfunction of several months' duration over the past year. Some 30 percent of women said they lacked sexual interest or desire for several months in the past year, while 30 percent of men complained about premature ejaculation as a problem. Nearly all these sexual difficulties could be shown to be associated with lowered levels of overall happiness and satisfaction with one's life. On the other hand, there was no simple relationship between the volume of sexual activity and general life satisfaction. Much more research needs to be done to clarify and elaborate on how people achieve positive sexual health, and its role in generating a good quality of life.

PART 2

Sexual bodies and behaviors

Introduction

Most people think of certain body parts as either sexual or not. We think of penises and breasts as sexual, for example, but probably think of feet as not sexual. Most of the time, we think that sexual body parts are sexual for natural or biological reasons. But in this part of the book we will be exploring the way that body parts *become* sexual through a variety of social forces. What counts as sex depends on how the body is defined or viewed.

You might say that in all societies there is a hierarchy of sexual bodies and behaviors. In America, this hierarchy has two important features. First, the penis is widely considered to be the most important sexual body part. The penis has been socially constructed to be the "actor" in the sex act. The erect penis is associated with virility, power, and masculinity. The body of the heterosexual, white, young, able-bodied male, poised and ready with his erection, is at the top of the social hierarchy of bodies in our society. Second, heterosexual coitus (the penetration of the vagina with the penis) is thought to be the most normal and natural sexual behavior. Everything from the education about sex we receive in high school to the way medical authorities talk about sex tells us that there is a natural "fit" between the penis and vagina.

Body parts other than the penis, and sexual behaviors other than heterosexual coitus, are socially judged to be less natural, less normal, and less sexual. The vagina, for example, is thought of as a sexual organ, but a passive, receptive one – with nowhere near the sense of virility and power of the penis. Anal sex violates the social norm that tells us that heterosexual coitus is the only natural way to have sex. In doing so, it has been constructed as dirty, unclean, and unnatural. Even heterosexual activities other than coitus are thought of as less important or sexual. Foreplay, for example, is constructed as something one does *on the way to* coitus, but not as a sexual end in itself.

So, in America, heterosexual men and their bodies are at the top. But not all heterosexual men. Some heterosexual men very definitely do not come to be thought of as sexual, much less virile, powerful, and masculine. Asian men, for example, have long been constructed in popular culture as effeminate, slight, and dainty – far less sexual and far less powerful compared to their white American, hypermasculine counterparts. Older men and men who have lost their ability to achieve an erection are constructed by the medical community and culture at large as having a "dysfunction." The medical community has created a "Viagra culture" to restore to these men what our society deems most important: the erection. So even heterosexual men can have their bodies marginalized and constructed as asexual by social authorities.

The hierarchy of bodies and behaviors we will talk about in this part is always open to challenge. Anal sex was once almost uniformly only associated with gay men and moral pollution, but has increasingly become an act that some heterosexuals participate in, too. Gay pornography that features anal sex sometimes challenges the idea that the penetrator or "top" is the most powerful partner in the sex act. Women, too, have challenged the idea that they are simply passive participants in the sex act. Not long ago, the vagina was considered the primary female sexual body part. But the women's movement of the 1960s and 1970s challenged this notion, and women have increasingly come to understand the clitoris as central to sexual behavior and pleasure. Feminists also encouraged women to "be responsible for your own orgasm," in order to challenge the notion that men do sexual things and women passively participate.

Sometimes the way we challenge the hierarchy of sexual bodies and behaviors ends up reaffirming the dominant norms. Many Asian men and gay men resist the depiction of themselves as effeminate and slight by going to the gym, "beefing up," in order to better fit into the dominant American mold of what a man should look like. But other times, challenges to this hierarchy appear where you might least expect them. The very Viagra culture that re-affirms the notion that the erection is all-important has also opened a door for older women to talk about their sex lives. Older women have long been thought of as asexual, and "dried up." But the cultural buzz surrounding Viagra has made possible new discussions about sex among the elderly, and especially the sexuality of older women.

So, taken together, these essays do what a sociology of sexuality should do: they show us how certain body parts have *become* sexual through a variety of interesting social processes. What is considered a sexual body part changes over time. What is considered a legitimate sexual act is not related to nature as much as to social forces. As you'll learn, even something as seemingly simple as an orgasm changes over time and is experienced in remarkably different ways in different cultures.

chapter 7

Medicine and the making of a sexual body

Celia Roberts

Sex and sexuality are inextricably bound up with medicine in the West today. Sexual desires, sexual health, and sexual identities are both subjects for medical practice and objects of extensive scientific study. This is evident in multiple ways. As a discipline, medicine has developed a detailed language to describe and discuss sexual issues, and has established numerous professional journals and societies to support the scientific and medical study of sex. The medical knowledge produced in these journals and relevant textbooks and clinical guidelines understands some sexual behaviors and identities as illnesses and produces treatments to address these. These treatments, including pharmaceutical and behavioral interventions, are offered to patients presenting with sexual problems in general practitioners' offices and specialized clinics. In public health campaigns around sexually transmitted diseases, members of the general population and specific targeted groups are given medical information and encouraged to change their sexual behaviors in order to protect their physical health. In all of these cases, particular versions of sex and sexuality are produced or performed in interactions amongst medical professionals, scientists, patients, and members of populations. Sex and sexuality, in other words, are not "natural" objects worked on or taken up by medicine, but are produced in these interactions in particular ways.

This combination of sex and medicine is a historically specific phenomenon, but one that has become very normal to most of us in the West today. It is also a model that is increasingly distributed within non-Western societies, particularly through sexual health education campaigns and medical products and services. In these countries,

Western scientific understandings of sex and sexuality interact and intersect with indigenous understandings in complex ways. The development of medical and scientific knowledge about sex has had profound global implications for how we experience our bodies and our sexual relationships, and indeed how many aspects of different societies operate.

Whilst historically there have been many societies in which religion or morality was the most important knowledge framework for understanding sex and sexuality, in the West today this is no longer the case. When someone demonstrates unusual or socially unacceptable sexual desires or behaviors today we are much more likely to consider them sick than merely morally corrupt. Although we may well punish them criminally, and even expect them to repent morally, we seek explanations of their behaviors and feelings from medicine and psychiatry, and may well provide them with medical treatments as well as legal punishments. On a more everyday level, those experiencing difficulties with sexuality are very likely to seek medical help – in the advice columns of popular magazines and health books, in doctors' surgeries, or in sexual health clinics – and to expect medical solutions to their problems. This provision of medical treatments in turn provides a profitable market for the pharmaceutical industry. The case of so-called "sexual dysfunction" is a case in point. Rather than being understood as stemming from a mix of psychological, biological and cultural factors and managed accordingly, the erectile problems of older men are commonly treated with Viagra™, a medication that increases blood flow to the penis. Providing a simple medical "solution" to a complex problem, Viagra™ is a sign of our sexual times, one whose popularity produces significant profits for its manufacturer.

This chapter discusses the nature of these multiple and deep connections between sex and medicine. Its aim is not to simply critique medicine, or to suggest that these connections are necessarily negative. Rather, the chapter explores the culturally and historically specific development of connections between medicine and sex and asks questions about the implications of these for the everyday lives of people in the West and across the globe.

Histories of sex

This strong association between sex and medicine developed in the West over the last two-and-a-half centuries was dependent on the growth of modern science. As Michel Foucault (1987) has argued in his important book, *The History of Sexuality: An Introduction*, the development of European modern science established sex as something central to our identity, our "core" or "essential" being. Rather than being only a set of activities or actions, from the nineteenth century sexual behaviors and feelings have become something that tells us about who we "really" are (see also Garton 2004; Weeks 1981). As such, they become subjects for scientific analysis and research. In the late nineteenth century, Foucault demonstrates, medicine and science established norms of sex and sexuality and began to measure individuals and groups against them. This happened at the level of biological bodies, at the level of sexual desires, and in relation to what have come to be known as sexual identities. Through these processes of medical classification, measurement, and discussion, individuals and groups came to recognize themselves as particular types of sexual subjects, and framed their experiences in culturally valorized ways (Garton 2004: 18). In turn this produced populations of people understood to need (and sometimes also desiring) medical treatment of what had come to be understood as sexual pathologies. These processes, as historian Jeffrey Weeks (1981) has shown, also produced forms of resistance against medicine and its practices of pathologization. Some sexual identities, such as homosexuality, were formed in part in resistance to Western medicine's insistence on the pathological nature of certain desires and behaviors (a pathologization that was also linked to criminalization in the case of homosexuality) (Garton 2004: 214). The categories of sexual pathology created by medicine, then, were always received by "passive victims" of pathologized subjects, but were developed in relation to active contestation and the formation of new sociosexual ways of being (see also Terry 1999).

Sexual desire and sexual identities

Social theorists argue that contemporary sexualities have been formed in relation to the production of medical and scientific knowledge. Even the very "basic" categories that we associate with sexuality today ("heterosexuality," "homosexuality," "libido," for example) are words and concepts developed within specialist medical fields. This argument has been made most strongly in the case of homosexuality, but is also valid in relation to the more normative case of heterosexuality.

The medical study of sexuality has long been interwoven with the social sciences. This is evident in the field of sexology, the scientific study of sex and sexual behavior. Historian Janice Irvine (1990) has documented the development of this field in her book *Disorders of Desire* (see also Garton 2004; Foucault 1987; Weeks 1981; Terry 1999). The term "sexology" was coined in 1907 by German physician Iwan Bloch to name a growing field established in Europe in the late nineteenth century, in particular by Austrian Richard von Krafft-Ebing and Englishman Havelock Ellis. The aim of this new science was to study the sexual life of the individual within the context of medicine and the social sciences (Irvine 1990: 5). Perhaps the most important role of sexology in the late nineteenth and early twentieth centuries was its painstaking cataloging of the known variety of sexual behaviors and desires. This work produced a population of subjects and patients for doctors and scientists to study and treat.

Irvine argues that early European sexologists "were a disparate group with conflicting professional and political agendas" (Irvine 1990: 6). Some wanted to use sexology to change society; others thought sexology should be a pure and nonpolitical science. Irvine suggests that the tensions between social and biological sciences in sexology have always been a problem – gradually sexology leaned more and more towards biology and medicine in an attempt to legitimate the field as a science. Accordingly, modern sexology (which after the Second World War was based in America rather than Europe) became highly biological and scientific, studying physical measurements such as hormonal levels and neurological patterns in connection with sexual behaviors and identities. The groundbreaking survey work of American Alfred Kinsey in the mid-twentieth century is a key example of this emphasis on the scientific study of sex. In more contemporary times, reliance on "objective" measures of bio-logical factors such as hormone levels establishes sexology's difference from both "nonscientific" sex therapies and humanities or purely social science-based sexuality research (Irvine 1990).

In the realm of treatments also, sexology has come to rely more and more on the biological and medical sciences. This tendency existed in the early twentieth century, when sexologists and doctors used sex hormones to try to change the sexual desires and drives of homosexual men. In some instances, these men were understood to have too much "female" hormones (estrogens) which were understood to be feminiz-ing, and so were given "male" hormones (androgens) in an attempt to "normalize" them. In other cases, homosexuality was seen as best treated by dampening sexual drive through the administration of "female" sex hormones. Both methods were unsuccessful in changing homosexual men's desires and behavior. Later, in the mid-twentieth century, even more severe methods were used, including the administra-tion of electric shocks. All of these "treatments" assumed that homosexuality was a pathology or illness. It was not until 1973 that activists were able to pressure psychia-trists and doctors to remove homosexuality from the official list of psychological pathologies (the Diagnostic and Statistical Manual of psychiatric disorders) and to stop attempting to change the sexual desire and behaviors of homosexual men and women.

In other arenas, however, sexologists and general practitioners continued to use hormonal and other pharmacological products to treat problems of desire and sexual behavior. The advent of Viagra™ in the 1990s is the most well-known example of this. This highly commercially successful medication assists men who have problems achieving or sustaining erections, providing increased blood flow to sustain an erec-tion that makes intercourse possible. Hailed as a "wonder drug" in popular culture, and well regarded in medical circles, this medication plays a key role today in main-taining a narrow understanding of sex as sexual intercourse. Rather than assisting aging men to come to terms with bodily changes or to explore forms of sexual practice other than intercourse, argues sociologist Barbara Marshall (2002), Viagra™ provides a short-term and narrowly focused "quick fix." One direct-to-consumer advertisement for Viagra™ broadcast on American television, for example, shows a middle-aged man brimming with confidence on returning to work after an evening of satisfying sex. Puzzled work colleagues ask if it is a new haircut, exercise regime, or suit that has made all the difference, but viewers understand that it is the pharmaceutical product that has turned this man's life around. Such advertisements reinforce connections between sexual drive, work-related performance and masculinity, clearly suggesting that Viagra™ can solve a multitude of life problems through making sexual inter-course possible.

Hormone replacement therapies (HRT) have also been used to treat sexuality-related problems encountered by older people since the 1960s, in women and more recently also in men. Medical and scientific discourses and pharmaceutical advertise-ments describe HRT as maintaining youthful sexual drive and desire and suggest that HRT can be a kind of elixir of youth (Roberts 2002). Pharmaceutical advertisements for HRT show unhappy, bad-tempered women being changed into smiling and receptive beings, and depict men taking androgens as strong and potent god-like creatures.

Maintaining sexual drive is described in the medical literature as essential to healthy aging, something that should be biochemically managed and supported. Like those around Viagra™, discourses around HRT reproduce narrow ideas of sex, sexuality, and gender relations, reinforcing culturally prevalent connections between sex, happiness, and success, and suggesting that medication can concretize or make real these connections for aging people. Such concretization, of course, also establishes a profitable and ever-growing market, as the proportion of older people in Western populations increases.

Sexual pathologies and biologies

The use of medical products to treat sexual problems relies on an understanding of sexuality and sexual drive as a biological, rather than social, force. Discourses around HRT, for example, assume that sexual drive comes from hormonal levels in the body: when these change as a person ages, the logical way to treat problems, according to contemporary medicine, is to supplement the body so that it has the hormonal profile of a younger person.

This biologistic way of thinking is also linked to understandings of sexual behaviors deemed pathological by medical discourse. Although, as discussed above, hormonal treatments of homosexuals are no longer acceptable in Western countries, some scientists continue to search for biological determinants of homosexuality (Irvine 1990: 246–52), and even in the late twentieth century some researchers, for example Gunter Dörner of Germany, have proposed hormonal interventions for pregnant women in order to avoid the birth of homosexual babies (Irvine 1990: 19). Male sex offenders – rapists and pedophiles, for example – are sometimes treated with anti-androgens and other hormones as well as being incarcerated. In all of these cases, sexuality is understood, at least in part, as a biological force that can be changed by the administration of pharmaceuticals. The assumptions here are that sexuality and sexual desire arise from the biological body, and that they can, in many cases at least, be medically altered.

The biological origin of sexual desire and drive is one that has troubled medicine and science since the nineteenth century. This question has always been linked with questions of sex and gender. Since the mid-eighteenth century, scientists and doctors have worked with a notion of sex that understands men and women as complementary opposites. Since the twentieth century, genes and hormones have been figured as the main biological causes of the physical (and in many cases also the psychological) differences between men and women. In human fetuses, the so-called "male" sex hormones (androgens) are understood to cause maleness, whilst the absence of significant amounts of these is seen to produce femaleness. At puberty, "male" hormones begin to produce a sexually mature man, and "female" hormones produce sexually mature women. This understanding of humans as having two "opposite" sexes underlies scientific and medical understandings of sexuality. Heterosexuality, which is seen as fundamentally linked to sexual reproduction, demonstrates that the two opposite sexes are also "complementary." The two sexes, in other words, are understood to be designed to come together for the purposes of reproduction and to "naturally" find each other attractive, so that the species will continue to reproduce and survive.

This model of sex and (hetero)sexuality is much troubled by the existence of individuals and groups who do not fit it. At the level of biological bodies, the model of two opposite sexes has been challenged at least since the 1930s, when it was discovered that male horses (and male humans) have "female" sex hormones in their bloodstreams. Although this famous finding contradicted an early idea that each sex has its "own" hormone only, it has since been incorporated by reference to relative amounts of hormones. Human males (and other male mammals) have "female" hormones as well as "male" ones, but they have less than females do. The model of the two "opposite" sexes has also been long disrupted by the existence of people born with what is known as "indeterminate sex," that is, whose genitals, genes or hormonal levels do not correlate clearly to either maleness or femaleness. These individuals, who are today referred to as "intersexed," have long been regarded as biological anomalies, with their bodies seen medically as faulty or pathological. Despite there being no medical need to intervene, most babies born intersexed in the West today receive hormonal and/or surgical treatment in an attempt to fit them into a "normal" male or female category (Fausto-Sterling 2000). Critics of this medical approach, such as biologist Anne Fausto-Sterling, have argued that decisions about which sex the baby should be "made into" are based on narrow ideas about heterosexual sex. The decisions to operate on a baby's genitals and to use hormonal medication are made according to whether doctors feel that, as an adult, the person would be capable of penetrating a vagina with his/her penis. If it is not felt that the penis would ever be large enough, it is "reduced" and a vagina constructed, if one is not present (Fausto-Sterling 2000). It is never considered that the baby may grow up to be homosexual, or indeed that s/he might want to have sex in other ways. This example demonstrates the deeply assumed link between biological sex (maleness and femaleness) and (hetero)sexual practice prevalent in medicine. If born not clearly male or female, a person is understood as in need of medical assistance, and this assistance is justified on the basis of imagined future heterosexual identity and behaviors. Unsurprisingly, in recent years there has been much political resistance to this kind of medical treatment, as documented in the work of Fausto-Sterling, amongst others. As in the earlier case of homosexuality, this resistance to medical practices and discourses is intimately intertwined with the development of a socio-sexual identity (intersexuality).

Biological theories about sex and sexuality also have a complex historical connection to ideas of racial differences. In his *History of Sexuality: An Introduction*, Foucault (1987) argues that modern racism was born alongside modern sexuality. Ideas about heterosexual reproduction are important here in different ways. In the late nineteenth and early twentieth centuries, many scientists and social theorists argued that reproduction should be controlled by the state, with some individuals encouraged to reproduce whilst others were discouraged or even prevented. These ideas were linked to understandings of evolution and to Darwin's notion of "the survival of the fittest," in which species' survival was related to the reproduction of characteristics best fitted to the organism's environment. Coming out of a period of massive Western expansion into non-Western countries, and the colonization of vast areas of Africa, Asia and South America, scientists in the eighteenth and nineteenth centuries had produced

Celia Roberts

theories of racial hierarchy in which white men and women were figured as superior to non-whites. With the development of the early-twentieth-century science of eugenics, these theories gained new medical weight. Given that this was also the time at which modern birth-control methods were beginning to be developed, this new medical attention to issues of race and reproduction was highly consequential. As is well known, this connection was taken to its most brutal extreme in Nazi Germany, where many individuals were sterilized and millions of others killed in order, supposedly, to promote the reproductive purity of the Aryan "race."

The connections between sex, race, and reproduction have remained important to Western medicine and science since the Second World War, despite global horror regarding Nazi atrocities. Evidence shows, for example, that women in the developing world continue to be exposed to more invasive and potentially dangerous forms of medical contraceptive technologies (such as implants and long-lasting injections) in the hope that the population of developing countries will be kept in a particular proportion to that of developed countries. Women of color in the United States and other Western countries have also experienced significantly different forms of reproduction-related healthcare than their white compatriots. Access to new reproductive technologies for infertile couples is also highly unevenly distributed across the globe and within individual countries.

Sex and reproduction

Since the 1970s, second-wave feminists have hoped that medicine might disentangle historical and seemingly oppressive connections between sex and reproduction, through the development of the contraceptive pill, for example, and to a certain extent this has happened. Many women in the West and across the world are now able to use one or more of a range of medical contraceptive technologies to have non-reproductive heterosexual sex and to engage in "family planning." The development of medical technologies of safe abortion and the morning-after pill have also helped in this regard. Many millions of women in the world do not have access to these technologies, or are exposed involuntarily to more dangerous versions of them.

Alongside this increasing control over reproduction, medicine has also developed a significant discourse and set of practices around infertility. It is now claimed that one in seven couples in the West will struggle to become pregnant when they stop using contraception. These problems have been linked to the use of hormonal contraception, to increasing levels of chemicals in our environment, and to social changes, such as couples wanting to have children at later ages. The solutions developed to address this problem have been chiefly medical. They involve new reproductive technologies, such as in-vitro fertilization (IVF), interuterine insemination, ovarian stimulation and intracytoplasmic sperm injection. These scientific techniques move reproduction from the intimate sexual sphere and place it within a medical, technical realm, promising a level of control that is not actually matched with pregnancy outcomes. Most of these technologies involve extensive failure and entail significant physical and psychological risks for women patients, as well as currently unknowable lifetime risks for the babies born through these procedures. Like the drugs discussed above, however, they are immensely popular and currently provide ever-increasingly profitable markets in medical services and pharmaceutical products.

More recently, new genetic technologies have been developed to assist couples whose fertility problems are linked with genetic disease, or who are at serious risk of giving birth to children who will suffer from severe genetic disease. These techniques can provide genetic testing of embryos made using IVF or of fetuses *in utero*, and are linked in the latter case to abortion technologies (women can decide to terminate fetuses that will develop certain genetic conditions). In the West today, it is standard for women over the age of thirty-five to be given prenatal testing for chromosomal conditions such as Down's syndrome as part of normal medical care. American anthropologist Rayna Rapp (1999) has studied the social impact of this development, arguing that women are given a historically unique role in deciding which babies should be born today. She calls pregnant women undergoing this type of testing (known as amniocentesis) "moral pioneers" (Rapp 1999: 306). In everyday life, then, pregnant women are making moral decisions about continuing with pregnancies or not according to information produced by medicine, thus demonstrating the depth to which medical knowledge now penetrates the intimate, daily life of "ordinary" people and the very constitution of society (who will be born and who will not).

In all of these examples, medicine and reproductive sex are deeply intertwined: medical interventions take over, replace or become substitutes for more "traditional" practices of impregnation and abortion. This is not to argue that processes of reproduction (impregnation, pregnancy, birth) were previously "natural," but rather that, in the West today (and increasingly, but in different ways, in non-Western countries as well), they have moved into the realm of medicine and become inextricably enmeshed with medical understandings of sex and biology.

Sex and disease

Medicine is also deeply intertwined with sex in the areas of disease and sexual health. The advent of the global HIV/AIDS epidemic in the mid-1980s is the most significant example of this in the current epoch. As many commentators have argued, HIV/AIDS has provided an enormous and enduring stimulus to medical and scientific work on sex and sexuality, fostering ever-deeper relations between these two fields of human life (see, e.g., Epstein 1996).

Faced with an initially untreatable, fatal disease that was transmitted via body fluids during sex (as well as by needle-sharing), social scientists, activists and policy-makers argued that it was important to learn more about contemporary sexual practices and how body fluids were actually shared. Research in both Western and non-Western countries since the 1980s have studied a full range of sexual practices amongst a wide variety of groups, asking who does what, when, and with whom. This work led to the development of what has come to be known as "safe" or "safer" sex, forms of sexual practice that minimize the risk of the transmission of the HIV virus that causes AIDS. These practices are widely promoted today, both in medical settings (doctors' offices, waiting rooms, sexual health clinics and hospitals) and in other public arenas (television, magazines, public transport, etc.). In many Western and non-Western countries today, these campaigns are linked to other sexually transmitted diseases, rates of which are rising even as HIV infection rates decrease (syphilis, chlamydia, and herpes, for example). In all of this work, medical research on the spread of disease within particular social groups and geographical areas, and on how specific diseases are transmitted, is linked with social scientific work on sexual behavior. Through the dissemination of public health advice on safe sex, then, medicine enters the most intimate spaces of our lives, as people take up (or fail, or refuse, to take up) this advice when they have sex.

Conclusion

Medicine and science have had profound consequences for how we experience sex today. In many ways, medicine has contributed to making sex safer and more pleasurable for many people. The possibility of treating sexually transmitted diseases and sexual dysfunctions, of preventing unwanted pregnancies and of diagnosing and treating reproductive problems and the genetic profile of future children, have arguably improved the lives of many who have come into contact with medicine. The development of medical categories for sexual desires and identities is perhaps a more mixed blessing: some social theorists have argued that categories such as homosexuality and heterosexuality, maleness and femaleness have produced severe limitations on sexual expression and the unnecessary pathologization of biological and social diversity, thus contributing to the production of societies characterized by intolerance of those who do not fit well into established categories. For many people, then, the combination of sex and medicine has produced spaces of fear, suffering, and unnecessary and painful "treatment."

However ambivalent, the connection between sex and medicine is profound and enduring. It is also constantly reinforced by the production of new pharmaceutical products to treat sexual problems; through the continued research on sexual biologies, behaviors, and desires; and through the development of medical treatments for sexually transmitted diseases. The social sciences have an important role to play in all of this: to describe and analyze what is happening in medicine and in broader society, and to continue to describe the diversity of human sexualities in order to promote better ways of living with this diversity. Medicine cannot take on sex and sexuality without the social sciences – it does not have the skills and resources to provide adequate accounts of the complexity of human behavior – so the uneasy relationship between medicine and social science will continue into the foreseeable future.

References

Epstein, Steven (1996) *Impure Science: AIDS, Activism and the Politics of Knowledge*, Berkeley: University of California Press.
Fausto-Sterling, Anne (2000) *Sexing the Body: Gender, Politics and the Construction of Sexuality*, New York: Basic Books.
Foucault, Michel (1987) *The History of Sexuality: An Introduction*, Robert Hurley (trans.), London: Penguin Books.

Garton, Stephen (2004) *Histories of Sexuality: Antiquity to Sexual Revolution*, London: Equinox Press.

Irvine, Janice M. (1990) *Disorders of Desire: Sex and Gender in Modern American Sexology*, Philadelphia, PA: Temple University Press.

Marshall, Barbara (2002) "Hard Science: Gendered constructions of sexual dysfunction", *Sexualities* 5(2), 131–58.

Rapp, Rayna (1999) *Testing Women, Testing the Fetus: The Social Impact of Amniocentesis in America*, Durham, NC: Duke University Press.

Roberts, Celia (2002) "Successful aging with hormone replacement therapy: it may be sexist, but what if it works?", *Science as Culture* 11(1), 39–59.

Terry, Jennifer (1999) *An American Obsession: Science, Medicine and Homosexuality in Modern Society*, Chicago, IL: University of Chicago Press.

Weeks, Jeffrey (1981) *Regulation of Sexuality since 1800*, London: Longman.

Celia Roberts

chapter 8

Polishing the pearl

Discoveries of the clitoris

Lisa Jean Moore

In the early 1990s, I worked on a national sex information switchboard for a couple of years. Much to my surprise, a majority of the callers were men, and their two most common questions were: "What is the normal penis size?" and "Where is the clitoris?" Trained to provide anonymous, non-judgmental, and accurate information to callers, I would respond that most penises when erect were between 5 and 7 inches long. I could almost feel the relief as these callers thanked me, quickly hanging up the phone to get on with their days, secure in the validation that they (and their penises) were "okay."

As for the clitoris question, I instructed callers to place their hands in a praying position, bend their knuckles slightly and imagine this as the vagina. If the area between the thumbs was the vagina opening, the clitoris was roughly located in the place above the tips of their thumbs, in the triangular area. I never felt as if this answer was quite as successful. Many callers fumbled or dropped the phone while trying to follow my instructions. Some callers were clearly confused by the model as they asked, "So it's a hole?" or "But what does the vagina really look like?" Furthermore, I was increasingly alarmed by the steady stream of female callers who asked for instructions on how to find their own clitorises or wanted suggestions on how to experience orgasms exclusively through vaginal penetration. "Is there something wrong with me?" they inquired when discussing how dissatisfying penis–vagina sex was, oftentimes explaining that they had never experienced an orgasm during sex. (Tellingly, decorating the office wall was a hand-drawn cartoon of a vagina that said "The clitoris. If you can't find it, you can't come.") Clearly there is something baffling and mysterious about the clitoris. According to a small sample of people calling a sex information line, even though size doesn't matter, location and purpose do. Where is it? What does it do?

And finding and exploring the clitoris is not just an intimate affair. Simultaneous to these personal concerns about one's own and others' sexual bodies, the management of the clitoris also figures prominently in international human rights, through debates about female genital cutting (FGC, sometimes also referred to as clitoridectomy, or female genital mutilation, FGM). According to the United Nations, "FGC/FGM refers to all procedures involving partial or total removal of the external female genitalia or other injury to the female genital organs for cultural or other non-medical reasons." Generally presented as a practice that is exclusively performed by "other" cultures,

> [F]emale circumcision has been practiced in the United States since at least the nineteenth century. Cases of its use in the late nineteenth through the early twentieth century were for the treatment of masturbation (by both women and girls) and nymphomania – a term used interchangeably with masturbation and with what was regarded as excessive amounts of sex.
>
> (Webber 2003: 65)

According to the Center for Reproductive Rights, it is estimated that, worldwide, 130 million women have experienced female genital cutting.

When one attempts to define the clitoris, it becomes increasingly apparent that the definitions are constrained by social and political forces. In other words, there is no universal or stable definition of the clitoris, and many of the definitions reveal anxieties about women's bodies and sexualities. How is it, then, that this piece of flesh has inspired such personal and cultural anxiety? Taking a look at some of the Western "experts" who have produced images of female bodies and sexualities, it is clear that the clitoris is a very elusive, dangerous, and complicated invention. Referring to the clitoris as an "invention" means that the definition and representation of this piece of flesh is something that changes through time and depending on who is defining it.

Histories of the clitoris

Anatomists, psychoanalysts, sexologists, and pornographers have all established their professional reputations by claiming expertise about the clitoris. "Anatomies of private parts are perhaps the most intently and minutely examined as they often provide us with some of the earliest available, 'most scientific,' and supposedly, therefore, neutral knowledge of body parts least visually accessible in contemporary Western daily life" (Moore and Clarke 1995: 256). Different male anatomical explorers dispute the "scientific" discovery of the clitoris. In 1559, Realdo Colombo wrote of discovering the clitoris, "the seat of women's delight," and he called it "so pretty and useful a thing" in his *De Re Anatomica*. But bio-colonizers Kasper Bartholin, Gabriel Fallopius and Ambroise Pare were also making claims to parts of women's bodies and challenged the crediting of Colombo with the clitoris. According to historian Thomas Laqueur (1990), prior to the mid-eighteenth century, scientific explanations of men's and women's genitalia were based on a one-sex model whereby women's genital anatomy was an inversion of men's. The clitoris and the uterus were internal, or inverted, versions of the penis and scrotum.

In the biomedical textbooks of the 1900s through the 1950s, the clitoris is depicted and described as homologous to the penis – that is, it is formed from the same evolutionary structure – but is also considered inferior to the penis. In 1905, Sigmund Freud, the father of psychoanalysis, published essays that argued for a differentiation between clitoral and vaginal orgasms. Clitoral orgasms were considered immature and, as women became properly socialized into their adult sexual orientation of heterosexuality, they would experience the "mature" orgasm in their vagina. Sexologists of the 1930s and 1940s, notably Havelock Ellis and Robert Latou Dickinson, read female genital physiology as evidence of their sexual experiences, often citing an enlarged clitoris as proof of prostitution or lesbianism. "Whether she chose under examination to reveal her 'sins' verbally or not, a woman's genitalia revealed her confession to the sexologist, her confessor. Her sex practices alone or with others, with men or women, in a normal or abnormal manner, thus entered the realm of the scientifically knowable. On the examining table, literally wide open under his scrutiny, Dickinson's subject could not hide her sexual secrets from him" (Miller 2000: 80). In this context, the clitoris can reveal a woman's transgression against patriarchal sexual norms. And the control of women's sexual expression and "perverted desires" is evident in other academic disciplines. During the 1930s, art criticism of Georgia O'Keeffe's flower paintings pejoratively labeled her a woman first and an artist second, generally dismissed her artistic contribution and wrongly described her paintings as male genitalia – a male critic wrote: "much of her earlier work showed a womanly preoccupation with sex, an uneasy selection of phallic symbols in her flowers, a delight in their nascent qualities" (cited in Mitchell 1978: 682).

In 1953, Alfred Kinsey and his research team published *Sexual Behavior in the Human Female*, which was comprised of 5,940 interviews with women. Kinsey and his colleagues interpreted this data to define the clitoris as the locus of female sexual sensation and orgasm. Despite this scientific evidence culled from women's own voices, the practice of labeling and describing the function of the clitoris was abandoned in anatomical textbooks during the 1950s–1970s. Importantly, a survey of lay and medical dictionaries found that definitions of the clitoris refer to the male body as a template or norm from which the female body is somehow derived (Braun and Kitzinger 2001). This definition process often implies that the clitoris is inferior to the penis. If one's knowledge were based on historical anatomical rendering and dictionary definitions alone, it would be possible to believe that the clitoris is small, purposeless, and subaltern to the penis.

Pornography is another realm where individuals get information about human genitalia that contributes to the confusion and mystique about the clitoris. In an issue of *Men's Health* magazine (2000), an article called "Sex Tricks from Skin Flicks" provides advice for readers from forty X-rated films. For example: "You know her clitoris needs attention, especially as she nears climax. But it's hard to find such a tiny target when both your bodies are moving. Use the flat of your palm to make broad, quick circular motions around the front of her vaginal opening. That way, you're sure to hit the spot." Clearly, some men and women are viewing pornography as an instructional aid in their genital and sexual exploration.

Whether it is in print, film, or online media, the clitoris (or "clit," as it is referred to almost exclusively in porn) has been depicted with great attention to detail and celebration of diversity of shape, size and color. That is not to say all renderings of the clitoris are intentionally feminist or particularly instructive. In 1972, in the most profitable movie in film history, *Deep Throat*, directed by Gerard Damiano, the actress Linda Lovelace's clitoris is nine inches down her throat. The only way for her to experience orgasm is to have her throat stimulated with a long, erect penis. Contemporary films feature the clitoris, such as director Jack Remy's *Pleasure Spot* (1986) plotted around a clitoral transplant, and *Papi Chulo Facesitting* (2005) presenting the main character "Luv" positioning her clitoris over the nose of Tom. Pornographic series such as *Tales from the Clit*, *Terrors from the Clit*, and *Pussy Fingers* each offer a variety of shots of the clitoris as part of female genital anatomy and female sexual expression.

Feminist insurgencies

During the 1970s, consciousness-raising groups of women equipped with plastic vaginal speculums, mirrors and flashlights taught one another how to explore their sexual and reproductive organs. These groups of women fueled the Feminist Self-Help Health Movement and created fertile ground for feminist reformation of anatomical texts. These self-examinations and group meetings revolutionized existing descriptions and renderings of the clitoris (Federation of Feminist Women's Health Centers 1981). "From minor homologue it is transfigured into the raison d'être of other organs. Deliberate, self conscious effort is made to present the clitoris as a 'functioning integrate unit'" (Moore and Clarke 1995: 280). The Hite Report on Female Sexuality published in 1976 was based on data drawn from 1,844 of 3,000 anonymous questionnaires distributed to American women aged between fourteen and seventy-eight. Although many questioned the methodological rigor of this study, the project amassed significant and compelling data about the importance of clitoral stimulation for female orgasm.

But these feminist insurgencies were met with great resistance from mainstream anatomical practices. Throughout the 1980s and 1990s, the backlash to feminism in anatomy reasserted women's sexual response as linked exclusively to reproduction, not sexual pleasure. For example, in *Human Anatomy and Physiology*, the author argues that "With the current emphasis on sexual pleasure and the controversy over the role of women (and men) as sex objects, it is easy to lose sight of the fact that a large part of a woman's body is adapted specifically for functions of conceiving, bearing and nurturing children" (Silverstein 1988: 740). Certain anatomical texts of this time seem to purposefully render the clitoris as useless or unnecessary (Moore and Clarke 2001).

Throughout the 2000s, video, CD-ROM, and web-based anatomies emerge as modes of viewing genital anatomy. These new ways of accessing images and descriptions of the clitoris do not necessarily change the definition of the clitoris. "Continuities with previous textual anatomies abound in new visual and cyber forms such as the heterosexual requirement, the female body as reproductive not sexual, and the biomedical expert as the proper and dominant mediator between humans and their own bodies" (Moore and Clarke 2001: 87). Notably, feminists still participate in research on women's genital anatomy. For example, Rebecca Chalker (2002), a pioneer of the Self-Help Health Movement, has established that the clitoris is made up of eighteen distinct and interrelated structures. Biometric analysis of a diverse sample of female genitals has "proven" that there is a great range of variation in women's genital dimensions, including clitoral size, labial length and color (Lloyd *et al.* 2005).

In sum

Mapping, representing and defining the clitoris is a political act. As a result, the clitoris has many competing and contradictory narratives that vary depending upon personal, cultural, political, and historical circumstances. So, based on who is defining the clitoris, it can be classified as an inverted and diminutive penis, a small erectile sex organ of the female, a love button, an unhygienic appendage to be removed, a site of immature female sexual expression, a key piece of evidence of sexual perversion, or a vibrant subject of pornographic mediations. These different definitions of the clitoris are constrained by the political and cultural context, including who is representing the clitoris, for what purposes, and under what conditions.

References

Braun, Virginia and Celia Kitzinger. 2001. "Telling it Straight? Dictionary Definitions of Women's Genitals", *Journal of Sociolinguistics* 5, 2: 214–33.

Chalker, Rebecca. 2002. *The Clitoral Truth: The Secret World at Your Fingertips*, New York: Seven Stories Press.

Colombo, Realdo. 1559. *De Re Anatomica*.

Federation of Feminist Women's Health Centers. 1981. *A New View of the Woman's Body*, New York: Simon Schuster.

Freud, Sigmund. 1905. *Three Essays on the Theory of Sexuality*, Standard Edition, London: Hogarth Press.

Hite, Shere. 1976. *The Hite Report: A Nationwide Study on Female Sexuality*, New York: Macmillan.

Kinsey, Alfred C. *et al.* 1953. *Sexual Behavior in the Human Female*. Philadelphia, PA: W. B. Saunders.

Laqueur, Thomas. 1990. *Making Sex: Body and Gender from the Greeks to Freud*, Cambridge, MA: Harvard University Press.

Lloyd, Jillian, Naomi Crouch, Catherine Minto, Lih-Mei Liao, and Sarah Crieghton. 2005. "Female Genital Appearance: 'Normality' unfolds", *British Journal of Obstetrics and Gynaecology* 112, 5: 643.

Men's Health. 2000. "Sex Tricks from Skin Flicks", 15, 7: 54.

Miller, Heather Lee. 2000. "Sexologists Examine Lesbians and Prostitutes in the United States, 1840–1940", *NWSA Journal*, 12, 3: 67–91.

Mitchell, Marilyn Hall. 1978. "Sexist Art Criticism: Georgia O'Keeffe, A Case Study", *Signs* 3, 3: 681–7.

Moore, Lisa Jean and Adele E. Clarke. 1995. "Clitoral Conventions and Transgressions: Graphic Representations of Female Genital Anatomy, c1900–1991", *Feminist Studies* 21(2): 255–301.

—. 2001. "The Traffic in Cyberanatomies: Sex/Gender/Sexualities in Local and Global Formations", *Body and Society* 7(1): 57–96.

Silverstein, Alvin. 1988. *Human Anatomy and Physiology*, New York: John Wiley and Sons.

Webber, Sara. 2003. "Cutting History, Cutting Culture: Female Circumcision in the United States", *The American Journal of Bioethics* 3, 2: 65–6.

chapter 9

Viagra and the coital imperative

Nicola Gavey

Anyone encountering Viagra for the first time through direct-to-consumer promotions of the drug could be forgiven for thinking they had stumbled onto a miraculous new elixir of relational health and wellbeing. Viagra, according to drug company advertisements, will generate not only sex, but also the restoration of closeness, romance, love and intimacy. It will, in fact, protect against the very breakup of relationships threatened by "distance" – a distance born, it is implied, of the ailing self-esteem and crumbling masculinity caused by "failure to admit" and therefore to overcome the condition of "erectile dysfunction" (see Gavey 2005). And what is the route to such happiness and harmony? It is the biotechnological production of a penile erection with all the qualities – of firmness and duration – required for vaginal penetration and "successful" intercourse.

As critics have pointed out, the promotion of Viagra as a magic-bullet remedy to this host of personal and relational troubles relies on a whole array of contemporary assumptions about sex and gender. So too, of course, does the construction of the very problem (erectile dysfunction) it is designed to fix. Most blatantly, the whole phenomenon of Viagra relies on a hard-core "coital imperative" (Jackson 1984). This is the widely shared presumption that heterosexual sex *is* penis–vagina intercourse; and that anything else is either a preliminary to – or an optional extra beyond – real sex.

In magazine advertisements targeted at potential consumers, notions like "satisfactory sexual activity" and "making love" are premised on the requirement of a penis erect enough for penetration that lasts (see Gavey 2005). (Hetero)sex, within the Viagra promotion industry, *is* penetration – of the vagina by the penis. And the penetrating penis must be capable of reliable and durable action to avoid pathologization. According to a "sexual health inventory" on the drug company's website, even the man who reports he is able to maintain an erection that is firm enough and lasts long enough for "satisfactory" intercourse "most times" and reports "high" confidence in his ability to "get and keep an erection" scores the advice that he "may be showing signs of erection problems" (see Gavey 2005). The possibility that sexual activity or making love could happen without penile penetration of the vagina – which conceivably might be an option that some heterosexual men with erectile changes (as well as some without), and their partners, might otherwise consider – is completely obscured within the promotional advice.

Of course drug companies did not invent the coital imperative. Contemporary culture is thoroughly saturated with the commonsense assumption that (hetero)sex is coitus. In fact, to question that mature heterosexual sex could be otherwise – that it might not require intercourse – is likely to generate bemused and/or dismissive responses emphasizing the power of *nature* to determine the proper form of sexual practices and desires. From this perspective, the coital imperative might be seen as simply the way things are; as a taken-for-granted feature of human nature. However, in this chapter I argue not only that the coital *imperative* in its current form is highly problematic, but also that it is neither simply natural nor immutable.

The dangers of the coital imperative

Feminists have long debated the symbolic meaning of intercourse. Some have portrayed it as a key site of women's oppression (e.g., Dworkin 1987), while others have sought to resurrect it as a viable sexual practice for heterosexual feminists (e.g., Segal 1994). However, despite these exchanges about the politics of coitus, the coital *imperative* which casts intercourse as an *essential* part of heterosexual sex, unquestionably has a downside – for women in particular. Heterosexual intercourse is a sexual practice that has life-changing implications, in particular pregnancy and the transmission of sexual infections (some of which have lasting complications and/or are life-threatening). While a myriad of techniques and technologies exist for circumventing potential consequences like an unwanted pregnancy or an STI, they are widely perceived and/or experienced as difficult or adverse in their own right. For example, the most technically effective methods of birth control, such as oral contraceptives and IUDs (intrauterine devices), are well known for their "dangerous or troubling side effects" that lead many women to discontinue use (e.g., Petchesky 1990: 189). Also, while many women report enjoying intercourse (see Segal 1994), others go through with it in the absence of their own desire or pleasure (e.g., Gavey 2005) because of the assumption it is normal and, therefore, required. Some women continue to have intercourse even despite routinely experiencing outright pain and discomfort. One 51-year-old woman, for instance, said she was sometimes unable to "disguise how much discomfort" she experienced during intercourse due to her own advanced illness; yet she persisted because of her belief that it was not good for men to go without regular intercourse (e.g., Potts *et al.* 2003: 706).

Given the potential for intercourse to have serious adverse consequences for (particularly women's) health and wellbeing, it would be reasonable to assume that it might be better regarded as a choice within sex rather than as a taken-for-granted act if "sex" is to occur. However, by and large this is not the case. Elsewhere I have discussed the poignant case of Romanian women who continued to engage in coital sex with their husbands, in the absence of their own pleasure, and despite the painful consequences associated with unwanted pregnancies, which were difficult if not impossible to avoid during the extreme pronatalist regime under Ceausescu. One woman, who had had seven illegal abortions, said: "When I was asked by my husband to make love with him I began to feel pains in my stomach because of fear" (cited in Gavey 2005: 123). Despite the especially harsh social conditions these women were living under, which exacerbated the stakes of engaging in unwanted intercourse, the fantasy of sexual and reproductive choice does not necessarily play out fully even in neo-liberal societies in which the notion of choice seems to be fetishized above all else. Girls and women commonly report having sexual intercourse even when they don't want it and/or gain no pleasure from it (e.g., Gavey 2005). Intercourse, it would seem, is part and parcel of sex; not an item that can freely be chosen *or* discarded from the (hetero)sexual menu. Sanders and Reinisch (1999), for instance, found that while virtually everyone in their study regarded penile–vaginal intercourse as constituting having "had sex," 60 percent were of the view that oral–genital contact (if it was "the most intimate behavior" they engaged in) would not.

The coital imperative is not natural

One of the interesting insights gained from historical studies of sex is the finding that some of the assumptions that currently operate as taken-for-granted truths about (hetero)sexuality are not in fact historically constant. For instance, historians write of a "sexual revolution" in the eighteenth century during which the whole nature of what heterosexual sex *was* changed radically. According to Tim Hitchcock (2002), drawing on data from England and Western Europe, it became increasingly phallocentric at this time, moving away from a set of practices that encompassed mutual masturbation, kissing and fondling, mutual touching, and so on. Instead, "putting a penis in a vagina became the dominant sexual activity" (Hitchcock 2002: 191). By the nineteenth century, "proper" marital sex in the United States not only centered on the act of coitus, but reference to noncoital sex was rare in publications of the era, and when it was mentioned it was always associated with prohibitions (Seidman 1991). Perceptions of women's sexuality also changed markedly over this period. From being seen as sexually aggressive (Hitchcock 2002), women came to be seen as sexually passive. Their pleasure during sex, and their orgasm in particular, became increasingly less important (see also Laqueur 1990). More recent changes over the twentieth century include the shift away from seeing (hetero)sex in primarily procreative terms. Through the "sexual revolution" of the mid to late twentieth century, women's sexual pleasure has come back onto the agenda – at least in theory.

It seems ironic, then, that at a time when the procreative function of sex has perhaps never been less important, the sexual act "designed for" procreation has not only persisted as the defining feature of hetero(sex), but, with the Viagra moment, it is increasingly being stretched across the lifespan. Most men using Viagra and similar products are beyond a procreating stage of life. Yet, while the reproductive function of coitus is no longer valorized, the particular heterosexual act for reproduction is. Apparently, in the nineteenth-century United States when the reproductive function of sex was still of primary importance (D'Emilio and Freedman 1988), and sex was based even more narrowly around the procreative act of coitus than it is today, it was assumed that sex between a husband and wife would generally diminish over the course of their marriage (Seidman 1991). By the age of fifty, it was thought, men's sexual life would be over: the "sex drive" being "either absent by that age or enfeebled to a point where it would have little significance in the marriage" (Seidman 1991: 25). Today, when men's bodies give up on producing the kind of rigid penile arousal required for "successful" intercourse, it is considered to be a sexual dysfunction (even though to some extent statistically normal, as the drug company promotions like to reassure people). Such trends might have been predicted by Jeffrey Weeks's (1985) diagnosis of the colonization of sex by capitalism since the beginning of the twentieth century. As part of a more general "commoditisation and commercialisation of social life," Weeks (1985: 22, 23, 24) pointed to an "expansion of perceived sexual needs, particularly among men." This was fertile ground for the "proliferation of new desires as the pursuit of pleasure became an end in itself." Not only the pursuit of pleasure; for sex has become increasingly entangled with all sorts of "higher" psychological and relational meanings, such as intimacy and identity (e.g., Seidman 1989). Intercourse is practiced not simply as a (possible) means to physical pleasure, but as an expression and/or confirmation of love and closeness (e.g., Gavey *et al.* 1999).

The coital imperative is not immutable

Attention to the historical antecedents of our contemporary sexual norms, as we have seen, suggests that there are no single cultural or biological determinants of human sexual behavior that are rigidly prescriptive over time and place. Further support for this contention exists in contemporary evidence that (at least) some people do act otherwise, to embody alternative forms of (hetero)sexuality (not to mention those who escape the strict confines of heteronormativity through lesbian, gay, or other forms of queer sexuality). One example of this comes from the accounts of women and men who have faced erectile difficulties only to find that it enhanced their sexual relationships (Potts *et al.* 2004: 497). As one man who did not have erections commented:

> Matter of fact . . . in some ways our sex life has been, in a *different* way, better since . . . It was a matter of adapting to suit the occasion rather than giving all away, which I suppose . . . some people give it all away, but we were determined not to . . . And she can get me to a climax and sort of keep me going, you know, far more than I used to before . . . so in that way the sex is . . . different and arguably better than what it was before.

Stories such as this – and there were more – disrupt the pharmaceutical company's uni-dimensional hype about the devastation that erectile difficulties (necessarily) cause for heterosexual relationships, as well as for sex itself.

Viagra's intervention

As part of the increasing medicalization (e.g., Tiefer 1995) and commercialization of sexuality, "Viagra" is a cultural phenomenon rather than simply a (set of) biotechnological product(s); a phenomenon that relies on, reinforces, and extends existing sociocultural norms. The impact of Viagra can be felt at several different levels, from the intimate lives of individual women and men to the broader public domain of popular culture. Given that the promotion, and presumably the appeal, of Viagra trades on the coital imperative, it is not surprising that it can intervene within people's private sexual lives in ways that directly (re)assert this imperative. For instance, a 48-year-old woman described how Viagra enforced the coital imperative within her sexual relationship, with the unwelcome extinction of noncoital sexual activities (Potts *et al.* 2003: 704–5):

> [Viagra use began] during a time when I was trying to impress upon him that foreplay would be a nice thing. After twenty-odd years of marriage, foreplay is one of those things that goes by the way; however, I was trying to maintain that this was, you know, quite an important part of making love, so when Viagra came along the whole foreplay thing just *vanished*, I mean it wasn't even a suggestion, it was: "OK, I've taken the pill, we've got about an hour, I expect you in that time to be acquiescent."

Not only does Viagra intervene in men's bodies, minds, and sexuality (and, therefore, in women's experience of heterosex and in relationships between men and women), but the Viagra phenomenon intervenes in culture itself. This phenomenon is more than just the chemical compound sildenafil citrate. It is the potent mix of the drug itself (as well as newer similar drugs) and their promotion within drug company marketing, professional endorsements, and various popular cultural representations. The promotion of Viagra as a biotechnological miracle for restoring men's potency, and with it personal and relational happiness, plays with culture. It shifts the meanings of intercourse – not by inventing new meanings, but by reinforcing and intensifying existing ones in ways that move to squeeze out any comfortable spaces for alternative meanings around having or not having intercourse. At the same time, it prescribes new norms for coitus by extending normative expectations for its place in the lives of aging men, and those with health conditions that threaten erectile reliability. In these ways the Viagra phenomenon shifts the cultural conditions of possibility for (hetero) sex, in ways that are both prescriptive and restrictive.

Some of the interviewees in Potts *et al.*'s research observed that the cultural phenomenon of Viagra involved the *construction* of a problem. That is, it represented the invitation to understand erectile changes as pathology rather than simply a natural change or as an expression of acceptable corporeal and sexual diversity. For example, as one 60-year-old woman explained (Potts *et al.* 2003: 712):

> Yes, it would definitely be different for everybody, I guess, but I think you'd probably find that . . . a large percentage of women in my age group would say that . . .

the desire decreases as you get older and . . . Possibly, if I think about it, it'll come up *because* Viagra has been brought up, right? Because I think Viagra has made a lot of people feel inadequate . . . everybody's on the defensive about how often they have sex and so on, in the older age group.

Even for women and men who already do see erectile changes as a problem to be fixed, Viagra delivers one solution (pharmaceutically restoring the erectile capacity) with such force that other potential "solutions" are either obscured or devalued. In the case of men for whom Viagra poses a serious health risk (e.g., those taking nitrates in medication prescribed for angina or those using recreational drugs that contain nitrates), this fixation with an erect penis and coitus *as* sex is potentially fatal. In these ways, we can see how the Viagra phenomenon works both prescriptively, to install new needs for intercourse, and at the same time restrictively, to close down other legitimate possibilities for sexuality.

In this chapter I have argued that the Viagra phenomenon reinforces and hardens the coital imperative. Not only does it potently work to re-naturalize and re-normalize the centrality of intercourse to heterosexual sex, but it extends its reach to areas of society that previously were able to slip it by (that is, men and women beyond middle age, and those with certain health conditions). And, on the way, it pathologizes bodies and people who cannot, or prefer not to, engage in sexual intercourse on every, or even any, sexual occasion.

In the midst of a Western cultural moment that is arguably open to all sorts of possibility for progressive social change around sexuality, the Viagra phenomenon is profoundly *disappointing*. Social constructionist perspectives (e.g., Foucault 1981; Tiefer 1995) which draw attention to the shifting and contextual nature of human behavior and experience have become highly influential within sexuality studies. Moreover, even recent trends within biology emphasize the co-constitution of organisms and their environments (see Gavey 2005). The convergence of these constructionist perspectives from biology, social science and history permits a cautious optimism that the plasticity of human sexuality might allow for shifting and less rigid norms that promote increased tolerance and an ethic attentive to difference and power. It is just possible that these trends within the academy, as well as within the queer margins of culture, might have signalled broader movements towards new cultural understandings and practices. Were such an ethic brought to bear on questions relating to health, wellbeing, and equality, the coital imperative would surely be due for some wider critical scrutiny. Instead, such potentially radical cultural shifts have arguably been stalled by the escalating medicalization of sexuality within the corporate thrust of pharmaceutical companies hungry for new markets in which to expand profit. Through their prominent co-option of the coital imperative, which is strategically necessary in order to create a new market for a costly erectile fix, the disappointing spin-off is that many men and women are likely to be deprived of the cultural conditions for realizing diverse sexual and reproductive choices that might have enhanced their health and wellbeing.

References

D'Emilio, John and Estelle B. Freedman. 1988. *Intimate matters: A history of sexuality in America*, New York: Harper & Row.

Dworkin, Andrea. 1987. *Intercourse*, New York: The Free Press.

Foucault, Michel. 1981. *The history of sexuality (Volume 1: An Introduction)* (R. Hurley, trans.), Harmondsworth, Middlesex: Penguin.

Gavey, Nicola. 2005. *Just sex? The cultural scaffolding of rape*, New York and London: Routledge.

Gavey, Nicola, Kathryn McPhillips, and Virginia Braun. 1999. "Interruptus coitus: Heterosexuals accounting for intercourse", *Sexualities* 2 (1): 35–68.

Hitchcock, Tim. 2002. "Redefining sex in eighteenth-century England." In Kim M. Phillips and Barry Reay (eds), *Sexualities in history: A reader*, New York and London: Routledge.

Jackson, Margaret. 1984. "Sex research and the construction of sexuality: A tool of male supremacy?" *Women's Studies International Forum* 7: 43–51.

Laqueur, Thomas. 1990. *Making sex: Body and gender from the Greeks to Freud*. Cambridge, MA and London: Harvard University Press.

Petchesky, Rosalind P. 1990. *Abortion and woman's choice: The state, sexuality, and reproductive freedom (Revised Edition)*, Boston, MA: Northeastern University Press.

Potts, Annie, Nicola Gavey, Victoria Grace, and Tiina Vares. 2003. "The downside of Viagra: Women's experiences and concerns", *Sociology of Health and Illness* 25 (7): 697–719.

Potts, Annie, Victoria Grace, Nicola Gavey, and Tiina Vares. 2004. "'Viagra stories': Challenging 'erectile dysfunction'", *Social Science and Medicine* 59: 489–99.

Sanders, Stephanie A. and June M. Reinisch. 1999. "Would you say you 'had sex' if . . . ?" *Journal of the American Medical Association* 281 (3): 275–77.

Segal, Lynne. 1994. *Straight sex: Rethinking the politics of pleasure*, Berkeley and Los Angeles: University of California Press.

Seidman, Steven. 1989. "Constructing sex as a domain of pleasure and self-expression: Sexual ideology in the sixties", *Theory, Culture & Society* 6: 293–315.

—. 1991. *Romantic longings: Love in America, 1830–1980*, London and New York: Routledge.

Tiefer, Leonore. 1995. *Sex is not a natural act and other essays*, Boulder, CO: Westview Press.

Weeks, Jeffrey. 1985. *Sexuality and its discontents: Meanings, myths and modern sexualities*, London and New York: Routledge & Kegan Paul.

chapter 10

Sex and the senior woman

Meika Loe

On a warm summer evening, a women's discussion group was underway at a senior community center in northern California. At this particular meeting, one longtime participant, Jerry, a short, white-haired woman in her seventies, made an announcement to the group. "After years of work, I just sent off my book manuscript . . . it is about my sexual relationship with a younger man, and the importance of society recognizing senior women and our sensuality." The room erupted in cheers. Afterwards, several women approached Jerry, wanting to share stories about their own sexual experiences and to hear more about hers.

As this story reveals, now more than ever seniors are expressing themselves as sexual beings. In the Viagra era, sexual desire and performance is more visible and more valued than ever – for men of a broad range of ages and ethnicities. Think about recent Viagra endorsers Bob Dole, Raphael Palmiero, and Pele. None the less, despite new public attention to the sexualized senior man, the stereotype of the asexual senior woman continues to prevail. Even in the Viagra era, nobody seems to be talking about women's sexualities, or asking senior women about their sexual desires. However, in the context of my research on Viagra, I found senior women who were eager to talk about how they view health, sexuality, and culture in the Viagra era.

I met senior women through two senior citizen organizations in Southern California: a singles social club and a seniors-only summer school. Agnes, Annette, Bette, Doris, Hilda, Nora, Pauline, and Sally are the focus of this chapter. At the time of their interviews, they ranged in age from sixty-seven to eighty-six years of age. Most were living either in Florida or Southern California, approximately half were Jewish, and all were white, heterosexual, middle- or upper-middle-class American citizens. They all had differing relationships to Viagra: four had partners who tried Viagra, others had friends who used the product, and a couple only knew of Viagra through news reporting or conversations with friends. Importantly, all but Bette, who was divorced, were widows. At the time of our conversations, Bette and Doris were actively dating, while the others were not. All names were changed to protect my informants. All interviews took place over the phone in October and November 2000. All were conducted by the author and tape-recorded.

Research on sex and senior women

Before interviewing senior women, I looked for existing research on sexuality and senior women. Unfortunately, the assumption that sexuality declines and disappears with age has led to gaps and silences in the few landmark national sexuality studies that have been conducted. Research by Kinsey in the 1950s and Masters and Johnson in the late 1960s are examples of such negligence, as there is little to be learned in these studies about senior sex. Such assumptions about lack of sex may have even informed the latest *Sex in America* survey (1994) which included only those aged eighteen to fifty-nine. One notable exception came in 1976 with Shere Hite's *The Hite Report on Female Sexuality* that received questionnaire responses from women aged fourteen to seventy-eight. According to Hite, one of the major findings was that age is not a factor in female sexuality, or in other words: "Older women are NOT less sexual than younger women – and they are often more sexual."

Bob Dole's erectile dysfunction was not the only senior Viagra story that existed for the women I interviewed. Indeed, for many, the public chatter created by the Viagra phenomenon marked an opportunity for women to weigh in on the larger social discourse on health, aging, and medicine, and the construction of their own sexual selves. In the pages that follow, senior women fill in the gaps left by centuries of sex research and Viagra promoters, by sharing their desires and viewpoints, and, in the process, revealing how social sex really is.

Senior women's views on sexual pleasure and partners

It is no surprise that, for most seniors, Viagra is viewed in the context of health and aging. For many, Viagra may represent the elusive pursuit of youth, reminiscent of the ways in which male consumers of the drug can construct Viagra as a fountain-of-youth pill, enabling them to "feel eighteen again." However, few of the women I spoke with longed to return to the sexuality associated with their teenage years. Instead, sexuality represented a means to feeling healthy and vital. For example, Bette, age sixty-nine, told me that she views sexuality as a "really good calorie burner." Another volunteered: "[Viagra] has allowed us to enjoy sex again – makes us mentally feel younger." In addition, Pauline, age eighty-one, was one of several women who volunteered that her "sexual prime" was post-menopause:

> Well, menopause made sex less risky for me, and I didn't have to put a diaphragm in every night or interrupt sex for that. The risks were much less, which made it more enjoyable.

As opposed to accounts calling sexuality "risky" for the elderly, Pauline found sex less risky when she didn't have to worry about pregnancy. Just as Pauline declared sex enjoyable later in life, several of her peers, some of whom were widows, confided to me that they had been feeling sexual desire in recent years. However, their stories reveal that such desires may not be acted upon in the context of social constraints.

For example, 74-year-old Nora's "sexual urges" were mitigated by concerns about appearing "oversexed" or disrespectful in the context of widowhood, or by frustration over finding a willing and able sexual partner in one's age group.

> I was appalled that, 6 weeks after my husband died, somebody would want to kiss me or I might want to respond, because I don't think truthfully that I was what I would call an oversexed woman. I had sexual urges but I never initiated love-making too much.

For senior women like Nora, acting on sexual desire may have been seen as risky or fruitless for a number of reasons. First, as Nora noted, expressions of desire fed into stereotypes about appearing "oversexed" as a senior woman of her generation. Second, Nora had to confront life expectancy patterns that result in a "partner gap," leaving four out of five women of seventy-five and older without male partners. Finally, a number of social factors including the idealization of youth may lead older men in Nora's age bracket to want to date younger women.

Doris, a witty, practical, sexually active 86-year-old, was similarly vocal about her sexual desires as well as her concerns about the lack of potential sexual partners in her age group. For Doris, men are not necessarily in short supply, but *healthy* male sexual partners are. In her comments below, Doris described her desire to have a sexual relationship at her age, as opposed to the platonic arrangements she saw her friends having.

> Bear in mind that I am eighty-six years old, and I am interested in sex under certain conditions. Clean bill of health is my number-1 priority. Protection is right up there with number-1, and I don't care if it does sound clinical . . . that's the world I live in. And I have to say that most of the men I have met have been inadequate in performance, so my conditions didn't either enhance or hinder the act . . . I have about given up on the whole thing . . . not worth the effort . . . at least at the moment. I am satisfied to have someone for company at movies, restaurants, concerts, short trips, etc. I find that the older I get, the less sex has to do with my happiness. And since I am financially independent, I really do not need anyone living with me, I can manage my daily life very well, and doing "wifely" things is not something I would care to do. If things get to be desperate, there is always a vibrator, which is ready to "go," providing the batteries are new. Who could ask for more?

Doris's pursuit of pleasure was thwarted by male partners she perceived as unhealthy, who do not use protection, or those that could not "perform." As a result, Doris considered giving up on finding a sexual partner, and turning instead to her vibrator for pleasure.

Perhaps these comments of sexual dissatisfaction are one reason we never heard from the likes of Elizabeth Dole and the other sexually frustrated partners of senior men. This is the side of the story that Pfizer (the manufacturer of Viagra) doesn't talk about – some women's desire for sex and men's inability to respond positively to these desires. These comments show the other side of impotency; that is, the sexual frustration for women. Again contrary to the ideas about sex that we are used to hearing, these women appear to be the sexual initiators in these relationships. Senior women like Doris remind us that sexual pleasure exists in the context of social rules and relationships. Rather than pleasure and desire being static and natural, Doris reveals how sexuality is socially contingent and fluid.

While several senior women confided in me that they turn to vibrators in place of sexual partners, other women, like 80-year-old Hilda, like the idea of a female Viagra, or a future pill for women's sexual pleasure.

ML: What would be your ideal drug?
H: I'd want to experience what I've read about. The ecstasy.
ML: Do you mean libido? Orgasm?
H: Yes. I have two friends who make reference to the fact that they have had wonderful sex lives. They are both widows. And both very unusual for my generation since they've had more than one partner. One told me that she never experienced with her husband what she had with another man. So maybe some guys do it better than others. I wouldn't know – I've only had one. And this is the way I'm going to finish.

Hilda's comments illustrate the role that social networks, or peers, play in the construction of sexual desires. Like most of us, Hilda based her sexual knowledge and ideals in relation to the experiences of friends. In the process, she highlighted one of the key differences between men's and women's desire for a Viagra-like drug. Generally, while men of Hilda's generation may need the drug to help them continue to pursue sexual pleasure, senior women of her generation may want a drug to discover sexual pleasure for the first time.

Clearly, Pauline, Nora, Doris and Hilda do not fit the "asexual" stereotype associated with generations of senior women. For them, like the rest of us, sexuality is complex, fluid, and social. Their sexual desires and pursuit of viable partners are mediated by perceived health and social risks, sanctions, and ideals. As individuals, then, these senior women reveal the role society plays in shaping their sexual identities and behaviors. In the next section, senior women directly confront the role that culture may play in constructing and reinforcing pressures to be sexual beings.

Senior women's concerns about sexualized culture

While some senior women are curious about a mythic "pink Viagra" that can enhance pleasure, others see both pink and blue Viagra pills as representative of a problematic quick-fix pill culture, and an increasingly sexualized culture. For example, senior women like 81-year-old Annette believe that sex is more often used to demonstrate physicality and efficiency, rather than romance and feelings.

> All of that preparation an hour in advance, it makes sex not grow out of a loving feeling. It becomes planned and purely physical. And I just don't like that. The whole idea of sex has become so physical. Such gymnastics involved! And while I'm not opposed to experimentation and variety – not at all – it's become only that. The love is missing. The affection!

For Annette and others, Viagra marketing was the instigator of, or the scapegoat for, changing sexual norms. Nora linked this cultural change to a generational shift in sexual discourse, which is "too open" today, leaving no sexual mystique. Concurrently, the marketing of Viagra-like drugs is to blame for an increasingly sexualized culture that promotes promiscuity. Nora commented, "It would be hard to be celibate today. Sex is idealized on the tv and in movies as perfect and acceptable and it's just not that way in real life." For women like Nora, a culture dangerously focused on the sexual fix is perceived not only as over-sexed, but also masculine, leading women to act "too much like men and ignore romance, intimacy, and emotions." A move toward goal-oriented, or masculine sexual ideals in the Viagra era was also implied by 67-year-old Agnes:

> What is important to me is being in love. I wouldn't be with someone just for the sex. This is a woman's point of view. That love and affection are more important than sex. A man would say the opposite. That sex is most important.

Together, Agnes, Annette, and Nora blame Viagra-like drugs for promoting new problematic cultural expectations and pressures related to sexuality. They construct women's sexuality as emotional, mysterious, and romantic, as opposed to male sexuality which is non-emotional and physical. In sum, these senior women claim that masculine sexuality has set new and dangerous standards for women and society.

Despite the cultural shift toward masculine ideals and sexual pressures, Sally, age seventy-five, and then Hilda, age eighty, also convey a sense of being "caught" in a pill culture that both promotes and benefits from people's limited tolerance for personal discomfort, as well as a culture that excludes people who cannot afford these solutions.

> I think the price is going to leave even the middle-classes behind. The insurance companies may not want to pay for some of these high-priced wonders. But I do think that the rich will have a greater advantage in all of these things.

> People's tolerance levels are really low. If it hurts, go get a pill. I'm not like that. I figure you should fight it. Like here at the pool, I tell people with arthritis to go in the pool, because water is good for it. But they'd rather take a pill. I wouldn't. It's too easy to take a pill. Even a diet pill. They'd rather take a diet pill than go to a gym.

Senior women such as Agnes, Annette, Sally and Hilda point to problems they see as exacerbated by the marketing of Viagra-like drugs, including the promotion of exaggerated sexual norms and expectations, prohibitively expensive prescriptions, a quick-fix ethic, and an under-emphasis on romance and emotions. In response, some actively resist such cultural pressures, choosing to associate sex with romance and to avoid quick-fixes.

What do senior women want?

In the Viagra era, particularly as pharmaceutical companies race to produce and market a potential blockbuster "female Viagra," senior women are slowly being acknowledged as sexual agents. But senior women's sexual lives are nothing new. As Agnes put it:

> These days, seniors are still falling in love and feeling young and sexually active again. Is this new? Probably not. It has probably been the case for some time now, but people didn't talk about it.

What do senior women want? At the very least they deserve to be included in public discussions on sexuality. In my interviews with medical practitioners I was troubled to hear some describe their "horror" as elderly patients began to ask for Viagra-like products. They were not used to imagining their parents or their patients as sexual beings.

Rather than dismiss or ignore senior women, I suggest that we learn from them. Talking to these women really opened my eyes. I knew that women had responses to the Viagra phenomenon, but I never imagined how rich, varied, and self-aware these responses might be, particularly from a group of women largely without sexual partners. Like all of us, between stories these women wanted to know if they were normal for having desires, fears, and doubts related to sexuality. At the same time, not having current sexual partners seemed to free them up to be able to reflect on their sexual lives, and even to make plans for the future.

Their stories reveal complex sexual identities and desires. These stories convey how sexuality can be mitigated and enabled by social expectations and constraints. They remind us that, just as everyone is a product of this culture, all of us have complex and conflicting ideas and feelings about sexuality in the Viagra era. Senior women, like all of us, are caught up in the social realities of our time, including medicalization, gendered and sexual oppression, and increased commercialization, perhaps even to a larger degree than men. At the same time, their lives also reflect vast generational changes in the social construction of gender, sexuality, medicine, and health. Most importantly, they remind us that, whether by taking a pill or talking about our desires, all of us are sexual agents, actively defining sexuality for ourselves and one another. In sum, they remind us of the "messy" social side of sex and sexuality that, as sociologists, we should care deeply about.

Bibliography

Hite, Shere. 1994. *Women as Revolutionary Agents of Change: The Hite Reports and Beyond.* Madison: University of Wisconsin Press.
Levy, Judith A. 1994. "Sex and Sexuality in Later Life Stages," in *Sexuality Across the Life Course.* Alice S. Rossi (ed.). Chicago, IL: University of Chicago Press.

chapter 11

The body, disability, and sexuality

Thomas J. Gerschick

> We do not express or even show our wishes, because we have learned that in our condition of disablement or disfigurement, no one could (or should) find us sexually attractive.
>
> (Zola 1982: 215)

People with disabilities face formidable challenges in establishing self-satisfactory sexualities; yet despite these challenges, they are increasingly doing so. This chapter conveys a range of scholarship from advocates, researchers, and other interested parties regarding the relationship among the body, disability, and sexuality. I begin with a brief contextualization of disability and then turn my attention to the role of the body in social life using the experiences of people with disabilities to highlight key social dynamics. Subsequently, I provide an overview of the challenges that people with disabilities face in determining self-satisfactory sexualities and conclude with a discussion of their active responses to those challenges.

Disabled bodies

Those who are characterized as disabled experience a wide range of medically defined conditions, some readily visible, others much less so. These conditions are conceptualized in a variety of ways by doctors and scholars, but generally they are grouped under physical and psychological conditions. Examples include deafness, blindness, spinal cord injury, multiple sclerosis, muscular dystrophy, developmental disabilities, bipolar disorder, and mental illness. These definitions serve to distinguish people with disabilities from the temporarily able-bodied in society. I intentionally utilize the term temporarily able-bodied to highlight the fact that aging is disabling and many of us will live long enough to develop a disability during our lifetime. Such language highlights the fact that human variation reflects a continuum, rather than a dichotomy of being disabled or not.

As many scholars have noted, it is exceedingly difficult to determine the size of the population of people with disabilities globally due to lack of consensus regarding definitions of disability and differential abilities within countries and regions to count their populations. One well-informed researcher, Gary Albrecht (2004), placed the number at approximately 500 million worldwide, the vast majority of whom live in the developing world. Reflecting our limited understanding of the scope of the population, there is much we do not know regarding the circumstances, conditions and treatment of people with disabilities. As a consequence of this, the bulk of this chapter will focus on the existing scholarship which largely attends to the West, especially the United States. Furthermore, given the relatively new attention to disability and sexuality, not much attention has been paid to the intersection of these with other social factors such as race, class, gender, sexual orientation, and ethnicity. Wherever possible, I include available understandings of these intersections.

The importance of the body in social life

The body is central in social life. People are privileged by the degree to which they approximate the cultural ideal. Bodies physically exist along a continuum. Given the large amount of human variation across time and culture and the array of expectations and standards, the body must be framed in terms of degrees of normativity: from more normative to less (Gerschick 2005). There are many ways in which a body can be less normative. Characteristics such as race, ethnicity, class, age, physique, weight, height, ability, disability, appearance, and skin color predominate. People can be less normative by being too light, too dark, too fat, too skinny, too poor, too young, too old, too tall, too short, too awkward, and/or too uncoordinated. Scholars have noted that the degree to which one is bodily-normative matters considerably because it helps place one in the stratification order. The degree to which bodily variation has been accepted has also varied across time and culture. The societal treatment one experiences, then, depends on the degree of normativeness, one's resources, and the particular historical, cultural, and structural contexts in which one lives (Gerschick 2005). For example, consider the resources available to the late actor, Christopher Reeve, following his injury in 1995, due to his celebrity and wealth. Although his injury was severe, he received the highest quality of care possible and became a cultural icon for his work on behalf of others with spinal cord injuries. Many other people with disabilities, lacking Reeve's status and resources, are treated much more poorly. Their opportunities are also much more limited.

The negative treatment experienced by most people with disabilities can be understood by considering how bodies are symbolic. One's body serves as a type of social currency that signifies one's worth. Consequently, people with less-normative bodies, such as people with disabilities, are vulnerable to being denied social recognition and validation. People respond to one another's bodies, which initiates social processes such as validation and the assignment of status. Summarizing the research, Patzer (1985: 1) observes:

> Physical attractiveness is the most visible and most easily accessible trait of a person. Physical attractiveness is also a constantly and frequently used informational cue . . . Generally, the more physically attractive an individual is, the more positively the person is perceived, the more favorably the person is responded to, and the more successful is the person's personal and professional life.

Thus, researchers maintain that to have a less-normative body, such as having a disability which is perceived by most to be unattractive, is not so much a physical condition as it is a social and stigmatized one.

This stigma is embodied in the popular stereotypes of people whose bodies are less normative. People with disabilities, for instance, are perceived to be weak, passive, and dependent. The English language exemplifies this stigmatization; people with disabilities are de-formed, dis-eased, dis-abled, dis-ordered, ab-normal, and in-valid (Zola 1982: 206). Having a disability can also become a primary identity that overshadows almost all other aspects of one's identity.

This stigma is embedded in daily interactions among people. People are evaluated in terms of normative expectations and, because of their bodies, are frequently found wanting. As demonstrated by the social responses to people with disabilities, people with less-normative bodies are avoided, ignored, and marginalized. They experience a range of reactions from subtle indignities and slights to overt hostility and outright cruelty (Gerschick 2005, 1998). This treatment creates subtle but formidable physical, economic, psychological, architectural, and social obstacles to their participation in all aspects of social life.

A hierarchy of bodies exists in any particular historical, cultural, structural, and global context. The degree to which one's body is devalued is also affected by other social characteristics including social class, sexual orientation, age, and race and ethnicity. The type of disability – its visibility, the severity of it, whether it is physical or mental in origin, and the contexts – mediate the degree to which a person with a less-normative body is socially compromised (Gerschick 2005, 1998). For instance, a severe case of Chronic Fatigue Syndrome can disable someone, thereby creating a less-normative body; however, typically the condition is not readily apparent and as a consequence does not automatically trigger stigmatization and devaluation. Conversely, having quadriplegia and utilizing a wheelchair for mobility is highly visual, is perceived to be severe, and frequently elicits invalidation. One of the challenges facing researchers is to develop a systematic theory to address the degrees of non-normativity and the circumstances that lead to different levels of stigmatization and marginalization and how these differ for different groups of people based on their gender, race, ethnicity, social class, sexual orientation and origin (Gerschick 2005).

People with less-normative bodies, such as people with disabilities, are engaged in an asymmetrical power relationship with their more-normative bodied counterparts, who have the power to validate their bodies and their identities (Gerschick 2005,

1998). An example comes from Jerry, aged sixteen at the time of his interview, who lived with Juvenile Rheumatoid Arthritis:

> I think [others' conception of what defines a man] is very important because if they don't think of you as one, it is hard to think of yourself as one or it doesn't really matter if you think of yourself as one if no one else does.
>
> (Gerschick and Miller 1994: 50)

In order to be validated, each person in a social situation needs to be recognized by others as appropriately meeting the situated expectations. Those with whom we interact continuously assess our performance and determine the degree to which we are meeting those expectations. Our "audience" or interaction partners then hold us accountable and sanction us in a variety of ways in order to encourage compliance. Our need for social approval and validation further encourages conformity. Much is at stake in this process because one's sense of self rests precariously upon the audience's decision to validate or reject one's performance. Successful enactment bestows status and acceptance; failure invites embarrassment and humiliation (West and Zimmerman 1987). This point is illustrated by Kit, one of researchers Shakespeare, Gillespie-Sells and Davies's informants:

> I actually think my being a disabled lesbian is a very . . . it's a struggle, I don't mean that it's a struggle in that I don't want to be a disabled lesbian, it's a struggle in that you are completely, you are completely insignificant and denied any identity or importance.
>
> (Shakespeare, Gillespie-Sells and Davies 1996: 154)

It is challenging to maintain one's dignity and sense of self under such circumstances.

Challenges to sexual satisfaction

Before turning my attention to the ways in which people with disabilities seek sexual self-determination, I want to focus on five particular challenges to developing self-satisfactory sexualities: the medicalization of disability, the attitudes of the temporarily able-bodied, internalized oppression, fetishists, and physical and sexual abuse.

The medicalization model of people with disabilities

Historically, disability has been defined in part in medical terms. It has been perceived as an individual, physical problem requiring a medical or mechanical solution. Scholars point out that the emphasis in this model is on deficiency, pathology, tragedy and loss that can, with medical intervention, be remedied. This mindset locates the problem solely in the individual, not in society. As such it is apolitical. The person with a disability is defined as passive, dependent and infant-like, one who needs others to care for them. It reinforces the power of others, especially care professionals, to define people with disabilities and their circumstances. While there is no doubt that medical

Thomas J. Gerschick

attention has significantly improved the lives of people with disabilities over the last several decades, the attendant mindset has also undermined disabled people's ability to self-determine their lives, including their sexuality.

Associated with this is the view that people with disabilities are asexual. As a consequence, scholars maintain that medical practitioners tend not to provide information to people with disabilities about sexual functioning or sexual healthcare. In denying them information about sexual pleasure, medical practitioners send a tacit but powerful message about how people with disabilities are perceived as sexual beings. They are, apparently, not entitled to this kind of pleasure, as explained by then 53-year-old essayist, Nancy Mairs:

> the general assumption, even among those who might be expected to know better, is that people with disabilities are out of the sexual running. Not one of my doctors, for example, has ever asked me about my sex life. Most people, in fact, deal with the discomfort and even distaste that a misshapen body arouses by disassociating that body from sexuality in reverie and practice. "They" can't possibly do it, the thinking goes; therefore, "they" mustn't even want it; and that is *that*. The matter is closed before a word is uttered. People with disabilities can grow so used to unstated messages of consent and prohibition that they no longer "hear" them as coming from the outside, any more than the messengers know they are "speaking" them. This vast conspiracy of silence surrounding the sexuality of the disabled consigns countless numbers to sexual uncertainty and disappointment.
>
> (Mairs 1996: 51–2)

One can easily imagine, then, how debilitating this mindset can be in cultures that emphasize sex and sexuality.

Attitudes of people with disabilities as sexual partners

Successfully creating and maintaining self-satisfactory sexualities and identities under these challenging social circumstances is an almost Sisyphean task. Consequently, sexuality is threatened when corporeal appearance and performance are discordant with cultural expectations, such as in the case of having a disability (Gerschick 1998). Depending on the degree of their difference, people with disabilities contravene many of the beliefs and expectations associated with being desirable and sexual. For instance, in the contemporary West, to be perceived as physically attractive is to be socially and sexually desirable. Due to their invalidated condition, however, women and men with disabilities are constrained in their opportunities to nurture and to be nurtured, to be lovers and to love, and to become parents if they so desire (Gerschick 1998). These dynamics are particularly acute in subcultures where a premium is placed on bodily appearance. Poet Kenny Fries, in his memoir, discusses what it is like to be a man with a disability within a gay culture that idealizes bodies:

> in bars I would plant myself at a table or on a stool at the bar and stay in one place as long as possible. When I saw someone I would like to get to know, I would stay put. And even when I had to go to the bathroom I would put it off for as long as I could to

avoid making my disability noticeable by standing up and walking. By deciding to remain stationary, I rarely met the men I wanted to meet, the men I was attracted to. Those I met would have to come over to me, or I would meet them by chance when they happened to take an empty seat near where I sat at a table or at the bar.

(Fries 1997: 131)

Thus people with disabilities, many with few social resources, face deeply entrenched prejudice and stereotypes when seeking to establish self-satisfactory sexualities. They rarely have the power to challenge the dominant discourse which infantilizes them and perceives them to be asexual (Shakespeare, Gillespie-Sells, and Davies 1996).

Internalized oppression

Sexuality and a sense of oneself as a sexual being are not created in a vacuum. Frequently people with disabilities internalize societal negative stereotypes and act on them as if they were true. In the following quote, writer and filmmaker Billy Golfus, who was disabled due to a motorcycle accident, illustrates the insidiousness of internalizing asexual stereotypes about people with disabilities when he discusses a woman for a potential relationship:

Even though she is attractive, I don't really think about her that way partly because the [wheel]chair makes me not even see her and because after so many years of being disabled you quit thinking about it as an option.

(Golfus 1997: 420)

The woman in this illustration was as invisible to him as his own sexuality was. This example reveals how deeply some people with disabilities internalize societal standards of desirability and sexuality, which then makes them complicit in their sexual oppression (Gerschick 1998).

Similarly, people with disabilities internalize the belief that their degree of function, attractiveness and desirability determines their self worth. Author and cartoonist John Callahan explained:

I can remember looking at my body with loathing and thinking, Boy, if I ever get to heaven, I'm not going to ask for a new pair of legs like the average quad does. I'm going to ask for a dick I can feel. The idea promoted in rehab of the socially well-adjusted, happily married quad made me sick. This was the cruelest thing of all. Always, I felt humiliated. Surely a man with any self respect would pull the plug on himself.

(Callahan 1990: 121)

The lack of self-esteem in this crucial human arena leads people with physical disabilities to limit themselves at times, as Nancy Mairs (1996: 52) describes:

my wheelchair seals my chastity. Men may look at me with pity, with affection, with amusement, with admiration, but never with lust. To be truthful, I have so

Thomas J. Gerschick

internalized the social proscription of libido in my kind that if a man did come on to me, I'd probably distrust him as at least a little peculiar in his erotic tastes.

As the following section demonstrates, Mairs has reason to be concerned.

Fetishists

One of the paradoxical issues facing people with disabilities are devotees: temporarily able-bodied people who are attracted to them because of their disabilities. Because most devotees are heterosexual males pursuing women with disabilities, especially women amputees, this section focuses on them.

There are many websites and magazines devoted to community, companionship, relationships, and picture and DVD exchange and sale between temporarily able-bodied men and women with disabilities. These forums provide locales where women with disabilities can meet and interact with their followers. They can run, or respond to, personal ads and arrange to meet potential suitors in person. Many of these forums are controlled by women with disabilities (Kafer 2000).

The social meanings and ramifications of these sites, communities, and behaviors are difficult to discern. In a society which does not value emotional, mental, or physical difference, relationships between people with disabilities and their devotees are created in an environment of vast power differentials. However, many of the women involved in these communities experience their participation as empowering. Additionally, if we define the attraction of devotee men as deviant, what does that say about the social desirability of women with disabilities? Is it problematic to find women with disabilities attractive? If we define these relationships in this way, are we defining women with disabilities as victims in need of protection, thereby further infantilizing them (Kafer 2000)?

Read another way, these communities challenge the dominant cultural stereotype of women with disabilities as being unattractive and asexual. Some women with disabilities report enhanced self-esteem, self-confidence, and comfort with their bodies since joining devotee communities. These communities and associated social gatherings can be a source of revenue as well, since they provide a market for women with disabilities to sell photos and DVDs of themselves. Supporters claim that this phenomenon allows women with disabilities more power to define and control their sexuality (Kafer 2000).

While some women with disabilities experience a positive effect, these communities simultaneously sexually objectify women with disabilities. The degree to which devotee communities challenge or alter the social structure is highly debated (Kafer 2000). This is especially true regarding power relations between people with disabilities and the temporarily able-bodied. As of now, these communities are relatively small and have had little apparent effect on the perceptions or actions of the temporarily able-bodied. Furthermore, one cannot ignore that devotees are almost entirely temporarily able-bodied men, most of whom are heterosexual, some of whom are gay. There are very few women devotees seeking men or women with disabilities (Kafer 2000). This raises further concerns about power differentials. For instance, these relationships cannot be understood outside of a patriarchal culture which empowers men at the expense of women. Thus, it would be difficult to create an egalitarian relationship when male devotees have cultural and structural power as men while women with disabilities are devalued.

Although women and men with disabilities share similar experiences of devaluation, isolation, marginalization, and discrimination, their fortunes diverge in important ways. One of these ways is in terms of the violence they face.

Physical and sexual abuse

Although there is much that we do not know regarding the extent of violence that people with disabilities experience, research suggests that children with disabilities are 70 percent more likely to be physically or sexually abused than their able-bodied counterparts (Crosse, Kaye, and Ratnofsky 1993). Researchers report that this abuse is more likely to be chronic than episodic and perpetuated by someone the victim knows, such as a family member or personal attendant. Furthermore, this abuse is gendered; females with disabilities are more likely to be sexually assaulted, whereas males with disabilities are more likely to experience physical abuse (Sobsey, Randall, and Parrila 1997). Thus, having a disability exacerbates one of the worst elements of oppression and does untold amounts of damage to disabled people's sense of and experience of their sexuality (Gerschick 2000).

Claiming their own sexualities

As the preceding pages have demonstrated, people with disabilities face formidable challenges to creating self-satisfactory sexual experiences and identities. However, we would be making a grave mistake if we did not simultaneously highlight the agency of people with disabilities to fight the beliefs and social dynamics that hinder the development and expression of their sexualities (Shakespeare, Gillespie-Sells, and Davies 1996).

Scholars point out that the Disability Rights Movement, while slow to address issues of sexuality, has for several decades championed a sociopolitical understanding of people with disabilities as a minority group with all the attendant human rights. Movement members have fought for the access and employment rights of people with disabilities. As a result, they have created a social space for activists and scholars to address sexuality by publishing books, educating, and advocating. Key to these efforts is reframing issues of bodily difference as problems with societal definitions, accommodations, and expectations, rather than with people with disabilities themselves. As a consequence, prejudice and discrimination towards people with disabilities are likened to other forms of political, cultural, and social oppression such as racism, sexism, and heterosexism. Thus, the emphasis in the Disability Rights approach is on the cultural, attitudinal, and structural barriers that people with disabilities face rather than on their physical differences. Physical differences, such as disabilities, are only limitations to the degree that society makes them so.

Activists' and scholars' work takes place on multiple levels. On the individual level, they are facilitating people with disabilities' redefinition of their bodies and their relationship with them. They encourage them to embrace their bodily differences and increase self-esteem about them. In so doing, they create positive images and role models that acknowledge, nurture, and promote self-esteem and sexuality for other people with disabilities. This redefinition is clearly illustrated by Penny, one of Shakespeare, Gillespie-Sells, and Davies's informants:

> For me, sex is about pleasure, humour and respect. It is with these factors in mind that I approach any seeming "difficulty" my impairments present me. Of course there are techniques and positions I will never manage to do. But I know this is true of most people, along that huge scale of human variety that in reality exists in human beings. Some activities I choose not to do, because I have no taste for them. This is as it should be. But I also know my open attitude to my sexuality, arising because I am a disabled person, often defines sex for me as a much more celebratory and explorative experience than for many non-disabled people.
>
> (Shakespeare, Gillespie-Sells, and Davies 1996: 205)

On an individual and societal level, scholars and activists challenge the limited definition of what constitutes sexuality and sexual behavior, especially the emphasis on heterosexual intercourse. People without genital sensation, from a spinal cord injury for instance, can have orgasms through the stimulation of other parts of their bodies. It is well known that the skin and the brain are two of the largest sources of sexual pleasure.

On a societal level, activists and scholars recognize that the formation of their own culture is key to developing their sexual freedom, for it is in this culture that they can develop their own images, beliefs, and standards, and from this social space they can challenge those of the dominant culture. They emphasize that the pursuit of sexuality and sexual happiness regardless of the condition of one's body is a fundamental human right. They argue that people with disabilities must have the power to define sexuality for themselves. Movement members also seek to shatter the stereotypes associated with people with disabilities, including that they are infantile and asexual. Finally, they are strong advocates for reproductive freedom and contraception for people with disabilities.

Conclusion

Disability has a profound effect on people's sexuality. The barriers are great, but so is the agency challenging them. Yet there is still much we do not know about this process. For instance, we have scant information regarding how disability intersects with other social characteristics like sexual orientation, race, class, ethnicity and gender to shape sexualities. Furthermore, we know little about global variations. As a consequence, there are many opportunities for scholars to add to our understanding. I close this chapter with encouragement to take up these issues, so that we may better understand the social factors and dynamics that shape the sexualities of people with disabilities today, and so that we may eradicate the social, cultural, and political barriers to their sexual self-definition and self-satisfaction.

References

Albrecht, Gary L. 2004. "Disability as a Global Issue", in George Ritzer (ed.), *Handbook of Social Problems: A Comparative International Perspective*. Thousand Oaks, CA: Sage.

Callahan, John. 1990. *Don't Worry, He Won't Get Far on Foot*. New York: Vintage.

Crosse, Scott B., Elyse Kaye, and Alexander C. Ratnofsky. 1993. *A Report on the Maltreatment of Children with Disabilities*. Washington, DC: National Center on Child Abuse and Neglect.

Fries, Kenny. 1997. *Body, Remember: A Memoir*. New York: Dutton.

Gerschick, Thomas J. 2005. "Masculinity and Degrees of Bodily Normativity in Western Culture", in Michael S. Kimmel, Jeff Hearn and R. W. Connell (eds), *Handbook of Studies on Men and Masculinities*. Thousand Oaks, CA: Sage.

—. 2000. "Toward A Theory of Disability and Gender", *Signs*, 25 (4): 1263–8.

—. 1998. "Sisyphus in a Wheelchair: Men with Physical Disabilities Confront Gender Domination", in Judith Howard and Jodi O'Brien (eds), *Everyday Inequalities: Critical Inquiries*. New York: Basil Blackwell.

Gerschick, Thomas J. and Adam S. Miller. 1994. "Gender Identities at the Crossroads of Masculinity and Physical Disability", *Masculinities* 2 (1): 34–55.

Golfus, Billy. 1997. "Sex and the Single Gimp", in Lennard J. Davis (ed.), *The Disability Studies Reader*. New York: Routledge.

Kafer, Alison. 2000. "Amputated Desire, Resistant Desire: Female Amputees in the Devotee Community". Paper presented at the Society for Disability Studies Conference, Chicago Sheraton, June 29–July 2.

Mairs, Nancy. 1996. *Waist-High in the World: A Life among the Nondisabled*. Boston, MA: Beacon Press.

Patzer, Gordon L. 1985. *The Physical Attractiveness Phenomena*. New York: Plenum.

Shakespeare, Tom, Kath Gillespie-Sells, and Dominic Davies. 1996. *The Sexual Politics of Disability: Untold Desires*. London: Cassell.

Sobsey, Dick, W. Randall, and Rauno K Parrila. 1997. "Gender Differences in Abused Children with and without Disabilities", *Child Abuse and Neglect* 21 (8): 707–20.

West, Candace and Don Zimmerman. 1987. "Doing Gender", *Gender and Society* 1 (2): 125–51.

Zola, Irving. 1982. *Missing Pieces: A Chronicle of Living with a Disability*. Philadelphia, PA: Temple University Press.

Thomas J. Gerschick

chapter 12

Orgasm

Juliet Richters

Orgasm can be defined from a physiological point of view as a reaction to sexual stimulation in both males and females. It consists of a series of muscular contractions in the pelvic muscles around the anus and sexual organs. It is preceded by increasing muscular tension and involves high blood pressure and rapid breathing and a visible red flush of the skin. In men, it is usually accompanied by ejaculation of semen.

This physiological description does not tell us much about what orgasm feels like. Orgasm is usually experienced as the climax, or high point, of a sexual event (either partnered sex or masturbation). It is preceded by an intensely pleasurable feeling of growing excitement and is usually followed by a feeling of delicious relaxation. However, these are generalizations. Rather than feeling calm immediately afterwards, people sometimes feel excited, elated or weepy, and orgasm need not signal the end of the sexual event. Erection of the penis and fullness of the vaginal area may disappear slowly or rapidly after orgasm. People vary in how soon after an orgasm they are ready to resume sexual activity: some people like to continue immediately or start again within minutes, and others may lose interest in sex for days or even longer. Some people may experience repeated orgasm or waves of orgasmic tension and pleasure without an apparent peak and collapse. "At best, an organ-moving cataclysm: my ovaries, uterus, breasts, and brain become one singing dark pulsating sea of the most exquisite feeling" (Hite 1976: 129).

Orgasm in social context

Describing orgasm as a physiological reaction makes it sound as though it is something that happens to humans everywhere, like digestion or sneezing. But this is not the case. The experience of orgasm varies greatly in different cultures and at different times in history. In all cultures it is usual for men to ejaculate during sex, and sex usually includes vaginal intercourse. None the less, it is possible for men to ejaculate after minimal stimulation – especially in a stressful situation – without feeling much or any orgasmic pleasure.

> Having orgasms is the most pleasant physical experience in my life, bar none, and as far as having sex without them, how can there be sex without orgasms? An orgasm is the logical culmination of sex, and the two, orgasm and sex, cannot be differentiated.
>
> *(Hite 1982: 468)*

Female orgasm is more variable. There have even been some cultures in which orgasm for women was virtually unheard of, generally ones with very restrictive sexual mores. A study of the sexual culture of mid-twentieth-century Inis Beag, an island off the west of Ireland, reported that the islanders had the view (shared with many Western peoples) that men were by nature far more interested in sex than women (Messenger 1971). Women were taught by the clergy and at home that sex with their husbands was a duty which must be endured, because it was sinful to refuse intercourse (Messenger 1971: 39). Inis Beag people were very shy about (even partial) nudity, about urination and defecation, and about heterosexual social interaction. They lacked a tradition of "dirty jokes," and even the men felt that intercourse would use up their energy or harm their health ("a common belief in primitive and folk societies," says Messenger). Although it was hard for the researchers to get details about people's sexual habits, they concluded that "intercourse takes place with underclothes not removed; and orgasm, for the man, is achieved quickly, almost immediately after which he falls asleep" (Messenger 1971: 41). Female orgasm appeared to be unknown. Other physiological processes such as menstruation and menopause were traumatic for women because local traditions had no explanation for them.

More sexually liberal cultures assume that women take at least as much pleasure in sex as men, and regard orgasms for men and women as a "natural" part of sexual interactions. We should not make the mistake of thinking that this is only a result of contemporary scientific knowledge and post-feminist liberalism in developed countries. In the *Kama Sutra*, a Sanskrit treatise on love-making that dates from about the fourth century CE (Vatsyayana 1963), the author does not refer to orgasm by a distinct name, but it is clear from the discussion that he regards women and men as deriving pleasure and satisfaction from sex.

> At the first time of sexual union the passion of the male is intense, and his time is short, but in subsequent unions on the same day the reverse of this is the case. With the female, however, it is the contrary, for at the first time her passion is weak, and then her time long, but on subsequent occasions in the same day, her passion is intense and her time short, until her passion is satisfied.
>
> *(Vatsyayana 1963: 122)*

People learn what to feel in sex as much as they learn what to do. For people to understand a bodily sensation as sexual, it needs to have a place in a script that labels and organizes it. As Gagnon and Simon put it in *Sexual Conduct*, "Without the proper elements of a script that defines the situation, names the actors, and plots the behaviour, nothing sexual is likely to happen" (1973, p. 33). In sexually repressive cultures it is even possible for people to masturbate to orgasm (defined physiologically), or have spontaneous orgasm while asleep or awake, without experiencing what is happening as sexual – they may experience it as emotional or religious passion, or some kind of fit or weird feeling. This can also happen to children before they know about sex. Even in recent years parents have taken small children to the doctor because of "fits" or "attacks," only to have the behaviour explained as masturbatory orgasm. Orgasm as a purely physiological event can occur without the person having any awareness of it *as sexual*. There is no direct correlation between physiological events and social ones – and sexual events are deeply social, even those that happen when we are alone.

A social constructionist view of sex places it firmly within the realm of culture. As anthropologist Carole Vance (1991) put it: "The physiology of orgasm and penile erection no more explains a culture's sexual schema than the auditory range of the human ear explains its music" (p. 879). By sexual schema she meant the patterns of sexual understandings and behaviour within which sex in that culture is organized. This shows us that a physiological definition of orgasm cannot tell us about the meaning of orgasm in people's lives. Sexual arousal or orgasm experienced by a person in a social situation is not equivalent to a single measurable physiological response. Physiology concerns itself with bundles of biochemical mechanisms that do not have meaning in themselves. We are unconscious of many of them. Only through our interpretation of sensations and their meanings do they become connected with sex in the social sense.

Having and not having orgasms

In medical circles orgasm is no longer seen as weakening or damaging to one's health, as it was by some experts up to the nineteenth century. However, many clinicians and researchers see variations of sexual practice or experience as dysfunctions. One could cynically observe that, if something is a medical dysfunction or problem, a therapist or drug manufacturer can make money out of fixing it. Yet most sexual "dysfunctions" are not due to illness or the failure of some part of the body to work properly (erectile dysfunction due to diabetes is an obvious exception). Rather, they are social failures to perform sex in a way that is socially acceptable (Morrow 1994). Many writers refer to orgasmic dysfunction (the inability to reach orgasm) or coital orgasmic dysfunction (the inability to reach orgasm through vaginal intercourse). This medicalization of sexual problems has been widely criticized (Kaschak and Tiefer 2001; Tiefer 2004; Potts *et al.* 2004).

Another way of interpreting this notion of dysfunction would be to say that what is seen as a problem reflects social expectations. The existence of "difficulty reaching orgasm" as a sexual problem tells us that, in contemporary Western sexual mores, each partner is generally expected to reach orgasm at least once in a sexual encounter. Thus a person may feel inadequate if they do not reach orgasm, and may even pretend that they have done so, rather than admit that they cannot. A person may also feel inadequate if the partner does not reach orgasm. This is another reason why someone may fake orgasm, to save the partner's feelings, perhaps fearing to cause offence by making them feel sexually unattractive or inept in technique. It is more often men who feel a duty to make the partner reach orgasm, as it is more often women who miss out on orgasm in heterosexual partnered sex. "My partner thinks I do when I show signs, like special hard breathing and body movements. But I never have orgasms – *never*" (Hite 1976: 156).

Experts have argued over whether repeated sexual stimulation and excitement not relieved by orgasm is harmful to health. Certainly many people find it irritating and disappointing, and a sense of frustration or of being used can lead people to avoid sexual arousal altogether. How they feel may depend largely on their perception of the meaning of the sexual acts which caused the excitement and the social context in which they occur. "I think orgasms are overrated. When I masturbate, it is to achieve orgasm, but with my lover I really don't care if I do or not. I just want to feel warm and close" (Hite 1976: 136).

People are less likely to have an orgasm during sex when they are young and inexperienced and when they are with a new, unfamiliar partner. It is statistically common for men in regular relationships to reach orgasm during sex while women often do not. Studies show that women who have frequent orgasms tend to enjoy sex more, have sex more often and report that they are satisfied with their sex lives (de Visser *et al.* 2003; Laumann *et al.* 1994; Haavio-Mannila and Kontula 1997).

In the past some writers have argued that upbringing, attitudes, religion, relationship issues, anxiety, previous traumatic experiences or even the woman's relationship with her father determined whether she would reach orgasm during sex (Andersen and Cyranowski 1995; Fisher 1973). Men's orgasms have rarely been seen as problematic in this way. A large survey in Australia showed that the likelihood of a man reaching orgasm at the last encounter he reported with an opposite-sex partner was high (over 95 percent) as long as the encounter included vaginal intercourse. This is an effective way for most men to reach orgasm, and it is widely regarded as the standard and expected sexual act that should be included in every sexual episode. Nearly 70 percent of women overall had an orgasm in the last encounter they reported with a male partner. However, the likelihood of having an orgasm varied considerably depending what sexual practices they engaged in. Women were more likely to reach orgasm (86 percent) in encounters that included both manual stimulation and cunnilingus. (Women were also more likely to have had an orgasm – 76 percent – at the last encounter they reported if their partner was a woman.) This is supported by earlier research showing that the change women wanted most in their sex lives was "more foreplay" (Davidson and Darling 1989).

For women, difficulty in reaching orgasm is a commonly reported sexual problem. Men rarely suffer from this problem. But it is not necessarily a great advantage for men that they have more and faster orgasms. Many men struggle during sex to avoid ejaculation that occurs too early, before they have had much chance to enjoy themselves. Women often complain, however, that men are too goal-oriented in sex and see it as a rush towards the reward of orgasm rather than enjoying the sensual pleasures of extended arousal.

More men than women report reaching orgasm "too early" – though we do not know whether men who say this in surveys actually reach orgasm faster than men who do not. It is possible that men who feel they come too fast are just more aware of a social expectation or requirement for them to "last longer." Women who reach orgasm rapidly are more likely to be praised for responsiveness; it is rarely seen as a problem. This highlights the difference in socially acceptable behaviour during sex. When a woman reaches orgasm during sex, it would be unusual behaviour if she were to immediately turn over and fall asleep, assuming the encounter to be over, even if the man had not had an orgasm.

The sexual politics of orgasm

What goes on in sex is therefore not neutrally negotiated between two equal parties. It is no accident that the dominant or most widely accepted sexual practice, vaginal intercourse, is one that reliably delivers sexual pleasure and orgasm to men but less reliably to women. In other chapters of this volume, we see that sexual practice is shaped by dominant discourses. Men and women bring to sexual encounters their enculturation as masculine and feminine, the injunctions of parents, school, the media, and wider society. Young men are more likely than young women to have experience of masturbation, and to be more familiar with what stimulation effectively brings about orgasm for themselves, and to be more confident that it is acceptable for them to openly seek orgasmic gratification in an encounter. Sex therapists and counsellors have tended to accept social norms and to enforce rather than challenge the idea that it is normal and preferable to experience orgasm through intercourse rather than through other forms of stimulation. This emphasis on intercourse is not "natural" or politically neutral: it is a way in which women have been required to serve or service men over the centuries. There are signs that this may be changing, however. Oral sex is becoming more acceptable and more widespread, and young people with access to explicit sexual information in magazines and on the internet may be less bound by the "coital imperative" than their parents were.

Unlike many heterosexuals, gay men do not assume that each sexual encounter will include penetrative intercourse; this usually has to be negotiated, and often does not occur. Even during anal intercourse, they do not assume that it will lead to orgasm for the insertive partner – they often stop and do something else, or stop after the receptive partner has had an orgasm. Without the traditional heterosexual script for practice, assumptions that are seen by many men as "natural" desires of the body – such as the need to reach orgasm during penetration – are shown to be socially variable.

Orgasmic variations

Humans rarely have sex with the primary or conscious intention of causing a pregnancy. Thus variations of practice in search of intense or extended sexual pleasure need not necessarily include ejaculation in the vagina.

One variation of practice is for the man to avoid orgasm so as to prolong intercourse and avoid pregnancy. This is technically called *coitus reservatus*. In the Oneida Community, a socially experimental commune in nineteenth-century United States, every man was regarded as the "husband" of every woman but reproduction was strictly limited. The men had to learn to have intercourse without ejaculating, and were said to be able to do so for an hour or more. The community believed that the "spilling" of semen led to the loss of men's energy or strength, so they presumably disapproved of men reaching orgasm by other means than intercourse. Men were supposed to lose their erections gradually after intercourse without having an orgasm.

One could regard any intercourse in which the man does not simply head for orgasm as soon as possible as a form of *coitus reservatus*. Extended intercourse may give a female partner more time and more chance of reaching orgasm. As in the Oneida Community, a man's control over when he ejaculates can also be used as a form of contraception, if he takes care to ejaculate well away from the vagina (and has the good fortune not to "leak" semen beforehand). Ejaculation may occur during some other sexual practice (such as oral sex or masturbation) or by withdrawing from the vagina just before ejaculation, which is technically called *coitus interruptus*. It is a less reliable form of contraception than modern methods such as the pill, but can be useful in cases where other methods are not available.

Some strands of Tantrism (a group of Indian mystic sects dating from the sixth century CE or earlier) include ritual sex in which the man is similarly required to avoid ejaculating while the woman is encouraged to have orgasms.

There is a great deal of debate about the definition and nature of the "multiple orgasm." It can be hard to distinguish mini-peaks in protracted high-level sexual arousal from multiple orgasms. Some experts define several orgasms separated by refractory periods (when sexual stimulation is unwanted or ineffective) in one sexual session as "repeated" rather than "multiple," while "multiple orgasms" are not separated by refractory periods. Although women are more likely than men to have trouble having orgasms at all, women who do easily have orgasms seem to have a better chance of having multiple ones, though even women for whom this is possible may only experience it occasionally. Men who want to experience several orgasms in a single sexual session of sex need to have a quick recovery period so that they can reach orgasm and regain their erection several times – this is easier for young men. Alternatively they may be able to train themselves to have multiple orgasms. This involves learning to have an orgasm without ejaculation. This sounds crazy to many men who equate the two, but it is possible for some men to learn to inhibit the ejaculatory reflex so that they can have a "dry" orgasm. (A man who has had an "accidental" ejaculation without the sensation of orgasm may be aware that the two do not necessarily go together.) Men can also train themselves to maintain a level of high arousal just before the moment when ejaculation becomes inevitable, to experience waves of orgasmic-level pleasure (Brauer and Brauer 1990).

There have been arguments over the years about whether women also ejaculate or release fluid at orgasm. In earlier centuries discussion of this topic was confused by lack of knowledge of the physiology of reproduction. In some cultures, the woman's vaginal moisture was thought to combine with the man's semen to bring about conception; thus an unaroused woman was assumed to be infertile. Once the ovum and sperm (as distinct from seminal fluid) were discovered and seen under the microscope, it became clear that conception depended on women's ovulation, not on their sexual fluids. The idea that women sometimes ejaculated – released whitish or clear fluid in spurts at orgasm or during high arousal – was ignored in sexual medicine, though it survived in pornography through the eighteenth and nineteenth centuries. Twentieth-century research showed that some women do ejaculate, and this fluid is different from urine as it contains high levels of a chemical that occurs also in male prostatic fluid (one of the components of semen) (Zaviacic *et al.* 1988). When the ejaculate is thin and copious it presumably contains urine as well, though the mechanism by which this occurs in someone who otherwise has perfectly good control of urination is not well understood. Indeed, some women who ejaculate have tried to stop themselves having orgasms so that they did not wet the bed. Some have been treated surgically for incontinence, as their sexual response was seen as a dysfunction. It is probably simpler to put a towel on the bed.

All these variations make it clear that human orgasm is a highly variable phenomenon, both in whether it occurs at all, and how it is experienced. People can live their whole lives without it, while others will risk their lives to achieve it.

Bibliography

Andersen, Barbara L. and Jill M. Cyranowski 1995. "Women's Sexuality: Behaviors, Responses, and Individual Differences", *Journal of Consulting and Clinical Psychology* 63: 891–906.

Brauer, Alan P. and Donna J. Brauer 1990. *The ESO Ecstasy Program: Better, Safer Sexual Intimacy and Extended Orgasmic Response*. New York: Warner.

Davidson, J. Kenneth, Sr. and Carol A. Darling 1989. "Self-Perceived Differences in the Female Orgasmic Response", *Family Practice Research Journal* 8: 75–84.

de Visser, Richard O., Anthony M. A. Smith, Chris E. Rissel, Juliet Richters and Andrew E. Grulich 2003. "Sex in Australia: Heterosexual Experience and Recent Heterosexual Encounters among a Representative Sample of Adults", *Australian and New Zealand Journal of Public Health* 27: 146–54.

Fisher, Seymour 1973. *Understanding the Female Orgasm*. Harmondsworth, Middlesex: Penguin.

Gagnon, J.H. and Simon, W. 1973. *Sexual Conduct: The Social Sources of Human Sexuality*. Chicago, IL: Aldine Publishing Company.

Haavio-Mannila, E. and O. Kontula 1997. "Correlates of Increased Sexual Satisfaction", *Archives of Sexual Behavior* 26: 399–419.

Hite, Shere 1976. *The Hite Report: A Nationwide Study of Female Sexuality*. New York: Dell.

— 1982. *The Hite Report on Male Sexuality*. New York: Ballantine.

Kaschak, Ellyn and Leonore Tiefer (eds) 2001. *A New View of Women's Sexual Problems*. Binghamton, NY: Haworth Press.

Laumann, Edward O., John H. Gagnon, Robert T. Michael and Stuart Michaels 1994. *The Social Organization of Sexuality: Sexual Practices in the United States*. Chicago and London: University of Chicago Press.

Messenger, John C. 1971. "Sex and Repression in an Irish Folk Community", in D. S. Marshall and R. C. Suggs (eds), *Human Sexual Behavior*. New York: Basic Books.

Morrow, Ross 1994. "The Sexological Construction of Sexual Dysfunction", *Australian and New Zealand Journal of Sociology* 30: 20–35.

Potts, Annie, Victoria Grace, Nicola Gavey and Tiina Vares 2004. "'Viagra Stories': Challenging 'Erectile Dysfunction'", *Social Science and Medicine* 59: 489–99.

Richters, Juliet, Richard O. de Visser, Chris E. Rissel and Anthony M. A. Smith 2006. "Sexual Practices at Last Heterosexual Encounter and Occurrence of Orgasm in a National Survey", *Journal of Sex Research* 43(3): 217–26.

Tiefer, Leonore 2004. *Sex Is Not A Natural Act and Other Essays*. Boulder, CO: Westview Press.

Vance, Carole S. 1991. "Anthropology Discovers Sexuality: A Theoretical Perspective", *Social Science and Medicine* 33: 875–84.

Vatsyayana 1963. *The Kama Sutra of Vatsyayana*. Trans. Sir Richard Burton and F. F. Arbuthnot. London: William Kimber & Co.

Zaviacic, M., A. Zaviacicová, I. K. Holomác and J. Molcan 1988. "Female Urethral Expulsions Evoked by Local Digital Stimulation of the G-spot: Differences in the Response Patterns", *Journal of Sex Research* 24: 311–18.

chapter 13

Anal sex

Phallic and other meanings

Simon Hardy

> It hits me like an iron fist . . . that in this global communications village . . . my father's going to see me getting a butt-fuck I didn't actually get. I hate the idea of having anal sex; as a woman it's a negation of your femininity. Most of all I hate being a fake.
>
> (Irvine Welsh, *Porno*, 2002: 374)

As can be seen in the above quotation, Welsh's novel of Scottish lowlife raises some important themes concerning the murkier aspects of contemporary experience rarely addressed by sociologists. However, the characterization of the female protagonist, Nikki, soon takes us far beyond what is likely in reality. She is more assertive, more in control and more "feminist" than it is possible for most female performers to be in the porn industry. This is evident in that she refuses to do anal sex, which is the very trademark of the do-it-yourself, gonzo pornography being described, and she even objects to a video edit that makes it appear as if she has. What arises here is not simply a question about the meaning of anal sex in modern culture, of why a woman might object to it, but also the issue of sexual truth, of personal identity and the role of sexuality and of sexual representation in its formation and authentication. Sexuality and pornography have become a means of existential assertion for modern-day men and women: "Look at me, see my body, see me fucking, see what I am, who I am, *that* I am."

This chapter will consider contemporary cultural constructions of anal sex. This may strike the reader as an unprepossessing theme for academic attention but it is a fact, and an increasingly common fact, of everyday social experience and conduct, which deserves our attention as much as any other. In fact it is arguable that anal sex represents the "final frontier" for many of the key themes that have defined modern sexual culture. These include the struggle for equality of gender and sexual orientation; the relationship between sexuality and self-identity; and the clash between a phallic model of sexuality, which is both normative and patriarchal, and a more diverse range of "perverse" sexualities.

It is important to be clear from the outset what we mean when speaking of "phallic sexuality." This is really shorthand for the dominant way of doing and thinking about sexuality in modern Western culture. It is a form of sexuality that centers around the penis and its penetrative role in coital intercourse, between a heterosexual, and traditionally married, couple. It is normative in that it is widely accepted as the normal and, perhaps, natural form that sexuality should take. It is also patriarchal because the act of intercourse is understood in terms of an anatomical dichotomy in which the penis is seen as "active" and the vagina as "passive," and therefore, at least implicitly, the male partner as superior and the female as inferior. The sources of this view of sexuality will be discussed further.

To a great extent our understanding of penetrative anal sex has been subsumed into this phallic model, with the anus becoming interchangeable, in the "passive" position, with the vagina. In such a case, of course, a male may take on the symbolically "inferior" role in the act, although phallic sexuality always accords the "superior" role to the owner of a penis. Certainly most academic commentaries on either male–female or male–male anal sex, whether in a contemporary or historical context, seem automatically to assume that it is an act of phallic domination by the inserting partner over the receptive partner. Yet, as we shall see, even if the phallic interpretation remains the most common, it is only one of a range of different ways of understanding the act. In fact, anal sex is an especially interesting case to consider on this point because the naturalizing discourse that underpins phallic sexuality cannot be so easily extended to the supposedly "unnatural" act of anal penetration.

Let us consider, then, the wider range of present-day constructions of anal sex, as we find them discussed in sociological, psychological and medical literature. We encounter anal sex in a variety of guises: as a method of contraception, as a health risk, as a heterosexual substitute, as a perversion, as a routine variation of sexual repertoire, as a special/ultimate intimacy, as a fashionable theme of cultural representation, as an obligatory pornographic number, and, yes, as an act of phallic domination.

A method of contraception

It is quite possible that in global terms the majority of instances of anal intercourse have no particular erotic meaning distinct from those already associated with genital intercourse. In many cases anal sex is practiced as a pragmatic method of contraception by heterosexual couples for whom genital–anal intercourse offers a direct substitute for vaginal intercourse, where other forms of contraception are unavailable or unacceptable. Such circumstances may not often apply in the USA but the practice has, for instance, been cited by public health agencies as a possible contributing factor in the rapid spread of HIV infection in parts of Africa.

A health risk

This leads us to a theme about which we have heard a good deal in recent years: anal sex as health risk. Anal intercourse is associated with a number of health issues, but it is above all the potential for the sexual transmission of HIV infection (especially from the inserting to the receptive partner) that has led to its being cited as a risk behavior by health educators.

Yet the medical profession no longer monopolizes the concept of risk, which has recently hopped from medical to erotic discourse. Sociological studies, such as D.T. Ridge's (2004) research on young gay men in Melbourne, Australia, show that the element of risk now associated with unprotected anal intercourse may sometimes heighten its erotic appeal. In this context the practice of "barebacking," as it is called, is often experienced as a daring and adventurous form of transgression that provides the individual with a sense of being carried away by an overwhelming male sex-drive, and thus provides a powerful affirmation of masculine identity.

A heterosexual substitute

In some institutional settings anal, male-to-male penetration can substitute for vaginal penetration, not, in this case, for the purposes of contraception but because of the absence of women. John Gagnon and William Simon's (1973) classic study of sexual conduct in prison shows that "homosexual" acts take place between "straight" men, not so much to release sexual tension but to affirm masculine identity. A large part of the prison population, they argue, is drawn from sections of society for whom the body and its performance of sex acts is the principal means of demonstrating a powerful, commanding masculinity. In prison this depends not on the sex of one's partner but on one's role in the act. Masculinity is affirmed by anally penetrating, or receiving fellatio from, a feminized male in scenarios that are frequently cohesive but always defined as "heterosexual."

A perversion

The status of anal sex as a perversion has a complex history, as the work of scholars such as Katz (1995) has shown. The Puritan settlers of seventeenth-century New England considered sodomy the most serious of a range of sexual sins. But the perversity of sodomy lay, like the other sins, in being a pleasure that wasted procreative potential in the context of communities that were struggling to survive and grow. Nor was sodomy seen as the proclivity of a specific, separately defined minority; anyone might succumb to any form of temptation, including sodomy with either sex.

The notion that the act of anal intercourse was a behavioral manifestation of a particular "type" of person, who was characterized by a perverted sexual nature, was the invention of nineteenth-century medical discourse. This tradition culminated in the psychology of Sigmund Freud (1977), who elaborated a developmental model of psychosexual identity. For Freud, the monogamous heterosexual whose sexual drive is directed to genital intercourse was the *normal* outcome of a process of individual development that involved an interaction of innate drives and social experience. However, getting to that stage was always a precarious process with, more often than not, a less-than-perfect outcome. Along the way, many individuals acquired a degree of perverse deviation from the straight and narrow course of normal development.

Freud made a distinction between sexual objects and sexual aims. Those who experience desire for a person-object of the opposite sex were classified as the "heterosexual" type, and those who experience desire for a person-object of the same sex were classified as the "homosexual" type. Thus the sexual feelings of the individual came to be a clue to his or her nature and identity. At the same time, Freud delineated a series of sexual aims that arise from the successive stimulation of the erogenous zones of the body through early development. The oral phase corresponds to breast-feeding; the anal phase to the acquisition of control over holding and releasing feces; and the genital phase to the subsequent discovery of genitalia and sexual difference. Adult interest or preoccupation with oral or anal themes therefore represented a throwback or "fixation" with immature sexual aims. Moreover, all aims had both "active" and "passive" variants, the former to stimulate or penetrate, and the latter to be stimulated or penetrated. The qualities of active and passive were associated respectively with masculinity and femininity and seen to inhere in the anatomy of sexual difference itself: penises and clitorises were active, and vaginas and anuses passive. Thus Freudian psychology helped to establish many of the hallmarks of *our* way of seeing sex acts. These include the idea that anal sex is a developmental perversion, largely but not exclusively associated with male homosexuality; and the idea that sex acts are inherently divided into active-masculine and passive-feminine roles, and that they express the inner essence of the individual.

A routine variation

The view of anal sex as perversion provides the background for another, more contemporary, meaning of this activity: anal sex as a routine variation of sexual repertoire. While Freud may have defined anal intercourse as "abnormal," in so doing he also said that its roots lie in universal processes of psychosexual development and acknowledged that it had behind it the same libidinal energy as "normal" sex. The effect of this was to, as it were, open the back door to its partial normalization. As a partially redeemed perversion, anal sex brings the erotic force of norm violation to bear as a routine variation of sexual repertoire, especially in the context of long-term relationships. Gagnon and Simon's (1973) research on heterosexual couples showed that sexual encounters early in a relationship followed a fairly strict "menu" of kissing, petting, oral sex and coitus, but that as relationships became more established anal intercourse was one of a number of variations that could be gradually integrated: typically by the male partner's suggestive use of his fingers followed by increasingly insistent attempts to penetrate, with the passivity of his female partner taken as assent.

There is strong evidence that this "routine variation" is increasingly widely practiced within the general and predominantly heterosexual community. A particularly authoritative survey of sexual behavior is *The National Survey of Sexual Attitudes and*

Simon Hardy

Lifestyles, carried out for the United Kingdom government, which found that the proportion of men to have experienced anal sex in the past year had risen from 7 percent in 1990 to 12.3 percent in 2000, while the proportion for women had increased from 6.5 percent to 11.3 percent over the same period. It should be noted that the report's authors caution that part of this change may arise because people are more willing to admit to such behavior in an increasingly permissive social environment. Yet the suggestion that the cultural climate has changed is also of interest.

A fashionable theme

Even allowing for the above figures, it is likely that anal sex fits into that category of those items in the collective imagination that are talked about far more than they are actually done. Anal sex, and the butt more generally, have become fashionable themes of cultural representation and sex talk, from "chick lit" to teenage banter. At the cinema we see Bridget Jones grin sheepishly as her lover tells her what they have just done is still illegal in many American states. At home we hear our teenage sons and daughters, sisters or brothers declare that anal is the only kind of sex anyone *they* know is interested in. The former porn actress Georgina Spelvin once said that boys in the part of America where she grew up had two great ambitions: first, to own a gun so they can kill Pepsi bottles; second, to get a blow-job. That was the 1970s; today we can be forgiven for thinking that the scope of teenage sexual fashion and fantasy has moved on. It would seem that anal sex has finally emerged from its closet into the cultural mainstream. Yet at the same time its current popularity depends precisely upon the last vestiges of taboo. The ass, long the locus of shame in the Freudian psyche, has become the symbol for a new cult of voluptuous sensuality. This trend is evident from Hip Pop videos to tv commercials, such as the advertisement for the Renault Megane, an automobile with a heavily built up boot(y), set to the Groove Armada lyric "I see you baby, shaking that ass."

A porno number

The form of popular culture most directly responsible for the current obsession with the anus is surely pornography. In her study *Hardcore*, Linda Williams (1989) notes that, in the 1970s heyday of pornographic cinema, anal sex was cited as one of eight generic numbers that a successful pornographic film would need to provide for the heterosexual market. Yet at that time the defining image of hardcore porno was the so-called "money-shot" of a man ejaculating onto the face or body of the female performer. This was crucial to the genre because it proved the authenticity of the moment, the truthfulness of at least the male performer's arousal, and it provided a sense that what the viewer was seeing was *real*. The task that pornography set itself was to uncover the truth of sex, to explore and document it in vivid detail; including, crucially, those aspects that Freud and others had proscribed as perverse. The pornographic lens sought out the secrets of the body, of sexuality, of orgasm and ejaculation. Porno became an expression of the modern *will to knowledge*; the desire to discover the "truth" about sexuality and, inevitably therefore, an important part of the truth about ourselves.

Today pornography is no longer made on film or distributed through cinemas, but its role as a means of discovering and defining sexual truth has been extended by new media technologies, such as video, the internet, webcams, email links and so on. Cheap, accessible and, especially, interactive media have enabled many more people to produce as well as to consume pornography. If engaging in sexual activity has long been an important way to prove our authenticity and identity as human beings, seeing ourselves represented in televisual media is another way to validate our existence. The burgeoning world of amateur porno has provided many people with the opportunity to combine the sexual and representational means of self-authentication by selling or exchanging images of themselves having sex. Even the – still large – proportion of pornography that circulates with a clear division between producers and consumers exhibits the rough and ready realism of the gonzo format in order to achieve the vital sense of authenticity.

At the same time one of the key features of this modern pornography is surely the obsession with anal sex. Although the "money-shot" is clearly still crucial, it has increasingly been joined at the top of the list of porno numbers by the "meat-shot" of anal penetration. This too is an expression of pornography's revelatory mission, whereby each "perversion" must be documented and recorded in live action; each orifice penetrated and explored in turn. Within this scheme anal penetration seems to have become the *coup de grâce* of the endlessly repeated "menu" of pornographic scenes: the phallic hunt of a man, or group of men, through the body of a woman: mouth, vagina, and anus; the last of these being penetrated repeatedly until it gapes wide open, while the camera zooms in to inspect the raw dark hole. The camera may not be able to capture female orgasm, to prove the truth of a woman's pleasure, which Williams (1989) argues was the ultimate goal of pornographers in the 1970s and 1980s. But modern pornographers have found that their camera can do something else instead: it can witness the impact of the phallus on the body of a woman, in the form of the temporary and extreme dilatation of her anal passage. If modern pornography has a defining moment or image, this is now it. It is as if, with the retreat of feminism, the dream of documenting female sexual pleasure has been abandoned in favour of the most brutal objectification. Recently we have had the still more extreme spectacle of double penile penetration of the female performer's anus, without regard to the limitations of bodily anatomy or the recent HIV/AIDS crisis in the Californian porno industry.

An act of phallic domination

For all the desire of pornography to break though conventional barriers and taboos, it has never really challenged those of gender hierarchy. It is notable that, in mainstream, heterosexual porn, amid all the prodding and probing of female orifices, the anuses of the men remain strictly off-limits.

While we have seen something of the variety of different ways of thinking about anal sex, pornography shows that the predominant meaning associated with the act remains that of phallic domination, in which the *one* individual asserts himself through the subordination of the other (*zero*). Yet it is important to avoid giving the impression that pornography should be seen as having created this conception rather than simply amplifying an idea that was already current. In a sense pornographic discourse reproduces, in simplified and literal form, the phallic interpretation of sex acts provided by the more authoritative discourse of post-Freudian psychology, which made them into a window on the soul, or the nature of the self, whilst dividing them into rigidly dichotomized relations of active and passive roles.

A special, ultimate intimacy

Since the sexual revolution of the 1960s there have been more or less conscious attempts to re-imagine the erotic connotations of anal sex. The idea of anal sex as the ultimate intimacy between a loving couple has appeared particularly as a theme in relationships between gay men.

One study (Sik and Kat 2000) of Chinese gay men in Hong Kong found that, since the period of de-colonization (1984–97), their relationships with British or other "European" men had become more equal. In many cases this included the adoption of the practice, common to gay men elsewhere, of reciprocating roles in anal sex, which was widely seen as the ultimate expression of gay love. Although these roles were still interpreted in terms of "top–bottom" or "zero–one," they became negotiable and interchangeable. A similar tension around issues of power and intimacy appears in an Australian study (Kippax and Smith 2001). Here, some gay men saw the receptive role as feminizing and submissive, and they therefore needed to reassure themselves by role swapping, while others felt that the power relations involved in the most intimate of acts were much more complex and less one-sided than is usually assumed. A Norwegian study (Middelthon 2002) found that most young gay men interviewed expressed anxieties about a loss of manhood that they associated with the receptive role. Some expressed the view that, while a woman can play the receptive part in the act of genital intercourse with the grace ordained by nature or tradition, this did not extend to men playing the receptive role in anal intercourse, which was seen as potentially humiliating. Sex acts, and the part played in them by the individual, were experienced as playing a crucial role in defining self and identity. Yet these anxieties could be counteracted provided some or all of the following conditions were met: that the act was erotically satisfying, reciprocal, face-to-face, and above all with a caring partner or preferably the love of one's life.

Conclusion

We have completed this brief overview with a glimpse of some pioneering attempts to re-imagine anal sex. The gay practice of reciprocal anal penetration has been seen as de-centering the phallus, which, since Freud, has been at the heart of normative sexuality. But it seems that as yet, for all the cultural veneer of newness and excitement, in the heterosexual, mainstream erotic imagination anal sex remains much as

Gagnon and Simon (1973) found it over forty years ago: an act generally understood in terms of a symbolic power relation. We have seen that, although there are many possible meanings for anal sex, the fashion for it in heterosexual pornography and practice, far from diminishing the power of the phallus, actually reasserts it with new emphasis through a motif of anal conquest. The multiple meanings and subversive potentials of anal "perversion" resolve themselves into the all-too-familiar male-dominant phallic form, featuring the same old symbolic dichotomy of active-masculine and passive-feminine. At a time when we have begun, at last, to get over the idea that a woman's receptive contribution to the act of genital intercourse makes her in any way inferior, the switch in emphasis from penetration of the vagina to anus seems to constitute a symbolic reaffirmation of phallic power. Maybe that is why the fictional porn actress Nikki, in Welsh's novel, would have refused anal sex as a negation of her femininity.

References

Freud, S. 1977. *On Sexuality: Three Essays on the Theory of Sexuality and Other Works*. London: Penguin.

Gagnon, J. H. and Simon, W. 1973. *Sexual Conduct: The Social Sources of Human Sexuality*. Chicago, IL: Aldine Publishing Company.

Katz, J. N. 1995. *The Invention of Heterosexuality*. New York: Dutton.

Kippax, S. and Smith, G. 2001. "Anal Intercourse and Power in Sex Between Men", *Sexualities* 4(4): 413–34.

Middelthon, A.-L. 2002. "Being Anally Penetrated: Erotic Inhibitions, Improvisations and Transformations", *Sexualities* 5(2): 181–200.

Ridge, D. T. 2004. "'It was an Incredible Thrill': The Social Meanings and Dynamics of Younger Gay Men's Experiences of Barebacking in Melbourne", *Sexualities* 7(3): 259–79.

Sik Ying Ho, P. and Kat Tat Tsang, A. 2000. "Negotiated Anal Intercourse in Inter-Racial Gay Relationships in Hong Kong", *Sexualities* 3(3): 299–332.

Welsh, I. 2002. *Porno*. New York: W. W. Norton & Company.

Williams, L. 1989. *Hardcore: Power, Pleasure and the "Frenzy of the Visible"*. Los Angeles: University of California Press.

PART 3

Gender and sexuality

Introduction

Feminists have changed the way we think about ourselves and our social world. Statements such as "we are just individuals" or "the social world is made up of individuals who are essentially the same" have been challenged. Such seemingly self-evident statements of truth are now suspect as feminists have argued that we are almost always thinking, feeling, desiring, and acting in gendered ways, as either men or women or against these gender statuses. In other words, being a man or woman is a significant part of us, a status we cannot easily, if at all, shake off.

Feminists have also taught us that our gendered status is social. We are not born men or women but acquire these gender identities beginning with our social designation as male or female. Our families, schools, popular culture and government help to produce gendered selves. Gender status, at least as its lived in many parts of the contemporary world, fashions our bodies and psyches to fit into the rigid boxes of male/female and man/woman.

Finally, feminists have taught us that the relationship between men and women is, in part, oppositional and hierarchical. In other words, the traits that define being a man are the opposite of those defining women. If women are expected to exhibit caregiving, nurturing, and accommodating behaviors, men are expected to either minimize these behaviors or give them a very different meaning. So, if women's caregiving is supposed to be expressed in tender communicative acts, men's nurturing takes the form of doing tasks such as making money or mowing the lawn.

Social roles are distributed based on these normative gender traits. For example, women are expected to be the primary parent and to do the lion's share of the housework. Furthermore, conventional gender roles, men in masculine and women in feminine roles, position men and women as unequal. In virtually every institutional sector in the United States and the world, from churches to schools and the government, men are disproportionately in positions of power, are paid better, and occupy positions of higher status than women. These patterns of gender difference and inequality are, feminists claim, socially created and reproduced; they are not dictated by nature but produced by history.

Does the social influence of gender stop at the door of sexuality? Clearly not. Sexuality is gendered as much as our work life. There is a considerable body of research and scholarship that shows the gender patterning of the meaning and social organization of sexuality and intimacies. For example, while both men and women look for sex and love in romantic relationships, men in general tend to value sexuality for its performative and erotic aspects while women emphasize its communicative, emotionally bonding aspects. Similarly, whereas women express love through tender, nurturing behavior, men will often speak of what they do for their partners, e.g. earn money or provide security. More dramatically, violence in intimate relationships is a decidedly masculine behavior. According to the World Health Organization, one-third of women report experiencing some form of physical or sexual violence from an intimate partner.

Of course, gender is not only about men and women. In the last decade or so, we have seen the rise of new gender styles that reject rigid binary gender norms and roles. From metrosexuals to queer straights and transgendered persons, gender is increasingly approached as a flexible aspect of identity and behavior. Many individuals are today struggling to step outside the gender binary, to rewrite the dynamics of intimacy in post-gender ways. In particular, young people are struggling to find ways to express themselves and to forge intimacies beyond the binary models of gender and sexual identity. But make no mistake. These new currents of self and intimate invention are occurring in social contexts still very much rooted in gender-binary norms.

chapter 14

Unruly bodies

Intersex variations of sex development

Sharon E. Preves

Distinctions between sex, gender, and sexuality

In *Doubtful Sex* (1995), medical historian Alice Dreger writes: "In any human culture, a body is never a body unto itself, and bodies that openly challenge significant boundaries are particularly prone to being caught in struggles over those boundaries." Let's begin with what we know to be true. There are two and only two sexes, right? And you know with certainty which one of the two you are, I'm sure. Have you ever stopped to consider *how you know* what sex you are? It sounds pretty simple; just a quick check of the genitalia is all it takes. It's actually not so easy to draw a binary distinction between the sexes, despite common belief, given that so much variation in genital and other sexual anatomy occurs with great regularity. Most often, as noted above, we consider external genitalia to be the unequivocal sign of anatomical sex. In fact, a cursory examination of the genitalia is typically how sex assignment occurs at birth.

What happens if the genitalia aren't typically female or male in their appearance, as occurs in roughly 1 of 2,000 births (Blackless et al. 2000)? Should we then turn to an examination of the sex chromosomes, gonads, or hormones? The state supreme courts of Texas and Kansas both ruled that sex is chromosomal; we know someone is a man if he has XY chromosomes and we know someone is a woman if she has XX chromosomes (Lum 2002). In Texas, this chromosomal definition of sex permitted a lesbian couple to be legally married in a state that didn't allow same-sex marriage, because one of the women was a male-to-female transsexual and had XY chromosomes (Koidin 2000).

Getting back to the sense of confidence you have about your own physical sex, do you know whether you have XX or XY sex chromosomes (or some other variation, such as XXY or XO)? What about your gonads? Are you certain that you have ovaries, testes, or some combination of the two? Moreover, have you ever had your levels of estrogen or testosterone assessed to see if you are producing these hormones at typically female or male levels? Those of us who don't know the answers to these questions because we've never had reason to really ponder them experience a gender privilege that is akin to the racial privilege of being Caucasian and relatively unaware of the ways in which racial categorization shapes one's existence. That is, while most of us are sexed as female or male at birth and gendered as feminine or masculine in later life, to do so without pause or difficulty is indeed a privilege, as is the ease with which many people enter and exit women's or men's lavatories, locker rooms, and the countless other gendered spaces we inhabit on a daily basis.

Some readers may find it surprising to know that babies are born with external genitalia that look neither clearly female nor male with great regularity. As noted above, conservative estimates suggest that children are born with intersexed genitalia in 1 or 2 of every 2,000 births (Blackless et al. 2000) – the same rate at which Down's syndrome and cystic fibrosis occur (Desai 1997; Dreger 1998; Roberts et al. 1998). I would venture to guess that most readers know of someone who has Down's syndrome or cystic fibrosis. If that is the case, then based on frequency data alone, most readers also know someone who is intersexed. Many readers may be dubious about this, as they are not aware that they know someone who has intersexed anatomy. Given the stigma and secrecy that frequently accompany variations of sex, gender, and sexuality, the lack of education and awareness about the continuum of sexual anatomy is understandable.

Why is there such a shroud of secrecy with regard to variations of sex development? Put simply, exceptions to the rule of two clearly distinct sexes (female and male) disrupt the very foundation of our social structure, thus creating a breach in social order. Not only are there predominant social expectations regarding two clearly distinct physical sexes, there is also a social expectation for one's anatomical sex (e.g. female or male) to be congruent with one's gender identity and role – as a clearly feminine or masculine person. Moreover, there is a social expectation for one's sexual identity to be attracted to the anatomy and gender "opposite" one's own. Thus, normalcy with regard to sex, gender, and sexuality is reliant upon having clear, causal, and linear connections between anatomical sex, gender identity and role, and sexuality (Butler 1990, 1993). Following this model, if a person's sexual anatomy is ambiguous, it will be difficult to know their gender, as a woman or a man, and nearly impossible to ascribe their sexual orientation within a framework that assumes binary sex. That is, if a person's genitalia, chromosomes, gonads, or hormones are not typically female or male, how can that person identify as hetero-, bi-, or homosexual, given that these categories presume female and male anatomies that are clearly distinct from one another?

Sharon E. Preves

Social expectations of sex, gender and sexuality

Binary sex and gender expectations surround us; everything from restrooms to clothing to identification cards to religious rites of passage and sporting events relies on a sex/gender binary. When the shared social expectation of this sex/gender binary is disrupted via anatomical sex or gender role variation, the social response typically revolves around attempts to decrease the uncertainty and proclaim the person in question as unequivocally female or male. Take the heart-wrenching 2009 investigation of then 18-year-old South African runner Caster Semenya's sex by the International Association of Athletics Federation (IAAF), the worldwide governing body for track and field. When Semenya won the 800 meter race at the World Championships in Berlin in August 2009, finishing nearly two and a half seconds before her closest competition, her record-breaking win was overshadowed by rumors that the IAAF had required her to undergo sex verification testing before the race (Levy 2009). Sure, Semenya's physical build and voice are more masculine than many women's, but it was her tremendous speed that drew speculation among her competitors and the IAAF that her sex may be in question.

Caster Semenya's eligibility to compete against women was challenged just six months before U.S. figure skater Johnny Weir's flamboyant behavior both on and off the ice at the 2010 Winter Olympics in Vancouver had two Canadian broadcasters suggesting that he should be subjected to sex verification testing (McKnight 2010) – something that has never been required of male athletes. Indeed, in an attempt to level the playing field, the International Olympic Committee (IOC) has used various means of weeding out "sex imposters" among female athletes since 1966 to disqualify genetic males from competing as women (Fausto-Sterling 2000a). After nearly a decade of protest from athletes, the IOC suspended mandatory sex verification of female athletes for the 2000 Olympic Games on a provisional basis (Newman 2001). As of this writing, Semenya's future as a competitive runner remains uncertain. The IAAF has yet to rule on whether they consider her "female enough" to continue the tremendously promising career that she only just began. That decision could be issued soon, as members of the IAAF and the IOC met in January 2010 with medical experts in "disorders of sex development" (DSDs) at a two-day private gender symposium to discuss recommendations for female athletes whose sex may be deemed questionable by medical standards (e.g. genitalia, chromosomes, hormones, and/or gonads that are not female-typical or congruent with one another). The IOC left this meeting with a recommendation to further medicalize variations of sex development by establishing world-renowned centers for excellence in the diagnosis and treatment of disorders of sex development, and requiring female athletes whose sex may be in question to seek hormonal, surgical, and/or psychological treatment from one of these medical facilities in order to be eligible to compete (O'Reilly 2010).

Cultural and historical variations on sex, gender and sexuality

This discussion of Semenya brings us back to a critical exploration of how sex, gender, and sexual normalcy are socially constructed. As the following examples illustrate, social expectations with regard to sex, gender, and sexuality are culturally dependent and vary significantly throughout history and across regions. Take homosexuality as an illustration. Being sexually attracted to others of the same sex or gender was considered a psychiatric disorder by the American Psychiatric Association until it was removed from the conditions listed in the *Diagnostic and Statistical Manual* in 1973 (Conrad and Schneider 1992). Claims of equality and human rights, spurred by the Civil Rights Movement, gave birth to the lesbian, gay, bisexual, and transgender (LGBT) movements that have flourished throughout the Western world in the last 40 years (Preves 2003, 2004). In contrast, institutionalized homophobia reigns supreme in some parts of the world. In Uganda, homosexuality is considered criminal behavior. In 2014, the Ugandan Parliament passed the Uganda Anti-Homosexuality Act punishing homosexuality with a life sentence in prison. The bill was condemned by the US, UK and European governments, but was only overturned for procedural grounds, opening the door for more such legislation in the future. It is feared that similar legislation will be adopted by other African countries.

Across the Indian Ocean on the South Pacific island of Papua New Guinea, behavior that would be considered homosexual (and criminal) throughout much of Africa is a mere right of passage for preadolescent boys. For the Sambia of Papua New Guinea, one of the country's 850 recognized tribes, men's ability to be fertile and develop male typical secondary sex characteristics, such as facial and body hair, a deep voice, fertility, and physical strength, is attributed to the ingestion of semen. Sambian belief holds that semen is not produced internally, but rather must be introduced externally through the ingestion of semen during fellatio rituals carried out as a standard rite of passage between men and boys (Herdt 1997). Behavior that would be condemned as illegal homosexuality throughout much of Africa or as criminal child abuse in the United States is socially constructed as not only normal but as necessary among this Papua New Guinean tribe.

Closer to home, we could reflect upon the variability in our own constructions of gender normalcy. Take, for example, the highly gendered colors of pink and blue. It might seem impossible to imagine either color being gender neutral, let alone associate the color blue with girls or the color pink with boys. However, a look into our rather recent history reveals the fickle (and social) nature of defining such colors as strictly gendered. It seems that pink was the preferred color for boys until after World War II, as it was considered a derivative of the color red, which was thought to be a fierce color. Similarly, the color blue was seen as a softer, gentler color, and thus associated with girls (Frassanito and Pettorini 2008). As evidence, *The Sunday Sentinel* advised Americans in 1914 "If you like the color note on the little one's garments, use pink for the boy and blue for the girl, if you are a follower of convention" (Frassanito and Pettorini 2008:881). In the same vein, in 1918, the *Ladies Home Journal* told its readership: "There has been a great diversity of opinion on the subject, but the generally accepted rule is pink for the boy and blue for the girl. The reason is that pink being a more decided and stronger color is more suitable for the boy, while blue, which is more delicate and dainty, is prettier for the girl" (Frassanito and Pettorini 2008:881).

Now that we have established distinctions between the terms sex, gender, and sexuality, illustrated social expectations about the binary and linear connections that

Sharon E. Preves

socially link these terms to one another, as well as cross-cultural and historical variations in social norms regarding gender and sexuality, it is time to return to the discussion of variations of sex development, with which this chapter began.

Societal reactions to ambiguous sexual anatomy

Just as views about homosexuality vary considerably across time and space, so do social responses to sexual anatomy that is deemed difficult to label as distinctly female or male. In societies where childbirth is medicalized, such as throughout much of Europe and North America, the response to a child whose genitalia seem ambiguous is a medical one. Despite the fact that the vast majority of infants born with variations of sex development exhibit no medical concerns (Diamond and Sigmundson 1997), most newborns with ambiguous genitalia are responded to as though a variation in sex development is a medical emergency. The American Academy of Pediatrics made this sentiment clear in their position statement on this topic:

> The birth of a child with ambiguous genitalia constitutes a social emergency. Abnormal appearance can be corrected and the child raised as a boy or a girl as appropriate. Parents should be encouraged not to name the child or register the birth, if possible, until the sex of rearing is established. Infants raised as girls will usually require clitoral reduction which, with current techniques, will result not only in a normal-looking vulva but preservation of a functional clitoris. [These children's] diagnosis and prompt treatment require urgent medical attention.
>
> (American Academy of Pediatrics 2000: 138)

The treatment protocol to make a child appear unambiguously female or male was created in the United States as recently as the 1950s. This model of surgically and hormonally "sexing" intersexed children is most closely associated with the late psychologist John Money and usually entails early surgery and hormonal intervention. The rationale for early intervention to decrease outward sexual ambiguity is to help children form gender and sexual identities that are congruent and to preclude intersexed children from experiencing stigma (Preves 2003; Karkazis 2008). Both motives are logical, given the overwhelming social expectation for sex, gender, and sexual normalcy.

To further the attempt to prevent or decrease stigma that might accompany variations of sex development, this treatment model not only attempts to physically erase the evidence of genital ambiguity, but to conduct "social surgery" as well, by encouraging parents and loved ones to keep the child's ambiguous anatomy a secret from the child her/himself. In short, the theory goes, a child's gender and sexual identity may develop problematically if s/he were to know about or suspect anatomical sex features which are incongruent with a binary female or male role. By intervening early and erasing visible sexually ambiguous features, both parents and child will respond to the "clarified" genitalia as the essential sign of gender and develop a healthy bond and normal gender and sexual identity in the future.

This model, while rooted in benevolence, has been widely criticized as creating rather than preventing feelings of stigma and shame. In the 1990s an alternative patients-rights model emerged via the mobilization of the first generation of adults who as children underwent sex "clarification" procedures. The most vocal and visible of these critics was Cheryl Chase, founder and executive director of the now defunct Intersex Society of North America (ISNA). In their early activism, Chase and "Hermaphrodites with Attitude" (the activist branch of the Intersex Society of North America) resorted to picketing at medical conventions to have their voices heard. Such was the case at the 1996 meeting of the Academy of Pediatrics in Boston after the group was denied a place on the meeting's agenda (Beck 1997/1998). Largely due to the effectiveness of her advocacy, just four years later Chase delivered a keynote address at the Lawson Wilkins Pediatric Endocrine Society's annual meeting in 2000, giving "the grand finale to a four-hour symposium on the treatment of [sexual] ambiguity in newborns" (Fausto-Sterling 2000b). That same year, Chase was invited to the table with the most prominent clinicians in the field to serve as a member of the North American Task Force on Intersex. This promising work group dissolved scarcely more than a year later due to heated disagreements about treatment options and research proposals (Preves 2003; Karkazis 2008).

A dramatic turn of events in the advocacy and treatment of intersex came in 2005, when a group of medical experts and intersex activists, including Chase, convened to attempt to overcome their seemingly insurmountable differences on how best to respond to physical sexual ambiguity. One of the main outcomes of this historic meeting was a change in the language used to refer to physical sexual ambiguity. More specifically,

> terms should be as precise as possible and should reflect the genetic etiology when available . . . The new nomenclature should be understandable by patients and families and should be psychologically sensitive. In particular, gender labeling in the diagnosis should be avoided, and use of the words "hermaphrodite," "pseudohermaphrodite," and "intersex" should be abandoned, as they either are confusing or have a negative social connotation that may be perceived as harmful by some patients and parents. The term "disorders of sex development" (DSD) was proposed and was defined as "congenital conditions in which development of chromosomal, gonadal, or anatomic sex is atypical."
>
> (Vilain et al. 2007: 66)

Shortly thereafter, this group published the 2006 "Consensus Statement on Management of Intersex Disorders" (Hughes et al. 2006).

Reaction to the shift in terminology from "intersex" to "disorders of sex development" has been mixed. Clinicians and parents largely seem to embrace the new DSD term, as it offers a welcoming distance from the highly politicized and sexualized terms "intersex" and "hermaphrodite." Some activists, however, are not so pleased. Many see the use of the word "disorder" as a giant step backward in their work toward destigmatizing variations of sex development. Perhaps the most outspoken faction against the term DSD is the international activist group Organization Intersex International (OII) that operates the "We are Not a Disorder" blog. In sharp contrast, Cheryl Chase, founder of the Intersex Society of North America and former "hermaphrodite with attitude", closed down operation of the Intersex Society of North America and started a new disorders of sex development non-profit called Accord Alliance, to work more closely with clinicians in her efforts to destigmatize variations of sex development. ISNA says on its the homepage of its (now archival) website about this change:

> In 2007, ISNA sponsored and convened a national group of health care and advocacy professionals to establish a nonprofit organization charged with making sure the new ideas about appropriate care are known and implemented across the country.
>
> This organization, Accord Alliance, opened its doors in March, 2008, and will continue to lead national efforts to improve DSD-related health care and outcomes. Accord Alliance believes that improving the way health care is made available and delivered is essential to ensure that people receive the services and support they need to lead healthy, happy lives.
>
> With Accord Alliance in place, ISNA can close its doors with the comfort and knowledge that its work will continue to have an impact. Archives of our historical documents and accomplishments will be preserved at the Kinsey Institute at Indiana University.
>
> This website will remain up as a historical artifact.
>
> (www.isna.org)

Activists and clinicians haven't been the only ones caught up in the struggle over nomenclature. Biologist Milton Diamond has argued against the word "disorders" and has proposed that the word "differences" be used in its place, to retain the acronym DSD, to mean differences, rather than disorders, of sex development (Diamond 2009). Others scholars have proposed VSDs rather than DSDs: "variations of sex development" (Tamar-Mattis and Diamond 2007). Throughout this essay and in its title, I have used the terminology with which I am most comfortable: "intersex" and "variations of sex development".

The case of intersex, and particularly a cross-cultural and cross-historical examination in the variations of its "treatment", brings to the fore the social processes of defining what is normal and what is deviant. The politicization of the terminology that surrounds intersex variations of sex development is merely a new twist to the enduring cultural battles to control and predict sex, gender, and sexuality. With surety, conflicts about how best to corral and respond to those deemed sex, gender, or sexual deviants will continue in perpetuity.

Further information

For an interactive overview of how some variations of sex development occur, see the website:
www.aboutkidshealth.ca/HowTheBodyWorks/Sex-DevelopmentAnOverview/pages/default.aspx

Readers may learn more about Organization Intersex International by visiting their website: www.oiiinternational.com

Readers can visit www.isna.org and www.accordalliance.org to learn more about both organizations.

References

American Academy of Pediatrics, Committee on Genetics. 2000. "Evaluation of the Newborn with Developmental Anomalies of the External Genitalia." *Pediatrics* 106(1): 138–42.

Beck, Max. 1997/1998. "Hermaphrodites with Attitude Take to the Streets." *Chrysalis: The Journal of Transgressive Gender Identities* 2(5) (Fall/Winter): 45–46; 50.

Blackless, Melanie, Anthony Charuvastra, Amanda Derryck, Anne Fausto-Sterling, Karl Lauzanne, and Ellen Lee. 2000. "How Sexually Dimorphic Are We?" *American Journal of Human Biology* 12(2): 151–66.

Butler, Judith. 1990. *Gender Trouble: Feminism and the Subversion of Identity*. New York: Routledge.

—. 1993. *Bodies That Matter: On the Discursive Limits of "Sex."* New York: Routledge.

Conrad, Peter, and Joseph W. Schneider. 1992. *Deviance and Medicalization: From Badness to Sickness*. 2nd edition. Philadelphia, PA: Temple University Press.

Desai, Sindoor S. 1997. "Down Syndrome: A Review of the Literature." *Oral Surgery, Oral Medicine, Oral Pathology, Oral Radiology, and Endodontics* 84(3): 279–85.

Diamond, Milton. 2009. "Human Intersexuality: Difference or Disorder?" *Archives of Sexual Behavior* 38: 172.

Diamond, Milton and Keith Sigmundson. 1997. "Management of Intersexuality: Guidelines for Dealing with Persons with Ambiguous Genitalia." *Archives of Pediatric Adolescent Medicine* 151 (October): 1046–50.

Dreger, Alice Domurat. 1995. *Doubtful Sex: Cases and Concepts of Hermaphroditism in France and Britain, 1868–1915*. Ph.D. dissertation, Indiana University.

—. 1998. *Hermaphrodites and the Medical Invention of Sex*. Cambridge, MA: Harvard University Press.

Fausto-Sterling, Anne. 2000a. *Sexing the Body: Gender Politics and the Construction of Sexuality*. New York: Basic Books.

—. 2000b. "The Five Sexes, Revisited." *The Sciences* 40(4): 18–23.

Frassanito, Paolo and Benedetta Pettorini. 2008. "Pink and Blue: The Color of Gender." *Child's Nervous System* 24(8): 881–82.

Herdt, Gilbert H. 1997. *Same Sex, Different Cultures: Exploring Gay and Lesbian Lives*. Boulder, CO: Westview Press.

Hughes, I. A., C. Houk, S. F. Ahmed, P. A. Lee and LWPES/ESPE Consensus Group. 2006. "Consensus Statement on Management of Intersex Disorders." *Archives of Disease in Childhood* 91: 554–63.

Karkazis, Katrina. 2008. *Fixing Sex: Intersex, Medical Authority, and Lived Experience*. Durham, NC: Duke University Press.

Koidin, Michelle. 2000. "Texas Ruling Allows 'Same Sex' Marriage." *Chicago Sun Times*, September 7.

Levy, Ariel. 2009. "Either/Or: Sports, Sex, and the Case of Caster Semenya." *New Yorker*, November 30: 46–59.

Lum, Matt. 2002. "'Slap in the Face': Christie Lee Littleton's Historic Texas Court Ruling Crosses State Lines to Deny Equality." *Texas Triangle*, March 22: 20.

McKnight, Peter. 2010. "Here's the Rule: Men are Men and Women are Ladies: Figure Skaters are Expected to Adhere to Strict Gender Roles, but that Doesn't Work for Everyone." *Vancouver Sun*, February 27.

Newman, Judith. 2001. "How Sexism and Bad Science Have Teamed Up Against Athletes." *SportsJones*. August 24.

O'Reilly, Ian. 2010. "Gender Testing in Sport: A Case for Treatment?" *BBC News*, February 15.

Preves, Sharon E. 2003. *Intersex and Identity: The Contested Self.* New Brunswick, NJ: Rutgers University Press.

—. 2004. "Out of the O.R. and into the Streets: Exploring the Impact of Intersex Media Activism." *Research in Political Sociology* 13: 179–223.

Roberts, Helen E., Janet D. Cragan, Joanne Cono, Muin J. Khoury, Mark R. Weatherly, and Cynthia A. Moore. 1998. "Increased Frequency of Cystic Fibrosis among Infants with Jejunoileal Atresia." *American Journal of Medical Genetics* 78: 446–49.

Tamar-Mattis, Anne and Milton Diamond. 2007. "Managing Variations in Sex Development." *Journal of Pediatric Endocrinology and Metabolism* 20: 552–53.

Vilain, Eric, John C. Achermann, Erica A. Eugster, Vincent R. Harley, Yves Morel, Jean D. Wilson, and Olaf Hiort. 2007. "We Used to Call Them Hermaphrodites." *Genetics in Medicine* 9(2): 65–66.

chapter 15

From transgender to trans*

The ongoing struggle for the inclusion, acceptance and celebration of identities beyond the binary

Joelle Ruby Ryan

In April 2015, Caitlyn Jenner (born Bruce Jenner) sat down with Diane Sawyer on ABC News for an in-depth, two-hour interview about her transition from male to female. The ABC interview was watched by over 17 million people and catapulted not only Caitlyn into the national consciousness, but the issue of transgender identity, gender transition and the overall acceptance of gender diversity in our families and communities. The Diane Sawyer interview was followed up by a cover story in *Vanity Fair* magazine featuring Caitlyn, for the first time seen dressed as a woman, and shot by well-known celebrity photographer Annie Liebovitz. The cover quickly went viral and garnered widespread support, condemnation, curiosity and fascination.

The response to Jenner within the transgender community was decidedly mixed. On the one hand, many were excited to have such a famous public figure come out so visibly and give the community a larger platform. With the exception of several other recent high-profile transgender personalities such as Laverne Cox, Chaz Bono and Janet Mock, the media attention given to Jenner has been unprecedented in the modern epoch, and it has generated many conversations and dialogues around the globe about what it means to be transgender. In fact, local news affiliates across the U.S. seized on Caitlyn's coming out as an opportunity to publish and televise sympathetic portraits of local transgender communities, further helping to lift up a marginalized population from the shadows of invisibility into the light. However, multiple critics within trans communities were quick to address the case of Caitlyn Jenner with caution due to her overall social location and political orientation. Issues of fame, privilege, wealth, race and whiteness, appearance, medical versus non-medical transitioning, femininity and mass media were among the many topics that surfaced in transgender communities in the blogosphere and on social media.

These debates made me think about the topic of diversity within the transgender community, both in terms of reflecting upon my own identities and my many years of transgender activism, as well as to analyzing Caitlyn Jenner and other high profile transgender people in relation to the binary gender system. In this chapter, I would like to, in the spirit of the second wave feminist mantra, "combine the personal and the political" in order to analyze the ways in which contemporary iterations of transgender identity have generally failed to expand options beyond the binary of "man" or "woman" in the mainstream culture. Despite lip service to the contrary, I assert that the "umbrella" formulations of "transgender", "trans" and most recently "trans*" have often served to relegate those of us with non-binary identities to the margins due to political expediency, internalized oppression within the trans community, and the desire for media validation and approval from mainstream culture. Greater acceptance for binary, medically transitioned transsexuals in the mainstream culture has caused GLBT advocacy organizations to center these experiences in their political work. The lack of non-binary visibility has often caused trans* folks who don't or can't "pass" to internalize dominant messages about their group. The impetus is strong to conform to mainstream narratives of transgender identity if one seeks any kind of socio-cultural acceptance, validation or encouragement.

To begin, I would like to reflect on my own history of coming out as transgender, and how my identities have affected my place within the political and activist spheres. Then, I would like to discuss how the media privileges famous, binary trans people and other privileged social identities in the new, supposedly more accepting cultural climate of gender and sexuality. Finally, I would like to proffer ideas for political, social and cultural interventions that move the conversation beyond the stale man/woman divide, to one that deploys an intersectional, queer, feminist approach in the fight for gender and sexual justice and liberation.

Transgender identities in the 1990s: personal and political awakenings

I creaked open the closet door at age 17 when I told my therapist that I thought I was a transsexual. Back in the early 1990s, there was not yet a "transgender" community, but a "TV/TS" (transvestite/transsexual) community. This meant that you were either a heterosexual male ("TV") who cross-dressed on occasion for personal fulfillment, or a transsexual who completely transitioned to the "opposite" gender through hormones and surgery and totally disavowed their assigned gender role. I knew that my gender identity was in permanent incongruence with my assigned gender and body, and that cross-dressing on occasion would not suffice. Therefore, I came to identify as a transsexual, as that was the only other option that was known to me. At the time, a transsexual was widely understood as a person who was "trapped in the wrong body" – i.e. a person who needed to make gender identity and body congruent through hormones, surgery and a seamless transition. As soon as possible, I wanted to jump up onto the nearest operating table to be able to get sex reassignment surgery to make mind and body line up in the expected way. This was more difficult in those early days because there were not as many young people who were transitioning, nor was the use of hormone blockers even a possibility (blockers were not a possibility until 2007 in the U.S.). When I went to my first transgender support groups and social events in my early 20s, I found that I was the youngest person in attendance and that many of the other transsexual women (there were seldom transsexual men in attendance) that were present were in their 40s, 50s and 60s. I believe that this is because transsexualism was so stigmatized and despised at the time that many people could not truly make the decision to come out as transsexual or to transition until middle-age or older.

In 1992, I first stepped foot onto the campus of my undergraduate institution, and I finally began to deal more intensely with my gender identity issues. I started to attend the GLBT group (which had just become trans-inclusive through my own efforts) and to talk seriously with my new therapist about my identity as a transsexual. However, my journey ended up being quite different than what I had previously thought or anticipated it would be.

In my sophomore year, I declared a Women's Studies major, and it truly transformed my life. It coincided with my discovery of the new emerging literature about gender diversity. Three of the first books that I discovered in the early to mid-1990s were *Gender Outlaw* by Kate Bornstein, *Stone Butch Blues* by Leslie Feinberg and *The Apartheid of Sex* by Martine Rothblatt. All three of these brilliant authors introduced the idea of living beyond the gender binary to me by bravely defending gender complexity, multiplicity and fluidity. Through fiction, memoir and theory, they discussed their desire to claim an identity that was neither man nor woman but something else altogether. Their texts revolutionized my own thinking as a member of the gender-variant community. Quite quickly, the "TV/TS" community was transforming into the *transgender* community. And what I found was the idea that there were more than two options (male OR female, cross-dressing OR complete medical transition), which was a startling and joyful revelation that prompted me to view my own identity in a very different fashion.

Through reading these and other authors and theorists, I discovered that it was possible to *not* identify as a man or as a woman, that there was a continuum and spectrum of infinite possibilities beyond our limited cultural concepts of gender and sexuality. I could take hormones, obtain surgeries or do neither. I could change my mind, and my identity could be fluid, shifting and transgressive. As soon as I read the work of Feinberg, Bornstein, and Rothblatt, as well as other authors writing cutting-edge gender theory like Judith Butler and Riki Wilchins, the idea of genders beyond the binary spoke to me in such an incredibly powerful way. This radical notion resonated with the very core of my being, and I knew that I was, in fact, a non-binary transgender person who melded aspects of masculinity and femininity in one being. Despite my sexed assignment, I knew quite clearly that I was not a man. In this culture, that meant I was then a woman by default. But maybe I was not a woman either but something completely different, a horse of a different color. Understanding non-binary gender identities enabled me to realize that I could express my gender however I wished, and I could customize my own transition in ways that resonated with my own complexity rather than conform to a cookie-cutter formulation of trans-sexualism created by non-transgender "experts."

However, what I have learned over time is that there is tremendous resistance to the notion of third, fourth, fifth or any number of genders beyond one and two. I think a lot of this has to do with the fact that people cannot "wrap their heads around" identities beyond the gender binary because as genderqueer people we continue to be so culturally illegible. While there may be a small amount of space now allotted to trans people who go clearly from one gender to the other, those who are both or nei-ther gender continue to be beyond the scope of many people's understanding. And sadly this misunderstanding and stigma happens in both the heteronormative society and within GLB communities. Non-binary, genderqueer, gender-fluid and neutrois identities, among others, represent a threat to the presumed tidiness of hegemonic categorizations. This "category crisis" may cause too much dissonance for some onlookers, the profound unintelligibility of our identities ultimately resulting in stigma, discrimination and even violence in the most extreme cases.

In the gay and lesbian community, which often glorifies masculinity, trans women and trans-feminine people in general are particularly stigmatized. Part of what was so powerful for me as a young trans woman coming into feminism and Women's Stud-ies was that it allowed me to connect the dots between my own marginalized identity and the discrimination I had faced my entire life. I was able to see that my identity as a trans-feminine subject was linked to the oppression that cisgender women and queer people face under a patriarchal system of gender and sexuality. Early trans-feminist voices like Susan Stryker, Sandy Stone and Beth Elliott wrote rich and ground-breaking texts that weaved the personal, political and theoretical strands of trans women's vibrant experiences into the feminist canon.

Becoming a feminist also helped me to begin to link gender oppression to other forms of oppression like racism, classism, and ableism. From my early 20s, intersec-tional feminism, particularly the work of women of color writers and theorists like Audre Lorde, Gloria Anzaldúa, bell hooks and Patricia Hill Collins, gave me critical tools to analyze power differentials in society and envision ways of mounting efforts for equality and social justice that were inclusive of multiple identities and cognizant of multiple axes of oppression. I feel lucky that from the very beginning of my feminist education, these authors were front and center. This helped me to see the problem of white, middle-class bias in feminism and Women's Studies and quickly deduce that there was a similar problem with cisgender privilege and bias. The work of intersec-tional feminists thus illuminated these ideological and political blind spots, but also demonstrated the need to fight on for inclusion of our marginalized groups to change the face of feminism and the future of feminism.

By the mid-1990s, the notion of a distinct "transgender community" started to solidify in a much more visible and systemic way. I think this was important because under the previous medical model of transsexualism, the entire idea was that people were programmed to essentially disappear into their target genders as seamlessly as possible. So, for example, if somebody was assigned male at birth the goal was to completely transition by jumping through the required bureaucratic hoops, obtain hormones and surgery, complete the "real life test", pass well as women and eventually be able to start an entirely new life for themselves, preferably in a new town, with a new job, and even abandoning previous social relationships. This was often referred to as "going stealth" or "woodworking." The older medical model of transsexualism essentially wanted people's trans-ness to be effectively erased. This required going from one closet to another, hardly a progressive political approach to managing gender diversity. The emergence of transgender liberation helped to drive home the idea that the previous model perpetuated shame and self-hatred, and that to be open, visible and "out" as transgender people helped to promote self-acceptance and pride, an idea that completely resonated with who I was as a person, as a feminist and as an emerging activist.

Tears in the umbrella: limits to trans diversity and inclusion

At that hopeful but naïve point in time of the nascent transgender movement, I believed that transgender would emerge victoriously as a truly inclusive movement with a "big tent" approach that would encompass all people who were in some way "gender outlaws." When I did education programs, for instance, I always talked about transgender as an umbrella term that included diverse gender constituencies like drag queens, drag kings, cross-dressers, transgenderists, transsexuals, bigender people, genderqueer folks and many more. In the beginning, transgender was very inclusive, at least rhetorically, of all of the various oppressed gender identities found in our society. However, even from the beginning, there were people who simply substituted "transgender" for "transsexual." Now, over 20 years into this social movement, what I find is that the transgender umbrella is seemingly not as inclusive as I had originally hoped, with more and more rips and tears appearing over time. As we have gotten more attention, and our issues have increasingly been taken up by popular media, the realities of people who live beyond the gender binary have been minimized in a race for trans acceptance and assimilation into mainstream society.

Just recently, my rural state of New Hampshire had an educational event on transgender issues with members of the state assembly. Within my state, I have been very involved with transgender community building, activism, and education since 1993. We currently do not have a law that prohibits discrimination in employment, housing, credit and public accommodations on the basis of gender identity and gender expression in our state. We are the only state in New England that still does not have such protections. In 2009, such a bill was introduced in the state legislature, but right-wing conservative and Christian fundamentalist activists took what was a simple nondiscrimination bill, redubbed it as a "bathroom bill" and made the spurious claim that the bill would enable transgender women to go into women's restrooms to assault girls and women with impunity. The atmosphere of fear mongering and misinformation was ultimately successful and promptly killed the bill.

In the intervening years, there has been a push to build trans community in the state to promote our visibility and to conduct education efforts at the local and state level to foster acceptance of trans people in the Granite State. When I heard about this educational program, I was excited that the groundwork was being laid once again to go forward with introducing a new nondiscrimination bill. I expressed my interest in being on the panel with the organizer, who was a cisgender gay man. As someone who has been involved in transgender politics for such a long time in New Hampshire, I wanted to provide context for the history of our community and our efforts to end discrimination. After not hearing about whether I was participating, I was finally told that as a non-binary person, my perspective would be too confusing for the people at the session, who were still struggling to understand transgender issues in the most basic sense. This was truly heartbreaking and infuriating to me. Approaches based in political expediency are very invested in particular outcomes and have a hyper-practical tactical strategy. Within political expediency, the end justifies the means. Often, the means are not ethical, principled or fair, with the idea being that politics requires constant compromise to reach desired objectives, thus legitimizing these problematic strategies. Needless to say, I find both the tactics themselves as well as their justification abhorrent and completely antithetical to the way in which I wish to engage in community and in social justice.

And it also felt like déjà vu. Back in my undergraduate days, many of us GLBT students would sit on educational panels for classes, in residence halls and in various departments across campus. There was a concerted attempt in those panels to put forward people who were gender conforming or "straight-acting." This meant that as a transgender person, I was frequently not invited. Likewise, my friends who were masculine lesbians, feminine gay men and other queers (including bisexuals) who did not conform to hegemonic gender norms and sexual binaries were also excluded. Sadly, this desire to hide or conceal the gender and sexual variance amongst us has a long history in the gay and lesbian community. My idealized notion of a utopic GLBT community was quickly dashed as I experienced the prevalence of biphobia and transphobia amongst many gay men and lesbians. "It is hard enough for people to understand being gay; bisexual and transgender people are just too confusing" was a frequent refrain that made many of my friends and I feel like outsiders even within the queer community.

Assimilationist politics are not new to the GLBT community, going back to the early days of the homophile movement in the U.S. Assimilationism refers to the political strategy of targeted social groups trying to conform as much as possible to the culture of the dominant group. The idea is that adherence to heteronormative culture and values will make GLBT more acceptable to the dominant society and encourage their integration into the mainstream. Assimilationism is also closely related to respectability politics, upholding the idea that if people from marginalized groups act as much as possible like their oppressor, they will be better treated and more easily accepted. Like political expediency, assimilationism is a deeply flawed tactic that will always leave people behind and implicitly and explicitly endorse the notion that the culture of the dominant group is superior, preferable and universal. The fact that now some parts of the transgender community are engaging in the same sort of assimilationist tactics of manufacturing a limited and conservatizing image of the community has been exasperating to me in so many ways. Clearly, we have not learned the lessons of our history that we can never throw enough people overboard, never jettison enough of the "different" people, to win approval from our enemies. For example, way back in 1973, radical trans woman of color and Stonewall combatant Sylvia Rivera was nearly booed off the stage of New York City Pride because of the assimilationist and anti-trans politics of gay and lesbian organizers. As I was completing this essay in June 2015, this tension was again perfectly exemplified by a GLBT Pride event held at the White House. While Obama was giving a speech to a bunch of well-heeled GLBT advocates, a transgender woman of color immigrant interrupted him to talk about the plight of immigrant transgender women and their horrific treatment in U.S. detention centers designated for men, by other detainees but also by Immigration and Customs Enforcement (ICE) officials. The woman, Jennicet Gutiérrez, was shushed, booed, and ultimately ejected from the White House. Obama gave her a thorough dressing down, to the applause of the many white, cisgender gays and lesbians present at the event. The media described the woman as a "heckler" rather than a transgender activist taking a principled stand against xenophobic, racist and transmisogynistic state-sponsored violence. Mainstream media, including some GLBT media, are complicit with this silencing and desire to erase and hide women like Gutiérrez from the public consciousness.

Dominant culture, mainstream media and the politics of assimilation

As the above examples of the marginalization of Sylvia Rivera and Jennicet Gutiérrez show, there has to be a unified community, a big tent approach in which no one is left behind. Despite working extremely hard for transgender human rights for over two decades, in many ways I find myself on the outside looking in of GLBT politics. As the trans community inches ever closer towards acceptance and civil rights, I find that this acceptance is predicated on certain basic assumptions, expectations and requirements. And we need only look once again to Caitlyn Jenner, to see how this so-called "acceptance" is actually quite limited and highly conditional.

If we're going to talk about public acceptance of trans people, I believe that Caitlyn Jenner is a particularly problematic person to focus on. Caitlyn Jenner, other than being a transgender woman, won the "privilege and power sweepstakes" and thus is hardly representative of the vast majority of transgender people. Caitlyn Jenner is white, wealthy, a former Olympic athlete, famous, camera-ready, thin, able-bodied, and a Republican. The vast majority of trans people in the United States are markedly different from Caitlyn Jenner along multiple vectors of difference. Many trans people in the US are people of color, poor or working-class, liberals, progressives and radicals, people who are unable to access proper medical care, including life-saving surgeries, people who are non-binary or unable or unwilling to "pass" and people whose marginality places them at risk of violence and severe discrimination at every turn.

While I saw many cisgender people seemingly acting like Caitlyn Jenner somehow invented transgender identity, it struck me that the desire to extend acceptance to Jenner was also because she was clearly locatable within the binary gender system. In fact, Jenner seemed to want to magically go from being a clearly masculine male to a clearly feminine female as is evidenced by the Diane Sawyer interview versus the *Vanity Fair* cover and 22-page article. While Jenner's transition has been many years in the making (and in fact the media and the paparazzi *did* notice that her body and appearance were changing), Jenner seemed to want a very unambiguous arrival to womanhood rather than easing into transition from male to female, thus concealing and making invisible any hint of gender ambiguity. This is, of course, her choice, and I do not mean to valorize one mode of transition over another. Rather, I am pointing out that it is vital to place Jenner's binary transition in the context of popular media culture, which has always privileged hyper-masculine men becoming hyper-feminine women, and vice versa, complete with the obligatory before-and-after photos. When I went to purchase the *Vanity Fair* magazine at my local drugstore, several of the employees could not wait to tell me how great they thought Caitlyn looked. While I appreciate that they indeed had something so positive to say about a transgender woman, I find it troubling that so much emphasis and attention has been placed upon Caitlyn Jenner's appearance, including her "passability" as a woman and ability to manifest adequate femininity.

I want to be clear that I unambiguously support every person's rights to their own unique gender expression. The most masculine man to the most feminine woman, and every unique and fabulous permutation in between and outside of hegemonic gender, should be fully embraced and celebrated. The problem has never been with people's gender expression, per se, including trans women who are high femme and trans men who are very masculine. The problem is the framing of certain trans identities within the media, within the medical establishment, and within the dominant, popular imagination. I also reject the old radical feminist canard advocated by ideologues like Janice Raymond that transgender folks conserve or reinforce conservative gender roles, as if such a disenfranchised and relatively small minority has the power to do that rather than the cisgender and heterosexual men and women who make up the bulk of normative gender subjectivities. The problem is not that some people fit into traditional binary gender roles but the assumption that everyone *can or should* fit into such roles. In addition, the notions that trans women must "pass" as cisgender women to be fully accepted as women and conform to dominant notions of feminine beauty illustrate a conditional acceptance that is hardly transformative.

We need to affirm and accept people's gender identities, including their names and pronouns, whether or not they are legible to us as members of the gender they identify with. Let me return to my own personal experience to underscore this point. I am a 6'6", 400 pound, asexual, genderqueer, gender-fluid, disabled, visibly trans woman. Due to these intersecting identities, people have perceived me as male, female, and something else throughout my entire life. In addition, I have struggled with self-esteem and with finding role models that affirm my beauty as a fat, non-passing and non-binary trans woman who is not hyper-feminine or high femme. I have already seen some of my trans women friends on social media who are remarking how they feel badly about themselves because they have not been able to achieve the femininity or the passability of Caitlyn Jenner. They also experience great sadness that hormone blockers or even early transition were not an option for them, further making it much harder to be perceived and accepted as women. The emphasis on passing, beauty and femininity can have a very damaging effect on transgender women, and it also leaves out people who are unable to transition or who do not want to medically transition.

So many trans folks are economically marginalized, under- or unemployed, and struggle for the most basic dignity and respect in their day-to-day life. In Diane Sawyer's interview of Jenner, the plight of transgender women of color was very briefly mentioned but not at all adequately fleshed out or elaborated. My hope was that the interview would be used as a kick-off to further the conversation about the experiences of the most marginalized trans people in the US and the violence and oppression they contend with each and every day. Unfortunately, as with what often happens in the media, Caitlyn's personal story took complete precedence over the realities of how our society is constructed in terms of not only gender identity, but race and class as well. It became about personal individual acceptance and acceptance from her family, but failed to look at the realities of systemic, institutional, macro-level discrimination and oppression like the fact that many transgender women must work in the underground economies to survive (sex work, dealing drugs, etc.) or face the violent horrors wrought by being put into men's units in gender-segregated facilities such as prisons, immigration detention centers, homeless shelters, etc.

I believe that this media interview resulted not only from the fact that Caitlyn Jenner is so incredibly privileged in multiple ways, but also because media likes to perpetuate the notion that we live in a society of equality and opportunity rather than one that is rife with bigotry, prejudice and systematic oppression. Emphasis is placed on whether one achieves self-acceptance and approval from one's family, as well as a "convincing" gendered appearance, rather than on the many societal barriers that lower trans people's life chances in multiple institutions from cradle to grave.

This new media hype includes trans men as well. Trans man Aydian Dowling recently made a splash by vying to become the first transsexual man on the cover of *Men's Health* magazine. This was preceded by a photo circulating of Dowling that features him in a pose that recreates nude photographs of musician and tv personality Adam Levine in *Cosmopolitan UK* magazine. In the original photo, Adam Levine is completely naked, save two entwined hands sporting bright red nail polish covering his genitals. In the new photo, we see a white man in the exact same pose, with similarly manicured and presumably female hands also covering his genital region. Many people might look at the photo and may not even know that Dowling is a trans man. The only possible giveaway might be the faint scars on his chest from chest surgery.

However, once again, as with Caitlyn Jenner, we see Dowling as having privilege in practically every other way except for his trans-ness. He is white, very masculine, medically transitioned through hormones and surgery, passable and he possesses the body and appearance which society considers "hot" (as with Levine) and therefore the confluence of these social identities make him of acceptable value in our patriarchal system. It is also easily understood as a part of assimilationist politics. "Look, he is just like a 'real man' except for his genitals!" The photograph also ironically re-centers the genitals and the body more generally as the determinant of gender, a notion that the trans community has been fighting against for decades. The media's love affair with Dowling's photo homage to Levine and his desire to be on the cover of *Men's Health* was capped off by a well-publicized appearance on *The Ellen DeGeneres Show*.

At a workshop I gave on weightism, lookism and appearance in the trans community, we talked about how images such as those of Caitlyn Jenner, Aydian Dowling and other high profile trans people like Chaz Bono, Laverne Cox and Janet Mock affect the lives and emotions of everyday trans people. This included extended discussion about how these images negatively affected self-esteem, self-worth and even hope for the future. Many trans people live in such dire economic jeopardy that they are not even able to access the health care that they need, including hormones and surgeries to alter their bodies in ways that can be life-sustaining in the face of persistent gender dysphoria. In addition, people of size and people whose appearance is not considered beautiful, handsome, "hot", sexy etc. suffer from these images in that it reinforces the dominant cultural ideal of what constitutes attractive people and even who is worthy of dating, love and sex. Weightism, lookism and transphobia can combine as a lethal force in trans people's lives, furthering vulnerability for depression, suicide, exploitation and even violence. This is not to demonize Caitlyn Jenner or Aydian Dowling or other public transgender people in any way as it is not really about them as individuals. Rather, it is about a social system that values certain bodies and certain identities while systematically devaluing, erasing and marginalizing other bodies and identities.

From transgender or trans we have now arrived at trans*. Trans* was specifically coined to call attention to non-binary identities under the trans umbrella. The desire is to reclaim trans* as a way that is not reducible to transsexuals or medically transitioning people firmly locatable within the binary gender system. Under the wide spectrum of gender-diverse, gender-expansive and gender-variant people, it was calling attention to and emphasizing those of us who are genderqueer, neutrois, gender nonconforming, multi-gendered, agender, gender fluid, etc. While I often now use trans* in writing and very much like the impetus behind its creation and usage, I once again fear that whatever moniker we use, transgender, trans, or trans*, that we will fail as a movement and as a society to truly be inclusive of non-binary gender identities. Moreover, we come up short of establishing gender multiplicity and fluidity as a foundational world view of the culture. Because of the confluence of corporate media culture and "reality" tv, the (often conservative) medical establishment, and increasingly assimilationist transgender politics, including within the GLBT nonprofit world, I am skeptical of genuine inclusion of non-binary genders anytime soon. Those of us who stand outside of male and female or even trans man and trans woman continue to be relegated to the margins. My goal in writing this chapter is to articulate an increasing frustration that I had as a transgender woman with feeling that even in my own LGBT community, a community which I have fought for and with for two decades, I and many others do not represent those who deserve liberation and civil and human rights because of entrenched political, social and ideological attitudes that devalue the most marginalized queer and trans* community members among us.

Conclusion: transforming trans* politics and celebrating queer differences

To conclude, I would like to sketch out a few preliminary ideas for interventions that push back against these trans- and homonormative tendencies and call for a renewed insurgence of queer and trans* militancy and radicalism. While there are no easy answers to these complex problems, I would like to suggest that we question the state of contemporary GLBT politics, and its emphasis on assimilation, normalization and respectability politics (see Warner 1999, for instance). Across the GLBT spectrum, there has been tremendous emphasis on marriage equality, military service, adoption of children and other issues that strived to assimilate GLBT people into mainstream heteronormative institutions and dominant cultural life. While I understand the need for these equal legal protections and institutional access, we must continue to stress that often this work benefits the sectors of the GLBT community that already hold the most power and privilege. The "top down" approach to equal rights prioritizes long and protracted political battles that benefit the few at the expense of the many. They privilege moneyed, white, cisgender gay men and lesbians while marginalizing people of color, poor and working-class queers and trans* folks. Rather than a top down approach, we need a bottom up model that works to empower and protect those who are most materially disenfranchised, including non-binary folks. Our visible queerness and gender nonconformity place us at the most risk for discrimination, economic jeopardy and violence.

Part of this is moving away from the single-issue, liberal approach that GLBT politics has often clung to. Intersectional, queer transfeminism can advocate for political strategies that are attentive to the heterogeneity of our communities and that proffer sharp and incisive *analyses* of power differentials. We need to embrace dissidents, nonconformists and outlaws and lift up their voices rather than rush to showcase the most normative among us to win respectability from our oppressors. From Compton's, to Stonewall, to Queer Nation, Act-Up and the Lesbian Avengers, we have a rich history of radical queer and trans* resistance to oppression to inform our current efforts. We need to acknowledge that while the "incrementalism" of the mainstream GLBT movement has benefit for some, many queers are struggling mightily from class oppression, homelessness, the criminalization of HIV/AIDS, the lack of culturally competent medical care, police profiling and violence, the prison system, immigration issues such as detention and deportation, hate crimes and much more.

We need to push back against a media that only allows people like Caitlyn Jenner and Aydian Dowling to narrowly represent the transgender community. In addition to demanding coverage of non-binary identities, we need to challenge the stale media obsession with medical transition and individualized acceptance from cisgender family members and society and demand that we look at macro-level societal discrimination and oppression and what we need to do to transform our society to one based in liberation and justice. In media and beyond, we need to push for genderqueer and non-binary inclusion and visibility, but we also need to demand that *everyone* look at the binary gender system and challenge it in their day-to-day lives. Issues of gender and sexuality are not only the province of LGBT people; they are issues for everyone and that matter to everyone. Beginning in kindergarten, we need to teach children that there is more to humanity than boy and girl, and that whatever their own identity, they can be and do whatever they wish in life. While the current transgender movement has made incredible strides towards creating greater gender and sexual freedom in our society, there is still tremendous work to liberate us all from the constraints of hegemonic gender scripts, sexual norms and traditional models of family, relationships and community.

While being an outsider and a misfit can be difficult and even painful, I also see it as the site of radical possibility that will continue to push the envelope of who we can be as human beings and the kind of world we can create. Too much of society is strait-jacketed by gray, unimaginative and crushing demands for conformity, muting the potential of humanity. As queer people, we have the rainbow as our international symbol of strength and pride, but we still have tremendous work to ensure that people represented by *all* of the beautiful and dazzling colors of the spectrum have the ability to self-actualize and live a life unencumbered by systemic hate, violence and oppression. While I struggle to engender such a world for myself and my comrades in struggle, I take strength from the resolve and perseverance of my trans* and queer warrior ancestors like Sylvia Rivera and Leslie Feinberg. It is up to us to continue their rich and revolutionary legacy. Are you ready to join me?

Bibliography

Bergado, Gabe. 2015. "Meet Aydian Dowling, the Trans Hunk Aiming for a 'Men's Health' Cover." *The Daily Beast*. 14 April 2015. Web. Accessed 10 July 2015.

Bissinger, Buzz. 2015. "He Says Goodbye, She Says Hello." *Vanity Fair*. July 2015. 50–69 and 105–106.

Bornstein, Kate. 1995. *Gender Outlaw: On Men, Women and the Rest of Us*. New York: Vintage Books.

Bornstein, Kate and S. Bear Bergman, eds. 2010. *Gender Outlaws: The Next Generation*. Berkeley, CA: Seal Press.

Bornstein, Kate (performer) and Susan Marenco (director). 1993. *Adventures in the Gender Trade*. Filmmakers Library, VHS.

"Bruce Jenner: The Interview." 2015. *20/20 with Diane Sawyer*. ABC News. 24 April 2015.

Butler, Judith. 1990. *Gender Trouble: Feminism and the Subversion of Identity*. New York: Routledge.

Collins, Patricia Hill. 1990. *Black Feminist Thought: Knowledge, Consciousness and the Politics of Empowerment*. Boston: Unwin Hyman.

Elliott, Beth. 1996. *Mirrors: Portrait of a Lesbian Transsexual*. New York: Masquerade Books.

Feinberg, Leslie. 1993. *Stone Butch Blues: A Novel*. Ithaca, NY: Firebrand Books.

Gendernauts: A Journey Through Shifting Identities. 1999. Dir. Monika Treut. Perf. Sandy Stone, Susan Stryker, Texas Tomboy, Annie Sprinkle. First Run Features.

Nestle, Joan, Clare Howell and Riki Anne Wilchins, eds. 2002. *GenderQueer: Voices From Beyond the Sexual Binary*. Los Angeles: Alyson Books.

Outlaw. 1994. Dir. Alisa Lebow. Perf. Leslie Feinberg. Women Make Movies.

Raymond, Janice. 1979. *The Transsexual Empire: The Making of the She-Male*. Boston: Beacon Press.

Rothblatt, Martine Aliana. 1995. *The Apartheid of Sex: A Manifesto on the Freedom of Gender*. New York: Crown Publishers.

Stone, Sandy. 1991. "The Empire Strikes Back: A Post-Transsexual Manifesto." Julia Epstein and Kristina Straub, eds. *Body Guards: The Cultural Politics of Gender Ambiguity*. New York: Routledge.

Stryker, Susan. 1994. "My Words to Victor Frankenstein above the Village of Chamounix: Performing Transgender Rage." *GLQ: A Journal of Lesbian and Gay Studies* 1.3: 237–254.

Warner, Michael. 1999. *The Trouble with Normal: Sex, Politics and the Ethics of Queer Life*. New York: Free Press.

Wilchins, Riki Anne. 1997. *Read My Lips: Sexual Subversion and the End of Gender*. Ithaca, NY: Firebrands Books.

chapter 16

Adolescent girls' sexuality

The more it changes, the more it stays the same

Deborah L. Tolman

Army girls gone wild!
Lesbian girls gone wild!
Girls gone wild in Dallas!
Barely legal sorority girls gone wild!
Korean Girls gone wild!
Anime girls gone wild!

> Results of a Google search on girls and sexuality (March 8, 2010)

At the last half of the twentieth century, not long after adolescence itself was invented, adolescent girls' sexuality was under heavy surveillance, and the root source of plenty of panic. An epidemic of teen pregnancy among African-American girls (not true); an epidemic of White middle-class girls giving boys oral sex in empty houses, in hallways and under table cloths (not true); an epidemic of teens rejecting relationships in favor of hooking up (not true). I suggest that one of the reasons these ostensible "epidemics" are grabbed, spun (and in essence created) by the media into the latest catastrophe is that they harbor possibilities of adolescent girls' sexual desire.

Good girls and bad girls

As we enter the next decade of the twenty-first century, the tightrope that girls walk separating good girls from bad has not been taken down but has in fact gotten tighter (Valenti 2008). Adolescent girls' sexuality is a fulcrum of contradictions: Girls want relationships, boys want sex, but everybody is just hooking up – no strings attached. "Virgins" can be reborn, but "sluts" can never shake the moniker that they still get. To be popular, with girls and with boys, girls are told to wear less and less to be more and more sexy, but girls who dress in skimpy clothes look like prostitutes. Girls are sexually aggressive, no longer sexual objects, but the coolest shirts are stamped with phrases like "Rub These for Luck" and "Who Needs Brains When You Have These?" "Sexting" is the latest supposed craze to incite panic among parents – and it's girls sending naked pictures of themselves to boys, never the other way around – but girls who "sext" are pathetic, not normal.

So what is it? Are girls now just as into sex, just as sexually assertive as boys or does the double standard still rule? Do girls (finally) just want to have fun? While the media saturates us with the fantasy or fear that deep down, girls are into being like porn stars, they are still as vulnerable as ever to being labeled and scorned for evidencing real sexual feelings and more than ever under pressure to appear – but not to actually be – sex kittens. Adolescent girls' sexuality is still not their own. And the landscape of what is normal sexuality for teenage girls, what "everyone" does or feels, is more confusing than ever.

The fundamental organizing principle of girls' sexuality remains firmly in place: if girls want to be considered good, nice or even normal, adolescent girls are not (really) supposed to have sexual feelings of their own. And there is much inequity for girls embedded in this division of teen girls into "good" and "bad." Stereotypes about African-American girls being hypersexual, Asian-American girls unlocking secret doors to male pleasure, Latina girls being hot, hot, hot make it very difficult (if they are middle-class or elite) and virtually impossible (if they are working-class or poor) for girls of color even to get on the "good girl" pedestal, and they bear the constant risk of being knocked off (American Psychological Association 2007).

Girls' sexuality development

This contradiction continues to obscure what is normal for girls' sexuality and its development. In fact, we know very little about how sexuality develops in adolescence. We do know that as the female body matures, sex hormones are released (Halpern et al. 1997). In addition to sexual development – i.e. getting breasts, hips, pubic and armpit hair – it is, on average, normative for girls to start to have sexual feelings in early adolescence. The new twist is that, as they go from early to middle to late adolescence, what they are actually supposed to do is *to seem to have them* – to "perform" sexual assertiveness, and not so much for their own curiosity or satisfaction, but as especially "good" objects of others' sexual desire. In other words they incite desire rather than express it.

The irony is that in fact, most girls do experience sexual feelings in their own bodies – embodied sexual desire. These feelings may surface when a girl sees someone to whom she is attracted or while she is kissing someone she loves – or not. Learning how to become a sexual person – what sexual desire feels like, how to think about making decisions about sex, who is sexually attractive – is a normative part of adolescent development for both girls and boys. This process, called sexual socialization, includes learning to find the "right" people desirable, the contexts in which it is "appropriate" – or not – to have or express sexual feelings, and what are acceptable "sexual scripts." These norms are conveyed by family, by peers, and by media. Girls continue to be sexually socialized into being sexy rather than being sexual, which results in girls and women learning not only that they are the object of another's desire, that they are to be looked at, but that they also come to experience their own bodies in this fashion. An object has no feelings of her own. This message stands in stark contrast to other domains of young women's lives, where they learn that they can be and do "anything," producing yet another confusing contradiction anchoring female adolescence.

Girls' sexual desire and the double standard

Given the escalation of the overt and in-your-face presence of sexuality in our social landscape, what's the big deal? Why is even the possibility that girls might have and act on their own sexual feelings such a problem? In fact, by the age of 19, the majority of girls have had sexual intercourse, more than half of girls have performed oral sex, and an increasing percentage have had anal sex (Advocates for Youth 2010). Some of these sexual encounters were protected, some of them were coerced; the little we know about young women's experiences of their own sexuality suggests that most of these encounters were not about young women's sexual desire or their sexual pleasure (Fine and McClelland 2007; Levy 2005; Tolman 2002, 2010). Why isn't *this* the problem?

Even as demands on teenage girls to be sexy have intensified and the sexualization of younger girls is now standard fare (APA 2007), young women's sexual desire is still not considered an anchor of young women's sexuality; dressed in heels, thongs and short skirts, in the end, it is desire for relationships that is (still) what girls are "supposed" to have (Bogle 2008). In fact, in order to keep boys – who are said to have uncontrollable sexual urges for which they cannot be held accountable – in check, the suppression of girls' sexual desire is required. If girls had or acted on their sexual feelings, the entire system would be in chaos – or so the panic goes. The norms and beliefs that sustain this conception, this construction of what normal and appropriate male and female sexuality are in adolescence, are institutionalized by the double standard. Without understanding or acceptance that girls too have and are entitled to sexual feelings, the double standard has not and will not budge. The interplay between these ideas is mutually reconstituting and reinforcing.

Resisting the double standard: sexual subjectivity

The good news is that in recent years, there has been some important and potent resistance to these constraining and unfair conceptions and norms. And some teenage girls

Deborah L. Tolman

refuse to be controlled by the regulating image of "the slut." That is, some girls claim their entitlement to their own sexual feelings, whatever they are. While few and far between, these resistant girls offer the outline of potential alternative stories of how young women might claim their own sexuality, and how social norms may be shifted. They are on the Web, writing zines, launching protests against being sexualized and objectified, creating communities where they can rant against this injustice, talk about how denying desire diminishes sexual and reproductive health, and gain courage and strength from knowing they are not alone. In unprecedented ways, teenage girls can take action not only in their personal relationships but in changing the "way things are." Bucking the system is hard work, and potentially socially and materially costly for many girls. But they have shown us that it can be done. They enact what researchers call "sexual subjectivity."

The concept of "sexual subjectivity" has recently been developed in relation to adolescent women's sexuality and its development (Horne and Zimmer-Gembeck 2006; Tolman 2002). Sexual subjectivity means having a sense of oneself as a sexual person who is entitled to have sexual feelings and to make active decisions about sexual behavior. It is the opposite of "it just happened," which is how many adolescent girls describe their sexual experiences, and has been identified as one of the only "stories" girls can tell about their sexual behavior (Tolman 2002). The phrase "It just happened" is passive rather than active; it literally has no people in it, no one who is responsible or accountable. Being a sexual subject is the opposite of being a sexual object – rather than solely being the target of someone else's desire, a sexual subject has agency, that is, she has her own desire as a compass in actively negotiating her sexuality. Sexual subjectivity offers an alternative to and denaturalizes the idea that it is normal for girls not to be only sexy but also to acknowledge and be acknowledged as legitimately sexual beings. This dissociation from one's sexual feelings remains a key part of how young women are socialized into their sexuality. Resisting this message is hard to do, but some girls do in fact do so. These girls have a sense of entitlement to their sexuality and also an awareness of the consequences of being a girl who has and acts on her sexual desire. These girls have figured out that if they do not let being labeled a "slut" affect them – that if they reject it as a viable way to think about girls' sexuality – the label will lose its power over them, at least psychologically. These girls may have a hard road to plow socially, but the resilience that can come with this choice can also enable these young women to lead the charge to resist dividing girls into good and bad, the very heart of what keeps desire so dangerous.

Another tension that is developing is around sexual identity or orientation. The "good girl" is assumed to be straight – not lesbian, bisexual or not sure if she is attracted to women. The fact that desiring girls is another "violation" is no accident. Heteronormativity – becoming a *heterosexual* person – has been considered what is normal and right. It is depicted on television as "the way things are" between young men and women, with a clear script for how everyone is supposed to behave (Kim et al. 2007). Many young women are rejecting this belief and claiming sexual identities that are not heterosexual, including having no label at all. Recently, both research and social changes have shown that having and acting on same-sex sexual desires is not uncommon for anyone, and for some people is the organizing principle of their sexuality (Russell 2005). Sexual fluidity – shifts and changes in whom women are sexually attracted to and/or with whom they have sexual experiences – has been documented in the last decade as a feature of female sexuality (Diamond 2009).

Wild girls?

The latest and most confusing notion about young women's sexuality appears constantly in the media, which is that all young women and teenage girls are sexually aggressive and want to go out and get sex just like guys do (Levy 2005; Zurbriggen and Roberts, 2012). This portrayal – and what is wrong with it – is best exemplified in the wildly successful *Girls Gone Wild* franchise. Primarily on location at spring break from college extravaganzas on beaches, this television series has created a spectacle of real young women performing male sexual fantasies – kissing other girls, having a threesome, masturbating for the camera, making it seem that young women are doing what they really want to do. In fact, young women will often say they want to bare it all and do it all, but a contradictory, ironic and very problematic slippage has actually occurred.

It is not an accident that virtually all of these young women are drunk when they take the dare to engage in a variety of sexual behaviors and exhibition of themselves. Many feel guilt and regret afterwards; virtually none of them describe these experiences as pleasurable or about their own sexual desire. It is about the desire to look and be seen as sexy. This is a desire that has been stirred, teased and aroused by the recent intensification of using sex – and sexualized girls' and women's bodies – to sell products. In fact, more than ever, sex has become something to give, to get, to trade and less about expressing emotions, a sense of connection to another person, or an embodied experience. It is not cool to want relationships – even when teenage girls (and boys) actually do. Perhaps this notion that relationships are toxic, risky or to be avoided is an unintended consequence of abstinence-until-marriage sex education, or the sensationalism of celebrity break-ups and heartbreaks which make relationships seem not worth the costs. Relationships require two authentic and complete people, which sexual objectification makes difficult. Constant exposure to images of girls and women who are portrayed only as sex objects is taking its toll on young women's sexuality development (Tolman 2010).

Reinforcing girls' sexual well-being

Why is it that the more things seem to change, the more they in fact stay the same? Having listened to many teen girls and also boys talk about their experiences with sexuality and relationships, I can hear it loud and clear. Teen boys are under pressure to embrace and "perform" ideas about masculinity that include being dominant *over* (and especially not dominated *by*) girls, wanting and trying to "get" sex (whether they actually want to or not) and showing that they are not gay (Tolman et al. 2003; Pascoe 2007). Girls are still split into two groups by adults, peers, the media, and social institutions into good and bad. This division is predicated on sexual restraint of themselves and of boys and being successful but being feminine at the same time. While there is a large and growing movement to demand and secure sexual rights for LGBT people (and teens), there is no social movement for girls' sexual rights – the right to be a sexual person, to have resources to make safe, healthy and fulfilling decisions, and to be safe from violence. Danger still trumps pleasure for women and girls (Vance 1994). Interestingly, in developing countries, such demands have taken hold, fueled by community groups and alliances of girls with others in their communities to demand these rights (Tolman and Costa 2010). In the United States, we can learn from the successes that have been achieved to begin to change how we think, talk about and thus experience and negotiate adolescent girls' sexuality.

Rather than focusing on risk reduction, we can start thinking about the development of sexual well-being as a part of our humanity that we do, can and should begin to develop in adolescence and then foster across our lifetimes. Sexual well-being includes: sexual and reproductive health (and access to required resources); comfort with one's own body and emotions; pursuing one's desires (barring harm to others); and being aware of and having the freedom to act (without threat of violence, material or social consequences) upon our sexual desires. Sexual well-being also includes the ability to identify risk, to make choices that diminish risk when possible, and to feel comfortable, happy and empowered in one's own body. The idea that all girls have a right to sexual well-being is predicated in part on sexual subjectivity, on resisting a system of dividing girls into categories of good and bad and pitting them against one another, and on recognizing, resisting and reframing the ongoing gender inequities that still characterize young people's sexual lives. Tackling demands for masculinity in boys that have harmful consequences for girls as well, refusing to tolerate homophobia, and enabling young women to be comfortable with their own sexual feelings, will be part of the task of articulating and securing sexual rights for teenage girls.

References

Advocates for Youth, accessed March 8, 2010. www.advocatesforyouth.org/index.php?option= com_content&task=view&id=30&Itemid=59.

American Psychological Association (APA). 2007. *Task force on sexualization of girls report.* Washington, DC: APA.

Bogle, K. (2008). *Hooking up: Sex, dating and relationships on campus.* New York: New York University Press.

Diamond, L. (2009). *Sexual fluidity: Understanding women's love and desire.* Cambridge, MA: Harvard University Press.

Fine, M. and McClelland, S. (2007). "The politics of teen women's sexuality: Public policy and the adolescent female body." *Emory Law Journal*, pp. 993–1038.

Halpern, C., Udry, J., and Suchindran, C. (1997). "Testosterone predicts initiation of coitus in adolescent females." *Psychosomatic Medicine*, 59(2): 161–71.

Horne, S., and Zimmer-Gembeck, M. (2006). "The female sexual subjectivity inventory: Development and validation of a multidimensional instrument for late adolescents and emerging adults." *Psychology of Women Quarterly*, 30(2): 125–38.

Kim, J., Sorsoli, C., Collins, K., Zylbergold, B., Schooler, D., and Tolman, D. (2007). "From sex to sexuality: Exposing the heterosexual script on primetime network television." *Journal of Sex Research*, 44(2): 145–57.

Levy, A. (2005). *Female chauvinist pigs: Women and the rise of raunch culture*. New York: Free Press.

Pascoe, C. J. (2007). *Dude, you're a fag: Masculinity and sexuality in high school*. Berkeley: University of California Press.

Russell, S. (2005). "Introduction to positive perspectives on adolescent sexuality: Part 2." *Sexuality Research and Social Policy: A Journal of the NSRC*, 2(4): 1–3.

Tolman, D. (2002). *Dilemmas of desire: Teenage girls talk about sexuality*. Cambridge, MA: Harvard University Press.

—. (2010). "It's bad for all of us: The impact of the sexualization of girls on boys', women's and men's sexuality." In E. Zurbriggen and T. A. Roberts (Eds), *The sexualization of girls and girlhood*. New York: Oxford University Press.

Tolman, D. and Costa, S. (2010). "Sexual rights for young women: Lessons from developing countries." In R. Parker and P. Aggleton (Eds), *Routledge Handbook of Sexuality, Health and Rights*. London: Routledge.

Tolman, D., Spencer, R., Rosen-Reynoso, M. and Porche, M. (2003). "Sowing the seeds of violence in heterosexual relationships: Early adolescents narrate compulsory heterosexuality." *Journal of Social Issues*, 59(1): 159–78.

Valenti, J. (2008). *He's a stud, she's a slut and 49 other things women should know about the double standard*. Seattle, WA: Seal Press.

Vance, C. (Ed.). (1994). *Pleasure and danger: Exploring women's sexuality*. New York: Routledge.

Zurbriggen, E. and Roberts, T. A. (2012). *The sexualization of girls and girlhood*. New York: Oxford University Press.

Deborah L. Tolman

chapter 17

"Guys are just homophobic"

Rethinking adolescent homophobia and heterosexuality

C. J. Pascoe

Teenage masculinity

Kevin, a high school student in suburban San Francisco, sits at an IHOP, short of money for dinner. His friend, Craig, agrees to lend him money, but only on the following condition – that Kevin repeat a series of confessional phrases which Craig can videotape and place on YouTube. Kevin buries his head in his hands asking, "You're going to take a video of this and post it on YouTube aren't you?!" Craig ignores Kevin's plea saying, "Anyway, repeat after me. I Kevin James Wong."

KEVIN	I, Kevin James Wong.
CRAIG	17 years old.
KEVIN	(WHO AT THIS POINT STARTS TO GIGGLE EMBARRASSEDLY):17 years old.
CRAIG	Senior at Valley High School.
KEVIN	Senior at Valley High School.
CRAIG	In Santa Clarita.
KEVIN	In Santa Clarita.
CRAIG	Am now confessing.
KEVIN	Am now confessing.

CRAIG   That I, Kevin Wong.
KEVIN   That I, Kevin Wong.
CRAIG   Am a homosexual male.
KEVIN   Am a homosexual male.

They dissolve into laughter as their friend Jesse jumps into the frame behind Kevin. Craig posted the video on YouTube and eagerly showed it to me as I interviewed him in a local Starbucks. He and his friends giggled as they continued to show me other YouTube videos, one of which featured them imitating men engaging in anal intercourse and then bursting into fits of laughter.

About two years before I watched Craig's video in that Santa Clarita coffee shop I found myself two hours away, at a high school in Riverton California, where a group of fifth graders had been bussed in for the day to participate in the local high school's performing arts day. As I looked around the outdoor quads decorated with student artwork and filled with choirs singing and bands playing, a student from River High, Brian, ran past me to the rear quad yelling to a group of the elementary school boys. He hollered at them, pointing frantically, "There's a faggot over there! There's a faggot over there! Come look!" The group of boys dashed after Brian as he ran down the hallway, towards the presumed "faggot." Peering down the hallway I saw Brian's friend, Dan, waiting for the boys. As the boys came into his view, Dan pursed his lips and began sashaying towards them. He swung his hips exaggeratedly and wildly waved his arms on the end of which his hands hung from limp wrists. To the boys Brian yelled, referring to Dan, "Look at the faggot! Watch out! He'll get you!" In response, the 10-year-olds screamed in terror and raced back down the hallway. I watched Brian and Dan repeat this drama about the predatory faggot, each time with a new group of young boys.

Kevin, Craig, Brian and Dan enacted similar scenes containing similar messages: men or boys who do not conform to normative understandings of masculinity and sexuality should be mocked, humiliated and possibly feared. I have spent the better part of the last decade interviewing teens about and observing their behavior around definitions of masculinity and sexuality. Across a variety of geographic settings, boys from a range of class and racial/ethnic groups report sentiments much like those expressed by Kevin, Craig, Brian and Dan. Conversations with and observations of these boys indicate that homophobic taunts, jokes, teasing and harassment are central to the ways in which contemporary American boys come to think of themselves as men.

The homophobia articulated by Kevin, Craig, Brian and Dan seems representative of many American youth. Nationally, 93 percent of youth hear homophobic comments at least occasionally and 51 percent on a daily basis (National Mental Health Association 2002). Interestingly, in one state, 80 percent of youth who have been targeted with anti-gay harassment identify as heterosexual (Youth Risk Behavior Survey – Washington 1995). While this harassment is primarily directed at boys, girls suffer from sexualized harassment as well. The American Association of University Women (2001) documents that 83 percent of girls have been sexually harassed at school. These cursory statistics point to an educational experience in adolescence characterized in part by sexualized and gendered aggression directed from boys at other boys *and* at girls.

This type of joking and teasing can have dire consequences. Ninety percent of random school shootings have involved straight-identified boys who have been relentlessly humiliated with homophobic remarks (Kimmel 2003). For instance, Michael Carneal and Andy Williams, both involved in rampage school shootings, had been harassed for being gay (Kimmel 2003; Newman et al. 2004). Michael Carneal's school newspaper actually published a report outing him as gay (though he did not self-identify as such) (Newman et al. 2004). Eric Mohat, a 17-year-old high school student in Ohio who enjoyed theater and playing music, shot himself in 2007 after hearing homophobic taunts. Similarly, Carl Joseph Walker Hoover, an 11-year-old middle school student in Massachusetts, suffered homophobic harassment from his classmates for performing well academically. He hung himself as a desperate response to the teasing. Lawrence King, having been bullied relentlessly since third grade for his non-traditional gender presentation, was shot and killed by a fellow student in 2008 whom he had asked to be his Valentine.

While certainly the sort of joking and minor humiliation exhibited in the two opening stories does not match the level of violence in these examples, a problematic intersection of gender and sexuality undergirds all of them. Practices that seem to reflect basic homophobia – imitating same-sex eroticism, calling someone queer or mincing about with limp wrists – are also about policing gendered identities and practices. Through making homophobic jokes, calling other boys gay and imitating effeminate men boys attempt to assure themselves and others of their masculinity. For contemporary American boys, the definition of masculinity entails displaying power, competence, a lack of emotions, heterosexuality and dominance. Says Kevin, for instance, to be masculine is to be "tough." The ideal man is "strong" and he "can't be too emotional" adds Erik. Maleness does not confer masculinity upon a given boy. Rather masculinity is the repeated signaling to self and others that one is powerful, competent, unemotional, heterosexual and dominant.

This signaling appears in two ways, through practices of repudiation and confirmation. Repudiatory practices take the form of a "fag discourse," consisting of homophobic jokes, taunts, and imitations through which boys publicly signal their rejection of that which is considered unmasculine. Boys confirm masculine selves through public enactments of compulsive heterosexuality which include practices of "getting girls," physically confining girls under the guise of flirtation and sex talk. For many contemporary American boys masculinity must be repeatedly proven, as one's identity as masculine is never fully secured. This essay unpacks adolescent boys' public enactments of homophobia and heterosexuality, examining them as sexualized as well as gendered processes which have ramifications for all teenagers – male, female, straight and gay.

The fag discourse

Boys repeatedly tell me that "fag" was the ultimate insult for a boy. Darnell stated, "Since you were little boys you've been told, 'hey, don't be a little faggot.'" Jeremy emphasized that this insult literally reduced a boy to nothing, "To call someone gay or fag is like the lowest thing you can call someone. Because that's like saying that you're nothing." Indeed, much like the boys terrorized by Brian and Craig, boys often learn long before adolescence that a "fag" is the worst thing a guy could be. Thus boys' daily lives often consist of interactions in which they frantically lob these epithets at one another and try to deflect them from themselves.

Many boys explained their frequent use of insults like queer, gay and fag by asserting that, as Keith put it, "guys are just homophobic." However, analyzing boys' homophobic practices as a "fag discourse" shows that their behavior reflects not just a fear of same-sex desire, but a specific fear of *men*'s same-sex desire. Many told me that homophobic insults applied primarily to boys, not to girls. While Jake told me that he didn't like gay people, he quickly added, "Lesbians, okay, that's good!" Now lesbians are not "good" because of some enlightened approach to sexuality, but because, as Ray said, "To see two hot chicks banging bodies in a bed, that's like every guy's fantasy right there. It's the truth. I've heard it so many times." So their support of lesbians is more about heterosexual fantasy than about a progressive attitude (Jenefsky and Miller 1998).

Furthermore, several boys argued that fag, queer and gay had little to do with actual sexual practices or desires. Darnell told me, "It doesn't have anything to do with being gay." Adding to this sentiment, J. L. said, "Fag, seriously, it has nothing to do with sexual preference at all. You could just be calling somebody an idiot, you know?" As David explained, "Being gay is just a lifestyle. It's someone you choose to sleep with. You can still throw a football around and be gay." David's final statement clarifies the distinction between popular understandings of these insults and teens' actual use of them. That is, that they have to do with men's same-sex eroticism, but at their core discipline gendered practices and identities (such as the ability, or lack thereof, to throw a football). In asserting the primacy of gender to the definition of these seemingly homophobic insults, boys reflect what Riki Wilchins (2003) calls the Eminem Exception, in which Eminem explains that he doesn't call people "faggot" because of their sexual orientation, but because they are weak and unmanly. While it is not necessarily acceptable to be gay, if a man were gay *and* masculine, as in David's portrait of the football-throwing gay man, he does not deserve the insult.

What renders a boy vulnerable to homophobic epithets often depends on local definitions of masculinity. Boys frequently cited exhibiting stupidity, femininity, incompetence, emotionality or same-sex physicality as notoriously non-masculine practices. Chad, for instance, said that boys might be called a fag if they seemed "too happy or something" while another boy expounded on the dangers of being "too smiley." Ironically, these insults are pitched at boys who engage in seemingly heterosexual activities. Kevin, when describing his ideal girlfriend said, "I have to imagine myself singing, like serenading her. Okay, say we got in a fight and we broke up. I have to imagine myself as a make-up gift to her singing to her out of her window." Kevin laughed as he said that when he shares this scenario with his friends "the guys are like, 'dude you're gay!'"

Because so many activities could render a boy vulnerable to these insults, perhaps it is little surprise that Ben asserted that one could be labeled for "anything, literally anything. Like you were trying to turn a wrench the wrong way, 'dude you're a fag.' Even if a piece of meat drops out of your sandwich, 'you fag!'" While my research shows that there are particular set of behaviors that could get a boy called the slur, it is no wonder that Ben felt a boy could be called it for "anything." In that statement he reveals the intensity and extent of the policing boys must do of their behaviors in order to avoid the epithet.

The sort of homophobic harassment detailed above has as much to do definitions of masculinity as it does with actual fear of other gay men (Corbett 2001; Kimmel 2001). Being subject to homophobic harassment has as much to do with failing at masculine tasks of competence, heterosexual prowess or in any way revealing weakness as it does with a sexual identity. Homophobic epithets such as fag have gender meanings *and* sexual meanings. The insult is levied against boys who are not masculine, even momentarily, and boys who identify (or are identified by others) as gay. This sets up a very complicated daily ordeal in which boys continually strive to avoid being subject to the epithet, but are simultaneously constantly vulnerable to it.

This sort of homophobia appears frequently in boys' joking relationships. Sociologists have pointed out that joking is central to men's relationships in general (Kehily and Nayak 1997; Lyman 1998). Through aggressive joking boys cement friendship bonds with one another. Boys often draw laughs though imitating effeminate men or men's same-sex desire. Emir frequently imitated effeminate men who presumably sexually desired other men to draw laughs from students in his introductory drama class. One day his teacher, disturbed by noise outside the classroom, turned to close the door saying, "We'll shut this unless anyone really wants to watch sweaty boys playing basketball." Emir lisped, "I wanna watch the boys play!" The rest of the class cracked up at his imitation. No one in the class actually thought Emir was gay, as he purposefully mocked both same-sex sexual desire and an effeminate gender identity. This sort of ritual reminded other youth that masculine men didn't desire other men, nor did they lisp or behave in other feminine manners. It also reminded them that men who behaved in these ways were worthy of laughter and derision.

These everyday joking interchanges, however, were more than "just jokes." For some boys, such as Lawrence King, the intolerance for gender differences espoused by these joking rituals has serious, if not deadly, consequences. Ray and Peter underscore this in their conversation. Ray asserted "I can't stand fags. Like I've met a couple. I don't know. The way they rub you. Gay people I don't care. They do their thing in their bedroom and that's fine. Feminine guys bother me." Peter, his friend, continued "If they try to get up on you. I'll kill you." Ray and Peter illuminated the teenage boys' different responses to gay and effeminate men as Ray espouses tolerance for the presumably gender normative former and Peter threatens violence against the latter. In this sense the discourse runs a continuum from joking to quite violent harassment. While boys said that the "fag" insult was more about failing at masculinity, than about actually being gay, it seemed that a gay and unmasculine boy suffered the most under this "gender regime" (Connell 1987).

As a talented dancer who frequently sported multicolored hair extensions, mascara and wore baggy pants, fitted tank tops and sometimes a skirt, Ricky violated norms of gender *and* sexuality. He told me that harassment started early, in elementary school. "I'm talking like sixth grade, I started being called a fag. Fifth grade I was called a fag. Third grade I was called a fag." Though he moved schools every two years or so, this sort of harassment continued and intensified as he moved into high school. At his school's homecoming game (for which Ricky had choreographed the half time show) he was harassed until he left after hearing things like "there's that fucking fag" and "What the fuck is that fag doing here? That fag has no right to be here." When watching him dance with the school's all female dance team other boys reacted in revulsion. Nils said, "It's like a car wreck, you just can't look away." J. R., the captain of the football team, shook his head and muttered under his breath, "That guy dancing, it's just disgusting. Disgusting!" shaking his head and stomping off. Even though dancing is the most important thing in his life, Ricky didn't attend school dances because he didn't like to "watch my back" the whole time. He had good reason for this fear. Brad said of prom, "I heard Ricky is going in a skirt, it's a hella short one." Sean responded with "I wouldn't even go if he's there." Topping Sean's response Brad claimed, "I'd probably beat him up outside."

The harassment suffered by Ricky featured none of the joking or laughter exhibited in other interchanges. Very real threats of violence undergirded boys' comments about him. Ricky told me that he walked with his eyes downcast in order to avoid guys' eye contact, fearing that they'd see such eye contact as a challenge. Similarly he varied his route home from school each day and carried a rock in his hand to protect himself. For many boys, in order to maintain a sense of themselves as masculine, they felt they had to directly attack Ricky, a symbol of what they feared most, of unmasculine nothingness.

Compulsive heterosexuality

If daily life for many boys entails running a gauntlet of homophobic insults, how do they avoid being permanently labeled as Ricky was? Boys defend against homophobic teasing and harassment by assuring others of their heterosexuality. By engaging in a number of cross-gender rituals, a boy can relatively successfully defend himself against ending up in Ricky's position, the object of harassment, derision and violence. In the same way that boys' homophobia is not specifically about a sexual identity, compulsive heterosexuality[1] is not only about expressing love, desire and intimacy, but about showing a sexualized dominance over girls' bodies. The sort of gendered teasing in which boys engage takes a toll on girls as well as other boys. In my research I found three components of compulsive heterosexuality: rituals of getting girls, rituals of touch, and sex talk.

Perhaps the most obvious example of "getting girls" is having a girlfriend. Having a girlfriend seems a normal teen behavior. For boys who are identified as feminine and teased for unmasculine practices, having a girlfriend functions as some sort of protection against homophobic harassment. Justin told me that some boys have girlfriends "so they look like they're not losers or they're not gay." David told me that a lot of the kids at his high school think that he is gay because of his preppy clothing choices and his lisp such that for him "it's better to have a girlfriend . . . because people think I'm gay. I get that all the time." In order to defend against teasing and harassment boys like David need to establish a sort of baseline heterosexuality by proving they can "get a girl." Because of the difficulty in avoiding all of the behaviors that might render one vulnerable to teasing, having a girlfriend helps to inure one to accusations of the "fag discourse."

Similarly, cross-gender touching rituals establish a given boy's heterosexuality. These physical interchanges may first appear as harmless flirtation, but upon closer inspection actually reinforce boys' dominance over girls' bodies. The use of touch maintains a social hierarchy (Henley 1977). Superiors touch subordinates, invade their space and interrupt them in a way subordinates do not do to superiors and these superior–inferior relationships are often gendered ones. Boys and girls often touch each other as part of daily interaction, communication and flirtation. In many instances cross-sex touching was lightly flirtatious and reciprocal. But these touching rituals ranged from playful flirtations to assault-like interactions. Boys might physically constrain girls under the guise of flirtation. One time in a school hallway a boy wrapped his arms around a girl and started to "freak" her, or grind his pelvis into hers as she struggled to get away. This sort of behavior happened more often in primarily male spaces. One day for instance, in a school weight room, Monte wrapped his arms around a girl's neck as if to put her in a headlock and held her there while Reggie punched her in the stomach, albeit lightly, and she squealed. A more dramatic example of this was during a passing period in which Keith rhythmically jabbed a girl in the crotch with his drumstick, while he yelled "Get raped!" These examples show how the constraint and touching of female bodies gets translated as masculinity, embedding sexualized meanings in which heterosexual flirting is coded as female helplessness and male bodily dominance.

While people jokingly refer to boys' sex talk as "boys will be boys" or "locker room" talk, this sex talk plays a serious role in defending against acquiring an identity like Ricky's. Boys enact and naturalize their heterosexuality by asserting "guys are horndogs" or by claiming that it is "kind of impossible for a guy" to not "think of sex every two minutes" as Chad does. Thinking about boys' sexual performance in terms of compulsive heterosexuality shows that asserting that one is a horndog and cannot help but think about sex is actually a gendered performance. Boys' sex talk often takes the form of "mythic story telling" in which they tell larger than life tales about their sexual adventures, their bodies and girls' bodies that do not reflect love, desire or sensuality, but rather dominance over girls' bodies. Pedro, for instance, laughed and acted out having sex with his girlfriend by leaning back up against the wall, legs and arms spread and head turning back and forth as he continued to say proudly "I did her so hard when I was done she was bleeding. I tore her walls!" The boys surrounding him cheered and oohed and aahed in amazement. Violence frequently frames these stories. Much like the touching rituals in which boys establish dominance over girls' bodies, these stories show what boys can make girls bodies do. Rich, after finishing lifting weights in his school's weight room, sat on a weight bench and five boys gathered around him as he told a story, after much urging, about sex with his now ex-girlfriend. He explained that they were having sex and "she said it started to hurt. I said we can stop and she said no. Then she said it again and she started crying. I told her to get off! Told her to get off! Finally I took her off," making a motion like he was lifting her off of him. He continued, "There was blood all over me! Blood all over her! Popped her wall! She had to have stitches." Boys start cracking up and moaning. Not to be outdone, other boys in the circle begin to chime in about their sexual exploits. Even those who don't have stories about themselves, asserted their knowledge of sex through vicarious experiences. Troy joined the discussion with a story about his brother, a professional basketball player for a nearby city. He "brought home a 24 year old drunk chick! She *farted* the whole time they were doing it in the other room! It was *hella* gross!" All the boys crack up again. Adam, not to be outdone, claimed "My friend had sex with a drunk chick. He did her in the butt! She s*** all over the place!" The boys all crack up again and yell out things like "Hella gross!" or "That's disgusting!" These graphic, quite violent stories detail what boys can make girls bodies do – rip, bleed, fart and poop.

To understand the role of sexuality in maintaining gender inequality it is important to look at sexuality, and specifically heterosexuality, not as a set of desires, identities or dispositions, but as an institution. Adrienne Rich (1986) does this when she argues that heterosexuality is an institution that systematically disempowers women. Similarly, compulsive heterosexuality is a set of practices through which boys reinforce linkages between sexuality, dominance and violence. This heterosexuality is a defensive heterosexuality, not necessarily a reflection of an internal set of emotions.

Conclusion

Many boys' school-based lives involve running a daily gauntlet of sexualized insults, as they simultaneously try to lob homophobic epithets at others and defend themselves from said epithets. In this sense masculinity becomes the daily interactional work of repudiating the labels of fag, queer or gay. Unpacking the definition of what appears to be homophobia clarifies the gender policing at the heart of boys' harassment of one another and of girls. Homophobic epithets may or may not have explicitly sexual meanings, but they always have gendered meanings. Many boys are clearly terrified of being permanently labeled as gay, fag or queer, since to them such a label effectively negates their humanness. As a part of boys' defensive strategy, girls' bodies become masculinity resources deployed in order to stave off these labels.

The practices of compulsive heterosexuality indicate that control over girls' bodies and their sexuality is central to definitions of adolescent masculinity. If masculinity is, as boys told me, about competence, heterosexuality, being unemotional, and dominance, then girls' bodies provide boys the opportunity to ward off the fag discourse by demonstrating mastery and control over them. Engaging in compulsive heterosexuality also allows boys to display a lack of emotions by refusing to engage the empathy that might mitigate against such a use of girls and their bodies. It is important to note that many of these boys are not unrepentant sexists or homophobes. In private and in one-on-one conversations, many spoke of sexual equality and of tender feelings for girls. For the most part these were social behaviors that boys engaged in when around other boys, precisely because they are less reflections of internal homophobic and sexist dispositions and more about constituting a masculine identity, something that is accomplished interactionally.

This gendered homophobia, as well as sexualized and gendered defenses against it, comprises contemporary adolescent masculinity. Fear of any sort of same-sex intimacy (platonic or not) polices boys' friendships with one another. The need to repudiate that which is not considered masculine leads to a very public renunciation of same-sex desire. Heterosexual flirtation becomes entwined with gendered dominance. What this means is that the public face of adolescent sexuality is rife with reproduction of gender inequality, through processes of the fag discourse and compulsive heterosexuality.

Note

1   This concept draws upon Adrienne Rich's (1986) influential concept of "compulsory heterosexuality" as well as Michael Kimmel's (1987) notion of "compulsive masculinity."

References

A.A.U.W. 2001. *Hostile Hallways*. Washington, DC: American Association of University Women.

Connell, R. W. 1987. *Gender and Power*. Stanford, CA: Stanford University Press.

Corbett, Ken. 2001. "Faggot = Loser." *Studies in Gender and Sexuality* 2(1): 3–28.

Henley, Nancy. 1977. *Body Politics: Power, Sex, and Nonverbal Communication*. Englewood Cliffs, NJ: Prentice-Hall.

Jenefsky, Cindy and Diane H. Miller. 1998. "Phallic Intrusion: Girl-Girl Sex in Penthouse." *Women's Studies International Forum* 21(4): 375–85.

Kehily, Mary J. and Anoop Nayak. 1997. "'Lads and Laughter': Humour and the Production of Heterosexual Masculinities." *Gender and Education* 9(1): 69–87.

Kimmel, Michael. 2001. "Masculinity as Homophobia: Fear, Shame, and Silence in the Construction of Gender Identity." Pp. 266–87 in *The Masculinities Reader*, ed. S. Whitehead and F. Barrett. Cambridge: Polity Press.

— . 1987. "The Cult of Masculinity: American Social Character and the Legacy of the Cowboy." Pp. 235–49 in *Beyond Patriarchy: Essays by Men on Pleasure, Power and Change*, ed. M. Kaufman. New York: Oxford University Press.

Kimmel, Michael S. 2003. "Adolescent Masculinity, Homophobia, and Violence: Random School Shootings, 1982–2001." *American Behavioral Scientist* 46(10): 1439–58.

Lyman, Peter. 1998. "The Fraternal Bond as a Joking Relationship: A Case Study of the Role of Sexist Jokes in Male Group Bonding." Pp. 171–93 in *Men's Lives*, Fourth ed., ed. M. Kimmel and M. Messner. Boston, MA: Allyn and Bacon.

National Mental Health Association. 2002. *What Does Gay Mean? Teen Survey Executive Summary*.

Newman, Katherine, Cybelle Fox, David J. L. Harding, Jal Mehta and Wendy Roth. 2004. *Rampage: The Social Roots of School Shootings*. New York: Basic Books.

Rich, Adrienne. 1986. "Compulsory Heterosexuality and Lesbian Existence." Pp. 23–74 in *Blood, Bread and Poetry*. New York: W.W. Norton.

Wilchins, Riki. 2003. "Do You Believe in Fairies?" *The Advocate*, February 4, p. 72.

Youth Risk Behavior Survey – Washington. 1995. Washington, DC: NYRBS.

chapter 18

Not "straight," but still a "man"

Negotiating non-heterosexual masculinities in Beirut

Ghassan Moussawi

Despite persisting cultural taboos and silence that covers the topics of sexuality and sexual nonconformity in the Arab Middle East, there has been a recent upsurge in studying sexualities and non-heterosexual identities in the Arab World (Whitaker, 2006; Khalaf and Gagnon, 2006; Habib, 2007). Still, there has been virtually no research on the ways that the normative status of heterosexuality creates gender and sexual divisions in the Arab World.

In this chapter, I will be looking at the ways that 10 self-identified non-heterosexual Lebanese men understand and negotiate their masculinities. I will argue that even though almost all the informants reject notions of "hegemonic masculinity," they also reject what they perceive as feminine men. I rely on my respondents' perceptions of what constitutes masculinity rather than imposing my own definition. Nonetheless, I assume that masculinity has varied meanings and that it is always defined in relation to a complex field consisting of varied ideas of femininities and masculinities. In addition, I assume that masculinity should be looked at as a performance; that is, masculinity "is more linked to something that one does, rather than what one is" (Whitehead and Barrett, 2001: 28).

It is important to note that even though all societies have ideas about gender, they do not all share a concept of masculinity. According to Connell, in many societies masculinity is understood as indicating a type of person rather than a type of behavior (Connell, 1995: 30). Based on my research, I believe that men and women in Lebanon are seen as quite different and are often regarded as polar character types. In addition, masculinity and manhood are highly regarded and often idealized in Lebanese culture.

Hegemonic masculinity in Lebanon assumes that homosexuality is the negation of masculinity. It is important then to look at the ways that these non-heterosexual men construct their masculinities. Homosexuality is officially criminalized and punishable by up to one year imprisonment. Thus, a public affirmation of a homosexual identity is quite risky and so I assume that these men would be more likely to highlight other aspects of their personal identity. Also, since being a man brings social privileges, I would expect these men to embrace masculinity and engage in what is considered normative masculine behaviour.

As I see it, any discussion of sexuality should consider gender to be central. In this regard, I argue that in Lebanon compulsory heterosexuality is enforced through enforcing dichotomous gender norms and roles. So, how do non-heterosexual men approach gender so as to affirm their masculinity?

For this research, I interviewed 10 men between 18 and 30 years old who were either currently enrolled in a university or had recently graduated. I chose this sample due to its convenience, since I relied on personal social networks and a snowball sampling, i.e. friends of those I interviewed. My interviews ranged between one and a half to two and a half hours and were conducted between September 2007 and April 2008. Almost all of them belonged to the middle or upper middle class of Beirut. Four out of the ten had their own apartments in Beirut and all were living in Beirut at the time except for one who had moved to the United States but was in Beirut for a vacation. Finally, almost all my interviews were conducted in both English and Arabic. Almost all of my respondents found it easier to talk in English when it came to discussing their sexuality. This preference is understandable since the Arabic "neutral" term for homosexuality, *mithli*, is rarely used.

I chose the term "non-heterosexual," rather than gay, because not all the men I interviewed identified as gay. The term non-heterosexual is an effort to keep in mind the complexity of sexuality. I also thought that using this term might capture a wider spectrum of individuals, including men who are not necessarily "out" or exclusively gay-identified. However, I do use the term "gay" in this essay when it is used by my informants. Finally, I am interested in the way that these men understand their sexuality and gender, rather than trying to impose categories of gay, straight or bisexual upon them.

Masculinities among non-heterosexual men in Beirut

In this section, I will consider the accounts these men give of their gender identity and ways that they conceive and define "Lebanese masculinities." I will attempt to look at how these men define and position their masculinities against the dominant notion which assumes that masculinity is an attribute of heterosexual men and which assumes that homosexuality is indicative of a feminine man. For example, in many television shows in Lebanon non-heterosexual characters are depicted and often mocked as extremely feminine, and overtly sexual.

Even though my informants had slightly differing conceptions of Lebanese masculinity, almost all of them claimed that Lebanese masculinity is characterized by the image of the *rijjal*; this is a man who is physically strong, well groomed, loud and proud of his sexual prowess. This type of man tells stories about women as sexual conquests and this is considered a way to demonstrate a sense of prideful manhood. These notions of masculinity were brought up on several occasions, especially when my respondents talked about strategies for "passing" as heterosexual in some situations.

Raed, a 23-year-old graphic designer, claimed that a Lebanese masculine man is always ready to pick a fight, highly interested in sports and cars, and publicly boasts about his sexual escapades with women. When it came to defining his own masculinity, Raed claimed that he does not believe in the concepts of masculinity and femininity, and that he does not think of himself in these terms. By contrast, Talal, a 22-year-old graduate student, asserted that a masculine man is someone who is responsible, "a man of his words" and someone that can handle stress and difficult situations. "Men are more adept at handling stress than women," he said. However, he also made it a point to distinguish between his own conception of masculinity and the "typical" Lebanese man. According to him, the stereotype of the Lebanese masculine man pretends to know everyone and everything, projects self-confidence, is very social, and goes out with many women. And, not least, "real" men are thought to be always strong, decisive and opinionated. Talal believed in a different notion of masculinity, one that emphasized respectability and responsibility. When asked whether he considered himself masculine, Talal claimed that indeed he is a man. "I am just naturally masculine. I don't do it on purpose." According to him, being masculine also means that he is not feminine. This is demonstrated when he further claims that "I don't walk or talk like a woman. Thus I am considered to be masculine."

Wael, a college student in his early twenties, made a distinction between two types of Lebanese men. One type of a masculine Lebanese man is muscular, has sharp facial features, and is always well groomed. The other type is considered "regular"; he keeps to himself in matters of the heart. Interestingly, Wael was somewhat critical of straight men. "Heterosexual Lebanese men," he asserted, "are very dull." This illustrates one of the ways by which non-heterosexual men can distance themselves from heterosexual masculinity by looking at it as more "rigid" than the masculinities of many non-heterosexual men. In this regard, Wael does not consider himself masculine in the rigid sense, but also he does not see himself as feminine.

Another young man I interviewed, Joe, also criticized straight Lebanese men as loud, too confident, and as making up stories about sexual adventures with women. "In Lebanon, masculinity is all about talking," he said. In particular, straight men boast about their sexual prowess in order to prove they are real men. Even though Joe claimed that he displays some feminine mannerisms, he insisted that he is not feminine. "I get angry when I see a feminine guy, I don't know why. I would never be with a feminine man," he added.

Khaled, who recently moved to New York City to pursue his graduate studies, described Lebanese masculine men as pride-oriented and a bit swaggering in the way they talk, walk and act. He told me that Lebanese men must always project strength, a sense of being decisive and dominant. Khaled was the only one who made a distinction between conceptions of masculinity in the Arab world and the "West." After having lived in NYC for a couple of months, Khaled felt more comfortable because he could express himself much more openly. In addition, he claimed that he is considered more masculine in NYC than he is in Beirut because in the latter city conceptions of appropriate masculinity are more rigid. In Lebanon, one has to know when to act "hyper-masculine" and when not to. This is less true in New York. Khaled does not consider himself masculine but also claimed that he doesn't really care about his gender presentation. He does think, however, that some people can tell he is gay by his body language.

Most of my interviewees shared similar notions of what were normative notions of masculinity in Lebanon. I found it interesting that when asked whether they consider themselves masculine, those who said no also insisted that they are not feminine either (even though I didn't ask. Most define their masculinity in terms of not being "typically Lebanese," but also not being feminine. They reject both the extreme ideal of masculinity and the "shameful" status as a feminine man. The hegemonic Lebanese man was seen as unnatural and rigid and boring. However, almost all the men were equally critical of "feminine" men. This prompted me to probe deeper into the ways that these men viewed gender non-conformity and their strategies to distance themselves from it.

Perceptions of femininity and gender non-conformity

Almost all my informants considered themselves broadly masculine, if not hypermasculine. They also expressed a decidedly negative view of feminine men, even those who identified with the "gay" community. These men seemed to be trying to negotiate a type of masculinity that was neither stereotypical masculine nor feminine. I want to focus a bit more on the notion of gender non-conformity. I use the term "gender non-conformity" to refer to any mannerism, way of talking, dressing or presenting oneself that does not necessarily conform to the gender ideals of a specific culture. In my interviews, gender non-conformity was often understood as men acting in a "feminine" way, but it also meant men departing from hegemonic norms of masculinity. In addition, extreme gender non-conformity is often understood in Beirut as indicating some form of sexual deviance. In a word, feminine men and masculine women are often perceived to be non-heterosexual. Interestingly enough, it was striking how most of my respondents embraced the conventional view that gender non-conformity expresses sexual non-conformity. Even though almost all of the men I interviewed claimed that they are gender nonconforming in their rejection of hegemonic masculinity, they expressed discomfort and even ridiculed feminine-acting men, including those who were gay-identified. The reasons stated for this discomfort was that these feminine men drew public attention to non-heterosexual men.

For instance, when I asked Tarek whether he considers himself to be masculine, he wondered whether I could tell he was gay. Tarek, like many other men, relied on his masculine demeanour to pass as "straight." On more than one occasion, many of my informants ridiculed feminine gay men in Beirut. "It is funny how gay men make fun of other gays in the community," Tarek stated. "Everyone is a tante." The labeling of feminine acting men as *tante*, the French term for auntie, illustrates this point. *Tante* is used among many Lebanese to refer to non-heterosexual men who are both feminine acting and who are generally interested in gossip (as explained to me by one of the informants).

Tarek was quite uncomfortable with effeminate men and claimed that he believes gay men should not be feminine. "If you want to be a woman," he said, "then be one." According to him, a guy's mannerisms are quite important and he considered it quite central for a man, whether gay or straight, to maintain gender conformity. He added that he does not have any feminine gay friends and that all of his gay friends are "straight acting." "I wouldn't be comfortable with a guy who is very feminine, especially in ordinary places" (i.e. places that are not "gay friendly"). Tarek expressed discomfort in "being seen" with feminine acting men, in routine social situations. Being seen with feminine men might make people suspect that he is non-heterosexual. Even though he believes that most Lebanese society view people who are gender non-conforming to be non-heterosexual, he himself does not believe that.

Salim also ridiculed feminine gay men on more than one occasion during the interview. Even though he said he doesn't mind feminine men, he still made a point of saying that he isn't sexually or emotionally aroused by them. He repeatedly used *tante* in reference to feminine gay men. Salim brought up an interesting point when he said that feminine gay men, whom he referred to as "queens," do harm to the gay community in Lebanon. Interestingly, he drew a parallel between the way "feminine gay men" project a negative image of the gay community and the way "hypermasculine" men project a bad image of straight men. The harm is linked to the fact that they present a stereotypical image of a gay man as lacking valued "masculine traits." "They are not doing well for the community and for its public image as a whole," he said. It is important to keep in mind, that it is the performance of gender by men that is evaluated as appropriately masculine or inappropriately feminine.

Joe's approach to gender was interesting because of his perception of his own gender difference. At the outset, Joe expressed outrage at the closeted gay men and extremely flamboyant men. Yet, he was aware that he displays some feminine attributes, most apparent in the way he walks and the way he gestures with his hands. He related that men, even after having sex with them, have distanced themselves from him in public. They apparently don't want to be seen with him because of his gender non-conforming behavioural traits. He related the following to me:

> I will be walking with a man on the streets after having been with him for the night, and he will constantly tell me how to act and how not to act. For example, he would give me comments on the way I move and walk by telling me to stop moving my hands or stop walking the way I do. So what if I moved a little bit feminine? Some men also walk in front of me or behind me, and refuse to walk next to me on the streets.

Joe added that even his sister used to get angry because of his effeminate mannerisms when, for example, they went out to nightclubs. At the same time, Joe said that even though he does not consider himself to be hegemonically masculine, he does not see himself as feminine either. In fact, he rejects feminine men. "Even though I am gay, I get pissed off and angry when I see a feminine guy. I don't know why. I just don't want to be with a feminine guy." When I inquired more into his perception of feminine men, Joe claimed that these are men who wear makeup and refer to each other in the feminine of *kifik*, for example ("How are you?" in Arabic). He believes that some people view him as gay not because he is feminine but because he is gentle (*na'im*). Still, even some of his fellow students at the university make fun of him and call him the "biggest fag" because of his gender non-conformity. He says that it never bothers him.

Almost all the men I interviewed agreed that there exists discrimination against feminine-acting men in Beirut. Karim claimed that there is a lot of discrimination against feminine men even within the gay community. "They are not very welcomed," he said, "because, if you're seen with someone who is feminine, you are directly associated with or thought of as gay. It makes many people uncomfortable." In fact, Karim thought that things are getting worse for feminine men in Beirut because today men are obsessed with their body image, and with being muscular and fit. "Part of it is reaffirming their masculinity. The image is very important. There's an obsession with being fit and looking good and being viewed as 'ordinary' (heterosexual)." Karim acknowledged that he too was once quite uncomfortable with feminine gay men, but that this attitude changed. "If I want people to accept me for who I am then I have to accept the other guys for who they are."

Raed and Wael also talked about how feminine men are excluded in the gay community. Wael terms this exclusion "sissyphobia." Of course it's even worse in the broader culture. Wael recalled being ridiculed at school for not being "typically" masculine. He was called names in high school, such as *tobje* ("fag"), even though he had not thought of himself as gay or non-heterosexual at that time. Finally, and most strikingly, Talal seemed to summarise the views of many of those I interviewed:

> In Lebanon, if you're gay, you're no longer considered a man. It is the closed-minded and illiterate people who think that. You're not considered a man, even if you are very masculine, as long as you are gay. It doesn't matter. There might be some exceptions, but generally this is the rule. If you're straight and feminine, you also have a problem.

Talal's fear of being viewed as "less of a man" is felt as real and widely shared by my respondents. Talal has known a few gay-identified feminine men, but his fear has meant that he is not close to them. "I don't mind them, but I don't understand why do they have to be so obvious or why they act that way. I am sure they're not doing it on purpose, but I still don't understand why." Despite knowing how Lebanese culture excludes feminine men, Talal himself avoids hanging out with them in public. When I asked him to describe a feminine guy, he said that it was a man who "acts like a woman, uses hand gestures, and body language, [and] is interested in makeup and shopping." So anxious is Talal of being exposed and rejected as not straight that he spoke of feeling very self-conscious when he is out in public. The fear of being "found out" as gay may be linked to the fact that he has only quite recently acknowledged his non-heterosexuality. He feels that straight people will respect him less if they found out. Khaled was the only one who claimed that he doesn't mind feminine-acting men. "I completely understand where they're coming from. They are very courageous. They have a lot of guts to do what their instincts tell them to do." Still, Khaled also used the derogatory term *tante* to refer to feminine-acting men.

Homophobia and anti-femininity

As I've argued, maintaining a masculine demeanour was deemed important by almost all of my respondents. In part, gender conformity concealed non-heterosexuality and conferred social privileges on these men. But a culture of masculinity and heterosexuality in Beirut was also sustained by a culture of homophobia. The anthropologist Sofian Merabet (2004) documented the way homophobia works in Beirut. For example, as non-heterosexual men began to gain a certain visibility, the police intervened by closing down businesses friendly to non-heterosexuals. Also, public homophobic behaviour almost always targets "overtly feminine men." Such homophobic behaviour is tolerated in part because feminine men are considered undesirable by both heterosexual and non-heterosexual individuals.

Recently, the controversial status of feminine men among Beirut's non-heterosexual community surfaced online. The controversy revolved around one of the few gay-identified bear bars in Beirut ("bear" is a term used to refer to hairy and masculine men in the gay community). A blog post in the Gay Middle East Blog titled "Beirut's Anti-Gay Gay Bar," described an incident where a man was barred from entering the bar because of his feminine demeanour. According to the blog, the owner of the bar admitted to having instructed the bouncer to turn away "overtly feminine" men, presumably to safeguard the desired "bear ambiance" of the bar (GayMiddleEastBlog, 2006). The author of the blog commented: "I will no longer frequent [this bar]. It's reprehensible for some gay men to reject others based on vague notions of masculinity. As gay men, we are all rejected by the larger society, and further segregation serves no positive purpose."

The sense of outrage that the author expresses is not necessarily widely shared by other men in the community. From my interviews, it is clear that feminine gay men have been routinely stigmatized and rejected within this small, fragmented "community," and by the larger Lebanese society. It is these feminine men, whatever their sexuality, that perhaps suffer the most in a culture that enforces a seamless norm of hegemonic masculinity and heterosexuality.

Conclusion

I attempted to look at how 10 non-heterosexual men define their own masculinity. As we've seen, these men resisted being associated with what they perceived as the stereotypical image of Lebanese masculinity. They also resisted being perceived as "feminine." All of the informants spoke of multiple masculinities and defined their own masculinity as neither a version of hegemonic masculinity nor male femininity.

Ghassan Moussawi

By way of a conclusion, I want to briefly return to the link between sexuality and gender. Even though all of the men I interviewed embraced their same-sex desires or claimed that they seek other men for emotional and sexual relations, a majority resisted defining themselves as "gay." For most of my respondents, the label "gay" was associated with having one's sexual identity as a core or defining identity. Although most of these men acknowledged that their sexuality was central to them, they refused to primarily define themselves as gay. This can be explained by the fact that in Lebanon there is currently no local positive conception of a gay identity. At the same time, as previously mentioned, the lack of commonly used neutral Arabic terms that refer to both heterosexual and non-heterosexual identities makes it harder for these men to talk about their sexuality.

However, it is interesting that most of my informants did not hesitate to refer to other non-heterosexuals in the community as "gay." My sense is that many of these men used this term because of its positive resonance, but we should not assume that its meaning is the same as in an American context. In order to comprehend the meanings people attribute to gender and sexuality the specific cultural contexts and local understandings must be taken into account.

Finally, throughout my interviews it was apparent that the performance of gender-conforming behavior was a central way in which the institutionalization of heterosexuality functions at the level of everyday life. Almost all of my informants were concerned with being regarded as "real men." I would argue that in projecting a conventional masculine self my respondents were also enforcing a norm of "compulsory heterosexuality." The latter is sustained not only by enforcing a norm of heterosexuality but by not tolerating gender non-conformity. By distancing themselves from the feminine man, these men were reinforcing the institution of heterosexuality. As long as heterosexuality is enforced though "the policing and shaming of gender and the damning of gay men as failed men and lesbians as not proper women," men and women will tend to reject the fluid and variable possibilities of gender (Jackson, 1999: 175).

Bibliography

Connell, R. W. 1995. *Masculinities*. London: Allen and Unwin.

GayMiddleEastBlog. 2006. http://gaymiddleeast.blogspot.com/2006/04/beiruts-anti-gay-gay-bar.html, retrieved April 2006.

Habib, Samar. 2007. *Female Homosexuality in the Middle East: Histories and Representations*. New York and London: Routledge.

Jackson, Stevi. 1999. *Heterosexuality in Question*. London: Sage Publications.

Khalaf, Samir and Gagnon, John (Eds). 2006. *Sexuality in the Arab World*. London: Saqi Books.

Merabet, Sofian. 2004. "Disavowed Homosexualities in Beirut". *Middle East Report* 23: Spring.

Whitaker, Brian. 2006. *Unspeakable Love: Gay and Lesbian Life in the Middle East*. London: Saqi Books.

Whitehead, Stephen. 2006. *Men and Masculinities*. New York: Routledge.

Whitehead, Stephen M. and Barrett, Frank J, (Eds). 2001. *The Masculinities Reader*. Cambridge: Polity Press.

chapter 19

How not to talk about Muslim women

Patriarchy, Islam and the sexual regulation of Pakistani women

Saadia Toor

In recent years, the status of the Muslim woman – often coded in the image of a veiled female figure – has become a major preoccupation of the mainstream media in the West, where it is framed as an issue of "Islam and gender." Regardless of whether the tone of the commentary is critical or sympathetic, the organizing logic is the same – that something called "Islam" exists and that it can explain all aspects of Muslim society. Note that the terms – "Islam," "Muslim society," "Muslim culture," etc. – circulating in this discourse are all in the singular, implying that there is one essential, monolithic thing called "Islam" which remains consistent across time and space, and that all Muslims are somehow essentially identical regardless of where they may come from geographically and culturally. The overwhelming conclusion of this discourse is that there is something uniquely sexist – even misogynist – about Islam, "the Muslim world," and thereby all Muslims, which in turn explains the low status of Muslim women.

The main thrust of this chapter is to show that this mainstream Western discourse on Islam is misleading insofar as it is premised on an essentialized and monolithic "Islam" emptied of history, diversity, complexity and dissent. I will show that, far from "unveiling" the insidious workings of an actually existing "thing" called "Islam," this discourse actually actively *constructs* it. Not only that, it does so in order to legitimize certain political projects. In other words, this discourse is deeply ideological.

In order to understand what I mean, let's turn first to the discourse and its history. In *Orientalism*, Edward Said (1978) argued that Western discourse on "the Orient" provided the ideological justification for European colonialism in Asia and in the "Islamic world" from the eighteenth century onwards. This justification included the idea that colonialism was, first and foremost, a "civilizing mission" rather than an exercise in the occupation of non-European lands and the exploitation of non-European peoples and their resources. It is also important to note that the concept of the "civilizing mission" came out of the ideology of liberalism which was on the ascendance in Europe at this time. Postcolonial scholars – particularly postcolonial feminists – extended this initial work on the ideological roots of European colonialism to emphasize the centrality of gender and sexuality to the colonial enterprise. Their scholarship has highlighted how non-Western women became cast in colonial discourse as victims of their oppressive culture(s) and tradition(s), in a way that allowed colonialism to emerge as their *savior*. The post-colonial feminist scholar Gayatri Spivak (1988) has captured this logic in her pithy reformulation of the colonial civilizing mission as "white men saving brown women from brown men."

Of course, white *women* also played an important role in the colonial enterprise. For example, many of the early British suffragettes were fervent supporters of imperialism and uncritically accepted their government's claims that the British imperial project was actually about protecting and furthering the rights of "native" women. This was paradoxical, given the fact that they were facing opposition from the same government with regard to their demands for the rights of British women. In fact, the discourse in Britain around the plight of native women served to undermine feminist claims domestically, since it allowed critics to argue that British women were much better off than women elsewhere in the world; therefore, they had no cause for complaint and no reason to demand greater rights. This support of imperialism in the name of native women's rights has come to be known as "imperial feminism."

A contemporary version of "imperial feminism" surfaced in the West in the immediate aftermath of 9/11, when George and Laura Bush – notoriously anti-feminist in their political and cultural agenda – invoked the very real plight of Afghan women under the Taliban to justify the attack on, and subsequent occupation of, Afghanistan. In this they were enthusiastically supported by well-known feminist organizations such as the Feminist Majority. The most familiar media image during this period became the *burqa*-clad Afghan (read: Muslim) woman; in fact the *burqa* itself became a symbol of Islam's attitude towards women.

Once more, white men – and women – were exhorted to save brown women from brown men. This was an ideological move designed to secure the consent of the American public for an unprecedented act of international aggression. Notably, after the initial rapturous accounts of newly liberated Afghan women shedding the *burqa*, wearing make-up and learning how to be beauticians, these women disappeared from the view of the American public.[1] So did the Revolutionary Association of the Women of Afghanistan (RAWA), an organization which had been ubiquitous in the American press during the key period before the attack on Afghanistan, and whose reputation as an authentic and fearless feminist organization was used to authorize the mainstream account of Afghan women's plight. After the occupation, however, RAWA was no longer useful for the United States' political agenda. In fact, it became downright *inconvenient*, since its bulletins make it clear that life for Afghan women not only did not improve under the new US-approved administration, but actually became worse.

What we had instead was an outpouring of "expert commentary" and "analysis" on women and Islam which argued that Afghan women's troubles under the Taliban were part of a broader problem of Islam's essential and unique misogyny. This is now an accepted part of popular Western discourse on Islam. One of the problems with this discourse, as Said (1981) argued in *Covering Islam*, is that it constructs a flattened and monolithic idea of Islam which is then used to explain the behavior of all Muslims regardless of their varied cultural, social and political contexts.

> "Islam" as it is used today seems to mean one simple thing but in fact is part fiction, part ideological label, part minimal designation of a religion called Islam. In no really significant way is there a direct correspondence between the "Islam" in common Western usage and the enormously varied life that goes on within the world of Islam, with its more than 800,000,000 people, its millions of square miles of territory principally in Africa and Asia, its dozens of societies, states, histories, geographies, cultures.
>
> (Introduction, x)

Said goes on to question the notion that this thing called "Islam" can explain complex behaviors, at the individual as well as the collective level:

> Is there such a thing as Islamic behavior? What connects Islam at the level of everyday life to Islam at the level of doctrine in the various Islamic societies? How really useful is "Islam" as a concept for understanding Morocco *and* Saudi Arabia *and* Syria *and* Indonesia?
>
> (Said 1981: xv)

Unfortunately, in the 30 years since Said penned his original critique of Orientalism, things have only gotten worse as far as the mainstream Western understanding of, and discourse on, Islam is concerned. Perhaps this is not surprising, given that Western – specifically US – political investment in parts of the world that are predominantly Muslim has also intensified during precisely this period. This neo-colonial project requires an ideological framework to legitimate it just as the earlier colonial project did. As before, this ideological discourse features a civilizing mission focused on the status of "native" women and on rescuing them from "their" men and "their" culture.

What are we talking about when we talk about "Islam"?

As the above quotes from Said indicate, there are serious problems with trying to use "Islam" to explain too much of the personal and social life of Muslims. In fact, any attempt to deploy the category in a meaningful or systematic way immediately reveals its fuzziness. When we use the term "Islam," do we mean the textual sources of Islamic tradition, namely the *Quran* and *Sunnah*? Do we mean the *shariah*, or system of Islamic jurisprudence, which is itself not a unitary thing? Do we mean the ways in which various political groups – and often the state – in Muslim societies deploy Islam? Or do we mean Islam as it is popularly understood and practiced, which changes every 50 miles or so?

These issues are not specific to Islam, obviously. Sociologically speaking, culture and religion are difficult, if not impossible, to separate in any context – even in the "secular" West. However, and ironically, Islam *does* pose a unique problem because of its decentralized nature. Unlike Christianity (and especially Catholicism) there is no single religious authority, and no institutionalized clerical hierarchy. Even Islamic law – the *shariah* that is so often invoked in the mainstream discourse as if it were one monolithic body of religious law – is interpreted differently by different Muslim communities depending on which *fiqh* – or school of jurisprudence – they tend to favor. Interestingly, Muslims can switch back and forth between different schools of jurisprudence depending on which orientation they prefer at any given time. This is a far cry from the idea of a unitary "Islamic law" popularized by the mainstream Western press.

Scholars have argued that instead of invoking Islam to explain behavior in "the Muslim World" we should look at historical as well as contemporary social conditions, relations and conflicts. In order to understand what this sort of analysis might look like, and what sorts of insights it might yield, let us turn to a specific Muslim country – Pakistan. Pakistan provides us with a crucial lens through which to examine the issues we are trying to grapple with here. It is a Muslim-majority country which officially designates itself an "Islamic Republic" and it has often been the subject of media attention in the West – not only for its role in the nine-year-old war in neighboring Afghanistan, but also because of the declining status of its women.

For our purposes here, I will focus on three important cases from Pakistan: first, the "Saima Love-Marriage Case"; second, the increase in the practice of "honor killings" in the 1990s; and last, the situation of women who are in state custody because they have been accused of *zina* (or illegitimate sex) by their families. Each of these will help us understand just how impossible it is to think of "Islam" as being the source of Muslim women's problems, and how complex the reality actually is. What I seek to demonstrate through these cases is that Islam is invoked very selectively even in so-called "Islamic societies," and even when the issue is the control of women's sexuality. In fact, sometimes the rights granted to women under Islamic law become inconvenient for the purposes of patriarchal control, in which case "Islam" is all too easily tossed aside in favor of "custom" and "tradition." This is an aspect of what I call "patriarchal opportunism," whereby patriarchal structures from families to nation-states strategically select elements from an ideological "toolbox" in their attempt to gain support for the sexual regulation of women.

Let us begin with what the Pakistani media referred to as the "Saima Love-Marriage Case." The pertinent details of the case were as follows: In February 1996, 22-year-old Saima Waheed married against the wishes of her parents, leading to a contentious legal battle which gripped the country. Saima was the college-educated daughter of an economically and politically influential family. Arshad Ahmad, the man she chose to marry, was a teacher at a government college in a small town. To give a sense of the class divide here, Ahmad supplemented his income of Rs5,000 a month (less than $60) by giving private lessons, while Saima's pocket money alone – which she received as a director of her father's company – was double that.

Saima informed her parents of her desire to marry Arshad, and his parents (following prescribed social norms) formally requested her hand for their son. However, when it became clear that her family had no intention of accepting the proposal, Saima took decisive action and married Arshad. She expected that her family would eventually accept the marriage. Instead, she was severely punished and then imprisoned in her parents' home. Saima finally managed to escape and to engage the services of Asma Jahangir, a prominent women's and human rights lawyer, in order to defend her right to marry without the consent of a *wali*, or legal (male) guardian.

Legally, the issue seemed fairly straightforward. A precedent-setting case had already established that an adult Muslim woman in Pakistan had the religious and legal right to contract marriage on her own behalf, without the intercession of a *wali*. Moreover, such "runaway marriages" are hardly news even – or perhaps especially – in socially conservative societies such as Pakistan where they are often the only means for young men and women to assert some modicum of control over their lives. However, in the legal discourse around the case, Saima's exercise of a right granted to her both by secular and religious law was still understood as a source of shame, both for her family and "the nation."

Ultimately, the Lahore High Court did validate her marriage on legal grounds. However, what is important to note is that Saima's case was argued, and ultimately judged, not within the terms of existing Muslim family law in the Pakistan Penal Code, or *shariah* law – both of which were unambiguous in their understanding of the rights of adult Muslim women with regard to marriage – but on the *general undesirability of filial disobedience*. In fact, both the judge who decreed the marriage legal under Muslim law, and the judge who wrote the dissenting opinion, expressed the wish that parental authority could be juridically enforceable.

Any close look at this case highlights the fact that despite ubiquitous references to "Islam," the *shariah* and even to Pakistan as the "Islamic Republic," it was in fact patriarchal control that was at issue here. Despite the conservative nature of her family, Saima was hardly a stereotypically oppressed or even a "traditional" young woman by Pakistani standards. She was active in intercollegiate (and therefore non-segregated) events; she first met Arshad at one such event. Her father was aware of her attendance at such events, and by all accounts he took intense pride in her achievements. She owned a car and a cell phone, both symbols of mobility and autonomy as well as wealth and social status. She and her female cousins were also not denied access to activities such as swimming and riding, both associated with the Westernized upper classes. Their dress code was also unconventional – they wore jeans and T-shirts at home and, even when outside, continued to wear them under the *hijab*. This is rather different from what we have learnt to expect of conservative Muslims, and shows in fact how important class is to any analysis of purportedly Muslim societies.

However, these accoutrements of capitalist modernity were given to Saima to enhance her *father's* social status, in particular by making her a more desirable item on the marriage market. Given that marriages in Pakistan are still very much about cementing relations between families, Saima's father expected to leverage his daughter's desirability to his strategic advantage. His anger, therefore, was not the result of a religious injunction – as we saw, religious (Islamic) law was squarely on Saima's side – it was anger at being deprived of a patriarchal privilege. Thus the minute she challenged his authority, all *her* privileges were summarily taken away.

What should be clear from our discussion of this case is that it is impossible – even in a country that calls itself an "Islamic Republic," where *shariah* law is institutionalized to some degree and when the issue is women's sexual agency – to claim that "Islam" is somehow the explanatory variable. If anything, the Saima case shows us that often the rights granted to women by Islamic law become *inconvenient* for local patriarchies. In such cases, any existing "Islamic" provisions are either "reinterpreted," finessed, tactfully ignored or even explicitly superseded by "custom" or "tradition." "Islam" should thus be understood as one out of several available tools in the ideological toolbox of patriarchies in Muslim societies.

The issue of "honor killings" in Pakistan provides a second illustration of "patriarchal opportunism." Contrary to the mainstream discourse in the West, honor killings are not "Islamic" either in the sense of being sanctioned by Islamic law or being popularly understood as such by ordinary people. Moreover, as a practice it is neither limited to Muslim communities – being prevalent in parts of the world as disparate as Latin America, South Asia and parts of North Africa – nor is it remotely universal *across* the Muslim world. Pakistan is one Muslim society where honor killings do exist; in fact, they have become more visible since the 1990s, prior to which they were limited to certain areas of rural Pakistan. The earlier version of the practice differs from its contemporary urban cousin in significant ways. For example, the older version was a highly ritualized and regulated mechanism by which specific communities policed the sexual behavior of its members, and the punishment for the transgression of sexual norms extended to both the man and the woman. By contrast, in the contemporary version, the victim is always a woman and the practice is increasingly "privatized" and "unregulated." One of the main reasons behind the rise of honor killings in Pakistan is the impunity with which the state allows family members – from parents to husbands and brothers – to get away with what is clearly understood as murder within both the Pakistan Penal Code and *shariah* law. This is the result of the increasing power of landed and tribal elites. In 1999, after a particularly high-profile case of "honor killing" which had shaken the country, a special session of the Pakistani Senate was called to address the issue. However, a resolution condemning the growing incidence of this practice was rejected under pressure from these elites in the Senate, who defended it as an essential part of their "culture" and "tradition." "Islam" thus has very little to do with the motive or justification of honor killings in Pakistan and is conspicuously absent from the discourse around them.

Lastly, I wish to turn to the issue of women who have been incarcerated under the *zina* laws in Pakistan. These laws are part of the Hudood Ordinances, promulgated by the military dictator General Zia ul-Haq as the cornerstone of his project of "Islamizing" the Pakistani state and society in the 1980s. The Zina Ordinance laid out various categories of sex crimes, from rape to adultery and fornication (pre-marital sex) which were all to be treated as crimes against the state. In order to entertain the charge of *zina* against an individual or individuals, however, the law required the testimony of "four adult male Muslim witnesses of good moral character" who had actually witnessed the act of penetration. The purported idea behind setting the bar for eyewitness this high was to prevent the abuse of this law through spurious accusations, and thereby protect the reputations of innocent men and women. On the surface, both men and women fell equally under the purview of the part of the law pertaining to adultery, and the law on rape appeared designed to protect women from sexual violence. However, the case of Safia Bibi soon made it clear that this law against sex crimes had serious implications for Pakistani women.

Safia Bibi was a blind teenaged girl in domestic service who charged her employer with rape; she had become pregnant as a result. Unsurprisingly, she couldn't round up the required witnesses to the crime. However, instead of simply dismissing the case for lack of evidence, the *shariat* court charged Safia Bibi with fornication because she was pregnant despite being unmarried.[2] This case galvanized a public outcry against the Zina Ordinance, led by the newly formed feminist group, the Women's Action Forum, which was joined by other secular pro-democracy groups as well as some Muslim clerics who publicly supported the defendant. The charge against Safia Bibi was ultimately struck down by the Supreme Court of Pakistan which makes it clear that *shariah* did not trump secular law in Pakistan even under the very martial law regime which had forcibly institutionalized this parallel legal system.

The high courts and the Supreme Court have continued to overturn the decisions of the appellate *shariat* courts in *zina* cases.[3] However, despite the efforts of Pakistani feminists, the Zina Ordinance remains on the books, and women continue to be its major victims. In fact, the majority of women incarcerated in Pakistani jails are there because they have been accused of *zina* by their families. In her critical ethnographic work with these women, Shahnaz Khan (2007) shows that far from being an expression of religious piety at the familial or state level, the *zina* laws are wielded as a potent weapon of control and extortion by families of "disobedient" women. The women are almost entirely from the lower classes. Men, who may also be charged with *zina*, rarely end up in jail since they are better able to negotiate a financial settlement with their accusers. It is clear then that, in its impact, this law is classed as well as gendered.

One of Khan's most surprising findings was that incarceration is actually seen by these poor women as a form of "protective custody" and thereby an *escape* from their families. The role of the state, Khan finds, is complicated in these cases – sometimes it sides with family, and sometimes with the woman, and Khan can unearth no discernible pattern to the variation. Complicating matters even further, Khan finds that the women themselves invoke the moral authority of Islam – and specifically what they understand as the rights it grants them – *against* their families. Islam also becomes a source of solace for them during this difficult period.

These facts disrupt the manner in which the mainstream media in the West constructs the role of Islam in the lives of Muslim women, and highlight the pitfalls of not distinguishing between the different forms and contexts within which "Islam" is invoked, and by whom. Among other things, a distinction must always be made between what I call "Islamization from below," within which we can slot the rise of (voluntary) public piety among Muslims such as the adoption of particular styles of facial hair by men and of various forms of *hijab* by women, and "Islamization from above," which refers to the ways in which structures of power – from families to states – deploy "Islam" in order to control women (and men) (Toor 2007). State policies imposing particular dress codes and enforcing gender segregation in public would be

Saadia Toor

examples of the latter. However, the adoption of the veil by female university students in Cairo in the late 1970s as a protest against the state would be an example of the former. There is, of necessity, a relationship between the two levels of Islamization, but it is complicated and certainly does not lend itself to easy generalizations. Moreover, ignoring this distinction and collapsing all forms of "Islamization" results in a serious misunderstanding of the social processes at work.

Khan's (2007) research on incarcerated women leads her to conclude that poverty is an important causal factor in the imprisonment of women under the charge of *zina* in Pakistan. She follows other Pakistani scholars in linking this poverty to the structural adjustment policies imposed on Pakistan by the World Bank and IMF from the 1980s on. The importance of this observation cannot be understated because feminist scholarship on structural adjustment across the world has shown a strong link between the deprivations created by these policies and a rise in violence against women. Khan's research thus allows us to connect something that appears to be a result of "Islamic law" (the incarceration of women under *zina* laws in Pakistan) to similar developments in other places, which are in turn the result of larger global political and economic processes. Needless to say, issues such as class and international political economy are never part of the explanatory framework when it comes to discussions around Muslim women in the West, since they do not fit into a framework in which everything to do with Muslims is explained by "Islam."

Structural adjustment is one aspect of globalization – defined as the increasing interconnectedness of different parts of the world at the economic, political and cultural levels – which has resulted in an intensification in the dynamics of social change across the developing or postcolonial world. Such rapid and intense social change produces anxieties in the societies and communities experiencing this change; anxieties which feminist scholars have shown to result in greater regulation of women. This was just as true of Europe during the period of capitalist modernization in the eighteenth and nineteenth centuries, and of colonized and decolonizing societies in the mid-twentieth century.

Issues related to women and gender in contemporary Muslim societies must be understood within the same framework. What passes for the victimization of women by "Islam" is all too often part and parcel of a more global phenomenon – an increase in the moral and sexual regulation of women by communities and kin-networks as a response to political, social and cultural anxieties; such anxieties have intensified under economic and cultural globalization. The regulation of women and their sexuality is, after all, a common feature of all patriarchal societies, traditional or modern, and certainly not simply Muslim ones. It is the discourse of Islamic exceptionalism – in essence the form of Orientalism operative today, which is defined by an exclusive focus on Islam – which prevents us from seeing the "family resemblances" between honor killings in the Pakistani or Jordanian Muslim communities and honor killings in Hindu and Sikh communities in India, between the violent protests against the celebration of Valentine's Day in Pakistan and India (led by the goon squads of the Muslim and Hindu religious right respectively), and between the attempts at the regulation of women by "Islamists" and the Christian Right in the United States alike.

The three cases from Pakistan discussed above illustrate just how difficult it is to understand the role played by Islam even in a single country. "Islam" can be, and often is, simultaneously a convenient ideological tool in the hands of the powerful, a source of spiritual succor for the powerless, and part of an identitarian response to the anxieties and ravages of an increasingly globalized world. Thus, instead of assuming that we already know what "Islam" means when we see it invoked in a particular context, we should actually always ask *how* it is being invoked, by *whom*, and for *what purpose*. We should also refrain from assuming that "Islam" is the only or even the best explanatory variable when it comes to understanding Muslim cultures, societies and individuals.

Conclusion

I have shown here that, unlike what mainstream discourse would have us believe, "Islam" is not the engine which explains all aspects of "Muslim" societies. When they prove inconvenient, even codified Islamic laws are summarily sidelined, ignored or glossed over. An obsessive focus on "Islam" alone misses the actual threats faced by women across the world. In postcolonial states – of which Muslim states are a subset – these range from local custom to colonial "family" and "sodomy" laws to policies promoted by international agencies which impoverish people (especially women) and make them more vulnerable to local (patriarchal) elites. We must also recognize that the conservative backlash that we see in the "Muslim" world and in the postcolonial world more generally can also be observed in the United States. Here, too, this backlash is articulated within a religious framework, and we can see a revitalized Christian movement gaining ground on issues such as a woman's right to choose and gay marriage.

Nuanced and thoughtful research on Muslim societies indicates that Islam itself should be understood as a deeply contested terrain. Like all ideologies, much of the form of its expression depends on the class or confluence of classes which wields it, and the historical context in which this expression happens.

In the absence of appropriate historical and sociological context it is impossible to come away with anything but a superficial and often incorrect understanding of the role Islam plays with regard to women. We should reject the idea that something stable and immutable called "Islam" exists anywhere. For example, the fact that Muslims in Pakistan, as elsewhere, invoke Islam in everyday discourse doesn't tell us anything about what they mean when they invoke it. The "Islam" invoked by the women imprisoned under the *zina* law and interviewed by Khan is not the same Islam featured in the discourse of Islamic political parties. We must therefore keep clear the distinction between Islamization-from-above and Islamization-from-below, and acknowledge Muslim women's agency even if it seems to contradict what we understand as "feminist" goals or politics and even if we understand this agency to be exercised within structural constraints. This is, after all, true of all agency, anywhere – there simply is no such thing as a "pure" freedom of choice unconstrained by social norms.

Thus, the concept of "Islam," whether deployed by state or private actors, needs to be something the researcher must unpack rather than assume a priori. The "Islam connection," when it is there, is complex and there is simply no shortcut around historically and sociologically nuanced analyses. And, finally, in the current geopolitical context in which the United States is at war with several Muslim countries, and where Islamophobia and racial profiling of Muslims across the world are growing concerns, the need for such methodological deliberateness becomes even more acute.

Notes

1 This equating of make-up with liberation is very common in mainstream discourse on Muslim women, as is evidenced by the titles of contemporary books and films such as *Lipstick Jihad* and *Kabul Beauty School*.
2 *Shariat* is the Urdu word for *shariah*; Urdu is the national language of Pakistan.
3 Many Islamic jurists and scholars at the time pointed out that the practice of using the juridical requirement to entrap and punish women (and women alone) for sexual transgression violated its intent, and was against the spirit of Islamic law. However, the fact that the law still stands, even if no other individual has since been found guilty under it, is a testimony to the ways in which Islam is opportunistically deployed in Pakistani politics.

Bibliography

Hussain, Neelam. 1997. "The Narrative Appropriation of Saima: Coercion and Consent in Muslim Pakistan." In Neelam Hussain, S. Mumtaz, and R. Saigol (Eds), *Engendering the Nation-State*. Vol. I. Lahore: Simorgh Publications.

Khan, Shahnaz. 2007. *Zina, Transnational Feminism and the Moral Regulation of Pakistani Women*. British Columbia, Canada: University of British Columbia Press.

Said, Edward. 1978. *Orientalism*. New York: Pantheon Books.

— . 1981. *Covering Islam: How the Media and the Experts Determine How We See the Rest of the World*. New York: Pantheon Books.

Spivak, Gayatri. 1988. "Can the Subaltern Speak?" In Cary Nelson and Lawrence Grossberg (Eds), *Marxism and the Interpretation of Culture*. Champaign: University of Illinois Press.

Toor, Saadia. 2007. "Moral Regulation in a Postcolonial Nation-State: Gender and the Politics of Islamization in Pakistan." Special issue of *Interventions: International Journal of Postcolonial Studies* 9(2): July.

chapter 20

Mis-conceptions about unintended pregnancy

Considering context in sexual and reproductive decision-making

Jennifer A. Reich

Half of all pregnancies in the United States are unplanned.

A college student who used a condom that broke. A 40-year-old woman who thought she couldn't get pregnant. A new mother who is breastfeeding and assumed that would prevent pregnancy. A married couple who are debating whether they are really done having children. A teenager who thought you couldn't become pregnant the first time. Break-up sex or make-up sex. Some who feel lucky, others who feel unlucky.

It is impossible to discuss reproduction without considering the social meanings of sexuality and gender that are always layered over it. For example, when I ask students to think of what kind of woman becomes pregnant without intending to be, students often visualize a woman who has multiple partners, routinely has unprotected sex, is generally irresponsible, or is ignorant of how to prevent pregnancy. The more generous ones sometimes explain that she is someone with low self-esteem or argue how schools should do more to institute comprehensive sex education with accurate information into their curricula. None think of these stories as funny; rarely do they condemn the men who also have sex that results in unintended pregnancy, though they might think of them as unlucky, even as they are suspicious of such women.

Yet when I ask those same students if there are any family stories of the "Drunk-on-New-Year's-Eve-Oops-Baby" or the other family legends of the unplanned but much loved child, most laugh and share such tales. Some have a sibling much younger than they – and sometimes they volunteer, "That story is me!" These stories are not embarrassing or perceived as stigmatizing, and no one condemns these drunken women for having unprotected sex. When women are married, unintended pregnancies are not viewed in the same light, and married women are spared the suspicion or contempt we so freely serve up to single women.

In fact, half of all pregnancies in the United States are unplanned. But as the above examples illustrate, the meanings of sexuality and reproduction shape perceptions and outcomes of these unintended pregnancies. In this essay, I describe the context in which unintended pregnancies occur, what sexually active people do to avoid pregnancy, and what we know about their choices about pregnancy outcomes. I do not devote space to considering the myriad ways reproduction also occurs that might not result from intercourse, or the challenges and choices faced by those who wish to become pregnant and experience difficulties in doing so. This in no way suggests that these experiences and decisions are less important. Rather, I have chosen to focus more specifically on reproductive decisions that arise from heterosexual intercourse – and that have remained controversial in US public policy.

Becoming sexual, avoiding pregnancy

Much of the concern about unintended pregnancy flows from a misguided belief that young people are becoming sexually active at younger ages. In fact, young people are waiting longer to have sex than in past years. In a survey of teens between the ages of 15 and 19, about 13 percent of never-married females and 15 percent of never-married males reported that they had had sex before age 15 in 2002, compared with 19 percent and 21 percent, respectively, in 1995 (Abma et al. 2004). When having sex, more than three-quarters of teen females report that their first sexual experience was with a steady boyfriend, a fiancé, a husband or a cohabiting partner.

This does not mean that all sex is welcome or freely chosen. When teens were asked how much they wanted their first intercourse to happen at the time it did, 13 percent of females and 6 percent of males really didn't want it to happen at the time, and 52 percent of females and 31 percent of males had mixed feelings about it. Ten percent of young women aged 18–24 who have had sex before age 20 report that their first sex was involuntary. The younger they were at first intercourse, the higher the proportion (Abma et al. 2004). Knowing the meanings of sex, the ability to plan for it, and the ability to feel secure in the choice, alters efforts to prevent pregnancy.

Today, most young people have sex for the first time at about age 17, but don't marry until their middle or late twenties. If we assume that these young people want to avoid pregnancy until marriage, this means that they are at risk of unwanted pregnancy (and sexually transmitted infections) for nearly a decade (AGI 2010). Even after marriage, challenges in pregnancy prevention remain. The average woman in the United States aims to have two children. To achieve this goal, she will have to use birth control for approximately 30 years of her life. As a result, estimates are that "virtually all women (98 percent) aged 15–44 who have ever had intercourse have used at least one contraceptive method" (AGI 2008a). Given that there are more than 62 million women of reproductive age, this represents a sizable need (Mosher et al. 2004).

Contraception in context

While birth control is common, so are controversies surrounding its use. For example, controversies surround questions of whether birth control should be paid for by insurance companies, whether teens should be able to access contraceptive services without parental consent, how the safety and efficacy of new methods should be reviewed and evaluated, and whether and how potential users learn about pregnancy prevention. Each of the policies and controversies around birth control has its own fascinating history and is worthy of further research and reading, beyond what I can provide here.

All these controversies reflect concerns about the appropriate role of sex more generally: broad support for easy access to birth control is seen by some as communicating that sex is primarily non-procreative, that is, not limited to efforts to have children, and occurs commonly outside of marriage. For some, this contradicts many assumptions about gender, marriage, and morality, which are often built around views of women's sexuality.

Although we often talk about the importance of pregnancy prevention, it is worth acknowledging that birth control is difficult to use consistently and effectively all the time. The effectiveness of birth control hinges in part on how much a user has to do and how motivated they are to avoid pregnancy. Approximately 5 percent of unintended pregnancies result from method failure. The rest are the result of inconsistent or incorrect use of contraceptives, or failure to use any birth control. When users have to do something every day or every time they have sex, they are less likely to do so successfully than those who use methods that require little effort on the part of the user. Successful use also seems to reflect how much women have to lose by becoming pregnant, and other changing needs. Although we think of women who become pregnant as careless or not trying to prevent pregnancy, about half of women who faced an unintended pregnancy report using birth control in the month prior to becoming pregnant (Finer and Henshaw 2006). As such, we can ask better questions about why women have gaps in usage. Women who have gaps in birth control use attribute these to lack of access, unpleasant side effects, infrequent sexual activity, or life transitions, like the beginning or ending of a relationship, changing jobs, or moving (AGI 2008c; Frost and Darroch 2008). Thus, birth control and pregnancy prevention rise and fall in priority based on what else is going on in women's lives, the context of their relationships, and their own understanding of risk.

The outcome of these transitions, choices, and challenges can be seen in Table 20.1, which shows the failure rates of theoretically perfect use of birth control next to the failure rate of actual use. Next to that is the frequency of use of that contraceptive method.

Women from all backgrounds experience unintended pregnancy, but some women are more affected than are others. Women between the ages of 18 and 24, women from low income backgrounds, women who live with their partners, and

Jennifer A. Reich

women from minority backgrounds, particularly Black women, are most affected. Education also seems to matter a great deal. Women without a high school diploma were about three times more likely to face an unintended pregnancy than were college graduates and were less likely to terminate that pregnancy. As a result, women without a high school diploma had about four times as many births from unintended pregnancies as did college graduates (Finer and Henshaw 2006). This likely underscores the importance of future goals in providing a reason to prioritize pregnancy prevention, and illustrates how the perceived risks unintended pregnancy presents shape sexual and contraceptive decisions.

Social location, including age, education, and income, also affects the kind of contraception you might use. For women younger than 30, the pill is the leading method. However, by the time women are 35, sterilization (tubal ligation) becomes the leading method. Use of sterilization is not evenly distributed; sterilization is the leading method among Black women and Hispanic women and for women with less than a college education, while the pill is the leading method for White women (Mosher et al. 2004). This may reflect delayed childbearing for women who complete college, but it also might suggest that low income women and women of color are offered different contraceptive services by healthcare providers than are White women who are disproportionately more likely to be seen by a privately funded healthcare provider (rather than by a publicly funded healthcare or family planning clinic).

Most data we have about unintended pregnancy come from health or survey data collected from women. As such, we know less about boys' and men's reproductive

Table 20.1   First-year contraceptive failure rates

| Method | Percentage of women experiencing an unintended pregnancy and popularity of method | | | |
	Perfect use	Typical use	Number of users (000s)	% of users
Pill (combined)	0.3	8.7	11,661	30.6
Tubal sterilization	0.5	0.7	10,282	27.0
Male condom	2.0	17.4	6,841	18.0
Vasectomy	0.1	0.2	3,517	9.2
3-month injectable	0.3	6.7	2,024	5.3
Withdrawal	4.0	18.4	1,513	4.0
Periodic abstinence		25.3	583	2.4
IUD (all)			774	0.2
Copper-T	0.6	1.0		
Mirena	0.1	0.1		
1-month injectable	0.05	3.0		
Patch	0.3	8.0		
Diaphragm	6.0	16.0	99	0.3
No method	85.0	85.0		

Source: Taken from AGI 2008a.

lives. What we do know is that young men (15–19-year-olds) are waiting longer than in previous years to have sex (meaning vaginal intercourse), but that three-fourths of men report becoming sexually active by the age of 20, with 96 percent having sex prior to marriage (AGI 2008b).

Seventy-one percent of 15–19-year-old men report using a condom the first time they had sex. However, fewer than half of sexually active young men aged 15–19 reported using condoms 100 percent of the time during the previous year (48 percent in 2002) (Mosher et al. 2004). Interestingly, condom use seems to decline with age. For example, in 2007, 76 percent of sexually active ninth grade boys used condoms at last sexual intercourse, compared with 60 percent of twelfth graders. At the same time, older male students were more likely to report that their partner used the pill at last sex (8 percent of ninth graders vs. 21 percent of twelfth graders) (AGI 2008b). Thus, it appears that over time, contraceptive responsibility shifts to women. Although most teens use contraception at least some of the time, teens who do not use contraception have a 90 percent chance of becoming pregnant.

In thinking about successful pregnancy prevention, we should consider where individuals receive accurate information and access to contraceptive technologies. One clear place is from healthcare providers. Nationally, 15.4 percent of Americans have no health insurance (about 46 million people) (DeNavas-Walt et al. 2009). While this is a significant barrier to reproductive healthcare, there is evidence that the picture is even worse for young men who are much more likely to be uninsured. Adult males aged 19–29 were the fastest growing age group among the uninsured between 2000 and 2004; 31 percent were uninsured in 2004, compared with 12 percent aged 18 and younger (Kaiser Family Foundation 2005). Lack of access to healthcare also serves as a barrier to access to information, contraceptive services, and treatment for sexually transmitted infections that might affect their future fertility or that of their partners.

Even when men do access healthcare, it is not clear they are offered reproductive health services. One government report found that although two out of three young men (aged 15–19) had a physical exam in the past year, fewer than 20 percent received counseling or advice from a healthcare provider about birth control, sexually transmitted infections, or HIV (Martinez et al. 2006). For older men, the data are similar. About one-half (55 percent) of all men 15–44 years of age received a health service in the twelve months before the survey, but only 11 percent of men received birth control counseling, 10 percent received advice about STIs, and 12 percent received advice about HIV in that same time period (Martinez et al. 2006). This suggests that as we aim to communicate greater need for men to share responsibility for pregnancy prevention and family planning, integrating opportunities to discuss and access contraception is important.

Unintended pregnancy and abortion

Even with perfect contraceptive use, abortion will always be a necessary option, as there is no method that can successfully prevent pregnancy 100 percent of the time. As mentioned, about half of all pregnancies are unintended and 40 percent of these (or 22 percent of all pregnancies) end in abortion. Estimates are that almost one in three women will have an abortion in her lifetime. However, because abortion is highly stigmatized, few of us know who those women are. Some celebrity women have come forth to share their experiences – for example, Whoopi Goldberg, Margot Kidder, Ani diFranco, Lil' Kim, Gloria Steinem, Ursula LeGuin, and Margaret Cho – but when women talk to other women, or when men listen to the women they know, we find that we all know someone who has chosen to terminate a pregnancy.

Pregnancy is calculated from the first day of a woman's last menstrual period and lasts about 40 weeks. Although conception occurs when a sperm and egg join and begin cell division (forming a pre-embryo or zygote), pregnancy does not occur physically until that zygote has implanted into the wall of the uterus. At that point, women often experience hormonal changes and associated physical changes.[1] Abortions in the first 12 weeks – when 90 percent of abortions occur – are exceedingly safe and have virtually no long-term negative effects on fertility or pregnancy complications.

All kinds of women seek abortions, but there are some trends. Of women who choose to terminate pregnancies, 56 percent are in their twenties; 61 percent already have one or more children; 67 percent have never married; 57 percent are economically disadvantaged; and 78 percent report a religious affiliation. When faced with an unintended pregnancy, women's reasons for choosing to terminate a pregnancy vary, but are also highly patterned. Most commonly, women expressed fear that having a child would interfere with their education, work or ability to care for dependents (74 percent). About 73 percent of women said they could not afford a baby now. Almost half of women (48 percent) expressed a desire to avoid becoming a single mother, or were "having relationship problems." Almost 40 percent of women terminated a pregnancy because they had completed their child-bearing. About one-third said they were not ready to have a child (Finer et al. 2005).

Focusing specifically on the 61 percent of women who already have children, one study found that women chose to terminate their pregnancies precisely because they aimed to be good mothers, and "believed that children were entitled to a stable and loving family, financial security, and a high level of care and attention" (Jones et al. 2008:79). This is a good reminder that the desire to be a good parent – to the children we already have or might have in the future – significantly drives reproductive decision-making.

We know less about men's roles in abortion. It is clear that some men never know about the abortion of a fetus they co-conceived or learned about it after the pregnancy was terminated. One study found that only about 22–25 percent of women who had abortions left the clinic with the man by whom they had become pregnant (Beenhakker et al. 2004). Although we cannot know how many of the absent men knew of the pregnancy or supported the decision to terminate the pregnancy, we can assume this suggests that there are some points of disconnect between men and women around abortion.

For men who were involved in the abortion experience, we see some patterns. In general, young men perceive unintended pregnancy to be negative and interfere with their activities, schooling, and future goals. In my own research, I looked at how men account for the decision to terminate a pregnancy of a fetus they co-conceived. Men often explained the decision to end a pregnancy in terms of their relative desire to reproduce themselves, whether they felt ready to take on the responsibilities of being financially supportive or a family man, or whether they felt they could have a traditional family and be a good father, as they defined it (Reich 2008). Men are bombarded with information about "taking responsibility." Some research suggests that adolescent and adult males identify responsibility as central to definitions of masculinity, and that the abortion experience may be an expression of responsibility.

In comparing research on men and women, both groups speak of their future goals and ambitions and their desire to feel better prepared to become parents, or to do a good job parenting children they already have. Women seem to speak more specifically of the challenges of day-to-day care of children or access to healthcare or childcare, while men tend to discuss more abstract concepts of how to become someone who plays catch or can meet their children's needs. In both cases, those facing unintended pregnancy voice a desire to feel prepared to parent.

Abortion is a highly divisive arena of public opinion. It is worth acknowledging how our assumptions about those who choose to terminate unintended pregnancies may be wrong. As the statistics show, almost 80 percent of women who seek abortions identify with a religious faith or tradition. Many women who object to abortion in the abstract seek out abortion services when it is their own pregnancies that cause a sense of crisis. Many women who support the right to safe, legal abortion services choose to continue unintended pregnancies. We also sometimes imagine that there are two kinds of women: those who have abortions and those who have babies. In fact, these are the same women, at different points in their lives.

Thinking about our family planning futures

Most of us have long reproductive lives. Although we may move in and out of relationships, become more or less sexually active, or change our goals for our future families as our lives change, we are all engaged in deliberate efforts to control, manage, and plan our procreative selves. How we feel about these processes reflects our cultural understandings of gender, sexuality, relationships, responsibility, morality, risk, and chance.

Even as this is an individual process, we see from research that there are also patterns. As we make choices, we do so from our social location and in interaction with the structures and resources that surround us. It is clear that education, age, ethnicity, and relationship status all matter in making decisions about reproduction and encountering unintended pregnancies.

In thinking about this as a near-universalizing experience that is experienced entirely differently by different men and women, I found the following statistic: by age 45, half of all women have experienced an unplanned pregnancy (AGI 2008c). This figure is so large that it is difficult to fully understand what it means. Yet what it does ask us to consider is, what do we mean when we talk about unintended or unplanned pregnancy? We should also understand that there are times women are not intending to become pregnant, but may not be actively working to avoid it. They may view intent, not just in terms of the presence or absence of contraception, but also in terms of the choices and statuses of their relationships (Barrett and Wellings 2002). Returning to our story of the "oops-baby" at the beginning, that baby is by definition unintended. But how does that pregnancy get discussed? How do women think of their own pregnancies? How do they define intent and accidents? How do they redefine those meanings throughout pregnancy? And how do those around them view their reproduction or sexuality: as normative or problematic? We should also remember that unplanned does not necessarily mean unwelcome or unwanted.

Finally, in thinking about the ways our reproductive desires change over time, we should also think of how our political and interpersonal discourse can be more respectful of each other's reproductive goals and experiences. Although there is political will to reduce rates of unintended pregnancy, there has been decreased support for access to comprehensive education on family planning in schools, a movement away from minors' abilities to access contraceptive and abortion services on their own (without parental consent), and laws in several states that ban the use of public and private insurance funding for abortion services. We also have inadequate support for women and men who choose to continue unintended pregnancies. Funding for children's health insurance, prenatal care, parental leave from paid employment, or affordable childcare have not been broadly supported and have in fact faced cuts across the country. As we work toward respecting each other's struggles around reproduction, we should also ask how we can support ways to help people make their reproductive plans and desires their reality.

Note

1   Estimates are that about 30 percent of conceptions or early pregnancies are lost before a woman knows she could be pregnant. Davidoff, Frank. 2006. "Sex, Politics, Morality at the FDA." *The Hastings Center Report* 36: 20–25.

References

Abma, J. C., G. M. Martinez, W. D. Mosher, and B. S. Dawson. 2004. "Teenagers in the United States: Sexual activity, contraceptive use, and childbearing, 2002." National Center for Health Statistics, Washington, DC.

AGI (Alan Guttmacher Institute) 2008a. "Facts on Contraceptive Use." edited by A. G. Institute. Washington, DC: Alan Guttmacher Institute.

—. 2008b. "Facts on Young Men's Sexual and Reproductive Health." edited by A. G. Institute. Washington, DC: Guttmacher Institute.

—. 2008c. "Improving Contraceptive Use in the United States." Washington, DC: Guttmacher Institute.

—. 2010. "Facts on American Teens' Sexual and Reproductive Health." Washington, DC: Alan Guttmacher Institute. On-line. Available at https://www.guttmacher.org/fact-sheet/american-teens-sexual-and-reproductive-health. Accessed April 16, 2016.

Barrett, Geraldine and Kaye Wellings. 2002. "What Is a 'Planned' Pregnancy? Empirical Data from a British Study." *Social Science and Medicine* 55: 545–57.

Beenhakker, B., S. Becker, S. Hires, N. Molano Di Targiana, P. Blumenthal, and G. Huggins. 2004. "Are Partners Available for Post-Abortion Contraceptive Counseling? A Pilot Study in a Baltimore City Clinic." *Contraception* 69: 419–23.

DeNavas-Walt, Carmen, Bernadette D. Proctor, and Jessica C. Smith. 2009. "Income, Poverty, and Health Insurance Coverage in the United States: 2008." U.S. Census Bureau, Washington, DC.

Finer, Lawrence B., Lori F. Frohwirth, Lindsay A. Dauphinee, Susheela Singh, and Ann M. Moore. 2005. "Reasons U.S. Women Have Abortions: Quantitative and Qualitative Perspectives." *Perspectives on Sexual and Reproductive Health* 37: 110–18.

Finer, Lawrence B. and Stanley K. Henshaw. 2006. "Disparities in Rates of Unintended Pregnancy In the United States, 1994 and 2001." *Perspectives on Sexual and Reproductive Health* 38: 90–96.

Frost, Jennifer and Jacqueline E. Darroch. 2008. "Factors Associated with Contraceptive Choice and Inconsistent Method Use, United States, 2004." *Perspectives on Sexual and Reproductive Health* 40: 94–104.

Jones, Rachel K., Lori F. Frohwirth, and Ann M. Moore. 2008. "'I Would Want to Give My Child, Like, Everything in the World'." *Journal of Family Issues* 29: 79–99.

Kaiser Family Foundation. 2005. "Health Insurance Coverage in America: 2004 Data Update Report." Henry J. Kaiser Family Foundation, Menlo Park, CA.

Martinez, G. M., A. Chandra, J. C. Abma, J. Jones, and W. D. Mosher. 2006. "Fertility, Contraception, and Fatherhood: Data on Men and Women from Cycle 6 (2002) of the 2002 National Survey of Family Growth." Washington, DC: National Center for Health Statistics.

Mosher, William D., Gladys M. Martinez, Anjani Chandra, Joyce C. Abma, and Stephanie J. Willson. 2004. "Use of Contraception and Use of Family Planning Services in the United States: 1982–2002." Centers for Disease Control and Prevention, Atlanta, GA.

Reich, Jennifer A. 2008. "Not Ready to Fill His Father's Shoes: A Masculinist Discourse of Abortion." *Men and Masculinities* 11: 3–21.

Jennifer A. Reich

PART 4

Sexual identities and sexual fluidity

Introduction

Sexual identity usually refers to how individuals think of themselves. Do you consider yourself straight? Queer? Asexual? Gay? Pansexual? Do you avoid sexual identity labels? Are you part of a group trying to come up with a new sexual identity name that better expresses your feelings and desires?

Sexual identity is thought to be deeply personal; we find our identities through a process of intense reflection in order to recognize our "true nature." In North American culture, we often think of sexual identity as something innate within the individual that needs to be "discovered." Or we think of sexual identity as a psychological "choice" that individuals must make.

However, most scholars who study sexuality have found that sexual identity is social. They make the case that sexual identity is socially constructed in a number of ways.

First, how do individuals come up with the idea that they should think of themselves as straight, gay, lesbian, or sexually fluid? Where do they get ideas about what a straight man or a queer woman should look like and act like? The very categories we use – and how we characterize the people within those categories – come from our society. For example, before the mid-1800s, there was no conception of being either gay or straight (or homosexual and heterosexual, in the language of the time). Yet people had same-sex sexual and/or romantic encounters. In the past, individuals who engaged in same-sex acts with one another were often married, had children, and were part of the traditional family structure. Perhaps they thought of their affairs as harmless or as sinful, but these acts did not define who they were as a whole person – as an identity.

People did not think in terms of having their identities organized around their sexual acts. Since the 19th century, social changes in Western society have made it possible to think about organizing identity around sexual preferences. These changes include: individuals becoming less economically and emotionally dependent upon family; more people living in cities where they could find many people into different sexual practices (without the watching eyes of family and neighbors); and the increasing importance of science for defining people in terms of "normal" and "abnormal" identities.

Given that our society places such an emphasis today on understanding identity in terms of sexual desire, behaviors and feelings, where does this leave people who do not feel sexual desires or romantic attractions? The very belief that one's sexual feelings and expression is important to knowing the self means that people who do not think of their lives in sexual terms also need a sexual identity label, "asexual," in order to be visible to others in a sexualized society.

Second, sexual identity is socially constructed in terms of the role it plays in relations between different groups. How do we know what it means to be a straight man in this culture? How do straight men come to define how they should act, dress, and look? Does this differ by racial or ethnic background? In the recent past, one could assume that one knew who was "gay" or "straight" by how men behaved – did they frequently touch one another or avoid most physical contact? Did they dress stylishly or unremarkably? Did they visit gay bars or sports bars? While these differences still might mark gay and straight men from one another, such distinctions are increasingly breaking down.

Third, as implied above, sexuality scholars think of sexual identity as social rather than innate because sexual (and gender) categories undergo constant change rather than remaining fixed. In the 1970s, one was likely to identify as *either* straight *or* gay (bisexuals were constantly regarded suspiciously as not choosing a side) – these identity categories were thought of as dichotomous, and were based on a binary understanding of people's sex and gender identities – female *or* male, man *or* woman. Three decades later, those who study sexuality do not think of sex, gender, and sexual identities as binary categories, but as *fluid*, perhaps as existing on continuums, which means that there are a diversity of human bodies, of possible ways to express genders, and of sexual expressions. Approaching sexual identity as social is messy, complicated, but interesting, as the chapters in this section demonstrate.

chapter 21

Introducing asexuality, unthinking sex

Ela Przybylo

In a portrayal of asexuality on Fox network's medical drama *House* originally aired on January 23, 2012, a couple enter the doctor's office. They are white, young, attractive, presumably able-bodied, heterosexual, and married. They also both identify as asexual. Getting caught in the orbit of Dr. Greg House (played by Hugh Laurie) and his team of doctors due to a simple bladder infection, the wife and her husband become promptly suspect in their asexuality and subject to a series of medical tests. As the episode unfolds, and Dr. House persists in his disbelief of asexuality, asexuality becomes undermined, erased, and misrepresented on two fronts. While the husband is found to have a brain tumor that "caused" his asexuality, his partner is found to be lying about her asexuality so as to make her husband happy. Together and asexual for ten years, *House* teaches its audience that the couple's asexuality is impossible. In the words of Dr. House, we learn only that sex is "the fundamental drive of our species, sex is healthy" and that "the only people who don't want it are either sick, dead, or lying" (*House*, 2012).

The goal of this chapter is to challenge these ideas of "compulsory sexuality." Recently, asexual or "ace" activism along with asexuality studies scholarship has begun to name and analyze the centralization of sex and sexuality in Western contexts. This centralization includes beliefs that sex is at the heart of a romantic relationship, that it is key to coming of age and maturation, and that it is vital to keeping bodies healthy across the lifespan. Sex is used in service of building intimacy, seeking pleasure and orgasm, playing and recreation, and creating and maintaining social bonds and companionship. It is widely talked about in the media as a source of pleasure and health. Similarly, sexuality features centrally in Western contexts as the innermost expression of who we are as individuals.

Terms such as "compulsory sexuality" explain the social expectation that sexuality is a universal norm, that everyone should be sexual and desire sex, and that to not be sexual or desire sex is inherently wrong and in need of fixing. In *House*'s pernicious portrayal of asexuality, we see "compulsory sexuality" at work. Sexual attraction and the pull to sex is portrayed as so central to human life, that asexuality is represented as impossible, as a fabrication, and as a problem to be resolved. Such representations erase the experiences of asexual people in a social context where sex and sexuality are understood as central to the self, to health, and to a meaningful relationship. As this chapter will outline, asexuality scholars and activists push back against such ideas of compulsory sexuality, arguing that asexuality is a viable form of self-identification that can foster new forms of communities, ways of relating, and vocabularies of understanding the self.

Asexual vocabularies, identifications, and community

As with many other sexual orientations, "asexuality" encompasses a broad range of practices, feelings, and self-narratives. The Asexual Visibility and Education Network (AVEN), an online gathering space of asexual knowledge and community formation, outlines "an asexual person [as] a person who does not experience sexual attraction" (AVEN). While sexual attraction is relative in terms of social, historical, and relational contexts, asexuality refers to the sexual orientation of those people who have low levels of interest in sex, in having sex with others, and in thinking of others in terms of sex. Asexuality, then, is an umbrella term for all individuals who have a disinterest or aversion to sex, sexual practices, and the role of sex in relationships. It cuts across other sexual orientations such as lesbian, gay, bisexual, pansexual, and straight as well as monogamous and polyamorous.

One way for thinking about asexuality is through an asexual-sexual spectrum, on which everyone can be placed, with a few people occupying the extreme ends (Storms 1980). Just as few individuals are strictly straight or gay, but rather manifest an intricate mixture of attractions, desires, and practices, thinking about an asexual-sexual spectrum moves us away from a binary model of "sexuals" versus "asexuals." Such an approach suggests that no one is categorically "sexual" and demonstrates that asexuality are relevant and salient for everyone. In this way asexuality is not separate from sexuality but the two rely on each other for meaning.

The asexual or "ace" community has generated a new vocabulary that contributes to our thinking on sexuality from an asexual perspective. Organized around the online platform AVEN, other virtual spaces such as blogs and Facebook groups, and through local gatherings, meet-ups, and conferences, asexual activists also coordinate an annual "Asexual Awareness Week," partake in Pride Parades in cities including Toronto, San Francisco, and London, and organize an International Asexuality Conference first held at World Pride 2014 in Toronto. One such term that has come out of online conversations in the asexual community is "gray-asexual" or "gray-A." Gray-asexual can be used by anyone who experiences some level of sexual attraction but for whom sexual attraction and desire for sex play a minor role (AVENwiki). Similarly, "demisexual" indicates an interest in sex that develops only sometimes and only after one feels very close and intimate with someone. Both gray-asexual and demisexual are identity terms developed by the asexual community to more fully account for the complexity of lived experiences of asexuality. They demonstrate that it is impossible to come up with a single definition that will work to explain people's unique engagements with asexuality across social contexts.

Another set of identity-related concepts that have flourished in and beyond the ace community are those of "romantic" and "aromantic" attraction. Romantic and aromantic, often neglected in discussions of sexuality, are indicators of whether and with whom one desires romantic closeness, which may include touching, kissing, and cuddling. Aromantic, on the other hand, indexes a disinterest in forms of romantic contact which may include touch, often instead prioritizing friendships, or being "friend-focused" (Chasin 2015: 176). This language takes the burden off of sexual attraction as the sole indicator of intimacy, desire, and closeness. For instance, while some asexual individuals are interested in romantic relationships, others are repelled or uninterested in romantic forms of physical intimacy. Asexuality studies scholar, Mark Carrigan (2011), observes that there are three general attitudes to sex among people who are asexually-identified. The first attitude, sex-positivity, sees sex as a positive and validating experience even while the person may not necessarily desire sexual activity. The second, sex-neutrality, marks a disinterest in sex. Finally, a sex-averse or anti-sex disposition is a visceral understanding of sex as gross and unpleasant.

Scholars who study the physiology around asexuality suggest that people who are asexual are capable of genital arousal but may experience difficulty with so-called subjective arousal. So while the body becomes aroused, subjectively—at the level of the mind and emotions—one does not experience arousal (Brotto and Yule 2011; also see Carrigan 2011). Based on the existing scientific body of literature, asexuality has been defined in a variety of ways including as a low level of sexual attraction, as not practicing sexual behaviours, or simply as self-identifying as asexual (Aicken et al. 2013; Van Houdenhove et al. 2014). In recent years, psychologists Morag Yule, Lori Brotto, and Boris Gorzalka have developed an "Asexuality identification Scale" (2015) that, through a series of 12 questions, can be used to assess whether or not someone is asexual. The questions ask, for instance, whether the person experiences sexual attraction to other people, whether they avoid situations where sex might be expected, and whether an ideal relationship from the person's perspective would have sexual activity (159–160). Quantitative studies cite prevalence rates of asexuality as between 0.4 to 1.05 percent of the general population (Aicken et al. 2013; Bogaert 2004), with some studies even indicating rates of up to 5.5 percent (Poston and Baumle 2010). At the same time, it is important to keep in mind that these studies draw on preexisting data and only draw on survey content from specific first world, Western countries (both Aicken et al. and Bogaert look at the UK; Poston and Baumle look at the U.S.).

Asexual stories

As feminist asexuality studies scholar, Karli June Cerankowski (2014) mentions, while asexuality is experienced and lived diversely, there is a tendency toward a singular narrative of asexuality fore-fronting portrayals of asexuality. As an example,

Anthony Bogaert in his book on asexuality talks about the "true asexual" as "the real deal—that is, a complete lack of sexual attraction and/or sexual interest . . .—not just a middle-age, on-again, off-again, malaise about sex [but] hard-core asexuality" (2012: 5). While Bogaert's work has been instrumental to public visibility around asexuality, this sort of statement provides an inaccurate and limiting sense of what asexuality might entail and what it means for people's lives. Namely, the dominant story that it presents to the general public relies on understandings of asexuality as being lifelong, absolute and constant throughout one's life, and as innate and categorically not a "choice" but rather as something one is "born with" (Hinderliter 2009; Przybylo and Cooper 2014). Such definitions reproduce a homogenized and inaccurate notion of what asexuality entails. For instance, it is unfair to hold asexual people to the standard of their identities being lifelong and unchanging because sexuality itself is likely to change throughout one's lifespan, as the conditions and contexts of our lives undergo change. Likewise, to assume that asexuality is never a choice and is something one is "born with" discounts the ways in which our sexualities are made sense of in socially situated contexts, where we choose what we do or do not do sexually based on what is available and possible for us. In other words, our sexuality is never strictly something we are "born with" or "a choice" but a mixture of both these components. Bogaert's sense of asexuality also undercuts people's authority to depict for themselves what sexual stance and identification makes sense for them at a certain point in time.

Finally, to assume that to be asexual one must self-identify is to rule out the many ways in which people might not even think of identifying as asexual, either because they have never heard the term or because they do not feel that the term is inclusive of the type of person they are. Bogaert's stance on asexuality, as exemplified by the above passage, makes people who identify as asexual vulnerable to having to "prove" that they are indeed asexual and that they are not undergoing a "phase" or "on-again, off-again" disinclination toward sex (2012: 5). This places stress on asexuals to have to "demonstrate" and "perform" their asexuality, a common discriminatory tactic that erodes the legitimacy of self-identification. Such a definition also serves to limit who can qualify as asexual, scaring away people who might otherwise meaningfully think of their sexualities in terms of asexuality. As queer theory scholars, Ela Przybylo and Danielle Cooper (2014) point out, statements such as Bogaert's come to function as part of the "truth archive" of asexuality, which, drawing primarily on physiological and quantitative studies, showcases a very specific story about asexuality and who can "count" as asexual. Such accounts function to push other lived experiences of asexuality to the margins of discourse and possibility.

Given that there are many ways to define, experience, and identify as asexual, it is possible to think of asexuality in the plural, as "asexualities" (Cerankowski and Milks 2014). A shift from singular asexuality to plural asexualities highlights the various experiences that are possible within the asexuality umbrella, such as those depicted by the terms gray-asexual, demisexual, romantic, and aromantic. Asexualities in the plural also better accounts for the ways in which sexual attraction is relative in terms of relational, social, and historical contexts. This makes the identity of asexuality highly contingent on the level of sexual attraction that is considered normal in a given social context. As such asexuality is necessarily a commentary on normative levels of sex and sexual desire and on who should be experiencing them. The following section considers asexuality in conversation with race, disability, and gender, demonstrating that these subject positions contribute to understandings of who is expected to be sexual, and conversely, who is barred from being sexual.

Discourses of compulsory sexuality

Discourses around "sexual normalcy" (Kim 2014) or "sexual normativity" (Chasin 2011) constitute a series of ideals around how people should relate to each other sexually. These discourses, or bodies of knowledge, are subject to flux and alteration across historical moments. For instance, contemporary Western culture emphasizes the "sexual imperative" or "compulsory sexuality," a technique that functions to prioritize both sex and sexuality, through (1) privileging sex over other forms of relating, touch, and other activities, (2) centralizing sexuality in the project of self-making and self-knowledge, (3) affixing sex to health, and (4) hinging sex to the coupled relationship, to love, and to intimacy. Together, these ideas about the role sex and sexuality should play in our lives comprise "sexusociety," or a society that is heavily organized around the conviction that sexuality is a universal element of our lives and relationships (Przybylo 2011). The presumption of compulsory sexuality is also interlaced with ideas around heterosexuality, race, gender, and ability.

Feminist critical disability studies scholar, Eunjung Kim (2014), demonstrates how the expectation of sexuality and the accompanying pathologization of asexuality arose in dialogue with racist, sexist, and ableist discourses. For instance, while we are encouraged to hold sex and sexual desire as a moral good, we are also encouraged to do so on specific terms, and certain forms of sex and sexuality are regarded as more appropriate, healthy, or good. In particular, coupled heterosexuality organized around the centerpiece of coitus (penis penetration of the vagina aimed at male ejaculation) is continually upheld as the most essential type of relationship and vital sex-act (Gavey 2005; Rubin 1984).

Ideals of "sexual normalcy" and levels of sexual desire are deeply bound to notions of normative bodies characterized not only by a promotion of heterosexuality, but also by whiteness, able-bodiedness, and androcentric sexual ideals (or male-focused sexuality). As such, "many individuals with disabilities, older people, children, intersex people, transgender people, lesbians, and ethnic, racialized, and impoverished others are often thought of as not being, or not being entitled to be, sexual" (Kim 2014: 250). People with disabilities are routinely met with the forced expectation of non-sexuality. If marked as disabled, you are denied sexual pleasure, presumed to not be physiologically and emotionally capable of sex, and dissuaded from sex as to discourage reproduction (Shuttleworth 2012: 63). Such a barring from sex is tightly linked with notions of whose life is deemed livable and whose life is considered worthy of reproducing. At its most extreme, people deemed "unfit" to reproduce by the state, such as people with disabilities as well as racialized people, have and continue to be forcibly sterilized (Lund and Johnson 2015; Davis 1983; Smith 2005).

As Kim (2010) outlines, "desexualization" is a forced imposition of nonsexuality resting on the assumption that some people should not desire and engage in sex and that sex is only for the able-bodied. This distinction between desexualization and asexuality is important because it allows us to perceive the difference between enforcing non-sexuality as a tool of marginalization, and the self-identificatory claiming of asexuality as a sexual orientation. Whereas with desexualization one is left without say or choice and is barred from sexual expression, claiming an asexual identity is an exercise in sexual expression. Writing on asexuality and disability, Emily Lund and Bayley Johnson indicate that "[w]hereas asexuality may be regarded with suspicion or disbelief in general society, the assumption of asexuality has been forced, usually inaccurately, on many people with disabilities. In other words, 'people' are assumed to be sexual while 'people with disabilities' are assumed to be asexual" (2014: 129). In contrast, many racialized groups are thought to be hypersexual, or "excessively" sexual, and thus are met with incredulity if they identify as asexual. Asexuality studies scholar, Ianna Hawkins Owen (2014), argues that asexuality is thus racialized as white and operates as a demonstration of white sexual ideals of self-mastery, morality, and sexual restraint. Ideals of compulsory sexuality are thus attached not only to particular sexual habits and intensities but also to certain ideas of whose body is most normal, healthy, vital, and socially valuable.

At the same time, because sexuality is taken for granted as necessary to normalcy and normative bodies (or those bodies who are expected to reproduce, to have sex, and to enjoy sex), asexuality is and has been historically diagnosed as a problem in need of medical redress and treatment. For example, there are and have been multiple diagnostic categories focused on pathologizing low levels of sexual desire. Since the late nineteenth century, low sexual desire has been categorized variously as frigidity, "sexual anesthesia" (Krafft-Ebing 1886/1922), "inhibited sexual desire" (Lief 1977), "hypoactive sexual desire disorder" (DSM-III-R 1987) and most recently as "female sexual interest/arousal disorder" and "male hypoactive sexual desire disorder" (DSM-V 2013) (also see Kim 2014). Such labels indicate that low levels of sexual desire were seen by sexology and continue to be regarded by scientific medicine as "unhealthy" and abnormal, reflecting more broadly on society's negative attitudes toward asexuality.

Women are especially vulnerable to being diagnosed as exhibiting low levels of sexual desire. A 2002 study reported that one-third of women in the United States could fall under the parameters of "hypoactive sexual desire disorder" (Warnock 2002; Kim 2014: 268). The study results suggest that low levels of sexual desire (asexuality included) are a common part of life, especially for women. Some feminist theorists argue that women might exhibit lower levels of sexual desire because they do not like the type of sex that is most often encouraged. Namely, feminist theorists have argued that within heteronormative contexts, sex continues to be organized around male orgasm, pleasure, satisfaction and the act of coitus (Irvine 1990/2005; Gavey 2005). In a sense, asexually-identified women challenge patriarchal discourses of women's sexual availability and notions that sex is necessarily enjoyable and life-affirming (Fahs 2010). Asexuality is also historically linked with femininity—and in particular to white, able-bodied, and wealthy femininity—through histories of assuming women's passionlessness while pathologizing female frigidity (Moore and Cryle 2012). For instance, in marriage advice manuals even into the 1950s, there was a general agreement that wives were more reluctant to have sex than their husbands (Bourke 2008: 435) and ideas of women's sexual passivity circulate even to this day (Gavey 2005).

Ela Przybylo

Yet in contemporary Western culture, to not be sexual is to be positioned as repressed and "frigid" and hostile to projects of sex-positivity both on individual and political terms. Moreover, asexual-identification also challenges gendered norms of masculinity since it puts a wrench in the "male sexual drive discourse" that holds that men are by default insatiably sexual, driven by the urge to have sex (Hollway 1984/1998: 231). To identify as asexual is to challenge ideas of what "being a man" supposedly means, including virility, health, and sexual aggression (Przybylo 2014).

Notably, contemporary asexual identification is also intertwined with transgender identity. For instance, many members of the asexual community identify as trans* and transgender, as genderqueer and gender variant. The Asexual Community Census, organized by the ace community in 2011, suggests that of 3430 respondents who completed the survey, only 60 percent identified as categorically "female" or "male." This is also confirmed in academic research with a recent study indicating that from 66 self-identified asexual participants, 18 chose a nonbinary gender identity such as genderqueer, gender-neutral, or androgynous (MacNeela and Murphy 2015: 799). As of yet there is no research that explores the intersections of transgender and asexual identification, and the ways in which these two identities are experienced in the context of compulsory sexuality.

Asexual discrimination

Because asexuality is commonly met with hostility, dislike, and bias, it is important to think about the ways people who are asexual or asexually identified are marginalized and discriminated against in various contexts. Feminist and social theorists have long expanded on the vitriolic prejudice against sexual practices and identities that fall outside the limits of what is considered normal. For instance, In "Thinking Sex," Gayle Rubin (1984) explored the "charmed circle" of monogamous, heterosexual, coupled, and reproductive sex practices and their reliance on marking other sexual practices as "deviant." Yet while Rubin called for a radical politics around sexuality that reevaluated routinely despised sex practices (i.e., promiscuity, masturbation, S/M) and sexual identities (i.e., lesbian or gay), she failed to imagine asexuality as a site of discrimination or as part of her radical theory of sexuality. This failure to imagine asexuality commonly marks the work of nearly all sexuality studies scholarship, crystallizing one of the common forms of discrimination leveled against asexual people: erasure.

Psychologists, Cara MacInnis and Gordon Hodson (2012), surveying 148 students at Brock University in Canada, found that "antiasexual bias" or "antiasexual prejudice" is a pronounced set of attitudes among college-age students. This is characterized by discriminatory intent toward asexual people including ideas of asexual people as "deficient," "less human, and disliked" (740). Asexuality studies scholars, Karli June Cerankowski and Megan Milks (2014), argue that "[t]he time has come to recognize the ways in which asexual people are marginalized" and unpack "the negativities attached to the word "asexual," so often seen as synonymous with pathology, dysfunction, repression, aloneness, antisociality, repulsiveness, unattractiveness, and inhumanness" (13). Recognizing asexual marginalization and discrimination is a significant political act that works against the widespread erasure of asexuality and directs our attention to thinking politically and socially about what makes asexuals vulnerable to negative intentions. To trace discrimination against asexual people is to recognize asexuality as a sexual identity and situate such discrimination in a socio-political context of compulsory sexuality.

For one, asexual people face obstacles to participating fully in both heteronormative and queer publics. Heteronormative publics are heavily guided by the assumption that most "normal" people, at specific times in their lives, must have sex in specific ways. In other words, to participate fully in social life, a person must perform both sex and a desire for sex. Sex, and sexual interest, become markers of "normality," peer group belonging, health and vitality, and a knowledge of the self. For instance, the assumption that a sexual urge is universal is foundational to everyday conversation. Personal disclosure about sexual experiences, evaluations of who is sexually attractive, and telling stories about one's personal sexuality are all mainstays of Western conversational bonding. As one participant from a study on asexual masculinity discusses, as an adolescent he had to "play along" with his male friends who "were all into porn mags" and checking out girls, feigning a desire for sex in order to fit in but ultimately "los[ing] out socially because [. . .] a lot of social activities seem to be [. . .] centered around sex" (Przybylo 2014: 229).

Queer countercultures, on the other hand, are committed to a radical politics of sex and to sex positivity, which seeks to bust open static sexual norms. This commitment to celebrating a whole host of bodily desires directly challenges heteronormative ideals around what sex looks like and around who should be having sex and experiencing sexual desire. Yet at the same time, queer publics, in assuming that sex is vital to queer relating, are often exclusionary of asexuality as an equally valid and radical mode of relating to others. Asexual people thus often feel unwelcome, inauthentic, or under investigation in queer communities because so much rests on sex as a practice of sex positivity, queer radicality, and social bonding (Cerankowski and Milks 2014). Thus, in both queer and heteronormative contexts, asexual people experience social exclusion and isolation as a result of the assumption that sex and sexuality are universal and inherent to interpersonal bonding.

Second, asexual people are particularly susceptible to unwanted or coercive sex, particularly when in relationships with nonasexual individuals. Asexual people experience the strain of maintaining their relationships through sex, of meeting their partners' sexual needs, and of doing performative work to convince their partners that they are enjoying sex. As a result, asexual people experience isolation and exclusion; while many may desire romantic relationships they may feel that the unwanted sex that will be expected of them is not worth the price (Przybylo 2014). Even with the recent changes to the DSM-V (2013), which exempts self-identified asexuals from diagnoses of low sexual desire such as "female sexual interest/arousal disorder" and "male hypoactive sexual desire disorder" (on the basis that asexual people are not "distressed" by their low interest in sex), asexual people are expected to compromise when in relationships with non-asexual partners (DSM-V 2013). Significantly, medical intervention is often leveled against asexual people in a coupled context, where a lack of sex can easily become understood as a failure of the relationship. Medical or therapeutic pressure is placed on the asexual partner to adapt and compromise their needs so as to maintain the relationship with their non asexual partner (Chasin 2015: 174). Pathologization—or the creation of medial diagnoses and concomitant treatments—is in itself a common form of marginalizing and discriminating against all types of sexual minorities. Asexual people are vulnerable to pathologization and medical treatment because they deviate from ideals of sexual normalcy in terms of levels of sexual desire. As Kristin Scherrer (2008) writes, "[f]or both LGBTQ and asexual people, one of the locations of discrimination is its historical and contemporary connection to institutions of mental and physical health" (623).

Finally, as already mentioned, asexual people are rendered unintelligible in a context where sex is so crucial to public and relational belonging. Asexuality is routinely disregarded as "a phase," and asexual people are culturally stereotyped to be any number of things including "prudes," "repressed," sexually unliberated, "in denial," unhealthy or in need of treatment. These common stereotypes are vivid in cultural representations of asexuality. For instance, as discussed in the introduction to this chapter, the portrayal of an asexual couple in the American medical drama *House* (2012), invalidated asexuality through portraying it as both a fiction (in the case of the character who "lies" about her asexuality) and as a medical condition in need of treatment (with the character in whom a brain tumor is identified). Such representations participate in an active erasure of asexuality through undertaking "denial narratives" (MacNeela and Murphy 2015) and invalidating asexuality as a valid sexual identity. Denial narratives by sexual people might include claims that asexuality is a disorder (pathologization), an immature phase, or something that can be fixed if the "right person" comes along (MacNeela and Murphy 2015: 803). Asexual people are regularly exposed to prying questions by skeptical listeners, who see asexuality as illegitimate and inauthentic, in order to "get to the bottom of this" unknown sexual manifestation (*The View*, a U.S. tv talk show, aired on January 15, 2006). Such questions include personal matters such as masturbation, sexual preferences and habits, and orgasmic capacities. Through denial narratives, harmful stereotypes, and interrogative questioning, asexuality is actively erased as a sexual identity and the difficult identity work undertaken by asexuals is invalidated.

It is important politically to recognize the discrimination asexual people experience because asexuality is so often held as an impossible site and erased from view. As we have seen, even sexuality studies scholarship has typically overlooked and failed to see asexuality as a viable sexual identity. By outlining the discrimination asexual people face, we can work against marginalization and against portraying asexual people as spectacles for consumption by a non asexual public (Cerankowski 2014). Shifting away from viewing asexuality as an individual abnormality to instead examining how sex is held in particular esteem marks a move toward understanding asexuality's marginalization. Such a move can push us to think about asexuality as a unique series of identifications worth celebrating and studying for the insight they bring to sexual and intimate life and also to sexuality studies scholarship.

Bibliography

Aicken, Catherine, Catherine Mercer, and Jackie Cassell. 2013. "Who Reports Absence of Sexual Attraction in Britain? Evidence from National Probability Surveys." *Psychology & Sexuality* 4(2):121–135.

American Psychiatric Association. 1987. *Diagnostic and Statistical Manual of Mental Disorders* (3rd edition, revised). Washington, DC: APA.

American Psychiatric Association. 2013. *Diagnostic and Statistical Manual of Mental Disorders* (V edition). Arlington, VA: American Psychiatric Publishing.

Asexual Awareness Week Team and Tristan Miller (aka Siggy). 2011. "Asexual Community Census 2011." http://asexualawarenessweek.com/docs/SiggyAnalysis-AAWCensus.pdf. Accessed July 1, 2015.

AVEN: Asexual Visibility and Education Network. 2012. www.asexuality.org.

Bogaert, Anthony. 2004. "Asexuality: Prevalence and Associated Factors in a National Probability Sample." *Journal of Sex Research* 41(3):279–287.

Bogaert, Anthony. 2012. *Understanding Asexuality.* Toronto: Rowman & Littlefield Publishers.

Bourke, Joanna. 2008. "Sexual Violence, Marital Guidance, and Victorian Bodies: An Aesthesiology." *Victorian Studies* 50(3):419–436.

Brotto, Lori and Morag A. Yule. 2011. "Physiological and Subjective Sexual Arousal in Self-Identified Asexual Women." *Archives of Sexual Behavior* 40(4):699–712.

Carrigan, Mark. 2011. "There's More to Life Than Sex? Difference and Commonality Within the Asexual Community." *Sexualities* 14(4):462–478.

Cerankowski, Karli June. 2014. "Spectacular Asexuals: Media Visibility and Cultural Fetish." Pp. 139–161 in *Asexualities: Feminist and Queer Perspectives*, edited by Karli June Cerankowski and Megan Milks. New York: Routledge.

Cerankowski, Karli June and Megan Milks. 2014. *Asexualities: Feminist and Queer Perspectives.* New York, NY: Routledge.

Chasin, CJ Deluzio. 2011. "Theoretical Issues in the Study of Asexuality." *Archives of Sexual Behavior* 40(4):713–723.

Chasin, CJ Deluzio. 2015. "Making Sense in and of the Asexual Community: Navigating Relationships and Identities in a Context of Resistance." *Journal of Community & Applied Social Psychology* 25:167–180.

Davis, Angela. 1983. *Women, Race, and Class.* New York: Vintage Books.

Fahs, Breanne. 2010. "Radical Refusals: On the Anarchist Politics of Women Choosing." *Sexualities* 13(4):445–461.

Gavey, Nicola. 2005. *Just Sex? The Cultural Scaffolding of Rape.* London and New York: Routledge.

"Gray-A/Grey-A." 2014. *AVENwiki.* www.asexuality.org/wiki/index.php?title=Gray-A. Accessed July 1, 2015.

Gupta, Kristina. 2015 "Compulsory Sexuality: Evaluating an Emerging Concept." *Signs: Journal of Women and Culture in Society* 41(1):131–154.

Hawkins Owen, Ianna. 2014. "On the Racialization of Asexuality." Pp. 119–135 in *Asexualities: Feminist and Queer Perspectives*, edited by Karli June Cerankowski and Megan Milks. New York: Routledge.

Hinderliter, Andrew. 2009. "Methodological Issues for Studying Asexuality." *Archives of Sexual Behavior* 38(5):619–621.

Hollway, Wendy. 1984/1998. "Gender Difference and the Production of Subjectivity." Pp. 227–263 in *Changing the Subject: Psychology, Social Regulation and Subjectivity*, Henriques et al. London and New York: Routledge.

Irvine, Janice M. 1990/2005. *Disorders of Desire: Sexuality and Gender in Modern American Sexology.* Philadelphia: Temple University Press.

Kim, Eunjung. 2010. "How Much Sex Is Healthy? The Pleasures of Asexuality." Pp. 157–169 in *Against Health: How Health Became the New Morality*, edited by Jonathan M. Metzl and Anna Kirkland. New York: New York University Press.

Kim, Eunjung. 2014. "Asexualities and Disabilities in Constructing Sexual Normalcy." Pp. 249–282 in *Asexualities: Feminist and Queer Perspectives*, edited by Karli June Cerankowski and Megan Milks. New York: Routledge.

Krafft-Ebing, Richard von. 1886/1922. *Psychopathia Sexualis with Especial Reference to Contrary Sexual Instincts: A Clinical Forensic Study*. 12th edn. Translated by Charles G. Chaddock. New York: Rebman.

Lief, Harold. 1977. "What's New in Sexual Research? Inhibited Sexual Desire." *Medical Aspects of Human Sexuality* 11:94–95.

Lund, Emily and Bayley Johnson. 2015. "Asexuality and Disability: Strange but Compatible Bedfellows." *Sexuality and Disability* 33(1):123–132.

MacInnis, Cara C. and Gordon Hodson. 2012. "Intergroup Bias towards 'Group X': Evidence of Prejudice, Dehumanization, Avoidance, and Discrimination against Asexuals." *Group Processes and Intergroup Relations* 16(6):725–743.

MacNeela, Pádraig and Aisling Murphy. 2015. "Freedom, Invisibility, and Community: A Qualitative Study of Self-Identification with Asexuality." *Archives of Sexual Behavior* 44:799–812.

Milks, Megan and Karli June Cerankowski. 2014. "Introduction: Why Asexuality? Why Now?" Pp. 1–14 in *Asexualities: Feminist and Queer Perspectives*, edited by Karli June Cerankowski and Megan Milks. New York: Routledge.

Moore, Alison and Peter Cryle. 2012. *Frigidity: An Intellectual History*. New York: Palgrave Macmillan.

Poston, Dudley L. Jr. and Amanda K. Baumle. 2010. "Patterns of Asexuality in the United States." *Demographic Research* 23:509–530.

Przybylo, Ela. 2011. "Crisis and Safety: The Asexual in Sexusociety," *Sexualities* 14(4):444–461.

Przybylo, Ela. 2013. "Producing Facts: Empirical Asexuality and the Scientific Study of Sex." *Feminism and Psychology* 23(2):224–242.

Przybylo, Ela. 2014. "Masculine Doubt and Sexual Wonder: Asexually-Identified Men Talk About their (A)sexualities." Pp. 225–246 in *Asexualities: Feminist and Queer Perspectives*, edited by Karli June Cerankowski and Megan Milks. New York: Routledge.

Przybylo, Ela and Danielle Cooper. 2014. "Asexual Resonances: Tracing a Queerly Asexual Archive." *GLQ: A Journal of Gay and Lesbian Studies* 20(3):297–318.

Rubin, Gayle. 1984. "Thinking Sex: Notes for a Radical Theory of the Politics of Sexuality." Pp. 267–319 in *Pleasure and Danger: Exploring Female Sexuality*, edited by Carole S. Vance and Kegan Paul. London: Routledge.

Scherrer, Kristin. 2008. "Coming to an Asexual Identity: Negotiating Identity, Negotiating Desire." *Sexualities* 11(5):621–641.

Shuttleworth, Russell. 2012. "Bridging Theory and Experience: A Critical-Interpretive Ethnography of Sexuality and Disability." Pp. 54–68 in *Sex and Disability*, edited by Robert McRuer and Anna Mollow. Durham: Duke University Press.

Smith, Andrea. 2005. *Conquest: Sexual Violence and American Indian Genocide*. Cambridge, MA: South End Press.

Storms, Michael. 1980. "Theories of Sexual Orientation." *Journal of Personality and Social Psychology* 38(5):783–792.

Van Houdenhove, Ellen, Luk Gijs, Guy T'Sjoen, and Paul Enzlin. 2014. "Asexuality: Few Facts, Many Questions." *Journal of Sex & Marital Therapy* 40:175–192.

Warnock, Julia K. 2002. "Female Hypoactive Sexual Desire Disorder: Epidemiology, Diagnosis, and Treatment." *CNS Drugs* 16(11):745–753.

Yule, Morag A., Lori A. Brotto, and Boris B. Gorzalka. 2015. "A Validated Measure of No Sexual Attraction: The Asexuality Identification Scale." *Psychological Assessment v.* 27(1), March: 148–160.

chapter 22

Sexual fluidity

Interview with Lisa Diamond

Lisa Diamond is a professor of psychology and of gender studies at the University of Utah. Her research concerns the psychological and biobehavioral processes underlying intimate relationships and their influence on emotional experience and functioning over the life course. She has published numerous articles on same-sex relationships and is best known for her book *Sexual Fluidity: Understanding Women's Love and Desire.*

Can you explain what you mean by sexual fluidity and how it's different from bisexuality?

I define sexual fluidity as the capacity for situation-dependent change in one's sexual attractions. The way I often explain it is as follows: We all have sexual orientations, but because of sexual fluidity, our orientations don't provide the last word on the range of attractions we may find ourselves experiencing over the lifespan, often triggered by particular relationships. Because of sexual fluidity, lesbians sometimes experience attractions for men and heterosexuals sometimes experience attractions for women. But that doesn't make them bisexual (bisexuality is a *consistent* pattern of attractions for women and men, whereas fluidity represents a capacity for situation-dependent flexibility).

You argue that the women you interviewed report a capacity and openness to changing the gender of their sexual partners. Do you understand this fluidity as socio-historically and/or biologically based?

I think that the capacity for fluidity may be probably biologically based, but it's typically triggered by social factors (and certain cultures and societies provide more opportunities for individuals to discover their own capacity for fluidity). Some individuals appear to be more fluid than others, and one possibility is that individuals are simply born with a large or small capacity for fluidity, in the same way that they are born with different sexual orientations. But if you are born into a culture that has extremely rigid ideas about sexuality, you might not ever have the chance to discover your capacity for fluidity.

Sexual fluidity among women, along with the "trans" phenomena, would seem to pose a challenge to a lesbian culture and identity. As a lesbian-identified person, do you agree and, if so, is a lesbian identity threatened?

I don't think so, and I think that the lesbian community has become much more open and accepting of more fluid conceptions of gender and sexuality over the years. A lot of this simply comes from first-hand experiences. Whenever I lecture about sexual fluidity, I end up meeting lesbians who say to me "you know, I had this odd experience a couple of years ago where I was attracted to this guy at work, and your work helps me understand this – it helps me realize that I am, in fact, still a lesbian, and being a lesbian is fully consistent with having those periodic, unexpected experiences ..."

Do you see any parallels between your research on sexual fluidity and Queer politics and theory, and the rise of the metrosexual and transgendered people?

I absolutely think it resonates with all of the insights that Queer theory has been bringing to our understanding of sexuality over the years. Queer theory has been instrumental in challenging our notions of the fixity and rigidity of sexuality, and has helped us understand how our own subjective experiences of our sexuality are fundamentally shaped by social forces. Fluidity represents one (of many) manifestations of that process, and I think that our increasing awareness of sexual fluidity helps to provide a scientific rationale for queer political approaches which try to move beyond rigid labels like gay, lesbian, and bisexual and which try to represent the true and dazzling diversity of sexual and gender identities.

Does your research findings regarding young women's sexual fluidity also suggest women's expanded gender flexibility? In other words, are women today exploring masculinity and femininity in ways that are challenging binary gender norms?

Absolutely – I have found that many adolescent and young adult trans individuals describe their gender identities in ways that are reminiscent of my earlier work on sexual fluidity. Twenty years ago, the conventional (but incorrect) wisdom on transgender experience was that trans individuals were "trapped in the wrong body," and that all of them wanted to undergo sex reassignment surgery in order to "switch" their gender. But now there are *so* many trans individuals who are speaking up and describing so many *other* forms of trans experience. Some feel that their gender is intermediate between male and female, and that they have no desire to "pick a category." Others feel that their gender transcends these categories altogether, and that they truly *have* no gender. Others feel that they are in a permanent state of flux between different positions on the male to female continuum, and they are perfectly comfortable with that sort of ongoing oscillation. So just as we have discovered the fluidity of sexuality, we are also discovering the fluidity of gender, for *both* women and men.

Has your research impacted on you in ways that you did not anticipate?

I think it has humbled me and made me aware of how much I don't know, and how much I still have to learn. I find that exciting and exhilarating. When I first started my research, I was utterly surprised to find so many trajectories of sexual identity, so many pathways, that were so different from my own experience, and the diversity of our community continues to amaze and fascinate me. I have also felt very gratified over the years to get so many emails and messages from individuals who have felt that my work has helped them to make sense of themselves. Many women have contacted me to say "I thought I was really weird and odd, but now I see that I'm not!" I always save those messages, they are precious to me. Being able to contribute to the well-being and self-acceptance of my fellow queers is so important to me, and has been one of the most gratifying things about my work.

chapter 23

Learning to be queer

College women's sexual fluidity

Leila J. Rupp, Verta Taylor, and Shaeleya D. Miller

In John Irving's novel, *In One Person*, the bisexual narrator, echoing a line uttered by his first love, the transsexual librarian Miss Frost, says "please don't put a label on me—don't make me a category before you get to know me!" (Irving 2012, 425). It is a sentiment increasingly shared by queer women college students on our campus, the University of California, Santa Barbara. Rather than call themselves "lesbian" or even "bisexual," many are embracing identities as "pansexual," "queer," or "fluid," or refusing to adopt any label at all. In this way these students reflect the research on and popular understandings of the sexual fluidity of women: women's openness to bisexual attractions and behavior; the lack of fit among desire, behavior, and identity; and the shifts in women's desires, behaviors, and identities across their lifetimes (Diamond 2008; Golden 2006). Although we set out to study women who identified as anything other than heterosexual, some of the students identify as "genderqueer" rather than as women, so technically the population consists of female-bodied individuals. We use the gender-neutral pronouns "ze/hir/hirs" or "they/their/theirs" for individuals who prefer to be referred to in that way. We analyze the stories of these college students from the perspective of queer theory, which emphasizes the anti-essential and fluid nature of gender and sexual identity (Butler 1990; Carrera, De Palma, and Lameiras 2012), and collective identity theory, which points to the ways that social movements and other groups create collective self definitions that draw boundaries between "us" and "them" (Taylor and Whittier 1992). We draw on these perspectives both to explore the meaning of fluid sexual and gender identities and to understand how these students come to embrace identities consistent with sexual fluidity or, in a few cases, to reject an identity altogether.

We find that women students call themselves "queer" and "pansexual" because their desires are expansive and include the possibility of attraction to transgender and genderqueer people; their identities shift and more fixed identities do not always fit; and their new fluid identities evoke a rejection of binary sexualities and have political meaning. Students come to these new collective identities when they arrive on campus through courses and literature on sexuality and queer theory and socialization in queer organizations and the campus queer community. This process reveals what Anthony Giddens (1987) has conceptualized as the double hermeneutic, in which social science research and the concepts of individuals and groups have a complex two-way relationship with each influencing the other. In this chapter, we demonstrate that the identities non-heterosexual women college students embrace are influenced by the scholarship on queerness and sexual fluidity, which itself originated in the increasingly fluid and non-binary sexual identities adopted by lesbian, gay, bisexual, and transgender individuals.

The setting

The University of California, Santa Barbara, is a stunningly beautiful campus of just over twenty thousand students, 85% undergraduates, perched on the edge of the Pacific. The undergraduate population is about half students of color and about a third first-generation college students. The relatively progressive Research I university is highly ranked as a party school in large part because of student life in the adjacent community of Isla Vista. Although Isla Vista is often not a friendly or safe place for queer students, there is a large, visible, and diverse queer community on campus, revolving around numerous student organizations serving various constituencies. The Resource Center for Sexual and Gender Diversity flyer announces that the Center provides a community space on campus for "self-identified lesbian, gay, bisexual, transgender, genderqueer, gender non-conforming, queer, questioning, two-spirit, same gender loving, as well as people with intersex conditions." Student organizations include the Queer Student Union and Associated Students Queer Commission; groups for different races and ethnicities, including Black Quare, La Familia De Colores, and Queer Asian Pacific Islanders (QAPI); more specialized groups, including Friendly Undergraduate Queers in it Together (FUQIT), Kink University: A Fetish Fellowship (KUFF), and Students for Accessible and Safe Spaces (SASS). There is a residence hall for queer students, Rainbow House; gender-inclusive housing for transgender and genderqueer students; and an LGBTQ studies minor, housed in the Department of Feminist Studies. The university has a top ranking as queer-friendly on the "campus pride index." Queer student activists are a diverse group in terms of gender identity, sexual identity, and ethnicity. Although not representative of all universities, there is no reason to think that UC Santa Barbara is unique in terms of the queer community on campus (see Rupp and Taylor 2013; Rupp et al 2014).

Our analysis is based on 125 interviews with women students who identify as anything other than heterosexual. As Table 23.1 shows, at UC Santa Barbara, as on campuses across the country, the vast majority of students identify as heterosexual (see Armstrong, England, and Fogarty 2012 for a description of the Online College and Social Life Survey). Our interviewees were about half white and half students of color (see Table 23.2), and they listed a variety of sexual identities, including bisexual, lesbian, queer, fluid, pansexual, gay, not straight, uncertain, and none (see Table 23.3). The three top identities for both white women and women of color were bisexual, lesbian, and queer, but with a reversed order, with white women most likely to call themselves bisexual and women of color most likely to call themselves queer (see Table 23.4). More women of color (48%) than white women (33%) adopted fluid identities (i.e., anything other than bisexual, lesbian, or gay), although this might be a result of more white women interviewed in the earlier phases of the project, when fluid identities were less common. In the interviews from 2006 to 2009, the racial/ethnic composition of the interviewees was 60% white women and

Table 23.1 Sexual identities of women students, total and UCSB, Online College and Social Life Survey, UCSB

Sexual identity	Total	UCSB
Heterosexual	92%	94%
Homosexual	3%	2%
Bisexual	3%	3%
Not sure	2%	2%

Table 23.2 Ethnicity of interviewees

Ethnicity	% of total
White ($n = 57$)	46%
Latina ($n = 27$)	22%
Asian American ($n = 19$)	15%
Bi/Multiracial ($n = 16$)	13%
African American ($n = 5$)	2%
Middle Eastern ($n = 1$)	1%
None claimed ($n = 1$)	1%

Table 23.3 Sexual identities of interviewees

Sexual identity	% of total
Bisexual ($n = 33$)	26%
Lesbian ($n = 31$)	25%
Queer ($n = 29$)	23%
Fluid ($n = 10$)	8%
Pansexual ($n = 8$)	6%
Gay ($n = 9$)	7%
Not straight, uncertain, none ($n = 5$)	4%

Table 23.4 Sexual identity by ethnicity

Ethnicity	Bisexual	Lesbian	Queer	Fluid/ Pansexual	Gay	None, Unsure, Not straight
White	35%	28%	19%	14%	4%	0
Women of color	19%	22%	27%	13%	11%	8%

40% women of color, and only 28% of the students as a whole adopted fluid identities. For the 2010–2012 interviews, women of color accounted for 58% and white women 42% of the interviewees, while 45% embraced fluid identities. The racial/ethnic shift is in part a result of an increasing student of color population on the campus and the growth of queer of color organizations. In any case, no pattern of difference emerged between white students and students of color in terms of their understandings of fluid identities.

Interviews were conducted by undergraduate students enrolled in a course on female same-sex sexuality in 2006, 2007, and 2012; by undergraduate and graduate research assistants from 2009 to 2011; and by Shaeleya Miller in 2011 and 2012 as part of her dissertation research. Students in the course located their own interviewees, and personal contacts and snowball sampling produced the students interviewed by research assistants. We utilize students as interviewers because we have found that similarity in age and status facilitates rapport. The semi-structured interviews were recorded and transcribed and covered desire, love, sexual behavior, relationships, identities, the coming out process, community participation, and political involvement. All the names used are pseudonyms.

Three stories

Omara is Mexican American, the daughter of a gardener and a teacher's assistant who grew up in a small coastal community not far from San Francisco. She identifies as pansexual or "just queer." She had a boyfriend in high school but found herself attracted to women, although it was not until her first year in college that she had a relationship with a woman. Acknowledging her desire, in high school she first identified as lesbian, then bisexual, and came to pansexual and queer only "after coming to college and being exposed to these different identities." Being in "this really diverse community with people that identify as transgender and genderqueer" opened up the possibility of having a relationship "with a person that identifies as, like, neither male or female or woman or man."

Sometimes, Omara says, she identifies as bisexual "to other people that don't really understand" the identity pansexual. She is not out to her family, which she describes as very traditional. One time she tried to explain bisexuality to her mother, who responded that bisexuals are confused. Referencing her Mexican heritage, Omara commented, "You know, it's just totally . . . I guess American, I don't know."

She found it easier to "figure myself out" when she came to UC Santa Barbara because the atmosphere was "way more open."

Aldara is a white queer student whose father came to the United States from Greece as a child. When she was sixteen, living in a town between San Francisco and Sacramento, she fell into a relationship with a girlfriend who shared her artistic interests, and they stayed together until her first year of college. At first she thought the relationship was "an exception," and she had no word for her identity. "Like I knew that I just was too open as a person" to identify as a lesbian, "because I knew that I had had real feelings for men before, too." She says, "I don't think I really understood, I just didn't understand a lot of the language that there was to identify myself with at all. So it was kind of difficult."

Aldara defines herself now as queer rather than bisexual because she's attracted to "FtM identifying people, to men, to women." Even so, she says she sometimes feels limited by the word queer "because I understand that it's privileged and I understand that a lot of people still find it offensive, and when it comes to that—I feel like I have to identify as bisexual. But, like for me, queer is what describes me best, because I really feel like I change every day. Like my sexual desire, who I find attractive, so queer is the word that works best for me."

She began using the word queer "since I started going here and heard the word. I started doing my own research on it," and when she googled "queer," the first thing she found was an article about how this was the word used at UCSB. She began to visit Rainbow House and went to Queerpalooza, a mixer where the leaders of all the queer organizations introduce their groups to new students. Then Aldara started going to all the meetings "and by the end of that year I was an officer for the next year and by the end of that year I was co-chair the next year, so I took on a lot of responsibility really fast." Aldara connects her queer identity not only to organizations on campus, but also to her classes. She recognizes how privileged she is to be exposed to academic work about sexuality. "And it's kind of crazy the way that education can change your view. I always think about that, I feel like if our whole nation had to take the classes I take, how different would the world be!"

Tee has a Taiwanese father and white Christian mother and identifies as queer and genderqueer. Ze grew up in a mostly Asian neighborhood in Los Angeles county and attended a high school ze describes as "very Asian and conservative and terrible." Ze sees hir Asian identity and queer identity as somewhat in conflict, explaining "there's no word for 'gay' in Taiwanese," although the Asian side of hir family is more accepting of hir queer identity than the white side. At UC Santa Barbara ze launched Queer Asian Pacific Islanders because there was no student organization for Asian queers.

When ze was a sophomore in high school, ze fell in love with a girl. It was a first for both of them, and ze likes to say "I thought I was straight for the first two weeks of my relationship with my first girlfriend." When ze came out to hir parents, hir mother kicked hir out of the house, and ze moved into an apartment with some queer friends.

Tee explains that ze identifies as queer "because 'lesbian' doesn't cover it. Because first off it makes implications about my gender identity. And also it makes implications about other people's gender identity, and I think trans and genderqueer people are super hot. So 'lesbian' is too exclusive, I think. So, yeah, but I mean it's taken awhile to get here." Ze majored in feminist studies, which clearly has had an impact on hir "getting here." Learning feminist and queer theory changed the way ze thought about hirself. "I went from straight, straight to lesbian, there was no bi, bisexual phase at all, because once I kissed a girl I, like, knew it." Despite shifting hir identity to queer, ze thinks the word is sometimes limiting, "and I wish it wasn't so academic." People out in the world "don't understand the whole umbrella concept."

The meaning of fluidity

Like Omara, Aldara, and Tee, students coming from different backgrounds use the terms "queer," "pansexual," or "fluid" to describe both an individual and a collective identity that signals expansive sexual desire, shifting and fluid sexual identities, and a political embrace of non-binary genders and sexualities. As these stories make clear, "queer" is both an umbrella term, covering a range of more specific identities, and also an identity that students embrace, so those who call themselves "pansexual" or "fluid" or other more traditional identity labels can also see themselves as queer. April, for example, a queer Vietnamese American student, says "I'm pretty solid about identifying as queer. It's just such a broad term, an umbrella term, so I feel like even if I was still, like, bi or trans or anything, then I would still fall into that category." Nicole, a Mexican American student, calls herself queer because it is "more broad and includes everything."

Expansive desire

Fundamental to fluid identities is not only at least the possibility of attraction to both women and men, but sometimes rapid shifts in sexual desire. Valeria, a Latina who identifies as a "lady-loving lesbian," or a "raging lesbian," describes thinking of herself for a time as pansexual but then realizing that "I'm really not pansexual because I don't think I could love everyone, like I can't really love men." In contrast, Aldara, as we have seen, explains that she is "too open as a person" to identify as lesbian because she had also had attractions to men and her desires "change every day." Other students, too, emphasize how quickly the direction of desire can change. Shae, a Korean American student, says that she sticks with "queer" "just because I think I'm just constantly like up and down and changing." Clara, a Latina, says "it's always changing" so she calls herself fluid. A white student, Phoenix, who identifies as fluid, also emphasizes shifting desire: "Sexual feelings for me change, you know, within a day, honestly. Sometimes I wake up and I'm like, 'I'm feeling extra queer today.' And like, 'I wanna get me some ladies. But then other days, I feel like I want a man in my life. I mean, a male-bodied person."

That qualification—"a male-bodied person"—points to another aspect of expansive desire: that it includes attraction to transgender and genderqueer individuals, sometimes just in theory, sometimes in practice. Omara, as we have seen, describes being able to see herself as being involved with "a person that identifies as neither male or female or woman or man," Aldara includes FtMs in her list of people she finds attractive, and Tee thinks trans and genderqueer people are "super hot." Biracial Emma, who is Mexican and white and identifies as queer, does so, she says, because "bi's not inclusive of trans people." Sara, also Latina, explains her acceptance of "queer" because "I am mostly attracted to women, but also to androgynous and genderqueer individuals." Jessica, who calls herself a "white-washed" Chinese American and who started a bisexual group on campus, says she is actually pansexual, which she defines as having "an attraction to men, women, and any genders that fall outside those two."

Shifting identities

Students describe not only fluidity of desire but also fluidity of identities. Emma connects the meaning of "queer" to changes in identities over time. "I used to think I was straight, and then I thought I was bi, and then I stopped having crushes on guys, so I thought I was a lesbian, then I got a crush on a guy and I dated him so then I was bi again, and I just say I'm queer." Emilia, a Latina student who identified as queer on her demographic sheet, also calls herself a lesbian in her interview. She explains, "I would say I identify as a lesbian because I'm attracted to other women but I also understand that it could be, sexuality could be fluid." If she fell in love with a man, then she supposes she would identify as queer. Many students listed the ways the identities they claimed had changed over time. Gabriella, a queer African American student, says, "I was straight. And then I was like, 'OK, I'm bisexual. I'm bi.' Then after that I guess I was like, I was fluid, kind of. And then it's lesbian, it was lesbian, and then I was fluid again. And now I'm just queer. Yeah, it does change all the time. But it's never heterosexual."

The fluidity that emerges from students' discussions of their desires and identities works against the adoption of more fixed identities such as "lesbian," even though some students call themselves that, and even against "bisexual," which they believe reinforces the sex and gender binary that dictates women's attraction to men. Vanessa, a white lesbian, is annoyed that "people think that lesbians don't exist sometimes cuz, like, women are supposed to be more fluid." Melissa, also white and identifying as fluid, distinguishes herself from lesbians as "people who knew since they were like two or like five years old" that they desired girls. Queer white Rachel does not like the "finality of the word 'lesbian'," "it seems like there is no going back from there." Tee, as we have seen, rejects "lesbian" because the term is too exclusive. April, who sees herself in the future with a woman, hints at the required fluidity of the identity queer when she says, "the thing is that, I don't want to, like, defeat the purpose of me labeling myself as queer because I'm open to any gender." Om, who is white, queer, genderqueer, and in a relationship with Tee, echoes Tee in saying, "if I were to describe myself as a lesbian that means I am a woman who desires other women. And that's not true because I'm a genderqueer dating another genderqueer."

Even more common is a rejection of the term "bisexual" as having negative connotations and as not sufficiently fluid. Gloria, who is white, refers to girls at her high school who did "the bisexual thing, like, for boys" and "make a bad name for all of us." She also dislikes the attitude that "Oh you just wanna fuck everything that moves because you're bisexual." So, she says, "that's why I like to use the word 'queer' instead because I wanna get away from the word 'bisexual.'" April describes bisexual as having "kinda a heavy stigma," and queer white Alex agrees, noting that "a lot of queer people really have an issue with bisexuality." Multiracial Missy (Mexican, Japanese, and white), also prefers "queer" to "bisexual," finding the word "not attractive" or "appealing" and also too binary, since she could imagine being attracted to a transwoman or transman. Jessica, who considers herself "actually" pansexual, deliberately adopts the term "bisexual" as a way to fight such stereotypes.

A number of interviewees emphasized the difference between their personal or individual identities and the collective nature of queer identities. Understanding what an identity entails and feeling that it is the right identity to embrace personally are two different things. Brittany, a white student who calls herself "bisexual queer," recognizes that "pansexual" or "omnisexual" might technically describe her sexuality, but "those don't feel like, I can't own those, it doesn't sit when I say it, like I don't feel like omnisexual." Likewise Phoenix can understand "queer" as an adjective meaning non-normative and as an inclusive umbrella term, but "the reason I don't understand it as a personal identity is because I don't feel it . . . And I think it takes feeling it to really understand what it means. And so I tried it on and it just didn't stick 'cause I don't feel it." Adrianna, a Latina student who refuses to identify because "I just like whoever I like," explains that adopting an identity, which she tried, "just didn't feel right . . . it didn't feel like it fit."

Beyond binaries

The inclusion of attraction to transgender and genderqueer people as part of a fluid identity makes it clear that moving beyond binary thinking about gender and sexuality is central to what it means to be queer, pansexual, fluid, or to even be "anti-identity." Shae says queer means to her, "in its simplest form, I guess I would say, just saying 'fuck you' to binaries. You know? Just basically 'fuck you' to everything." As that sweeping statement suggests, "queer" also connotes a political commitment. Om calls hirself queer "because I am also, you know, anti-oppression, anti-establishment, anti-racism, anti-sexism." Phoenix says that queerness "definitely involves, like, my political identity." Om started using queer "when I understood better the political implications of it." Elena, a queer Puerto Rican/Salvadorean, says, "I like to think about it as like very political, . . . I would just say it's, like, very all-encompassing as well." A Chicana, Amaya, considers queer a "political statement." She loves telling people she is queer because it shocks them and is "a really nice way of taking something that was once used against me . . . The term 'queer' has given me a lot of power."

As this suggests, the umbrella sense of queer can be a very unifying one, making clear how powerful it is as a collective identity. As Om says, "It's collective. It's including everyone, like, with their own personal identities in a larger group." Another white student, Amelia, makes a similar point when she says that "it's easier to identify with the community if there's one, like, singular identification."

"Queer," as an umbrella term, then, encompasses a range of identities, some more fixed and some more fluid. The students who call themselves queer, pansexual, fluid, or who reject an identity do so to signal their expansive desires, shifting and fluid identities, and as a political move beyond binary genders and sexualities. Our analysis reveals that both their activist and academic experiences at the university play an important role in the process of learning to be queer.

Learning to be queer

As Omara's, Aldara's, and Tee's stories makes clear, both coursework and the impact of the vibrant queer community on campus facilitate the move to fluid sexual and gender identities. Whether students are already out or experience same-sex desire for the first time in college, the impact of classes and queer groups is evident. Melissa refers to Lisa Diamond's 2008 book, *Sexual Fluidity*, in explaining that she has sex only with girls and wants to have sex only with girls but identifies as fluid rather than lesbian because she is attracted to guys and has dated them and made out with them but would not have sex with them or want to be in a relationship. Regina, a white queer student, says simply, "When I got to college I learned about the term 'queer' and its meaning to incorporate all sexualities that are not heterosexual." She stopped calling herself a lesbian and adopted "queer." Likewise, Tee says that "through many feminist studies classes" ze realized that "'lesbian' obviously didn't work anymore" so "I'm sticking with 'queer.'" Emilia, like so many others, dated her use of the term "queer" to her first year of college: "I think I was just getting more involved in the queer community and I was learning more about what it meant—what it means—to be queer." Brittany says "I've always been bisexual queer" but explains that at a recent queer student conference "I think I just started letting go of the identity bisexual" and started saying "I'm queer." Elena sometimes uses queer interchangeably with bisexual because "at least here people seem to be more positive when I say queer." She describes going to a first big queer meeting and "they're like, 'Well, we use queer on this campus 'cause it's a political term.'"

As we can see in Tee's story, students learned how to describe their gender identities as well as their sexual identities through involvement in the queer community and language learned in feminist and queer studies courses. Tee describes having always been gender non-conforming but having "reached a place where I feel pretty confident about who I am" because "I'm more educated, or at least more educated in feminist and queer theory," which allowed hir to learn "more about myself." The potential of "queer" to allow for multiple gender identities made it a preferred sexual identity for genderqueer students as well. Om suggested that queer was the most appropriate sexual identity for hir "because the word 'queer' doesn't have any gender connotation to it." For students like Om, who suggested that "my sexuality sort of led me to queer theory and feminism," theories and concepts learned in coursework provided them with new ways of describing their own experiences in more representative ways. Kacy, who is black and genderqueer, described learning in college that gender identity was different from sexual identity and subsequently questioning whether or not they were transgender. Through conversations with other queer students, Kacy reports that "I think I'm more questioning my gender identity . . . I feel more ok with it."

Some had never heard the term "queer" before, while for others it had only a negative association. Mackenzie, a white lesbian, had a hard time with the word "'cause where I come from the word 'queer' wasn't used positively." Vanessa also says that "Where I come from queer is like a horrible insult." Om "never considered it before coming to UCSB because I really only knew the, you know, negative connotations of it." At Queerpalooza, Vanessa reported, "they kept saying queer queer queer-this . . . I was, like, bombarded with it" and "slowly I got used to it." Madison, a Taiwanese American bisexual, had "never heard the word 'queer' until I came to college." It was at a meeting of Queer Asian Pacific Islanders (QAPI) that her friends "were all laughing at me and explaining it to me afterwards."

Sometimes students feel pressure to adopt the identity queer, either from individuals or from the community in general. Sandra, a white bisexual student, tells of the woman with whom she had her first sexual relationship announcing "'So you're queer now. You know that right? No more exercising your heterosexual privilege. You're queer. You need to stick with us and you need to take a political stance.'" Alexandra, the bisexual daughter of Russian immigrants who was co-chair of the Queer Student Union, says sometimes she had to use the label "queer" because "part of your duty is to be a really public face." Jessica called herself bisexual and queer "because I identified strongly with the Queer Student Union and the umbrella term . . . for the people that go to the school and talk about this in academia and stuff." The influence of theory is evident through a student-led seminar, "The Judith Butler Experience," that delved deeply into gender and queer theory. The undergraduates who participated in the informal course identified strongly as queer and tended to police the use of other sexual identities such as lesbian, gay, and bisexual.

Like Aldara, who calls "queer" a privileged term, students define it as a word for educated people, not necessarily appropriate for their families and friends back home, especially in communities of color or strongly Christian white families. Kacy explains that queer "encompasses every single type of identity but it is geared for the more educated individuals, "cause if you are educated you get to know what it means." They say that "back home if I'm talking with my friends who aren't college educated and who aren't gay they wouldn't understand what I mean by queer." Emma makes the same point, saying "I know a lot of people not in college aren't comfortable with 'queer.'" Esthela, who is from Shanghai, calls herself queer but also would not use the term at home because people wouldn't know it "and I don't wanna be, like, 'Oh, I learned it from somewhere else.'" Sara references her economically disadvantaged Mexican American background in saying that "'queer' was way more predominant here than it was at home" in San Bernardino county.

As a result, students also adopt different identities in different contexts. Esthela explains that "officially I'll say I just identify as queer, but once it came to close friends I would say, maybe, lesbian," suggesting how valorized the identity queer is among activist students. White queer Abigail says that how she identifies depends "on who I'm talking to, depending on, like, what's easiest I guess. I feel like queer is mostly how I identify but, like, I can fall into lesbian, bi, pan, queer, whatever." Likewise Gesa, from Germany, identifies as both queer and lesbian, using terms in both English and German depending "on what I think the other person understands and thinks when I say certain things, when I use certain terms."

For all these students, coming to the university and encountering or seeking out the queer community, queer organizations, and classes on queer topics helped to verify their desires and behaviors and often shifted their individual identities to accord more closely with the collective identity of "queer."

Conclusion

Women students at the University of California, Santa Barbara, call themselves "queer" or "pansexual" or "fluid" as both individual and collective identities that connote expansive desire, including for transgender and genderqueer people, shifting and fluid identities, and a political commitment to non-binary genders and sexualities. They may come to campus with non-heterosexual desires, experiences, and identities, but they tend to encounter the concept of queer through activist organizations, coursework in queer studies, and other queer students. Here we see Giddens' double hermeneutic at work. The concept of sexual fluidity is based on academic research on queer individuals and communities; and, in turn, queer scholarship, coursework on sexuality and gender, and queer campus organizations influence students to embrace fluid desires, behaviors, and identities. We do not mean to imply that the students we studied are blindly accepting the identity labels advocated by queer activists and theorists. Elsewhere, we have argued that the acceptability of same-sex sexual behavior in the college hookup scene, specifically women kissing and making out with other women and threesomes, provides opportunities for women to explore fluid sexual identities (Rupp et al 2014). The fact that so many women students reported that a whole host of sexual identity labels—whether queer, gay, lesbian, or bisexual—just do not feel right shows that there is individual agency at work in the process of forming and embracing sexual identities. Other scholars have pointed out the close connection between the anti-identity and anti-essential politics of queer activists and academic queer theory, in part because most of the early proponents of queer theory were themselves activists (Eleftheriadis 2014). Our analysis here suggests that the impact of queer theory may, in fact, be more significant than has been recognized because it offers up a collective identity that is being embraced by student and other activist groups. We find that the increasingly complex relationship among women students' individual sexual desires, behavior, and identities and their willingness to claim fluid identity labels is often the result of commitment to the queer community and to the tenets of queer academic research, all of which allows them to learn to be queer on campus.

References

Armstrong, Elizabeth A., Paula England, and Alison C.K. Fogarty. 2012. "Accounting for Women's Orgasm and Sexual Enjoyment in College Hookups and Relationships." *American Sociological Review* 77: 435–62.

Butler, Judith. 1990. *Gender Trouble: Feminism and the Subversion of Identity*. New York: Routledge.

Carrera, Maria Victoria, Renée De Palma, and Maria Lameiras. 2012. "Sex/Gender Identity: Moving beyond Fixed and 'Natural' Categories." *Sexualities* 15: 995–1016.

Diamond, Lisa. 2008. *Sexual Fluidity: Understanding Women's Love and Desire*. Cambridge, MA: Harvard University Press.

Eleftheriadis, Konstantinos. 2014. "Transnational Gender and Sexual Politics in Europe: Queer Festivals and their Counterpublics." Dissertation, European University Institute.

Giddens, Anthony. 1987. *Social Theory and Modern Sociology*. Cambridge: Polity Press.

Golden, Carla. 2006. "What's in a Name? Sexual Self-identification among Women." In *The Lives of Lesbians, Gays, and Bisexuals: Children to Adults*, edited by R.C. Savin-Williams and K.M. Cohen. Fort Worth, TX: Harcourt Brace.

Irving, John. 2012. *In One Person: A Novel*. NY: Simon & Schuster.

Rupp, Leila J. and Verta Taylor. 2013. "Queer girls on campus: New Intimacies and Sexual Identities." *Intimacies: A New World of Relational Life*, edited by Patricia Clough, Alan Frank, and Steven Seidman. New York: Routledge.

Rupp, Leila J., Verta Taylor, Shiri Regev-Messalem, Alison Fogarty, and Paula England. 2014. "Queer Women in the Hookup Scene: Beyond the Closet?" *Gender & Society* 28: 212–35.

Taylor, Verta and Nancy E. Whittier. 1992. "Collective Identity in Social Movement Communities: Lesbian Feminist Mobilization." In *Frontiers in Social Movement Theory*, edited by Aldon D. Morris and Carol McClurg Mueller. New Haven: Yale University Press.

chapter 24

The bisexual menace revisited

Or, shaking up social categories is hard to do

Kristin G. Esterberg

What is bisexuality? Is it an identity that a person holds, something one *is*? Is it a behavior, something one *does*? Is it stable? Or does it shift and float and change? Is bisexuality distinct from heterosexuality and homosexuality? Is it a little bit of both, or neither? Does bisexuality have the potential to end sexual categories altogether, or does it constitute a new, third category?

In the early part of the twenty-first century in America, bisexuality seemed to be both everywhere and nowhere. Popular magazines like *Newsweek* and *Essence* proclaimed that bisexuality is "coming out" and "out of the closet," and movies like *Kissing Jessica Stein* increasingly experimented with bisexual flirtation. At least in some quarters and on some college campuses, bisexuality seemed highly visible, chic. Yet at the same time many bisexuals themselves argued that they were almost completely invisible – socially erased. While to some commentators and social critics the "bisexual menace" might seem to be knocking at society's door, bisexual invisibility may be far more common.

Talk about bisexuality abounds. Bisexuality is seen by some as the "natural" state of sexuality – what everyone would "naturally" be before society has its way with you. Yet others argue that bisexuality doesn't exist. Bisexuals are "really" straight or gay or something else – or would be, if society hadn't had its way with them. In popular discourse, bisexuals are often seen as a menace. Called "vectors of disease," bisexuals are blamed for bringing AIDS and sexually transmitted diseases to "innocent" wives and children, and as polluting the "purity" of the lesbian community. Bisexual desire is seen as raging out of control, as bisexuals are portrayed as sexual swingers having multiple, simultaneous erotic relationships with "anything that moves" (as the title of one bisexual journal ironically put it). Bisexual sex is inevitably seen as group sex – a tangle of sweaty, unidentified body parts engaged in multiple perverse acts. And bisexuals are seen as hopelessly confused: fence-sitters, unable to make up their minds about what they "really" are.

At the same time, in at least a few quarters, bisexuals are lauded as post-modern, chic, and truly queer. In an historical moment in which traditional concepts of identity are increasingly being challenged, bisexuality seems to fit the bill. Unlike more vanilla monosexuals – lesbians, gay men, straights – bisexuals have the ability to "mess with" dualistic thinking about sexual identity. Because bisexuality does not fit neatly into the dominant categories – neither homosexual nor heterosexual, but both/and – bisexuality is sometimes seen as the sexual category to smash all sexual categories.

A series of oppositions

In popular discourse, bisexuality has primarily been defined as a series of oppositions. In one formulation, bisexuals and transgenders are seen on one side, the "queer" side, versus gay men and lesbians on the others. In this version, lesbians and gay men are seen as more conventional – monogamous, more like straights. The move toward same-sex marriage and civil unions for same-sex partners in Massachusetts and other states serves to highlight this divide. Same-sex desire as practiced by married same-sex partners is socially conventional; bisexual desire is seen as perverse. Sometimes this perversity is lauded, as when queer activists seek to deconstruct social labels, seeing them as oppressive and a source of social control. At other times this queerness is criticized as perverted and wrong – not only by right-wing activists but also by gay men and lesbians themselves.

Another scenario, promoted at least at times by the mainstream lesbian and gay movement and by many bisexuals themselves, sees lesbians, gay men, and bisexuals as having many interests in common. In this formulation, bisexuals are presumed to share a common base of oppression with lesbians and gay men. Bisexuals are lumped together with lesbians and gay men (lesbigays), who must unite against heterosexist oppression. Because all three desire – at least potentially, in the case of bisexuals – those of the same sex, and because this desire is socially stigmatized and legislated, the common interests of lesbians, gays, and bisexuals in ending oppression are emphasized over potential sources of difference.

In yet another scenario, lesbians are counterposed with all of those who "love men." From the vantage point of lesbian feminism, bisexuals are seen as trading on heterosexual privilege and selling out the lesbian movement. In a patriarchal and sex-obsessed world, lesbians alone (and primarily feminist lesbians) are seen as standing firm against patriarchy.

Finally, in an opposition that is far more often put forward by bisexual people themselves than by others, monosexuals – lesbians, gays, and straights – are counterposed to bisexuals. Here, monosexuals are seen as rigid, overly focused on gender as a basis for relationship, while bisexuals are seen as truly flexible and able to overcome differences based on gender.

Kristin G. Esterberg

Why are these oppositions important? First, they reflect deeply held assumptions about the dualistic nature of Western thought. In modern Western thought, the individual, who is presumed to have something called a self, reigns supreme. Prior to the mid-to-late nineteenth century, individuals simply did not *have* something called a sexual identity. Some time around the latter part of the nineteenth century, the terms homosexual and heterosexual entered into common parlance in Europe and the United States, and by the end of the twentieth century became the predominant way in which sexual desire was organized. By the late twentieth century, a Western man who experienced desire for men could hardly resist being labeled homosexual.

In addition, we tend to see things in terms of binaries: male/female, hetero/homo, black/white, dominant/subordinate. Because of the binary structure of Western thought, we tend not to recognize intermediate categories like bisexuality or transgenderism. When we do, we tend to interpret them in terms of the dominant category (Ault 1996). Thus, bisexuality is often treated in conjunction with homosexuality or lesbianism and rarely considered in its own regard.

These oppositions also reflect people's fears about bisexuality. For lesbians, gays, and straights, whose understandings of themselves are rooted in a clear separation of homosexual and heterosexual, male and female, bisexuality can raise powerful fears. For straights, bisexuality raises the dangerous specter of the pleasures of same-sex desire. For lesbians and gays, bisexuality raises the possibility of having to rethink one's own sexuality, acceptance of which is often hard-won. Especially for those who are immersed in a lesbian or gay community and politics, the loss of identity can be devastating.

These oppositions, too, tell us about shifting political alignments. Debates about the nature of bisexuality reflect political questions as much as empirical ones. They force lesbians and gays to revisit the question of political strategy. Contemporary lesbian and gay organizing reflects what some have called an "ethnic" model of identity. According to this model, lesbians and gays are an identifiable, relatively "fixed" percentage of the population and, like other "minority" groups, in need of civil rights protection (Duggan and Hunter 1995). The recent task of the lesbian and gay movement has been to develop a community and politics along ethnic community lines, with relatively firm boundaries between members and nonmembers, and to press for civil rights – especially in the areas of marriage and employment discrimination. Bisexuality poses a challenge to this model. If sexual identities are neither rigid nor fixed, then what are the implications for a unified lesbian and gay community?

Race, culture, bisexuality

The debates about bisexuality also highlight that sexual categories are essentially social constructions and, especially in the case of bisexuality, fuzzily constructed ones at that. The emphasis on identity in modern Western culture raises particular questions in thinking about race, culture, and bisexuality. Different societies in different time periods clearly organize sexuality differently. When we look cross-culturally, we find ample evidence of what we might call bisexual behavior. Yet we find relatively few examples of bisexual identity. So, for example, anthropologist Gilbert Herdt has extensively documented same-sex behaviors among the Sambia of Papua New Guinea (1997). In this society, all adolescent males experience a period of ritual same-sex expression with an older male. As adults, the males sexually initiate adolescent boys into adulthood, and most adult males also enter into sexual relationships with women. Are all Sambian men bisexual? Not according to the concepts of their culture. What does it mean to use such a term outside of its cultural context?

Similarly, many sociologists and anthropologists have documented what some have called a Latin model of homosexuality (or sometimes Latin bisexuality). In many Latin American societies, men may engage in sexual behavior with both men and women. As long as the men play an active ("insertive") role, they are not considered homosexual or bisexual. They are, simply, "normal" men. Yet the men who play a "passive" role are seen as homosexual – even if they also engage in sexual behavior with women. In this model, males who engage in sexual activity with other men are not considered homosexual, as long as they otherwise play culturally approved masculine roles. On strictly behavioral grounds, one might call those who play an "active" role bisexual, for they are often married or have relationships with women. But again, no word for bisexuality exists in this socially structured form of sexuality.

In the contemporary United States, African-American and Latino men who engage in sexual relationships with other men may be more likely than European American men to also maintain relationships with women. They may be less likely to think of themselves as gay or bisexual or to participate in a gay men's community. There are a number of reasons why this may be so. Racism within white gay men's communities is surely one reason. At the same time, in a racist society men of color may need and desire to retain connections to their families of origin and to their racial/ethnic communities. These kinds of connections are crucial for the survival of people of color.

The HIV/AIDS epidemic highlighted the gap between identity and behavior for many men of color, as men who had never identified themselves as gay or bisexual were stricken by the disease. Men who were "in the life" may or may not have disclosed their romantic and sexual relationships with men to others. Yet most rejected the label "gay" or "bisexual" as having far more to do with whites. Does this make the men bisexual, even if they do not think of themselves that way?

Class, too, is surely important. Poor and marginalized men and women are far more likely to be imprisoned or to engage in prostitution than the affluent and whites. The prison experience brings with it opportunities for same-sex sexual behavior for both women and men (something some social scientists have called "situational" bisexuality or "secondary" bisexuality). Yet prisoners and male prostitutes may very well not think of themselves as bisexual. Again, what does it mean to call someone bisexual who does not think of him or herself in that way? On the other hand, what does it mean to think of bisexuality as mainly a "white" phenomenon?

Bisexual identities

Debates around race, culture, and sexuality inevitably lead us to question what it means to be bisexual. If we define bisexuality as simply behavior – sexual desire or activity with both men and women – then we miss something important. Is a lesbian who occasionally sleeps with men "really" bisexual even if she continues to think of herself as lesbian? Is a married man who occasionally fucks men really bisexual, even if he thinks of himself as straight? What about a gay man and a lesbian who have sex with each other on occasion? Is theirs queer sex? Bisexual sex? Straight sex? What about virtual sex? If a woman exchanges sexual email with someone she thinks is female but is "really" male and writing from a female persona, is that straight sex? For whom? What is sex, anyway? What particular combination of body parts and desires have to come together in order for something to be called sex?

It's far more fruitful to think about the question of identities and to acknowledge fully the slippages between identities, desires, and behaviors. How do people come to think of themselves as bisexual? What does bisexuality mean to the people who think of themselves in that way? How might these change over time? Instead of seeing bisexuality as indelibly rooted in behavior, it is important to think about how individuals come to understand themselves as bisexual – and to consider how individuals reshape those understandings over time and context. Just because one is bisexual today, one might not be tomorrow.

When we shift to a focus of identity, we can begin to challenge the notion that sexual identities are fixed, essential, or unchanging. In my earlier research (Esterberg 1997), for example, I examined the identity accounts, or stories, that bisexual women in a Northeast community in the United States used to understand their experiences. Rather than seeing identities as fixed or essential parts of the person, I argued that identity accounts arise within the particular communities and social settings in which women (or, for that matter, men) find themselves. As women make sense of their desires, attractions, and relationships, they come to see themselves in culturally available terms. As a bisexual movement developed through the 1980s and the 1990s, women who experienced desire for both men and women could increasingly think of themselves as bisexual. This was a social category that simply didn't exist in other cultural times and places.

In the particular community I studied, I identified four dominant accounts of bisexual experience. Some of the women I interviewed thought of themselves as "not quite heterosexual." Their bisexuality consisted of an openness to experiences with women, even though they had primarily had erotic and romantic relationships with men. Others saw themselves as openly, sometimes proudly bisexual. These women tended to be active in creating a politicized bisexual presence within the lesbian/gay community. A third account was expressed by women who came to see bisexuality from the vantage point of lesbian feminism. These women had previously thought of themselves as lesbian; in coming to understand their desire for men, they came to think of themselves as bisexual. A final group of women rejected the impulse to label their identity at all, preferring to see their sexuality as fluid, in the moment. Labels – even seemingly expansive ones like bisexuality – felt restrictive.

Bisexuality, monogamy, and choice

If bisexuality is socially constructed, what does this say about the question of choice? Although heterosexuals, lesbians, and gay men also have the capacity to exercise choice in acting on their sexual desires, the question of choice retains greater significance for bisexuals. Even if individuals do not necessarily choose *desire*, a position many formerly lesbian bisexuals claim, they can certainly choose to act on it or not. They can choose whether to embrace the identity or not. This is not all that much different from others. Married couples, after all, typically don't have sex with all those whom they might like to (at least not if they wish to remain married). But the questions of choice and monogamy are inflected differently for bisexuals.

Social conservatives seize upon the question of choice and argue that a same-sex choice is a sinful one (or, in more secular terms, an antisocial one). Issues of choice are tricky among the left as well, and especially among feminist lesbians. As a political ideology, lesbian feminism valorized women's political, social, and economic relationships with other women. Lesbian feminism held out the possibility to heterosexual women that they, too, could become lesbian and move out from under men's patriarchal domination. In this way, bisexuality became perceived as a threat to lesbian visibility and solidarity, and bisexual women were seen as traitors. In the face of the mainstream lesbian/gay movement, too, which has built a political strategy on the claim that sexuality is biologically based, immutable, and fixed, bisexuals raise the possibility that sexual orientation is not so fixed after all, a position that many in the lesbian and gay movement see as undercutting their political position.

By its very nature, bisexuality also raises the issue of monogamy. Although, of course, there need be no necessary relationship between the potential for relationships with both sexes and actually having them, this distinction is not often made. Some critics go so far as to argue that bisexual monogamy is, by definition, impossible. In my earlier study, one interviewee argued that one's a lesbian if one's involved with a woman, straight if involved with a man. One could only be bisexual, in this schema, if one were involved with both a man and a woman at the same time.

Kenji Yoshino (2000) argues that gays and straights alike have an interest in defining themselves in opposition to bisexuals through the institution of monogamy. First, monogamy is a societal norm. And although straights, with their access to legal marriage, have perhaps greater investment in that norm than gays and lesbians do, monogamy has in recent years become a social norm among many American lesbians and gay men – especially as gay marriage and civil partnerships become legal in a few states. Some gays, Yoshino argues, distinctly wish to "retire" societal stereotypes of gay promiscuity.

Bi politics, bi movements

Where does this leave us, in thinking about bisexuality, visibility, and bisexual action? The 1980s and 1990s saw a flowering of bisexual organizing in the United States, as bisexuals sought to counter their invisibility. This period saw the creation of a number of autonomous organizations, groups, networks, and newsletters. Several path-breaking anthologies were published, and bisexuals – many of them movement-affiliated – appeared on numerous daytime tv talk shows (Gamson 1998).

One strategy bisexual activists used extensively entailed alignment with the lesbian/gay movement, and an attempt to force lesbians and gays to include bisexuals in their organizing. This strategy has been successful, at least to a limited extent,

Kristin G. Esterberg

as many mainstream lesbian/gay activists added the word "bisexual" to their organizations and activities, and others moved to names such as "Spectrum" or "Rainbow Coalition" that at least on the face of it included bisexuals. Still, the inclusion of bisexuals under a lesbigay umbrella is by no means certain.

Others sought to organize under a queer umbrella. The rise of queer politics in the 1990s may have been a more welcome home for those bisexuals who valued the transgressive nature of their sexuality. If queer activists sought to challenge traditional dichotomies of gay/straight, male/female, then bisexual activists fit right in. Queer organizing also represented a more youthful "in your face" style of activism, anathema to some within the more staid lesbian and gay movement. Yet the queer umbrella, while it may have sheltered a diverse group of practices, individuals, and organizations, also functioned as a "cloaking device," serving to render bisexuality invisible (Ault 1996).

Especially within these conservative times, bisexual organizing holds enormous challenges. Despite repeated public "discoveries" of bisexuality, the issue of bisexual invisibility is paramount. In becoming visible, however, bisexuals run the risk of creating a fixed identity. Identities, as queer and post-modern theorists have argued, are inherently limiting and subject individuals to social regulation. Yet they are also at least potentially liberating, by enabling like individuals to mobilize around shared concerns. The attempt to organize around bisexual identity thus poses the danger of fixing boundaries and limiting possibilities at the same time as it creates possibilities for women and men to articulate their desires and create a public space for them.

Learning from some of lesbian feminism's mistakes, bisexual organizers have sought to remain open about inclusion and the nature of bisexual identity. As a group that has been most subject to erasure, bisexual organizers are sensitive to the needs for individuals to define themselves. But can bisexual organizing ultimately avoid an ethnic model of social movement organizing? That remains to be seen. And over the last few years, as the nation moves further to the right, there seems to have been relatively little bisexual organizing.

Bye-bye binary? The missing potential of bisexualities

What are the chances that sexual identities as we know them today will actually disappear? Will bisexuality usher in an era of unlabeled sexuality? Are we at the brink of just such a queer moment, in which the hetero/homo divide collapses into an unlabeled ambisexuality, in which gender plays no more role in sexual choices than eye color or the way someone walks or cuts their hair? The existence of those who prefer not to take an identity, who prefer to remain unlabeled, might hint at such a possibility.

More than ever, however, I remain skeptical. We are deeply mired in a period of prolonged conservatism, in which play around gender boundaries seems increasingly anachronistic. Queer organizing seems distinctly a thing of the past, and there seems little social movement organizing that celebrates anything queer or transgressive. The phrase "queer nation" itself sounds hopelessly last century, and I see little on the horizon to take its place. The most prominent lesbian/gay social movement organizing seems focused on the issue of marriage and civil unions – an issue that seems, at least on its face, designed to solidify the differences between bisexuals and others.

If there's any hope for change in our thinking about bisexuality, it may come from the greater visibility of transgendered individuals and activists. Because their bodily existence shakes up the categories of male and female, masculine and feminine, transgender men and women may shake up sexual identities as well. Yet even here I remain skeptical. The tenacity with which heterosexuals hold onto heterosexual privilege and the deeply institutionalized nature of heterosexual life, on the one hand, combined with the deep investments that lesbians and gay men have made in their sexual identities and movements, on the other, lead me to believe that the collapse of binary thinking is not imminently on the horizon. Perhaps the best we can hope for is the realization that sexuality is far more complex than previously recognized. That, by itself, would be no small thing.

References

Ault, Amber. 1996. "Ambiguous Identity in an Unambiguous Sex/Gender Structure: The Case of Bisexual Women", *Sociological Quarterly* 20(3): 107–22.

Duggan, Lisa and Nan D. Hunter (eds). 1995. *Sex Wars: Essays in Sexual Dissent and American Politics*. New York: Routledge.

Esterberg, Kristin. 1997. *Lesbian and Bisexual Identities: Constructing Communities, Constructing Selves*. Philadelphia, PA: Temple University Press.

Gamson, Joshua. 1998. *Freaks Talk Back*. Chicago, IL: University of Chicago Press.

Herdt, Gilbert. 1997. *Same Sex, Different Cultures*. Boulder, CO: Westview Press.

Yoshino, Kenji. 2000. "The Epistemic Contract of Bisexual Erasure", *Stanford Law Review* 52(2): 353–461.

Kristin G. Esterberg

chapter 25

Beyond bi

Sexual fluidity, identity, and the post-bisexual revolution

April Callis

Ice identifies his sexuality as either gay or bicurious, but hopes that I might be able to tell him what he "really is." Lady identifies as trisexual, or as open, or as bisexual – depending on who is asking. Michaels tells me that he identifies as queer, but then adds that the more correct label might be "straight queer." Fruit identifies as pansexual, but tells me that no one understand what that means. Finally, Sydney refuses to take any sexual identity label at all, and instead makes a dismissive noise when asked.

While conducting pilot research in 2006, I spent several months interviewing undergraduate students involved in Purdue University's LGBTQ community. The detail that stuck out to me most about these interviews was the prevalence and variety of non-binary sexualities – self-identities that were neither gay nor straight. While some students I interviewed labeled themselves as bisexual, several labeled themselves as queer, pansexual, or refused to take sexual labels at all. To these people sexuality was not a binary structure, but rather a fluid, multi-faceted and individual enterprise that could change within a lifetime (or within a week), and could never totally be pinned down by any label.

My curiosity about non-binary sexualities such as these led me to undertake an ethnographic research project in Lexington, Kentucky. Through 80 interviews, archival research, and seventeen months of participant observations between 2008 and 2010, I analyzed how sexual identity was articulated by individuals claiming a variety of identities. Specifically, I looked at how identities that were neither gay nor straight (such as bisexual, pansexual, and queer) were talked and written about. I looked at various aspects of this issue – for example, what discourses (media, religious, scientific) participants called on when discussing these sexualities, as well as how representations of these non-binary sexualities had changed in local publications since the 1970s. This chapter will focus on just one aspect of my larger research project: non-binary self-identities other than bisexual.

Of the 80 individuals interviewed for this project, 37 (or 46%) identified in some way that was neither gay nor straight. However, only five of those were using "bisexual" as their primary self-identities at the time they were interviewed. The remaining 32 individuals utilized a combination of 21 different terms and phrases to describe their sexual identities. This chapter touches on just a few of these identities, explaining what they meant to the individuals that used them. I will then discuss how two issues, bisexual stigma and the increase in trans awareness and gender fluidity, have impacted how individuals label sexual attraction.

A researcher's dilemma: identifying identities

The 80 participants for this project were located through listservs and flyers hung at coffee shops, universities, bars, bookstores, and churches in Lexington. These materials explained that I was looking for participants that were willing to discuss sexual identity, both their own and in general. Interviews would be confidential, and I would only know interviewers by their chosen pseudonyms. I assumed that I would get responses from individuals labeling with a variety of different sexual identities, which is what I was hoping for. This would allow me to compare understandings of sexuality by gays and straights to individuals who labeled themselves in other ways.

However, even I was not prepared for the variety of answers I received when I asked participants how they labeled their sexual identities. While some individuals had a simple, single-word answer, many others self-identified using a phrase, a paragraph, or a five-minute story. Some participants were unable to put just one label on their identity, and gave elaborate descriptions of how they identified to their parents versus their spouses versus the people with whom they worked. Other individuals refused to label their sexuality at all, and expounded on why labels could never encapsulate their identity. Two women drew pictures of their sexuality: one was a bell curve, the other an x and y axis with a circle sketched onto it. More than one participant described their sexual behaviors and fantasies and then asked how I would define their identities, assuming that I would be able to tell them what they "really" were.

For the sake of comparative research, I decided to divide participants into two categories: "binary" versus "non-binary," based on their self-described sexual identities. Individuals that labeled as gay, lesbian, or straight would be categorized as binary, while everyone else would be non-binary – simple enough. I planned on prioritizing sexual self-identity, rather than sexual behavior and/or desire. I used Valentine's (2007) study as a model, where he explores the usefulness of the category "transgender" in light of the fact that many of the MtF individuals that he interviewed did not identify with this term. Valentine found that using the category in a situated, nuanced fashion allowed social recognition and political activism for gender-variant individuals while still allowing space for personal identification. Likewise, I planned to use the categories "binary" and "non-binary" to group a diverse set of participants without stripping them of their chosen identity labels.

However, I quickly found that even these two broad categories were not fluid enough to encapsulate the responses I was receiving. In some cases, participants used sexual identity labels that contrasted with their sexual behaviors. For example, Scott Red considered himself straight, but had occasional anonymous sex with men that he met online. Despite this sexual behavior, Scott only referred to himself as straight during our interview. I considered placing Scott Red into the category of non-binary, based on his sexual contact with both men and women. However, to identify him in this way missed the importance of Scott's self-identity as a straight man, even though his performance of straightness went against culturally normative definitions of the term. Therefore, Scott Red and the six other individuals who self-labeled as heterosexual but who admitted sexual behavior and/or desire for same-sex individuals were counted as having binary sexualities. Similarly, the three gay/lesbian self-identified individuals who had opposite-sex sexual experiences after coming out as homosexual were likewise categorized as having binary sexualities. That more than one-third of the individuals who identified their sexualities as binary in fact had fluid desire speaks to the importance of the sexual binary in our culture, as well as to the arbitrariness of sexual classification.

On the other side of this, many of the individuals whom I eventually placed in the non-binary category had identities that were more binary than I had expected. Jenn, who identified as a "lesbian accidentally married to a man" is an excellent example of this. Her identity could be read as homosexual (because she identified primarily as a lesbian), or heterosexual (because she was sexually exclusive with her husband at the time of the interview). However, I placed Jenn in the category of "non-binary," because her self-stated identity of "lesbian accidentally married to a man" was neither straight nor gay.

Finally, what was I to do about individuals who changed their sexual identities after I interviewed them? Because I was in Lexington for two years after I finished interviewing, I occasionally bumped into my research participants at community events. In one case, I found out that a participant who had self-identified as a lesbian at the time of our interview had, a year later, come out as a transman, and now sexually identified as queer. In another case, a woman who was married to a man and uncertain of her sexual identity at the time of our interview had later divorced and come out as lesbian. In these cases, as I did not have longitudinal information on everyone, I chose to use the sexual identities, gender identities, and pronouns that participants had given me at the time of our interviews. Thus, this research is just a snapshot of a single moment in time.

Non-binary/non-sexual

In the last decade, several studies have been conducted on the use of alternative sexual identity labels, with multiple academics noting that their use is steadily increasing. Jacobson and Donatone found that "increasing numbers of queer youths are identifying as bisexual, omnisexual, pansexual, women-loving, man-loving, person-loving, homoflexible, and heteroflexible" while still other youth were refusing to take sexual labels at all (Jacobson and Donatone 2009: 227). Horner found that youth are increasingly using identities such as "queer" and "questioning" (Horner 2007). Russell, Clarke and Clary found that in a survey of 2,560 middle and high school students, twelve percent identified as bisexual, two percent identified as queer, five percent as questioning, and three percent as some other label (Russell et al 2009: 887).

What all of the above studies agreed upon is that non-binary labels (particularly those other than "bisexual) are often used by LGBTQ youth. Non-binary labels have also been linked to gender, with more self-identified women taking these labels than men (Savin-Williams 2005). Of the individuals I interviewed in Lexington, non-binary identities were taken by individuals ages 18 through 63, but were mostly found in individuals in their 20s. Further, self-identified females did outnumber males in taking non-binary identities, with 23 out of the 37 non-binary individuals being biologically female.

Bisexual identities

Of these 37 individuals with non-binary identities, what labels were they using? Surprisingly to me, given its visibility in the media, only five participants used "bisexual" as their primary self-identity at the time of the interview. However, three others used "bisexual" as a secondary self-identity, and two more privately identified as bisexual, but publically identified only as heterosexual (one was out as bisexual only to his lover, while the other was not out to anyone). Twenty other individuals had labeled themselves as bisexual at some point in their lives, though they did not at the time of our interview. Finally, four individuals I interviewed talked at length about how they hated the term bisexual, but thought that it might be the best label for themselves. Thus, though only five people self-identified primarily as bisexual, the term was or had been integral in sexual identification for over forty percent of participants.

Queer identities

Outside of bisexuality, the most popular term that individuals used to describe their non-binary sexualities was "queer." Seven participants identified primarily as queer, with an additional six using queer as one of their multiple self-labels. When asked what queer meant to them, many queer-identified individuals discussed the term as a move away from the gender binary. Scout stated that she identified as queer because "she is attracted to more than one gender," going on to state that while she is mostly a part of the lesbian community, there is "transphobia found in the term lesbian, and also in gay and bisexual," that she wanted no part of. Rosario also defined queer as the potential to be "attracted to any gender," following that with "I've dated men, I've dated women, I've dated trans people, and I would be okay with dating intersex people." This mimics the findings of Peters (2005), who noted that individuals chose the label queer because it was "more inclusive of non-normative gender performances" (106).

The idea of queer as an umbrella, or as a space for fluidity, came up in several of the interviews with queer-identified participants. Lucy stated that she liked queer because "it doesn't necessarily have a definition . . . everyone can make it into what they want." She went on to refer to queer as "an umbrella to shove all of my shit under." Logan began to identify as queer because she felt that "there's enough ambiguity there to let me figure stuff out." Jean preferred queer to her other self-identities (pansexual and bisexual) because "it's hard to stereotype something that is purposely amorphous. Michaels referred to taking the label of queer as "shedding yourself of the things that might restrict you."

This understanding of queer was one that I also encountered during field research. As part of my research I volunteered several times a week at the University of Kentucky's OUTsource, which billed itself as a GLBTQQIA (gay, lesbian, bisexual, transgender, queer, questioning, intersex, and ally/asexual) resource center. In 2010, they kept a book on the back table where students could write their thoughts on sexuality, and/or answer questions from other students. On the fourth page, someone had posed the question "What do you think about the label 'queer'?" One student wrote that s/he loved the term queer, because "it is universal, embracing all people who accept and belong to what some see as aberrations from the 'norm' . . . Queer is open-ended, [and] inviting." In this and many of the above quotes from informants, there is the notion that queer allows for more variation than most sexualities because of its lack of an exact definition.

However, the term "queer" was not embraced by everyone. For many, the use of "queer" as a derogatory term was something that they could not overlook. Many gay-identified informants in particular spoke out about their dislike of the term, sharing stories of being called a "queer," or bullies playing "smear the queer" while they were growing up. A second problem that participants had with the term was the very lack of definition that others applauded. Though this allowed the term to retain fluidity, it also meant that participants had to define it over and over again to each person they talked to. A third issue that individuals had with the term "queer" was its perceived roots in academia. Jason, who identified as both gay and queer, stated that people who identified as queer were often "people with privilege and access to college education." Logan told me that she self-identified as queer, but told people she was a lesbian while working a summer job at a local fast-food restaurant, because queer "felt way too intellectual, too 'oh, she goes to this fancy college.'" Scott Robert, who identified as gay at the time of our interview, wanted to use the label "queer," but struggled both with the pejorative use of the term and that academic nature of it. For these individuals, sexual self-labeling was tied not just to personal desire, but also to issues of class and education.

Pansexualities plus

Beyond bisexual and queer, "pansexual was a term that ten individuals referenced, but which only two people took for themselves. Fruit, the only person to label solely as pansexual, tied this to her desire not to discriminate against any group of people. Jean, who identified as pansexual, bisexual, and queer, felt that pansexual was the most accurate label for herself because it meant that she was open to dating more than two genders. It seems that, for both informants, pansexual was similar to queer in its breakdown of the gender binary, but it had more of a set definition. This was the exact reason that queer-identified Lucy chose not to use it – because pansexual had a definition, it felt confining to her. However, it should be noted that this definition was not one that other participants understood, with several stating in interviews that they found the label confusing. Liz, for example, said that she "couldn't be pansexual because it confuses me." Jean used "bisexual" more often than "pansexual" when talking about her own sexuality because people didn't understand pansexuality. This is a similar finding to Gonel's (2013: 46) study, where many pansexuals felt that they had to use other identity labels to describe themselves because "people don't know what pansexuality is."

There were other terms that a limited number of my participants used to describe their sexual identities. Lady used the term trisexual, meaning that she would "try anything once." She went on to state that to her, this meant that she would "fall in love with people for who they are, not what they are." Sarah identified as heteroflexible, which to her meant that she had pretty much "stayed in the heterosexual realm but that does not mean I haven't ventured out." Other informants also used terms/phrases to denote that they were something slightly different from heterosexual. Three women identified themselves as "mostly heterosexual," while one other said that her sexuality was "on a spectrum between straight and bisexual." However, it is important to note that all of the women with these "slightly different from heterosexual" sexualities would generally identify as heterosexual, or would not correct people who assumed that they were. Thus, they were read by general society as part of the sexual binary.

Five of the individuals that I interviewed stated that they would prefer to have no sexual label, though they all stated that this was nearly, if not entirely, impossible in current U.S. society. Emma identified her sexuality as "I'm with her" (pointing to her girlfriend) and said that it was "the person, not the genitalia," that was important when she was looking for a partner. When asked what her sexual identity was, Sydney made a dismissive noise, and followed that with "any label that there is, is limiting." Kitty said that he did not like labels, but also stated that "to make things easier, I identify as gay. If I didn't feel like I had to, I wouldn't." Opren, who identified primarily as bisexual, stated "the problem with not taking an identity is that people demand an identity. [People want] a cute little label I can give you so you can be on your way." This caused her to continue to label as bisexual, despite her reservations with the term.

Beyond bisexuality

As stated previously, I was initially surprised by the number of individuals in Lexington that were using non-binary labels other than bisexual to describe their desires for more than one sex/gender. Beyond gay and straight, bisexuality is the most visible sexuality in current U.S. culture. Within Lexington, bisexuality began to be regularly mentioned in local publications in the early 1990s, with articles discussing the meaning of bisexuality and the creation of a local bisexual group. In 1992, the "Gay and Lesbian Pride Committee" became the "Gay, Lesbian, and Bisexual Pride Committee" in Lexington. In this same year, the Gay and Lesbian Service Organization newsletter (which has been in publication since the 1970s) began to refer to the "gay and lesbian community" as the "lesbigay community." This was explained in the publication as "lesbian (les) + bisexual (bi) + gay male (gay) = lesbigay" (Smith and Jones 1992).

By the late 1990s, lesbigay had become the initialism GLBT, which was used through 2010 in GLSO News publications.

This movement towards bisexual visibility in Lexington in the 1990s mimicked a similar movement in the U.S. media. In 1991, *L.A. Law* debuted an openly bisexual female character, and *Homicide: Life on the Street* followed in 1998 with a male primary character coming out as bisexual (Tropiano 2002). By the mid-2000s, several Nielsen top-rated prime time shows had bisexual characters, including *Grey's Anatomy* and *House M.D.* As of 2014, there are ten bisexual female characters and two bisexual male characters in scripted primetime television shows (GLAAD 2014).

In contrast, visibility of other non-binary sexualities is limited on both a local and national level. Nationally, there are currently no "pansexual," "trisexual," or "heteroflexible," characters on scripted primetime television. *Torchwood's* Jack Harkness comes the closest, as he is referred to as "omnisexual" in one novelization spin-off from the show (Adams 2009). In Lexington, the initialism "GLBTQQIA" is used at the University of Kentucky's OUTsource, which does include "queer" as an identity possibility. However, labels such as "pansexual" and "queer" have been used very infrequently in local publications, and only in the last decade. I was unable to find any local publication using alternate terms such as "heteroflexible" and "trisexual."

With the visibility of "bisexual," and relative invisibility of other non-binary identities on a local and national level, why were more individuals not using "bisexual" as their self-identities? For research participants in Lexington, this seemed to be the result of two phenomena: the stigma surrounding bisexuality, and the increased awareness of gender fluidity and trans identities.

First, bisexuality in Lexington was a contentious label. Bisexuals were articulated by informants as being hypersexual, as more likely to have sexual diseases, as being more likely to "break your heart," and as being confused about their "true" sexual identities (Callis 2013). Similar stigma has been found in several other studies of bisexuality. Perhaps the most often written about has been the association of bisexuality with deviant and hypersexuality, including the stereotypes that bisexuals are not capable of being monogamous, and are more likely to participate in swinging, threesomes, and sexual experimentation (Rust 2000; Bower et al 2002; Israel and Mohr 2004). The notion that bisexuals are more likely to leave their partners and/or to infect them with an STD is also prevalent in the literature detailing biphobia (Ochs 1996; Zaylia 2009).

Four of the individuals I interviewed told me that they might be "technically bisexual," but that they did not use this as their sexual identity. All four of them were explicit in tying this into the stigma surrounding bisexuality. Jenn, who identified as a "lesbian married to a man," said that if she identified as bisexual, people would assume that she could not be monogamous, or that she was just taking the label to be cool. She said that "people assume that bisexuals want to join in on all of these group things, which I'm not offended by, but I don't want that to be my identity." She went on to state that she felt that telling people she was a married bisexual was the same as saying "I'm married but I want to have sex with everything that moves." She ended by saying "I just can't handle those connotations – I just don't like them. So I prefer not to be bisexual." Sydney, who did not label her sexuality in any particular way, said that she had considered labeling herself as bisexual, but was uncomfortable with the "bad rep" that bisexuals had as people who "will sleep with anyone anytime, and can never be with one person." Ice referred to bisexuality as a "weak label" and bisexuals as "slutty." Cary said that the negativity surrounding bisexuality led to her continuing to self-label as a lesbian even while dating a man, calling bisexuality an "uncomfortable label."

The explicit connection between the stigma surrounding bisexuality and corresponding unwillingness to use "bisexual" as an identity label was articulated in several of my other interviews as well. Queer-identified Rosario had identified as bisexual before coming out as queer. She said that the biggest problem with labeling as bisexual was "being hypersexualized and people assuming that I would sleep with anything, or that I was slutty." Jason, who identified as gay and queer, said that the gay community thought of bisexuals as trying to "have the best of both worlds." He said this led to people having bisexual experiences but not considering themselves bisexual. Scott Red, who identified as straight, agreed with this. He said that he had known "people who have sex with men and women . . . but they would never identify themselves [as bisexual]." He went on to describe the stereotypes of bisexuality as women who would "sleep with anybody . . . just a slut" and said that bisexuality "might as well be called 'threesomes' instead of bisexual, as far as what people are hearing."

A second reason that many of my non-binary identified informants labeled in ways other than bisexual was trans awareness. As mentioned previously, the "lesbigay" community label used in Lexington in the early 1990s shifted to "GLBT" in the late '90s, showing an increase in transgender visibility. Further, the 1999 Fairness Ordinance (Local Ordinance 201–99) that was passed by the Lexington-Fayette Urban County Government provided protection to individuals with non-standard gender identities, as well as homosexual and bisexual persons. The media coverage of this ordinance increased trans awareness in the area. On a national level, several highly rated television shows and movies have included trans characters and storylines since the 1990s, including the Academy Award winning movie *Girls Don't Cry*, and the television shows *Ugly Betty* and *Degrassi*. A 2011 study found that over 66% of Americans were able to define the term "transgender," and felt that they were well-informed about trans issues (PPRI 2011). Thus, on both a local and national level, transgender individuals have become more visible, in turn impacting individuals' usage of the word "bisexual."

Thirteen of the women who used non-binary identity labels for their sexuality were "post-bisexual," meaning that they had at some point in their lives identified as bisexual. Of these thirteen women, nine of them explicitly tied their post-bisexual status to their desire to have a trans-positive identity label. For example, Andy stated that identifying as "queer instead of bisexual [means] I'm more inclusive to people of all genders." Blu used the term "queer" to label herself because "it doesn't exclude trans people." Queer-identified Katie said that:

> more people who might have called themselves bisexual are identifying as queer or pansexual. I think . . . it has to do with transgender people and their acceptance in the queer community. I think there are more people seeing that bisexual doesn't necessarily include attraction to people who are genderqueer or third gender.

The increase in trans awareness had impacted bisexual-identified individuals as well. Opren, was conflicted about her decision to self-label as bisexual because of the duality implied in the term itself, stated that "people don't fit into two categories."

The perceived disconnect between the term "bisexual" and transpeople and gender fluidity has been noted in several studies. Bower et al noted that "bisexual" was rejected by some of their participants because it "provides only two sexual object choice alternatives, either male or female" (2002: 32). Ochs found the same thing in her research, with women rejecting the label "bisexual" because "the 'bi' in 'bisexual' reifies the binary sex/gender system" (2007, p. 79). However, it is interesting to note that in a 2011 online survey of almost 3,500 trans people, 32% identified their sexual orientation as bisexual (Beemyn and Rankin 2011). A 2012 study found that out of 292 online trans participants, 14% currently identified as bisexual, and 51% had identified as bisexual at one point (Kuper et al 2012). Thus, the disconnect that many non-trans individuals felt between bisexual and trans identities was not one that all trans individuals felt.

Conclusion

During the 17 months that I was interviewing and conducting participant observation in Lexington, Kentucky, I encountered a variety of sexual identities. Moving beyond bisexuality, participants with non-binary sexualities self-labeled as trisexual, pansexual, queer, heteroflexible, mostly heterosexual, or chose not to label their sexualities at all. Some individuals labeled with phrases rather than words, such as one man who identified his sexuality as "being tangled in a post-structuralist debate." Other individuals used more than one identity to encapsulate their sexualities, with seventeen individuals using two or more identities regularly.

Two reasons for the plethora of non-binary identity labels being used is the increased visibility of trans and non-binary gender identities, and the stigma surrounding the label "bisexual." When bisexuality is thought to indicate hypersexuality, an increased likelihood of disease, and a decrease in relationship stability, it is no wonder that individuals would choose to label their attractions in other, less contentious manners. This also helps to explain the nine individuals who continued to label as gay or straight after experiencing attractions and sexual behaviors to more than one gender/sex. Further, with the root of bisexual implying "two," individuals with attractions outside of a single gender chose labels that seemed less restricting, such as pansexual (with a root that indicates "all" attraction).

However, there are certainly other possible reasons for this multiplicity of sexual identities. One is the increasing awareness of identities that comes with the internet and social media. Another, related possibility is a cultural shift in sexual discourse. Michel Foucault theorized that the power to label sexuality shifted in the late 1800s from the church to the medical and scientific communities. After the 1860s, science was where individuals increasingly turned to find the "truth" of their sexual urges and actions, and to have these urges labeled (Foucault 1978). However, it seems that now we are shifting away from an authority-based identity model (where we look for answers to our identity from the scientific or medical communities) towards a period of self-identification, often with the help of internet searches and social media. As this shift continues, it is likely that we will see even more letters and terms added to the "alphabet soup" of sexual identities that currently exist.

References

Adams, Guy. 2009. *Torchwood: The House that Jack Built*. London: Random House UK.

Beemyn, Genny and Susan Rankin. 2011. *The Lives of Transgender People*. New York: Columbia University Press.

Bower, Jo, Marcia Gurevich, and Cynthia Mathieson. 2002. "(Con)Tested Identities: Bisexual Women Reorient Sexuality." *Journal of Bisexuality* 2(2/3): 23–52.

Callis, April. 2013. "The Black Sheep of the Pink Flock: Labels, Stigma, and (Bi)Sexual Identity." *Journal of Bisexuality* 13(1): 82–105.

Foucault, Michel. 1978. *The History of Sexuality: Volume One*. New York: Vintage Books.

GLAAD. 2014. *Where We are On TV Report. 2014–2015 Season*. www.glaad.org.

Gonel, Ayisigi Hale. 2013. "Pansexual Identification in Online Communities: Employing a Collaborative Queer Method to Study Pansexuality." *Graduate Journal of Social Science* 10(1): 36–59.

Horner, Evalie. 2007. "Queer Identities and Bisexual Identities: What's the Difference?" In Beth Firestein (ed.), *Becoming Visible: Counseling Bisexuals Across the Lifespan*. New York: Columbia University Press.

Israel, Tania and Jonathan Mohr. 2004. "Attitudes Toward Bisexual Men and Women in the United States." *Journal of Sex Research* 39(4): 264–274.

Jacobson, Brian and Brooke Donatone. 2009. "Homoflexibles, Omnisexuals, and Genderqueers: Group Work with Queer Youth in Cyberspace and Face-to-Face." *Group* 33(3): 223–234.

Kuper, Laura, Robin Nussbaum, and Brian Mustanski. 2012. "Exploring the Diversity of Gender and Sexual Orientation Identities in an Online Sample of Transgender Individuals." *Journal of Sex Research* 49(2/3): 244–254.

Ochs, Robyn. 2007. "What's in a Name? Why Women Embrace or Resist Bisexual Identity." In Beth Firestein (ed.), *Becoming Visible: Counseling Bisexuals Across the Lifespan*. New York: Columbia University Press.

—. 1996. "Biphobia: It Goes More than Two Ways." In Beth Firestein (ed.), *Bisexuality: The Psychology and Politics of an Invisible Minority*. Thousand Oaks: Sage Publications.

Peters, Wendy. 2005. "Queer Identities, Rupturing Identity Categories and Negotiating Meanings of Queer." *Canadian Women's Studies* 24(3/4): 102–107.

Public Religion Research Institute (PPRI). 2011. *Strong Majorities Favor Rights and Legal Protections for Transgender People*. Publicreligion.org.

Russell, Stephen, Thomas Clarke and Justin Clary. 2009. "Are Teens 'Post-Gay'? Contemporary Adolescents' Sexual Identity Labels." *Journal of Youth and Adolescence* 38: 884–890.

Rust, Paula. 2000. "Bisexuality: A Contemporary Paradox for Women." *Journal of Social Issues* 56(2): 205–221.

Savin-Williams, Ritch. 2005. *The New Gay Teenager*. Cambridge: Harvard University Press.

Smith, Kristen and Jeff Jones. 1992. "A Word on Words." *GLSO News*, October: 3.

Tropiano, Stephen. 2002. *The Prime Time Closet: A History of Gays and Lesbians on TV*. New York: Applause Theatre and Cinema Books.

Valentine, David. 2007. *Imagining Transgender: An Ethnography of a Category*. Durham: Duke University Press.

Zaylia, Jessie. 2009. "Toward a newer Theory of Sexuality: Terms, Titles, and the Bitter Taste of Bisexuality." *Journal of Bisexuality* 9(2): 109–123.

chapter 26

Shrinking lesbian culture

Interview with Arlene Stein

Arlene Stein is a professor of sociology and a member of the Women and Gender Studies Program at Rutgers. Her recent publications include "What's the Matter with Newark? Race, Class, Marriage Politics, and the Limits of Queer Liberalism," in M. Bernstein and V. Taylor, eds. *Not the Marrying Kind*, University of Minnesota, 2012; "Therapeutic Politics: An Oxymoron?" *Sociological Forum*, March 2011; and "Sex, Truths, and Audiotape: Anonymity and the Ethics of Exposure in Public Ethnography," *Journal of Contemporary Ethnography*, October 2010.

Your first book, Sex and Sensibility, *traced the decentering of lesbian-feminism in the 1990s. Has there been a parallel decentering of the broader lesbian culture in the last decade or so?*

Lesbian culture in the United States has always operated under the radar to a great extent, and has taken varied forms, depending upon its location in space and time. My earlier work looked at how feminism offered many lesbians of the baby boom a unifying ideology. It was supremely sexy and radical to be a lesbian for a brief moment in the 1970s, at least in the context of the feminist counterculture. To be very honest, I am not sure whether there is such a thing as a "lesbian culture" at all still. In small and medium sized towns, there are friendship networks comprised in part of women who have affectional preferences for other women. In cities and university towns, where there are more opportunities for institution-building, lesbian women may flock to softball leagues, volunteering at battered women's shelters, or parenting groups. These networks tend to be highly segmented by age—and often by class and race as well. Because sexual subcultures, including lesbian subcultures, skew toward the young, I have to admit that I'm no longer the best person to serve as an analyst of them. When I wrote *Sex and Sensibility* as my dissertation at UC Berkeley in the late 1980s, I was myself a young person who was very much a part of the community I was studying. I am now in my 50s, and most of the lesbians I know are also roughly my age, other than those whom I encounter as a professor. My friends and I constitute a subset of the larger lesbian world, to be sure, but we're certainly not on the cutting edge.

How would you characterize the younger generation of Americans who are identifying as lesbian? Has the meaning of being a lesbian changed for these younger women?

My impression is that today many younger women do not identify with the term "lesbian" at all. Many identify as queer, some as gay, some as trans. Many relegate "lesbian" to the past, associating it with a separatist impulse which they don't particularly admire. But others, perhaps a smaller minority, are nostalgic for that movement's radical imagination. A friend of mine, an academic who is more than ten years younger than me, and who appreciates lesbian feminism for its cultural manifestations—women's land, women's music, Tee Corinne drawings of vulvas, and so forth—makes large format photographs of still-existing feminist women's land groups. She and others, some of whom identify with a cultural movement called "deep lez," love the take-no-prisoners attitude of radical lesbian feminism, and they embrace elements of it without a hint of irony! Like other younger lesbian-identified women, particularly those who see themselves as artists, they identify with feminism's DIY spirit, as well as with the more postmodern tendency toward cultural appropriation—and they don't see these impulses as being at odds with one another. As the trans singer/performer Antony Hegarty said in an interview recently, "sincerity is the new punk."

Do you think that current lesbians will continue a tradition of community building that separates lesbians from gay men and straight women?

I'm not sure. I suppose that as long as women who love other women are excluded from certain avenues of respectability and mobility, and as long as they experience homophobia and sexism, there will be a place for lesbians who organize as lesbians, even if they don't necessarily use that term to describe themselves. My sense is that fewer and fewer women, and fewer men for that matter, experience the deep sense of fear and shame that once accompanied the recognition of having same-sex desires. Younger people grow up with images of homosexuality on television. They're rather sanitized, and typically white/middle class/male images, but who would have imagined the day when Ellen DeGeneres, a middle-aged lesbian, could be everyone's favorite girl-next-door talk show host? Things have changed, to be sure. Still, as we know, there are young women (and men) who live in parts of this country, and not only in rural areas or religious communities, who face tremendous challenges in claiming their desires. But at least they have the Internet and can form communities online. That doesn't insure their physical safety, but at least it gives them a lifeline, and the knowledge they are not alone.

Interview with Arlene Stein

There's been a wide-ranging discussion of late on sexual fluidity, especially among women. What's your sense of how this theme is playing out among younger and older lesbians?

Sexual fluidity, and the possibility of bisexuality, has long been an elephant in the room. Lesbian feminists embraced fluidity when it worked to their advantage, when it brought many new women (including previously married housewives!) into the ranks of the lesbian nation. But when fluidity led in the other direction, toward heterosexuality, they castigated those who decided, after spending years as happy little lesbians, to go back to men. My sense is that queer women today are much more keenly aware of the prevalence of sexual fluidity and aren't quite as threatened by bisexuality as my generation was. Seventy years after Kinsey, we are better informed that sexuality is a spectrum. Younger women study this stuff in college, and they read magazine articles about it—and have access to girl-on-girl porn, for better or for worse. Older women? I suppose many of them—us!—have also been changed by the dominant culture's flirtation with bisexuality. But some continue to see bisexuality as a threat.

What has been the impact of the emergence of transgenderism and transexualism on the lesbian community?

It's pretty huge, I think. I'm doing research now on trans men and top surgery. I became interested in this project because it seemed to me that more and more female-assigned individuals who might have been butch lesbians twenty years ago are now bypassing the lesbian label and identifying as trans. Why is this the case? Certainly the decline of the lesbian feminist world and the rise of the trans community has a lot to do with it. These communities create cultural scripts that make it possible for people to construct lives that make sense to them. But there's more to it than that, I think. Trans medical procedures, such as top surgery, are now more widely accessible, and knowledge of them circulates on the Internet. There's a commercial element, to be sure, as surgeons have come to see this as an increasingly attractive, and lucrative, specialty. Unlike some lesbians, who fear what I've called the "incredibly shrinking lesbian world," I don't really have a unified political or emotional response to this development—which makes me want to know more. Right now, I see the rise of trans as rooted in late modern reflexivity and restlessness, and our desire to constantly work on, and become the best possible version of ourselves. Of course the impulse toward self-improvement is very American. But it's also a product of our neoliberal age, in which we all want to become masters of our own little universe, in this case our bodies. While I certainly do not share the opinion of some feminists that female-assigned individuals who wish to live as men are by their very existence antifeminist, I do see transgender as, at least implicitly, a critique of radical social constructionism and a recognition of the materiality of the body.

In your view has a trend towards the "normalization" of homosexuality affected lesbians differently than gay men?

Again, it's difficult to generalize outside of particular class, geographic, racial, and age contexts, but on the whole, gay men continue to enjoy a great deal more power than lesbians in American society, as evidenced by the fact that there are still gay male neighborhoods and commercial spaces, however weakened, and that there are a considerable number of gay men who are economic and political elites. Lesbians still experience gender discrimination. Today, the highest-ranking woman in corporate America is someone who was born a man, who transitioned later in life. Collectively, men simply enjoy greater opportunities than women do in many spheres. At the same time, heteronormativity also structures society, allocating rewards to those who get married and construct families in which the couple is at the center. It's no wonder many of us who can do so are choosing to enter that system, particularly as alternative forms of intimacy may be on more tenuous ground.

chapter 27

Straight men and women

James Joseph Dean

Introduction

From Alfred Kinsey's studies of sexual behavior of men and women in the 1950s to current studies of heterosexual behavior such as *Sex in America: A Definitive Survey*, heterosexuality has been assumed to be a natural occurring phenomenon outside social forces and without historical variance (Kinsey, Pomeroy, and Martin 1948; Kinsey et al. 1953; Michael et al. 1994). Heterosexuality has not been conceptualized as an identity in need of social explanation or empirical investigation. It is just assumed to have always existed, as it is today and since the beginning of the human race. It was not until recent work on the social construction of heterosexuality that a critical stance was taken toward heterosexuality as both an identity and a norm.

This chapter examines the social construction of straight identities. First, I briefly sketch the historical development of straight identity over the last 150 years and then explore the diverse gendered character of straight identities through the narratives of straight men and women. Through these stories, I illustrate how straight masculinities and femininities vary in their practices of projecting a straight identity status in everyday life. I argue that the development of straight identities must be understood in the context of the changing relations and status of gay and lesbian life today. If straight identities are always defined in opposition and relation to homosexual ones, then what are the implications of the increased visibility of gays and lesbians for straights today? How does gay visibility and social integration shape straight men's and women's identities?

A history of heterosexualities

In the early part of the Victorian era, from about 1820 to 1860, heterosexual identity did not exist in the United States among White middle class Americans. Rather, the social organization of sex was based on notions of a true manhood, a true woman-hood and spiritual love. During this time, the major division was whether sex took place within or outside of marriage. Sex was only permissible as an act of procreation in marriage. All non-procreative sex, as well as sex outside of marriage, was culturally prohibited. Marriage was the cornerstone of Victorian life. A proper womanhood, manhood and their progeny – not an erotic heterosexual love based on pleasure or carnal desire – were the organizing principles of intimate life among Victorians in the early part of the 19th century. Basically, sex was an instinct aimed at reproduction, not the basis of an identity (Katz 1996; Seidman 1991).

However, a shift occurred during the latter part of the Victorian era, roughly from 1860 to 1890. During this period, the concepts of heterosexuality and homosexuality emerged out of developments in literary, legal, psychiatric, medical-scientific and other expert and popular knowledge domains. Non-procreative heterosexual sex was still seen as deviant, but now alongside a deviant, though non-procreative homosex-uality. Only heterosexual sex aimed at procreative purposes could claim cultural legit-imacy. Heterosexual sex that was lustful and non-procreative was seen as pathological, as were acts of homosexual sodomy.

Examining the role of heterosexuality in the making of gender boundaries for the middle classes of the late 19th and 20th centuries, historical research shows the important part heterosexual identities played in reinforcing "opposite" gender roles for men and women. The norms and conventions of gender identities were central to the construction of heterosexual identities since gender norms and conventions were and continue to be a primary way straights project their identities in everyday life. The development of a homophobic culture was the result of both gay visibility and straight dominance, which repressed and stigmatized homosexuality as pathology, deviance and gender inversion (Chauncey 1994; D'Emilio and Freedman 1988).

Nineteenth-century society exhibited a clear delineation in the worlds of men and women, where men dominated the public worlds of work and politics and women were confined to the home as wives and mothers. Dramatic changes occurred, how-ever, during this time. The early 20th century witnessed women struggling for civil and political rights, particularly the right to vote, as well as joining the workforce and attending college in large numbers. On the other hand, men were moving from farm and blue-collar occupations to white-collar ones, where the key qualities for white-collar jobs were "feminine" ones, such as the ability to communicate well, to cooperate and to be professionally well-dressed. The gender division was changing. Men were becoming "feminized" through white-collar occupations while women were entering into the previously exclusive bastions of men such as college, the workforce and pol-itics (Chauncey 1994; D'Emilio and Freedman 1988; White 1993).

Historians argue that heterosexuality played a key role in the ideological justifi-cation of a traditional gender order, reinforcing the social differences between men and women as naturally and rightly different. Heterosexuality made gender differ-ences between men and women supposed necessities of nature, justifying gender

James Joseph Dean

divisions through a procreative need. Heterosexual men and women were thus necessarily different in order to reproduce the family, the nation and the human species as a whole.

The importance of these historical accounts in understanding heterosexual identity is in how they demonstrate the socially constructed nature of heterosexuality and its changing formations over the last 150 years. Today, straight identity is defined as sexual attraction towards the other sex. And procreation, while still used as a justification for heterosexual naturalness and dominance, has less and less justificatory resonance, especially since reproductive technologies like artificial insemination make procreative heterosexual relations unnecessary.

Today, a straight identity does not have to include a desire to marry or to have a family. It can simply mean other-sex attraction. In short, heterosexuality, like homosexuality, is increasingly viewed as a distinct identity neither reducible to procreation nor simply the opposite of homosexuality. Straight identities are like other identities, such as being Black or White, a man or woman, and entail their own cultures, patterns and styles. Shifting our attention from the history to the sociology of heterosexuality, I empirically examine the stories of straight men and women, looking at the ways these individuals project a sexual-gender identity in everyday life.

The straight men and women whose voices appear in this essay live in the northeastern region of the US. I interviewed 60 straight men and women in 2005 for the larger study of which this essay is an excerpt. All of the respondents' names are pseudonyms. The larger study is based on interviews with 15 Black men, 15 Black women, 15 White men and 15 White women. These straight individuals range from 20 to 68 years of age. While many of the respondents came from working-class backgrounds, many were middle-class professionals working in a variety of public and private sector jobs. As a group, the White heterosexual individuals were more highly educated than the Black respondents (see Dean 2014 for a fuller description of the study).

Straight masculinities and femininities

In this section on straight masculine and feminine identities, I map a continuum of straight identity practices from hegemonic to counter-hegemonic, showing a range of straight masculinities and femininities that employ homophobic practices in their establishment to those that contest homophobia through their own counter-hegemonic identity practices. By hegemony, I mean practices that claim dominance both through force and consent over subordinate persons and groups. In this section I focus on how straight individuals' homophobic practices stigmatize lesbians and gay men and assert claims to straight privilege.

Homophobic straight masculinities and femininities

As illustrated through the first interviewee, William Russo, hegemonic straight masculinities rely on exaggerated gender conventional practices to project and secure a clear straight masculinity that is often overly sexual and aggressive. Homophobic practices are the central way he projects a straight masculinity. However, even in the case of William, I show that gay visibility is reshaping heterosexual masculinities and in part making homophobic practices less central to some hegemonic masculinities. Paradoxically, William, while viewing men's relations with women as part of sexual domination, expresses some egalitarian views towards gays. Homophobia, then, takes on more complicated forms for those straights who endorse some egalitarian views that respect gays and lesbians but at the same time reinforce homophobic practices to various extents.

William Russo is a 38-year-old White male who grew up in Queens, New York. He joined the Army right after high school, serving two years of active duty and was in the reserves until 1990. He has a shaved head and a solid jock-like build and attitude. William projects a hegemonic straight masculine identity through trying to be dominant over other men and women. In particular, through hyper-competitive alpha male practices of trying to beat other men in any possible activity and in his attempts to win women's sexual attention, he is constantly trying to secure hegemonic masculinity.

William's hegemonic straight masculinity is constructed through a sexual objectification of women that reduces their sexualities to his instrumental needs. For example, at the very beginning of the interview, he tells me, "Honestly, in regard to relationships with women, bisexual is preferred. I like two girls." He explains to me that what he means by his preference for "bisexual" women are women who will have sex with him and another woman at the same time but only have relationships with men. While he says that he has found women in the northeast to be less open to this, he says that the most of the women he dated in Las Vegas, Nevada had less reservations about his preference for group sex. He explains,

> Living in Nevada, most women will do that. It's different than here. People here, my friend said it once where a woman will go out with a woman exclusively and then go out with a guy exclusively. In Nevada, I would go out on a date with my girlfriend, my girlfriend would want a lap dance. We'd go to a strip bar and we'd have a lap dance just so she could hang out with a girl. Sometimes the dancer would go home with you. Of the women I dated in Las Vegas, probably 75% of them were bi, but not bi in the sense that you're thinking where they'll have a relationship with a woman. They have a relationship with men, but they play with girls just because it's the way Vegas is.

William's preference for women who are willing to have group sex with another woman reinforces his straight masculinity as a form of hypersexual virility. In his experience in Las Vegas, these women were basically sexual play toys for straight men like himself.

William's hegemonic heterosexual masculinity, however, entails pernicious behaviors that have become even apparent to him over time, whether it is the danger of competitive aggressiveness leading to potential incarceration or his inability to emotionally relate to women in relationships. For example, while William prides himself on the ability to be competitive with other men, he also realizes the danger in this. He says,

There is that competitive thing there. You either chose to step up to it or you don't. Who's more of a man? That's it, who's more of a man? I'll go A, I'll go C. You'll go D. What? Motherfucker. I just went Z. That's what it's about. Anywhere you go. It's the ability to go from A to Z in less than thirty seconds flat when everyone else is going B. And that's, either you chose to do it or you don't and if you do it every single day of your life, you'll end up in prison. It's something you gotta ratchet yourself down [from]. But it's the ability to do that when you want to.

Since William has never been married and is single and straight, this status creates some tension for him. He knows that others sometimes view being single at his age, 38, as suspect of being gay, and this creates some anxiety for him. In general he maintains clear social and physical boundaries between himself and openly gay individuals to actively project a hypermasculine gender identity that reinforces straight masculinity. As a result of the boundaries he establishes between himself (as straight) and gay men, William generally avoids going into gay bars and fears having a man flirt with him. He openly acknowledges this,

I think as a heterosexual guy you have a phobia of being hit on by another guy. That's largely why we don't like to go, like myself, I don't feel comfortable going to The Pub [a gay bar] for a drink. I've been in there before. My friend Alicia dragged me in there one night. I didn't mind. I was there with two chicks, but I felt anxious the whole time. It was a sense of anxiety for me. But you just deal with it. I managed it. I mean I came out in one piece and I was fine. But it's not like, from my perspective, I wouldn't choose to go in there, sit down and have a beer because I wouldn't feel comfortable.

More interesting, however, is that while William maintains a hegemonic heterosexual masculine identity in many ways, he does not express a rabid homophobia. Gay visibility has contradictory effects. While some straights refuse to associate with gay men and lesbians entirely, others like William integrate them to various extents in their lives. For example, although William feels uncomfortable going to a gay bar, does not associate with gay men and lesbians in general and views bisexuality in women as synonymous for women who are open to group sex with a man and another woman, he does support gay marriage and has a gay male friend that he considers close. William, then, represents straight men who, while exhibiting a hegemonic masculine identity, no longer feel the need to construct their straight masculinity through strong homophobic attitudes. That is, gay visibility at times has the effect of uncoupling hegemonic masculinity and a virulent homophobia. As gays are viewed as increasingly good and normal, straight men negotiate the establishment of straight masculinity through a variety of identity practices that no longer necessarily depend on strong homophobic attitudes for its establishment.

Like William, Nia Gray also employs homophobia and boundaries of social distance to project her straight status and privilege in everyday life. Nia is a 21-year-old Black woman who is a graduate student. She was raised by her working-class Jamaican mother, along with her twin sister and nine other siblings in Brooklyn,

New York. Illustrating the significance of straight identity, Nia views heterosexuality as a central aspect of her self-identity. When I asked why heterosexuality is "very" important to her, she stated,

> Because considering the fact that I want to have children. I want to have the whole ideal family life. I want to get married. I want to have a husband there who will rub my back, my feet and all of that stuff. I think that it will create more of a balance in my life. I think being with a female would create an imbalance.

In this quote we hear how Nia codes heterosexual identity as including marriage, children and the "ideal family life" while viewing homosexual identities as excluding those possibilities.

Although Nia has gay and lesbian acquaintances, she feels that homosexuality is socially and morally inferior to heterosexuality. For example, one of the first individuals to come out to her was a close childhood friend, Lori, who she considered to be like family since they had grown up together since infancy. Nia told me that when Lori came out to her that she let Lori know that she would still be her friend. I asked Nia if she had become more supportive of lesbian and gay people because of that experience. This is how she responded.

NIA: I think it just made me question where I stood as far as that issue was concerned, considering that, OK, this is somebody who's like my sister. Am I so close-minded that I'm just gonna say forget her? Forget all that we've been through? I was like nah, nah, I'm not going to do that. And I just decided that I don't exactly support it, but I tolerate it. I tolerate it.
ME: What's the difference for you between support and tolerate?
NIA: Support, meaning I endorse it. Tolerate is like, OK, I don't like it, but I'm willing to put up with you because you're family or because we've been through so much. I wouldn't cut you out of my life just for that. So like I said, I wouldn't endorse it. I wouldn't be a supporter, like, ya, gay and lesbian rights. They should get married and all that stuff. I wouldn't do that. No.

However, the issue of how Nia "successfully" projects a heterosexual identity in everyday life is an anxious topic for her. Since she says that she cannot tell if a woman is a lesbian unless the woman is extremely stereotypical, Nia says that the only way another individual would know that she is heterosexual would be through her verbally telling them or through talking about men. Nia is a petite and attractive young Black woman, who by her own admission prefers to dress casually in jeans and tennis shoes and to forgo wearing skirts, high heels or cosmetics. Nia has also had several different women express sexual interest in her. And as a result, her main way of projecting her heterosexuality is through drawing boundaries between straights and gays in her social circles. Consequently, she has a strictly straight group of other Black friends. Furthermore, by condoning her friends' homophobic jokes, she reinforces her status as straight.

For example, she and her friends joke that one of their male friends, Toby, is gay or bisexual. She says that they joke around with Toby by telling him that he is a "homo." Although she says they do this just for fun, it also because Toby is a friend to a group of openly gay Black men. While Toby denies being gay, his friendship with gay men is a clear sign for Nia and their friends that Toby might be gay. She says that in their circle of friends, straights do not socialize with openly gay men and women. And to do so is to have one's straight identity questioned and doubted.

Nia does not generally include gays and lesbians in her social circles, says she would not go to a gay bar and notes that Toby was an object of jokes among her friends because he did. She stated that in their dorm room in college that, "when those guys [the gay friends] would come over, they wouldn't chill with us. They would go in their room and talk or whatever. And then after they'd leave, then we would start teasing him. Well, it wasn't really me, but I was there too. And I would laugh at it. I was kind of a part of it."

Nia's story illustrates an individual who does not want to reject lesbians and gays entirely but feels uncomfortable accepting homosexuality due to her family's and friends' strong aversion to it. For her, heterosexuality is important for achieving the ideal family life she wants. However, since she neither projects a clear straight feminine identity in everyday life nor wants to be viewed as possibly lesbian, she establishes her heterosexuality through maintaining a strictly straight group of friends as well as by condoning the homophobic jokes they tell among themselves.

Non-homophobic straight masculinities and femininities

Although straight privilege and status is still central for how men and women achieve respect in everyday life, straight men and women also secure their straight status through practices that avoid stigmatizing homosexuals. These straights, then, are models of respect, equality and justice in a multicultural society where differences of sexuality continue to matter in everyday life and in political battles for inclusion.

Born in 1979, Jason Watkins is an attractive young Black man. While average height, he has a lean muscular build and is wearing loose-fitting blue jeans and a windbreaker jacket during the interview. His hair is grown out into a small Afro and he has a dark-skinned complexion. Jason is a congenial person who is easy going but quiet and intensely private. He grew up in Queens and Long Island, New York. He was primarily raised by his Jamaican-Indian mother and grew up around his aunt and female cousin. Jason graduated from college two years ago and is working in an administrative job in Albany, New York.

Jason's straight masculine identity is refracted through the racial lens of his Blackness. And this racial lens means that Jason experiences being a (heterosexual) Black man as his most salient identity. Jason says,

> Me being a man and just me being Black just automatically throws out the vision of Black man. So that would be my identity, the strongest identity I have. It's not something I try to figure out how to portray to everyone that, "Heh, I'm a Black man." It's just something that they see me as. So I just let people see me as what they want to see me as until they find out who I am.

Although Jason says that he exhibits some stereotypical feminine behaviors, such as having manicured nails and crossing his legs when sitting, he says that other straight men never notice the clear polish on his nails nor do straight women question his heterosexual masculine identity because of it. However, they do jokingly tell him that he is a "metrosexual." Nevertheless, after a series of questions about whether Jason has ever found himself attracted to men, in which Jason says that he never has, he becomes defensive in answering questions about his masculinity. For example, when I asked him, "How do you think your mother shaped your sense of masculinity?" He says,

> Well I grew up with her. So I was around her all the time and I didn't turn out feminine. I grew up with my cousin, who's a girl. So I pretty much grew up around women my whole life and I never turned out acting feminine in any way. I guess just the way she acted and the way she portrayed herself. She [his mother] never really, she never really acted like a girl. She never acted sappy or she didn't show that much emotions to a lot of things.

Similarly, not only does Jason say that he does not act feminine in general, but he does take advantage of his heterosexual male privilege. He says,

> Actually, I'm happy I'm the guy. That does matter to me. We get more advantages. There are so many more things we can do that girls can't do, whether it's hooking up with girls or walking out on the street late at night or just being a guy, not having to be pregnant and going through all those hormones that they do.

Race is always central in the construction of Jason's heterosexual masculinity, and he says that his Black racial identity positions him within an array of racial stereotypes. Whether it be women acquaintances jokingly inferring he has a large penis, male friends insinuating he's good at basketball because he's Black, or male friends assuming that his associations with women are sexual, not platonic, in nature, his Black racial identity hypersexualizes and exaggerates his heterosexual masculinity.

Jason says, for instance,

> I mean if you see me around a lot of times you see that I always hang around with girls. They [straight men] never questioned my [straight] sexuality. A lot of people just assume that I have a lot of girls, both guys and girls.

I ask him, "But most straight guys wouldn't hang around with just girls, right? That would be a stereotype for gay men?" Jason says,

> That could be a stereotype for gay men, but in my case a lot of people seem to just think I have a lot of girls and I'm hooking up with all these girls that I'm hanging out with. Friends think, "Man, you have all these girls. All these girls like you." They never assume that I'm gay because I hang out alone with girls.

While Jason's straight masculine identity practices are generally conventional, his Black racial identity acts as a kind of inoculation against suspicion of being gay and instead it exaggerates his straight masculinity and sexual prowess, as seen through his friends' assumptions that he has "all these girls." Jason thus reproduces hegemonic straight

James Joseph Dean

masculine identity practices through both letting other men think he has sex with his women friends as well as by his general demeanor of remaining emotionally detached.

Although Jason wants to maintain his straight masculine privilege, he is egalitarian in his views toward women and homosexuals. For example, some of Jason's closest friends are straight and bisexual women and gay men. When I asked Jason why he was not homophobic, for example, he related his experiences of being a racial minority in a racist society and his desire to not be discriminated against because of who he is. He extends this idea to other minorities in society. Jason explains,

> Because I'm Black and if you look at it from the standpoint of the one time Black people were discriminated against by everyone. Why would you discriminate against somebody else? Just put yourself in their shoes because you actually can. Because Black people are still discriminated against. So just go to some place else and see how a gay person feels. It's that they can hide it and a lot of times they do hide it and that messes them up inside. So just let them be who they are because you can't hide who you are.

Jason illustrates how gay visibility and rights have successfully framed discrimination against homosexuals as similar to the experiences of racial discrimination that Blacks face and have faced in the past. Moreover, Jason views gays and lesbians as friends and social equals, thus illustrating how straights do not have to exclude gays and lesbians from their social circles to feel secure in projecting their heterosexual masculinity.

Even more pro-gay than Jason, I interviewed straight women like Erica Harris who routinely break down boundaries of normative heterosexuality, blur identity practices of straight femininity, and enact an active anti-homophobic practice in daily life. Erica is a 22 year-old black woman who manages a restaurant. In everyday life, Erica challenges boundaries between gays and straights in two main ways. First, her straight, lesbian, and gay friends and coworkers are integrated into her personal and professional lives. Second, in public Erica regularly holds her straight, lesbian, and bisexual female friends' hands and often greets them with a kiss on the lips. She says that she hugs, kisses, and holds the hands of both her male and female friends in public, and she makes no distinction between whether the women are straight, lesbian, or bi.

As a result of her intimate and affectionate practices in public that blur sexual identity boundaries, some of Erica's acquaintances jokingly and non-jokingly question her heterosexuality. However, even in these situations, Erica avoids disclosing that she is straight and allows others to assume that she might be lesbian or bisexual. Erica tells me about a situation where this happened:

> An example of a situation would be me sitting in public with a friend and a girlfriend of mine coming over and greeting me. We greet each other with hugs and kisses and maybe even her sitting on my lap while I'm having a conversation with somebody else. And the other person that I'm with, if they're not aware of the relationships that exist between me and these other people, might make a joke, "I didn't know you liked girls," "I didn't know you had a girlfriend," or "I didn't know that you were on that side of the fence." Some kind of lame, silly statement like that, which I usually chuckle at. I like the fact that people are confused or they

don't know; because I think it's silly to try to put everybody in a box. I guess part of that ambiguity . . . I must push it. I think I push it sometimes. I think I allow for people to question it. I don't snap back and say, "I'm a heterosexual! What are you talking about?" So, I don't defend it.

Instead of becoming defensive by suggestions that her physical intimacy with other women identifies her as seemingly lesbian, Erica courts the ambiguity and plays with lesbian/straight identity codes. Her antihomophobia condemns coding identity and intimacy practices as uniformly heterosexual or homosexual, challenging both hetero-sexual privilege and binary constructions of heterosexual/homosexual identities as mutually exclusive.

It is, perhaps, not surprising that Erica openly discusses her own same-sex encounter without a sense of shame. Growing up post-Stonewall and in contexts of LGBTQ cultural visibility seems to have laid the groundwork for her to feel comfort-able talking about the encounter without much anxiety.

I'm the kind of person who's willing to try anything and again try to not box every-thing into this is the way it is. This is the way it should be. This is the way it's gonna be. I'm able to be malleable, and I'm also somebody who does not view same-sex relationships as wrong. What I did was fine. It's a piece of my life story now.

As well, she says that this experience caused her to rethink her own straight identity and how an identity category reduces the complicated and messy nature of one's experiences. Erica describes sexual identities as fluid, contextual, and dependent on the circumstances one finds oneself in:

I consider myself heterosexual. Just the same way, like I said before, politically, I consider myself black. But I'm more than that in terms of my ethnic makeup. Just as in sexuality, I'm more than just a straight female. I'm attracted to different things. I don't make myself any promises that I'll never change. I believe that a lot of things are based on the individual person. Give me a woman who does every-thing right for me and we'll see. This particular woman did not.

Erica's antihomophobia extends beyond blurring sexual identity practices and giving up her heterosexual privilege: her identity practices demonstrate a queering of straight femininity. A queered heterosexual identification contests essentialist and unified conceptions of heterosexuality and replaces them with a fluid, contextual, and dynamic conception of sexualities. That is, Erica's anti-homophobic practices are also aimed at changing the worldview of her unenlightened acquaintances and friends. For exam-ple, she takes some of her homophobic straight male friends to gay bars to show them that gays are just as diverse, "normal," and often unremarkably ordinary as heterosexuals:

For example, going to a place like The Pub [a gay bar], some friends, if I even bring that up, they're like, "What am I? Fresh meat?" I'm like, "Honey, you're not that cute." And I think it's that they are not able to understand that there's not one kind of gay person. Not everybody is going to be threatening to you. That threatening persona, that threatening gay man [who's effeminate and aggressively flirtatious] . . . That's what my friends think they are going to encounter anytime they go into a place that is not completely heterosexual, which is unbelievable to me. So, what do I do? I drag them in there anyway.

Conclusion

This chapter has sketched a range of straight masculinities and femininities. While I showed that hegemonic straight identities rely on homophobic practices for their establishment, I also demonstrated that counter-hegemonic straight identities are antihomophobic while still using gender conventional identity practices to project a straight identity status. That is, the association of gender conventional behavior with straightness is one of the main ways straight individuals aim to project their sexual identity in everyday life. My general point, though, is that straight identities do not automatically have to include practices of homophobia. Rather, we need to separate out gender conventional identity practices from practices of homophobia. While gender conventional identity practices project heterosexuality and its privileged status, they do not necessarily entail homophobic practices of domination. In short, we must account for the diversity and changing enactments of straight masculinities and femininities that exist in America's dynamic sexual landscape today.

References

Chauncey, George. 1994. *Gay New York: Gender, Urban Culture and the Making of the Gay Male World, 1890–1940*. New York: Basic Books.

Dean, James Joseph. 2014. *Straights: Heterosexuality in Post-Closeted Culture*. New York: NYU Press.

D'Emilio, John and Estelle Freedman. 1988. *Intimate Matters: A History of Sexuality in America*. New York: Harper & Row.

Katz, Jonathan Ned. 1996. *The Invention of Heterosexuality*. New York: Plume Book.

Kinsey, Alfred, Wardell Pomeroy and Clyde Martin. 1948. *Sexual Behavior in the Human Male*. Philadelphia: Saunders.

Kinsey, Alfred, Wardell Pomeroy, Clyde Martin and Paul Gebhard. 1953. *Sexual Behavior in the Human Female*. Philadelphia: Saunders.

Michael, Robert, John Gagnon, Edward Laumann and Gina Kolata. 1994. *Sex in America: A Definitive Survey*. New York: Warner Books.

Seidman, Steven. 1991. *Romantic Longings*. New York: Routledge.

White, Kevin. 1993. *The First Sexual Revolution: The Emergence of Male Heterosexuality in Modern America*. New York: NYU Press.

chapter 28

Sexual narratives of "straight" women

Nicole LaMarre

When it comes to sexual identity, nothing is as "straight" as it seems. Today, when someone asks about a person's sexuality, more often than not they are referring to whether the person is straight, bisexual, or gay. However, sexual orientation, or self-identification of sexuality based on the gender/sex of preferred partners, is only one aspect of sexuality. Recent research suggests that, although people may identify as one orientation or another, their narratives have a fluidity that challenges the notion of fixed sexual identities. Sexual fluidity refers to sexual experiences, desires, and fantasies that contradict static heterosexual or homosexual identities. For instance, many women report engaging in sexual encounters with, or some level of intimacy, fantasy, or desire for, other women during their lives. This essay will explore sexual fluidity by exploring the sexual histories of several women. My interviews suggest that a critical rethinking of how heterosexuals negotiate sexual identities is vital to understanding the social organization of sexuality in contemporary American society.

The trouble with sexual identity

Many social groups and institutions are organized around sexual orientation. For example, "Focus on the Family" is established on a shared belief in the normalcy of heterosexuality and conventional, two parent households. Other family rights organizations, such as the now defunct "Love Makes a Family," are centered on lobbying for same sex marriage rights for LGBTQ families. Despite the fact that these two groups have vastly different goals, they share a common foundation; they each construct individuals and families around fixed sexual identity categories. One group advocates for the advancement and privileging of heterosexual families and the other promotes equal rights for LGBTQ families. While grouping people together by sexual orientation may be politically useful, as it unites people through their common goals, it is a strategy that raises some troubling concerns.

For instance, gay and lesbian organizations have had an often tenuous relationship with bisexuals, whose goals sometimes differ from that of homosexuals. Lesbian and gay organizations have sought to gain rights by presenting homosexuality as a biological trait that cannot be changed. Contrarily, bisexual organizations have fought to make room for multiple desires and to blur the boundaries between heterosexuality and homosexuality. Furthermore, groupings based on sexual identity are problematic because its members may not agree on key issues. For example, not all heterosexuals argue for the exclusion of homosexuals, and some homosexuals view same sex relationships as a conscious choice, others as a biological trait, and still others as a combination of both (Whisman 1996).

In a heteronormative society, where heterosexuality is institutionalized and naturalized to the point where it is seen as the basis of family and society, sexual identities become highly politicized because they act as a gateway to social privileges (Warner 1993). By asserting that heterosexuality is a natural condition, and by promoting this notion in the media and other institutions, heterosexuality is left unexamined. How often do we assume people we meet are heterosexual? Today, many people believe that heterosexuality has been the norm "since the dawn of time." However, heterosexuality as a sexual identity only emerged in the twentieth century (Katz 1996). Before this time, sexual acts between individuals of different genders were understood simply as a behavior. Today, sexual behaviors are almost always associated with a particular sexual identity. For instance, many of us would see anal sex as probably something that gay men do, while vaginal sex is something heterosexual women do. Yet these sex acts can be experienced by anyone, heterosexual, homosexual, or otherwise.

If heterosexuality is socially constructed and its definition historically specific, what are the understandings of heterosexuality today? Do individuals who we think of as heterosexual also have fantasies or behaviors that contradict this identity? Are there significant differences among "heterosexuals" in terms of their experience of desire and sexual satisfaction? Do all heterosexuals have the same perception of sexual identity and similar sexual experiences? Is sexual orientation significantly more complicated than social discourses allow?

Heterosexuality and heteroflexibility

Researchers have explored women's sexual narratives to uncover the wide range of sexual experiences of heterosexual and homosexual women (Chandra, Mosher, and Copen 2011; Diamond 2008; Hoburg, Konik, Williams, and Crawford 2004; Savin-Williams 2005). Studies have shown that women are likely to engage in an extensive array of sexual behaviors throughout their lifetimes, some of which transcend categorization as heterosexual or homosexual. Take the Madonna and Britney Spears kiss on MTV's 2003 VMA show, Katy Perry's hit "I Kissed a Girl," or even Lady Gaga's popularized song "Poker Face," which references bisexuality. Are any of these women, or at least their performances, strictly heterosexual? Some feminists and sociologists argue these instances are exemplary of heteroflexibility, where the political context of sexual decisions is glossed over by explanations of idiosyncrasy and personal choice (Diamond 2005; Essig 2000). Rather than witnessing an era of increased sexual freedoms and visibility, some argue that heteroflexibility presents the illusion of progress and sexual freedom. Other researchers have adamantly argued that sexual fluidity and the resistance to identity categories is perhaps an indicator of a larger, social rejection of gender/sexual binaries. For these individuals, we are witnessing a generation which is characterized by sexual autonomy and fluidity. It is possible that for some individuals and groups the former is true, and others the latter.

How do heterosexual women understand and experience heterosexuality? Furthermore, how are "straight" women using the categories of sexual orientation to interpret their sexual desires? Does heterosexuality serve to accurately describe individual sexualities when sexual behaviors and fantasies are explored? Do some women have the "freedom" to reject sexual orientation altogether? In order to explore these questions, I conducted a qualitative study in 2008 that examined how young adult, self-identified heterosexual women accounted for their heterosexuality. The interviews centered on analyzing the relationships between women's sexual behaviors, desires, fantasies, and personal definitions of heterosexuality.

Exploring heterosexuality: fluidity between sexual identification, acts, and desires

My study focuses on the sexual narratives of young adult (18 to 28 years old), self-identified "straight" women. The analysis shifts between the sexual desires of participants and the accounts they provide of their sexual identity in order to explore the contradiction in their sexual narratives. These women's narratives are vital in shedding light on how contemporary sexualities are limited by social constraints at the same time that some individuals may be experiencing expanded sexual freedoms.

It is my observation that while many women continue to rely on binary sexual categories (hetero/homo) to understand their sexual orientation, there are some women who refuse to identify as gay, straight, or otherwise. Moreover, they do this regardless of whether or not they would be socially defined as heterosexual, homosexual, or bisexual. This finding is especially significant because it suggests that some women's overall sexualities are transcending the expectations of normative heterosexuality (and normative homosexuality). Furthermore, regardless of how the women interviewed self-identified, their narratives underscore a level of sexual fluidity that challenges rigid identity categories. For many of these women, the label of "heterosexual" did not reflect the depth of their sexual experiences and desires.

I will present a sampling of narratives in order to suggest that sexual orientation is not sufficient for categorizing sexuality when the complexity of women's experiences are considered. The beginning excerpts reflect the contradictory character of heterosexual narratives. The final narrative examples suggest that, for some, sexual identity holds less importance than other facets of their intimate lives. They also illustrate the possibilities that exist when sexual orientation is abandoned as a social category altogether.

When I first spoke with Alice she was in a long-term relationship with her boyfriend of four years. I met up with Alice, a 22 year-old teacher, in her apartment to talk about her personal approach to sexuality. After self-identifying as a heterosexual, I asked Alice what, in her opinion, would make someone a homosexual. She responded, "I don't think you can be gay unless you have sex with someone of the same sex." She used actions, rather than desires or fantasies, as the basis for establishing a heterosexual/homosexual identity. Alice noted that even though a person may fantasize about a person of the same sex, it does not make them a homosexual unless they act on that desire.

Later in the interview, Alice specified that her favorite and most satisfying sexual act was oral sex. She said that she does not orgasm or enjoy sex with her boyfriend without oral sex, and would not continue to date him (despite their long history) or anyone else if they would not engage in cunnilingus. She went so far to say that she does not enjoy penetration (penile) with her boyfriend and cannot orgasm through penetration alone. When I asked her why oral sex was her favorite act, she said, "It's just really important to me, I don't know if it's the power or the control, but I really don't like penetration and don't get anything out of it. I really need [oral sex] to orgasm."

In terms of her sexual fantasies, Alice spoke about how she had a recurring fantasy of a woman "going down" on her. She further disclosed that the fantasy of oral sex with a woman was a source of eroticism for her; "I usually just picture a female going down on me [while having sex with her boyfriend], not a specific person just someone of the same sex going down on me." She also described watching lesbian pornography to turn her on. Despite the fact that she had often thought about being with a woman sexually, Alice had never had an intimate encounter with a woman. Although Alice initially identified as a heterosexual, after we had discussed her fantasies and desires she modified her statement, saying, "OK, how about this? I'm a heterosexual with bisexual tendencies. Until I have sex with a female I will still consider myself a heterosexual."

Alice's sexuality was not limited to heterosexual desires or normative heterosexual acts (as she expressed distaste and even an aversion to penetration), despite her self-identification as a heterosexual. Even though she found women desirable and erotic in a way she did not express about men, she relied on binary, restrictive definitions of her sexuality based on the gender/sex of her partners. While it is arguable whether or not Alice is truly "straight," the importance of her narrative lies in exemplifying the complexity of sexuality in a person who holds to a rigid sexual identity.

Diane also identified as a heterosexual. She was 23 years old and a graduate student in cultural studies. What I found most interesting in talking with Diane is that, unlike Alice, Diane detailed having intimate encounters (short of "going all the way") with several women. Although she identified as a heterosexual, her understanding of sexuality was less constricted by normative heterosexual expectations. She explained that sexuality

> depends on who the person is, what their sexual history is. For me personally, I see myself as a straight woman, but I think that really for anyone if the right person came along it wouldn't matter what sex or gender or anything they were. And I feel the same way about myself. I do find women attractive, you know I've never particularly met one who you know, tickled my fancy . . . I'd say sexual identity is just one part of my personality.

Although she identified herself as heterosexual, she spoke at length about a woman who she had "made out" with on several occasions, and with whom she almost had a sexual relationship. While she never had sex with the woman, she "totally would have." Now she asserts that not having sex ultimately saved their friendship.

Diane went on to discuss sex acts that satisfied her, as well as the fantasies that she had and how they played out in her sexual relations. She enjoyed penetration (penile, finger, and sex toy), and oral sex the most because it "sort of feels like you're more in control sometimes, like they're doing you a service. It's somewhat of a power issue." Power and control were important to her sexual satisfaction, particularly when engaging in oral sex and in BDSM (Bondage, Domination, Sadism and Masochism) activities, including tying up and whipping her partners.

I asked Diane about her sexual fantasies. She talked about "voyeurism" and "exhibitionism" in the form of public sex. She used an example of a sexual encounter on a vacation:

> I recently went on a [trip] and the last night I was there I ended up meeting this guy and we went for a walk and ended up having sex in the branches of some low growing trees. Essentially it ended up being a walled off section, so we were kind of in the tree so yeah, we'd hear someone walking close by and we'd freeze, but you know someone looking from where we were you could see the lights of a club on one side and signs for restaurants on the other and yeah that was just cool.

Part of the construction of normative heterosexuality is that sexual acts are not only between two consenting adults, but also that sex occurs in the private sphere. Diane breached these norms by engaging in public sexual acts that were integral to her overall sexual satisfaction and identity. Not only did Diane breach the heterosexual contract by partaking in public sex, but also by specifying that exhibitionism and "light bondage" were more fundamental to her sexual satisfaction than the gender/sex of her partner.

For Diane, her attraction to a person could not be reduced to a person's gender/sex alone. Diane expressed being attracted to both men and women. The types of sexual acts the person engaged in were at times more important than what her sexual partner had "underneath their clothes." While she also identified as heterosexual, the label did not hold particular meaning for her. Another participant, Claire, similarly found sexual acts to be, at times, more important than the gender/sex of the person she was having intimacies with.

Claire, a 25 year-old counselor, discussed her involvement in a local BDSM community. She talked about the clubs she had frequented, specifying that, "the whole thing is a real turn on and it's something I've thought about often. I really just like being submissive, not having to think and just being told sometimes it's just nice not to think . . . I mean not nice but hot when someone tells you what and where to do stuff." When asked what the most important facet of her sexuality was, Claire did not hesitate when answering that her submissive fantasies and involvement in the BDSM community were essential to her conceptualization of sexuality. However, while having experiences with female dominatrix, she still had not had "full on sex" with a woman and "look[s] for men when having sexual relations."

In both of these cases, sexual orientation did not capture the fluidity that Diane and Claire experienced. Despite expressing her occasionally strong attraction for women, Diane continued to define herself as heterosexual. Claire, while having BDSM experiences with women, self-identified as heterosexual. In doing so, Diane and Claire adopted a label that failed to incorporate the multiplicity of their desires and rendered some of their desires (public sex, BDSM) invisible. Overall, Diane and Claire were open to experiencing non-normative sexual acts (bondage, exhibitionism, and intimate encounters with women), but fell short of rejecting binary, exclusionary sexual categories.

An interesting finding during the interview process was that even women who had not had sexual intercourse (they identified themselves as virgins) detailed fluid conceptions of sexuality. Jackie, 19, and Laura, 21, were both undergraduate students when I spoke with them. Neither reported having a long-term or "significant" relationship. When asked about her identification, Jackie categorized herself as being predominately attracted to men, noting, "I don't really know why . . . It generally isn't a conscious decision. I think it's just what I feel physically and emotionally. It's a comfort thing for me I think." Jackie had only "made out" with men and had not gone "past second base" (foreplay not involving genitalia). Although her limited sexual experience was prototypically heterosexual, her personal understanding of sexual orientation was beyond normative constructions:

> I don't believe that the normal classification system is an effective or meaningful way to describe or categorize people. Our society is so ordered it likes to be able to put things in an organized group, including people. There is very little room for gray area. But I think people are dynamic and different and they generally don't fit into categories or even the gray area. The three main categories of like homo, hetero, or bi can be used as a guide for someone trying to describe themselves I guess, but are by no means the only ways that people can be described. Sexual identity is just like a *part* of your identity.

On the surface, Jackie's experience of sexuality was normatively heterosexual. Further discussion, however, unveiled a more nuanced and fluid view of sexuality. This fluidity was not built on her own personal experience of sexual intimacies, but rather on her perceptions of the people she knew and observed.

Laura considered herself to be "75% [heterosexual] and 25% gay because I don't think anyone is 100% straight. I guess someone might say I'm bicurious, but I don't really talk to people about that." Due to her "really bad habit of falling for people who are [unavailable]" she had not had any significant intimate or sexual relationships (only "kissing and cuddling" with "a handful" of men). In discussing the fantasies that were important to her sexual gratification in the absence of physical relationships, Laura discussed hentai pornography (a subgenre of Japanese anime) that often involved "hot women." Because of her fantasies, Laura questioned her identity: "I don't know if I think I'm straight because it's like an assumption that's been made for me and I just don't have experience to contradict it." In the end, sexual identity for Laura "doesn't have a whole lot of bearing . . . I realize they're terms people use and feel comfortable with and for that purpose they'll be used but for me they don't mean a whole lot beyond the fact conservative people feel more comfortable with those terms and stuff."

Jackie and Laura had surprisingly intricate understandings of sexual identity even though they identified as virgins. Although initially identifying her desires and experiences as heterosexual, Jackie's overall understanding of sexuality exceeded categorization. Her acknowledgement of fluidity and problematizing of sexual labeling challenged normative heterosexual scripts. Laura's narrative displayed fluidity in her own self-identification ("bicurious" and "25% gay"). Additionally, her enjoyment of hentai pornography and the female characters therein highlighted a desire that was unable to be captured by sexual identity categories. Because our desires and fantasies are not necessarily dependent upon acting them out in order to provide sexual gratification, fluidity thrives in many women's sexual histories.

Hannah's interview provides an interesting departure from the aforementioned narrative examples. While the women thus far have identified as heterosexual, the following women actively and purposefully rejected sexual categorization. Hannah, at the time of the interview, was a 21 year-old college student who majored in business. When I asked Hannah how she self-identified sexually, she said,

> I'm pretty open I guess. And we [my brother and I] were actually talking about this . . . I would be like oh she's really pretty and my brother would be like oh no no no, you're not gay at all [implying that I was]. So I don't, well like I think about it but I never actually dated a woman um, but like, well, I don't know if there's a name for it. Because I'm attracted to both men and women and usually to men that are more masculine but sensitive, and females that are more masculine. So I don't know.

She stated that "it's usually easier to say that I'm straight" because she has only had sexual experiences with men. When I asked her what she would say if someone asked if she was heterosexual or homosexual, she responded, "I'll tell pretty much what I just told you; that I'm attracted to both [men and women] but I've only hooked up with guys. I'm actually not that shy about it."

Unlike Alice or Diane, rather than purposefully portraying a "straight" identity, Hannah often found herself annoyed when people assumed her heterosexuality:

> Sometimes I get annoyed with people's assumptions about me and I'll be like what's wrong with that because I have a lot of friends who have gone through a lot of crap and so when people talk about sexuality I try to correct their assumptions. I think that's important . . . I try to correct [people's assumptions] as soon as I'm comfortable . . .

In terms of her favorite sexual acts, Hannah identified choking, submission, and the use of sex toys as important to her sexual satisfaction. As she often found herself in an aggressive role in her public life, playing a submissive role in her erotic life was exciting for her.

Hannah only had a few intimate encounters with women, none of which went "all the way," but she often thought of being with another woman while masturbating. Hannah's personal fantasies and erotic desires for other women were an integral part of her sexuality. She went on to explain that, "It wouldn't matter to me if it [having sex] was with a guy or a girl actually." If she were to be labeled as heterosexual, Hannah felt that she would have had to "give up expressing my desires for other women." Hannah was not comfortable identifying as a heterosexual because she felt it would limit her freedom of choice. Her discomfort with restrictive labels led her to reject binary categories. Similarly, Hannah expressed uneasiness with a bisexual label, as many bisexual women she knew eventually ended up with men and denied their desires for women.

I asked her at the end of the interview if she felt it was possible to draw borders around sexual identities. She replied, "I think it is too complicated. I mean I'm not attracted to every man, just like I'm not attracted to every woman. So, I don't think I put much stake in it [sexual orientation] because I don't think it's possible [to categorize people]. I mean you may be surprised – you haven't met everyone in the world." Hannah actively sought to correct people's presumptions of her identity because she felt sexuality was too complicated to be captured by any one orientation. The transgression of sexual categorization was an attempt to maintain her freedom to experience her desires however she wanted.

Hannah was not alone in her rejection of sexual identity categories. Madison, 23, described her sexuality as changing over time; "Yeah, I used to be super gay kid, from like 16 to 18, and then I dated a trans guy. And then after that I guess I'm just queer, I sleep with whoever I'm attracted to. I don't have those blinders or anything to be like this is not a good idea sexually. If it feels good and doesn't involve . . . anything illegal . . . I'm a pleasure seeker, so I don't think I'm going against anything that's natural or anything." Madison specified, "As far as finding my sexuality I don't know if I feel like I have to have a definition, if people ask me it depends on the person. I'll either say I'm sexually ambiguous or queer or bi. It just depends on the person [and their capacity for] understanding." Unlike Hannah, Madison had numerous sexual encounters with women. However, the discomfort with sexual labels was a recurring theme throughout the interviews, much as it was during my time speaking with Felicity.

Felicity was the final woman I had the privilege of interviewing. At 22, she had recently graduated with her BA and was working at a local not-for-profit organization. When we spoke, Felicity was dating a man after having been in several long-term relationships with women. The negotiation of her identity was complicated for her now that she was in a "straight" relationship. Felicity elaborated on her sexuality, saying:

> If asked or something like that I'd say I'm a lesbian. But now, it's very interesting, I don't know what to say anymore . . . You know, I've only dated women in the past. I'm dating a boy now, so it's different. But yeah I would definitely still say gay . . . I definitely hold on to some things that . . . are very much a part of the lesbian community I appreciate and don't want to let go of . . . just little things that are the things you hang onto because that's the little niche of community you have . . . I mean I'm always, you know, I identify with a more queer understanding of sexuality.

The dissonances Felicity experienced in her identity led her to adopt a "queer" perspective on sexuality that allowed for fluidity in experiences and identities. Her sexual history clearly made it difficult for her to rely solely on gender/sex preference in order to understand her sexuality. While she did label herself as a lesbian in a "symbolic" sense, her overall sexuality presented a rejection of the binary status quo.

In the end, all of these narratives portray women who experience a wide variety of sexual desires, fantasies, and behaviors. While all of their stories strayed from normative expectations of heterosexuality, only Hannah, Madison, and Felicity actively distanced themselves from being labeled sexually. As this research suggests, women's experiences and understandings of heterosexuality vary greatly from person to person. For some, heterosexuality is a matter of a dominant sexual attraction to the "opposite" sex. Yet for others, heterosexuality is contingent upon the gender/sex of the people you actually have sex with; sexual desires need not be limited to one sex. Some heterosexual women fantasized about other women but said they had no desire to act on their fantasies. Interestingly, a number of heterosexual women interviewed were very open to having sex with women but lacked the opportunity. No two accounts of heterosexuality were the same in the twenty interviews I conducted. When we look past the political meaning and organization of heterosexuality we see that no two heterosexuals are alike. Moreover, a handful of women in the study actively distanced themselves from sexual labels. What does this renunciation and transcendence of sexual orientation mean?

Conclusion

A thorough exploration of women's sexual narratives demonstrates that many heterosexuals have desires and experiences that contradict their sexual identity. Although socially perceived as a static identity, the category of "heterosexual" describes very little about an individual's overall sexuality. Heterosexual women do not necessarily experience an absence of same sex desires or sexual encounters. Furthermore, "straight" women may have very different interpretations of what heterosexuality means. This underscores the complexity of sexuality and the narrowness of contemporary discourses regarding heterosexuality. On the one hand, these interviews show the ongoing reliance on sexual binaries in order to interpret individual sexualities in contemporary society. On the other, the interviews demonstrate that some women are able to experience desires and fantasies that are not limited by normative expectations of heterosexuality. Based on sexual orientation alone, "straight" women have little in common sexually aside from their self-identification as heterosexuals.

These interviews dispel the notion of heterosexuality as a fixed identity. Thinking back to the organizations mentioned earlier, today, heterosexuality is less a static identity than it is a means of politically organizing groups of people. Through its organization around normative heterosexuality, "Focus on the Family" maintains the illusion of the fixity and constancy of heterosexual identities. The illusion has the effect of naturalizing monosexual attraction and making it a basic organizing principle of Western societies. This accounts for the continuing reliance on sexual orientation because it continues to have meaning in social institutions. But heterosexuality tells us little about individual sexualities. Today, heterosexuality maintains its privilege on an institutional level.

Nicole LaMarre

Certainly there are some women who may kiss other women solely for the benefit of teasing or stimulating men. Scholars often dismiss these women's experiences as examples of heteroflexibility, or argue they exemplify the heterosexualizing of female same sex desires. To some extent this may be true. However, women like Hannah are actively working to challenge the rigidity of sexual identity categories. Hannah's (as well as Madison and Felicity's) narrative suggests the possibility of creating a society that values personal choice and experience over sexual conformity cloaked by an appearance of sexual freedom.

While identity politics have been important in gaining sexual rights in our society, the underlying problem may not be the privileged status of heterosexuals. The true difficulty lies in society's reliance on oppositional, dualistic categories that pit groups of people against one another. Rejecting sexual identities may be the key to "undoing" oppression based on sexual orientation.

References

Chandra, A., W. Mosher, and C. Copen. 2011. "Sexual Behavior, Sexual Attraction, and Sexual Identity in the United States: Data From the 2006–2008 National Survey of Family Growth." National Health Statistics Reports 36: 1–35.

Diamond, Lisa M. 2005. "'I'm Straight, but I Kissed a Girl': The Trouble with American Media Representations of Female-Female Sexuality." *Feminist Psychology* (15): 104.

Diamond, Lisa. 2008. *Sexual Fluidity: Understanding Women's Love and Desire.* Cambridge: Harvard University Press.

Essig, L. 2000. "Heteroflexibility." From Salon.com 15 November. www.salon.com/2000/11/15/heteroflexibility/. Accessed June 23, 2015.

Hoburg, R., J. Konik, M. Williams, and M. Crawford. 2004. "Bisexuality among Self-Identified Heterosexual College Students." *Journal of Bisexuality* 4: 26–36.

Katz, Jonathan Ned. 1996. *The Invention of Heterosexuality.* New York: Plume Books.

Savin-Williams, R. 2005. *The New Gay Teenager.* Cambridge: Harvard University Press.

Warner, Michael. 1993. "Introduction." From *Fear of a Queer Planet: Queer Politics and Social Theory* ed. by Michael Warner. Minneapolis: University of Minnesota Press.

Whisman, V. 1996. *Queer by Choice: Lesbians, Gay Men, and the Politics of Identity.* New York: Routledge.

chapter 29

Men's sexual flexibility

Eric Anderson and Stefan Robinson

A group of undergraduate British rugby players are out celebrating their latest victory at a club inhabited solely by college students. The men dance with each other, and in the center of the dance floor, two stop dancing, embrace each other, and kiss solidly on the lips for a second or two. The question we have for our readers is: what is their sexual orientation?

Popular perceptions of sexuality normally maintain that there are just two types of sexual orientation: heterosexual and homosexual. This is changing, however, and scholars are arguing that a marked expansion of identity labels is occurring to accommodate the range and variability of behaviors, feelings, and identities that men report in contemporary culture (Kuper, Nussbaum and Mustanski 2012).

Bisexuality, for example, is increasingly understood as a legitimate sexual orientation for men. Others define themselves as pansexual, or just sexual. But the two rugby players described above are neither gay nor bisexual, they identify as heterosexual; they are just more flexible in their approach toward understanding heterosexuality than men have traditionally been.

In this chapter we provide evidence that young, heterosexual men are increasingly more flexible in the types of sexual and pseudo-sexual behaviors that they engage in with other men; even if it does not result in a change of sexual orientation. We relate these new behaviors to a decrease in stigma about many types of sexual practices, but principally, we argue that it is declining homophobia which permits otherwise heterosexual men to engage in same-sex interactions in absence of sexual desires for men. This is because heterosexual men are no longer assumed homosexual for engaging in such behaviors.

What we investigate with this chapter however concerns flexibility and not sexual fluidity. We define sexual fluidity as the notion that one's sexual orientation is not necessarily fixed; that one can vacillate between whom one is sexually (not romantically) attracted to; that today one might be attracted only to women, and tomorrow one might be attracted to both women and men, or only men (Diamond 2009). Sexual fluidity is not the same as bisexuality, however. Bisexuals recognize within themselves an enduring sexual desire for both males and females.

We are not concerned with sexual fluidity in this chapter for several reasons, primarily because we—largely—don't believe it exists. We use the word "believe" because there is surprisingly little research into this. While a great deal of research examines adolescent sexuality, we would not consider this "fluidity" and more a matter of figuring out one's sexuality. Of the research that does exist into the stability of adult sexualities, most examines women's sexual fluidity—with the underlying assumption that men's sexual orientations are more stable.

Concerning longitudinal studies, Mock and Eibach (2012) examined reports of sexual orientation identity stability and change over a 10-year period, drawing on data from the National Survey of Midlife Development in the United States (MIDUS I and II), testing for three patterns: (1) heterosexual stability, (2) female sexual fluidity, and (3) bisexual fluidity. The average age was approximately 47 years, and 54% of the 2,560 participants were female. At the time of the first study, 97.42% reported a heterosexual identity, 1.25% a homosexual identity, and 1.33% a bisexual identity. At wave 2 (10 years later), a little over 2% reported a different sexual orientation identity. Thus, although some support for each hypothesis was found, sexuality proved to be mostly stable. When one considers that some of these will have been closeted with their homo/bisexuality earlier, it speaks to the staying power of sexual orientation.

Kinnish, Strassberg and Turner (2005) used a retrospective analysis of 762 adults' sexual orientation (aged 36–60) over five-year increments of their lives. They examined sexual orientation (attraction) and behaviors, finding that when fluidity occurred, it did more so for non-heterosexuals and mostly in women. This makes sense, as sexual minorities come to terms with their sexuality. However, for heterosexuals 97% retained their heterosexual sexual orientation throughout the life course.

More evidence for the lack of sexual fluidity among men comes from "conversion therapy." These "therapies" are historically, and still today, levied upon gay men through fundamentalist religious organizations. Those attending them are highly religious and strongly desire to rid themselves of their sexual desires. Although no reputable scientist has shown that such "treatments" are effective (one found it was "possible" but later retracted his findings), it does not stop organized religion from postulating that, "through the Lord," anything is possible.

People who attend these conversion therapies tend to be highly motivated to become heterosexual, yet even among these religious, dedicated self-loathers, there is remarkably little success (LeVay 2011). Any shift to heterosexuality is likely exaggerated, with subjects submitting to the same societal pressures that keep many gays closeted in the first place. The history of ex-gays is complete with multiple leaders later coming out of the closet and denouncing the "therapy." We argue that the failure of gay conversion therapies is evidence of the stable nature of sexual orientation. Accordingly, we do not see (or at least see enough) scientific evidence to suggest that male sexual orientation, at least, is anything other than a relatively fixed component; that it is unchangeable—we recognize that we could be wrong.

Notions of heterosexual men's fluidity aside, in this chapter we are interested in heterosexual men who are flexible in their approach to heterosexuality. We articulate the difference between fluid (being able to change in sexual orientation) and flexible heterosexual men who engage in same-sex behaviors without being sexually attracted to males. While conflicting definitions of flexibility exist, in this chapter we thus refer to sexual flexibility as the willingness of otherwise heterosexual men to engage in sexual (or pseudo-sexual) behaviors with other men.

This type of flexibility is not new: it is just that it has, traditionally, been thought the domain of heterosexual women. For example, recent research has shown that approximately half of all heterosexual women have engaged in same-sex sexual experimentation (Katz-Wise 2015). Cultural perceptions of women's sexual flexibility are abundant in popular media, and particularly in pornography. However, until recently, heterosexual men have been socially constructed to understand that their sexualities are not flexible. Men have lived by what Anderson (2008) calls "the one-time rule of homosexuality" in which any discovered or revealed same-sex sexual behavior (like the two men kissing on the dance floor) has socially made them out to be entirely gay. This one-time rule, however, is beginning to change and we argue that the primary cause for this change is found in decreasing homophobia.

The influence of decreasing homophobia

In the 1980s and 1990s heterosexual masculinity was constructed against a backdrop of homophobic social stigma that delivered a blanket condemnation of all sexual or pseudo-sexual activities with other men. This is because these behaviors were associated with homosexuality. But the extreme homophobia of the 1980s and 1990s reflected more than just the dislike of men having sex with other men: male homosexuality was also disparaged by others because it was conflated with a perceived lack of maleness and the adoption of feminine traits. In other words, masculinity was associated with heterosexuality. Because of this conflation, those wishing to be perceived as masculine by their peers have considered it necessary to disengage from those behaviors that have been socially coded as feminine, and thus gay. Homophobia had become a benchmark for masculinity.

At such times and in such cultures men maintained emotional and physical distance from one another through the subordination of alternative identities, with any physical demonstrations of intimacy between males being generally confined to specific culturally approved activities, such as playing team sports. Conversely, acts of soft tactility and emotional intimacy, such as holding hands, softly hugging, crying, or non-sexual kissing were not permitted whatsoever (Anderson 2009). Indeed, sexual desire is often perceived as the traditional missing link between a friendship and a romantic relationship (Thompson 2006). Thus, to ensure the separation of sexual desire from their lives, men also avoid homosocial emotional and physical intimacy.

However, homophobia is on the rapid decline among men (Clements and Field 2014; Weeks 2007). A survey of over 200,000 undergraduates finds that 65% of US freshmen support same-sex marriage (Pryor et al. 2012)—a number that will be considerably higher for university students today. Anderson (2014) also identifies this trend with qualitative work, showing that—not long ago—it was homosexuality that was socially stigmatized, whereas youth today stigmatize homophobia. McCormack (2012)

Eric Anderson and Stefan Robinson

suggests that part of this acceptance concerns the disconnect between the phrase "that's so gay" from what it used to mean. Where at one time the phrase signified homophobia, today it is used as a general statement of discontent without intent to imply homosexuality whatsoever. This, and multiple other social improvements for homosexuality, suggests that the conservative project of same-sex sexual control is unraveling. Yesterday's common-sense values become the ignorance of today.

Declining homophobia has a positive impact on more than just gay and bisexual men as well. It also benefits heterosexual men. For example, as homophobia declines, heterosexual men value feminine expression among men (both gay and straight) more. This is something that Anderson (2009) calls "inclusive masculinity." He argues that male youth no longer fear being thought gay for the wrongdoing of gender (homosexualization). Alternatively, through the performance of femininity or homo-social intimacy, they are increasingly engaging in it. In other words, increasing cultural homophobia influences heterosexual men to police their gendered behaviors, while decreasing cultural homophobia has the opposite effect. We posit that when homophobia decreases, if enough men adopt a behavior (such as wearing pink clothing) that behavior then loses its feminine associations. In other words, we argue that sexual attraction is not fluid for men and that the socially valued forms of men's gendered expression (masculinity) is fluid—that it changes, greatly, in response to varying levels of cultural homophobia.

Conservative sexual forces and their decline

Our sexual freedoms have traditionally been habituated to align with certain legal, religious and "moral" narratives that govern our daily lives; at least until recently. This means that institutions have regulated who we have sex with, what type of sex we have, when we have it, where we do it, and the status of our relationship when doing it (Anderson 2012). As Duggan (2003) eloquently explains: "Conservatives argued to privatize most of collective life . . . advocating state regulation of marriage, reproduction, and sexuality" (p. 51). The principal mechanism at work is the demonization of sexuality which has been embellished in order to gain social control (Rubin 1984). Controlling sexuality, controlling our most innate emotional instincts, is a way of controlling people.

Modern governments also control sex (legally and/or culturally) because they think they will promote the healthy functioning of their societies or protect individuals from emotional harm. Canaday (2009) argues that it's also about drawing boundaries between us and them—and declaring who the moral citizen is. When citizens buy into this governmental control, they sacrifice their agency for the belief that the government knows what is best for the functioning of their own lives. Schwartz and Rutter (2000: 72) therefore say, "most societies are not organized to help people have a good sex life. Sex drives are not extolled and encouraged by governments."

However, there have been comprehensive changes to our sexual and gendered society over the last two decades. A new age of liberationist values has ushered in the democratization of sexual desire (Attwood 2010). For the younger generation today, love and sex are progressively being understood as separate constructs (Anderson

2014). This is perhaps an effect of our gradual but increasing divorce from religiosity, our enhanced sense of self-liberty, the advancement of birth control, the achievements of feminism (women's egalitarian and increasing financial independence), and (for gay men and lesbians) the growing acceptance of homosexuality. All of these trends have led gay and straight men to reinvent and re-understand their sexual lives (Savin-Williams 2005), albeit in different ways.

Furthermore, the explosion of pornography has reshaped and greatly expanded our cultural/sexual palette of opportunities: gone is the expectation of heterosexual missionary sex (McNair 2002). The Internet has sparked a revolution of sexual practice, but it has also sparked a revolution in the liberation from oppressive norms. For the first time in history, rather than simply looking at an erotic drawing, reading an erotic text, or salivating over an erotic photo, today it is possible to interact with the subjects of our desire via pornography and web-camming sex in all its forms.

We have seen social improvement in attitudes toward pre-marital sex, hooking up, oral sex, gay and lesbian sex, anal sex, masturbation, threesomes, the use of apps to find strangers for sex, sexting, phone sex, and web-cam sex. Today's young readers will likely be aghast to find out that men could not readily admit to masturbating until the turn of the 21st century, lest they be thought gay. Today, young straight men openly discuss masturbation with each other (Anderson 2014). Even public discussion of kinky sex is perhaps more prevalent than it has ever been (Weiss 2006). We can upload our own pornography to amateur web sites and take delight at knowing that others are fantasizing about us.

Thus, whereas religion and governments used to control porn in a misguided attempt to prevent it from unduly influencing its citizens' minds into sexual deviance, today's western governments have very little control over it. The Internet has ended such prohibition—efforts to the contrary are mostly futile. We are rapidly running out of sexual taboos and "It is increasingly difficult, these days, to find any area of consensual adult sexual conduct that most people will unequivocally say is wrong" (Jackson and Scott 2004: 238), with the exceptions, perhaps, of cheating—even though undergraduates do plenty of that (Anderson 2012)—and incest.

With the rapid decline of homophobia in Anglo-American cultures, the untangling of religious control from sexuality, and the softening of heterosexual men's masculinities, a new wave of being a heterosexual sexual being has been ushered in (in the West) and it looks nothing like what your father's masculinity and heterosexuality looked like.

The heterosexual kiss

In a newly prevailing liberal environment, young men are now free to engage in physically intimate behaviors that controvert the avoidance behaviors of previous decades. When two men kiss each other today, we do not definitively classify them as homosexual, nor condemn them for being so. Throughout America's universities, particularly in sports teams and nightclubs, there is a rapid and increasing frequency by which straight-identifying men are kissing their friends on the cheeks and lips, all without the fear of homosexual persecution. Statistical evidence for this comes from Anderson

Eric Anderson and Stefan Robinson

and some of his colleagues who, in 2012, found this number to be 40% kissing on the cheek and 10% on the lips, among heterosexual men studied at eleven US colleges. Another research team found 29% of heterosexual male undergraduates had kissed another man in Australia (Filiault et al. 2014) and in Europe it is much higher. In the United Kingdom, a multi-institutional survey found that nine out of ten heterosexual male undergraduates kiss their male friends on the lips (Anderson, Adams and Rivers 2012).

In all of these countries the men studied do not proclaim to be acting out of sexual desire, or even to consider a same-sex kiss a sexual act. Instead they embrace these behaviors as symbols of affection for one another; as a sign of their platonic love for their heterosexual friends. This is heterosexual flexibility.

In interviews conducted by Anderson, Adams, and Rivers (2012) one participant, Tim, said, "It's no more a sexual act than kissing your father." Tom argued, "It's like shaking hands. Well, it's more than that, but it's the same attitude." For the young men in this study, this type of kiss had been socially stripped of sexual significance. Whereas kissing a male friend on the lips would once be coded as a sexual act, the symbolic meaning of kissing has been interpreted differently by these young men.

Here, kissing is consistent with a normal operation of heteromasculine intimacy. Highlighting this, when Pete was asked about which friends he kisses and which he does not, he answered, "I wouldn't kiss just anyone. I kiss my good mates." He continued, "It's not that there is a system to who gets it or not. Instead, it's a feeling, an expression of endearment, an act that happens to show they are important to you." Like Pete, many others spoke of loving their friends and the significance of a kiss in showing this. Tim agreed, "Kissing other guys is a perfectly legitimate way of showing affection toward a friend." Ollie, a third-year engineering student, added, "You do it sometimes when out having a laugh with your mates, yeah. But I suppose it's also a way to show how much we love each other, so we do it at home, too."

Kissing can also transcend the spatial context of partying and celebration. Matt highlighted how important emotional intimacy was to him, telling a story about breaking up with his girlfriend. "I was really lonely, really depressed. So one night, I asked my housemate who is one of my best friends if I could sleep in the bed with him. He looked at me, smiled, and said, 'Come on,' opening the covers to invite me in." Matt continued, "He kissed me, and then held me. It was nice . . . I sent him a text the next day saying, 'I've got the best friend in the world.'"

Cuddling and spooning

Matt's story shows that there are also other ways of showing affection for a close friend. Beyond kissing, our research informs us that heterosexual undergraduate male athletes in Britain engage in more prolonged intimate activities including cuddling, hugging, spooning, and bed sharing (Anderson and McCormack 2015).

All of these men said that they had shared a bed with another man not out of homosexual attraction, but heterosexual affection. Jack's experience was representative of most of the participants: "Basically, my house is in the nearest town," he said. "When we go for a night out, those that haven't pulled [found a woman to take home] come back to mine and we share a bed. We don't have spare sheets and shit like that, so it's just least hassle." Thus, bed sharing can often be a pragmatic response to a particular social situation and, as Jamie says, "just not a big deal."

But it's not just bed sharing: of the 40 athletes that Anderson and McCormack interviewed, 37 had spent the night in bed with a heterosexual male friend and cuddled him. Mark McCormack is working on research that shows this is also a normal part of fraternity culture in at least one Ivy League university, too.

Without being prompted, Jarrett repeatedly stressed the amount of cuddling he and his mates engage in: "We're always cuddling, my lot. We're all comfortable with each other." Others highlight that cuddling occurs during the day and will often be described as "a quick cuddle." John praised these short interactions, saying "I love a quick cuddle, just so you remember your friends are about and are there for you." Similarly, Matt said, "I don't see anything wrong with sleeping in the same bed, or even showing that love in a club or even just at uni during the day." Sam also said, "I spoon, yeah . . . It is very common for us to go out [late], and then the next day after class receive a text from someone saying something like 'do you want to come and nap?'" Stephen explains, "You can rest your hand on his leg, or his hand, or wherever. There are no limitations."

For Pete and Tom, their bed sharing is a nightly occurrence. "We have shared beds loads of times last year, and we thought why not save money and just share a bed this year." When asked how often they cuddle, Pete says that they spoon most nights.

Threesomes

Male-male-female threesomes are another act that can be found occurring amongst university-aged heterosexual friends. In research conducted on two groups of collegiate athletes (Anderson 2008), it was found that 40% of the 49 men he interviewed had engaged in a male-male-female threesome where some physical contact occurred between the men. The willingness for two men to engage in such activities was told by Patrick to be at the behest of the female involved. He explained, "Well, for the most part it would be about getting it on with her, but like we might do some stuff together, too." Patrick said he would also allow himself to receive oral sex from a man but was not sure if he would give oral sex. He then smiled and said, "It depends on what she wants." While this threesome occurs with a foundation of heterosexuality present (a female), the heterosexual participants show consideration for engaging in same-sex sex as part of the pursuit for heterosexual sex.

Stuart goes further, informing us of his group sex experience. "My friend was fucking her and I was making out with him while he was doing it." Similarly, Stuart's teammate Tim said that "I made out with a guy once and I would let a guy blow me. I'm not gay but I think all guys wonder what it would be like. And I bet guys do it better anyhow." Ben said that he, Sam, and another heterosexual teammate once shared a room with Aaron (an openly gay athlete). "We let Aaron give the three of us a blow job," he said without hesitation, and then added, "And we're not the only ones who've done stuff with guys." Tom clarifies for us, "Just because one has gay sex, doesn't mean one is gay."

Eric Anderson and Stefan Robinson

Some might ascribe these sexual practices similar to other research of men who exist in such highly homophobic cultures that they are reluctant to identify as gay. When these men have sex with other men they are known as being on the down-low (Boykin 2005; King 2004); this is something particularly germane to Black men in the US. However, we argue that the behaviors described among these college athletes are not undertaken out of sexual urges for other men. Instead, they are described as occurring in a liminal state in which celebrations of sexual diversity occur. They happen "just because" and not because they desire sex with men.

While this type of activity is not widespread its representation in movies and discussion in popular culture has de-stigmatized these activities, particularly among undergraduates. In work Anderson is currently undertaking on 30 heterosexual male athletes, almost all report that they would engage in a threesome with two men and a woman, and almost three-quarters have had a threesome with another male and female. These threesomes are seen as a novel way of having heterosexual sex, as long as the male participants are not expected to sexually interact with the other man.

Conclusion

Decreasing cultural homophobia is an uneven social process. Not every reader in every college/university in America will relate to these findings—though we suggest that support for homosexuality is likely to be the vast majority in most. It is this changing perception of homosexuality as stigmatized to *homophobia* as stigmatized which has fuelled a reconceptualization of what it means to be both masculine and heterosexual for men. Men today are given a much greater range of gendered and sexual behaviors that they can partake in, while remaining socially heterosexual.

Anderson's (and his colleagues') collective body of research documents a significant shift in the need to perform an overtly heterosexual identity through expressing homophobia. Through the enactment of kissing, cuddling and other pseudo-sexual behaviors, young men are evidently embracing a much more flexible, organic and go-ahead attitude to sexual and pseudo-sexual conduct. This compliments the wider consensus in contemporary studies of sexuality which maintains there has been a marked expansion in the social and political landscape for gays, lesbians and the sexually flexible (McCormack 2012).

This progressive evolution has allowed men to engage in emotional and physical intimacy with their friends without risking their socially perceived heterosexual identity. Simply put, whereas college students' dads would have shamed any same-sex tactility, many college students today value the freedom to physically embrace one another. They express their fraternal love through the actions of kissing, cuddling and sharing sexual adventures, all supported by a newfound emotional intimacy with their friends. Even if one exists outside this culture, it is likely that the explicit love for a bro, and the concept of "bromance," is not alien. All of this is because of decreasing stigma against same-sex sex, and the diminishment of the one-time rule of homosexuality. Young men today are thus less concerned with regulating gender than they used to be.

None of this is to imply that men are becoming more fluid in their sexual attraction; rather, they are just more flexible in their approach to heterosexuality than men have traditionally been allowed to be. The expression of femininity and embracing of gendered and sexual behaviors that were (not long ago) taboo have set this generation of young, heterosexual men apart. It is a form of social change unique to millennials.

References

Anderson, Eric. 2008: "Being Masculine is Not About Who You Sleep With": Heterosexual Athletes Contesting Masculinity and the One-Time Rule of Homosexuality." *Sex Roles* 58(1–2): 104–115.

Anderson, Eric. 2009. *Inclusive Masculinity: The Changing Nature of Masculinities*. London: Routledge.

Anderson, Eric. 2012. *The Monogamy Gap: Men, Love, and the Reality of Cheating*. New York: Oxford University Press.

Anderson, Eric. 2014. *21st Century Jocks: Sporting Men and Contemporary Heterosexuality*. New York: Palgrave Macmillan.

Anderson, Eric and Mark McCormack. 2015. Cuddling and Spooning: Heteromasculinity and Homosocial Tactility among Student-athletes. *Men and Masculinities* 18(2): 214–230.

Anderson, Eric, Adi Adams, and Ian Rivers. 2012. "I Kiss Them Because I Love Them": The Emergence of Heterosexual Men Kissing in British Institutes of Education. *Archives of Sexual Behavior* 41(2): 421–430.

Attwood, Feona. 2010. *Porn.com: Making Sense of Online Pornography*. New York: Peter Lang.

Boykin, Keith. 2005. *Beyond the Down Low: Sex, Lies, and Denial in Black America*. New York: Carroll and Graf.

Canaday, Margo. 2009. *The Straight State: Sexuality and Citizenship in Twentieth-Century America*. Princeton: Princeton University Press.

Clements, Ben and Clive Field. 2014. Public Opinion Toward Homosexuality and Gay Rights in Great Britain. *Public Opinion Quarterly* 78(2): 523–547.

Diamond, Lisa. 2009. *Sexual Fluidity: Understanding Women's Love and Desire*. Cambridge: Harvard University Press.

Duggan, Lisa. 2003. *The Twilight of Equality? Neoliberalism, Cultural Politics, and the Attack on Democracy*. Boston: Beacon Press.

Filiault, Shaun, M. Murray, J. Drummond, Eric Anderson, and David Jeffries. 2014. Homosocial Intimacy Among Australian Undergraduate Men. *Journal of Sociology* 51(3): 643–656.

Jackson, Stevi and Sue Scott. 2004. Sexual Antimonies in Late Modernity. *Sexualities* 7(2): 233–248.

Katz-Wise, Sabra L. 2015. Sexual Fluidity in Young Adult Women and Men: Associations with Sexual Orientation and Sexual Identity Development. *Psychology & Sexuality* 6(2): 189–208.

King, James. 2004. *On the Down Low: A Journey into the Lives of "Straight" Black Men Who Sleep with Men*. New York: Broadway Books.

Kinnish, Kelly K., Donald S. Strassberg, and Charles W. Turner. 2005: Sex Differences in the Flexibility of Sexual Orientation: A Multidimensional Retrospective Assessment. *Archives of Sexual Behavior* 34(2): 173–183.

Kuper, Laura, Robin Nussbaum, and Brian Mustanski. 2012. Exploring the Diversity of Gender and Sexual Orientation Identities in an Online Sample of Transgender Individuals. *The Journal of Sex Research* 49(2–3): 244–254.

LeVay, Simon. 2011. *Gay, Straight and the Reason Why: The Science of Sexual Orientation*. New York: Oxford University Press.

McCormack, Mark. 2012. *The Declining Significance of Homophobia: How Teenage Boys are Redefining Masculinity and Heterosexuality*. New York: Oxford University Press.

McNair, Brian. 2002. *Striptease Culture: The Democratization of Desire*. London: Routledge.

Mock, Steven E., and Richard P. Eibach. 2012. Stability and Change in Sexual Orientation Identity over a 10-year Period in Adulthood. *Archives of Sexual Behavior* 41(3): 641–648.

Pryor, John H., Kevin Eagan, Laura P. Blake, Sylvia Hurtado, Jennifer Berdan, and Matthew H. Case. 2012. *The American Freshman: National Norms Fall 2012*. Los Angeles: Higher Education Research Institute, University of California.

Rubin, Gayle. 1984. Thinking Sex: Notes for a Radical Theory of the Politics of Sexuality. In *Pleasure and Danger: Exploring Female Sexuality* (pp. 267–320), edited by C. Vance. London: Routledge and Kegan Paul.

Savin-Williams, Ritch C. 2005. *The New Gay Teenager*. Harvard: Harvard University Press.

Schwartz, Pepper and Virginia Rutter. 2000. *The Gender of Sexuality*. Walnut Creek, CA: AltaMira Press.

Thompson, Elisabeth. 2006. Girl Friend or Girlfriend? Same-Sex Friendship and Bisexual Images as a Context for Flexible Sexual Identity Among Young Women. *Journal of Bisexuality* 6(3): 47–67.

Weeks, Jeffrey. 2007. *The World We Won*. London: Routledge.

Weiss, Margot. 2006. Mainstreaming Kink: The Politics of BDSM Representation in US Popular Media. *Journal of Homosexuality* 50(2–3): 103–132.

PART 5

Intimacies

Introduction

If we could transport ourselves to America or England in 1900, we would likely find ourselves in both a familiar and foreign environment. Familiar because most Americans or Brits, then and now, were married, had children, and lived in their own households independent of their family of origin. The link of intimacy and marriage was tight and celebrated by rituals of engagement and weddings, just as we often do today. Also, some of these marriages ended in separation and divorce, and some of these divorcees would remarry. All this would feel familiar and perhaps comforting to us.

Our time traveler would, however, feel like a stranger, even a foreigner, in some important ways. In Victorian America or England, the different aspects of intimacy were all bundled into the institution of marriage. That is, sexuality (meaning hetero-sexuality), love, companionship, and parenthood, were expected to occur entirely within the institution of marriage. There may have been sex outside of marriage, or same-sex intimacies, or even children born out of wedlock, but all of these practices would have been stigmatized and likely resulted in scandal or worse. The institution of marriage was the only legitimate, respectable social context for romantic intimacy for our Victorian ancestors.

In the last 100 years, however, these different dimensions of sexual intimacy are no longer necessarily bundled together. Today, in most Western nations, individuals, espe-cially the young, have choices about whether and how to combine the different aspects of intimacy. You can choose to marry but you can also cohabit with your partner without ever marrying; while most Americans marry after a period of cohabitation, many West Europeans are in fact choosing to not marry. The same Americans and Europeans may today choose a non-heterosexual intimacy, for example, same-sex intimacy or a roman-tic bond between two trans persons. While same-sex couples cannot marry in America, they can in many European nations. Today, marriage may or may not involve children, while same-sex couples may decide to adopt or to have children through alternative forms of insemination. And while love remains the center of romantic intimacy, as it did for our Victorian ancestors, its meaning has changed. Sexual compatibility, a deep sense of soulful connection, and the dense intertwining of personal and social lives are central to romantic love today. In Victorian times, love was expected to develop after marriage, and it had more to do with fulfilling gender roles and maintaining mutual respect than self-realization and communicative solidarity.

In short, individuals today, at least in America and across much of Europe, have a wide range of intimate choices available to them. We can choose whether or not we want to forge an intimate relationship, with whom, whether to marry, have children, be monogamous, and even whether we want to live together. And, of course, we can choose to dissolve our intimate bonds when we are no longer happy or satisfied. The sphere of romantic love has become for many of us a primary site of freedom and self-fulfillment through forging a transformative intimacy with our soul mate.

As a result, intimacies exhibit a diversity of forms and meanings, flexibility and openness, that is unique to our present age. Some critics may assail this intimate diversity for weakening the institution of marriage and the family, or for tolerating too much individual choice, but there is no going back to our Victorian ancestors. Our challenge today is to figure out how to balance our desire for choice and self-fulfillment with our equal need for intimate security and solidarity. This challenge will almost certainly mean that the sphere of romantic intimacy will continue to be a site of enormous hope, promise, and conflict for decades to come.

chapter 30

Romantic love

Interview with Eva Illouz

Eva Illouz was born in Morocco and moved to France when she was ten. She went on to get a PhD in Communications at the Annenberg School of Communications at the University of Pennsylvania. Since 1991 she has lived in Israel, where she teaches at the Hebrew University of Jerusalem. She is the author of four books, *Consuming the Romantic Utopia* (University of California Press, 1997), *The Culture of Capitalism* (Israel University Broadcast), *Oprah Winfrey and the Glamour of Misery* (Columbia University Press, 2003), and *Why Love Hurts: A Sociological Explanation* (Polity Press, 2013).

Is romantic love a natural feeling or is it a product of social and cultural life?

When sociology and anthropology took up the subject of emotions – some twenty years ago – they rejected *en bloc* the psychological and biological view that emotions are pre-cultural, individual, and not subject to historical forces. In short they rejected what we may call an essentialist view of emotions, the view that emotions are things that exist in themselves and are permanent. My own work is very much influenced by the opposite view, the constructivist view, which holds that the experience of emotions is shaped by language and that the rules governing their expression and exchange are essentially social.

But if it is now well established that ideas pertaining to God or to sexuality are subject to cultural and historical variations, we are less inclined to think that emotions can and do change and that they are subject to the influence of culture. Like anger, love[1] is often thought to be a universal emotion. To make things more difficult for us, there seems to be evidence that falling in love takes similar characteristics in different periods of time and in different cultures. For example, in many cultures, sight plays an important role in the activation of emotion (many languages have an equivalent of the expression "love at first sight"); the feeling of falling in love is sudden and is experienced as a disruption of one's routine and daily life; it is overwhelming and often takes an obsessive character; finally, the emotion of falling in love is experienced as overpowering the person's will. All of these characteristics can be found in the sixth-century Arabic legend of Majnoun and Leyla, in the thirteenth-century German epic by Gottfried von Strassburg "Tristan und Isolde," or the early thirteenth-century French fable "Aucassin et Nicolette," in William Shakespeare's sixtenth-century *Romeo and Juliet*, as well as in contemporary Hollywood cinema. And to top it all, contemporary research in neuropsychology seems to confirm the existence of specific brain regions which are activated when falling in love, which would in turn suggest that falling in love is grounded in biology, not culture, and therefore likely to be universal rather than bound by culture and language.

Contrary to some of my colleagues, I think it is unproductive to engage in a head-on collision with the biological research paradigm. Instead of arguing about the biological versus contextual nature of emotions, we should try to understand exactly just which aspects of the life of emotions, each paradigm – biological or constructivist – can or cannot account for. The question which I have thus tried to address in my work is: what can constructivists, like me, account for in love which the essentialists can't? I think that the biological approach to emotions cannot say anything about the social rules which activate emotional experiences and the fine-grained meanings contained in them.

The emotion of romantic love cannot be separated from social rules pertaining to the control of women's and men's sexuality, the regulation of marriage, and the ways in which property is transmitted. Without knowing something about these topics, we cannot understand which mental scripts fill people's heads when they say they are in love, nor can we understand whether and how love is encouraged or prohibited in a given society. For example, I would argue that falling in love is an importantly different experience whether women's virginity is defined as a condition for marriage or whether sexual experimentation before marriage is encouraged. When women's sexuality is closely regulated and limited to marriage, as was the case, say, in nineteenth-century America, romantic love takes the form of an all-encompassing narrative engulfing the self, expressing an absolute emotion and total commitment. Because sexual love was to be entrusted to one person only, such a conception of love emphasized the irreplaceable uniqueness of the love object. When, after the 1960s, women's sexuality became more a matter of individual desire and choice, romantic love took the form of a narrative of self-exploration; the link between sex, love, and marriage was weakened.

Let me take another example. In Ancient Greece, the supreme form of love was that between a mature man and a young boy. What preoccupied Greek culture was not to formulate a life-long commitment or to translate love into the institution of marriage, but rather, who penetrated whom. The older man had to be the one to penetrate, not be penetrated. He was to be active because the love between them was an affection between the mature man and the younger man in which the mature man was to guide the younger man and be a sort of substitute father to him. All this is done at the same time that the older man is married, has a legitimate wife, and children.

So we see in these examples that the biological approach to emotions cannot account for the social rules that guide the expression and social organization of emotions, and more importantly, biological views cannot explain the changing meanings of emotions and love. *of love*

Many of us think of the world of romantic love and the world of the marketplace as different and antagonistic. Is this a mistaken view?

Let me answer this question with a literary, but historically accurate, example. In his memoirs, Casanova, the eighteenth-century adventurer and seducer of a large number of women, recounts how, on being introduced to a lady of quality, a countess, he is taken by her beauty and charm. The day after meeting her, he goes to call on her in her house. He finds himself in a sitting room furnished with "four rickety chairs and a dirty old table." This sad and surprising spectacle is not improved by the countess's appearance, for, when she arrives, Casanova is struck by the misery and uncleanliness of her déshabillé. Understanding his dismay, she appeals to his pity and explains that, although of noble extraction, her father receives only a very small salary which he must share with his nine children. Casanova's immediate and unapologetic reaction deserves to be quoted: "I was not rich myself, and, as I was no longer in love, I only heaved a deep sigh, and remained as cold as ice."

Casanova, the reckless adventurer and charming seducer, turns out to have the soul of a cold-blooded accountant. His ardent love evaporates as soon as he is confronted with the countess's shabby economic situation. In the thoughts and feelings Casanova lets his reader take a peek at, economic interest breathes naturally through sentiments. Contrary to what a modern reader would think today, Casanova's thoughts were far from immoral. Quite the opposite; in a pre-capitalist world, to be moral implied one knew to choose an object of desire by taking into account his or her social standing. In an economy with restricted labor markets and circulation of commodities, property and inheritance were crucial to one's social standing, and property could be maintained or increased mostly through marriage. In a pre-capitalist world, the conduct of private life was thus subservient to economic strategies, interests, and modes of evaluation. If in non- or pre-capitalist societies, economic decisions were based on moral meanings (for example, who could work where on the basis of their religious membership; who could engage in banking activities, etc.), by the same token, sentimental or emotional decisions were always colored by economic considerations.

In contrast, and contrary to conventional wisdom and even contrary to some strands in sociological thought, I would claim that capitalism has been a great separator of sentiments and economic calculations.

By taking economic production out of the household, by making people less dependent on inherited property, and by making the family into an emotional – rather than an economic – unit, capitalism made marriage out of love entirely legitimate and even commendable, affirmed the sovereignty of individuals' emotional choices, and radically separated sentiments from interests. In capitalism, people could sell their labor on an open market, and thus became less dependent on inheritance for their economic survival, making them better able to choose according to their inclination. Moreover, by taking economic activity out of the household, capitalism made the family specialized in emotions, rather than in economic production.

Engels, Marx's famous collaborator, thought that in bourgeois marriage the desire to preserve or transmit private property was simply too strong to override disinterested love and sentiments, but Engels was wrong, for in many ways the reverse has happened: because capitalism made economy into a specialized activity – independent of sexual reproduction and marriage – it also made the family into a non-economic unit, an emotional hothouse in which men and women would become increasingly preoccupied with their mutual love, sexuality, individual self-development and parental affection. The norm of love that has been made possible by the capitalist economy has disturbed the rules by which people came to choose a partner and which governed what they could expect from marriage.

Thus, I am saying that capitalism has instituted a divide between interests and emotions, channeling each of them into a distinctive institutional sphere. The ironical conclusion of this is that the market and the social organization of capitalism are intricately intertwined with the fact that love became defined as a strictly disinterested emotion, that is, one without an a priori consideration of the partner's economic assets and social standing. So there is a paradox here, for it is the market society which has made possible the separation between interests and intimate relationships.

What are some of the social forces that create a culture of romantic love?

First, let us establish what a culture of romantic love means. It is a culture whereby the definition of the good life includes finding a person able to generate long-lasting and yet exciting feelings, and being able to extend the experience of love throughout one's life. In other words, a culture of love is a culture where the experience of love plays a central role in the definition of self and in which actors engage in a wide variety of symbolic practices to create, experience and maintain the emotion of love. Moreover, this love is not just any kind of love: it is heterosexual but not necessarily oriented toward child-bearing and child-rearing; it is connected to marriage, but can very well thrive without it; it privileges intensity and excitement, yet aims or claims to be long-lasting; finally, it is individualistic both in the sense that it gives expression to the innermost unique and authentic aspects of the self and in the sense that it is closely associated with the idea of self-realization.

Contrary to a naive view of modernity as a heartless and bureaucratized era, I would say that modernity has made love into our categorical imperative, the experience without which we do not feel fully accomplished as human beings.

A number of factors have contributed to creating such culture: the most important is the public/private divide I mentioned earlier. Without the creation of an institutional and cultural divide between the public and private self and a massive cultural shift making the private self the sole repository of authenticity, meaning, and commitment, a culture of love as I defined it would not be possible.

Moreover, love flourishes in individualistic cultures. Individualism is the social transformation without which we cannot understand the rise of a culture of love. Individualism has many institutional sites (legal, economic, moral, etc.). But in the twentieth century it was the culture of consumption which shaped most significantly the individualist search for love. It is the individualism promoted by consumption which has perhaps most contributed to institutionalize a culture of

Interview with Eva Illouz

romance. Contrary to conventional wisdom, I would say that consumer culture is not a materialist culture, but rather a deeply emotional one. Consumer culture caters to and elicits some deeply rooted emotions – as love or the need for security – through scenarios of the good life and models of self-realization. Consumer culture has used extensively the image of the couple in love to promote its goods (a man and a woman engaged either explicitly or implicitly in a romantic interaction is probably the most widespread image in advertising culture). Moreover, at the end of the nineteenth century, the leisure industries, avid to expand their economic and social reach, catered to men's and women's search for intimacy. Thus what we call dating implies both that the couple meet outside the home and that they purchase together a leisure good: to go to a movie, to a bar, or to a restaurant – which have all become normal arenas for romantic meetings – is to engage in a consumer activity which gives expression to an individual's inner self and search for pleasure and happiness.

For these different forces to coalesce into a coherent cultural model which can in turn guide the self, experience must be organized in a cultural form which expresses and gives shape to a new way of feeling. If, during much of the eighteenth and nineteenth centuries, it was the novel which offered to the self a narrative model of love (especially to its female readers), in the twentieth century this role was assumed (and even amplified) by the movie. In this way Hollywood transformed the culture of love in a few significant ways: if, until then, love had been connected to the rhetoric of religious devotion, it now became more radically secular and a project for its own sake; whereas the nineteenth-century novel contained sexuality in a euphemized and implicit way, Hollywood, using the obvious characteristics of the visual medium, abundantly depicted romantic kisses, embraces, and petting, and explicitly alluded to sexual interactions and naturalized the association of love and sexuality. More than any other cultural medium, the movies defined romantic interactions in visual terms: a romantic moment would now be defined not only by culturally explicit scenarios of sexual interactions, but also by a certain kind of "atmosphere" containing specific props (for example, a romantic dinner or the proximity of the sea). Finally, contrary to literary strands which had preceded it, Hollywood built a strong association and equivalence between love, marriage, and happiness. Thanks to the movies, love became a powerful motive in the modern cultural imagination.

What do you mean by the idea of romantic love as a kind of utopia?

A utopia is a narrative through which societies think out loud about and formulate their preferred social arrangements. This is why utopias typically erase contradictions: to dream that the lamb and the wolf will coexist (as the Book of the Prophets envisioned) negates nature and the state of scarcity to which the human condition has often been submitted to. The romantic utopia describes how self-fulfillment, authenticity, meaning and happiness are reached in the experience of heterosexual love. Similar to other utopias, it negates a number of contradictions particularly rife in modern societies, such as the contradiction between marriage and the non- or anti-institutional love that is implied by the traditional ideal of love. But this does not mean that utopias are a form of false thinking. On the contrary: utopias must be distinguished from ideology

– even if this distinction is tenuous and open to argument. Utopias make us dream about a better world, about alternative arrangements, and even if those dreams often degenerate in control and manipulation, we still must account for the hope and creativity they contain and often generate. Utopias inspire change.

Moreover, utopias shape our thoughts or dreams through specific means of expression and communication. The romantic utopia is essentially a visual one, combining ideals of beauty, models of masculinity and femininity, visual scenarios of romantic scenery, with models of sexual manners and courtship.

What I find particularly interesting in the romantic utopia is that it reproduces ideals of masculinity and femininity, yet it is simultaneously a genderless ideal. Historically, we observe that the greater the injunction to love inside marriage, the higher the status of women. But the romantic utopia went one step further, in that it "feminized" men, that is it drew them inside the purview of domesticity, and offered to merge men and women in a genderless model of intimacy. Through the ideal of intimacy, men and women are enjoined to foreground similar selves centered around the verbal expression and sharing of their emotional inner self. In fact, the tension which haunts modern couplehood can be understood precisely as a tension between genderless ideals and the persistence of gender differences and inequalities.

You argue that the idea of dating didn't become widespread until the 1930s. What do you see as the significance of dating for the development of romantic love?

At the end of the nineteenth century, dating was a word reserved for the working class because it implied that the couple would meet outside the confines of the domestic sphere. By and large, members of the middle class met inside the home, and commercial amusements were not considered as appropriate venues to meet. Dating was inappropriate because, let us remember, it implied two different things: one is an interaction that has a potentially romantic character in a public space, not guarded or defined by middle-class values; the second is that this interaction takes place in the sphere of commercial entertainment. Dating could become widespread and common when leisure consumption became generalized – reaching all social classes – and institutionalized. For example, going to a fancy restaurant or on a vacation in a faraway location becomes the privileged site for the experience of romance. Thus we may say that dating is the outcome of a romanticization of commodities (the refrigerator becomes romantic when associated with a couple dining by the light of candles) and a commodification of romance (experiencing romance becomes increasingly connected to being able to purchase leisure goods). Dating is an outstanding example of how the interaction between a new technology, images, gender definitions, and economic changes converge to create a new social form, in the Simmelian sense of that word.

But what exactly does this entail? Many would argue that this entails a severe degradation of the romantic bond. I am not convinced that commodities and consumption as such debase human relationships. In fact, meeting in such consumption-oriented places as restaurants, or going on a weekend in a luxurious resort, often end up generating (or regenerating) intense feelings. Commodities have the power to ritualize interactions by making clearer their spatial and temporal boundaries, that is by making them mark off the conduct and objects of daily life.

Moreover, in the culture of dating the idiom of pleasure becomes dominant and the anonymity afforded by public spaces entails a perceived greater freedom, which in turn leads to one of the processes Seidman and Giddens have described, namely a progressive disconnection of romance from marriage. So, if from the eighteenth century onward we see a close association of marriage and love, in the twentieth century we see a progressive separation of these two modes of conduct.

Between the nineteenth century and World War Two the meaning of love changed from spiritual edification to personal happiness. Have there been any significant changes in the meaning of romantic love since World War Two?

I don't think the changes have been as dramatic as those we observe in the passage from the nineteenth century to World War Two. Still, they are important changes which are related to the transformations undergone by sexuality. I am going to set aside the question of the transformation of sexuality during that period. Seidman's work explores this question thoroughly and I have very little to add to it. I think that two cultural persuasions have massively altered the meaning of love: one is psychologism – the broad cultural worldview and language derived from various schools of clinical psychology, especially dynamic psychology; the other is feminism – the view inspired by political liberalism, a view which calls on granting men and women equal rights and status inside the private and public spheres. How have these two formations altered the romantic bond?

Both contributed to what we may call with Max Weber a disenchantment of the romantic bond. By this I mean a new ironic detachment from the idea of love and a reflexive attitude vis-à-vis its psychological and sociological underpinnings. Psychology, for one, put forward the idea that love is never quite what it looks like. For psychoanalysis, the psyche is deeply ambivalent, and thus love turns out to be a close cousin of its opposite, hatred. Moreover, the culture of psychology invites us to doubt how seriously we should take our feelings. Where the romantic tradition suggested that love was an inexplicable recognition of a unique person destined to us, psychology explains love as the need to reenact losses and painful aspects of our past relationships with caring characters.

Feminism also has put love under the microscope. Contrary to popular mythology, radical feminists argue, love is not the source of transcendence, happiness, and self-realization. Rather, romantic love is one of the main causes of the divide between men and women, as well as one of the cultural practices through which women are made to accept (and "love") their submission to men. For, when in love, men and women continue to perform the deep divisions that characterize their respective identities: in Simone de Beauvoir's famous words, even in love men retain their sovereignty, while women aim to abandon themselves. Or, in her *Dialectic of Sex*, Shulamit Firestone argues that the source of men's social power and energy is the love women have provided and continue to provide for men, thus suggesting that love is the cement with which the edifice of male domination has been built. Romantic love not only hides a sex segregation, but in fact it makes it possible.

I think that the two cultural persuasions of feminism and psychology have thus made us deeply suspicious of love, or at least ironic vis-à-vis its most conventional aspects.

In the popular media, romantic love is viewed as something we all experience in more or less the same way. But is romantic love truly experienced in a classless way and is it the same between men and women?

Well, yes and no. If romance and love are such powerful utopias, it is precisely because they are genderless and classless. In a way, this is why romantic love has been a transgressive social force, precisely because it often disturbed class boundaries and mechanisms of transmission of property: for a prince to fall in love with a poor shepherdess means to relinquish a great source of power. In our popular representations, love makes men leave the competitive realm of power, and draws them in the emotion-filled female sphere of care and nurturance. It is true that capitalism was responsible for locking men and women in separate gender spheres – relegating women to what Hannah Arendt has dubbed "the shadowy realm of the interior," and throwing men into the harsh and competitive arena of the market – but in making romantic love an intrinsic component of bourgeois marriage it also increased the status of women and in fact slowly eroded male supremacy inside the household. It is also true that modern marriages are not as far from arranged marriages as one would like to think (statistics show we often end up marrying somebody socially and economically compatible with us). Yet, the norm of love has changed importantly how people choose a partner and what they expect from marriage.

In that sense, romantic love has been an anti-institutional force, if not destroying then at least disturbing class and gender divisions. The connection of consumer culture and love in a way only reinforced this "oecumenical" appeal of the romantic utopia.

Yet, things are not that simple. Let's take the gender dimension. Past the stage of courtship, women tend to be the ones who monitor the relationship and who bear the burden of doing "emotional work." Or, take the class dimension: in many subtle and not-so-subtle ways, people's cultural tastes and ways of talking – which are deeply connected to one's education and socioeconomic level – affect how they express their emotions, how they are able to draw other people into their emotional life, and whether they are able to create moments of intense bonding, those precise moments where you forget another's socioeconomic status. Quite often, in order to be able to do that – that is, to create moments of pure bonding – two people need to be in harmony together, but such harmony of the hearts is quite often a social harmony, predicated on common cultural and social references. Finally, I would say that romance has been and continues to be an upper-middle-class way of life because it presupposes a not inconsiderable amount of resources in time and money.

So Lady Chatterley might be attracted for a while to the raw sexuality of her working-class lover, but when she needs expressions of love and emotions, she will most likely be flustered by the social and economic gap that normally separates them.

In American culture, the first date often involves going out to a restaurant. Are there sociological reasons for this?

The restaurant is the quintessential consumer space: it is both public and private, in that it caters to a large number of people, yet it also enables two people to isolate themselves and feel thoroughly individualized in their experience. Moreover the

Interview with Eva Illouz

restaurant mobilizes a vast array of artifacts (food, light, tablecloth, music, general design); this is why it is able to ritualize the meeting, by which I mean, following Durkheim, that it enables two people to withdraw from daily conduct and to (re)generate intense feelings. What enables a couple to do that is the fact that a restaurant makes the activity of eating into a formal and aesthetic one (food, clothes, light, music, all conspire to make the meeting stylized), sharply distinct from daily life. The typical imagery of a romantic restaurant involves soft light (candles), langorous music, exotic and luxurious food presented in beautiful dishes, and an elegant décor. All of this creates an esthetic experience which de-familiarizes and enhances daily life. The restaurant thus enables a ritualization of the romantic bond. Moreover, given that a restaurant represents a small expenditure in the income of middle- or upper-middle-class people, the experience can be renewed frequently. The restaurant is thus the perfect meeting between consumer and romantic culture, whereby pleasure of the gustatory and olfactory senses and a wide variety of artifacts combine to create privacy, intimacy, and novelty, easily purchasable and renewable.

(By the way, in the era of internet dating, the restaurant is no longer likely to be the place where people meet on their first date.)

There is a trend in the United States for individuals to experience romantic love but remain single or cohabit. Why do you think this is happening, and will this trend continue?

Capitalism produces contradictions. I think that one of the most salient and less discussed contradictions is between the idea that forming long-lasting intimate bonds is of the utmost importance for the self, and the idea that the individual must strive for self-affirmation, autonomy, self-reliance, and self-realization. The culture of individuality from which romantic love emerged and in which it flourished has produced a culture in which men and women are increasingly self-reliant, take their own self as the object and center of their life narrative and life goals, and are thus less willing to engage in the kind of Other-oriented (what some view as self-sacrificing) practices demanded by family and marriage. This is especially true of women, who are less inclined to want to face the sometimes difficult tasks of having to combine work and children. Also, marriage has been and to a certain extent still is a primarily economic institution. Given that many women do not feel the need to marry for their economic survival, the necessity of marriage also fades.

But again, things are not simple, because even if marriage as such is on the decline, the norm of monogamy – which has been historically enforced as the prerogative of married people – seems to pervade heterosexual (nonmarried) relationships as if one of the main characteristics of marriage had been thoroughly internalized.

Note

1   This chapter deals with heterosexual love. Unless otherwise specified, use of the term "love" should be understood in this sense.

chapter 31

Sexual capital and social inequality

The study of sexual fields

Adam Isaiah Green

The study of collective intimate life—including everything from with whom we "hook up" to whom we marry—has been rather devoid of sociological imagination. This is not to suggest a lack of insightful work on sexual identities, communities and practices; indeed, the last forty years have seen a proliferation of probing sociological research on these topics, beginning at least as far back as 1974 when Gagnon and Simon developed a social constructionist approach to the study of sexuality that moved beyond the frameworks of deviance and social control. Rather, I suggest that desire and desirability have been understood, with too few exceptions, in a manner that reduces them to either idiosyncratic properties of subculture, or altogether outside the scope of what concerns most sociologists of intimate life—marriage markets (but for a few important exceptions, see Epstein (1991) and Whittier and Melendez (2004)). But in-between these two polarized positions is a meso-level domain of collective sexual life for which most individuals in the modern world are familiar and which operates via sociological principles to shape and transform the very things we want and desire in a partner. *Here* is a sociology of collective sexual life, a structured domain of interaction oriented around the pursuit of partnership that I call the *sexual field*.

A sexual field is a social domain anchored to physical and virtual sites and inhabited by individuals with potential romantic interest in one another. For example, a college fraternity party can be thought of as an event that generates a sexual field where individual participants seek out partnership by orienting themselves toward one another according to norms of desirability that are specific to that particular social domain (Green 2014). Such norms often attach sexual value to particular physical characteristics, such as height, weight or skin color, along with forms of self-presentation, including choice in clothing, hairstyles, and affect (Armstrong et al., 2006). These norms of desirability, in turn, produce a system of stratification that make some actors more desirable than others. A sexual field, then, is a social space where actors with different degrees of desirability (i.e., what I call "sexual capital") convene to find intimate partnership but where status is unevenly distributed, thus lending the field a degree of competition. While stratification in a sexual field cannot be reduced to race, class, gender, age and ethnic hierarchies, sexual fields are, nevertheless, social orders that reflect and produce social inequalities, and are therefore an important topic of sociological investigation.

Below, I provide an overview of the sexual fields framework, including its core concepts and its key theoretical insight. Along the way, I use sexual fields research in order to illuminate its concepts. I conclude by highlighting the role of social inequality in collective sexual life, and suggest some lines of inquiry that call out for future sexual fields analysis.

The sexual fields framework

The post-World War II era has been characterized both by the increasing autonomy of the sexual sphere from traditional sources of social control (e.g., the family, the Church), and the increasing specialization of sexual subcultures (D'Emilio 1983). Hence, when compared to the 19th century, actors today have both more autonomy in directing their intimate lives and more specialized options to consider in the pursuit of intimate relations (Giddens 1992; Weiss 2012). Indeed, in the 20th and now 21st centuries, we enjoy, *en masse*, a semblance of intimate life designed to accommodate highly specific preference structures around partnership to a degree perhaps unrivaled in historical terms. Websites designed to accommodate everything from a fling to a marital relationship make this point especially clear. Today online, one may select from racial, ethnic and religious preferences (e.g., Jdate.com, Asia FriendFinder.com), class preferences (e.g., Sugardaddie.com, MillionaireMatchmaker.com), age preferences (e.g., SeniorMatch.com, Cougarlife.com), body type preferences (BigMuscleBear.com, Chubbychasersdating.com) and relationship type preferences (AdultFriendFinder.com, Fling.com), among still others. Similarly, queer-oriented websites and social apps abound along with real-time brick and mortar sites such as bars, bathhouses, gay-designated neighborhoods, nightclubs, circuit parties and bookstores. Here, non-heterosexual individuals partake in collective sexual life to cultivate a variety of intimate partnerships and friendships. In total, when one considers the contemporary sociosexual landscape outside the bedroom of the monogamous couple, one finds a staggering array of different kinds of collective sexual life that illustrate their growing independence from traditional institutions of social control, such as the family and the Church.

In recent years, scholars of sexuality have sought to makes sense of this proliferation of erotic worlds by building on former social constructionist research, conceiving of collective sexual life as a particular *kind* of social life in its own right (Green 2008b; 2014). Drawing from Bourdieusian field theory (1977; 1990) (see below), this work understands the search for intimate partnership to occur in the context of a sexual field, each field with its own particular logic of desirability and accompanying distribution of sexual capital (Farrer 2011; Farrer and Dale 2014; Green 2008b; 2014; Martin and George 2006). As I draw out in greater detail below, the sexual fields approach entails an analysis of the ways in which partnership preferences, including preferences around sexual, economic and social attributes, are forged in the context of sexual fields whereby the field organizes both what we desire in another and how we understand ourselves within the sexual status order.

Field theory and the sexual fields framework

Bourdieu's analysis of routine practice, as developed in field theory (see Bourdieu 1977; 1990) is the basis for the development of the sexual fields framework (Green 2008b; Martin and George 2006). The chief theoretical insight of field theory is the notion that actors exist relationally in social space, their distinct positions arising as the consequence of differential resources (i.e., the distribution of capital) within the field. Like field theory more generally, key concepts of the sexual fields framework include the concepts of field and capital—and add to these the concepts: sexual sites, structures of desire, and sexual circuits. These concepts are useful to the extent that they help to identify how the things sexual actors want in an intimate partner, and the things that sexual actors need in order to attract such an intimate partner—are, in part, *field effects*, a product of ecological, social learning, and social psychological processes associated with the field. But before exploring this insight I first review the component parts of the sexual fields framework below, beginning with an elaboration of the concept of the sexual field.

In Bourdieu's (1977; 1990) work, *two guiding metaphors* capture the field with relevance for collective sexual life (Martin 2011), including the field as a "fields of force" and as a "field of struggle". Like a field of gravity that brings into alignment the otherwise diverse elements that enter its orbit, the metaphor of a field of force suggests that we consider how collective sexual life is shaped by the structures and processes of any given field, be it an online dating website, a debutante ball, a gay leather bar, a college keg party, or a big-city speed-dating event, to name only a few. That is, upon entering and becoming a participant in any of these sexual fields, one finds that certain lines of action are required to be a relevant "player," to occupy social space and command the rewards of the field. These lines of action may include self-presentation, such as style, behavior, and the cultivation of a particular body type, along with social practices related to how to approach another, deference, demeanor, the enactment of courting practices, sexual repertoires, nightlife and lifestyle preferences. One need only consider the contrasting environments associated with a college keg party and a swanky Martini bar to imagine how distinct sexual fields require that individual participants align their actions and self-presentation to the logic of desirability specific to each field. As well, sexual fields may require additional individual characteristics and group associations for participation, including one's occupation, income, race and ethnic background, with whom one socializes, where, religious affiliations, and the like. Websites designed to facilitate long-term dating or marriage, for example, will generally require much more detailed consideration around partner characteristics—including characteristics such as religion, race and occupation—than the hook-up bar with the weekly drink special located in every large college town in North America. This is because the marriage-oriented website and the local pick-up bar represent two distinct sexual fields with their own particular logic of desire and desirability.

To the extent that fields are domains of organized striving, they may also be seen as a field of struggle, like a battlefield or an athletic field. In this sense, field participants occupy social space on account of their distinct, relative positions to one another which are often determined by different degrees of sexual capital between players. These positions confer a "sense of one's place" within the field along with a corresponding repertoire of lines of action appropriate to their status (Martin 2011). In more common parlance, this idea relates to the notion of being outside of or within the same "league" as a desired other. Thus the observation, "s/he is way out of your league!" suggests that a desired female has much more sexual capital than the desirer.

In a sexual field—say the downtown heterosexual city nightclub—not all men will have access to the most desirable women, and *vice versa*. To the extent that men and women may vie for the same subset of potential intimate partners, or even simply for significance in this social space (e.g., a sense of visibility and esteem), the downtown city nightclub can be regarded as a kind of battlefield whereby one's status is determined by and relative to other players in the field. Put in the terms of the sexual fields framework, we might say that nightclub scene participants operate with differential degrees of sexual capital that stratify sexual actors in their pursuit of field esteem and its rewards, the latter of which include securing partnership (or just a phone number) with a partner of one's choosing. One's relative status within this field will, in turn, bear on self-assessment, who will approach whom and how, and subsequent practices related to self-presentation and the management of self.

A second key concept in the sexual fields framework—*sexual capital*—is that type of capital (among other types, including economic, cultural and social capitals) associated with attractiveness and desirability. Sexual capital confers advantage upon those who possess it within a sexual field. As noted above, the precise attributes that determine sexual capital vary across sexual fields as different fields are organized by distinct characteristics of desirability. In this sense, sexual capital is not simply a characteristic of individuals—e.g., having a fit body or pleasing facial features—but rather, is simultaneously a property of individuals *and* a property of the sexual field. Thus, within the context of a given field, individuals possess more or less sexual capital, yet they do not "own" sexual capital (Farrer and Dale 2014). Rather, sexual capital is a relational resource that signals the relationship an actor has to others in the field and to the field's standards of attractiveness—what Martin and George (2006) call the field's "hegemonic system of judgments". In this sense, sexual capital indexes one's power relative to other players within the sexual field.

However, because desirability in a partner is not reducible to *sexual* desirability, sexual fields must accommodate a broader notion of what makes someone attractive, including cultural and economic capital. In this sense, it is often helpful to think about how fields legislate not just sexual desirability but a broader kind of *capital portfolio* possessing different degrees of capitals. Like sexual capital, valued capital portfolios cannot be determined in advance but, rather, take shape differentially between communities, social strata, and sexual fields. While in some instances actors may convert economic, cultural or social capital into sexual capital (Martin 2005), in other instances these capitals are desirable in a partner but not themselves sexy. They are thus considered separate from sexual capital, but may be as or even more important in terms of providing field status. As a simple example, Buss et al. (2001) shows how women and men, on average, desire a different combination of capitals within the capital portfolio of desired partners, with women placing more value on economic and cultural capital than men, and men putting greater emphasis on sexual capital than women. Interestingly, as women have become more economically enfranchised over time, these differences have diminished, though not completely disappeared (Buss et al. 2001).

A third core concept, *structure of desire*, captures desire as an aggregate of individual wants and attitudes—i.e., the field's collective judgments of desirability. Collective judgments of desirability materialize at the site of the sexual field and are observable in the representations and patterned interactions of the field. For example, sexual fields often communicate a sexual status order through broadcasting idealized images of what is and what should be important to the clientele, including representations of the perfect "couple" on the front page of a dating website (e.g., characteristics related to race, age, class, affect, body type, presentational style, etc.), the appearance of the bartenders (e.g., including characteristics related to race, age, class, affect, body type, etc.), the décor (e.g., compare the gay leather bar with the upscale Martini bar), the name of the site (e.g., the Ramrod), patterns in the fronts of patrons (e.g., dress, adornment, affect), and the patterned written content of website profiles, including descriptions of the likes and dislikes of website members (e.g., "no Asians"; "no daddies"; "under 30 only"; "no fats or fems"). Structures of desire are also observable in field interactions, including the talk about who is desirable and who is not, observable patterns in who is favored and who is ignored (i.e., who is popular), who is bought drinks and who is left paying for one's self, who gets let in first by the bouncer (and who is stalled or denied entrance altogether), and who earns the most hits, hearts, flowers or kisses on a dating website.

Taken together, these elements of a structure of desire both reflect and align how individuals understand desirability, including the attractiveness of others and the relative desirability of themselves. That is, to the extent that individuals in a sexual field have an intuitive awareness of the relational nature of "the game", they are bound to engage in comparison processes whereby they assess the degree to which a given person of interest possesses sexual capital within the field, along with the degree to which they themselves possess the required capitals to hold the attention of such desired person. Rather than understand desirability in purely idiosyncratic or essentialist terms, players in the sexual field act as lay social scientists who are obliged to construct theories around others' desirability and their own. Hence, structures of desire become crucial to the extent that individual players understand them as determining their opportunities for partnership, including dominant standards of desirability against which they themselves are judged. Moreover, as I explore further below, structures of desire can have the effect of resocializing our desires, such that the things we originally desire change over time following repeated exposure to the field.

The comparison processes by which actors determine the field's structure of desire, including the sexual status of others and themselves, are usually made in reference to recurring networks of actors who share the field sites we occupy and, in turn, provide the social basis upon which we construct a theory of sexual value. These networks—*sexual circuits*—are made up of those with whom we regularly "rub elbows" in the field but with whom we lack stronger ties of dependence, such as friends, family members or coworkers (Adam and Green 2014). Sexual circuits represent patterned flows of individuals and groups that populate particular sexual sites. In Toronto, for instance, Adam and Green (2014) use surveys from Gay Pride attendees and discover ten distinct circuits. These circuits are comprised of patterned groupings of individuals who report attending particular combinations of sites in the prior year, including a distinct subset of fields connected to bars, bathhouses, nightclubs, public restrooms, parks, social apps and websites. Thus, circuits represent network members with shared interests in particular sexual fields over others, shared lifestyle practices, and in many cases a similar range of sociodemographic characteristics, including most notably, age and race.

Having reviewed some of the major concepts of the sexual fields framework, I turn below to a brief discussion of the framework's central theoretical insight concerning the transformation of desire and desirability in collective sexual life.

Desire and desirability in collective sexual life

The core theoretical premise of the sexual fields framework holds that desire and desirability are transformed over time as individuals enter collective sexual life and become resocialized in the context of the field. To date, Green (2014) has identified three central ways in which fields "act back" on desire and desirability such that both may be regarded, in part, as changed on account of the field. These include: 1) the popularity tournament; 2) socialization; and 3) aggregation and intensification processes. I explore each one individually below.

One of the simplest processes by which a sexual field may transform sexual desire and desirability is through the popularity tournament (Green 2014; Martin and George 2006; Waller 1937). In the context of a popularity tournament, one's relative standing in the sexual field has the tendency to reinforce and even intensify one's subsequent social status. Thus, Waller (1937) finds that at college co-ed parties, "nothing succeeds like success"—i.e., the popular become even more popular. Conversely, one may infer that the unpopular become even less so over time. Put differently, individual partner preferences in a sexual field are not reducible to pre-existing, individual desires prior to field participation but, rather, are transformed, to varying degrees, upon entering the "gravitational pull" of the sexual field (Green 2014). Thus one's initial field status is consequential for one's future field standing.

A second core way in which sexual fields act on sexual desires and desirability relates to general processes of socialization. Here, exposure to a given sexual subculture within a sexual field can resocialize sexuality such that we acquire a deeper taste for that which we were previously only mildly interested, or even an aversion to things we previously desired. Weiss' (2012) ethnographic account of the "pan-BDSM" scene of San Francisco makes this point explicitly clear. In this sexual field, novitiates enter the erotic world of BDSM, often with prior interest in bondage and sadomasochism but without a full appreciation for the relationship of pleasure to pain, the erotic power of a well-skilled "top", or the erotic potential of "play" scenarios—such as "child molestation" and "slavery"—which, in other contexts, might be quite un-erotic. In a somewhat different vein, in Shanghai, Western Caucasian men favor local Chinese women who participate in the sexual fields of key "ethnosexual contact zones" (Farrer and Dale 2014). Chinese women who seek out these fields are typically younger, on average, then their Western expat-sisters, and hold expat men in higher esteem. Here, the desires of expat men are resocialized to favor local Chinese women and, as a consequence, they lose interest in their Western female counterparts, the latter perceived to be less deferential and more demanding. In this context, we have an instance of the transformation of racialized desires—toward local Chinese women and away from Western expat women—within a sexual field that encourages expat men to cultivate a taste for ethnicity. And at a transwoman bar, otherwise "heterosexual" men encounter highly feminized and flirtatious transgender women and develop an erotic taste for them that overcomes the disjunct between anatomy and gender such that the trans women's hyper-sexualized feminine affect becomes a source of sexual desire (for more, see below) (Weinberg and Williams 2014).

Finally, a third central field effect can be seen in an amplification/intensification process that draws from Fischer's (1975) ecological theory of urbanism and subcultures. With respect to collective sexual life, individual desires are collectivized at the sites of a sexual field such that they obtain a critical mass, exceeding the desires of any given individual to constitute a new, intensified structure of desire. Put differently, structures of desire amplify the individual desires of field participants to produce an intensified, "hyper" realized structure of desire. Levine's (1998) analysis of the clone sexual subculture of the 1970s and 1980s provides a superior example of this process. Then, the post World War II gendered sensibilities of gay male participants pooled together as the clone sexual subculture took form, magnifying, amplifying and intensifying the individually held desires and sensibilities of each man's construction of masculinity. What resulted was a hypermasculinized "clone" sexual subculture—a "super masculinity"—that intensified their individually held masculine scripts in all aspects of the subculture, from sexual practice to presentation; indeed, even the names and décor of the bars and bathhouses were hypermasculine (Levine 1998). Both the desires and desirability of the clones were transformed as actors entered the gravitational field of the clone sexual field.

Having considered three central ways a sexual field may "act back" upon desire to shape how we think about and experience our own desire and our sense of desirability to others, I turn below to some concluding lines of inquiry for future sexual fields research.

Future directions in sexual fields research

Research from the perspective of the sexual fields framework is in its infancy, and much work remains to be done. For instance, at the broadest macro-historical vantage point, we may ask how sexual capital in any given field is shaped by histories of colonialism, slavery, state-building, globalization, and the like. As well, if Kimmel (2008) and other sociologists are correct about the extension of adolescence into the late twenties of contemporary young adults whereby changes in the economy of the developed Western world render both women and men ever more dependent upon parents later into the life course—i.e., "emerging adulthood"—we might wonder how these changes will impact intimate life and the sexual field. Indeed, with fewer opportunities for earning a living wage, higher demands for post-graduate credentials and training, and prolonged internal struggles around identity and self-mastery, college-age adults of today will delay marriage and child rearing, and establish careers later in the life course than their parents. These kinds of macro-level socio-demographic shifts will undoubtedly bear on the sexual social life that young adults pursue, the latter of which call out for sexual fields analysis.

Of course, the late modern information age, including the introduction of social apps and Internet sites that cater to sexual life, has radically transformed the social organization of collective sexual life, increasing both the development of highly specialized sexual fields and ease of access to them. This transformation has facilitated intimate connections, extending possibilities for partnering well beyond the traditional boundaries of time and space. Yet virtual sites, be they dating websites or social applications with GPS technologies (e.g., "Tinder"; "Grindr") are also social in the sense that they are comprised of actors who become visible to one another and who must navigate status expectations in ways not altogether different from real-time sites of sociality. Moreover, because many websites and social apps allow users to search on particular criteria, they facilitate the development of ever-narrower preference structures around age, race, class, ethnicity, religion, body type, relationship type, and so on. This fact is likely to transform how actors, *en masse*, think about and construct desirability in ways that will surely shape future sexual fields and the ways in which its participants produce and negotiate sexual stratification.

Finally, the relationship of the sexual field to sexually transmitted infections is a substantive line of inquiry that demands immediate attention. Among men who have sex with men (MSM), for example, the introduction of promising HIV pre-exposure prophylactic medications (PrEP) and emerging data on the success of anti-retroviral treatment (ARV) in preventing HIV transmission are likely to transform the social organization of collective sexual life as new sexual identities, such as the HIV "positive but undetectable" and "PrEP user" change the assessment of sexual risk and the subsequent patterning of intimate partnership. But precisely if and how the successful treatment of HIV will bear on collective sexual life, on attributions of desirability, and on the norms of acceptable and "underground" sexual practices, remain as yet unknown and call out for sexual field analysis.

Bibliography

Adam, Barry D. and Adam Isaiah Green. 2014. "Circuits and the Social Organization of Sexual." In Green, Adam Isaiah (ed.), *Sexual Fields: Toward a Sociology of Collective Sexual Life* (pp. 123–142). Chicago: University of Chicago Press.

Armstrong, Elizabeth. 2010. "Sluts." Paper presented at "Bringing Bourdieu to Sexual Life." University of Toronto.

Armstrong, Elizabeth, Laura Hamilton and Brian Sweeney. 2006. "Sexual Assault on Campus: A Multilevel, Integrative Approach to Party Rape." *Social Problems* 53: 483–499.

Bourdieu, Pierre. 1977. *Outline of a Theory of Practice*. Cambridge: Cambridge University Press.

—. 1990. *The Logic of Practice*. Stanford, CA: Stanford University Press.

—. 1998/2001. *Masculine Domination*. Translated by R. Nice. Stanford, CA: Stanford University Press.

Bourdieu, P. and Wacquant, L. 1992. *Invitation to a Reflexive Sociology*. Chicago: University of Chicago Press.

Buss, David M., Todd K. Shackelford, Lee A. Kirkpatrick and Randy J. Larsen. 2001. "A Half Century of Mate Preferences: The Cultural Evolution of Values." *Journal of Marriage and Family* 63: 491–503.

D'Emilio, John. 1983. *Sexual Politics, Sexual Communities: The Making of a Homosexual Minority in the United States, 1940–1970*. Chicago: University of Chicago Press.

Epstein, Steven. 1991. "Sexuality and Identity: The Contribution of Object Relations Theory to a Constructionist Sociology." *Theory and Society* 20: 825–873.

Farrer, James. 2011. "Global Nightscapes in Shanghai as Ethnosexual contact Zones." *The Journal of Ethnic and Migration Studies* 37: 747–764.

Farrer, James and Sonja Dale. 2014. "Sexless in Shanghai: Gendered Mobility Strategies in a Transnational Sexual Field." In Green, Adam Isaiah (ed.), *Sexual Fields: Toward a Sociology of Collective Sexual Life* (pp. 143–170). Chicago: University of Chicago Press.

Fischer, Claude. 1975. "Toward a Subcultural Theory of Urbanism." *American Journal of Sociology* 80: 1319–1341.

Gagnon, John and William Simon. 1974. *Sexual Conduct. The Social Sources of Human Sexuality*. New York: Aldine.

Giddens, Anthony. 1992. *The Transformation of Intimacy: Sexuality, Love & Eroticism in Modern Societies*. Stanford, CA: Stanford University Press.

Green, Adam Isaiah. 2008a. "Erotic Habitus: Toward a Sociology of Desire." *Theory & Society* 37: 597–626.

—. 2008b. "The Social Organization of Desire: The Sexual Fields Approach." *Sociological Theory* 26: 25–50.

—. 2011. "Playing the (Sexual) Field: The Interactional Basis of Sexual Stratification." *Social Psychology Quarterly* 74: 244–266.

—. 2013. "Erotic Capital and the Power of Desirability: Why 'Honey Money' is a Bad Collective Strategy for Remedying Gender Inequality." *Sexualities* 16: 137–158.

—. 2014. *Sexual Fields: Toward a Sociology of Collective Sexual Life*. Chicago: University of Chicago Press.

Hakim, Catherine. 2011. *Honey Money: The Power of Erotic Capital*. London: Allen Lane.

Kimmel, Michael. 2008. *Guyland: The Perilous World Where Boys Become Men*. New York: Harper Collins.

Levine, Martin. 1998. *Gay Macho*. New York: New York University Press.

Martin, John Levy. 2003. "What is Field Theory?" *American Journal of Sociology* 109: 1–49.

—. 2005. "Is Power Sexy?" *American Journal of Sociology* 111: 408–446.

—. 2011. *The Explanation of Social Action*. New York: Oxford University Press.

Martin, John Levy and Matthew George. 2006. "Theories of Sexual Stratification: Toward an Analytics of the Sexual Field and a Theory of Sexual Capital." *Sociological Theory* 24: 107–132.

Waller, Willard. 1937. "The Rating and Dating Complex." *American Sociological Review* 2: 727–734.

Weinberg, Martin S. and Colin Williams. 1975. "Gay Baths and the Social Organization of Impersonal Sex." *Social Problems* 23: 124–136.

—. 2010. "Men Sexually Interested in Transwomen (MSTW): Gendered Embodiment and the Construction of Sexual Desire." *The Journal of Sex Research* 47 (4): 374–383.

—. 2014. "Sexual Field, Erotic Habitus, and Embodiment at a Transgender Bar." In Green, Adam Isaiah (ed.), *Sexual Fields: Toward a Sociology of Collective Sexual Life* (pp. 57–70). Chicago: University of Chicago Press.

Weiss, Margot. 2012. *Techniques of Pleasure: BDSM and the Circuits of Sexuality*. Durham, NC: Duke University Press.

Whittier, D.K. and R.M. Melendez. 2004. "Intersubjectivity in the Intrapsychic Sexual Scripting of Gay Men." *Culture, Health and Sexuality* 6: 131–143.

chapter 32

Identities, inequalities, and the partners of trans folks

Carey Jean Sojka

People often use the acronym LGBT to signify the identities *lesbian*, *gay*, *bisexual*, and *transgender*. Sometimes in addition to LGBT there might also be a Q for *queer*, a second Q for *questioning*, a second T for *transsexual*, an I for *intersex*, a P (or two) for *pansexual* or *polyamorous*, or an A for *asexual*. We have expanded this alphabet soup of identities beyond *gay* and *lesbian*, but even as we try to add letters to include more people based on their identities, we often leave some groups out.

The partners of transgender (or trans) people are one such group. Their lives are often somewhat invisible in gender and sexual diversity communities. Perhaps this is because of the diversity of ways that partners of trans people identify. Some may be straight, lesbian, gay, queer, bisexual, pansexual, transgender, cisgender, genderqueer, or may have any other number of identities. Because of this, there is no one word or identity that can encompass this group.

For some, partnering with a trans person does not mean anything different than partnering with others with whom they may have had relationships throughout their lives. For instance, a lesbian cis woman might find herself partnered with a transgender woman. To her, the attraction is about being with a woman whether that person is transgender or cisgender. For others, the attraction might be predominantly understood as an attraction to trans people, and they may even identify their desire with terms such as *transamorous* or *transensual*.

Partners of transgender people are sometimes called *partners*, *significant others* or *SOFFA*s (significant others, friends, family, and allies), or even *tranny chasers*,

People have different kinds of attractions

the latter of which is often considered a derogatory term but in some situations is reclaimed in ways similar to the reclamations of *queer*, *dyke*, or *fag*. Some partners of transgender people were in their relationship before their transgender partner disclosed a trans identity, and others may partner at some stage during or after a transition. Given the diversity of backgrounds of this group and the myriad ways that partners of trans people identify their desires, their sexualities, and their genders, it may be difficult or impossible to find one term to describe this group as a whole.

Research which focuses on the experiences of the partners of transgender people is becoming more prevalent, though there are still many unanswered questions. Two areas addressed in current research involve the negotiation of identities and the influence of inequalities on these relationships.

Identities of transgendered partners

Sonya Bolus, a cisgender woman partnered with someone who transitioned during their relationship, wrote about her own experiences as the partner of someone who is trans. While she felt some confusion about the transition and how it was affecting her own life, she also had positive feelings about her partner's gender changes. For instance, she wrote that at times "I feel like part of an ancient, unspoken tradition, as one who is particularly 'wired' to partner with a transperson" (Bolus 2002:117). During her partner's transition, Bolus' own identities shifted as well. While not all partners of trans people identify their desire based on the fact that their partner is transgender, Bolus's comment suggests that her own transitioning desire might be shaped by her partner's trans status. Bolus continued by noting,

> there are stray moments when I stop in my tracks, suddenly realizing my own transition, how I have also changed. How I am changing even now. On one such day I make a word for myself: *transensual*. And in naming myself, I feel substantial – connected.

> (Bolus 2002:118)

Bolus is not alone as a cis person who frames her story as a transition of sorts; other people who have partnered with a trans person during gender changes have noted that their identities and desires may change or that their understandings of these may become more complex over time. Although the partner may not go through the same type of transition as their trans partner, their own experiences can alter their lives and understandings in significant ways that they come to understand as their own transition.

While some studies note that transgender people's sexual desire does not necessarily remain fixed throughout a transition and does not inevitably seem to be heterosexual after transition (Cromwell 1999; Devor 1997; Hines 2007), few studies have focused on the ways that a transition may be related to a partner's potential shifts in identity. Bolus identified as a lesbian earlier in life, but she came to find new terms to better describe herself and her desire such as *transensual*; she also found empowerment through the act of naming herself and her desire. She is not the only one to describe her desire this way, and the identities *transensual* and *transamorous* are becoming better known in trans and queer communities. The desire of people who are transensual or transamorous is neither based on attraction to someone of the supposed "opposite" sex nor attraction to someone of the supposed "same" sex as themselves; in this way, these identities move beyond the heterosexual/homosexual binary toward desire that is defined by attraction to someone who transgresses gender boundaries. Not all partners of transgender people understand their desire in these terms, but it is important to note that some partners choose to define their desire in this way.

Partners' reconsiderations of their own sexual identities are often directly influenced by their relationships. Lenning (2009) found that gender changes prompted the reconsideration of gender identity and sexual orientation among the significant others of trans people (53). In her work, she noted that the significant others of trans people "more often [than trans people] gave a response [for sexual orientation] that reflected their partner's transgender identity" (49). Thus, when trans people responded to questions about their sexual orientation, they mostly referred to themselves but not their partners, while cis partners often referred to their trans partner's identities to confirm or complicate their own.

Partners may sometimes struggle to understand or to define their sexuality when they are partnered with a transgender person, especially when they feel pressured to define their identities for others. Tiffany, a white cisgender woman who is partnered with an Asian heterosexual trans man, identifies herself as a lesbian. However, when it comes to sharing this information with other people, she finds that her identities can become complicated:

> People are wondering what your sexuality is and, even on quizzes, I get asked on surveys and things like that and I really don't know what to put because I can't put that I'm heterosexual and I can't put that I'm a lesbian. I almost feel like I'm compromising him by saying that I'm a lesbian because he's still female and I don't want to do that.
>
> (Pfeffer 2008:338)

Although Tiffany considers herself to be a lesbian, she is aware of many dynamics that influence her identity, including her partner's gender and sexuality. She does not want her identity as a lesbian to discredit her partner's gender identity as a man, but she does not feel that she can identify as heterosexual either. Tiffany feels connected to her lesbian identity and may not want to abandon it; for her, the identity may not discredit her partner's gender, but she worries that others will interpret her identity in such a way. This can make it difficult to explain the complexity of her identities to others outside the relationship.

As Tiffany suggests, relationships with transgender people may often be difficult to define, even by those in the relationship. However, some people seem less concerned about what labels are used to define their relationship. Bernadette, a trans woman, spoke of her relationship with her cisgender partner. When the interviewer asked "Do you think some people see your relationship as a lesbian relationship?" she responded,

Carey Jean Sojka

Oh, some people might, but that is their concept of it. I have a relationship with my wife, which is very intimate and loving and has been for the past umpteen years – 40 years – and it isn't any different now than it has ever been and it's very good.

(Hines 2007:130)

For Bernadette and her partner, the quality of their relationship was more important than their genders or the classification of their relationship. She did not see the necessity of defining their relationship in one particular way.

Partners of trans people also sometimes express an awareness of the ways that their own gender presentation affects their partner. Michele, a white, cisgender, self-identified dyke who was partnered with a trans man, said,

The more I look like a girl and present as a heterosexual girl, the more likely [my partner] is to pass as a boy. And sometimes that makes me uncomfortable because I don't like having my queer identity elided over – especially since I've owned it for so long. . . . It makes me angry. It makes me feel invisible. It makes my queer identity feel invisible.

(Pfeffer 2008:334)

At this point in time, Michele had identified as a dyke or a lesbian for 14 years, and her queer identity had become important to her. While she believes that her gender presentation affects the ways that her partner's gender may be read in public, she also feels uncomfortable being read as heterosexual. Michele is thus left to negotiate this complicated tension between her own desire to be understood as queer and her seemingly heterosexual relationship.

Partners of transgender people who were a part of queer or LGBT communities before their relationship may feel a sense of loss when their relationship is read by others as heterosexual. In similar ways, partners in relationships which seemed heterosexual before a transition may also feel a sense of identity loss when their relationship is no longer read as heterosexual. Our identities can become very important, and people may begin to feel that their queer or heterosexual identities are invalidated if others interpret their relationships to be something other than what they had been in the past. For people like Michele, the feelings of queer invisibility can thus be linked to a sense of community and a fear of losing that community.

This tension between preferred and perceived identities may occur in many relationships with a transgender person. However, in relationships where this is the case, not all partners feel the need to resolve this tension. Some may feel comfortable with their identities and the way that the relationship may be read by others even if these seem to conflict.

There is often the misconception that trans people transition to become "straight," but this is a problematic perspective because it sexualizes trans people's motivation for gender changes and because it simply isn't true for many trans relationships. Many trans women partner with trans or cis women and many trans men partner with trans or cis men. Gabriel, a cisgender man who partnered with a trans man, said,

I met a handsome man who I wanted to get to know. Then I was told that he is not just a man but an FTM man. He is still the same attractive and quality person I met.

(Cromwell 1999:133)

not always doesn't what the person is but how they are

For Gabriel, the trans identity of his partner did not matter as much as the attraction he felt toward his partner, and their relationship was not heterosexual. While research on relationships with trans people tends to acknowledge that trans women can partner with women or men, cis or trans men partners of trans men are less researched.

Another trans man, Danny, explained what it was like to have sex with men as a man. The interviewer asked him "What's the difference . . . between having sex with men now and having sex with men before [transition]?" Danny's response was:

> I didn't really. If I did it was oral sex . . . it was already gay sex . . . umm . . . that was a new area. It depends upon your partner's perception. If a man thought I was a woman, we didn't do it.
>
> (Halberstam 1994:212)

For Danny, the significant aspect was that when he had sex with a man, that person understood him as a man and understood their encounter as "gay sex." When people confuse gender with sexuality, they may not comprehend why a trans man would be attracted to men; however, if we analytically separate gender identities from sexual identities, it becomes clearer that these may or may not be linked for individuals. Thus, it makes sense that Danny would only have sex with men when his identity as a man was also validated.

It is also important to remember that trans people sometimes partner with other trans people; these relationships, like those that often seem from the outside to be gay or lesbian relationships involving transgender people, are often unexamined in research. Trans men partner with other trans men, trans women partner with other trans women, and trans men partner with trans women. C. Jacob Hale commented on some of these dynamics:

> What is it when a transfag and a transdyke get together and make magic together with their bodies and hearts? . . . Whatever else it is, it isn't lesbian or gay or bisexual or heterosexual, because all of those miss the crucial fact that his transsexuality and queerness, her transsexuality and queerness, are a major part of what gets them together in the first place . . . .
>
> (Cromwell 1999:133)

Hale notes that in some of these relationships, trans and queer identities may play a large part in the attraction that brings people together. These partnerships, like many involving at least one trans person, may seem difficult to define. However, the difficulty often arises when others try to fit the relationship into our common categories for sexuality.

Inequalities in trans relationships

Inequalities and issues such as intimate partner violence can occur in all types of relationships, including those that include trans people. Researchers such as Brown

(2007), Pfeffer (2010), and Ward (2010), have focused on important concerns raised by feminists about gender inequality in relationships. Although these particular studies focus on the relationships between trans men and cis women, their work can reveal connections between identities, social inequalities, and broader social structures.

Both Pfeffer (2010) and Ward (2010) address work inequalities in relationships between cis women (Pfeffer 2010) or cis femmes (Ward 2010) and trans men. Both found that cis women partners of trans men often do a significant amount of work, including housework, emotion work, and medical work, for their trans men partners. Pfeffer (2010) specifically addressed emotion work in relationships between trans men and cis women. She noted that a number of her participants discussed the extra emotion work and household labor in which they engage in order to draw their partners out or to care for them, particularly around areas where the trans men were being stereotypically masculine such as messiness, carelessness with others' feelings, not being able to process or discuss important issues, and lack of self-care (Ward 2010:175). This worked to validate their partner's masculinity.

Brown (2007) addresses the issue of intimate partner violence and found that for some cis women, it was often a fear (and sometimes the explicit threat) of being understood as poor allies to the trans community that kept them from speaking out about abuse that they experienced within relationships. They were sometimes threatened with exclusion from the trans community or were accused of being transphobic because they didn't "understand" that trans men experience an adolescence, one that was said to include aggression, violence, or abuse as part of masculine behavior. In this way, some of their trans men partners used the idea of their "adolescence" as an excuse for abusive behavior. Some cis women partners also worried that by speaking out about abuse, they would be hurting trans men who are already fighting against structural discrimination and violence. These dynamics are not unique to trans relationships and have been documented in relationships dealing with other marginalized identities as well.

These studies on inequality all center on the relationships between cis women and trans men, and yet the themes of gender labor and intimate partner violence are likely to be important in trans relationships with other gender configurations as well, though perhaps in different ways. For instance, there are many accounts of violence in relationships that involve trans women, particularly those between trans women and cis men, and this violence, when occurring against trans women, seems to be perpetuated by sexism, trans-misogyny, and fetishization in intersection with other factors. Further research is needed to uncover more about these challenges to healthy relationships and how different types of identity configurations influence these issues.

Making sense of experiences

As we can see, the lives of partners of transgender people are quite diverse. Despite this diversity, one important thing to note across these differences is that the experiences of partners are valid in their own right. Partners are not just witnesses to a transgender experience; they also bring their own understandings into their relationships and they potentially encounter changes in their own lives throughout these relationships.

While a cisgender partner of a trans person does not experience what it is like to be transgender, they may have insight into transgender perspectives. Cromwell writes about the *transsituated perspectives* that trans people have because of living in the world as someone who is trans. He also writes that "nontransgendered people can and do have transsituated perspectives" (Cromwell 1999:129). Thus, a cisgender partner of a trans person may understand a trans experience in distinctive ways even though they may not go through a gender transition in the same way as their trans partner. Similarly, Halberstam notes that partners are often "a part of the enactment of 'trans-sex' rather than its object or incidental partner" (1994:220), suggesting that partners' experiences are more than periphery; understanding a partner's perspectives is essential to understanding the dynamics of their relationships. Therefore, centering partners, cis or trans, is just as important as centering trans people when addressing these relationships.

While further research is needed to conceptualize these experiences and while this work may prove to be complex, it is helpful that some of the voices in this diverse group of people are included in research on trans and queer communities. We may be at the beginning stages of bringing these experiences to light in our communities, but as we begin to identify factors that are important to their identities and relationships, we will ultimately have a clearer picture of what it means to be a partner of a transgender person.

Bibliography

Bolus, Sonya. 2002. "Loving Outside Simple Lines." Pp. 113–119 in *GenderQueer: Voices from Beyond the Binary*, edited by Joan Nestle, Clare Howell, and Riki Wilchins. Los Angeles, CA: Alyson Publications.

Brown, Nicola. 2007. "Stories from Outside the Frame: Intimate Partner Abuse in Sexual-minority Women's Relationships with Transsexual Men." *Feminism and Psychology* 17(3):373–393.

Cromwell, Jason. 1999. *Transmen and FTMs: Identities, Bodies, Genders, and Sexualities*. Urbana, IL: University of Illinois Press.

Devor, Aaron. 1997. *FTM: Female-to-Male Transsexuals in Society*. Bloomington, IN: Indiana University Press.

Halberstam, Judith. 1994. "F2M: The Making of Female Masculinity." Pp. 210–228 in *The Lesbian Postmodern*, edited by Laura Doan. New York: Columbia University Press.

Hines, Sally. 2007. *TransForming Gender: Transgender Practices of Identity, Intimacy and Care*. Bristol, UK: Policy Press.

Lenning, Emily. 2009. "Moving Beyond the Binary: Exploring the Dimensions of Gender Presentation and Orientation." *International Journal of Social Inquiry* 2(2):39–54.

Pfeffer, Carla. 2008. "Bodies in Relation – Bodies in Transition: Lesbian Partners of Trans Men and Body Image." *Journal of Lesbian Studies* 12(4):325–345.

Pfeffer, Carla A. and Ralph LaRossa 2010. "'Women's Work'? Women Partners of Transgender Men Doing Housework and Emotion Work." *Journal of Marriage and Family* 72(1):165–183.

Rubin, Henry. 2003. *Self-Made Men: Identity and Embodiment among Transsexual Men*. Nashville, TN: Vanderbilt University Press.

Ward, Jane. 2010. "Gender Labor: Transmen, Femmes, and Collective Work of Transgression." *Sexualities* 13(2):236–254.

Carey Jean Sojka

chapter 33

Gender and the organization of heterosexual intimacy

Daniel Santore

Popular images of romance tend to suggest an idyllic bond between partners; intimacy, as portrayed in movies, television, books and other media, is a spontaneous, mutually fulfilling experience. Yet few of us would dispute that romantic intimate relationships can be more complicated than that. It is difficult for individuals to agree about what a "good relationship" entails, and who should be responsible for which kinds of duties. For all the carefree pop-culture imagery, the fact remains that intimacy is not free of conflict and involves tough decisions.

Sociology seeks out social explanations for the ways couples resolve disagreements and negotiate intimate life. Research on heterosexual intimate relations has found that *gender* is one resource upon which people rely when arranging their relationships. Cultural ideas about gender roles, as well as the different social positions occupied by women and men, are key social forces shaping our intimate relationships. This chapter explores how gender organizes heterosexual intimacy. Attention is paid throughout to power dynamics and inequalities between women and men in intimate relationships.

The claim of gender difference

Why is gender an important concept in understanding intimate relationships between women and men? One explanation, often associated with feminist perspectives, is that there are fundamental differences between women and men. These differences are of the utmost importance in patterning all of our social experiences, including intimate relationships. Throughout the 1970s and 1980s, feminist social science and theory was rich with accounts of the salience of "gender difference" (Connell 1987). Gender-difference arguments posited essential differences between women and men based not on biological, but on *social* conditions. For example, one strand of gender-difference argument claims that women and men have different social experiences by virtue of living within a patriarchal capitalist system. Historically, capitalism has placed women in the private sphere (the home), and men in the public sphere (the workplace). The fact that women and men occupy systematically different social positions means that they experience social life in different ways. This arrangement has implications for heterosexual intimate life. A man oriented around his role as a capitalist worker assumes a practical, unemotional disposition toward intimacy that corresponds with the structural and cultural demands of such a role. A woman, on the other hand, placed in charge of maintaining the emotional well-being of the private realm of home and family, is expected to function primarily as a caring supporter of the man/worker. These different dispositions, then, rooted in the structure of capitalist society, are relevant to the intimate lives of women and men; the images of the emotionally closed-off man and the emotionally driven woman speak to the different social roles of men and women.

To continue with our example, these opposed gender roles (that is, the worldly, active man and the domestic woman), so prevalent in industrial capitalism, also structure sexual scripts for women and men. The man is expected to be the more aggressive initiator of sexual activity, while the more passive woman, whose own interests in or demands for sex are considered "bad form," merely supports (sexually) one more of the man's needs. Note that the differentiated experiences conditioned by capitalism are not *merely* differences; relations between women and men are characterized by inequality or relations of dominance and subordination. Gender inequality in intimacy is in this way bound up with the social structure of capitalist society.

Gender-difference arguments have been challenged on a number of grounds. For example, asserting essential *social* differences between women and men may be as damaging as assuming essential *natural* or *biological* differences. Why might that be so? The attempt to homogenize women's experience – according to any characteristic – leads to uniform accounts of women's lives, inattentive to differences among women. To assume broad similarities across so wide-ranging a group inevitably privileges certain characteristics and obscures others, none of which are representative of all women. The lives of women with variable sexual identities, of women of color, and of other marginalized women are obscured in a "capital-W" concept of woman. Moreover, many of the characteristics attributed to women (and men) in gender-difference arguments are not so easily spread around (Kimmel 2004). Warmth and sensitivity, perennial "feminine traits," are not the exclusive province of women, any more than assertiveness is the province of men. To the extent that gender-difference arguments assume a socially produced gender dichotomy, women and men alike are pigeonholed. Differences between the genders are highlighted, while differences within are ignored.

　　　　　　　　　　　　　　　　　　　　　　　　　　Daniel Santore

Is gender disappearing?

The idea that different, "gendered" experiences shape intimate relationships relies in part on an understanding of the social conditions that exist alongside gender. What does this mean? It means that, to understand the way ideas about gender develop, attention must be paid to the broader social context that shapes the lives of women and men. This idea can be illustrated by looking briefly at two periods in American heterosexual intimacy. We can think of America in the early 1800s as a setting in which intimate relationships between women and men were approached in a practical manner, as material needs weighed heavily upon the intimate relationship. Far from being barred from productive labor, women during this period often had an important if limited role in economic production. Not only men but women too had a hand in producing subsistence for the family, through farming, crafts, and other labor. Material survival during this period demanded that everyone pitch in, women and men alike.

In the late 1800s and early 1900s, at least in the middle classes, only the man was needed as a producer of material subsistence for the family. Women's roles shifted. To be sure, women's roles retained some responsibilities such as household maintenance, care-giving, reproducing healthy workers, etc. Yet women's participation in explicitly economic production (for example, making goods to be sold) was reduced. Along with these material changes, cultural ideas about gender also changed. In the early 1800s, when women and men performed similar labor, an ideology that women were unsuited for "real work" was less defensible. Yet such an ideology flourished during the end of the nineteenth century, when women were relieved (forced out) of many sectors of the labor market; it is in this period that American cultural ideas about "women's place is in the home" really became prominent. A new ideology declared that women's appropriate place was in the private sphere of the household, while men's was in the public world of work and government. This was justified by the idea that men were seen as decision-makers and leaders whereas women were viewed as caring and submissive. The point here is that the interaction of gender, culture, and economic structure is complicated and undergoes change.

Today we can observe new social shifts. It appears that major social changes in Western capitalist countries have profoundly affected the contemporary landscape of heterosexual intimacy. There is lessened dependence by women on men's wages, as more women attend college and go out to work. As a result, women have a reduced material need to be involved in intimate relationships. What people expect out of intimacy also changes. Intimate relationships become more romantically based, rather than based on survival; intimate desires can expand to include emotional and spiritual fulfillment. Finally, it is no longer only men who are encouraged to strike out and live a personally fulfilling life. Women too are increasingly advised not to feel forced to decide between emotional fulfillment through intimacy, or a fulfilling career. Women are encouraged to blaze their own path, much more so than they were before the 1960s.

These changes potentially mean real improvements for heterosexual intimacy. In particular, they promise to place women and men on more equal footing in their intimate relationships. This is the spirit in which Anthony Giddens (1991) has articulated the idea of the "pure relationship." To Giddens, intimacy between women and men in contemporary society points to a more democratized, mutually fulfilling relationship. As women's and men's lives and goals begin to look more similar, and women's right to a personally fulfilling intimate life is given equal weight, the chance emerges for an "intimacy of equals." Pure relationships leave behind many of the patterned gender differences that created inequality in relationships; now, women and men can openly discuss their needs and desires, and assess their relationship in terms of their personal fulfilment.

Gender, intimacy and (in)equality

There is a rich body of sociological work that indicates the jury is still out regarding the reality of egalitarian relationships. Even if cultural ideas about gender are changing, and ideals of intimacy emphasize equality, it does not necessarily mean real equality. For example, a culture of egalitarianism may lead men and women to agree to openness about communicating their needs and wants. But if there are still persisting *structural* gender inequalities, if men make more money and if their careers are more highly valued, men may still have more power in intimate decision-making.

So, what does the empirical record indicate about the status of gender equality in heterosexual intimacy? A lot of research has been done on heterosexual marriage. While married men do more housework than they did during the 1950s and 1960s, they still don't do nearly as much as their wives. Survey research conducted during the late 1980s found that married women perform almost 80 percent of all housework duties (Berardo *et al.* 1987). And even as gender disparities in *amounts* of housework shrink somewhat, the *types* of tasks performed by wives and husbands remain gender-role specific. Men tend to perform physical tasks like mowing the lawn, but not "administrative" tasks like arranging the family holiday dinner. The gender roles extend further, into the more "personal" realm of physical intimacy between women and men. Before marriage, young men in America typically enjoy freedom of sexual activity; monogamy is an expectation that comes along only *with* marriage. Women have not traditionally enjoyed such liberation. Indeed, it is only recently that women's bachelorette parties – a symbol of relinquishing sexual privileges – have sprung up, indicating a measure of women's own sexual freedom (Montemurro 2003).

Inequality in intimate relationships can have less obvious negative consequences for women. To the extent that women come to expect equality in intimacy, the failure to actually achieve this can lead, unsurprisingly, to frustration. Women may feel that they have to at least present their married lives – their divisions of housework, depth of emotional connection, and ideas of what's fair – in a manner consistent with popular expectations. This promises tension for women whose intimate lives fall far short of equality. For example, interviews with married women found that it can be a daily effort to construct a narrative of an egalitarian intimate life when actual practice is otherwise (Dryden 1999). When actual relationships do not measure up to what is expected, married women may engage in a complicated string of justifications and denials in order to fashion their "square-peg" intimate relationship into the "round-hole" ideal. Of course, this should not be interpreted as a reason why women should alter their expectations! Rather, it should be viewed as one more reason to redouble efforts to engage the deeper roots of gender inequality and male dominance in intimate relationships. If women are frustrated in their desires for equality in intimate life, it is not the expectations but the cultural and material causes of inequality that need fixing.

It is important to note that ideals of equality do exist in relationships – commitments to equality are no myth. Difficult though it is to shed gender when we step into an intimate relationship, there are heterosexual couples who consciously strive to do just that. Couples who actively reject gender as a resource in decision-making processes have succeeded to some extent, if only in small numbers (Risman and Johnson-Sumerford 1998). These couples commit to an ideal that women and men need not relinquish careers, hobbies, and friendships, simply because they enter into a romantic bond. For women this promises to be a liberating condition, as this privilege has not always been so readily extended to them. Moreover, this egalitarian ideal holds that the couple should strive for a fair division of jobs and responsibilities, and try to not use gender to determine who does what. Finally, these couples stress deep communication, a commitment to be attentive to each other's personal histories (often negatively referred to as "baggage") and to each other's individual aspirations and goals.

While an egalitarian ideal of intimacy may be widespread in American society, research suggests that the couples who are most likely actively to try to arrange their lives in this fashion tend to be dually employed, often professionals, and possess high levels of education. This means that many couples who do not have these economic and cultural resources will be at a structural disadvantage in trying to pursue and realize an egalitarian ideal.

The research suggests that this egalitarian ideal is elusive even for women in the most advantageous position. Even in couples where each person holds a high-status occupation, women may still defer to men's interests and wishes. For example, women employed as university faculty members have been shown to live within gendered patterns when it comes to decisions about professional and leisure activities. This is the case in part because the professional couples are more likely to live in "long-distance" relationships. Along with distant relationships come a number of issues to be addressed (for example, who goes to see whom; how often; how does each party make use of their valuable free time?). Research indicates that more often than not women visit men, not the other way around, putting aside work at their own jobs (Holmes 2004). And to the extent that women in distant relationships tend to spend more time at their male partners' residence/community than do men at women's, men need not cope, as women surely must, with the lack of friends and acquaintances associated with traveling in unfamiliar circles.

Conclusions

Intimate relationships between women and men change. Intimacy today looks different than it did 50 years ago, and looked different then than it did 50 years before that. There are cultural and structural reasons (for example, changes in economic production, and in gender roles and expectations) why relationships between women and men look the way they do at any given period. For all the large changes, however, we have durable, persistent themes on which to focus our analyses of intimate life. Gender, inequality, and power are core topics in any discussion of heterosexual intimacy, and have been since relationships between women and men were first considered by social science.

Whether we have moved to a place where intimacy between women and men is an "intimacy of equals" is a complicated question, Anthony Giddens's portrait of the pure relationship is neither accurate nor inaccurate. It is clear that women are a larger presence in the male-dominated public sphere; it is also clear that women's personal goals are often held to be as important as men's, and many relationships provide space for the pursuit of those goals. As a result, in many relationships women's needs and desires are more diverse, and are taken more seriously, than ever before. Yet gender inequalities persist within intimate relationships. It seems that the "gender revolution" – in heterosexual intimacy and myriad other areas – still has its work cut out, as has been the case since its beginnings.

Contrary to popular culture representations, romance between women and men does not guarantee equality; love, it turns out, does not conquer all. Even men and women's best intentions (for example, dividing chores, stressing emotional engagement, sharing child rearing) to erase a gender-ordered relationship are likely to remain incomplete fixes in the struggle for equality, *so long as institutional obstacles remain in place*. As many sociologists have noted, personal solutions alone are not enough to combat structural inequalities. Gender disparities in wages, lack of child-care, and sex-segregated labor markets, all pose problems for equality in heterosexual intimacy. A culture of equality in intimacy gets us part of the way; naming and fixing social-structural disadvantages for women are necessary for fuller equality.

References

Berardo, Donna Hodgkins, Constance L. Shehan, and Gerald R. Leslie. 1987. "A Residue of Tradition: Jobs, Careers, and Spouses' Time in Housework." *Journal of Marriage and the Family* 49(2): 381–90.

Connell, R. W. 1987. *Gender and Power*. Stanford, CA: Stanford University Press.

Dryden, Caroline. 1999. *Being Married, Doing Gender: A Critical Analysis of Gender Relationships in Marriage*. London: Routledge.

Giddens, Anthony. 1991. *Modernity and Self-Identity: Self and Society in the Late Modern Age*. Cambridge: Polity Press.

Holmes, M. 2004. "An Equal Distance? Individualization, Gender and Intimacy in Distance Relationships." *The Sociological Review* 52(2): 180–200.

Kimmel, Michael S. 2004. *The Gendered Society*. Oxford: Oxford University Press.

Montemurro, Beth. 2003. "Sex Symbols: The Bachelorette Party as a Window to Change in Women's Sexual Expression." *Sexuality & Culture* 7(2): 3–29.

Risman, Barbara J. and Dannette Johnson-Sumerford. 1998. "Doing it Fairly: A Study of Post-gender Marriages." *Journal of Marriage and the Family* 60(1): 23–40.

chapter 34

Interracial romance

The logic of acceptance and domination

Kumiko Nemoto

With globalization and an increasing immigrant population in the United States, the surge in interracial relationships might not be a surprising trend. In fact, the increase in intermarriage and interracial relationships should be a welcome sign in the changing landscape of love, romance, and family, as it fits America's racial-melting-pot image and atmosphere of steadily greater multiculturalism. However, interracial relationships are still far from the norm. While many Americans date someone of another race, fewer marriages cross racial lines. While about 92 percent of all interracial marriages include white partners, only 4 percent of married whites have non-white spouses (Qian 2005:34). In fact, many white Americans remain uncomfortable about interracial intimacy and tend to disapprove of their family members' interracial relationships (Qian 2005:33). Skin color also greatly influences patterns of interracial marriage. The lighter the skin color, the higher the rate of intermarriage with white Americans (Qian 2005:35). Hispanics who label themselves as racially "white," Asian Americans, and American Indians have high rates of marriage with whites compared to those of African Americans. Also, there are distinct gender patterns: 74 percent of the black–white couples involve a black husband and a white wife, and 58 percent of the Asian American–white couples involve an Asian American wife (Qian 2005:36).

The increase in interracial relationships gives the impression that racism and discrimination are lessening in our society. However, the types of interracial couples that are deemed acceptable and desirable continue to be shaped by society's dominant racial and gender beliefs. An increase in dating and marrying across racial lines may not be explained entirely by a decline in racism. Patricia Hill Collins (2004:250) writes, "Crossing the color line to marry interracially challenges deep-seated American norms, yet such relationships may not be inherently progressive." By the same token,

Henry Giroux (2006:32) argues that some seemingly oppositional or counter-normative behaviors in fact reveal the logic of domination more than they represent the logic of protest or resistance to the system, much less the logic of liberation. So, what are the dominant images of interracial relationships? What are the ingrained messages in them? In this chapter, I will examine some popular images and interracial relationships and how they express dominant ideologies. Then, drawing on my research on Asian American–white couples, I will explore the racial and gender ideologies that shape these couples and the challenges that are faced by them.

Whiteness and images of interracial couples

Popular culture daily sells hypersexualized racial images and offers aesthetic consumption of racial differences as if such consumption were synonymous with the end of racism and sexism. The cultural images are ambiguous, blurring the line between oppression and nuanced celebration of racial diversity. The images of interracial romance continue to be shaped by traditional themes of white normalcy, whites' exoticization of people of color, male authority, and distinct differences between masculinity and femininity. In many images, white manhood and womanhood continue to represent the norm, with people of color portrayed alongside in an exoticized way.

Even though the popular media claim that "racial mixing" represents an ideal of racial integration, it has also denoted whiteness as a sign of normalcy and ascendancy. In 1993, a multiracial female cyborg appeared on the cover of *Time* magazine as "The New Face of America." Her image metaphorically characterized a future America as increasingly comprising multiracial individuals and couples. At the same time, this young female cyborg represented future multicultural citizenship in a state that would continue to enforce conventional norms of heterosexuality, family values, and white privilege. The "white-enough" appearance of the cyborg, as the face of America, evoked the image of "the future as what will happen when white people intermarry" (Berlant 1997:207), and insinuated that whiteness would remain central to America's race relations. Also, by highlighting race within the private realms of "love," "sex," and "marriage," the cover ensured the continuation of heterosexual unions and family love as solutions for the "problems" of race and immigration (Berlant 1997). Almost 15 years later, media portrayals of interracial couples and multiracial families still reflect what the female cyborg represented at that time: interracial relationships depicted in terms of their approximation to heterosexual unions and the ideal white middle-class family in which traditional male authority figures rule and female caretaker figures serve.

Recent images of interracial couples have apparently gained wide media attention not just because these couples transgress racial lines, but also because they express exotic yet traditional versions of femininity and masculinity. Couples in the media often consist of a white partner with a light-skinned partner of color such as Halle Berry or Jennifer Lopez (Childs 2009). Nonwhite partners often appear to mirror the white fantasy of hypermasculine or hyperfeminine racial minority images. By portraying interracial couples that represent traditional gender and racial messages, these popular images tell us that interracial couples can be acceptable when they embody attractive racialized femininity and masculinity in which male authority is embraced, whiteness is retained, and American middle-class ideology is sustained.

In addition, images of interracial romance, while aesthetically and romantically appealing in terms of their potentially positive effect on race relations, can erase realities of racial violence and racial hierarchy. They reduce racial differences to a matter of physical appearances and conventional heterosexual romantic norms. Instead of challenging hierarchies and inequalities, these interracial images re-order signs of race and gender according to traditional ideologies, and perpetuate the display of white manhood and white womanhood as dominant – in other words, white men and women as figures served by men and women of color.

Considering the fact that over 90 percent of screenwriters are white (Childs 2009:70), it might not be surprising that images of, and storylines about, interracial relationships in television and film reflect white male desires and fantasies. Interracial relationships are also often portrayed as "race-less" in white-dominated settings (Childs 2009), and race is often represented as a matter of superficial physical differences. Such color-blindness or race-less-ness is a unique aspect of American multiculturalism, and it often entails the exoticization of racial minorities or white-centered assimilation messages (Perry 2002). Neither approach critically engages the issue of power (Nylund 2006). Also, the analysis of interracial couples in contemporary films (Childs 2009) finds repeated instances of the message that white people are not racist; it is racial minorities and their communities, not whites, who oppose and complain about interracial relationships. In many tv programs and films, interracial romances are represented as doomed to fail, thus perpetuating the safe normalization of white couples and same-race unions. The images are also gendered: interracial relationships that appear in the media reinforce white male heroism, with white men depicted as liberal and progressive, certifying their goodness, kindness, and superiority over others (Childs 2009:87).

Popular discourses about Asian American women

Given the dominant hierarchies of race and gender implicit in popular images of interracial relationships, this section looks at how racial and gender ideologies have been historically played out in Asian American–white relationships. Compared to African Americans, a higher number of Asians and Asian Americans marry whites. There are various social factors that could explain the high rate of intermarriage between Asian American women and white men: Asian Americans' overall high education and income, compared to whites and other racial minorities, may be one. But such factors do not explain why Asian American women have a higher intermarriage rate than Asian American men. Also, while Asian Americans are often seen as a "model minority," the question of how Asian American men and women fare as intimate or marital partners of whites has not been much discussed.

Racial stereotypes play a critical role in the dynamics of gender in interracial relationships. Like the stereotype of black men's hypermasculinity, long-existing stereotypes of Asian women as submissive, subservient, passive, and/or hypersexual may serve as critical components in heterosexual attraction. Also, in a culture that automatically equates long dark hair and a thin body with being "feminine" regardless of race, images of the

Asian female body are easily marked as representative of a non-threatening femininity. In contrast, Asian men have been often de-sexed and feminized, or hypermasculinized as martial artists or oriental villains. As many researchers have discussed (e.g. Espiritu 2000), these stereotypes of hyperfeminine Asian women and de-sexed Asian men contribute to the maintenance of conventional orders of race and gender centered on the normalcy of whiteness and the dominance of men.

Exotic and hyperfeminine images of Asian American women have long flourished in the United States. Images of Asians and Asian Americans as hyperfeminine have been popular precisely because they complement social and cultural beliefs about American manhood and American family values, in which white men serve as the dominant patriarchal figures and women serve as caretakers of the family. Images of subservient Asian women were repeatedly circulated on military bases in Asian countries during World War II, the Korean War, and the Vietnam War. When a large number of Asian military brides entered the United States in the post–World War II period, interracial marriage was still banned in many states; the images served to reduce racial anxieties stemming from the large influx of Asian women and facilitated these women's assimilation. Hyperfeminine and sexual images of Asian women continue to play a critical role in the transaction of desires and fantasies in cross-border marriages (Constable 2003).

In the 1970s, the model minority stereotype took hold. Asian Americans were viewed as educated and upwardly mobile. Asian and Asian American women, still imagined as submissive, were increasingly viewed as upwardly mobile and therefore as desirable. These women were good substitutes for white women (who were often viewed as challenging) (Koshy 2005). As a result, Asian American women emerged as exemplars of an alternative femininity which could help men regain the confidence they lost after feminism marked white femininity as more independent and masculine (Koshy 2005).

Subservient images of Asian immigrant women have also complemented America's paternalistic images of nation. That is, these women are welcomed in part because they celebrate America while condemning the patriarchal and non-democratic countries they left. Immigrant women are valued for having the courage to pursue freedom and to escape from their home country's patriarchal constraints (Berlant 1997:195). The women, with few distinctions among them with regard to whether they are "immigrants," "aliens," "minorities," "illegal," or whatever, and who want to "escape" the constraints of their patriarchal families, are seen as suitable markers of model migrant citizens who will be devoted to America (Berlant 1997). Such a gendered immigration discourse has long framed Asian female–white male sexual relationships, especially in the context of military brides who have entered the United States. Thus, the stereotypes associated with Asian women and the immigration discourse have historically served to validate Asian American female–white male couples as "acceptable" gendered unions that can sustain the traditional orders of gender, nation, and family in the United States.

Asian American–white couples

In order to understand the impact of race and gender on the dynamics of interracial relationships, I conducted interviews with 42 Asian Americans and whites who were either in interracial relationships at the time of the interview or had previously been involved in such relationships (Nemoto 2009). I explored couples' race consciousness and social receptions, racialized desires, and gender dynamics. The Asian Americans I interviewed included Chinese, Filipino, Japanese, Korean, and Vietnamese Americans. The individuals ranged in age from their early twenties to their early fifties, and all were heterosexual.

White men interviewed for the study often viewed Asian American women as ideal partners because of their racialized femininity and model minority traits. The stereotypes of Asian American women as hyperfeminine and subservient were frequent responses I received. Likewise, white women referred to Asian American men as having model minority traits or as being domineering. But there are some interesting differences among the couples consisting of an Asian American woman and a white man, relating to whether the woman was a native-born or foreign-born Asian American. Foreign-born Asian American women who lack class mobility, language skills, and a thorough knowledge of US racism and sexism were more likely to adhere to traditional gender arrangements in their dating or marriages, while second-generation Asian American women who date white men often have more education and/or a higher socioeconomic status than their white partners. The second- and higher-generation young Asian Americans saw themselves as upwardly mobile and independent, and different from stereotypical Asians. They expressed a preference for white men who possess "egalitarian" traits, which they mentioned were often lacking in Asian American men. Interestingly, many Asian American women, including young second- and higher-generation women who described themselves as being egalitarian and independent, projected highly gendered images onto white men, describing them as being protective breadwinner figures or liberators. Thus, it seems that racial and gender hierarchies have greatly influenced Asian American–white couples. But stereotypes could also be surmounted. For example, Asian American men who possess high class status could repudiate negative stereotypes by exercising power over white women.

In the following section, I discuss some of the findings of my research, with a particular focus on the ways Asian American–white couples were received by family and friends. The Asian American female–white male couples I interviewed reported little social hostility or familial opposition, especially when compared to Asian American male–white female couples; in other words, Asian American women coupled with white men seemed to be much more socially accepted than Asian American men with white women. Some men stated that having an Asian wife was not a problem because of their reputation as good wives. Gary, a 58-year-old businessman who is married to a Korean woman, said, "American men like Asian women. . . . I think there's a great acceptance of the Caucasian man marrying an Asian woman. In fact, many of my friends, non-Asian friends, actually say that they envy me because they understand that Asian women are very good wives and very nice ladies." His comment demonstrates the culturally shared notion that Asian women possess the qualities of good wives and also, therefore, reinforce men's sense of masculinity. Gary said, "I think [Asian women] respect the [traditional] values and they tend to be pretty loyal. They exhibit qualities that a lot of American women don't seem to have [such as being] family oriented. [They are] good mothers and good parents."

Some white men noted that the Asian American woman's exotic appearance and small physique is part of their attraction. Peter, a 27-year-old, said that he likes dark-skinned women, and Asian women often caught his eye because of their distinct physical features which he described as "more beautiful than those of whites." Peter associated his second-generation Chinese American girlfriend's thin body with stylish urban femininity, which he thought suited his lifestyle as a musician who performs underground electronic music. Possessing a young Asian woman was a sign of cultural hipness. Peter added, "If you are dating Asian girls, probably it is cooler than if you are dating black girls."

Some men mentioned that, even though they were attracted to Asian women, they were not attracted to other women of color. Patrick, a 28-year-old engineer, had dated a variety of Asian women whom he met in Asian countries when he traveled for work. "I kind of acquired the taste for or the inclination of liking Asian woman," he said. "Black women and Mexican women are different, too. But for some reason, I'm never attracted [to them]." In all likelihood, he has never been attracted to other women of color because his interest lies not in their color but rather in racialized images of traditional womanhood. Of his Filipino engineer wife, Patrick said, "Her nature is [to] try to take care of her husband. I don't think that most American women I've met have been that way . . ." Foreign-born Asian American women were often characterized by their white partners as being family-oriented, loyal, and caring. These characteristics apparently played a critical role in some men's attraction to them. The image of Asian women as enhancing men's masculinity bolsters their sense of themselves as authority figures and also contributes to the positive social reception of Asian and Asian American women.

In addition to the stereotype of hyperfemininity, the stereotype of the model minority also adds to the positive image of Asian American women. In my interviews, Asian American women, especially those born in America, associated being Asian with being a disciplined "model minority" and believed this is the reason why they are welcomed by whites. Victoria, a second-generation 26-year-old Chinese American medical student, pointed out that Asian American female–white male couples are extremely common. She said, "All the Asian girls I know have gone out with white guys, basically . . . because it's almost popular for white guys to go out with Asian girls." Victoria emphasized that Asian women are desirable for white men. "I know my boyfriend's parents are happy because I'm a lot different from the girls he's gone out with before . . . I don't think American girls are quite as respectful as far as how [they] treat another person's family." Victoria's comment illustrates that Asian American women are not merely associated with domestic femininity but also are exemplars of disciplined, respectable womanhood. Peter, a 27-year-old white man, said, "A lot of white women are like spoiled brats. . . . A lot of the white women I dated have had codependency issues. They were just overly demanding." Peter says his current Chinese American girlfriend is from an intact family and is professionally ambitious and tenacious, qualities that his white former girlfriends lacked. While these descriptions of model minority traits are well-meant, some of the descriptions, such as "not overly demanding," "not complaining too much," or "not sexually promiscuous," indicate that these men value a conservative, somewhat submissive image of womanhood. They apparently feel that they have more control in their intimate relationships than with white women.

Kumiko Nemoto

While the white men I interviewed reported few negative responses from their family and friends with regard to their Asian or Asian American girlfriends, many of them did note that things would have been different if they had brought a black woman home. Peter, a 27-year-old multimedia designer, said, "No one ever said anything about Vivian [his Asian girlfriend] . . . But had I come home with a black girlfriend, then some . . . of my uncles or somebody might have said something about not liking it." Thus, it is not that race does not matter in interracial relationships; it is just that certain racialized femininities, ones that adhere to more traditional gender roles, are more acceptable than others.

Many of the Asian American women I interviewed expressed a preference for white men over men of other ethnic and racial groups, including Asian American men. A 58-year-old first-generation Korean woman believed that American husbands treat women better than Korean husbands do. Similarly, a 38-year-old first-generation Filipina American, who is a mother of two biracial children whom she referred to as "white," talked about her childhood dream to marry a white man. White men, she believed, embody an authentic American middle-class ideal. Considering the fact that whiteness (and its associated Anglo-Saxon middle-class lifestyle) has been circulated globally as a sign of power and an object of desire (Kelsky 2001), foreign-born Asian women's preference for white men over men of other races might not be surprising.

However, most second- or higher-generation Asian American women also explicitly expressed their aversion to Asian and Asian American men, sometimes much more strongly than foreign-born Asian women did. Victoria, a 24-year-old medical school student, was adamant that she would never date anyone other than a white man. She said, "I never dated an Asian guy. . . . I think that Asian guys are not courteous to women." Grace, a 26-year-old engineer, also never dated Asian men. Grace described them as incapable of dealing with "independent women" like herself. "I am not attracted to Asian guys. . . . They are not gentlemen. . . . They are not affectionate. At least the ones I've met. I think my personality clashes with a lot of them. Because I think I'm too independent. I'm too outgoing. A lot of Asian guys like Asian women. . . Either they are dainty or they are pretty or they are. . . . submissive . . . " Second- or third-generation Asian American women portrayed white men as being egalitarian, tall, and capable of providing them with what they deserve. Many Asian American women were particularly willing to date or marry white men because they believed these men could provide evidence that they are assimilated, authentic "Americans" who are also independent. Thus, Asian American women's valuing whiteness and white manhood has promoted a mutual attraction between them and white men, bolstering existing racial stereotypes and gender hierarchies.

In the relationships between Asian American men and white women, some of the more successful couples adhered to very traditional gender arrangements. In many of these cases, the Asian American men possessed professional jobs, class status, or career prospects. When minority men exhibit or possess class privileges, and follow the male breadwinner model, they are likely to exercise leverage and power in their relationships with white women, and possibly repudiate the negative racial stereotypes associated with them. However, many negative stereotypes of couples consisting of Asian/Asian American men and white women persist. In contrast with the social acceptance of Asian American female–white male couples, a few white women

Asian women are more accepted than black women by white male's family

stereotype on asian men

dating Asian American men reported negative reactions from their families and friends. Emily, a 38-year-old schoolteacher married to a Cambodian American man, used to invite her friends to their home, but eventually stopped. "We had made friends from work, then tried to invite them to dinner. But there's always an air of uncomfort-ableness that we both detect from these people." Emily has been disowned by her family members since she married her husband; he has rarely met her kin. Karen, a 20-year-old student coupled with a Chinese American man who is studying engi-neering, remembered her parents mentioning something about their future child. "It wasn't extremely derogatory, but I didn't really like it. They said something like, our children may have a hard time because they will be half-white, half Asian." Karen's friends also expressed concern about her boyfriend. "I said, you know, I am dating somebody and he is Asian. One of my friends made fun of it, and made an Asian joke. The other one said OK. They didn't say oh, that's great. They just said OK. One of them asked me how my parents felt about it." Tracey, a 26-year-old waitress married to a 29-year-old Japanese man, remembered her friends' comments. "They asked me if he had a bad temper or drank too much."

These experiences show that white women coupled with Asian American men encounter less social acceptance than Asian American women with white men. How-ever, this does not mean that Asian American women do not encounter racism. In the same study, most Asian American women described individual encounters with rac-ism, such as name-calling or being dismissed as "foreigners." But the long-popular stereotypes of subservience combined with the logic of patriarchy, in which white men are imagined as protectors and authority figures, validate Asian American female–white male couples and provide them with far more social acceptance than is granted to other types of interracial couples. As I mentioned previously, the public presence of white husbands serves as a buffer or reduces general suspicion toward these women, reducing the likelihood that they will be seen as immigrants, foreigners, or racial minorities (Nemoto 2009:71). Meanwhile, white women with Asian American men are deemed most acceptable when they follow traditional gender arrangements – and even then they might be seen as deviant because they haven't adhered to the logic of white male authority.

In this chapter, I have argued that the dominant racial and gendered ideologies embedded in images and discourses of interracial relationships make certain couples more socially acceptable than others. Even though the rise of interracial dating and marriage gives the impression that racism and sexism are in decline, our images of interracial romance continue to be constructed by traditional ideologies of race and gender. Discourses and the realities of interracial romance do not signify a public welcome for random cross-race relationships. In the case of Asian American–white couples, the high intermarriage rate of Asian American women may largely derive from the dominant stereotype of these women as hyperfeminine and subservient. This stereotype reinforces men's authority, and traditional norms of marriage and the family. These unions therefore do not contradict the dominant ideologies of white-ness, white privilege, or gender inequality. Seen this way, interracial romances may be a more exotic version of the traditional heterosexual union that sustains white privi-lege, male authority, and America's traditional norms of heterosexual marriage and family values.

Kumiko Nemoto

References

Berlant, Lauren. 1997. *The Queen of America Goes to Washington City: Essays on Sex and Citizenship*. Durham, NC and London: Duke University Press.

Childs, Erica Chito. 2009. *Fade to Black and White: Interracial Images in Popular Culture*. Lanham, MD: Rowman & Littlefield.

Collins, Patricia Hill. 2004. *Black Sexual Politics: African Americans, Gender, and the New Racism*. New York: Routledge.

Constable, Nicole. 2003. *Romance on a Global Stage: Pen Pals, Virtual Ethnography, and "Mail-Order" Marriage*. Berkeley: University of California Press.

Espiritu, Yen L. 2000. *Asian American Women and Men: Labor, Laws, and Love*. Walnut Creek, CA: Alta-Mira Press.

Giroux, Henry A. 2006. *The Giroux Reader*, ed. Christopher G. Robbins. Boulder, CO: Paradigm.

Kelsky, Karen. 2001. *Women on the Verge: Japanese Women, Western Dreams*. Durham, NC: Duke University Press.

Koshy, Susan. 2005. *Sexual Naturalization: Asian Americans and Miscegenation*. Stanford, CA: Stanford University Press.

Nemoto, Kumiko. 2009. *Racing Romance: Love, Power, and Desire among Asian American/White Couples*. New Brunswick, NJ and London: Rutgers University Press.

Nylund, David. 2006. "Critical Multiculturalism, Whiteness, and Social Work: Towards a More Radical View of Cultural Competence." *Journal of Progressive Human Services* 17(2): 27–42.

Perry, Pamela. 2002. *Shades of White: White Kids and Racial Identities in High School*. Durham, NC and London: Duke University Press.

Qian, Zhenchao. 2005. "Breaking the Last Taboo: Interracial Marriage in America." *Contexts* 4(4): 33–37.

chapter 35

Inventions of hetero-sex in later life

Beyond dysfunction and the coital imperative

Linn Sandberg

"Do you know how 80 year-old people fuck?" After sex, when the 60 year-old Inga is lying naked in bed, entangled together with her 76 year-old lover Karl, he suddenly asks her: " Do you know how 80 year-old people fuck?" "How?" Inga replies and Karl says " She's standing on her head and he dips it from above." They both laugh. This scene, from the German film *Cloud Nine* (2008) about a romantic and sexual relationship in later life, evokes the popular image of sexuality in old age as defined by impotence. But the scene, through jokes and laughter, also challenges the pervasive idea that older men's impotence is the end to sex in later life. The couple have just had intercourse and Karl is only four years away from 80 and a possible expiry date for his erectile function. But instead of mourning and dreading a future of impotence, Karl and Inga laugh about it and merrily present playful alternatives when penetrative sex becomes difficult or even impossible.

This playfulness and inventiveness of later-life sexualities, which does not necessarily involve heterosexual intercourse, rarely makes it to the spotlight. Instead, a coital imperative – the idea that "real" sex always necessarily involve penile-vaginal intercourse – increasingly informs mass media and medical discourses of ageing and sexuality and assumes that impotence is a dreadful fate for senior men. However, when listening to the narratives of some older partnered heterosexual men and women, alternatives to sexual intercourse such as intimacy and touch emerge as important themes, not as substitutes for intercourse, but as enjoyable in their own right.

This chapter discusses the question of how old men and women "fuck" from existing qualitative research on later-life sexuality. The examples are primarily taken from my own study on older heterosexual men, masculinity and sexuality and for this reason a particular focus of the chapter is on men and masculinity (Sandberg 2011).

Changing discourses on later-life sexuality

Older persons have historically been understood as largely asexual, and when the sexualities of older people have been acknowledged, they have generally been discussed as a source of disgust, ridicule or simply dysfunctional (Andersson 2009; Vares 2009; Calasanti and Slevin 2001). These longstanding dominant discourses of later-life sexuality are also largely gendered, with older women more often associated with being asexual. In contrast, the negative stereotypes of older men are linked to "over-sexualisation" such as in stereotypes of "the dirty old man" (Calasanti and Slevin 2001; Sandberg 2011). More recently, however, it is possible to trace a shift in discourse of later-life sexuality. Ideas that sexuality vanishes as one ages are increasingly being challenged and giving way to understandings of sexuality as lifelong and a positive aspect of later life (Gott 2005; Marshall and Katz 2002; Sandberg 2013). Also, today there are significantly more representations of romance and sex among older people in films, newspaper articles and scientific literature (Vares 2009).

Who are the new "sexy seniors" and why have they arrived? If the earlier understanding of old age as asexual was based on a negative and ageist understanding of old people as undesirable it may seem as if this "new" focus on sexuality in later life is a positive challenge to ageism. However, one should perhaps be careful to uncritically praise the new positive approach to later-life sexuality as it is largely defined through biomedicine and "pharma-scripts" formulated by pharmaceutical companies distributing erectile drugs such as Viagra (Marshall 2010). In these scripts, later-life sexuality is largely defined through the function or dysfunction of the male penis and its potential to engage in heterosexual intercourse. Being able to perform a functioning sexuality through engaging in penile-vaginal penetration thus becomes the hallmark of successful and heteronormative sexuality, and essentially what it means to be a successfully ageing human being.

This new Viagra-induced later-life sexuality is problematic and ageist in how it promotes agelessness and overlooks the realities of physical ageing bodies. Not all older men can or wish to use sexuo-pharmaceuticals to maintain lifelong erections. For older women, continued heterosexual intercourse may be outright painful due to vaginal dryness and sensitivity (Potts et al. 2006; Potts et al. 2004). The shift to sexuality as lifelong could thus be criticized for not only maintaining but also reinforcing a coital imperative as suggested by Nicola Gavey in this volume, and it puts further pressure on ageing men and women to engage in penetrative sex.

It may then seem self-evident to start with the anxieties and problems of older men and women with regards to sexuality. However, in my qualitative research on older men, sexuality and masculinity in Sweden I was fascinated with how several men, aged 67 to 87, presented stories about (re)inventing sex, pleasure and desire as a result of both changes in attitudes over their life course and their changing bodies (Sandberg 2011). These stories, emerging in qualitative interviews and body diaries, not only challenged coital imperatives by prioritizing intimacy and touch as wider notions of sexuality, but also, in some cases, reconfigured meanings of masculinity and male sexual bodies. The narratives on sexuality in my study also resonate with other qualitative work where older men and women, rather than mourning lost erections and emphasizing ailments and problems from ageing, pointed to extended sexual repertoires and experiences of freedom and lust as they aged (Fileborn et al. 2014; Potts et al. 2006; Vares et al. 2007; Ménard et al. 2014).

To explore the question of "how old people fuck" I will start with the notion that ageing bodies hold capacities for pleasure and later life is a time where one has learned about sex and has more time to engage in it. These narratives neither fit neatly with "decline discourses" of later-life sexuality nor success discourses where ageing men and women maintain youthful bodies through invigorating coital sex as presented in the marketing for sexuo-pharmaceuticals.

Beyond dysfunction: ageing bodies' capacities for pleasure

In many ways the 83 year-old Jakob, interviewed for my study, embodies dominant ideals of masculinity. He is a former member of the military and emphasizes his body's strength and stamina. He understands himself as a man who has matured over the years and come to increasingly care for others, including his sexual partner. Late in life he recouples with an old female acquaintance from when he was young. At first they are very sexually active and are having intercourse. However, as a result of their ageing embodiment, health issues, as well as other changes from ageing, they are at the time of the interview "less sexually active," which he seemingly understands as having less intercourse. But he also simultaneously challenges the understanding that sex = intercourse, which may seem surprising given his general investments in dominant masculinity. He says: "Being together doesn't have to end with or lead to intercourse. A lot of warmth can be given just by bodily contact really." Jakob is not alone to express this; several of the men interviewed in my study pointed to how sexual intimacy was about touch, about "feeling the whole of the body" and "just feeling a naked body next to you." For many, the appreciation and enjoyment men experienced from touch and cuddling was partly a consequence of changing embodiment as they were ageing – changes that further directed them to touch. This is distinctly expressed by the 74 year-old Nore:

> Well it changes – it's probably like that for all older couples. It gets drier and the man has more difficulties in getting an erection. So it isn't just like in the old days, and maybe that's a good thing in some ways, 'cause then there is a different technique sort of. It's not just to – You have to touch each other in a different way. I add lubricant and if I can't get an erection the whole thing is a way of getting [an erection]. It becomes part of the foreplay. So in a sense that's good.

A lot of focus in the research on later-life sexuality is about sexual problems and most notably about men's erectile function (Ménard et al. 2014). However, as suggested from the men in my study and distinctly expressed in the account by Nore above, changes in erectile function are not necessarily always understood as a problem, but also as a possibility to touch more. This also resonates with the experiences of older women interviewed in other studies, where the absence of erection in some cases expanded the sexual repertoire to include cuddling and touch that did not have to lead to intercourse (Fileborn et al. 2014; Hurd Clarke 2006).

Moreover, when the men participating in my study discussed changing embodiment related to ageing and the consequences of this it was not only erections that were the focus. Stiff joints, aching backs and knees were also some of the aspects of ageing embodiment that changed the sexual repertoire, but not necessarily for the worse. In two interviews the experiences of breast changes relating to ageing and illness were discussed. In one example, Nore tells of how he grew breasts as a result of a prostate cancer treatment, something he at first feels is a "blow to masculinity." But his experience changes when he learns that his wife finds them "sexy" as they are soft and sensual to touch. In another example, 84 year-old Owe tells how his wife, when they were in midlife, was diagnosed with breast cancer and she was forced to have a double mastectomy. To begin with, they both feared this would be a loss in their sexual and intimate life since breasts are "nice to caress and touch." But Owe and his wife found other ways of experiencing pleasure after the mastectomy and other things replaced sexual experiences with her breasts. He explains:

> There was a deeper feeling of other things that could be pleasurable. Just caressing the body and to feel each other, that this works out, this works fine . . . It could possibly have been something that could have disturbed, but this was 1983. And there was probably no big difference before and after.

The stories of Owe and Nore differ in the sense that one is about gaining breasts and the other is about loss, but they are similar in that both point to how changes in ageing bodies are not all about loss, but of bodies' potential for unforeseen pleasures. It is interesting how the cases of Nore and Owe also point to how changes may also lead to new experiences of gendered embodiment, in that women without breasts and men with breasts may experience sexual and intimate pleasure despite not conforming to normative ideas of what is a male or female body.

One may argue that the experiences of touch, cuddling and intimacy, which extend the repertoire of sex beyond a narrow focus on intercourse in later-life sexuality, are substitutes for heterosexual intercourse. But the stories of intimacy and touch seemingly point to cuddling and touch as an "enjoyable end in itself" without having to lead to intercourse (Hurd Clarke 2006:136). For women belonging to generations where engaging in intercourse was understood as a "marital duty," they may sometimes experience less pressure when their partners no longer have an erection and they can enjoy sex further outside of coital imperatives (Fileborn et al. 2014; Gott and Hinchcliff 2003). And, although not explicitly expressed in my research on older men, the pleasure and enjoyment older men seem to get from non-coital sex suggest that not having to perform through erection and penetration could take some pressure off men as well.

Great lovers are made not born: time, experience and learning

Ageing is not only about the ageing bodies; it is just as much about socio-cultural aspects that could include things such as going into retirement, bereavement and the accumulation of life experiences. Changing life circumstances and becoming more experienced could also impact sexual experiences. Similarly to how the elderly couple Karl and Inga discussed at the chapter's beginning, laughed and joked about sex, Edvard, interviewed in my study, argues that sexuality is more carefree in later life. Edvard is a social dancer and when he speaks of the attraction and the sexual feelings in dancing he says:

> It isn't that different really, with people of different sexes and interests meeting and holding each other . . . But it's more carefree now in comparison to when you were younger. . . . At that age things were embarrassing, you blushed real easy and those things. But now you've been around an entire life and maybe had several relationships, so we're sort of laughing and joking about things, right?

Although Edvard in this quote does not specifically speak of sex but instead of sexuality in relation to social dancing, he points to how being more experienced with relationships in later life makes things more relaxed and less serious. Also, a more carefree attitude may not only be about being more experienced but also about unlearning and overcoming negative attitudes and destructive messages about sex, something that could take a long time (Ménard et al. 2014).

Being more experienced could also contribute to becoming more sexually skilled. When the men in my study spoke about themselves sexually, they emphasized that they had learned things about sex throughout life. They had also matured and become more attentive to the needs of their female partners. In one interviewee's case, he came to learn about sex after his wife had left him for another man and he realized that sex was partly to do with it, that he had not been observant of her sexual pleasure. Men, both in my study and other studies, perceived that sex in youth was mainly about "empty out and move on" whereas in their mid- to later-life they were more focused on mutual pleasures and the satisfaction of their partners (Potts et al. 2006:316; Sandberg 2011). Certainly, it is hardly likely that all men become great lovers as a result of ageing and these kinds of narratives can also be understood as ways of constructing a desirable masculine self in later life. That men are not always improving is, for example, visible in studies with older women. As an older female interviewee of Fileborn et al.'s (2014:7) study express:

> He couldn't see that I had sexual needs. He couldn't see that I didn't need a penis . . . Because once he'd done his bit that was it. He'd roll over and go to sleep. And I'd be left going "What the fuck?"

Still, although not all men improve sexually as they age, the narratives of the men in my study, as well as other research, suggest that increasing experiences throughout the life course and learning about sex could contribute to challenging coital imperatives and a one-sided focus on men's erections and orgasms. Studies also suggest that women sometimes experience more confidence when they age and felt that they were better at expressing and negotiating what they enjoyed and desired sexually (Fileborn et al. 2014; Vares et al. 2007).

Other changes associated with ageing pertain to time and being in a life stage when the pressures of working life and raising family are gone. Frank, 71, for example, remarks that sex earlier in life had to happen "when it fits the schedule" and how now when he is retired he can take more time. No longer having children living at home is also an aspect of later life which sometimes is perceived as giving more freedom and time to engage in and enjoy sex. This seems to be particularly the case for women who traditionally hold more responsibilities in child rearing (Hurd Clarke 2006; Fileborn et al. 2014).

Not having to worry about becoming pregnant was also discussed as giving a particular freedom to later-life sexuality, both by the men in my research and in other studies with older women. In my research, I was struck by men who discussed freedom of sex beyond reproduction, something that is more often related to women's experiences (Hurd Clarke 2006). The interviewee Edvard discusses how sexuality in youth is about "urges" and "instincts" that have the aim of making us reproduce. Sex outside of reproductive time is experienced, however, as less goal-oriented and more linked to intimacy and touch. Edvard argues:

> Sexuality exists for people to reproduce, and for us [older people] this is not the case anymore. It's quite natural that this is not the case anymore, things change character, there's warmth and things are different, I don't know how to say it. Like, when you're young intercourse is the goal of sexual activities, right? But that's not the case anymore, it could happen but it doesn't have to . . . That's not what's important, there's a lot more. There's the closeness. Some kind of trust in having a close friend that you may share even a naked body with, so to speak.

So ageing bodies in some ways reorient older men and women to sexual practices that focus more on non-coital intimacy and touch. But orientations to intimacy and touch may also come from experiences of being in a particular life stage that is outside of work, child rearing and reproduction. This enables more sexual freedom, in the sense of having more time for sexual and intimate practices and to explore sex beyond the coital imperative.

Fuck like you're 80 years old

How do 80 year-olds fuck? Sex is complex no matter the age, and there is obviously no "one-size-fits-all" kind of model for how people have sex, regardless of if you are in your 80s, 60s, 40s or 20s.

However, there are persistent societal discourses that try to state how later-life sexuality happens or does not happen. Existing stereotypes of desexualized oldies (most notably "old crones"), "dirty old men," or more recently "sexy seniors," are narrow and disempowering to old people (Hinchcliff and Gott 2008). Negative decline discourses on later-life sexuality, on the one hand, rely largely on asexual stereotypes that disregard that older people continue to have sex far beyond midlife. To the extent that later-life sexuality is acknowledged, it is mainly discussed in terms of dysfunction and unsatisfactory sexual experiences. This contrasts with what several quantitative studies actually suggest (Tessler Lindau et al. 2007; Beckman et al. 2008; Trompeter, Bettencourt and Barrett-Connor 2012).

On the other hand, more affirmative discourses on later-life sexuality buttress stereotypes of "sexy seniors." In these discourses, the focus is often on narrow binaries of sexual function/dysfunction, where those who maintain sexual function through erections are deemed successful and those who don't are failures. Embracing the sexy senior, moreover, risks reinforcing a new norm where sex is necessary to be a healthy, positively ageing older person. This overlooks those who, for various reasons, cannot or do not wish to pursue sexual and intimate relationships.

By presenting my own and other qualitative studies on the voices and experiences of older heterosexual people, this chapter presents later-life sexuality as neither faulty nor dependent on a Viagra-induced forever-functioning sexual machinery, but as involving reinventions and negotiations of sexuality. Older men narrated their experiences of sex as very much focused on the significance of intimacy and touch as they were ageing. Although some felt that their ageing bodies – in particular changes in erectile function – was a hardship, the very same men were also pointing to the great pleasures they experienced from being intimate with and touching a partner. This was also something many women voiced when interviewed in other studies: an end to penetrative sex could in fact be an opening for long-sought intimacy that involved cuddling. This chapter does not suggest that all oldies want are cuddles and caresses. Certainly both older men and women may enjoy intercourse as Meika Loe suggests in her chapter in this volume. But intercourse was not all there was to sex, for women or men.

More time, more experience and less duties could enable better sex as people age. As Ménard and colleagues (2014:6) suggest in their research on "optimal sex," "great lovers are made not born" and instead of looking at older people as always having sexual problems, we should also highlight how learning over a lifetime, including greater sexual experience, could contribute to great sex for older adults. My own research, as well as other studies, point to how sexuality may be less determined by conventional sexual scripts such as a coital imperative (Simon and Gagnon 2003, cited in Ménard et al. 2014). Intimacy and touch are practices that involve the entire body rather than being narrowly focused on genital pleasure. Still, they should not necessarily be understood as substitutes for "real sex," as men and women are clearly enjoying these practices in their own right. In this sense, intimacy and touch may exist in a borderland between the sexual and the non-sexual.

However, since intimacy and touch may not readily fall into dominant notions of sex – which is often assumed to involve intercourse – narratives of intimacy and touch can sometimes be overlooked and downplayed as not really being about sex (Sandberg 2011; Fileborn et al. 2014). Doctors, social workers, researchers and others working with older people should thus stay open to the significance of the broad spectra of sexual intimacy that challenges a coital imperative. Moreover, gender relations in later-life sexuality must also be thoroughly acknowledged. If men's sexualities are prioritized before women's, as gender and sexualities scholars have suggested, then possibilities of negotiating and reinventing sex are notably different for men and

Linn Sandberg

women in heterosexual relationships (Jackson 1999; Ramazanoglû and Holland 2002). Narrating oneself as a more intimate, considerate and better lover as an older man may be a way for men to come across as desirable without necessarily changing their sexual practices.

Feminist disability scholar Alison Kafer (2013:42) uses the concept "compulsory nostalgia" to describe the idea that we are always assumed to mourn the past, more specifically able bodies of the past "that perhaps never were". "Compulsory nostalgia" takes able-bodied, and in the case of age, youthfully able bodies, as the default position for which we should all strive. However, as I have shown in this chapter, older men and women are not primarily mourning the past, but experiencing pleasures thanks to their ageing. Eighty year-olds may not necessarily stand on their heads to pursue sexuality in later life as joked about in the film *Cloud Nine*, but stories of older men and women point to an inventiveness and possibility of rethinking sex that is rarely discussed in medical accounts or mass media portrayals.

Bibliography

Andersson, Åsa. 2009. "Från fula gubbar och liderliga gummor till virila casanovor och glada änkor?: om 1900-talets förändrade synsätt på äldres sexualitet." *Tidskrift för genusvetenskap* 4:49–69.

Beckman, Nils, Margda Waern, Deborah Gustafson and Ingmar Skoog. 2008. "Secular trends in self reported sexual activity and satisfaction in Swedish 70 year-olds: Cross sectional survey of four populations, 1971–2001." *BMJ* 337: a279:1–7.

Calasanti, Toni and Kathleen Slevin. 2001. *Gender, social inequalities and aging.* Oxford: Altamira Press.

Fileborn, Bianca, Rachel Thorpe, Gail Hawkes, Victor Minichiello, Marian Pitts and Tinashe Dune. 2014. "Sex, desire and pleasure: Considering the experiences of older Australian women." *Sexual and Relationship Therapy.* DOI: 10.1080/14681994.2014.936722.

Gott, Merryn. 2005. *Sexuality, sexual health and ageing.* Berkshire: Open University Press.

Gott, Merryn and Sharron Hinchcliff. 2003. "Sex and ageing: A gendered issue." In: Arber, Sara, Kate Davidson and Jay Ginn. (eds.), *Gender and Ageing: Changing Roles and Relationships*, Maidenhead: Open University Press, pp.63–78.

Hinchcliff, Sharron and Merryn Gott. 2008. "Challenging social myths and stereotypes of women and aging: Heterosexual women talk about sex." *Journal of Women & Aging* 20: 65–81.

Hurd Clarke, Laura. 2006. "Older women and sexuality: Experiences in marital relationships across the life course." *Canadian Journal on Aging* 25:129–140.

Jackson, Stevi. 1999. *Heterosexuality in question.* Thousand Oaks, CA: Sage.

Kafer, Alison. 2013. *Feminist, queer, crip.* Bloomington: Indiana University Press.

Marshall, Barbara. 2010. "Science, medicine and virility surveillance: 'Sexy seniors' in the pharmaceutical imagination." *Sociology of Health & Illness* 32:211–224.

Marshall, Barbara and Stephen Katz. 2002. "Forever functional: Sexual fitness and the ageing male body." *Body & Society* 8:43–70.

Ménard, A. Dana, Peggy J. Kleinplatz, Lianne Rosen, Shannon Lawless, Nicholas Paradis, Meghan Campbell and Jonathan D. Huber. 2014. "Individual and relational contributors to optimal sexual experiences in older men and women." *Sexual and Relationship Therapy*, DOI: 10.1080/14681994.2014.931689.

Potts, Annie, Nicola Gavey, Victoria Grace and Tiina Vares. 2003. "The downside of Viagra: women's experiences and concerns." *Sociology of Health & Illness* 25:697–719.

Potts, Annie, Victoria Grace, Tiina Vares and Nicola Gavey. 2006. "'Sex for life?: Men's counter stories on 'erectile dysfunction', male sexuality and ageing." *Sociology of Health & Illness* 28:306–329.

Potts, Annie, Nicola Gavey and Ann Weatherall (eds.). 2004. *Sex and the Body*. Auckland, New Zealand: Dunmore Publishing Limited.

Ramazanoglû, Caroline and Janet, Holland. 2002. "Women's sexuality and men's appropriation of desire." In: Plummer, Ken. (ed.), *Sexualities: critical concepts vol. 1*, London: Routledge, pp.401–420.

Sandberg, Linn. 2011. *Getting intimate: a feminist analysis of old age, masculinity & sexuality*. Diss. Linköping: Linköpings universitet.

Sandberg, Linn. 2013. "'Just feeling a naked body close to you': Men, sexuality and intimacy in later life." *Sexualities* 16:261–282.

Simon, William and John H. Gagnon. 2003. "Sexual scripts: Origins, influences and changes." *Qualitative Sociology* 26:491–497.

Tessler Lindau, Stacy, Phillip L. Schumm, Edward O. Laumann, Wendy Levinson, Colm A. O'Muircheartaigh and Linda Waite. 2007. "A study of sexuality and health among older adults in the United States." *New England Journal of Medicine* 357:762–774.

Trompeter, Susan E., Ricki Bettencourt and Elizabeth Barrett-Connor. 2012. "Sexual activity and satisfaction in healthy community-dwelling older women." *The American Journal of Medicine* 125:37–43.

Vares, Tiina. 2009. "Reading the 'sexy oldie': Gender, age(ing) and embodiment." *Sexualities* 12:503–523.

Vares, Tiina, Annie Potts, Nicola Gavey and Victoria Grace. 2007. "Reconceptualising cultural narratives of mature women's sexuality in the Viagra era." *Journal of Aging Studies* 21:153–164.

chapter 36

Sexual politics in intimate relationships

Sexual coercion and harassment

Lisa K. Waldner

Todd meets Jan at a party and flirts while playing a drinking game. He is feeling the effects of too much alcohol and lies down in an adjacent bedroom. Jan enters and begins kissing him and taking off his clothes. Todd does not want to have sex with Jan. Besides feeling sick, he has a steady girlfriend. However, he lets Jan unzip his pants and has sex with her because he can hear his friends cheering him on from the living room. To leave without having sex would have meant losing face with his friends and enduring taunts of "pussy" and "fag."

Linda is taking a sociology class at a local community college. One of her female classmates frequently asks her out and makes sexually suggestive comments in front of the other students. This made Linda uncomfortable but she hoped that ignoring Tammy would encourage her to stop. The last straw was when Tammy followed Linda into the women's restroom, pushed her up against a stall, and grabbed her breasts. Linda dropped the class.

Nancy and Tom are engaged but have not had sex because Nancy wants to wait until her wedding day. This annoys Tom because he thinks he has waited long enough. One evening, after too many drinks, Tom initiated sex but after Nancy refused his advances Tom became angry and physically forced her to have sexual intercourse. Tom told her afterwards that he wanted to make sure they were sexually compatible and not to worry because she was "great." Nancy was devastated that someone she loved and trusted violated her. While she has broken off the engagement, she was too ashamed to call the police.

Labels such as date rape, sexual harassment, and sexual coercion may be applied to some of the situations described above, yet there are important distinctions along dimensions of power, sexual meaning, and behavior. Unlike sexual harassment, rape, and date rape, sexual coercion is less widely reported by the media. The first three have become part of the American lexicon due to widespread news coverage of events such as the Anita Hill/Clarence Thomas hearings or Kobe Bryant's legal troubles. Yet most of us have probably experienced some form of sexual coercion at one time or another. Social scientists have been studying aspects of sexual coercion between intimates since the 1950s, yet it has only been within the last twenty years that the multidimensional nature of this concept has been actively explored. By comparing sexual coercion to the more well-known concept of sexual harassment, we can better understand the common denominator of power.

Rape, sexual coercion, and sexual harassment all have in common the use or abuse of power. "Imposing one's own will, even against opposition" (Weber, in Runciman 1978: 38) is a classic sociological definition of power and an example of what feminists term "power over." Sexual coercion, which encompasses rape as well as a continuum of milder behaviors, is a type of interpersonal power grab similar to sexual harassment. What differentiates harassment from coercion is that labeling an incident as harassment requires neither evidence of forced sexual behavior, nor a sexual interest in the victim.

Types of sexual harassment

Any setting where interaction is guided by professional rules of conduct, whether written or unwritten, such as the workplace, university classroom or a physician's office, needs to prevent both "quid pro quo" and "hostile environment" sexual harassment. These types of harassment differ in terms of the behaviors experienced and the social position of the harasser. All share in common the misuse of power to sexually degrade and humiliate.

We more often think of sexual harassment as something done *by* persons with power *to* their subordinates. Different kinds of socially superior positions have in common the requirement to exercise power over others. We expect professors to assign homework, physicians to prescribe medical treatment, and bosses to give orders to their employees. We understand that, if we refuse to comply, there may be serious consequences such as being fired or failing a class. We may not like it, but rarely do we question the "right" of persons in these positions to dictate our behavior, so long as what we are told is within the boundaries of what is socially considered acceptable. Max Weber terms the legitimate exercise of power "authority," in order to distinguish it from illegitimate power exercised through brute physical force or other types of coercion.

Pressurizing or forcing a subordinate into sexual interaction in exchange for promotion, more favorable work assignments, or keeping a job, is inappropriate and is an example of "quid pro quo" sexual harassment. If Linda's professor rather than her classmate had insisted on a date or sexual contact in exchange for a better grade, not failing, or staying in the class, this would also constitute quid pro quo harassment. Note that quid pro quo in this context usually involves two persons in an unequal power exchange. Professors, employers, doctors, and ministers, by virtue of their professional roles, have power and influence over their students, employees, patients, and parishioners.

Lisa K. Waldner

In the example of Linda and Tammy, both are presumably in equal student roles. Tammy does not have the means to engage in quid pro quo harassment, as she does not determine Linda's grade. However, Tammy's persistent requests for a date and inappropriate sexual banter is an example of "hostile environment" harassment or creating an uncomfortable setting through off-color jokes, sexual innuendoes, or other sexually charged behavior aimed at degrading the intended target. Tammy is using her influence among her classmates to informally exercise power through her sexual degradation and humiliation of Linda.

Hostile environment harassment can also be used by those occupying formal positions of power. In fact, professors, employers, and the like usually have more control over the environment than their subordinates. My geology professor would pull down the video screen to show slides, and act surprised to find a *Playboy* centerfold taped to it. When this continued to happen we realized it was intentional. Some students thought it was funny and told their offended classmates to "lighten up." This type of harassment is often disguised as humor where the offended often find themselves on the defensive for being "too" sensitive, serious, unsophisticated, sexually repressed, or other (insert character flaw here). This "turn the tables" strategy of defending inappropriate behavior enables harassers to avoid acknowledging their degradation of others.

Finally, subordinates may create a hostile environment as a means of destabilizing or reversing a power imbalance deemed inappropriate based on cultural expectations of who *should* be dominant. For example, a male student who intentionally writes inappropriate sexual comments in an essay for his female professor is also creating a hostile environment. While it is possible for a female student to make a male professor uncomfortable by engaging in similar behavior, this strategy is more commonly used by those who expect to be in control by virtue of being male, white, or heterosexual, but find they are subordinate to a female, person of color, or homosexual (or perhaps someone who is all three). Although a female boss or professor has more formal power, being male gives these subordinates more cultural power and thus is an example of what is called *contrapower harassment* (Grauerholz 1989, cited in Gratch 1996).

In quid pro quo sexual harassment there is pressure on the subordinate to be sexually or romantically intimate with a superior. Documenting a hostile environment does not require providing evidence that the harasser has a sexual interest in the victim. As a result, same-sex harassment is possible even if the parties differ in sexual orientation. In other words, a heterosexual man or woman can sexually harass a gay man or lesbian and vice versa. While we assume Tammy had a sexual interest in Linda because of her persistent requests for a date, her unprofessional behavior rather than her sexual interest is the key determinant. In contrast, sexual coercion involves someone with a sexual interest in a more resistant partner.

Defining sexual coercion

Depending upon the type of sexual harassment, exercising "power over" someone may come from formal or more informal power sources. While no one occupies a formal position of power within a romantic or sexual dyad, American culture historically has supported the "right" of husbands to force sex on their wives. For the unmarried, including gays and lesbians, exercising "power over" someone through sexual coercion is likely to be based on informal power.

Stranger rape is an example of extreme sexual coercion, but the focus here is on the activity that takes place between two people who know each other more or less, and who have been interacting with each other in a romantic or sexual way. Sexual coercion occurs whenever one partner pressures or forces the other to engage in any sexual behavior, ranging from kissing to various types of intercourse (oral, anal, vaginal). Because pressure or force is used, the outcome is unwanted by the resisting partner. Rape, or physically forcing sexual intercourse, is the most severe form of sexual coercion; unwanted kissing achieved through verbal and/or emotional manipulation is at the milder end of the continuum. The introductory scenario including Tom and Nancy would usually be recognized as an example of rape, because Tom physically forced Nancy to have sexual intercourse. What becomes more difficult to determine is the boundary between milder versions of sexual coercion and acceptable seduction strategies.

Because the milder pressure used by partners is similar to socially acceptable seduction strategies, the line between coercion and seduction can be blurry. In American culture, candlelight, wine, and music are all thought to enhance the mood and render sexual activity more likely. Indeed many of us have planned the perfect "romantic evening" for a special partner, hoping that the night would end in physical intimacy even if just a prolonged kiss. However, someone who sneaks a shot of vodka into his date's drink with the intent to take sexual advantage has crossed the line. Where does gentle persuasion end and coercion begin?

Clarifying this boundary are three factors that must all be present to label an experience as sexual coercion: (i) a sexual outcome, (ii) an active agent, and (iii) a victim perception of the experience as unwanted. The range of potential sexual outcomes and coercion strategies will be discussed subsequently, but note that this definition only includes situations when pressure is directly attributed to the actions of an aggressive partner. There are situations when a person feels pressure or has subsequent regrets but sexual coercion, as currently defined, did not occur.

An initial query is, when was the sexual outcome defined as unwanted? Everyone has experienced second thoughts or buyer's remorse: "I wish I had not made out with the blonde at the party." Even if the "blonde at the party" initiated the saliva exchange, it is not sexual coercion if both parties desired physical contact at the time. An exception to this rule is in situations when the initiator deliberately lies to or otherwise manipulates the partner. Lying about being in love in order to have sex is coercion, because some individuals would only choose to be sexual within the context of a loving relationship. Because the facts were misrepresented, the sexual outcome was potentially unwanted. In this latest example, the third criterion, an active agent or individual who misled the partner is also present. Unwanted sex does not require an active agent, but coercive sex does.

In the opening scenario including Todd and Jan, only two of the three conditions for sexual coercion were met: a sexual outcome and Todd's perception of unwanted sex. While it is true that Todd did not want to be sexual with Jan, there is no active agent because neither party was pressuring or coercing the other. While Jan initiated

Lisa K. Waldner

sex, she did not deliberately get him drunk, use physical force, or employ any coercion technique. She never calls him "pussy" or "fag." What compels him to have sex despite being uninterested is his fear of what he perceives his friends *might* do or say. Furthermore, there is no evidence that Todd communicated in any manner his reservations to Jan. Todd's unwanted sexual experience was more the result of sharing his friends' definition of masculinity, including pursuing every available sexual opportunity. Women defining femininity as taking care of their partner's sexual needs, even when they do not coincide with their own, may also find themselves feeling pressure. Neither of these situations are examples of sexual coercion. Although the sexual outcome was unwanted, there was no deliberate manipulation or pressure from a partner. To label Todd's situation as sexual coercion would necessitate Jan taking responsibility for Todd's beliefs on masculinity and her inability to read his mind.

While Todd's situation is not sexual coercion, this is not to say that we should be unconcerned with external influences such as cultural values. Given the potential negative consequences of unwanted sex, situations where individuals feel societal pressure to be sexually intimate because of gender roles, homophobia, concerns about popularity, or perceptions of peer pressure, are problematic yet fall outside the scope of interpersonal sexual coercion. However, partners that actively use cultural ideologies as a coercion tool do fall within the current definition. Examples in American culture include questioning someone's masculinity, femininity, or sexual identity for turning down heterosexual sex. If Jan had threatened to tell Todd's friends that he turned her down, questioned his masculinity or sexual identity by name-calling, or questioned his ability to perform sexually, she would have been guilty of using verbal sexual coercion strategies. While the verbal attacks can be gender-specific (accusing a man of being impotent, or calling a woman cold), the motivation for both is similar, wanting sexual interaction from a resistant partner.

Coercion strategies and sexual outcomes

Sexual coercion has two dimensions, the target sexual outcome and the tactic used by the aggressor. Women have reported being coerced into a variety of outcomes (kissing, fondling, and various forms of intercourse) by male perpetrators using a range of tactics including verbal-emotional and physical strategies (Christopher 1988). Verbal strategies may or may not contain some aspect of emotional pressure or manipulation. Common strategies include: telling lies ("I love you"); making false promises ("we'll get engaged"); blackmail (threatening to disclose negative information that may or may not be true); and saying things to make a partner feel guilty ("If you really loved me, you would"). Rape is the most severe form of coercion because the more extreme sexual outcome of intercourse is obtained through the use of physical force or threat of force.

Not all physical strategies include the use of force associated with rape. For example, persistent physical attempts by continual touching or being "handsy" is also a form of refusing to take no for an answer. Other physical strategies include encouraging partners to drink excessively or use drugs, physical detainment (blocking a car door, not letting someone leave), physically holding someone down, threatening to use force, using physical force (slapping and hitting), or physical force with a weapon. Even with physical strategies there is a continuum, with physical detainment and persistent touching being less aggressive than holding someone down or using physical force. Encouraging someone to drink too much is less aggressive than spiking a drink with vodka or Rohypnol (a date-rape drug). This is not to say that we should ignore milder forms of coercion, but we must acknowledge that tactics can differ by the degree of force or pressure applied. Furthermore, situations are complicated and any coercion incident might include several different tactics.

Because women usually lack the physical capacity to force sex on men, coercive women rely more on verbal-emotional strategies. Threats of disclosing real or imagined problems with sexual functioning have long been associated with things said to women ("What's the matter; are you frigid?"), but men too are vulnerable to verbal attacks that question masculine ("Can't you get it up?") and heterosexual ("You must be gay") identities. Social scientists know very little about the content of the "parting shots" that men and women fire at each other to humiliate, degrade, and verbally pressure partners into sexual activity. We do know that the lies men tell women to manipulate and deceive tend to revolve around feelings about caring, and promise of commitment (DeGue and DiLillo 2004).

Current findings on sexual coercion

A basic question is, how much sexual coercion is occurring between intimate partners? Sociologists often use surveys to answer this question. Reported rates from surveys differ because of how coercion is defined, the wording of questions, and the time period under study. For example, surveys that focus only on instances of coerced intercourse will report lower rates than those that include questions measuring instances of unwanted kissing and fondling. Additionally, physical force may be the only tactic studied, or one of several including verbal strategies. Asking individuals if they have experienced sexual coercion without some sort of behavioral checklist that defines what we mean by targeted outcomes (intercourse, kissing, fondling) and tactics (intoxication, physical force, verbal pressure, etc.) is likely to yield a smaller number of affirmative responses. The target time period may also have an impact on reported rates. Sometimes we want to know "lifetime prevalence rates" by asking individuals "have you ever experienced" some form of sexual coercion, while in other studies we focus on a narrower time period, such as within the last twelve months. Because of these differences, rates for heterosexual women with a coercive male partner range from 83 percent (Waldner-Haugrud and Magruder 1995) to 27.5 percent (Larimer et al. 1999). These same studies suggest the proportion of heterosexual males with a coercive female partner ranges between 73 percent and 20.7 percent.

For both heterosexual men and women, unwanted kissing or fondling happens more often than does intercourse (this is not true for gays and lesbians). Physically aggressive tactics such as force or holding someone down are reported less often than less aggressive methods such as making false promises or telling lies. Tactics commonly reported by both heterosexual male and female victims include intoxication, persistent touching, and lies.

Lisa K. Waldner

Although both heterosexual men and women report sexual coercion, these experiences are not equivalent. Numerically, there are more women than men who report being pressured or forced into sexual interaction. The context of the experience also differs between men and women in two important respects. First, women are much more likely than men to report the use of physical force (Struckman-Johnson 1988; Waldner-Haugrud and Magruder 1995; Larimer *et al.* 1999). Second, men are much more likely to report stopping the coercion at kissing or fondling. In contrast, women are more likely than men to report sexual intercourse as the eventual outcome (Waldner-Haugrud and Magruder 1995).

Same-sex sexual coercion

Compared to heterosexuals, we know a great deal less about the lives of gays and lesbians, and sexual coercion is no exception. Prevalence rates for gay men and lesbians vary for the same reasons previously discussed. Currently, it appears that lesbians (30–50 percent) are more likely than gay males (12–29 percent) to have a sexually coercive partner (Waldner-Haugrud 1999). Yet, compared to heterosexual women, lesbians are less likely to experience sexual coercion. Recall that heterosexuals are more likely to experience coerced kissing and fondling than intercourse. In contrast, both lesbians and gay men are more likely to report penetration (oral, anal, vaginal) rather than kissing or fondling as the eventual sexual outcome (Waldner-Haugrud and Gratch 1997). The reason for this difference is unknown, but possibly fear of pregnancy may inhibit heterosexuals who would otherwise pressure their partners into intercourse. Similar to heterosexuals, gays and lesbians report that milder coercion strategies (lies, persistent touching) are more frequently used against them than being held down or other types of physical force.

Risk factors

More attention has been paid to describing outcomes and tactics than identifying what types of characteristics or situations increase the likelihood of being involved in sexual coercion. What is known is the connection to alcohol. Gay or straight, male or female, victim or aggressor, those who drink excessively are more likely to report being victimized or perpetrating unwanted sexual contact even when other tactics besides intoxication are used. What constitutes excessive drinking is somewhat subjective, as some individuals can tolerate higher levels of alcohol consumption than others, but the definition of binge drinking can serve as a useful benchmark. Binge drinkers are women who consume four drinks or more per drinking occasion and men who consume five or more drinks. Individuals who engage in binge drinking are at a higher risk for coercion than those who abstain or consume less.

The attitudes and beliefs of rapists have been compared to those of men who are not sexually aggressive. Rapists tend to have more negative attitudes towards women and more traditional ideas about gender, including the meaning of masculinity and the role of women. For example, they are more likely to agree that men should be the ones to initiate sex, and that women who drink and flirt are "asking for it." This latter belief is called a rape myth, or a false belief used to justify rape. Widespread acceptance of rape myths gives men more cultural power over women.

Men who are not rapists but use verbal methods of sexual coercion are also different from non-aggressive men. Coercive men have less empathy for women, more experiences with child abuse, a stronger adherence to rape myths, a higher level of acceptance for relationship violence, and a greater level of distrust and anger towards women. None of these factors necessarily causes sexual coercion but may help us better to understand both the social (cultural attitudes towards women, rape myths, male dominance, homophobia, gender ideologies), familial (history of child abuse, experiences with relationship violence), and interpersonal (lack of empathy, distrust and anger towards women) conditions that foster sexual coercion.

Not crossing the line

We can reduce but not completely eliminate our chances of becoming a victim of sexual harassment or coercion. What is completely within our own power is the choice to live a sexually ethical life by choosing not to use harassment or coercive strategies in our interpersonal interactions. While avoiding more blatant violations such as quid pro quo sexual harassment and rape seems clear, milder sexual coercion strategies and sexual banter (that may or may not be labeled as hostile environment harassment) are less clear. What further complicates matters in the case of sexual harassment is that both the workplace and the classroom are often a meeting place for marriage and dating partners. The key to distinguishing whether or not something is sexual harassment or harmless sexual banter is how *wanted* the behavior is perceived by the recipient (Gratch 1996). Asking a co-worker or classmate out on a date is not going to be labeled as sexual harassment if the one asked was hoping for such an opportunity. Neither is someone apt to label their partner sexually coercive if they wanted to be kissed or to have sex. This ambiguity between actual wants and what others perceive creates the potential for conflict, because some of us are better at correctly interpreting situational cues than others. However, all of us need to be truly committed to listening to those we interact with and not using historically acceptable excuses to justify offensive behavior. This doesn't mean that we should never ask colleagues out on dates, refrain from sexual banter, or avoid making sexual advances.

Putting aside the question of Linda's sexual orientation, Tammy's request for a date need not have been an example of sexual harassment. It was Tammy's *persistent* requests despite Linda's lack of interest, communicated by ignoring Tammy, that constituted harassment. Sexual banter in the workplace need not be sexual harassment if the parties involved are comfortable interacting with each other in this way. Linda's ignoring of Tammy should have been a signal that her sexual comments were unwelcome. The same rules also apply for sexual coercion. Resistance should always be taken as a sign that a sexual invitation is not wanted unless the parties involved have negotiated a different understanding. This is more practical than the approach of requiring parties to receive verbal consent at every level of sexual intimacy, because people communicate in both verbal and non-verbal ways. Making a sexual pass at someone and being turned down is not sexual coercion unless the initiator refuses "to get it" by *persistently* making sexual overtures or resorting to name-calling and other sorts of bullying behavior.

Max Weber defines "life chances" as the likelihood of experiencing a phenomenon connected to one's position within the social hierarchy. The likelihood of experiencing sexual harassment or sexual coercion is always higher for those with low social power. Yet power is not always connected to a formal position. Understanding the different avenues for acquiring and exercising power allows for a fuller, more complicated picture of social reality that defies easy categorizations or simplistic solutions.

Bibliography

Christopher, F. S. 1988. "An Initial Investigation into a Continuum of Premarital Sexual Pressure." *Journal of Sex Research* 25: 255–66.

DeGue, Sarah and David DiLillo. 2004. "Understanding Perpetrators of Nonphysical Sexual Coercion: Characteristics of Those who Cross the Line." *Violence and Victims* 19: 673–88.

Gratch, Linda Vaden. 1996. "Recognizing Sexual Harassment: Problems Caused by Labeling Difficulties." In Bernice R. Sandler and Robert J. Shoop (eds), *Sexual Harassment in the University*. Boston, MA: Allyn & Bacon.

Grauerholz, E. 1989. "Sexual Harrassment of Women Professors by Students: Exploring the Dynamics of Power, Authority and Gender in a University Setting." *Gender Roles* 21:789–801.

Larimer, M. E., A. R. Lydum, B. A. Anderson, and A. P. Turner. 1999. "Male and Female Recipients of Unwanted Sexual Contact in a College Student Sample: Prevalence Rates, Alcohol Use, and Depression Symptoms." *Sex Roles* 40: 295–304.

Runciman, W. G. 1978. *Weber: Selections in Translation*. Cambridge, MA: Cambridge University Press.

Struckman-Johnson, Cindy. 1988. "Forced Sex on Dates: It Happens to Men Too." *Journal of Sex Research* 24: 234–40.

United States Equal Employment Opportunity Commission. 2004. "Discriminatory Practices." Available online at www.eeoc.gov/abouteeo/overview_practices.html (accessed 22 March 2006).

Waldner-Haugrud, Lisa K. 1999. "Sexual Coercion in Lesbian and Gay Relationships: A Review and Critique." *Aggression and Violent Behavior* 4: 139–49.

Waldner-Haugrud, Lisa K. and Brian Magruder. 1995. "Male and Female Victimization in Dating Relationships: Gender Differences in Coercion Techniques and Outcomes." *Violence and Victims* 10: 203–15.

Waldner-Haugrud, Lisa K. and Linda Vaden Gratch. 1997. "Sexual Coercion in Gay/Lesbian Relationships: Descriptives and Gender Differences." *Violence and Victims* 12: 87–98.

PART 6

Sexual lifestyles

Introduction

The notion of sex as the basis for a lifestyle would likely have sounded odd, if not bizarre and unintelligible, to your grandparents and great-grandparents. Theirs was a world very different from those of us in the West. How so?

Let's take 1900 as the baseline. America was becoming an industrial and urban nation, indeed a global power. Social diversity increasingly characterized city life. Small-town folk migrated to cities for jobs; many blacks migrated from rural towns to cities in hopes of more freedom; immigrants from China, Ireland, Italy and many other nations flooded our cities. Also, women were beginning to participate in public life, not only in paid work but café life; same-gender subcultures and networks began to surface in cities such as New York, Chicago, Atlanta and San Francisco. People of different genders, classes, nationalities, and races were intermingling in public life in a way that was new. In many ways, it was an exciting time. And yet, when it came to intimate and sexual life, America was still under the cultural influence of nineteenth-century Victorianism. Women's lives still were centered in the domestic sphere; sexual and intimate choice was severely restricted. For example, interracial marriage was illegal; same-gender desires were being defined as a polluted identity to be criminalized and persecuted by the state.

At the heart of American culture in 1900 was the institution of marriage. Adults were expected to marry. Marriage was exclusively between a man and women, and available only to members of the same race. Marriage was a state institution. One married before the state and ending marriage required the official approval of the state. Further, the state recognized specific spousal roles: men were expected to be the providers and protectors of the household; women were to be wives and mothers and to defer to men's authority. Marriage was lifelong, not only in intent but often enough in reality since divorce was not easily granted and most women simply did not have the economic capacity to live on their own—not to mention that being a single woman was stigmatized. There were, in effect, no acceptable alternative life-styles to marriage.

Furthermore, marriage was an enveloping institution. Sex, love, companionship, and parenthood were all knit together. One was to marry the person you loved; the ideal was to be a virgin until marriage and after to be monogamous; and only in marriage was it appropriate to have children. Marriage and family was said to create a special companionship and social bond; all other relationships either lacked intimacy or were considered secondary. One's personal life revolved around marriage and children. Even socializing was now imagined to be couple based and what spare time was available was devoted to the kids. In a word, marriage encompassed wide stretches of individuals' lives.

In order for sex to be recognized as a lifestyle, there would need to be an environment in which women were able to be more or less economically and socially independent; the institution of marriage would have to have loosened its control over individuals; simultaneously, there would have to be a culture that tolerated differences in sexual and intimate arrangements. All of these things were absent until, roughly speaking, the 1960s and 1970s. At this point, women were participating in the market economy, going to college, establishing their own households, and, not least, were claiming, largely because of feminism, a right to sexual-affectional freedom.

Think of how sex changed between then and now. Today, sex carries various meanings—pleasure, love, intimacy, self-expression, a way to validate gender identity, and so on. Sexual expression is tolerated in a variety of social arrangements, from hook ups to dating, friends with benefits, cohabitation, or marriage. Note: sex is no longer linked to love or marriage or procreation. Indeed, neither love nor childbearing is no longer necessarily tied to marriage. Today, romantic love can and does occur in a variety of social relationships, from short term to long term, from monogamous to polyamorous. Similarly, becoming a parent is no longer tied to being married. Some 40 percent of births in the US today occur outside marriage. In short, in the past few decades, American intimate culture has changed dramatically. A marriage-centered culture is giving way to or paralleled by a relationship-centered culture in which the idea of sexual lifestyles makes sense.

Sexual lifestyle means individuals can choose what it means to have sex—with whom, how, when, and how they wish to relate sex to social arrangements. Straight, gay, bi, trans, hooking up, fuck buddies, single parent households, singledom, polyamory, cohabitation and even celibacy—this is the world of sexual lifestyles. In this cultural environment, apart from the norm or rule that sex be between two or more consenting adults and be free of coercion, many of us believe that individuals have a right to choose their sexual lifestyle.

chapter 37

Contesting the culture of monogamy

Consensual nonmonogamies and polyamory

Christian Klesse

Consider the following scenario in which Chris, Natalie and Kitty talk about their lives and their non-orthodox views on monogamy and nonmonogamy in a documentary titled *Polyamory*, produced by Simon Anderson as his Journalism Major Project at the University of Technology in Sydney (Anderson 2012).

> *Chris, Kitty and Natalie, all in their 20s, all based in West Sydney, form a polyamorous relationship. They are in two interconnected couple relationships – a 'hinge relationship' (also often referred to as a V relationship) – in which Chris maintains a loving erotic relationship with both Natalie and Kitty, but Kitty and Natalie are not lovers with each other. However, according to the understanding of all partners, everyone is allowed to enter equally committed relationships elsewhere. Kitty and Chris are both involved with a woman called Selena, who does not currently reside in Sydney and with whom they form a three-way triangle.*

> *Chris, Kitty and Natalie have come to polyamory after being in monogamous relationships. Kitty was dissatisfied with the restrictions of dealing with multiple attractions in monogamous relationships. Chris was frustrated with keeping up 'artificial barriers' regarding the degree of intimacy with people outside his monogamous relationships whom he felt close to. His partnerships got strained whenever he did not ensure that*

barriers were maintained. Natalie formed a closer bond with Chris after a period of hooking up, in the full knowledge of his other relationships.

None believes in the romantic myth that only one person can make you happy. They reject the conventional marriage script, but speak of truly loving each other. They are committed to one other and would like to grow old together as a family. Of course, the open nature of their arrangement means that the constellation of this family may change. Kitty dreams of living in a house with a large family with maybe four or five adults (not all of whom may be primary partners) and a number of kids.

Kitty and Natalie hate it if their relationship is represented as a 'patriarchal trap' in which Chris (the only man in the current set up) is privileged by maintaining relationships with two women. They highlight that they, too, have other relationships and that rights and responsibilities are spread evenly within their relationship structure. Believing in the power of honesty and communication, they are all confident that they have found feasible ways of dealing with occasional instances of jealousy.

Chris, Natalie and Kitty are comfortable using the language of polyamory to talk about their intimate lives. Most people who were interviewed on the streets by the documentary maker, however, had never heard the term. Media reports on polyamory (including documentaries) have burgeoned over recent years. While mainstream media coverage tends to foreground problems or finds it hard to avoid stereotypes, titillation or exoticisation, Anderson's documentary is an example of a more recent wave of non-judgemental positive media representations of polyamory (Antalffy 2011). These changes are the result of a growing interest by polyamorous people to create visibility for their distinctive ways of life and to engage in activism to challenge on-going discrimination.

What exactly is polyamory? Polyamory stands for a relationship arrangement, which is open to all partners to enter loving and/or sexual relationships with other people. Because it describes a situation in which everybody agrees that the relationship is (at least potentially) nonmonogamous, polyamory is an example of the wider category of consensual nonmonogamy. Polyamorous communities have blossomed in many countries within Europe, North America and Oceania, and also, albeit to a much smaller extent, in other parts of the world, including some countries in South America, Asia and the African continent. Polyamory does not reflect any particular gendered partner choice. Moreover, people of different sexual preferences (or 'orientations') engage in polyamorous relationships. Despite polyamory's emphasis on long-term commitment, it is often dismissed by critics (just like other consensual nonmonogamies, such as swinging, group sex, cruising, casual sex, etc.) because it rejects the widely shared value of monogamy.

This chapter explains polyamory by first discussing the *culture of monogamy*, and its components couple-ism and familialism. Then I discuss a few forms of consensual nonmonogamies (including polyamory) that form relational alternatives to monogamous couples.

The culture of monogamy

Monogamy – defined here as both emotional and sexual exclusivity with one partner at a time – is deeply engrained in many Western societies. Historically speaking, monogamy is a core element of the 'culture of bourgeois (sexual) respectability' that rigidified in the process of nation-state building in the Europe and western settler societies in the late eighteenth and throughout the nineteenth century (Mosse 1985). Proper sexual conduct became scrutinised with the confluence of bourgeois morality and the culture of patriotism.

Monogamy is also an integral and important element of the culture of romantic love. According to Karl Lenz (1998), the ideal of romantic love emerged in European literature in the eighteenth century and encompassed the following characteristics: (1) the unity of sexual passion and affectionate emotionality; (2) the unity of love and marriage; (3) the integration of parenthood; (4) the values of commitment and faithfulness; (5) the intensification of a sense of individuality and uniqueness of the beloved partner; (6) the promise of unique happiness; (7) a new ideal of cross-gender mutuality and gender equality (which implied a more 'androgynous' tendency) (pp. 267–272). Monogamy is evoked here in the references to faithfulness and the uniqueness of a chosen life partner.

Couple-ism, familialism and the culture of monogamy

At the heart of the culture of monogamy lies the idea of the *couple*. The culture of monogamy structurally privileges couples, sustaining an ideology that creates a hierarchy between different types of intimacies (for example, the idea that partners or spouses should come before friends). Monogamy fosters patterns of strategic resource accumulation within the couple, through joined property, a division of labour, mutual networking and alliances in interpersonal politics. Taken together, this forms the basis of a distinctive form of 'couple power' (Steiner 1976).

The endorsement of couple relations is at the heart of social policies that advocate for marriage and childrearing within the core family. In the UK, both Labour and Conservative governments (plus political coalitions) have promoted stable families, primarily those organised around the heterosexual couple. They thereby follow an ideological doctrine that could be characterised as an articulation of both couple-ism and familialism. The recent introduction of same-sex marriage and equal access to same-sex couples in adoption laws signals changes in UK discourses on familialism and couple-ism, indicating greater flexibility and a less rigid policy fixation on heterosexual relationality. However, polyamorous families were not considered in this socio-legal shift.

Family diversity and serial monogamy

Despite society's strong investment in the nuclear family, reality often looks different. In culturally and ethnically diverse societies there are many alternatives to the romantic or conjugal (nuclear) family model. Family practices have undergone major transformations in most societies. Experiences in the UK are a case in point. There are fewer marriages, and cohabitation has been increasing. The same applies to so-called live-apart-together relationships in which intimate partners do not live in the same household (Roseneil 2006). Singlehood, too, has been on the rise (Budgeon 2008; Reynolds et al. 2007). In 2013, 29% of all 26.4 million households in the UK were single households (ONS 2013). Divorce rates have also risen steadily; it is now expected that 42% of marriages will end in divorce.

Rather than practising lifelong monogamy, most people nowadays engage in what can be dubbed *serial monogamy*. Serial monogamy signifies a pattern in which people may opt for monogamy in committed relationships for as long as the relationship may last. After a break up they may enter a monogamous relationship again, either immediately or after a period of singlehood (during which they may or may not be dating).

Many children are raised in several households or by at least some caretakers different from their biological parents. The profound transformation of family life in Western societies has been captured with terms such as 'blended families' (Baxter et al. 1999), 'family fragments' (Smart and Neale 1999) 'postmodern families' (Stacey 1996), 'post-familial families' (Beck-Gernsheim 1998) and 'families of choice' (Weston 1991). Some have argued that we should abandon the term 'family' altogether, because it is strongly associated with certain kinship constellations and fails to represent the diversity of lived family life (Morgan 1999).

Mono-normativity and compulsory monogamy

The fixation on monogamous couples and family relations by the state, as well as by ethnic, religious and national communities' policies and cultural values, can be described as an oppressive system. Some poly people use the term *mono-normativity* to describe this form of power.

> Mono-normativity is based on the taken for granted allegation that monogamy and couple-shaped arranged relationships are the principle of social relations per se, an essential foundation of human existence and the elementary, almost natural pattern of living together. From this perspective, every relationship which does not correspond to this pattern, is being ascribed the status of the other, of deviation, of pathology, in need of explanation or is being ignored, hidden, avoided and marginalized.
>
> (Bauer 2010: 145)

Mono-normativity has been key to civilisational narratives and notions of (white) European supremacy. For example, Krafft-Ebing's famous book *Psychopathia Sexualis* (1886) established a close link between Christianity, monogamy, and whiteness to argue the superiority of Christian Europe above so called 'polygamic races'. Anti-Islamic sentiment was an important feature of the rejection of multi-partner marriage (also referred to as polygamy):

> [T]he love of man, if considered from the standpoint of advanced civilization, can only be of a monogamic nature ... From the moment when woman was

Christian Klesse

recognised the peer of man, when monogamy became a law and was consolidated by legal, religious and moral considerations, the Christian nations attained a mental and material superiority over the polygamic races, and especially over Islam.

(Kraft-Ebing, quoted in Willey 2006: 531)

Drawing upon Adrienne Rich's (1983) famous article 'Compulsory Heterosexuality and Lesbian Existence', many poly folks have called pressures to be in a monogamous couple relationship 'compulsory monogamy' (Heckert 2010). Compulsory monogamy is reinforced by laws, including anti-adultery laws, legal prohibitions on polygamy, and discrimination against nonmonogamous and poly parents in custody cases (see Emens 2004 for a discussion of US laws).

Mono-normativity and compulsory monogamy contribute to discriminatory attitudes towards non monogamous people. At the individual level, monogamy is taken to indicate a person's 'true commitment' to their partner/spouse, and is a symbol of love and dedication. In regard to personal character, the capacity to be monogamous symbolises that one has dignity, maturity, reliability, self-control, reason, balanced equilibrium, the capacity for true love, etc. Those who fail to behave monogamously or who reject monogamy risk forfeiting all of these character traits, and the respect that accompanies them. People who are identified as nonmonogamous may fall into disregard by their circle of peers, friends or family members and jeopardise their standing in the wider community.

Polls have shown a strong condemnation of nonmonogamy among the US population for decades. In 1973, 70% of survey participants considered adultery to be 'always wrong'. In 2004, 82% described such acts as 'almost always wrong'. A Gallup poll in 2006 showed most respondents considered adultery to be worse than polygamy or human cloning (see Druckerman 2007: 15). Polls in other countries, too, indicate the centrality of monogamy and coupledom to contemporary sex and relationship ethics. The survey *Sexual Behaviour in Britain* demonstrated widespread condemnation of nonmonogamy among British citizens (Wellings et al. 1994). Only one person out of fifty thought that extra-marital sex is 'not at all wrong'. Four out of five respondents held the view that extra-marital sex is always or mostly wrong (78.7% men and 84.3% women). Two-thirds of men and more than three-quarters of women rejected sexual activities outside of a domestic partnership. Monogamy, marriage and long-term couple status thus provide core criteria for the perception of the legitimacy of sexual acts.

Anti-promiscuity discourses and the double standard

Mono-normativity is further sustained by anti-promiscuity discourses (Klesse 2007). 'Promiscuity' is a negative and degrading label used against people who are thought to have 'too much sex'. Promiscuity allegations go hand in hand with moral value judgments, framing such persons as indiscriminate, hedonistic, irresponsible, selfish and/or incapable of building caring and loving relationships. Anti-promiscuity discourses have been key to many oppressive thought systems such as sexism, racism, anti-Semitism, hatred and disgust towards the poor and the working classes, homophobia and biphobia. The accusation of promiscuity has often served as a justification for discrimination against oppressed social groups.

Along those lines, due to a 'double standard' of sexual morality, women are more likely to be subjected to anti-promiscuity discourses than men. Slurs such as 'slut', 'slag' or 'whore' are powerful weapons for those who wish to attack a woman's reputation through 'slut shaming'. Promiscuity allegations function as a means of regulating women's sexual agency, stigmatise women and legitimise male sexual violence and abuse (Tanenbaum 1999). Furthermore, since women's virtue plays a significant role in representations of the 'nation', 'race' or 'community', women's sexual behaviours tend to be strongly scrutinised by self-declared guardians of ethnic, nationalist or religious interpretations of the 'common good' (Anthias and Yuval-Davis 1989).

Historically, anti-promiscuity discourses have been particularly effective when aimed at specific groups of women. Working-class women, and racialised or ethnicised women (such as Black or Jewish women) have been represented as hyper sensual and over-sexualised (Bhattacharyya 1998). Racist and classist sexual stereotypes have been mobilised to undermine the moral reputation of certain groups of men as well. For example, stereotypical representations of both Black men and working-class men insinuate over-sexualisation, lewdness and sexual assertiveness.

Against this backdrop, it is not surprising that many feminists have been highly critical of monogamy. This includes representatives of 'second wave' of western feminism, such as Shulamith Firestone, Germaine Greer, Betty Dodson, Juliet Mitchell and Lee Comer. Marriage, monogamy and also cohabitation (with men) were seen by many (heterosexual and bisexual) feminists as risky because of the possibility for manipulation, control and restriction by male partners. Feminist critiques of monogamy are slightly less prominent nowadays, but survive in queer and sex-positive currents of feminism, such as in the work of Gayle Rubin, Carol Queen, Dossie Easton or Ummni Khan. Since the 1990s, queer politics have provided fertile ground for critiques of monogamy as a form of cultural assimilation into a heterosexual, heteronormative, culture of romanticism (Warner 1999). Monogamy has also been critiqued as an expansion of bourgeois property relations in counter-cultural and/or revolutionary movements (Red Collective 1978). Some feminists, such as Stevi Jackson and Sue Scott, draw on these traditions in their contemporary critique of monogamy.

The cheating system

While cultures of love have undergone significant changes, the value of monogamy remains an integral part of many contemporary notions of love. Infidelity is still a frequent cause of relationship break-ups and legal divorce proceedings, even if the overall percentage of adultery as the cited cause for divorce has been declining (Shorter 2005). The experience of being cheated upon in a presumed monogamous relationship can deeply unsettle trust in the relationship.

The fact that the heteronormative cultures of sexual respectability endorse monogamy does not mean that all people who claim to value monogamy actually *behave* monogamously. Research indicates that 'cheating' is endemic in many societies. In the US, 60% of men and 50% of women reported having extra-marital affairs

(Jeffries 2012). Surveys often indicate higher rates of adultery for men than women. Depending on cultural context, this adultery gap may be small or quite significant (see Druckerman 2007: 61–63). Nonetheless, women also cheat, as indicated for example by adultery-oriented online dating services such as *Ashley Madison* in the USA or *Marital Affair* and *undercoverlovers.com* in the UK (see Rambukkana 2015; O'Meara 2012).

In Eric Anderson's (2012) research into monogamy/nonmonogamy involving 120 gay and heterosexual male college students in the UK and the US, 79% of the research participants disclosed that they were cheating on their partners. Anderson suggests that for many, cheating is a routinised way of dealing with cognitive dissonance, i.e. a clash between desire and temptation (which is felt to be overwhelming), and internalised moral objections towards nonmonogamy and unfaithfulness. Due to the prevalence of cheating, in 2004 Poly blogger and activist Pepper Mint (see https://freaksexual.wordpress.com/) speaks of a 'monogamy/cheating system' – meaning that cheating is so widespread that it has to be seen as an integral, 'systemic' part of the culture of monogamy. This raises serious questions about why monogamy is so highly valued. Many advocates of polyamory describe it as an 'ethical form of nonmonogamy' because of its open relationship approach rather than a nonmonogamy based on cheating, dishonesty or misguidance.

Consensual nonmonogamies

In contrast to cheating, consensual nonmonogamy is based on sharing knowledge of the nonmonogamous nature of the relationship. The type and scope of nonmonogamy permitted depends on negotiation among partners. Different kinds of arrangements may range from 'anything goes' (no sharing of details and no consultation necessary) to highly detailed contracts and regulations. Consensual nonmonogamous arrangements differ widely and include: single people's engagement with multiple sexual partners (short term and/or long term); open couple relationships (in which one or both partners are open to flings, affairs, one-night stands, sex with friends or fuck buddies – or maybe even long-term lovers of a slightly lower degree of intensity); open or closed multiple partner relations such as triads, quads etc.; and other multi-adult relationships or families with or without children, etc.

Consensual nonmonogamies are usually based on an attempt to find an agreement, settle conflicts and engage with problems to resolve difficult emotions. There are many styles of consensual nonmonogamies, including polyamory, multi-partner marriage (polygamy), swinging, BDSM group play, etc. (see Barker and Langdridge 2010). People of all walks of life feel drawn towards nonmonogamy, yet certain cultures and movements have been more supportive in creating social and discursive spaces for experimenting with relational alternatives to monogamous couplehood.

Nonmonogamy in lesbigay and queer communities

Research indicates that non-heteronormative sexual cultures have often had a more relaxed approach to questions of nonmonogamy. This is because many non-heterosexual people design their relational life conscientiously contesting the heteronormative status quo.

For example, US and UK research on gay men has demonstrated the high prevalence of nonmonogamous arrangements. The creation of nonmonogamous relationship styles has frequently been described as one of the most *distinctive* features of gay male partnerships. For many gay men, love, commitment and intimacy is not dependent on sexual monogamy; therefore they may create spaces for optional sex outside of the core couple (Weeks et al. 2001). A popular US study from the mid-1980s stated: 'The expectation for outside sexual activity was the rule for male couples and the exception for heterosexuals' (McWhirter and Mattison 1984: 3). Later research confirmed this trend. Research into bisexuality, too, has shown that a large number of members of bisexual communities are involved in nonmonogamous relationships (Rodriguez Rust 2000). Nonmonogamous practices are also common in lesbian, bi and queer women's communities, in particular within BDSM-oriented, sex-positive and queer- and trans-feminist currents (Munson and Stelboum 1999; Deri 2015). However, nonmonogamous practices within women's cultures tend to be less visible – and certainly less institutionalised – compared to gay men's culture.

It is important to qualify that it would be wrong to conflate lesbian, gay, bisexual and queer identities with nonmonogamous communities. Misguided stereotypes such as the belief that 'gay men have a natural proclivity towards promiscuity' or 'bisexuals are by necessity nonmonogamous' have been central to homophobic and biphobic discourses. Not all gay men, lesbians or bisexual people are nonmonogamous. However, I think it is important to recognise the more conscious and relaxed attitudes within lesbigay and queer cultures towards nonmonogamy. This is because they have created (sub-)cultural spaces which have been more open to experimentation. These communities have also been more inclined to form critical and politicised sexuality discourses and practices – including monogamy/nonmonogamy. These spaces and discourses have sustained experiences that could serve as an inspiration for novel and reflexive dealings with monogamy/nonmonogamy within mainstream heterosexual cultures, too.

Polyamory and poly culture

Debates about polyamory are shaping new language to discuss alternatives to monogamy. Variants of the term 'polyamory' have been in usage since the 1950s, gaining momentum in US counter-cultural settings in the early 1990s and became more globally popular through discussions on the Internet. Polyamory designates a distinctive style or philosophy regarding nonmonogamous practice. Broader definitions of the concept interpret polyamory as an umbrella term and synonym for consensual non-monogamy. For example, Lano and Parry (1995) suggest that polyamory stands for all 'ethical forms of nonmonogamy' – ethical here means consensual. According to *The Oxford English Dictionary*, polyamory consists of 'the custom or practice of engaging in multiple sexual relationships with the knowledge and consent of all partners concerned' (Polyamory 2007). More narrow definitions suggest that these (consensual) 'multiple sexual relationships' are – ideally – based on mutual love and long-term commitment. These qualities are further supported by a set of polyamorous core values, such as commitment, integrity and communication (Emens 2004).

Polyamorous relationships come in different forms and shapes. A distinction between primary, secondary or tertiary relationships helps many polyamorous people manage boundaries of complex relational networks and signals distinctions in terms of precedence, intensity, or commitment. Polyamory can thus be described as a kind of 'patterned multiplicity'. It is also common in polyamory cultures to refer to geometrical shapes or letters as a shorthand for the description of certain relationship constellations. For example, the terms 'triangle' or 'quad' are used for multi-partner relationships in which all people are closely involved with one another. The letters V, Y, Z, W or X signify for multi-partner relationships, in which only certain people in the group have an erotic or sexual connection to one another. Polyamorous relationships can also be seen as a prime example of the 'chosen families' phenomenon (Weston 1991). Many people in poly relationships raise children, and parenting arrangements frequently exceed traditional biological kinship models. Children thus may have multiple parents, including those with whom they do not have a biological link (Pallotta-Chiarolli 2010; Sheff 2014).

People who are monogamous often find it difficult to imagine how it is possible for others to consent to nonmonogamy. A major issue of concern for those who struggle to understand polyamory is how poly people manage to come to terms with jealousy. Although some people claim not to be jealous at all, there is in fact a great deal of discussion about jealousy among polyamorous people. A lot of advice literature for those in poly relationships (or who wish to explore polyamory) addresses the subject of jealousy. Yet in contrast to mono-normative contexts, jealousy is considered to be a set of emotions and responses that can be worked upon with the aim of controlling and modifying them, maybe even making them an unnecessary or superfluous reaction. In poly culture, jealousy does not assume the quasi-naturalised status that it holds in mono-normative contexts where it is often evoked to legitimise fits of rage and even acts of violence. Rather, it is considered to be a problem that can be dealt with, an obstacle, an unfortunate legacy of mono-normative emotionality, which can be resolved within a relationship through creativity and imagination (Deri 2015).

Poly culture fosters an atmosphere of openness that permits sharing jealousy-related anxieties, worries and fears without necessarily putting partners in the wrong for having some fun or if they have been seeing other partners. At least, this is the ideal. Jealousy can be taken as the starting point for self-exploration and changes in one's own emotional responses. Many people in nonmonogamous and poly relationships also set up rules (when, where, with whom) to create safe spaces and establish more secure ground (Wosick-Correa 2010).

Conclusion

Reflections and stories on the experiences that people make in their attempts to build polyamorous relationships, families and communities now circulate more frequently in the public sphere. On one hand, polyamory is gaining popularity within mainstream media. Media representations have become more diverse, but too often still remain steeped in misrepresentations and exoticism. Yet polyamorous people have also developed stronger voices of their own. Their media (blogs, internet pages, publications, etc.) and political actions provide less distorted insights into an exciting terrain of social experimentation to explore alternatives to heteronormative and mononormative patterns of intimacy. (See, for example, Pepper Mint's blog 'freaksexual': https://freaksexual.wordpress.com/.)

Yet positive images do not automatically translate into access to material rights. Changing laws and policies depend on long-standing and concerted efforts of activism and advocacy. The culture of monogamy still goes strong, even if it may display cracks and presents itself – in certain contexts – in less rigid and monolithic ways.

We need to be aware that complicated structures of privilege mediate the perception of different styles of non-monogamy (Rambukkana 2015). While polyamory has recently moved into the limelight, other forms of non monogamy keep carrying the grave stigma of promiscuity. For non-heterosexual, kinky, queer non monogamies it is more difficult to pass as 'sexy' and acceptable in the mainstream. Bearing the brunt of perversion, they are more frequently demonised. Polygamy, too, continues to provide targets for the projection of social anxieties. We can see this with regard to the scandalisation of Mormon polygamy in North America and Muslim polygamy across the global North. Sexual cultures are in flux and the culture of monogamy shows fissures, but we are far from a situation of benign acceptance of relational and sexual diversity. This is why the critique of mono-normativity is an important issue within gender and sexuality studies.

Bibliography

Anderson, Eric. 2012. *Polyamory – Journalism Major Project*, University of Technology, Sydney, Semester 2, documentary film, available at: www.youtube.com/watch?v=zMvyXTsEtU4 (accessed 9 December 2014).

Antalffy, Nikko. 2011. 'Polyamory and the Media', *SCAN – Journal of Media, Arts and Culture*, Vol 8, October 2011, available at: http://scan.net.au/scan/journal/display.php?journal_id=157 (accessed 30 January 2015).

Anthias, Floya and Yuval-Davis, Nira eds. 1989. *Woman-Nation-State*. London: Macmillan.

Barker, Meg and Langdridge, Darren eds. 2010. *Understanding Non-Monogamies*. London: Routledge.

Bauer, Robin. 2010. 'Non-Monogamy in Queer BDSM Communities: Putting the Sex Back into Alternative Relationship Practices and Discourse.' Pp. 142–153 in M. Barker and D. Langdridge (eds.) *Understanding Non-Monogamies*. London: Routledge.

Baxter, Lesley A., Braithwaite, Dawn O. and Nicholson, John H. 1999. 'Turning Points in the Development of Blended Families.' *Journal of Social and Personal Relationships* 16: 291–313.

Beck-Gernsheim, Elisabeth. 1998. 'On the Way to a Post-Familial Family – From a Community of Need to Elective Affinities.' *Theory, Culture, and Society* (special issue on Love and Eroticism) 15 (3/4): 53–70.

Bhattacharyya, Gargi. 1998. *Tales of Dark-Skinned Women: Race, Gender and Global Culture*. London: UCL Press.

Budgeon, Shelley. 2008. 'Couple Culture and the Production of Singleness.' *Sexualities* 11(3): 301–325.

Deri, Jillian. 2015. *Love's Refraction: Jealousy and Compersion in Queer Women's Polyamorous Relationships*, Toronto: University of Toronto Press.

Druckerman, Pamela. 2007. *Lust in Translation: Infidelity from Tokyo to Tennessee*. London: Penguin Books.

Emens, Elizabeth F. 2004. 'Monogamy's Law: Compulsory Monogamy and Polyamorous Existence.' *New York University Review of Law & Social Change* 29: 277–376.

Heckert, Jamie. 2010. 'Love without Borders? Intimacy, Identity and the State of Compulsory Monogamy.' Pp 255–266 in M. Barker and D. Langdridge (eds.) *Understanding Non-Monogamies*. London: Routledge.

Jeffries, Stuart. 2012. 'The Sex Issue: Is monogamy dead?' *The Guardian*, Saturday 10 November. Available at: www.theguardian.com/lifeandstyle/2012/nov/10/sex-is-monogamy-dead (accessed 7 January 2015).

Kinsey, Alfred C., Pomeroy, Wardell B. and Martin, Clyde E. 1948. *Sexual Behavior in the Human Male*. Philadelphia: W.B. Saunders Company.

Kinsey, Alfred C., Pomeroy, Wardell B., Martin, Clyde E. and Gebhard, Paul, H. 1953. *Sexual Behavior in the Human Female*. Philadelphia: W.B. Saunders Company.

Klesse, Christian. 2007. *The Spectre of Promiscuity. Gay Male and Bisexual Non-Monogamies and Polyamories*. Aldershot: Ashgate.

Krafft-Ebing, Richard von. 1924/1886. *Psychopathia Sexualis: With Especial Reference to the Antipathic Sexual Instinct: A Medic-Forensical Study* (trans. F.J. Rebman). New York: Physicians and Surgeons Book Company.

Lano, Kevin and Parry, Claire. 1995. 'Preface.' Pp. v–vi in K. Lano and C. Parry (eds.) *Breaking the Barriers to Desire. New Approaches to Multiple Relationships*. Nottingham: Five Leaves Publications.

Lenz, Karl. 1998. *Soziologie der Zweierbeziehung. Eine Einführung*. Wiesbaden, Deutschland: Westdeutscher Verlag.

McWhirter, David P. and Mattison, Andrew M. 1984. *The Male Couple – How Relationships Develop*. Upper Saddle River, NJ: Prentice Hall.

Mint, Pepper. 2004. 'The Power Dynamics of Cheating: Effects on Polyamory and Bisexuality.' Pp. 55–76 in S. Anderlini-D'Onofrio (ed.) *Plural Loves: Designs for Bi and Poly Living*. London: Harrington Park Press.

Morgan, David. 1999. 'Risk and Family Practices: Accounting for Change and Fluidity in Family Life.' Pp. 13–30 in E. B. Silva and C. Smart (eds.) *The New Family?* London: Sage.

Mosse, George L. 1985. *Nationalism and Sexuality*. New York: Howards Fertig.

Munson, Marcia and Stelboum, Judith P. eds. 1999. *The Lesbian Polyamory Reader. Open Relationships, Non-Monogamy and Casual Sex*. London: Harrington Park Press.

O'Meara, Sarah. 2012. 'Why Women Are More Likely To Cheat On Their Husbands (Particularly When It's Raining).' *The Huffington Post*, 18 May. Available at: www.huffingtonpost.co.uk/2012/05/18/health-women-cheat-more-than-men_n_1526652.html (accessed 7 January 2015).

Office for National Statistics. 2013. 'Statistical bulletin: Families and Households, 2013.' Available at: www.ons.gov.uk/ons/rel/family-demography/families-and-households/2013/stb-families.html) (accessed 9 December 2014).

Pallotta-Chiarolli, Maria. 2010. *Border Sexualities, Border Families in Schools*. Lanham, MD: Rowman & Littlefield Publishers.

Polyamory. 2007. *The Oxford English Dictionary Online*. Available at: http://dictionary.oed.com/ (accessed 8 June 2007).

Rambukkana, Nathan. 2015. *Fraught Intimacies: Non/Monogamy in the Public Sphere*. Toronto: University of British Columbia Press.

Red Collective. 1978. *The Politics of Sexuality in Capitalism*. London: Red Collective and Publications Distributions Cooperative.

Reynolds, Jill, Whetherell, Margaret and Taylor, Stephanie. 2007. 'Choice and Chance: Negotiating Agency in Narratives of Singleness.' *The Sociological Review* 55(2): 331–351.

Rich, Adrienne. 1983. 'Compulsory Heterosexuality and Lesbian Existence.' Pp. 212–241 in A. Snitow, C. Stansell and S. Thompson (eds.) *Desire. The Politics of Sexuality*. London: Virago.

Rodriguez Rust, Paula C. ed. 2000. *Bisexuality in the United States*. New York: Columbia University Press.

Roseneil, Sasha. 2006. 'On Not Living with a Partner: Unpicking Coupledom and Cohabitation.' *Sociological Research Online* 11(3). Available at: www.socresonline.org.uk/11/3/roseneil.html (accessed 30 January 2015).

Sheff, Elisabeth. 2014. *The Polyamorists Next Door. Inside Multiple-Partner Relationships and Families*. New York: Rowman & Littlefield.

Shorter, Edward. 2005. *Written in the Flesh. A History of Desire*. Toronto: University of Toronto Press.

Smart, Carol and Neale, Bren. 1999. *Family Fragments?* Cambridge: Polity.

Stacey, Judith. 1996. *In the Name of the Family. Rethinking Family Values in the Postmodern Age*. Boston, MA: Beacon Press.

Steiner, Claude. 1976. 'Coupleism.' Pp. 127–135 in Hogie Wyckoff (ed.) *Love, Therapy, and Politics*. New York: Grove Press, Inc.

Tanenbaum, Leora. 1999. *Slut! Growing Up Female with a Bad Reputation*. New York: Seven Stories Press.

Warner, Michael. 1999. *The Trouble with Normal: Sex, Politics and the Ethics of Queer Life*. Cambridge, MA: Harvard University Press.

Weeks, Jeffrey, Heaphy, Brian and Donovan, Catherine. 2001. *Same-Sex Intimacies. Families of Choice and Other Life Experiments*. London: Routledge.

Wellings, Kaye, Field, Julia, Johnson, Anne M. and Wadsworth, Jane. 1994. *Sexual Behaviour in Britain: The National Survey of Sexual Attitudes and Lifestyles*. Harmondsworth: Penguin.

Weston, Kath. 1991. *Families We Choose: Lesbians, Gays, Kinship*. New York: Columbia University Press.

Willey, Angela. 2006. '"Christian Nations", "Polygamic Races" and Women's Rights: Towards a Genealogy of Non/Monogamy and Whiteness.' *Sexualities* 9(5): 530–546.

Wosick-Correa, Kassia. 2010. 'Agreements, Rules and Agentic Fidelity in Polyamorous Relationships.' *Psychology & Sexuality* 1(1): 44–61.

chapter 38

The time of the sadomasochist

Hunting with(in) the "tribus"

Darren Langdridge

Sadism and masochism were unknown medical terms until the late nineteenth century, when the psychiatrist Richard von Krafft-Ebing introduced these labels to refer to the very particular, and indeed sometimes quite peculiar, behaviors of some of his patients. Later still, Freud (1905) brought the terms together to produce the label of sadomasochism, which remains in widespread use today to describe sexual activity involving bondage and/or the infliction or receipt of pain or humiliation: a sadist preferring to bind the other, inflict pain and/or humiliation, whilst a masochist preferring to be bound, receive pain and/or humiliation. These acts of description had a much more profound impact than simply drawing public attention to behaviors that have been known for many hundreds of years, however. For with recognition by the medical profession, the people engaged in these practices were at once demonized and subject to the control of the state through the twin arms of the medical and legal professions. Of course, some of the behaviors described by Krafft-Ebing and Freud were nonconsensual acts of violence, perpetrated on unwilling victims. But others were not, instead being fully consensual acts sought out for the pleasure they afforded. This crucial distinction remains at the heart of the dispute over the legitimacy of sadomasochism as a sexual practice/identity that may be pursued by consenting adults.

In this chapter I outline the ways in which sadomasochists have forged new sexual sub-cultures in the US and UK; that is, distinct communities of people engaged in similar practices. With this in mind, I highlight the way in which safe, sane, and consensual practice forms the basis for membership of most sadomasochistic sub-cultures. First, however, it will be necessary to provide some context to the discussion of S/M as a sub-culture through consideration of the way in which S/M has been the subject of medical and legal attention.

The medical gaze and the resistant sadomasochistic subject

Since 1886 the medical profession has continued to describe, theorize about and "treat" people who engage in sadomasochistic sex. Most often this has involved the medical profession working with people engaging in non-consensual acts of sexual violence. However, work with this population has then often been applied to all people who engage in S/M. This is rather unfortunate since this particular process serves to conflate consensual and non-consensual practices (and people), with research priority invariably given over to that which is non-consensual. Only rarely has the medical profession sought to explore the meaning of such practices amongst people happily and consensually engaging in them for the pleasure they afford, fully cognisant of what they are doing. Sadism and masochism are still classified as psychiatric disorders within the Diagnostic and Statistical Manual of the American Psychiatric Association (DSM V – 2013) and the International Classification of Diseases of the World Health Organization, the two most widely used psychiatric diagnostic manuals. Like homosexuality some thirty years ago, consensual sadism and masochism are considered alongside rape and child sexual abuse as individual psychopathologies. The inclusion of these diagnostic categories and the continuing difficulties encountered with the medical profession are in large part due to the influence of early psychoanalytic understandings of sadomasochism, which considered it a developmental disorder along with homosexuality and indeed pretty much anything other than heterosexual sexual intercourse. There are, however, ongoing campaigns in both the US and the UK to have these diagnostic categories removed from future editions of DSM and ICD.

As mentioned above, the medical categorization of sadomasochism operates to do much more than simply describe a group of sexual behaviors. The power of medicine to pathologize has long been recognized, and this is particularly apparent with sadomasochism, where the voice of the participant has been drowned out by the voice of the medical professional. But whilst participants' voices have historically been silenced, this appears to be changing, as sadomasochism becomes a sexual story (cf. Plummer 1995), gaining wider recognition and acceptance. More recently, there has been a growth in sociological and psychological research that has sought to give voice to practitioners themselves with the aim of understanding the meaning of these practices/identities. Unlike much medical research, this work does not attempt to impose a pre-determined, culturally and morally conditioned, theoretical framework on people, but rather seeks to give priority to the voices of practitioners themselves so that their own meanings are prioritized.

Darren Langdridge

Operation Spanner and the legal battle for the sadomasochistic body

Opposition to S/M has not only been medical but also legal, and "Operation Spanner" serves as a key example of the way in which the state has sought to mark off what is and what is not acceptable, with regard to consensual sexual practice, in the UK at least. In December 1990, sixteen gay men were convicted for engaging in consensual sadomasochistic sex – in an operation codenamed "Spanner" by the police investigating the case. The men were either fined, or imprisoned for up to four and a half years, depending on the perceived severity of the acts in which they were involved. Even though none of the men required medical treatment, the injuries were deemed serious enough to warrant prosecution. They appealed to the House of Lords (Regina v. Brown and others, 1994) and the European Court of Human Rights (Laskey v. United Kingdom, 1997, 24 EHHR 39), both of which turned down their appeals. In the UK High Court the defence of consent was denied since, according to Mr. James Rant QC, the presiding judge, it was the role of the law to draw the line "between what is acceptable in a civilised society and what is not." Furthermore, it was decided that sadomasochism, unlike decorative piercing, tattooing, or contact sports (such as boxing), should not be exempt from the law of assault. Whilst these men have now been released from prison, the campaign to clear their names and prevent the imprisonment of others engaged in consensual sadomasochistic sex continues (see online at www.spannertrust.org (accessed March 17 2006)).

The Spanner case raises a number of important issues and, in particular, the importance of the intersection of gender, sexual identity, and sexual practice. All the defendants were gay men, and there is evidence to suggest that this may have been an important factor in their prosecution. In another similar case, where a husband branded his initials on his wife's buttocks (Regina v. Wilson, 1996), the court accepted the defence of consent in spite of the act being serious enough to fall under the legal category of assault occasioning actual bodily harm, as it did in the Spanner case. In this case, the courts stated that consensual activity between a husband and wife in the matrimonial home was not a proper subject for criminal prosecution. One wonders what the view of the court would have been if the wife had branded the husband, or if two lesbians had branded each other with their initials. The implications of even more complex intersections, with for instance race and ethnicity, nationality or disability alongside gender, sexual identity and sexual practice, are also worth considering. For there is not one set of sadomasochistic behaviors but many different sadomasochistic behaviors; not one sadomasochistic practitioner but many different sadomasochistic practitioners; not one sadomasochistic community but many different sadomasochistic communities. S/M citizens may be white, male, middle-class and able-bodied, or black, female, lesbian and disabled, and every variation in between. Privilege may be accrued with one aspect of a person's identity or practice whilst simultaneously denied by another. With so much diversity, state authorities will find it increasingly difficult to regulate such practices/identities but, as the Spanner case demonstrates, they may well try, even if it involves the gross oversimplification of such diversity in the pursuit of prosecution, for the spurious desire to draw the line between what is and what is not acceptable in a civilized society.

Sadomasochistic sub-cultures

A number of factors have led to the growth of new sadomasochistic sexual sub-cultures, including, of course, the simple desire to meet others with similar sexual interests/identities. However, a number of other factors have coincided in recent years to bring about the rise of these new communities in the West, including: the growth of urbanization and industrialization enabling autonomous personal lives to develop; oppressive state interference in people's personal lives and the resistance that this engenders; changes in communication and the mass media; the emergence of individual stories of personal suffering, pain, and then triumph; the (very recent) rise of positive psychotherapeutic and medical professionals encouraging the story; and the development of an interactive social world ready to hear the story (cf. Plummer 1995). These factors have been similarly identified as key elements in the emergence of the lesbian and gay movement and the attempts of lesbians and gays to gain equality and social justice. Indeed, the rise of S/M has in many, though not all, ways followed a similar path to the rise of the lesbian and gay movement in the 1970s and 1980s. Furthermore, Giddens (1991) argues that in these late-modern times we are witnessing a transformation of intimacy. One consequence of this is the emergence of "plastic sexuality" – sexuality with a focus on pleasure rather than on either reproduction or romantic love. The recent prominence of S/M may be viewed as part of a culture of sexual pleasure.

Sadomasochism, as a new sexual story, certainly appears to be in the ascendancy. S/M has appeared in: film ("9 and ½ Weeks," "Blue Velvet," "Crash," "Quills," "Tie me up, Tie me down," "Sasayaki (Moonlight Whispers)," "Wild At Heart"); television (advertisements, including Calvin Klein and Häagen-Dazs, and programs such as "Buffy The Vampire Slayer," "Twin Peaks," and numerous "late-night" documentaries); music (from "The Velvet Underground" and "REM," to "Twisted Sister," and from "Robbie Williams" and "Kylie Minogue," to "Eminem" and "Marilyn Manson"); literature ("Coming to power," "Consensual Sadomasochism," "Leatherfolk," "Public Sex: The Culture of Radical Sex," "Screw the Roses, Send me the Thorns," "SM101," "The Topping Book: Or, Getting Good at Being Bad") and the popular *Fifty Shades of Grey* books and film. The list is almost endless, and continually growing. Much of this represents a watered-down version of S/M, but still it seems that the public appetite is there, as is a media willing to feed this hunger.

But sadomasochistic communities are complex things. As noted previously, there is not one S/M community or sub-culture but a myriad of communities serving a myriad of purposes. Unity and division can be seen within and between such communities, and radical differences in identity work and practice witnessed. Some communities consist of members relating to each other much like family members, caring for each other and ensuring that all involved feel a sense of belonging. Other communities will be much more transient, driven primarily by desire and fueled by a commercialism similar to that within many contemporary lesbian, gay, and bisexual communities.

Indeed, there has been tremendous growth in the commercial S/M scene, with clubs emerging in major cities catering for pretty much every desire. Cutting across these different communities will be structural variations. In particular, communities are more often than not structured by sex and sexual orientation. Distinct scenes exist for gay men and lesbians, as well as straight men and women. Bi and trans people may find a home in one or both of these communities, or instead create an alternative queer space in which such binary divisions matter much less. Other structural factors, such as class or race, may also play a part. Research shows that, on the commercial gay S/M scene at least, there remains a dominant white, middle-class male population, although it is worth noting that this appears to be changing with increasing numbers of working-class, black and Asian men inhabiting previously white, middle-class spaces. Finally, people engaged in S/M may embrace or resist S/M as an identity at different times and in different places. For some, S/M is their primary identity, with man or woman, gay or straight, working-class or middle-class, all secondary or sometimes not important at all. For others, S/M describes all or part of their sexual practice rather than their identity, and membership of S/M communities may or may not be important as a consequence. This complexity makes it difficult to speak of S/M as a distinct sub-culture, and instead I argue S/M communities are better understood as "neo-tribes" (Maffesoli 1996).

The concept of the "neo-tribe" has been growing in popularity in cultural studies as a heuristic for understanding the ways in which nebulous communities might serve the needs of their members in a time still dominated by a culture of individualism. Sadomasochistic subcultures provide very clear examples of neo-tribes. Unlike sub-cultures, S/M communities are fluid and dynamic, coming together through a sense of sexual belonging rather than through structural or political factors. S/M practitioners will enter a community for the sense of belonging it engenders, and then leave it in search of another. Many will also be members of multiple communities, living out multiple (sometimes competing) identities. Maffesoli (1996) seeks to re-work the notion of a tribe, moving away from traditional anthropological understandings, through a consideration of the way the individual has increasingly served to function as *the* key feature of social life, in the West at least, for the last half century. There have of course been communities in recent years in which the individual gave way to the group, but these communities have tended to be fixed, structured by race or class. Very recently, however, we have witnessed the rise of new forms of communities in which people come together for "mutual aid, conviviality, commensurality [and] professional support" (Maffesoli 1996: 69). That is, these communities function to enable people to bind together, fulfilling the deeply felt need to experience a sense of belonging in countries where individualism dominates. Weinzierl and Muggleton (2003: 12) describe the "*tribus*" (collection of neo-tribes) thus:

The "tribe" is also "without the rigidity of the forms of organization with which we are familiar; it refers more to a certain ambience, a state of mind, and it is preferably to be expressed through lifestyles that favour appearance and 'form'" (Maffesoli 1996: 98). Tribes do not therefore exhibit stable practices of inclusion and exclusion – they are integrative and distinctive at the same time. These new network socialities seem to encourage plural, fluid, and part-time rather than fixed, discrete, and encompassing group identities – individuals are able to flow between multiple signs of identity conceptions.

S/M communities provide very good examples of neo-tribes in the making. Here there is little that is static, with much that is played out in terms of appearance and form: two key characteristics of neo-tribes (Maffesoli 1996). Motifs appear and disappear, are changed and manipulated, as new desires emerge and take center-stage. Surface appearance and form is emphasized through bondage, leather, rubber or metal, along with the skin, of course, as the final material to be enjoyed by practitioners. Tattooing, branding, and other forms of body modification also play an integral part in many S/M communities. Membership of most S/M communities is also not fixed, with practitioners moving within and between communities as they seek out acceptance and support along with the gratification of desire. What is crucial, however, is the attitude of the practitioner, and in particular their desire (or not) to subscribe to the norms of the neo-tribe they seek to join.

In the following section I draw on recently published work on S/M (Beckman 2001; Langdridge and Butt 2004, 2005; Taylor and Ussher 2001), along with publicly accessible material written by S/M practitioners on the internet, to highlight the ways in which S/M practitioners produce and refine rule systems for the neo-tribes they have created. In particular, I focus on the active maintenance of a robust notion of consent in S/M communities, and the ways in which community members regulate this through advice, support, and active intervention. At all times the focus will be on giving voice to practitioners themselves, in stark contrast to much previous work on this topic where the theoretical perspective of the researcher has led to the silencing of the researched.

Negotiating safe, sane, and consensual S/M

"Safe, sane, and consensual" is a phrase very familiar to S/M practitioners, for it has emerged as *the* central rule for most, though not all, S/M practice. Indeed, for many within S/M communities any sex which is not safe, sane, and consensual is abusive and to be avoided at all costs. Safe play involves safety at a number of levels. First, there is the physical safety of the people involved in the "scene" (the term for any situation where people are engaging in S/M sex). This often involves careful negotiation before a scene, ongoing discussion throughout a scene, the use of "safewords" (an agreed code word/s which means the scene must stop or slow down), the provision of equipment to aid safe play (like condoms, gloves, strong scissors) and so on. Safe play is also likely to involve careful negotiation around mental safety to avoid those involved in a scene panicking or feeling used or abused. This may include considerable "aftercare," where people spend time soothing any injuries and ensuring that there is no unwanted emotional aftermath. Sane play is in many ways connected with safe play, especially where emotional safety is concerned. This particular feature of S/M has arisen, at least in part, as a response to pathologizing medical understandings of S/M which suggest that the people involved are in some way psychologically damaged and therefore unable to consent in an informed way. Practitioners take care before and during scenes to check out the mental health of partners as best they can. In public spaces, like S/M clubs, many of those present will act as arbiters of what is sane play and will often intervene if it is thought the scene is going too far. This is more difficult to regulate in private settings, but responsible S/M practitioners will take care of each other and seek to ensure their play is sane – real and grounded – at all times. Finally, most S/M practitioners will only play if it is fully consensual. This means playing only with adults and actively negotiating consent at all stages of a scene. Maintaining a robust notion of consent is particularly important within most S/M communities for both the safety of practitioners as well as the perception from much mainstream sexual culture that S/M involves abuse. However, consent is a complicated issue and, as will be shown below, considerable thought and discussion is given to the meaning of consent within the context of sadomasochistic sex.

Langdridge and Butt (2004) investigated websites produced by S/M practitioners with the aim of exploring the stories being told therein. They found two main discursive themes in their analysis: one concerned with rejecting pathological understandings and therefore ensuring the play was sane; and another was concerned with the explicit negotiation of consent. Safety was also a key issue identified for practitioners, in line with safe, sane, and consensual practice. The theme concerned with rejecting pathological explanations was particularly focused on countering the beliefs that S/M is the product of childhood trauma and that people engaged in S/M cannot form satisfactory loving relationships; both ideas psychoanalytic in origin. Unlike early discourses of homosexuality, there were few attempts to identify a cause (or causes) for one's sadomasochistic behavior, but rather a simple rejection of pathological psycho-medical discourses. This discourse served to offer up a notion of pluralistic sexuality, where S/M was not seen in opposition to, but rather as an extension of, "vanilla" sex. This, along with the increasingly public nature of sexual identities, may play an important part in practitioners feeling little need to search for causes for their behaviors.

The second major theme identified by Langdridge and Butt (2004), which was concerned with the explicit negotiation of consent, involved the active explication of oral and written contracts serving to establish the psychological boundaries for safe, sane, and consensual sex. Sadomasochistic sex, unlike most other forms of sexual activity, often employs explicit contracts between practitioners. These contracts offer up a particularly powerful challenge to institutionalized power inequalities through parody, as contracts are constructed to undermine masculine hetero-normative understandings of sex and sexuality by, for instance, mimicking the traditional marriage ceremony. Parody has been a particularly powerful tool for queer activists and it appears that S/M-ers also employ this strategy in an attempt, deliberately or not, to undermine the structural inequalities that form the foundation of institutionalized oppression. The way in which safe, sane, and consensual practice is practically employed can be vividly seen in the following "submissive Bill of Rights" (reproduced only in part here), which is being continually modified, updated, and reproduced across the web and then used within D/s relationships (Dominant/submissive relationships):

> You have the right to be treated with respect. Not only do you have this right, you have the right to demand it. Being submissive does not make you a doormat or less of a person than anyone else. The word "submissive" describes your nature and in no way diminishes you as a human being. You have the right to respect yourself as well.

You have the right to be proud of what you are. Being a submissive is nothing that should ever bring you shame or feelings of reproach. Your submissive nature is a gift and should always be a source of pride and happiness.

You have the right to feel safe. Being a submissive should not make you feel afraid, insecure or threatened. Submission is not about living on the edge or flirting with fear. In any situation you should feel safe or there can never be true surrender. . . .

You have the right to say NO. Being submissive does not take away your right to have dislikes or negative feelings about things. If something is happening or about to happen that you feel strongly opposed to, it's your duty to speak up. Remember, failing to communicate the word NO is the same as saying YES. . . .

You have the right to be healthy. Health involves your physical, mental and emotional wellbeing. Any relationship, D/s or otherwise, that causes you to suffer physically, mentally or emotionally, beyond your limits, is abuse. . . . Being a submissive does not give anyone the right to harm or injure you in any way. The D/s community will stand behind you if you should encounter such a situation but you are the one who has to make them aware before they can help.

There are many similar documents employed within S/M communities. Contracts are drawn up for D/s relationships where the parties explicitly contract all aspects of their relationship. This will include all aspects of safe, sane, and consensual practice, with statements about playing safely and respecting limits, commitment to each other, and agreement around specific sexual practices. As Langdridge and Butt (2004) point out, these contracts may also serve to parody other contractual relationships, most often the marriage contract but also employment contracts and business service contracts. This playful aspect of S/M, along with the loving commitment that practitioners will often have for each other, is often lost on those looking from the outside, who see only violence and pain. Beckman (2001) and Taylor and Ussher (2001), in their qualitative studies with S/M practitioners, similarly stress the centrality of consent. One participant in Taylor and Ussher's (2001: 298) study described the process of negotiation thus:

We'll write to one another at some length and then we'll probably sketch out some kind of sequence of events . . . everything is pretty well planned out not in chapter and verse but so we'll have a rough idea of what's likely to happen and where the respective limits are.

(E)

This kind of explicit negotiation around a scene and consent are common in longer-term S/M relationships, although, of course, not the same for all S/M encounters. Indeed, in many S/M scenes, especially in commercial S/M venues, the partners may never have met before and may engage in very little conversation. However, even in these situations consent continues to be negotiated, though often non-verbally. For instance, a submissive may move into a sling, voluntarily indicating their consent to be fucked or fisted, and often then voice or signal to the dominant to get condoms or gloves. Ongoing interaction between the practitioners will also involve the active negotiation of consent, as a dominant moves to fist and a submissive moves their hips away to indicate their refusal. So, even here, in the most casual of sexual encounters, we can see boundaried play that is at once safe, sane and consensual – the central requirement for membership of most, if not all, S/M neo-tribes.

Conclusions

This chapter has sought to highlight the growth of S/M neo-tribes and the way in which these communities have developed new rule systems to both protect members and challenge negative stereotypes. In spite of the considerable efforts by those engaged in consensual S/M, however, there is ongoing resistance to these particular sexual sub-cultures from the state, principally through the twin arms of the legal and medical professions. In spite of this, or perhaps in part because of this, there has been the proliferation of S/M communities in which members can come together for mutual pleasure and the support that belonging can engender. These emerging neo-tribes highlight the ambiguity, fluidity, and complexity of belonging, and the way in which communities give themselves boundaries through the active creation and maintenance of rules and regulations. To this end, S/M neo-tribes provide a place for people outside the mainstream sexual culture to fulfill their desires in a way that is safe, sane, and consensual – surely the *sine qua non* for good sex, regardless of the form it takes?

References

American Psychiatric Association. 2013. *Diagnostic and Statistical Manual of Mental Disorders* (5th ed.). Washington, DC: American Psychiatric Association.

Beckman, A. 2001. "Deconstructing Myths: The Social Construction of 'Sadomasochism' Versus 'Subjugated Knowledges' of Practitioners of Consensual 'SM'". *Journal of Criminal Justice and Popular Culture*, 8 (2): 66–95.

Freud, S. 1905. *Three Essays on the Theory of Sexuality*. Standard Edition, Vol. 7 (ed. and trans. J. Strachey). London: Hogarth Press.

Giddens, Anthony 1991. *The Transformation of Intimacy*. Cambridge: Polity.

Langdridge, D. and T. Butt 2004. "A Hermeneutic Phenomenological Investigation of the Construction of Sadomasochistic Identities". *Sexualities* 7 (1): 31–53.

—. 2005. "The Erotic Construction of Power Exchange". *Journal of Constructivist Psychology* 18 (1): 65–73.

Maffesoli, M. 1996. *The Time of the Tribes: The Decline of Individualism in Mass Society*. London: Sage.

Plummer, K. 1995. *Telling Sexual Stories: Power, Change and Social Worlds*. London: Routledge.

Taylor, G. W. and J. Ussher 2001. "Making Sense of S&M: A Discourse Analytic Account". *Sexualities*, 4 (3): 293–314.

Weinzierl, R. and D. Muggleton 2003. "What is 'Post-Subcultural Studies' Anyway?" In D. Muggleton and R. Weinzierl (eds), *The Post-Subcultures Reader*. Oxford: Berg.

chapter 39

Dominatrixes and the BDSM scene

Interview with Danielle J. Lindemann

Danielle J. Lindemann is Assistant Professor of Sociology at Lehigh University. Her work focuses on issues at the intersection of gender, sexuality, culture, and work. Specifically, she is interested in how non-normative practices can shed light on social life "at the center." Her 2012 book, *Dominatrix: Gender, Eroticism, and Control in the Dungeon*, explores how relationships between professional dominatrixes and their clients can illuminate broader dynamics of gender, power, labor, and intimacy.

It seems like the BDSM scene uses a fair amount of special terms. Could you tell us about some of the terminology, like what BDSM stands for, as well as terms like dommes, subs, and safe words?

"BDSM" stands for "Bondage, Discipline, Sadism, and Masochism." "Domme" is short for "dominatrix": a woman who plays out the "dominant" (for lack of a more appropriate word) role in sadomasochistic and/or fetishistic scenarios, while the person who is the "submissive" (or "sub") takes the more passive role. The acts that occur during these erotic encounters vary widely and can include things like physical and verbal humiliation, flogging, spanking, and caning. These women also do things like urinate on their subs, "forcibly" put male subs in women's clothing, and put them on leashes and treat them like pets. Dommes and subs refer to their interactions as "scenes" or as "playing," and paid encounters are generally referred to as "sessions." A "dungeon" is the place where a pro-domme does her sessions with clients.

A "safe word" is a word that, when called out by the submissive during the interaction, indicates that he does not wish to continue. Safe words are necessary because words of distress such as "stop" may be misinterpreted by the domme as being part of a particular role-playing scenario rather than as unambiguous pleas for help. The dommes and subs I interviewed often spoke of using the word "red" as a safe word to mean "stop" (whereas "yellow" meant "slow down").

One thing that's interesting about the terms used in BDSM is that they seem to have withstood the test of time. Other aspects of the scene have changed (for instance, the internet now plays a large role in dommes' self-promotion), but the core terminology that participants use within this social word has pretty much remained consistent. For example, Weinberg, Williams, and Moser published a study of erotic sadomasochism in 1984, and much of the lingo their research subjects used was the same my respondents in 2007–2008 used to describe their activities.

It's not uncommon in the media to encounter occasional references to BDSM and there's also the recent popularity of the book 50 Shades of Grey. *To what degree do you think BDSM is a common sexual practice and to what degree is it considered a "fringe" sexual lifestyle?*

First, I want to be clear that my research only looked at people who engage in commercial BDSM encounters, so based on that alone I have no frame of reference for how prevalent these activities are in the general population. However, other studies have shed light on this. In fact, not only is BDSM a prevalent theme in popular culture, but research going back nearly a century suggests that the predilection for sadomasochistic sexuality is somewhat prevalent as well. Sigmund Freud, for instance, saw sadism as existing in "the normal individual" (1938:569), and one of the Kinsey studies found that 55% of females and 50% of males had a "sado-masochistic response" to being bitten (1953:677–678). Studies like these seem to problematize the notion of erotic sadomasochism as a "fringe" practice.

Another interesting point: some work has suggested that a predilection for erotic sadomasochism and participation in these practices are more common among individuals of higher socioeconomic status (Eve and Renslow 1980). I found evidence of this as well in my research, with my respondents' overall level of education being relatively high. Among the pro-dommes I interviewed, all had completed a high school degree, only one's highest level of education was high school, and in fact 39% had received training toward a graduate degree.

Your book Dominatrix *gives the impression that there's a BDSM subculture with a scene of clubs, workshops and a social network of regulars. Could you describe that scene?*

Pro-dommes often talk about the BDSM "scene." Typically, they use this term to describe the public world of BDSM—BDSM-related interactions that do not take place in a private residence or in a commercial dungeon. However, sometimes they do apply the term to all BDSM-related activities, including commercial encounters, whether in public or private.

The public BDSM subculture consists of "play parties" (at which attendees engage in BDSM) and "fetish parties" (where these acts may occur, but where the focus is more on socializing while dressed in fetishistic attire). In New York, where I mostly did my fieldwork, there is also a group called The Eulenspiegel Society (or TES, pronounced "tess") that runs discussion panels and workshops with titles like "Traditional Discipline: Spanking That Special Playmate." Finally, there was "the club," which was how respondents referred to a club called Paddles. As of the time of my fieldwork, Paddles was the only permanent BDSM-themed club (versus traveling party) in the city.

What happens at the club and at these parties that comprise "the scene"? Not only do participants engage in BDSM, but these parties may also involve demonstrations, during which elements of BDSM are displayed and admired. "It's nice to show off," one of my respondents told me. I should emphasize that "sex" (as in intercourse or oral sex) rarely occurs at these public parties, and many have nudity restrictions. Also, as you point out, there is a group of "regulars," who appear often at these events. In the New York City scene, one domme explained, "Everybody knows everybody."

In your book, you discuss different types of dominatrixes, from "lifestyle dommes" to "dungeon dommes" to your focus on "pro-dommes." What are the similarities and differences between these different dominatrixes?

In the book, I use the word "pro-domme" (which is a term used by the participants themselves) to refer to women who are paid by clients (who are almost always male) to participate in these encounters. In contrast, "lifestyle" dommes engage in unpaid BDSM interactions for erotic pleasure in their personal lives. However, I did find that many pro-dommes are *also* lifestyle—that is, they engage in these acts with clients for money but also for their own pleasure in their non-work lives. Fifty-nine of the sixty-six pro-dommes I interviewed also self-identified as lifestyle. Many, but not all, lifestyle pro-dommes are also "in the scene"—that is, they attend public events and parties. A minority are only lifestyle with their partners in private.

A lot of the people I interviewed talked about the rift between people "in the lifestyle" and those who engage in BDSM practices for money. In actuality, I found that these two worlds are enmeshed in many ways. As I've mentioned, many pro-dommes are in fact also players in the lifestyle scene. And the club in New York adjoined a commercial dungeon. The dungeon's pro-dommes spent time at the club as a way to bring in new clients.

Another rift that many of my respondents mentioned was between "dungeon dommes" and "independent dommes" (or "indies"). Dungeon dommes are women who work at the larger dungeons (or "Houses"): spaces owned by managers who hire women to work there, provide their equipment, schedule their appointments (or hire someone to do that), and take a cut of the money the women earn. In contrast, indies rent or own their own spaces and work for themselves. Indies often perceive dungeon dommes negatively as being younger, less experienced, less skilled, less safe in their practices (putting their clients at greater risk), more interested in money, and more likely to perform sexual "extras" (such as oral sex and hand jobs) on their clients. Dungeon dommes and indies also share some similarities, in that they both engage in these practices for money and indies often begin their careers as dungeon dommes in the larger Houses before branching out on their own ("going indie").

There's a distinction in Dominatrix *between sex work and erotic labor. What is the difference? And how would you describe the labor conditions of working as a dominatrix?*

"Erotic labor" is a term coined by Wendy Chapkis (1997), and it is a broader term than "sex work." It encompasses a variety of erotically oriented commercial practices, ranging from exotic dancing to prostitution. "Sex work" is often (though not always) used to describe erotic labor that includes penetration or oral sex, and pro-dommes seldom engage in these practices. Interestingly, the New York pro-dommes I interviewed were adamant about not being labeled "sex workers," whereas those in San Francisco were less likely to draw this distinction (for a variety of reasons I discuss in the book).

Vis-à-vis other types of erotic labor, pro-dommes' labor conditions are pretty favorable. Because these women seldom engage in sexual "extras," the risk of disease transmission is relatively low (compared with, for instance, prostitution). Clients are to some degree screened before sessions, and dungeons are indoors and relatively clean.

However, I do not want to downplay the fact that working as a pro-domme entails some risk. While most women told me that they had never feared for their safety because of their work as pro-dommes, some did, or they had heard stories of others who had been assaulted during sessions. However, I found it telling that when asked about safety, many pro-dommes discussed the physical risks to their *clients*, rather than themselves. This aspect of their narratives seems to make commercial BDSM unique among forms of erotic labor.

I should point out that there are also legal risks to this work. In New York most of what pro-dommes do is legal, but in San Francisco the same acts are not legal. (I go into this in greater detail in the book.) None of the women I interviewed had ever been arrested for engaging in commercial BDSM, but some felt that the threat was still there.

There probably aren't a high percentage of people in the general population who visit professional dominatrixes (pro-dommes). You make the case that the social dynamics between pro-dommes and their clients (who usually play the role of submissives) tells us something about power dynamics of the larger culture. Could you tell us a little about that?

Sociologist Lynn Chancer argues that a variety of relationships in everyday life are "sadomasochistically oriented," "whether between a particular teacher and student, or a worker and boss, or in other highly charged encounters between partners caught in symbiotic enmeshments of power and powerlessness" (2000:1). Along these same lines, I make the point that dynamics such as dominance and submission, and love of giving pain and love of receiving pain, are not features of social life that are unique to the dominatrix's realm. On the contrary, we can look at commercial BDSM as a kind of microcosm for better understanding the ways that these basic principles manifest themselves in daily life.

For example, pro-dommes illuminate the power dynamics involved in relationships between service providers and their clients more broadly. These women use the expression "topping from the bottom" to talk about submissives who are not "really" submissive in the sense that they attempt to overly control the ways in which they are dominated. The concept of topping from the bottom is useful for considering the dynamics of negotiation within other occupational contexts as well. Imagine an interior decorator, for instance, attempting to wrangle a demanding client who repeatedly attempts to "top from the bottom" by interjecting his own opinions and tastes.

Typically, pro-dommes are usually women and their clients are usually men. What do you think the typical gender dynamics of pro-dommes and their clients says about gender relations in the larger culture?

I think that the dynamics between pro-dommes and their clients have much to tell us about gender relations in the larger culture. For one thing, although this is a "deviant" subculture, certain normative expectations related to femininity and masculinity filter into this realm. For instance, some of the standards of beauty for pro-dommes align with beauty standards found in the larger culture. So this realm teaches us about the "stickiness" of these norms, even in a supposedly subversive context. Similarly, although this is a context that ostensibly represents an inversion of the gender-power hierarchy (with the woman in control), in fact I find that males do not necessarily abdicate control in this realm. I view the interaction between dommes and subs as a more nuanced jockeying for control.

Second, as you mention, this is a commercial enterprise in which, largely, women are the service providers and men are the clientele. The fact that males are the consumers of eroticism is reflective of erotic labor more generally (with some exceptions) and ties into the cultural notional of woman-as-commodity. In many ways pro-dommes do upend the gender-power hierarchy, but in other ways they expose normative conventions and ideals.

Those in the scene often refer to BDSM as erotic "play" and enjoy the aspect of costumes and role play. What is it about the erotic do you think that lends itself to "play"?

Much of the time, when scholars write about "play" it is in relation to a very specific stage of early childhood, before children are old enough to engage in more complex games that have rule structures and winners and losers (Mead 1967). Think about a toddler playing dress up, for instance. But, as you mention, there is also a "play" element to adult eroticism—particularly within this kinky subculture—that I do not think has been fully explored by scholars. Elizabeth Wilson makes an interesting point when she muses that perhaps "individuals find an outlet for the playful" in the "sexual games" associated with BDSM: "After all, for adults in our society there is no place where they can really 'play' other than in the intimacy of a relationship that is designated 'sexual'" (1983:38). It is fascinating to me that, while play is for the most part socially unacceptable in everyday adult life, the erotic realm seems to provide access to it.

BDSM seems particularly prone to providing access to play. Maybe this is because the practice of BDSM and the practice of play both inherently involve the production of fantasy and the changing-up of social roles. I think that in the dominatrix's dungeon in particular, participants are able to use play in order to explore alternative parts of their personalities that are suppressed in their daily lives.

For example, one type of session in which pro-dommes and their clients engage is a "cross-dressing" session (or "forced femme") in which the client dresses in articles of women's clothing. One pro-domme told me that she enjoyed "seeing if I can bring the female persona out, which gives [the client] a break from his regular life." Within examples like these, there is a sense that the erotic play involved in these encounters allows clients to experience elements of masculinity that are subordinated to compulsory expressions of masculinity (e.g. male as dominant) in their day-to-day lives. This also ties into pro-dommes' contention that clients tend to be white men in relative positions of power in their non-dungeon lives.

How did conducting research on BDSM impact how people viewed you as a researcher? What are the challenges, as a researcher, of exploring a topic that some see as controversial?

On one level, this is a difficult question to answer, because I don't think one can ever fully know how one is being perceived. However, I do muse on this a bit in the book. Other researchers such as Chancer (earlier) and Elizabeth Bernstein (2007:201) have touched upon the notion that researchers who study sexuality are uniquely "contaminated" by their scholarship in ways that other researchers are not. Readers are more likely to eclipse researcher and researched, and if they feel negatively about your research population then you inherit some of that negativity as well. I experienced some of that.

On the other hand, one benefit of studying something like this is that it forces you to be meta-critical of your own object of study and its importance. People I met outside of academia seemed to find this topic inherently fascinating, but academics tended to need more convincing that this was not a frivolous area of study. I'm not sure that researchers who study other less controversial things have the onus on them to validate their objects of study to the extent that sexuality researchers do. And sexuality studies need to be more validated—sex is a central component of human life! But I do think that in some ways it is a productive burden that we have as sex researchers. For example, thinking about pro-domme/client interactions in the context of scholarship on work and occupations—and, specifically, the micro dynamics of professional/client interactions—ended up being very helpful for a central claim I made in the book about "topping from the bottom" and the negotiation of power within these commercial encounters. In that case, branching out to imagine the ways in which this topic could be relevant to non-sexuality subfields actually enhanced my argument.

So my experience has been that, as a sexuality researcher, you often need to be able to explain, cogently and articulately, why your topic should be interesting to people, for reasons including but also beyond how it informs broader scholarship relating to gender and sexuality. That was one of my primary goals in the writing of my book, and I'd like to think I've accomplished that.

Bibliography

Bernstein, Elizabeth. 1999. "What's Wrong with Prostitution? What's Right with Sex Work? Comparing Markets in Female Sexual Labor." *Hastings Women's Law Journal* 10(1): 91–119.

Bernstein, Elizabeth. 2007. *Temporarily Yours: Intimacy, Authenticity and the Commerce of Sex.* Chicago, IL: University of Chicago Press.

Chancer, Lynn. 2000. *Sadomasochism in Everyday Life: The Dynamics of Power and Powerlessness.* New Brunswick, NJ: Rutgers University Press.

Chapkis, Wendy. 1997. *Live Sex Acts: Women Performing Erotic Labor.* New York: Routledge.

Eve, R.A. & D.G. Renslow. 1980. "An Exploratory Analysis of Private Sexual Behaviors Among College Students: Some Implications for a Theory of Class Differences in Sexual Behavior." *Sexual Behavior and Personality* 8: 97–105.

Freud, Sigmund. 1938. *The Basic Writings of Sigmund Freud.* Translated and edited by A. A. Brill. New York: Modern Library.

Kinsey, Alfred C., Wardell B. Pomeroy, Clyde E. Martin, and Paul H. Gebhard. 1953. *Sexual Behavior in the Human Female.* Bloomington, IN: W. B. Saunders Co.

Mead, George Herbert. 1967. *Mind, Self, and Society.* Chicago, IL: University of Chicago Press. First published 1934.

Weinberg, Martin S., Colin J. Williams, and Charles Moser. 1984. "The Social Constituents of Sadomasochism." *Social Problems* 31(4): 379–389.

Wilson, Elizabeth. 1983. "The Context of 'Between Pleasure and Danger': The Barnard Conference on Sexuality." *Feminist Review* 13: 35–41.

chapter 40

The racial and sexual stereotypes of the "down low" on Craigslist.org

Salvador Vidal-Ortiz and Brandon Andrew Robinson

White cocksucking DL DDF bottom looking for black tops – Straight acting, DL White male 5'11. 170 looking for Brothas needing a good blow n go. Love to swallow that nut. Will do two or more as well. Maybe stretch my booty hole. Call tonight, tomorrow, next week, whenever you need a quick relief. I am always looking to service black cock.

> Atlanta Craigslist > Men Seeking Men, Date: 2008-11-10, 11:05 AM EST

The previous advertisement on Craigslist.org is a good illustration of this chapter's focus: we examine the "down low" (DL) construction in order to explore the intersections of sexualities with race and gender. The thread of this chapter is threefold. We first illustrate how masculine white men seek masculine black men to be these white men's sexually aggressive sex partners. Second, we show how white men extend their racial desire to other non-white men (on the DL), and thus construct a newer version of the "down low" that continues to stigmatize black men, but now adds other men of color. It is important to note that both the expansion of desire to include other men of color, combined with the exclusion of desiring other white men – even if on the DL – is in operation in these ads. Third, because the association of the "down low" is often conflated with blackness, white men who self-categorize as DL do not carry the burden or stigma that is attached to black men and other men of color who are perceived to be on the DL. This third point is central, as DL men of color are often portrayed as having internalized homophobia, for not "coming out" as gay, and as being deceitful toward the women that they are presumably in a relationship with. White men continue to escape these stereotypical portrayals.

Constructions of the "down low"

The "down low" is a slang term used to describe masculine men who often identify as heterosexual and who are having discreet sex with other men. It has been linked to the rise of HIV infections, first through a raceless discussion of bisexuality in the 1990s (Mukherjea & Vidal-Ortiz 2006), eventually becoming linked mainly to black men's sexual behaviors (Denizet-Lewis 2003; King 2004). In popular and social scientific readings of the DL, men on the "down low" are considered to not be honest about their sexual lives, to be closeted and selfish, and also as men who may be spreading HIV within black communities, in particular to black women (Ford et al. 2007).

However, the meanings of the "down low" are actually in constant flux. For some scholars, it is a negotiated choice between being a black man in the United States and wishing to have same-sex intercourse (McCune 2014). For others, it is a way to discipline black bodies that just amplifies fears of sexual HIV infection within their lives (Phillips 2005; Snorton 2014). Yet for others, the "down low" "reflects a particular desire to participate in Black hyper-masculinity, relationships with women, and heterosexual culture" (Ward 2007: 34). As a result, black men are confined to hyper-visible sexual stereotypes such as having uncontrollable bodies (Ward 2008), where a spectacle is made of their sexual lives and practices, ignoring the complexities of black men's sexualities. These constructions of the DL have signs of hegemony (masculinity, heterosexuality) while being a racial minority, suggesting a more complex understanding – really, a mutual constitution – of sexualities, race, and gender.

Based on hundreds of ads posted on Craigslist.org in two U.S. regions, we conduct an analysis of the types of messages conveyed on the site. We pay attention to the racialized appropriation of the "down low" by (presumably) white posters (one never knows, for sure, that the posters' self-identification on the posts matches, outside of the Internet sphere, such ethno-racial – and even gender – categorization). Subsequently, we notice how not only do white men insert themselves in a discourse that undoubtedly carries more stigma for black men, but that white DL men in these ads are simultaneously lumping, in the DL imaginary, all desirable DL men into a "non-white" homogeneous categorization.

Moving from the popular media constructions discussed elsewhere (Denizet-Lewis 2003; King 2004; Boykin 2005), we situate the "down low" within historical racial understandings of black gender expressions and sexualities, and how sexual stereotypes of black individuals are possibly being reconfigured with the construction of the "down low." We discuss the major themes present on Craigslist.org while connecting these themes to theories about black sexual stereotypes and the linking of these stereotypes to other non-white people as well. We ultimately suggest that the "down low" is a complex site of intersecting modes of race, gender, and sexualities that needs to be fully unpacked in order to adequately understand the circulation of DL discourses today.

Researching the DL on Craigslist.org

This research was conducted in 2008 and 2009 by analyzing advertisement postings on the website Craigslist.org in the East coast and Midwest regions of the United States. We selectively chose advertisements by postings that explicitly said DL or "down low" within the advertisement title or within the advertisement itself. Since we were surveying men who categorized themselves as being on the "down low," we wanted to limit the data to advertisements that stated "down low" and not assign this label to other advertisements that may be straight men seeking other straight men but who do not label or identify as being on the DL. We perused for indicators of race, sexual identity, sexual acts, descriptions of the posters themselves, and the people that they were seeking to have a sexual encounter with. Through this process, we narrowed the findings to 357 postings. These posts appeared in two specific sites of Craigslist.org: the general men seeking men section and the casual encounters (men seeking men) section.

Collecting "down low" advertisements on Craigslist.org provides an avenue of examining the DL and its constructions. By analyzing the advertisements and the people that the advertisements claim that they are desiring, one will have a better understanding of the "down low" construct within this website's context. Because we are focused on the DL construct (or the discourse, the common narrative, the collective representation of what the DL is), we take the poster's identity to be what they post, but the "real" identity of the person is less relevant to this work than the messages circulating and the specific mutual constitution of masculinity, sexualities, and race within these messages.

A few notes on the posts and selection are important: First, this research is based on what was originally a content analysis of the advertisements of men who sought to have sex with men on the "down low" from Robinson's undergraduate senior capstone research; while portions of this research have already been published (Robinson & Vidal-Ortiz 2013), we draw a newer analysis here. Second, some ads had pictures, and we omitted them for brevity in this chapter. Third, all misspellings, incorrect grammar, erroneous punctuation, and the like have been left intact so as to see how these postings are actually shown on Craigslist.org. We take the specific data presented as evidence of our claims (for total number of advertisements coded with the specific themes presented below, see Robinson & Vidal-Ortiz 2013), and we see this chapter as giving the reader a glimpse of the main narratives constructed by many of the advertisements analyzed. Our concern is less with the amount of advertisements than it is with the messages and potential impact such posts may have. We only show excerpts of a larger pool of advertisements as an indication of these themes in the broader DL discourse on Craigslist.org.

Sameness/difference: DL white masculine men seeking DL black masculine men

Much of the discourse and research about the "down low" has focused on black men who are presumably having sex with other black men (Denizet-Lewis 2003; King 2004; Ford et al. 2007). In this first section, we seek to complicate this portrayal by turning to white men who claim to be on the DL, but who are using the term to seek sex with black men – and that they do so by not only seeking black men who are masculine, they claim to be masculine as well. By adding white men to this portrait of the "down low," we seek to add a nuanced lens to a predominant racial discourse of the DL that is presumed in popular and academic work to be just about blackness. We also think through the complexities of white DL men seeking sexual encounters with men of color.

We turn our discussion to the advertisement at the beginning of this chapter, where there are a few relevant themes that help illustrate this interwoven dynamic of race, sexualities, and gender. As it was evident in that first ad, white men who are claiming to be on the DL may be appropriating this term in order to have sexual encounters with black men (and as shown in the next section, other men of color). The example above was very common among many of the advertisements posted by white men (see Robinson & Vidal-Ortiz 2013); these men seem to use mainstream DL terms to perhaps try to attract black men while at the same time appropriating the DL discourse to themselves. White men like the one in the opening post claim to be seeking a "brotha" or a "thug" to play with on the DL. The implicit sameness of their masculinity (being a white, straight acting DL man seeking a black DL man) combined with white men seeking to have black cock complicates previous analyses of the "down low." This post is not a straight black man seeking sex with another straight black man, but a white masculine man seeking sex with a black masculine man on the DL.

In *Black Sexual Politics*, Patricia Hill Collins (2004) sets out to examine how racism operates through ideologies about black sexualities. White elites created the image of the "black buck" in order to depict black men as human animals and as intellectually inferior to white men. Black men were reduced to their bodies, where their muscles and penises were seen as defining their subjugated humanity. This image of the black buck depicted black men as sexually unrestrained and as inherently violent. The historical representation of the black buck becomes manifested today through black men being cast as criminals, who are unruly, violent, hyper-sexual, and who do not submit to white men's authority. In the advertisement opening this chapter, black men are also reduced to their penises. The black man is the "brotha" who does not submit, but oppositely, this white man wants to submit to the black man (or at least to his cock). These white men then may be re-constructing the sexual stereotype of the "black buck," where this "thug" is now being erotically desired by some white men. There is also a reduction of black men to their genitalia in the following ad:

> *MASC/STR8 BEEFY BTTM LOOKIN FOR THOSE HUNG DL BLK TOPS* – real masculine, straight acting wht beefy bttm here lookin to host those MASC DL HUNG TOPS TONIGHT. love to suck big blk dick and get my tight hole stretched out by a nice chocolate fuck stick. i'm 29, five' ten'', 210 lbs, brn/hzl, buzzed head/stache, goatee, jawline beard, stocky/beefy build, 46chst, 36wst, 6cut avg cock, hairy, very masculine, very straight acting. lookin for those MASC cats who are HUNG and HWP. i have poppers. hosting only. hit me up for pics.
>
> Washington, DC Craigslist > Men Seeking Men,
> Date: 2008-11-16, 12:53 AM EST

S. Vidal-Ortiz and B. A. Robinson

This post reduces black men to certain stereotypes, where black men with large penises ("hung") will presumably sexually penetrate ("top") the masculine, straight white bottom with the use of the black men's "chocolate fuck stick." It is similar to the opening post in that it establishes a black top preference, where black men are often seen as being "authentically" sexually aggressive, and hence, assuming the penetrator role during sex. The post's message also suggests a type of aesthetics (HWP means height-weight proportionate) that suggest a stereotypical kind of black man who is "naturally" lean and muscular, where the white poster is stocky and beefy. Yet it is masculinity or the "straight acting" claim of this poster that glues his opposite race desire through both men's presumably same gender expression/presentation. Thus, their masculinity and public heterosexual performance separate them from any public perception of them as gay men. And the fact that being fucked is present in the post does not seem to threaten this claim of masculinity. Indeed, Dowsett and colleagues (2008) show that sexual acts like being penetrated can reinforce masculinity in some same-sex encounters, where the macho talk of "taking it like a man" might be seen as an expression of manhood. Masculinity, then, appears to bind these men together across inter-racial lines; however, race is still prevalent within these advertisements as a marker of difference, despite the notion that these men may have much in common since they are straight acting and masculine. The following post also reifies this narrative:

> *Any slim straight or dl black guys want to get sucked now by white guy* – Looking now, u be tight bodied (not necessarily a gym rat), negative, verbal is great, hung thick, just want to sit back and get drained. Age open if the body and dick are right, looking before 10 am, 2 blocks from Key Bridge – sorry, no thick or heavy guys. Must be African-American, though. Eight inches plus preferred. Me: white, very clean, negative, 160lbs., ready to empty that pipe.
>
> Washington, DC Craigslist > Casual Encounters,
> Date: 2008-11-14, 8:15 AM EST

Like in the previous two posts, a white guy is seeking to service a straight black man. The black man is again reduced to his presumably large penis (a "pipe"), where "eight inches plus" is preferred. Physical descriptors are also given to delineate what type of masculinity this white man is seeking. He wants a slim, tight-bodied black man – no one thick or heavy. These bodily descriptors are associated with larger cultural notions of "thug" bodies and of black men being "naturally" muscular. This desire for masculinity may again dissociate their sexual acts from being read as gay because being gay is often conflated with effeminacy.

Some white men's use of the DL on Craigslist.org is based upon racial stereotypes of black men being muscular, sexually aggressive, and having large penises. This specific use of the DL may be a way in which these white men desire and attract black men to presumably penetrate them. Historically, black men's portrayal as the "black buck" (i.e., as violent and hyper-sexual) was used in order to justify enslaving and lynching black men. These stereotypes live on today to also justify the large mass incarceration of black men through painting these men as rapists and criminals. However, on Craigslist.org, these same stereotypes, which are often used to subjugate black men in the larger society, are actually being sexually desired by some white men on the DL. Although there appears to be a shared sameness among all of these DL men because of their masculine presentation, as explored later, this appropriation of the DL by white men may also work to re-inscribe white hegemony, as these white men's use of the DL is not pathologized in the same way that blackness and the DL is still today.

Expanding the repertoire: seeking other non-white DL masculine men

In this section, we illustrate how white men's use of the DL includes desire for other men of color besides black DL men. We set out to uncover how such use works to homogenize racial difference, where all non-white men get lumped into a similar category of desire: being on the DL and being non-white. We show how the DL comes to stand in for certain stereotypes – non-white, masculine, and hyper-sexual – for white men to consume on Craigslist.org.

> *HORNY DL WHITE BOY THUG* – Masculine guy here looking to play late night tonight. The door is unlocked. The room is dimly lit, the manhole is lubed and my mouth and throat are open. Just walk in and ANONYMOUSLY fill me with your CUM. BLACK GUYS ARABS MEXICANS ALL TO THE FRONT OF THE LINE NO WHITE BOYS I LIKE TO FEEL HUMILATED.
> Detroit Craigslist > Casual Encounters, Date: 2009-03-04, 3:07 AM EST

This poster continues the thread of seeking men of color to fuck him, with the poster self-claiming to be a DL white boy thug who is masculine. The use of Arabs (not of a specific nationality or place of origin) and Mexicans (a reductionist stereotypical expression for all groups of the same region/descent), together with black guys, offers up though a clear indication of stereotyping. After 9/11, "Arabs" are commonly associated with violence and terrorism in the U.S. imaginary; Mexicans (and, presumably, other Latinos) are generally linked to illegality (including undocumented immigration) and gangs; and black men are stereotyped as violent and hyper-sexual criminals. To the poster, it is not important who these men of color are or what their background is, as "all" follows these terms. This use of "all" suggests *any* of these men of color, irrespective of where they come from, are lumped into the same stereotypical desires of being the hyper-sexual aggressor during the sexual encounter.

What this post also introduces is the idea that non-white men are inherently capable/willing to humiliate this horny DL white boy thug, and hence, these men of color are thus more desirable. The poster stated a desire for a fantasy where he services men of color, and he specifically says "no white boys." The poster insists on being in a submissive interaction, and for him, humiliation is associated only to non-white men. But we cannot be fooled by thinking about power in simplistic ways, and assume black men, or men of color, will have power over this poster; the subtlety of saying he wishes to be humiliated is a game of power that intertwines race, class, and status. The poster – presumably a white man – is getting exactly what he wishes by claiming to be on the DL – he is getting to have sex with particular men of color, live his fantasy, and consume that set of exoticized elements. However, this DL discourse will not impact this white man once he leaves his apartment or goes to work the next day, in the very same way the DL discourse will still be associated in the larger society with men of color. Likewise, the common perception that men of color do not come out of the closet is also inherent in this white DL man's desire. This white boy thug's claim to humiliation can be read as self-loathing – a common description often made of men who have sex with other men but are not willing to publicly admit being gay. In that, one could read his desire of physical humiliation as a quest for very real domination in all other social and symbolic spheres, through the very single act of claiming humiliation.

In the following post, one sees how the use of the DL gets linked to seeking Mexicans and other Latinos:

> *21 yo looking to get down with a yng guapo* – Hey Mexican/Latinos welcome 18-30. Must be fit, around my age, full latino, hung and a top. Be clean on the dl, and masculine as well. My stats: 5foot8 140 white, bottom, clean masculine and on the dl. I am lookin for now. No endless emails. Stats/pic in first email. I can host or travel.
> Chicago Craigslist > Men Seeking Men, Date: 2009-03-08, 6:56 PM CDT

The notion of the DL is being used here to activate a sense that Latinos, and not just black men, can offer the same set of sensations and interactions as black men did in previous posts. Interestingly, Latinos (individuals coming from potentially two dozen countries) are reduced to Mexican, both in the explicit mention (Mexican/Latinos) but also in the use of the "young guapo" phrase – a phrase applicable in Mexico, but not in most other Latin American places, and certainly not among U.S. Latinos. These Latino men must be "full Latino," suggesting that a mixture with non-Latino-ness (or perhaps, more specifically, a mixture with whiteness) may make the person as not "authentically" DL and masculine. This racialized "young guapo" also gets associated with similar stereotypes of black men in that they are seen as just "fit" tops, who have large penises (i.e., "hung"). In previous DL literature, González (2007) noted the use of the DL among Latino men, yet in this instance, we can notice how the discourse of the "down low" is being used by white men to have sex with Latino men, whom they categorize as masculine, just like them, but non-white. These white men's use of the "down low" moves the label beyond blackness to other bodies of color; however, it still maintains certain notions of masculinity and fit bodies that supposedly binds these DL men together across racial lines.

Lastly, one sees Latino and black get lumped together within this "down low" advertisement:

> *Cute European looking for latino or black dick* – I am cute European guy in mid 20's and would love to play around with hung dl or thug latino or black man who is hung and tough. . .My stats are 5.11, 150 with nice smooth ass. Looking for tonite and I can't host!!!! Reply with stats and a pic!!!
> New York Craigslist > Men Seeking Men, Date: 2008-11-15, 8:45 PM EST

In this advertisement, the use of the "down low" is not just used to attract black men but also Latino men. These men of color are reduced to their hung dicks, and their hyper-masculinity is re-inscribed with notions of seeking a tough thug. The cute European guy (where European stands in for whiteness, and phenotypically the poster is white in his pictures) mentions his nice smooth ass, suggesting that he wants to also be penetrated by a Latino or black man. The discourse of the "down low" moves beyond blackness, but it does so by just applying black racial stereotypes to other men of color – homogenizing them as all being masculine, hung thugs.

Conclusion

Desire is a complex web that reflects the social worlds in which we live. It is a site of contestation – a terrain not only of pleasure but also of power and the mutually con-stitution of race, class, gender, sexuality, body size, and ability. People meet, and in that encounter, meanings are exchanged. Values are placed on a person's body parts, ethno-racial background, gender presentations, and sexual positions and enactments. Desire is never innocent. It carries elements of worth, where race, gender, and embod-iment are often used in this battlefield to either value or reject certain people and experiences (Robinson 2015). Desires matter, and desire is never just about one thing, but a multiplicity of elements. Within Craigslist.org DL advertisements, desire is no different from many other social identity/location negotiations present in modernity around notions of intimacy and sex.

Roderick Ferguson's (2004) queer of color critique may help though in illuminat-ing how the "down low" may be a re-working of the sexual stereotypes about men of color that still uphold whiteness as the norm while subjugating bodies of color, even if these men of color are sought to be the ones to humiliate white men during the sexual encounter. In *Aberrations in Black*, Ferguson reveals how racist regulations are through gender and sexual regulations. Black sexualities, non-heterosexual sexuali-ties, and other non-normative sexualities have to be constantly pathologized and reg-ulated in order to maintain white heterosexuality as the norm in society. In this regard, the "down low" can be seen as a new way to police certain forms of sexualities. It relies on the notion of the black buck, in that men on the DL are seen as hyper-sexual (e.g., having sex with men and women) and violent (e.g., spreading HIV). However, along with this construction of the black buck, these men are seen as failing to uphold dominant notions of the family through not being "properly" heterosexual. Also, these men of color are seen as failing to be "proper" gay subjects, since they do not "come out" and disclose their sexual practices or claim a bisexual or gay identity. The "down low" then can be situated historically through the image of the "black buck," that is now intersecting with notions of improper same-sex sexual behavior (i.e., notions of HIV infection and not "coming out").

Oppositely, white men are identifying as being on the DL and using the language. These white men are having sex with men of color; however, they are not being dis-cussed as having internalized homophobia, or demeaned psychologically, nor sym-bolically dissected through public health for supposedly infecting women with HIV. They can use the term to find sexual enjoyment and fulfillment, reifying stereotypes about people of color's sexualities in the process, and not have their sexual choices and practices pathologized or even discussed. In fact, their use of the "down low" is furthering stereotypes about people of color's sexualities as being hyper-sexual, deviant, marginal and even "closeted" (and thus, exotic), while allowing these white men to go unnoticed in their reification and deployment of these DL portrayals. Of course, we do not know if these men are not gay, appear to be more feminine than they claim, and are willing to do all they say in the advertisement. But we ought to revisit the construction of non-whiteness as something to be consumed in these ads: while common narratives may assume power to be something held by the one "dominating" or "humiliating" (which we cannot always assume means penetrating, although some posts make it explicit), here we seek to turn the eye back to the production of whiteness in these posts as a privileged place from which to activate fantasies of the other (sexually and racially) while attempting to create bonding between them (as DL, as masculine). In the end, white DL men do not face the structural challenges that men of color do.

This chapter begins to show a contribution to the limited amount of scholarship on the DL and web interactions. We show that the DL on Craigslist.org is not just black and Latino men, but there are also white representations of this sexual and social experience. However, racial stereotypes of people of color's sexualities shape how white men are using the DL to search for black men and/or other men of color. These stereotypes form how masculinity is constructed around a hyper-masculine man of color for a white man to have a sexual encounter with. The hyper-masculinization of men of color is deployed to re-affirm the hegemony of white masculinity within this space, showing how the "down low" is part of a product of a long historical construction of pathologizing people of color's sexualities. But because this research also shows that many white men are now deploying DL terminology to claim it for themselves, we need to understand what this use of "choosing" to be on the DL for white men actually means. Further exploration of how shared masculinity presumably brings these men together inter-racially is also needed. White men are on the DL; however, they escape the negative stereotypes associated with the construction of the DL in the larger society. These white men's privilege remains maintained, while still pathologizing people of color's sexualities. Nonetheless, we need to move beyond simplistic notions of the "down low" and begin to more fully illuminate how it is a site to stereotype people of color and reify white hegemony, and how that happens in all spheres of life – even (and perhaps most centrally) within the intimate, sexual realm.

References

Boykin, Keith. 2005. *Beyond the Down Low: Sex, Lies, and Denial in Black America*. New York: Carroll & Graf.

Collins, Patricia Hill. 2004. *Black Sexual Politics: African Americans, Gender, and the New Racism*. New York: Routledge.

Denizet-Lewis, Benoit. 2003. "Double Lives on the Down Low." *The New York Times*, 3 August.

Dowsett, Gary W., Herukhuti Williams, Ana Ventuneac and Alex Carballo-Dieguez. 2008. "'Taking it Like a Man': Masculinity and Barebacking Online." *Sexualities* 11: 121–141.

Ferguson, Roderick A. 2004. *Aberrations in Black: Toward a Queer of Color Critique*. Minnesota: University of Minnesota Press.

Ford, Chandra L., Kathryn D. Whetten, Susan A. Hall, Jay S. Kaufman and Angela D. Thrasher. 2007. "Black Sexuality, Social Construction, and Research Targeting 'The Down Low' ('The DL')." *Annals of Epidemiology* 17(3): 209–216.

González, Alfredo M. 2007. "Latinos on Da Down Low: The Limitations of Sexual Identity in Public Health." *Latino Studies* 5: 25–52.

King, J. L. 2004. *On the Down Low*. New York: Broadway Books.

McCune, Jr., Jeffrey Q. 2014. *Sexual Discretion: Black Masculinity and the Politics of Passing*. Chicago: University of Chicago Press.

Mukherjea, Ananya and Salvador Vidal-Ortiz. 2006. "Studying HIV Risk in Vulnerable Communities: Methodological and Reporting Shortcomings in the Young Men's Study in New York City." *The Qualitative Report* 11(2): 393–416.

Phillips, Layli. 2005. "Deconstructing 'Down Low' Discourse: The Politics of Sexuality, Gender, Race, AIDS, and Anxiety." *Journal of African American Studies* 9: 3–15.

Robinson, Brandon Andrew. 2015. "'Personal Preference' as the New Racism: Gay Desire and Racial Cleansing in Cyberspace." *Sociology of Race & Ethnicity* 1(2): 317–30.

Robinson, Brandon Andrew and Salvador Vidal-Ortiz. 2013. "Displacing the Dominant 'Down Low' Discourse: Deviance, Same-sex Desire, and Craigslist.org." *Deviant Behavior* 34(3): 224–241.

Snorton, C. Riley. 2014. *Nobody Is Supposed to Know: Black Sexuality on the Down Low*. Minneapolis: University of Minnesota Press.

Ward, Jane. 2007. "Straight Dude Seeks Same: Mapping the Relationship Between Sexual Identities, Practices, and Cultures." Pp. 31–37 in *Sex Matters: The Sexuality and Society Reader*, Second Edition, edited by Mindy Stombler et al. New York: Allyn and Bacon.

Ward, Jane. 2008. "Dude Sex: White Masculinities and 'Authentic' Heterosexuality Among Dudes Who Have Sex With Dudes." *Sexualities* 11(4): 414–34.

chapter 41

Sexual liberation and the creative class in Israel

Dana Kaplan

The story of the history of sexuality is often told as a shift from a traditional, repressed sexuality to a contemporary liberated and hedonistic sexuality. But this conventional view ignores the importance of class in shaping sexual cultures. By and large, during the nineteenth century in many Western societies, there were two opposing ideologies of sexuality. There was a middle-class, "respectful" sexuality, and, from the perspective of the middle class, there was a lower-class, deviant, permissive sexuality. In the course of the twentieth century, however, this division has been reversed. Today, working-class sexuality is often considered conservative and restrained while a culture of sexual fulfillment and intense sexual pleasures have been idealized by the middle class. For this class, sexuality has gradually become an important way for selves to express their individuality.

In this chapter I explore the way social class shapes sexuality. Specifically, I examine the significant role pleasure and notions of liberation play in middle-class sexuality. The common view is that the sexual revolution of the 1960s had the effect of blurring class boundaries, and sexual liberation became universal. I have my doubts. In any event, I will explore everyday understandings of sexuality among the new, creative middle class in Israel. I will argue that notions of liberated sex invoke a sense of individuality and entitlement among this class. By describing sex as a "fun" leisure activity and by endorsing sexual experimentation, members of this class express their individual personalities in the context of a post-industrialized Israel.

Israel is usually described as a society which is undergoing a shift from collectivism to individualism. From a society unified around a hegemonic Zionist pioneering ethos, Israel is increasingly becoming a pluralistic and globalized society. This change is evident in the economic, cultural and ideological spheres. In the economic sphere, a state-centralized economy has, from the mid-1980s, undergone a profound process of privatization. This economic liberalization has encouraged a service economy and a flourishing hi-tech industry. In the cultural sphere, consumerism has become a new way of life for many Israelis. Middle-class Israelis have turned out to be enthusiastic consumers of the new leisure and lifestyle goods provided by a new culture industry. For example, the media environment is saturated with new privately owned tv channels, airing global and commercial content. Similarly, many Israelis have begun shopping in American-style malls, enjoy an elaborate dining scene (from global fast food chains to exquisite restaurants), and carefully design and decorate their homes.

The post-industrialization of Israel is also apparent in a shifting value system, from collectivist to individualist values and from traditionalist to modernist values. This shift is expressed also in a relaxation of sexual norms. By and large, there has been a normative shift from sexual Puritanism to more liberal views regarding sex and homosexuality in particular. Yet, despite a growing sexual individualization, Israel remains a family-oriented society with a positive attitude towards procreation, as is evidenced by high marriage and birth rates compared with similar, post-industrial societies. This mixture of family values and relative sexual tolerance makes Israel a remarkable case study for examining the relationship between sex and class. Further, this tension between the more traditional inclination towards family life and the tendency to experiment with sex reinforces the ways in which my interviewees interpret their sexuality as a true exploration of an individualized self.

My point of departure draws from the sociologist Pierre Bourdieu's analysis of the new French middle class. He claims that this class has shifted from a "duty to [a] fun [sexual] ethic" (Bourdieu 2010: 365). In Bourdieu's analysis, sexual freedom and sexual satisfaction are seen as essential for flagging membership in this class. Intense sexual pleasure is a marker of class status. Yet there has been relatively little research into the class aspects of the quest for intense sexual pleasure. In general, social research on sexuality emphasizes the role of gender rather than class. Furthermore, the sexual culture of the privileged, which is based on a discourse of liberation and self-realization, is not usually seen as class-distinctive. Consequently, the specific ways in which sex is enmeshed in the class experiences of the middle class remains under-explored. This chapter reports on my preliminary research into the role of sexuality in the new middle classes in Israel.

Based on in-depth interviews with middle-class heterosexual men and women in Israel, I will explore two ways in which this class expresses itself through its approach to sexuality. First, sex is approximated to art and to a bohemian way of life. Sex is given an artistic, avant-garde and transgressive meaning. Second, sex is said to indicate a "well connected" person and someone who endorses a "fun" lifestyle. Both the view of "sex as art" and "sex as a lifestyle" accentuate a middle-class culture that puts a premium on individualism and self-expression.

Sex as art

Shusterman (2006) argues that art and sex have been unjustly assigned to separate spheres. He argues that sex is an everyday kind of aesthetic experience. My interviewees also approached sex and art as interconnected.

An insight into sex as art is given by a middle-aged academic man, a BDSM (bondage, domination, sado-masochism) master. His sexual journey has taken him to the canon of Western S&M erotic literature. He has also read psychoanalytic scholarship as well as surfed "the cage," an Israeli BDSM website, and watched artistic erotic movies for inspiration and knowledge. This has helped him to contextualize his new found sexual taste within a sophisticated, artsy, libertine heritage. But BDSM is also related to another form of artistic outlet – writing. Examining the largest Israeli BDSM virtual community reveals that members express cultural know-how by writing erotic literary pieces. Writing beautifully, that is, being witty, kinky and racy, is the most common activity in this site. In the BDSM world, writing is also a bodily practice, as when the "master" writes on his "slave's" skin. Our BDSM interviewee is apparently in the habit of writing aphorisms as well as verbal abuse all over the body of his long-time "slave." The aesthetization of BDSM is related both to its aristocratic social history but also to its distinctive theatricality.

> This theatricality, that was always there [in my sex life], and it is meant to create some kind of a drama in sex. Many times this drama surpasses sex and it is not directly sexual. It can even be a simple thing, like abstaining from getting naked. As far as I'm concerned, sex should not necessarily start or even continue with nudity.

Theatricality is a way to make sex a powerful aesthetic and erotic experience.

BDSM practitioners are not the only sex artists I discovered. Apparently, one can consider oneself a creator of a superior kind of life even by practicing a more normative – if quite kinky – sexuality. A sense of transgressiveness can be achieved by the simplest means, for example, by not having sex in a bed or preferring "a more disorganized atmosphere," as a male interviewee says. Many of the interviewees perceive some sexual acts as less acceptable and hence more risky and interesting. For example, both women and men report engaging in anal sex, which until recently has been culturally associated with the stigma of homosexuality. Thus, when a senior manager in the NGO (non-governmental organization) sector says she "recently became interested in the ass," this speaks not only to the expanded tolerance of homosexuality but to an ethic that aims to push the sexual envelope. For the new middle classes in Israel, gay culture has come to epitomize coolness. The construction of anal eroticism as a positively "dangerous" and "risky" adventure and its incorporation into heterosexual lives can therefore be interpreted as part of the middle-class politics of "cool."

Artistic creativity is shown in the aesthetization of sex and the elevation of the sexual act to the level of art. One interviewee considered the sexual encounter itself as an out-of-the-ordinary experience. For him, the enactment of a "good fuck" is like the creation of a masterpiece for an artist. Sex assumes a kind of transcendent, almost "sacred" value. "Now [when we come] is a good time to die. Like, if I'd died, I would die happy." The aesthetization of sex is also related to a heightened awareness of one's own and one's partner's body. Men and women of the creative class are familiar with their personal turn-ons and turn-offs, and can easily verbalize them. Moreover, they are aware of the fine-tuning of their bodies when they feel sexual, and are reflexive in identifying the specifics of their desire. A woman says: "Sometimes [when] I'm exhausted, there is something in the weight of [my] body that arouses me sexually." Another interviewee spoke of "sexual competence" as "acknowledging the ability to extract from the body fun and pleasure and to really connect to it. . . . [it's] the way you conduct yourself, [your] thoughts, speech, etc."

In these examples, we can see that feeling sexual is a capacity originating from a heightened awareness of one's body and potential bodily pleasures (to feel aroused when exhausted, or to be aware of one's erotic potential). For the creative class, genuine sexual pleasure entails going against conventional sexual norms or scripts. Sexual excitement is often triggered by being acutely aware of one's specific erotic desires and a willingness to transgress social norms. Like an artistic creation, sexual excitement and pleasure emanate from within the self.

The experience of liberated sex is understood as an expression of authenticity, as it is premised upon an ability to connect body, mind, and self expression when being sexual. Being a sexual person is constructed as an experience of mind/body release and uninhibited flow. For example, a woman says,

> There is the satisfaction [per se], but there is also everything that surrounds it. It's a kind of a satisfaction-package. . . . This satisfaction is definitely related to having a good orgasm, but it is also so much more. It's not only about coming. I also gain satisfaction from the situation, from the totality of what's happening.

For this woman it is more exciting and fulfilling to be in a sexual mood and to plan a sexual scene than it is to just "come." Sexual satisfaction is thus related to building up to the thrill (such as having a get-away weekend) and not just the act of having sex or the orgasmic moment. In this respect, it is significant that the individual is responsible for generating sexual excitement. One of the clearest expressions of this tendency is being able to be clear about one's sexual needs and to communicate them. Sexual sophistication is thus not about possessing a special skill or technique; nor is it synonymous with being sexy and desired by others. It is a particular disposition towards the body and its pleasures. For the interviewees, sex is not an instinctual drive or act. Rather, it is a learned capacity, which can be cultivated and developed. For example, many interviewees reported that they have gradually learned how to touch and be touched in more pleasurable ways.

The "cultivated" sexual disposition – rather than the "natural" sexual instinct – is similar to what Bernstein (2009) describes in her study of educated, middle-class female sex workers. This new kind of prostitute, she contends, professionalizes her sexual labor by perfecting her sexual skills, such as giving a better massage or becoming a certified sex therapist. But sexually pleasing customers is not the only thing that matters. In fact, in order to successfully market the sexual commodity they offer, these women also strive to perfect an authentic sexual experience. As professional middle-class women, they want to get aroused and experience sexual pleasure with customers. In this regard, and similar to many other service-oriented occupations, they bring their class-based cultural capital to work. But even in a much less "service" oriented atmosphere, cultivating and perfecting one's own pleasure capacities is a serious task.

Dana Kaplan

If "sex work for the middle classes" simulates real-life intimacy, then "non-commercialized" middle-class sex may take the shape of a game. Most of the interviewees emphasize the pleasure of fantasizing, flirting, being "players." They may be sincere – but they are still only players. For example, a female photographer says that her favorite part of intimacy is the falling in love phase, and the sweet agonies that go along with it. Then, she is "horny for days and days" and so she comes "in a second."

Interestingly, there is a gender difference in cultivating the capacity for sexual pleasure. Whereas men stress that, over time, they have learned to please their partners, women talk of becoming more attuned to their sexual needs. In the interviews, men express their masculinity by saying that they are now better lovers than before, more attuned to the "female body," and can make women come better or faster. For example, an academic described how his wife has helped him to be a better, more considerate partner in their marriage. When asked if she was as dominant in their sex life, he replied that "No, [not] in sex. It was something *I* have started exploring and investigating, [it was important for me] to see what makes *her* feel good . . ., that the point in having sex would be to make her come, that she would feel good with it." Women, on the other hand, tended to construct the ability to take pleasure in sex as a "long forgotten" and reawakened capacity, usually (but not always) as a consequence of a love affair outside marriage. But both men and women underscore their ability to create a pleasurable sexual act, indeed to construct sex as a total pleasure-experience. This is understood as a sign of a sophisticated, avant-garde self.

Sex as lifestyle

As we have seen, being sexually skillful and playful is understood as an expression of a unique and creative self. But an interest in sex is also the backdrop against which they, as typical members of the creative class, can demonstrate their market skills and ability to relate to people. For example, a male interviewee who is a senior insurance agent admits to sometimes closing large-scale deals in a *ménage à trois* with a customer and his wife. Others say their friends know all about their active, fulfilling sexual life, and that they openly discuss "their good sex life" with friends, as well as with business acquaintances. By talking of sex they also increase their reputation and status.

But sex doesn't have to mix with business to be valuable. Interviewees portray sex as part of an endless endeavor of self-improvement. The association of sex and self-care is not surprising, given that fitness and health are essential in the lifestyle of the middle classes. In particular, men emphasize the importance of a culture of self-improvement through bodily and sexual fitness and health. They stress the importance of smelling good, going to the gym, having tattoos, eating well, and, of course, having good sex. In their discourse, sex is not constructed, however, in terms of sexual health or sexual functioning, but rather as taking good care of oneself. Similarly, sex is not discussed as a luxury but rather as a matter of living a high "quality" and sophisticated life. Thus, a highly successful lawyer identified himself as a dedicated and expert host. He enjoys inviting friends over for a tasteful, freshly self-cooked dinner made from the best, freshest and most exquisite ingredients. "I live intensively. If I entertain friends, then I entertain with a million things. I'm constantly stressed out, in my life, in my demand for quality," he says. However, he states, "when I entertain as I like to, I do it for myself. I enjoy the experience of creating it." For him, the attraction lies in being able to create a fine dining experience.

The analogy between food and sex connoisseurship is a recurrent theme in many of the interviews, especially for the men. These "new men" like to cook for their families, go out to ethnic as well as expensive restaurants, invite friends over and experiment with sex, whether anal sex, group sex or attending sex clubs. In this vein, a revealing fantasy of a male interviewee is one in which he cooks dinner for two secretaries and, eventually, "something [sexual] happens." Similarly, when asked to explain what "sexual enjoyment" means for him, another male interviewee compared sex to a range of other lifestyle options that bring pleasure, such as eating out, buying clothes and owning a car.

> What is it that you gain from dining in a nice restaurant? Go have McDonald's! What is it there to gain? In the morning I purge it anyway! What did I gain? More calories? [But] do you enjoy!? Why would you buy a beautiful piece of clothing? Why would you have a nice dinner? Why buy a nice car – and [yet] you don't see the rewards of the most important thing – physical pleasure.

These examples show that sex is placed in the sphere of the everyday and is not formulated as something "sacred" and apart from the "profane." Whereas the importance of sex lies in that it brings pleasure, this is not a crudely bodily pleasure. Instead, sex is conceived of as an opportunity for self-exploration and expression. Similar to the consumption of food or fashion, sex is implicitly divided into more and less sophisticated kinds of pleasures.

In contemporary Israeli life, a refined taste no longer relies only upon the consumption of highbrow cultural products. Rather, it is more often a creative process, whereby consumers interact with cultural forms. Instead of simply purchasing commodities, consumers are increasingly active in creating their own, exciting consumption experience. Thus, going to the gym, drinking coffee in the local Italian-looking café or spending a few hours in the flea market looking for vintage clothes is no less important than the actual body, cup of coffee or piece of clothing one purchases. This, I believe, is why the sex/food analogy is so prevalent in the interviewees' discourse. Food and dining have become a total consumer experience in contemporary times. In many ways, sexual activity can also indicate a playful, creative self.

An interest in sex is sometimes presented as part of a "total" lifestyle of self-refinement and sophistication. The ordinary and easy way in which my interviewees discuss their sexual lives entails considerable cultural wit and social sophistication. The willingness, even enthusiasm with which they share intimate details from their lives is related to what Hey (2005) describes as a distinctive, new middle-class disposition of "excitation." Hey argues that a flexible occupational market blurs "the market/self-interest/social/sexual interest nexus." In the creative occupations, workers are expected to express a very strong yet controlled "shameless pushy" personality (Hey 2005:863). It appears, then, that being a sexually oriented person is a way of relating to people and presenting such a strong personality.

Dana Kaplan

Conclusion

I have argued that sexual liberation is part of the culture of the creative class in contemporary Israel. In this sense, class shapes sexuality. The categories of "sex as art" and "sex as a lifestyle" are related to two significant capacities of the creative class. One is the ability to evaluate sexuality in aesthetic terms; the second is the capacity for self-promotion. These two capacities are extremely significant and beneficial to those who hold them within a capitalist order. In contemporary societies, and this is true of Israel, there has been a shift from corporate, organized capitalism to a global, networked capitalism in which culture itself is a huge business. From a society of producers, we have turned into a society of consumers. The market offers a variety of lifestyles and identities to choose from or construct. However, even in the face of such transformations, class has not disappeared from the social landscape. To a large extent, the freedom to choose and nurture individual lifestyles is a class-based privilege (Bottero 2004).

In consumer-oriented capitalism, unlike industrial capitalism, artistic hierarchies, gender roles, and the separation of labor from leisure and the private from the public sphere are constantly shifting, if not eroding. In this new reality, class differences are ever more subtle. For example, sociologists of culture convincingly show that popular and everyday cultures are more significant than highbrow and canonical cultures in differentiating between classes. Thus, in the past, a privileged social position was related to the conspicuous consumption of high art. But in contemporary capitalism, class-based tastes are largely expressed through skills such as the appreciation and interpretation of art, rather than owning expensive art. More importantly for the current discussion, the aesthetic sphere expands from the artistic to broader social terrains and new cultural forms. In this regard, my interviewees constructed sex as a form of art. For them, sex is one such social sphere of everyday aesthetization.

The creative class also signals its privileged social position by emphasizing self-promotional skills. I explored this notion through the category of "sex as a lifestyle." Here, sex is more than a sign of an artistic sophistication. It also enables social interactions, or strengthens social ties and demonstrates one's communicative skills. In contemporary Israel, where employment flexibility requires flexible workers, the demand from the creative class to present an "authentic self" (unique and special) is institutionalized in the sphere of work. Yet the search for authenticity expands to society at large. For example, according to Bauman (2007), acquiring social value and recognition increasingly depends on the ability to cultivate "subjectivity." By this he means that social standing is strongly related to being communicative and unique, and to projecting a distinctive self-identity to others.

The men and women I interviewed talked about sex using terminology taken directly from the culture of contemporary capitalism. Corporations and people alike are supposed to not only "look sexy" on the outside but also to "be sexy" on the inside. People are expected to project and convince others of their "creative and romantic subjectivity" (Adkins 2008:187). Certain subjective states, like "ease," "flow" or "audacity" may prove personally and economically advantageous. In other words, creativity, sophistication, flexibility, and self-promotion are not only indicators of a "good" sexual citizen but a potentially "good" economic prospect.

It was not long ago that sex was considered a private, personal matter, at least normatively. Sex has now entered the public sphere, and it is commodified in a variety of ways. For instance, sex is commonly used by the media to promote and sell commodities. Sex is also a commodity in itself, part of a global economy of cyber-pornography, sex tourism, trafficking or sex work. Yet, sex does not only promote consumption. More significantly, having sex can feel like shopping. When there are more sexual options to choose from, sex becomes a site for cultivating a sense of individual identity and a social lifestyle. We may have more sexual partners during our lifetime than in the past. We may also experience a "consumerist" type of sex life in which we continuously expect new and exciting pleasures. In this marketplace logic, "we are urged to resist prior (conventional/oppressive/just plain boring) forms of intimacy in much the same way that we are urged to throw out or update last year's wardrobe" (Blum 2002:853). Yet if sex is similar to modern consumer culture and indeed part of this culture, then, like consumer culture itself, sex is also organized along class lines.

Finally, against the backdrop of a "sex industry," the creative class can associate themselves with an elevated kind of sexual experience. By conceiving sex as both aesthetic and a type of social interaction, rather than a merely "biological" act, they can approach sex as a form of self-expression and authenticity. These men and women move easily in the world of aesthetic objects and intense experiences, as they refine their capacity for sexual pleasure. This capacity is class-based.

Bibliography

Adkins, Lisa. 2008. "From Retroactivation to Futurity: The End of the Sexual Contract?" *NORA: Nordic Journal of Women's Studies*, 16(3): 182–201.

Bauman, Zygmunt. 2007. *Consuming Life*. Cambridge: Polity.

Bernstein, Elizabeth. 2009. "Sex Work for the Middle Classes." *Sexualities*, 10(4): 473–88.

Blum, Virginia L. 2002. "Introduction: The Liberation of Intimacy: Consumer-Object Relations and (Hetero)Patriarchy." *Antipode*, 34(5): 845–63.

Bottero, Wendy. 2004. "Class Identity and the Identity of Class." *Sociology*, 38(5): 985–1003.

Bourdieu, Pierre. 2010 (1984). *Distinction: A Social Critique of the Judgment of Taste*. Cambridge, MA: Harvard University Press.

Gershuny, Jonathan. 2005. "Busyness as the Badge of Honor for the New Superordinate Working Class." *Social Research*, 72(2): 287–314.

Hey, Valerie. 2005. "The Contrasting Social Logics of Sociality and Survival: Cultures of Classed Be/Longing in Late Modernity." *Sociology*, 39(5): 855–72.

Shusterman, Richard. 2006. "Aesthetic Experience: From Analysis to Eros." *Journal of Aesthetics and Art Criticism*, 64(2): 217–29.

chapter 42

Wikisexuality

A new category of sexuality in the virtual world

L. Ayu Saraswati

What do you call a man who, when online, would have sex with men but in the offline world, he would only have sex with women? A study by health scientist Michael Ross shows that heterosexual men who have sex with other men online would still claim themselves as heterosexuals because for these "straight" men, the experiences of the body in the physical world are more privileged than the virtual one when it comes to constructing their identity (Ross 2005: 345). This labeling of one's sexuality that only considers one's expression of sexuality in the offline world while disregarding online encounters is problematic. We need a new category of sexuality to help us understand the complexity of sexuality in this era of the digital world. I call this new category of sexuality *wikisexuality*.

Wikisexuality is a new formation of sexuality that takes into account the fluidity of sexuality as it traverses various layers of reality—the physical and virtual worlds. It is a collaborative- and interactive-based sexuality, rather than an essence-based sexuality. An essence-based sexuality hints at absolute truth and fixed sexuality without any external interactions. Wikisexuality allows us to see the constant formation and re-formation of sexual identities. It reflects the non-linear and chaotic formation of sexuality that moves us beyond the mono (i.e., homosexual, heterosexual) versus multiple (i.e., bisexual, pansexual) categories of sexuality and beyond the nature versus nurture debate by evoking the notion of sexuality as constantly shifting with every encounter.

In naming this new construction of sexuality in virtual space as "wikisexuality," I purposefully adopt the word "wiki" to draw on its meanings and usages in cyberspace.

In the Internet world, wiki is employed to signify a collaborative website. According to c2.com, website of a company by Ward Cunningham, the person who first hauled this Hawaiian term into cyberspace, the idea of wiki suggests that the website is always a work in progress and that the "conversation" on the wiki website happens in the "timeless now." An example of a very well-known website that employs a wiki concept is Wikipedia, where various users can add, edit, and delete information. By calling sexuality in cyberspace wikisexuality, I suggest that sexuality in cyberspace is something that is editable (even by strangers)—it is unfixed, fluid, and thereby non-essentialist. This is one of the aspects of wiki that I am borrowing here: sexuality as a (collaborative) work in progress.

Offering a new category of sexuality allows me to redress what psychologists Kelly Brooks and Kathryn Quina refer to as "unlabeled" sexuality: women who in their study refused to be called lesbians or bisexuals because these women consider their sexuality more fluid than these categories may suggest; they claim that when it comes to sexual orientation it is the "person, not the gender" that matters (Brooks and Quina 2009: 1031). Psychologist Lisa Diamond calls this "sexual fluidity": "situation-dependent flexibility in women's sexual responsiveness" (Diamond 2009: 3). None of these studies, however, look at the Internet and its influence in further complicating the fluidness of sexual expressions and experiences in this digital moment of time.

Cyberspace is an important site of analysis to study sexuality. As media studies scholar Wendy Chun argues, cyberspace is "marked as a heterotopia of compensation—as a space for economic, social, or sexual redress that simultaneously represented, contested, and inverted all other 'real' spaces" (Chun 2006: 55). For Dennis Waskul and Mark Douglass, cyberspace is "a hyperreal technology of social saturation that dislocates space, time, and personal characteristics as variables of human interaction" (Waskul and Douglass 1997: 381). Sue Thomas even boldly celebrates the power of the Internet: "the Internet is my body. It's an extra set of senses, an additional brain, a second pair of eyes" (Thomas 2004: 18). Nonetheless, as sociologists Mike Featherstone and Roger Burrows (1995: 8) have pointed out, cyberspace has been represented as "overly utopian." Most of these "playful" sexual interactions that allow people to be whatever gender and sex they want to be online tend to be text- or chat-based (Gauntlett and Horsley 2004). There are, however, many expressions of sexuality in cyberspace that are beyond these text-based encounters and therefore challenge these existing studies. This essay, for example, focuses on examining Tantric sex websites. The category of wikisexuality is applicable in understanding different expressions of sexuality in the cyberworld generally. In this chapter, I use 75 websites of American Tantric goddesses (sexual and spiritual women healers) as a case study to further explain the term wikisexual. In analyzing these websites as important sources of information and data, I view them the way modern philologist Antonio Gómez views personal weblogs, i.e., "the means whereby people in general and adolescents in particular can self-express and discursively construct their self" (Gómez 2010: 29).

A word of caution is necessary here. I recognize that a website analysis cannot stand for my claiming that these are the "real" experiences of people interacting in cyberspace. Carefully reading these websites simply allows me to understand the *discourses* (a systematic way through which people can define, think about, and represent a topic, and how knowledge and subjectivity related to that topic can be produced) of sexuality and gender that are at play. Arguing so, I nonetheless do not frame the "real" world and the world of "representation" as two distinct and separate worlds. As cultural studies scholar Stuart Hall argues, "reality does not exist outside the process of representation" (Jhally 1997). This is also the stand that I take in this chapter.

In what follows, I will ground my discussion about Tantric goddesses by providing a brief context for Tantra. Then, using Tantric goddess websites as a site of analysis, I will explain how the sexuality of these Tantric goddesses as they represent themselves online exemplifies wikisexuality: (1) as non-essentialist, interactive, and collaborative sexuality; and (2) as playful and performative sexuality.

Grounding Tantra in history

Tantra is a spiritual practice found in Hindu, Jain, and Buddhist traditions (Barratt and Rand 2007: 7). It has been around since the fifth or sixth century CE (Barratt and Rand 2007: 7). Tantrism as we know it today is a construction of nineteenth-century Orientalist scholars and a commodified and commercialized version of Tantra produced and circulated by Tantric gurus including Osho-Rajneesh (Urban 2003: 2, 236). In the United States, Tantra could be found as early as the 1900s, although the "western appropriations" of Tantra existed since the late nineteenth century (Urban 2003: 208). By the 1960s and 1970s, Tantra had been popularized by celebrities such as Jimi Hendrix and Mick Jagger (Urban 2003: 203–204). By the end of the twentieth century, Tantra was known mostly for its teachings that squarely locate desire at the epicenter of liberation (Shaw 1994: 195; Urban 2003: 229; White 2003: 15). It is seen as a spiritual practice that considers "sexual activity [a]s a rich form of prayer" (Barratt and Rand 2007: 8; see also Bullis 1998: 112). Sex is thus seen as a "gateway to heaven" (Feuerstein quoted in Urban 2003: 8).

In this chapter, I specifically focus on Tantric goddesses; in present-day American society they are referred to as spiritual *and* sexual healers who guide their worshippers by means of their sensuality. My specific focus on women who are spiritual and sexual teachers and healers is partly driven by the fact that dominant narratives of religious teachings often devalue women who take pleasure in sexual activities and that spirituality or "mysticism" is most often attached to celibacy or "asceticism" (Hutchins 2010; Jackson 1992: 86).

Wikisexuality as non-essentialist, interactive, and collaborative sexuality

Wikisexuality as non-essentialist sexuality suggests that sexuality is not something that one is born with and therefore remains fixed throughout one's lifetime. I propose that subjectivity is performed and constructed at the moment of encounter: who we are and how we perform that identity (i.e., as a mother, a student, etc.) depends on whom we interact with. There is no essence in one's identity or sexuality. We are not bisexual or heterosexual *prior* to the encounter.

Sexuality in this sense then becomes a verb, a doing. It is not an essence, a fixed entity, or a being. Cyberculture scholar Dennis Waskul pointed out that in cyberspace, "self is not something that we 'have'; instead, it is something that we communicate" (Waskul 2003: 13). Identity as a "verb" suggests that identity is "something that we *do* in a process of communication" (Simpson 2005: 123; Waskul 2003: 15). Enlisting this understanding of identity to further help us understand wikisexuality, I argue that wikisexuality is sexuality as it is expressed at a particular moment, something that one does, rather than an essence or a *being* in itself.

On their websites, American Tantric goddesses represent their sexuality as "open." On sacredsensualist.com, for example, a Tantric goddess advertises that she will welcome "men, women, transfolk, and couples (of whatever gender makeup) onto [her] table." Such openness seems to be the norm on these websites and suggests a fluidity of sexuality that registers beyond existing categories of sexuality. Depending on whoever comes to their "table," these Tantric goddesses express their sexuality and the sexuality of their clients in fluid ways. There is no essence to these postmodern Tantric goddesses' sexuality. Some have indeed used the term "heteroflexible" to move away from the limiting categories of heterosexuality or bisexuality.

From these websites, sexuality as a collaborative and interactive project can be seen from the ways in which these Tantric goddesses claim that they can help and *work with others* to "liberate" and "empower" women in their sensual life journey. For example, in a two-day session called "Sexual Healing: The Next Step, A Workshop for Women" women are invited to "unpack [their] history, and with [the Tantric goddess's] skill and gentle guidance, take the next healing step in [their] journey toward wholeness." They will "receive the support to explore the obstacles in [their] physical, emotional and spiritual body that keep [them] from [their] full feminine expression. When we do that, freedom is the next step!" This and other similar websites function as an invitation, indeed a public one, for the audience to interactively and collaboratively formulate and articulate their sexuality with the guidance of these Tantric goddesses. That is, these goddesses will help women to better articulate their sexuality. Their sexuality is in formation at the moment of collaborative encounter.

Thus, sexuality is and involves a (social) process. It even necessitates an audience (the Other) for it to be fully articulated. Mary Bryson and Lori MacIntosh, in analyzing queer youth's articulation of their sexuality online, argue that it is indeed the stranger and/or the public that "orient the subject" (Bryson and MacIntosh 2010: 116). They point out, "The act of always performing oneself with an audience's potential response in mind and the need for a reciprocal exchange are products of a social and technological persistence, the exigencies of a posthuman life, a public life" (Bryson and MacIntosh 2010: 115). Thus, the Internet allows for a new mode of encountering others: through interactivity that creates an audience-oriented subjectivity (Dawson 2005: 31; Lövheim and Linderman 2005; Slevin 2000: 70, 78ff.).

Wikisexuality can then be thought of as audience-oriented sexuality. It is produced *for* and *with* others. Wikisexuality is a sexuality that relies on the public, or on others, to complete its articulation. This in some ways reflects the nature of new media: "[U]nlike traditional media, which positioned users as receivers, the new media participant must consciously construct an identity for others to evaluate. This may be as basic as choosing a 'username' or as detailed as constructing an avatar and customizing an interactive profile" (Jones 2010: 263). In Anna E. Ward's study, "self-display" such as on Facebook or the Beautiful Agony website that she observed has become "a necessary precondition for identity creation. Self-discovery is now interchangeable with self-expression, specifically, self-expression that demands an audience" (Ward 2010: 162). That is, our presentation of ourselves often depends on how we perceive how others might view us, and in gaining that understanding of how others would react to us we begin to have a better understanding of ourselves (Zhao 2005: 387). Wikisexuality here is something that one works at and mostly with and for others.

Wikisexuality as playful and performative sexuality

If wikisexuality is an interactive and collaborative sexuality, then its mode of interaction and collaboration is play. Play is indeed one of the dominant modes of encounter in cyberspace. Cyberspace is even considered a fertile "playground" for identity formation (Downes 2005: 91). Analyzing text and webcam cybersex and erotic rate-my-picture websites, Waskul and Vannini argue that Internet sex play can be considered a form of "ludic" relationship in that "it is generally playful, casual, distant, noncommittal," and "ludic(rous)" when it is "laughable—even hilarious—due to apparent absurdity or incongruity" (Waskul and Vannini 2008: 242). They provide an example of how playful cybersexting functions as ludic—a man pretending to be a woman while having an outercourse with a woman who pretends to be a man. However, whereas Waskul and Vannini see these Internet sex-play activities as more ludic and ludic(rous), "fleeting," or reflecting "a lack of concern for depth, solemnity, seriousness, civility, and respect" (2008: 259), I see them as formative. Internet sex play is more than simply a playful mimicry or a laughable activity. Even in those moments of laughable encounters, people are nonetheless expressing and experimenting with their sexuality. They are engaged in the process of wikisexuality. Moreover, play provides a suitable discourse for understanding wikisexuality particularly because, as Sartre claimed, "play is the characteristic mode of being of a being that has no Being, understood in the sense of a stable and essential metaphysical presence" (quoted in Küchler 1994: 17).

The word "play" itself is very common and used in many of these Tantric websites, suggesting the ways in which the discourse of play deeply permeates the Tantric goddesses' world. On some websites such as partnerplayshop.com and tantradakini.com, the word "playshop" is used instead of "workshop." A Tantric goddess even calls her session a "Tantric playground," a space for people to "div[e] into. . . play to expand who [they] are." She claims that play provides spaces for "explorations [that] are great for total true wellness and happiness. As a lifelong student of psychology, [she has] an appreciative intelligence of role-play and a true talent for it." Thus, here, play and role-play are evoked as an avenue for self-exploration and ultimate happiness.

As a space for playful performance of one's sexuality, Tantric spaces, as these goddesses represent them online, can then be considered as liminal space. Matthew Jones (2010: 255) defines it as "experimental zones where social roles and relationships are tested and redefined." For example, Miss Christina, a Tantric practitioner of

10 years, offers a goddess training for men who would like to cross-dress. She claims that, "in Miss Christina's Goddess Training, there is only celebration, play, and education—never ever humiliation. With a flick of [her] wand, [she] will help you transform into the bombshell you want to be—if only for an hour or two." On her website, she offers her services for a "gentleman" who has

> never explored [his] feminine side but would like to with someone whose [sic] discreet and enthusiastic, wants to learn the arts of being a Goddess, loves receiving a "full make-over"—from make-up to garter belts, seeks a Personal Goddess Shopper who will help [him] pick out the finest fashions—from head to toe—so [he] can feel [his] best, would love to share [his] passion for "everything feminine" with a sexy gal who gets it.

First, in reading this, it is important to remember that this is not simply an "advertisement" as such, but rather a discursive act to provide meanings for (fluid) sexuality and sexual encounter. This is in and of itself an articulation of sexuality. Second, in addition to all of these, she will also help the man find his "feminine walk, voice, name, and attitude." This kind of "playful deviance" can become a safe site for these men to experience "self-validation" (Redmon 2003, quoted in Jones 2010: 257). As Daniel Downes (2005: 91) argues, "[P]lay allows us to leave the bonds of the social order for a while. The play space is safe; we can experiment without fear of extreme consequences. Play is distinct from ordinary life not only in locality but in duration." The Tantric clients are thus invited to come out and play with their sexuality, hence articulating their wikisexuality, even "if only for an hour or two."

Articulation of sexuality in this corner of the virtual world therefore seems to be about employing various modes of play and playing with various modes of being (sexual). Play is, according to James Hans, "a *structuring* activity, the activity out of which understanding comes" (Hans 1981: x). Play functions as a system of knowing, an epistemological act and activity that affects the lives of the players in all significant ways. Play thus requires that we constantly pay attention to the changes that would influence our mode of living and playing.

Play is also a site where power is exercised, articulated, and struggled over. It is through play that new reality and change occurs (Boulding 1988: 103; Edwards 1998: 6). On these websites, the play that these goddesses perform aims to heal, change, empower, and liberate. For example, the Tantric goddess of templeoftantra.com claims, "One of my specialties is working with women's issues for healing and empowerment. A place you can be seen, heard and 'held' by another sister." Similarly, another website advertises her service for women with "healing issues around sexuality and body image, undergoing a major transition such as marriage, divorce, motherhood, new career, seeking clear direction, feeling stuck in a life she knows she has outgrown, looking to gift herself with a healing, blissful journey with the Goddess."

Another purpose of play that these Tantric websites suggest is the breaking of taboos. For example, a session called dark tantra offers an absolute play experience that asks the client to leave their everyday roles and step into their non-essential self while being interactive and collaborative with the Tantric goddesses and surrendering to their power. This session starts with opening discussions over light repast and sparkling water, candle lit bath ceremony and then we will disappear into Dark Tantra either blind folded or not, depending on the client and his or her comfort level with me during Dark Tantra. THIS is of the utmost importance. We co-create the scenario together, experiment with role play, fetish and fantasy . . . (client must be the submissive . . . this is a requirement), and must easily be able to drop the "macho" masculine image or "frilly" feminine side carried with you on a daily basis, and turn it over to your Goddess . . . I require input from clients wishing Dark Tantra, and a letter of what you seek is of the utmost importance. These types of scenarios must be planned together, so speaking on the phone or even meeting in person to discuss your fantasies and explorations is vital for a successful session.

This example certainly highlights and provides evidence for how sexuality that is artic-ulated through play assumes a non-essentialist subject position. The client is invited to collaboratively co-create the scenario together with the goddess; his or her partici-pation is "vital" for having a successful and satisfying session. The goddess is open to working with people of all genders who must let go of their everyday role as "macho" or "frilly feminine," thereby further emphasizing the non-essentialist aspect of sexual-ity and gender. Lastly, the goddess explicitly uses the word "role-play" in describing the session, once again highlighting the important role of play and role-play as a mode of encountering others sensually.

These examples certainly show how play can be a method through which power is exercised. That is, the narratives constructed surrounding the rules of the game justify who and how one can play and who and what gets excluded (Nagel 2002: 1). For Miss Christina, her rule is "Only kind, upscale, attentive gentlemen admitted." Upscale is indeed the correct word; her advanced training costs about US$350 per hour. The average fee charged by these goddesses ranges from US$200 to US$350 per hour, or US$1000 per day. Workshops that are held in some popular tourist des-tinations (such as in Costa Rica, Bali, or Hawaii) usually run about US$2000 per person for about a week, not including airfare. What this suggests is that power and access to capital matters and determines even the question of who can play. Only people who have hundreds or thousands of disposable income dollars can participate in the play and feel the ultimate sensual happiness offered by these goddesses. This does not only provide us with an example of how the Internet "facilitates a capitalist framework for the management of sexual expression" but also how—although play has a possibility for leveling the playing field—there still exists inequality within the field of play (Jones 2010: 268). In other words, class may provide more possibilities in one's experimenting with their (sexual and gender) identity construction.

Conclusion

In this chapter, I have explained the concept of wikisexuality and how it can help us better understand complex sexuality in the digital era. But another, just as important, question that needs to be asked is: Do we need a label at all? Queer theorists argue that categorizations matter in the performances that they signify and the relationships and realities they create (Hemmings 2002: 8). Hence, it is obvious that because language matters—we make sense of the world through language—we do need a new category of sexuality such as wikisexuality that allows us to capture the fluidity of sexuality when we transgress these layers of virtual and physical realities.

Yet, another question follows: What happens when we claim and label ourselves as "wikisexuals"? In cyberspace, it is always easier to use readily available stereotypes to present ourselves to others because others can then easily construct who we are based on these existing stereotypes (Simpson 2005: 127). Sexual mapping has been rendered important, for it allows us to know where we or others are positioned within existing sexual categories so that we can proceed and create meanings of our encounters (O'Brien 1999: 84). The fact that wikisexual is not readily intelligible or understood will simply make it unknown to the other. To say that we are wikisexuals, to refuse to be known as a heterosexual, homosexual, bisexual, asexual, and so on, therefore upsets this sexual mapping and the encounters that follow. This is so because wikisexuality always suspends and fails to provide meanings to one's performative utterance (here, à la Austin, 1962). That is by saying "I am wikisexual," I do not perform my sexuality, nor do I wish to deny it. If at all, it only makes visible the performative tensions of such an utterance. In other words, when I proclaim myself to be wikisexual, the person hearing this statement cannot know whether I am interested in women or other genders. It can only invite more questions and conversations about sexuality and its fluidity. What I suggest here, therefore, is considering wikisexuality as a subversive mode of articulating and playing with one's sexual identity within the structure of cyberspace.

Moreover, wikisexuality also speaks to the anxiety some people might have about categories of sexuality in general. It is an anxiety that comes from having to *know* what our sexual orientation is and stick with it. And if we don't happen to be the normative heterosexuals, we have to prepare a narrative to explain why not. It is a similar anxiety that happens in the dating world when someone has to figure out if the person they are dating is "the one." When we challenge the myth of "the one," we release the pressure to somehow *know*, and simply focus on the process and playfulness of dating, the need to know if that person is "the one" becomes less significant. Similarly, framing sexuality as wikisexuality allows us to escape this anxiety because there is no essence (or "the one") to one's sexuality.

Certainly I am aware that suggesting wikisexuality as a new sexual category runs the risk of erasing, if not undermining, multiple narratives of sexuality in the mainstream arena. In some ways, this is precisely the point that I am working against. I do not propose this term as another homogenizing sexual category—that all human beings are similarly wikisexuals: to do that would betray the very notion of wikisexuality, a sexuality that is in constant formation and produced in collaboration with others and hence unique and context-specific. However, it is in being able to playfully claim that I am wikisexual that I can then challenge existing categorizations of sexuality and make visible the fluidity of sexuality. It is a hopeful start.

Note

A fuller, more definitive version of this paper has been published in Sexualities 16 (5/6), 2013: *587–603 by SAGE Publications Ltd. All rights reserved. © L. Ayu Saraswati.*

Bibliography

Austin, John. 1962. *How to Do Things With Words*. Oxford: Clarendon Press.

Barratt, Barnaby, and Marsha Rand. 2007. "On the Relevance of Tantric Practices for Clinical and Educational Sexology." *Contemporary Sexuality* 41(2): 7–12.

Ben-Ze'ev, Aaron. 2004. *Love Online: Emotions on the Internet*. New York: Cambridge University Press.

Boulding, Elise. 1988. *Building a Global Civic Culture: Education for an Interdependent World*. New York: Teachers College Press.

Brooks, Kelly, and Kathyrn Quina. 2009. "Women's Sexual Identity Patterns: Differences among Lesbians, Bisexuals, and Unlabeled Women." *Journal of Homosexuality* 56(8): 1030–1045.

Bryson, Mary, and Lori MacIntosh. 2010. "Can We Play Fun Gay? Disjuncture and Difference, and the Precarious Mobilities of Millennial Queer Youth Narratives." *International Journal of Qualitative Studies in Education* 23(1): 101–124.

Bullis, Ronald. 1998. "Biblical Tantra: Lessons in Sacred Sexuality." *Theology and Sexuality* 9: 101–116.

Chun, Wendy. 2006. *Control and Freedom: Power and Paranoia in the Age of Fiber Optics*. Cambridge, MA: MIT Press.

Dawson, Lorne. 2005. "The Mediation of Religious Experience in Cyberspace." In M. Højsgaard and M. Warburg (eds) *Religion in Cyberspace*, pp. 15–37. New York: Routledge.

Diamond, Lisa. 2009. *Sexual Fluidity: Understanding Women's Love and Desire*. Cambridge, MA: Harvard University Press.

Downes, Daniel. 2005. *Interactive Realism: The Poetics of Cyberspace*. Montreal: McGill-Queen's University Press.

Edwards, Brian. 1998. *Theories of Play and Postmodern Fiction*. New York: Garland Publishing.

Featherstone, Mike, and Roger Burrows, eds. 1995. *Cyberspace/Cyberbodies/Cyberpunk: Cultures of Technological Embodiment*. London: Sage Publications.

Gauntlett, David, and Ross Horsley, eds. 2004. *Web.Studies*. London: Arnold.

Gómez, Antonio. 2010. "Competing Narratives, Gender and Threaded Identity in Cyberspace." *Journal of Gender Studies* 19(1): 27–42.

Hans, James. 1981. *The Play of the World*. Amherst: University of Massachusetts Press.

Hemmings, Clare. 2002. *Bisexual Spaces: A Geography of Sexuality and Gender*. New York: Routledge.

Hutchins, Loraine. 2010. "Bisexual Women as Emblematic Sexual Healers and the Problematics of the Embodied Sacred Whore." *Journal of Bisexuality* 10(1/2): 191–207.

Jackson, Roger. 1992. "Ambiguous Sexuality: Imagery and Interpretation in Tantric Buddhism." *Religion* 22: 85–100.

Jhally, Sut. 1997. *Stuart Hall: Representation and the Media*. [videorecording] Media Education Foundation.

Jones, Matthew. 2010. "Mediated Exhibitionism: The Naked Body in Performance and Virtual Space." *Sexuality & Culture* 14: 253–269.

Küchler, Tilman. 1994. *Postmodern Gaming: Heidegger, Duchamp, Derrida*. New York: Peter Lang.

Lövheim, Mia and Alf Linderman. 2005. "Constructing Religious Identity on the Internet." In M. Højsgaard and M. Warburg (eds) *Religion in Cyberspace*, pp. 121–137. New York: Routledge.

Nagel, Mechthild. 2002. *Masking the Abject: A Genealogy of Play*. Lanham, Maryland: Lexington Books.

O'Brien, Jodi. 1999. "Writing in the Body: Gender (Re)Production in Online Interaction." In M. Smith and P. Kollock (eds) *Communities in Cyberspace*, pp. 76–104. London: Routledge.

Redmon, David. 2003. "Playful Deviance as an Urban Leisure Activity: Secret Selves, Self-Validation, and Entertaining Performances." *Deviant Behavior* 24: 27–51.

Ross, Michael. 2005. "Typing, Doing, and Being: Sexuality and the Internet." *The Journal of Sex Research* 42(4): 342–352.

Shaw, Miranda. 1994. *Passionate Enlightenment: Women in Tantric Buddhism*. Princeton: Princeton University Press.

Simpson, Brian. 2005. "Identity Manipulation in Cyberspace as a Leisure Option: Play and the Exploration of Self." *Information and Communications Technology Law* 14(2): 115–131.

Slevin, James. 2000. *The Internet and Society*. Cambridge: Polity Press.

Thomas, Sue. 2004. *Hello World: Travels in Virtuality*. York: Raw Nerve Books.

Urban, Hugh. 2003. *Tantra: Sex, Secrecy, Politics and Power in the Study of Religion*. Berkeley: University of California Press.

Ward, Anna. 2010. "Pantomimes of Ecstasy: BeautifulAgony.com and the Representation of Pleasure." *Camera Obscura* 25(1) 73: 161–195.

Waskul, Dennis. 2003. *Self-Games and Body-Play: Personhood in Online Chat and Cybersex*. New York: Peter Lang.

Waskul, Dennis, and Mark Douglass. 1997. "Cyberself: The Emergence of Self in On-Line Chat." *The Information Society* 13: 357–397.

Waskul, Dennis, Mark Douglass, and Charles Edgley. 2004. "Outercourse: Body and Self in Text Cybersex." In D. Waskul (ed.) *net.seXXX: Readings of Sex, Pornography, and the Internet*, pp. 13–33. New York: Peter Lang.

Waskul, Dennis, and Phillip Vannini. 2008. "Ludic and Ludic(rous) Relationships: Sex, Play, and the Internet." In S. Holland (ed.) *Remote Relationships in a Small World*, pp. 241–262. New York: Peter Lang.

White, David. 2003. *Kiss of the Yogini: "Tantric Sex" in Its South Asian Contexts*. Chicago: University of Chicago Press.

Zhao, Shanyang. 2005. "The Digital Self: Through the Looking Glass of Telecopresent Others." *Symbolic Interaction* 28(3): 387–405.

Websites

(All websites cited here were last accessed on 13 June 2011.)
http://c2.com/doc/etymology.html
www.sacredsensualist.com/about.html
www.awakenedloving.com/honoring-the-wisdom-of-the-yon/
www.partnerplayshop.com/OmSweetHome.html
http://tantradakini.com/events.htm
www.christinasecret.com
www.templeoftantra.com/forWomen.html
www.wayofbliss.com/Sessions.html
www.forevertantra.com/sessions.php
www.stardancertantra.com/lunalodge.html

chapter 43

"The thorn in my side"

How ex-gays, ex-ex-gays, and celibate gays negotiate their religious and sexual identities

S. J. Creek

It's no secret that religion significantly influences how many people understand and express sexuality. Countless sociologists have explored the extent to which our sexual behaviors, our identities, our relationships—all of these things—can be mediated by religion. Similarly, our religious identities, beliefs, and behaviors can also be impacted by our sexuality. Perhaps one of the clearest examples comes from the lives of women and men who have been a part of the ex-gay movement in North America.

The ex-gay movement is a network of para-church ministries, support groups, residential programs, supportive churches, and Christian therapists, aimed at helping people rid themselves of unwanted same-sex sexual attractions. The first professionalized ex-gay organization was created in 1976, a backlash against the sexual revolution and the gains of the gay and lesbian rights movement (particularly the de-pathologization of homosexuality by the American Psychological Association). Ex-gays believe that people can change their sexual orientation through the right combination of therapy and prayer. People who have same-sex attractions are not actually gay or lesbian, from this point of view. They are heterosexual at their core but through some set of childhood circumstances were knocked off course. In the face of "misguided" feelings, they have made the moral decision to claim a gay or lesbian identity and to act upon their same-sex sexual attractions. Though it has taken some decades to gain recognition within the Christian Right, the movement has arguably been a significant factor in changing how evangelicals talk about homosexuality (Stafford 2007).

Ex-gay ministries and other counselors who use therapeutic means to eradicate same-sex sexual attractions have been widely denounced by countless professional organizations, including the American Psychological Association, the American Psychiatric Association, National Association of Social Workers, and the American Medical Association (Lambda Legal 2011). Over the years there have also been a number of very public departures from the movement. Leaders like John Smid (Wong 2014), John Paulk (Schlanger and Wolfson 2014), Alan Chambers (Steffan 2013) and numerous others (Rhodan 2014) have left and denounced the movement. In 2012, the largest ex-gay organization, Exodus International, publicly apologized and shut its doors, though a smaller organization, the Restored Hope Network, has since taken the leadership reigns (Throckmorton 2012).

Through my own research of this movement, I spoke to both people actively involved and to people who left. I began my study by attending a week-long annual, national ex-gay conference, hosted by Exodus International. My days at this conference were full of praise sessions, workshops for women hoping to reclaim their "true femininity" and lose their same-sex desires, panels exploring compassionate pastoral response to ex-gay individuals, and speeches by leaders rallying members for the larger "battle" against homosexuality.

The second part of my research involved one-on-one interviews (across the U.S. and Canada) with people who had, at one point in their lives, sought help from an ex-gay ministry. While initially, I thought I would talk to two kinds of people—those who identified as ex-gay and remained involved in the movement and those who no longer identified as ex-gay and left the movement—I quickly realized I needed to add a third group. This group featured people caught in between, marginally connected to the movement and still avoiding same-sex sexual activity, yet identifying as gay and feeling they had nothing to "fix." For each of these groups, the balance of religion and sexuality was keenly felt and central to how they understood themselves. In the sections to follow, I explore the varied ways each grappled with religion and sexuality.

Of the seven women and eleven men, all but three were white. Two identified as Chinese, and one identified as Colombian. Research participants lived in the Southeastern United States, the Midwestern United States, or Eastern Canada, and all identified as Christian. Participants ranged in age from 19 to early 60s. Most were in their 30s or 40s. Each ex-gay individual in this study was affiliated with an ex-gay organization at the time. More identified as "a struggler" than "ex-gay," though they labeled the larger movement as "ex-gay." Thus, I will use that language interchangeably throughout this essay.

Ex-gay Christians: "The opposite of homosexuality is holiness"

In many ways, strugglers have their own "coming out" stories. Unlike the typical coming out stories that document and legitimate the process of claiming a lesbian, gay, bisexual, or queer identity, strugglers' stories do the opposite. Strugglers, often in conjunction with an ex-gay therapist and/or support group, tell their own story of *"coming out" of homosexuality*.

The primary focus for strugglers is finding their "root." The "root" is the circumstance or set of circumstances, usually in childhood, that pushed an individual onto the "wrong" track, (i.e. off course from their divinely designed heterosexuality). Any number of things can do the trick: a too-distant mother or father, a too-close mother or father, physical abuse, emotional abuse, mental abuse, sexual trauma, "inappropriate" messages about femininity or masculinity, irreligious parents, family instability, familial drug/alcohol abuse, neglect, or bullying by peers. "Digging up" the "roots" in a Christian therapeutic setting, according to strugglers, allowed them to address the issues head on, and, through that work, to diminish or even eradicate their same-sex attractions.

In the wake of sometimes traumatic pasts, strugglers reported the emergence of same-sex sexual attraction, usually in adolescence. Most, though not all, reported "acting out" on these feelings. For some, "acting out" refers to actual physical intimacy with a person of the same-sex, but it also can mean consuming gay pornography or masturbating to same-sex sexual fantasies. A few even had romantic gay or lesbian relationships. Those who engaged in sexual activity or relationships called this "entering the lifestyle."

Rather than finding relief or freedom from "entering the lifestyle," ex-gays noted intense feelings of shame, revulsion, emptiness, and isolation. Most of the ex-lesbians, like Lisa and Anise, emphasized how "unhealthy" and "codependent" their romantic female relationships were. Some, like Arthur and Miguel, were unhappy with their promiscuity and inability to maintain a relationship. Perhaps, the largest challenge was feeling "very far from God" (Gus). Nearly all of these relationships and sexual trysts were hidden from family, friends, and fellow church-goers. Ex-gays simmered silently in shame and isolation, a metaphorical ex-gay "closet."

Nearly every struggler's story contained a point where they were discovered. A friend, a spouse, a church-member, or spiritual leader learned that they were "acting out." This moment of reckoning usually coincided with a personal reflection that strugglers had "hit bottom"—that is, that they had reached a nearly unbearable level of depression, shame, and unhappiness. However challenging this reckoning and confrontation may have been, they reported relief at their secret being "out."

> You can't even imagine the shame that you will go through when you're in something like this . . . 'Cause, I mean, I would never ever . . . I would never do something like that. I could never sleep with a woman. Oh my gosh. You know, that's like a cardinal sin . . . And so I told my one friend, and I threw up when I told her. It was just like I had to tell someone and it just came out.
>
> (Annette: interview)

Shortly after the relief of this secret, a friend, relative, or pastor connected them with an ex-gay ministry. Through counseling, support group sessions, church support, and prayer, strugglers located their "roots" and moved away from shame. Even as they experienced the "mortification" of confessing their darkest secrets (Kanter 1972) their new religious therapeutic framework simultaneously promised them the opportunity to "transcend" (Kanter 1972) and "heal" from their homosexual pasts.

They met other people like them, which lessened their isolation. They also experienced community with other Christians. Many also discussed how "God's healing" manifested in their lives. Those who were married to partners of another sex indicated a greater love for their spouse. Some talked about diminished same-sex attractions. Others did not indicate a lessening of same-sex attraction, but spoke of the tools to deal with that attraction. When asked how they identified their sexual orientation, a bulk of participants said something like the following two passages (Creek and Dunn 2012: 315):

> What I can say is I'm a child of Christ; I'm a woman of Christ.
>
> (Constance)

> I guess it's more about receiving the grace of the Lord, and you know these things have been all washed away, and that your true identity really is Christ.
>
> (Timothy)

Both of the previous excerpts reflect the underlying meaning of a saying attributed to former ex-gay leader, Alan Chambers: "The opposite of homosexuality is holiness" (2009: 23). That is, homosexuality and Christianity are antithetical, and, yet, the point of seeking help from an ex-gay ministry is *not* necessarily to achieve heterosexuality. Rather, strugglers claim a religious identity in place of a sexual identity. To "change" orientation from this view point is not to flip a switch from "gay" to "straight" but from "gay" to "Christian."

Ex-ex-gays: "At the end of all the emotional hype, I was still gay"

For many people seeking help from an ex-gay ministry, a primary motivator is the desire to have a heterosexual marriage with kids. This was especially true for participants who eventually left the movement. These nine men and two women all identified as gay, except for one man who identified as a "Kinsey Scale 6 Queer." Nearly all were white, with one man identifying as tri-racial and one man identifying as African American. Most lived in the Midwest, though a few resided in the Mid-Atlantic, the Southeastern or the Western U.S. Nearly all were in their 20s to 30s, with one participant in his 60s.

Like the ex-gays in the last section, these individuals sought out an ex-gay ministry to help them eradicate their same sex desires. They attended support group meetings, visited ex-gay therapists, and took part in retreats. Most became heavily involved in online ex-gay communities. Some, like Taylor, did not spend even a full year working with an ex-gay ministry. Others, like Eric, Jonas, and Eli, spent several years working with an organization to change. Collaborating with others, they revisited their biographies, located their "roots" (with varying degrees of success), and tried to craft their own ex-gay "coming out" narratives.

As they continued in the movement, though, most were troubled by the growing nuance from leaders regarding the meaning of "change." Ex-ex-gays commonly shared feeling that leaders had pulled a "bait and switch," promising them a change in orientation in the beginning, but later emphasizing "holiness" instead. Taylor, who sought help from an online ministry for about eight months with little success, finally emailed the leader of the ministry to ask for guidance:

> [S]he told me it was about holiness, not orientation. That's when I got really confused . . . the term ex-gay in itself, say you're ex something, and gay meaning an orientation, means you're ex that orientation. So now if you tell me it's not about the orientation, then I have an issue 'cause you've been telling me all along by the very term that it's about orientation . . .
>
> (Creek 2014: 146–147)

Taylor's words reflect a common frustration among ex-ex-gays, a sense that the change being offered was not nearly as effective as initially promised. This was compounded by experiences at ex-gay conferences, where participants reported meeting people who claimed to be "changed," but whose behaviors suggested otherwise.

Seeing no change in orientation over time, many ex-ex-gays reported experiencing depression, unhappiness, isolation, and uncertainty. One participant, Jonas, became suicidal, which caused him to very seriously reflect on his relationship to the ex-gay movement.

> I meditated on a very simple thing that was written that Jesus said about trees and fruits. You can judge a tree by the fruit that it bears. A good tree bears good fruit, a bad tree bears bad fruit. And in that analogy, I thought I'm surrounded by bad fruit, a pile of rotting fruit. But I didn't understand why, I was doing everything I thought was right, you know? I hadn't touched any men . . . Something is wrong here. I don't know what's wrong here, but something I'm doing here is wrong. So I wrote a letter to my counselor and said I can't come back to counseling until I've got myself stabilized. I returned to grad school in the fall, and wasn't doing the counseling thing. Just kind of holding the ex-gay thing at arm's length. Not truly rejecting it . . . And then, boy meets boy. I met Jeff. But it was different this time. Every other time I had a thought, I shut it down, I aborted it as sin. But this time, "I've been doing this all my life," I thought, "let's see where this goes."
>
> (Creek 2014: 148–149)

Eventually, each of these eleven participants left the ex-gay movement. They were unable to change their orientation, despite sometimes years of prayer and therapy. They had come to doubt the success stories touted at ex-gay conferences, and more than a few felt they had been lied to by ex-gay leaders. As Eli put it: "At the end of all the emotional hype, I was still gay."

For the ex-gays in the previous section, their conservative Christian identities were the most salient identities they held. When asked their sexual orientation, they often pointed instead to their Christian identity. For ex-ex-gays, though, religious identities simply would not serve as a substitute. By leaving the movement, ex-ex-gays had to accept that a "change" in orientation was not coming. By admitting that "change" was not coming, ex-ex-gays had to consider that they may indeed be gay. Taking on a gay identity, then, meant reassessing their conservative Christian identity. For Rocky, that reassessment led him to an LGBTQ-friendly denomination, Metropolitan Community Church. Jonas found a Quaker church. Erik began exploring postmodern Christian writing and the emergent church movement. Nathan reported having a hard time finding a new "spiritual home." Ex-ex-gays in this study offered a compelling example of sexuality informing how individuals understand their religious identity and beliefs. A religious identity that cannot fully explain or make room for unceasing same-sex attractions was simply "unlivable" (Nathan).

Gay celibate Christians: "Nobody gets us"

Between the two poles of "ex-gay" and "ex-ex-gay," there was a third, smaller group: celibate gay men and women. These participants held to conservative Christian ideology, believed acting upon same-sex sexual attractions was morally wrong, and identified as gay. At the time of their interviews, two were affiliated with an ex-gay organization, two were affiliated with a ministry that helped people manage their sexual attractions but condoned gay identities, and one had since renounced such ministries entirely. All identified as Christian, and all eschewed same-sex sexual activity. All were white, ranging in age from late 20s to early 40s. These four men and one woman resided in the Midwestern U.S. or in Eastern Canada.

Time with one or more ex-gay ministries led these individuals to conclude that their sexual orientation was not going to change. Yet, unlike most people who leave the movement, they continued to believe that acting on their attractions was wrong. Thus, three remained single and celibate. One man, Walter, had long been married to a woman. Another man, Allen, married a woman who also struggled with same-sex attraction. He explained the rationale underpinning their decision to marry: "[I]f the choice is being celibate alone, or celibate together, I'd rather be celibate together, and if sex doesn't work in the relationship, I still want to spend the rest of my life with you."

Allen and Walter were better able to deflect criticism of their gay identification because they were married to women (though this was not true across the board, as I will discuss later). For the other three participants, Erin, Jack, and James, claiming this identity in conservative Christian spaces presented some challenges. All three worked to counter pre-existing ideas about what "gay" meant, or even avoided disclosing their identity, if necessary. James, for instance, shared, "I tend to categorize myself as a gay, celibate Christian, but I am very hesitant using that because. . .in evangelical Christian subculture it [gay] means: 'sleeps with everybody five days a week. Might take a couple of nights off just out of sheer exhaustion'" (Creek 2013: 131).

Each of the gay celibates in this study had relationships with both ex-gay and ex-ex-gay people, a circumstance that offered community and conflict. On the one hand, both ex-gays and ex-ex-gays understand a significant part of the dilemma faced by gay celibate Christians, and this mutual understanding was the basis of many friendships. "They continue to be some of the most important significant relationships. And even those that are in very different spaces from me," Allen shared.

On the other hand, at times, both ex-gays and ex-ex-gays challenged gay celibate Christians on their sexual identities and behaviors and their religious beliefs. In ex-gay settings, for example. Allen sometimes found his identity attacked on theological grounds.

> [T]hey would say, the charismatic ones would always put it in, "It allows entry into evil spirits." . . . Or others would say, "It's the language of bondage." "It's idola- trous language." And I'm like, "It's no more idolatrous for me to say 'I'm gay'— it's describing a situation of my life—anymore than me saying, 'I'm American' is idolatrous." And, you know, yeah, it's an important part of my identity, that doesn't mean that it's the central part. You know? They always seem to say, "If you say that you're gay, then that means that you're sinner, that's the center part of your identity."
>
> (Creek 2013: 129)

Similarly, in ex-ex-gay or gay settings, gay celibates were also questioned. Jack lamented problems he and others have encountered on a gay Christian online forum.

> [Non-celibate gays] will come into the [gay celibate] forum and ask a very honest, but loaded question. Two or three of us will respond, and then they'll start the debate. "I disagree because, dah, dah, dah.". . . And we say, "Wait a minute, this is our safe space." I even said to [a friend] the other night, "Well, sometimes I just wish that there was a place just for us"
>
> (Creek 2013: 130)

Each of these settings—ex-gay and ex-ex-gay—remained crucial to gay, celibate Chris- tians because of the connections and relationships they represented. Celibacy met a variety of their needs and complemented their identities, while also creating a lack of intimacy and companionship. In the absence of this kind of contact, friendships, par- ticularly friendships rooted in an understanding of the struggle between religion and sexuality, were extremely important.

Conclusion

Each participant in this study had to balance the expectations of conservative Christi- anity with their very real same-sex sexual attractions. How they ultimately managed this balance held significant implications for their sexual identities, sexual behaviors, and religious identities. The groups explored in this essay represent three possible paths.

Ex-gay women and men argued that their "identities in Christ" were the most important identities they held, and, regardless of the degree of cessation of unwanted sexual attraction, they were unwilling to identify as "gay" or "lesbian." To do so, they believed, would directly compromise their religious identities. This group was older than the other two groups, and less likely to have engaged with online ex-gay minis- tries. They were more willing to embrace nuanced understandings of "change" and to accept that they might never be free of same-sex sexual attraction.

Ex-ex-gays, or people who left the ex-gay movement, were ultimately frustrated with the lack of change in their orientation. Despite prayer and therapy, their attractions did not abate, and heterosexual marriage and kids remained an elusive goal. Eventually, they embraced their sexual attractions and a "gay" identity, and instead begin to reframe their religious identity. Some abandoned the label "Christian" altogether, while others reworked the meaning of the label "Christian" to one that had room for their changing sexual identities and behaviors.

Finally, celibate gay Christians were unwilling to let go of both their conservative Christian identity and their belief in the immorality of acting on same-sex attractions. Yet, they also believed identifying as gay was an honest reflection of who they were. It was not, as ex-gays contended, "idolatrous."

The lives of these women and men are of interest to sociologists of religion and sociologists of sexualities, because they are such a clear example of how religious and sexual identities inform one another. While their experiences of these men and women may seem extreme to those unfamiliar with the ex-gay movement, the experience of juggling the demands of religion with the realities of one's sexuality is a widespread experience that transcends time and cultural context. Be we devout or atheist, a closer examination of our own sexual identities and behaviors (and of public policy and laws that regulate those very behaviors and identities) will undoubtedly show the influence of religion. Such an examination might also yield the knowledge that our shifting views on sexuality have, at one time or another, influenced our religious beliefs, behaviors, and labels.

References

Chambers, Alan. 2009. *Leaving Homosexuality: A Practical Guide for Men and Women Looking for a Way Out*. Eugene, OR: Harvest House Publishers.

Creek, S. J. 2014. "'Mindful of the Words Spoken': The Shifting Narratives and Identity Work of Former Ex-Gay Young Adults" in *Queering Religion, Religious Queers* edited by Ria Snowden and Yvette Taylor, pp. 137–157. New York: Routledge.

—. 2013. "'Not Getting Any Because of Jesus': The Centrality of Desire Management to the Identity Work of Gay, Celibate Christians." *Symbolic Interaction* 36(2): 119–136.

Creek, S. J. and Jennifer L. Dunn. 2012. "'But Be Ye Transformed': The Sexual Storytelling of Ex-gay Participants." *Sociological Focus* 45(4): 306–319.

Kanter, Rosabeth. 1972. *Commitment and Community: Communes and Utopias in Sociological Perspective*. Cambridge, MA: Harvard University Press.

Lambda Legal. 2011. "Health and Medical Organization Statements on Sexual Orientation, Gender Identity/Expression and 'Reparative Therapy.'" Retrieved February 1, 2015 www.lambdalegal.org/publications/health-and-med-orgs-stmts-on-sex-orientation-and-gender-identity).

Rhodan, Maya. 2014. "9 Ex-Leaders of the Gay Conversion Therapy Movement Apologize." *Time* July 31. Retrieved on February 1, 2015 (http://time.com/3065495/9-ex-leaders-of-the-gay-conversion-therapy-movement-apologize/).

Schlanger, Zoe and Elijah Wolfson. 2014. "Ex-Ex-Gay Pride." *Newsweek*, May 1. Retrieved February 1, 2015 (www.newsweek.com/ex-ex-gay-pride-249282).

Stafford, Tim. 2007. "An Older, Wiser Ex-gay Movement." *Christianity Today* October, 51(10): 48.

Steffan, Melissa. 2013. "Alan Chambers Apologizes to Gay Community, Exodus International to Shut Down." *Christianity Today* June 21. Retrieved February 3, 2015 (www.christianitytoday.

com/gleanings/2013/june/alan-chambers-apologizes-to-gay-community-exodus.html? paging=off).

Throckmorton, Warren. 2012. "A Look Inside the Restored Hope Network." Retrieved February 3,2015 (www.patheos.com/blogs/warrenthrockmorton/2012/08/03/a-look-inside-the-restored-hope-network/).

Wong, Curtis M. 2014. "John Smid, Former 'Ex-Gay' Leader, Marries a Man in Oklahoma." *The Huffington Post* November 19. Retrieved on February 1, 2015 (www.huffingtonpost.com/2014/11/19/john-smid-ex-gay-wedding-_n_6186524.html).

PART 7

Sexuality, media, and commerce

Introduction

"Sex sells." We hear this often and we can see ample evidence of how it has become the norm. In the media (whether in magazines, television, or websites), we constantly encounter sexualized images (usually *hetero*sexualized images) meant to sell everything from clothing to cleaning products. Check out the blog "The Society Pages" and type "sex sells" into the search box – you will see posts about sexy-looking M&Ms, women athletes portrayed primarily in terms of their sexy appearance, and even CPR promoted as sexy.

This raises the question – who sells sex to whom and under what conditions?

The media is the key social institution that uses sex to sell. Television programs, films, magazine articles, and best-selling novels all produce stories that script the expression of romance in a relationship, how a sexual encounter is supposed to unfold and how individuals are supposed to act when they are turned on. While the media should not be assumed to accurately represent what *most* people think or do, media stories can reveal the social dynamics of the dominant sexual culture, as in who has power to tell which sexual stories to a large audience.

The film industry that produces movies, television shows and music videos is a capital-intensive industry which puts a high price of admission on who can tell stories because of the high cost of filming and distribution; not just anyone has the ability to make a feature film that will reach a mass audience. Thus it's useful to ask, who is positioned in the media's sexual stories as *subjects* – those who make decisions and have others catering to their needs? Who is positioned as *objects* – people who are acted upon in a sexualized way, gazed at for pleasure and scripted to act in ways that please those with more status and power? Most film (including porn) and television stories feature straight white upper-class men in positions of power whose desires are fulfilled (usually) by white women with particular "ideal" body types and looks. Not coincidentally, this reflects the demographics and perspectives of film executives and screenwriters. Cisgender heterosexuals are usually positioned as normal and central to most media stories, while those who identify on the GLBTQIA spectrum are often secondary characters. Likewise, in our racialized society, most media sexual stories view white bodies as more desirable and worth of respect.

What about digital media – Twitter, websites, YouTube videos, blogs, or Instagram? Unlike the film industry, the cost of participation is low for producing sexual stories and images; getting a domain name and/or starting an account on Tumblr is relatively low-cost and correspondingly a greater diversity of people participate. The Internet has been key for sharing diverse perspectives from queer folk of color, trans* identities, genderqueer, gender fluid, sexually fluid, and asexual individuals who post videos, photos, and tell their stories. The LGBTQIA presence on the Internet has helped carve out more social space for alternative sexual and gender voices. But digital media is also a place where the dominant (hegemonic) culture is reinforced – for every queer person of color posting on Tumblr, there are probably a dozen young white straight women posting sexy photos of themselves on Instagram. Thus, digital media both reinforce and challenge the dominant sex-selling culture.

Relatedly, we can ask, who is asked to sell sex? Who labors in the sex industries and under what labor conditions? The porn industry – like the mainstream film industry – tends to reflect the same social dynamics with cisgender men as subjects and women as objects, and white bodies more highly valued than people of color. People who are employed in the sex industries find ways for their work to be meaningful, just as in other industries, with some even leaving the mainstream porn industry to present alternative perspectives and stories.

As capital-intensive media and digital media co-exist, they will continue to influence one another, with digital media continuing to both reinforce and challenge dominant sexual stories. The chapters in this section explore this tension between reinforcing and challenging the culture's dominant sexual stories.

chapter 44

Popular culture constructs sexuality

Interview with Joshua Gamson

Joshua Gamson is a Professor of Sociology at the University of San Francisco. He is the author of *Claims to Fame: Celebrity in Contemporary America* (University of California Press, 1994), *Freaks Talk Back: Tabloid Talk Shows and Sexual Nonconformity* (University of Chicago Press, 1998), *The Fabulous Sylvester: The Legend, The Music, The Seventies in San Francisco* (Henry Holt, 2005), and *Extraordinary Kin: Inside the New World of Unconventional Family Creation* (NYU, 2015).

You wrote two books on popular culture. What is it about popular culture that fascinates you?

I'm first of all just interested in everyday life, and so much of everyday life gets its texture from popular culture – whether it's from commercial culture, or from more organic, self-created forms of culture. Pop culture is a common currency, and in this society there aren't that many things the whole population shares; the United States is so diverse, and just so huge, that commonalities are relatively rare, and mostly they come from pop culture. I also find thinking about popular culture challenging, because it so often combines social significance with tremendous superficiality. It's important almost by definition – it's the sea in which we swim, and to a large degree it sets the terms and boundaries of imagination; it is where discussions central to social life take place. But often the experience of pop culture, especially commercially produced culture, is thin, fleeting, and not that deeply felt or thought through. I find that combination intriguing. And finally, I'm interested in the politics of pop culture. There's this interesting tension between a sort of "top down" version of popular culture, in which people who control major cultural institutions create and manage what gets out there, and a "bottom up" version of popular culture, in which people at a more grass-roots level make up their own stuff. I think those dynamics are important and interesting to understand.

In general, how do you see popular culture influencing or shaping sexuality?

There are a few ways this happens. Sexual statuses, populations, behaviors, and so on, all get processed through popular culture. Some become visible in it, others are rendered invisible; some are celebrated or treated as legitimate, others are denigrated or delegitimated. So popular culture affects who and what gets on the cultural map in the first place, and proposes ways of thinking about sexualities. (Some people think popular culture *determines* how people think about sexuality, but I don't think that's quite right.) So, for instance, for a long time there were just very few stories being told publicly about homosexuality, and those that were – in movies, in novels, and so forth – were mostly about the tragic lives of people presented as diseased. Obviously, gay people are now far from invisible in popular culture – gay and lesbian lead characters are now routine on television fiction and gay people have been fixtures on reality television for a long time now. Advertising explicitly targets lesbians and gay men. We have a critical mass of openly gay celebrities and entertainers, and I cannot possibly keep track any longer of all the films and books with gay content. Before that change in the popular culture, it was hard to make the argument for gay rights and respect, since people who don't exist don't get rights, and people who are sick are usually put away. Now, with the change in popular culture, we face a radically different environment with a different set of challenges: the conservative backlash against gay visibility; the commercialization and sanitizing of a lot of lesbian and gay life as it becomes mainstreamed in pop culture; the attempt to set off "good" gays (monogamous, gender-normative) from "bad" ones (promiscuous, gender-nonconforming).

Popular culture also is the main site of public discussion of sexualities, whether in the form of fictional or nonfictional representations – a CNN report on same-sex marriage or an episode of *Modern Family* – or in the sorts of public controversies that are a cultural constant. Pop culture is a kind of forum – a structured one, in which only some people get to speak, but a forum nonetheless. Ideas about sexuality are proposed, and people take those into everyday life. Even things that might appear trivial, like the "leaking" of nude celebrity selfies or speculation about an actor's homosexuality, can be significant moments when people are publicly debating whether and how sex should be publicly visible, battling out sexual norms. These discussions are also important for affecting what gets on the policymaking agenda around sexuality, and often also in how policy decisions are resolved. How sexuality is framed is especially crucial here, I think. So when poor African American women's sexuality is framed in popular culture as "out of control," for example, it is easier for policymakers to justify something like forced sterilization; when the frame of "gayness is a natural difference" is dominant, it is harder to justify discriminatory policies. In fact, advocates and political actors are well aware of the significance of cultural framing, and often seek to shape it to their advantage.

I also think popular culture is simply a central source of how people imagine themselves as sexual beings: they see images and hear stories about what sex can or should look like, what kinds of relationships are available to be had, and so on, and these become the source material for building their sexual identities and practices. For example, in recent years popular culture has involved much, much more open discussion of women's sexuality, and not just of women as passive servants to male sexual needs. It's one thing for a woman to grow up with the "happy homemaker pleasing her man" images and stories that dominated pop culture of earlier decades, and quite another for a woman to see hookups on reality tv shows from *The Real World* to *The Bachelorette*, or reruns of *Sex in the City* in which women discuss masturbation and orgasms, and are shown, literally, pursuing their own pleasure, or even the polyamorous, in-control sexuality of female vampires on a show like *True Blood*. This has been met, not surprisingly, by images in pop culture that amount to what many people call "slut shaming," in which women are criticized for sexual agency, but the point remains that images of female sexual agency are now more available both for public debate and as fodder for people's identities and practices.

What do you think are some of the big changes in the way popular culture views sexuality over the last few decades?

It's been a strange few decades. On the one hand, there has been a massive opening up of pop-cultural images and discussions of sexuality, to the point where homosexuality – while still obviously controversial – is presented on television, for instance, in a diverse set of genres, with an increasingly diverse range of gay and lesbian characters, and in storylines or formats that are quite flattering to gay people. This is a huge dramatic change, given that in the fifties and sixties homosexuality was barely visible in popular culture, and when it was, it was usually presented as a sad, sick, stigmatized existence. Homosexuality is out of the pop-culture closet, to the degree that we've had entire tv shows – from *Will & Grace* to *Modern Family* and pay cable series like *The L Word*, *Queer as Folk* and *Looking* – and even entire tv networks, built around gay life. Now, with shows like *Orange Is the New Black* and *Transparent*, we're seeing a parallel emergence of pop culture in which transgender people are visible as self-possessed, three-dimensional characters. Similarly, as I suggested earlier, while a few decades ago the idea that women could be sexual subjects rather than only objects, that women could be in control of their own sexuality, was not all that prevalent in popular culture, now, images of women making decisions about who and how to be, sexually, are commonplace. On the other hand, the last few decades have also seen both a huge backlash – with consistent attempts to desexualize popular culture, to re-closet the ideas and images that have become part of pop culture – and a major expansion of exploitation of sexuality, especially women's sexuality, for selling.

Of course, the Internet has also radically changed the dynamics of pop cultural representations of sexuality. In many ways cultural production has been decentralized, and the costs of making and disseminating pop culture have been vastly reduced, so that one doesn't need to be a well-resourced production company to make pop culture that represents sexual practices, identities, ideas, and communities. That widened range of ideas and images about sexuality – including stuff that most television would never consider due to regulation, advertiser concerns, and risk aversion – is now so easy to access. To me, the pop cultural view on sexuality has become much more fragmented and anarchic – in many ways (though I hesitate a bit in saying this) the Internet appears to have liberated sexual imagery from the confines of pop cultural organizations that, as businesses, are inherently cautious.

You studied daytime talk shows in Freaks Talk Back. *Why? What did you find in your research?*

Mainly because daytime talk shows were among the first significant sites of consistent discussion of lesbian, gay, bisexual, and transgender issues in popular culture, and also because they are places where people actually speak for themselves – sometimes edited, always constrained, often distorted, but at least speaking. I thought the talk shows of the 1970s to 1990s would be a great place to go to understand how stigmatized sexualities became visible in popular culture, what kinds of visibility were available and why, what happened to the sexuality discourse when the genre changed (becoming, in the case of talk shows, more "tabloid"), and just how public discussions and spectacles of sexuality operated.

I found that, although there was certainly plenty of degrading and exoticizing and stigmatizing content in the shows, that was neither the most significant nor the most interesting aspect of them. After just a little while into the research process, I began to take the exploitation of sexual and gender minorities as a starting premise. Of course, shows built on conflict, taboo subjects, sensationalizing, and so on, were using their guests for entertainment purposes. But one of the most interesting findings was that exploitation and voice were not mutually exclusive, and that the people presented on the shows as "freaks" were often given, and took, plenty of space to talk back, and they often got a lot of support from the studio audiences for doing so. In fact, in the earlier version of the genre, the more middle-class debate shows like *Donahue*, people were invited to testify and demystify their sexual identities, and were treated as experts on their own experience. Even in the newer version of the genre, the louder, scrappier, nastier shows like *Springer*, oftentimes the anti-gay bigots were the ones who really got raked over the coals. Another interesting finding was that the kind of gay, lesbian, bisexual, and transgender visibility on the more tabloid shows was much, much more diverse in terms of race and class than on the older, more staid shows, which were almost exclusively white and middle-class. Sexual minorities also became, oddly, more incidental, mixed into programming that was about something else. For instance, a show on "You stole my boyfriend!" would have a gay storyline thrown into the mix. Finally, I found that, when I looked more closely at just who was being degraded and treated as bizarre, it was really not sexual minorities in general, but people who departed from conventional gender norms or monogamy norms. None of this means we should celebrate talk shows as advocates for sexual minorities, but that the picture was much more complicated than degrading or bizarre portrayals.

Some researchers argue that the media today promotes stereotyped views of gay men and lesbians; others argue that the media champions images of gays and lesbians as normal or ordinary Americans. What view is supported by your research?

As I implied in my response about talk shows, it seems obviously to be both, and the important question – at the center of a lot of my research – has to do with the conditions and forces that drive in one direction or the other. You have to break it down, I think: how the stereotype vs. normalized process plays out has to do with which particular medium and industry and genre you're looking at. For instance, various wings of the media have clearly discovered that images of gays and lesbians can be profitable, for attracting both a gay niche audience and straight audiences. But there are different strategies for doing so. If you look at advertising images aimed directly at gays and lesbians, you see more "normal" images, partly because advertisers have an interest in seeing lesbians and gay men as normal and predictable consumers; if you look at films marketed to teenaged boys, you still see a fair amount of gratuitous and old-fashioned gay stereotyping, since that's familiar and comfortable to the market being pursued. If you look at programming on a network like Logo, which makes its money by targeting a core LGBT audience, you find shows like *RuPaul's Drag Race*, which presents its own unapologetic, gender-transgressive, queer world.

Oftentimes, you get both normalization and stereotyping at once. For instance, openly gay men are abundant in reality television, especially in the style and makeover genres. Those shows have none of the sick-and-self-hating stereotypes, no interest whatsoever in the closet, and the gay men there are emulated by the straights they're in charge of transforming. Their sexuality itself is uncontroversial. But the shows also often promote certain old stereotypes (gay men are more "cultured" than straight ones) and generate new ones (gay men are in charge of instructing straight people in how to be good consumers). The news coverage of gay marriage countered the stereotype of lesbians and gay men as "different," while also further stigmatizing those gays and lesbians who choose different relationship frameworks than monogamous coupling. All that complicated stuff aside, though, I think the overall trend has been towards images of certain gays and lesbians (gender-conforming ones, in particular) as normal, ordinary, even possibly boring.

What are your chief criticisms of the way the mass media presents sexuality, and especially sexual minorities?

My chief criticisms are just that the mass media have not yet made enough room for all kinds of sexualities to be visible and thoughtfully considered; that they still proceed, for the most part, from a heterosexist worldview, in which they speak to their audience as if everyone were heterosexual; and that the images of sexual and gender minorities currently available remain quite narrow racially and class-wise. The coverage still often centers around sexual minorities as sources of controversy and conflict (always a good way to attract an audience, but not always so in touch with the actual experience being presented), or on "good gays" versus "bad gays."

As someone who wrote a book on celebrity culture, can you comment on the relationship between celebrities and sexual politics? Has it changed in the past few decades?

I do think there have been some major changes in this arena, though less when it comes to feminist sexual politics than when it comes to LGBT politics. Female celebrities, especially from the music world, have been challenging ideas about female sexuality, and female power more generally, for decades – I'm thinking of people from

Janis Joplin to Tina Turner to Joan Jett to Madonna to Beyoncé, who in various ways have embodied or articulated, if not always without contradiction, a version of female power that is assertive and sexual. That tradition, and the controversies it generates, continues. I think the changes are more pronounced when it comes to the relationship between celebrities and LGBT politics, in part simply because of the mainstreaming of lesbian and gay, and to a lesser degree bisexual and transgender, politics, and the liberalization of attitudes towards sexual and gender difference in younger generations especially. Celebrity is often built and maintained through identification, so that the fan has a sense of affinity and intimacy with the celebrity; the public image is managed and controlled in order to attract and sustain loyal attention. One element of this is public support for causes. Over the past few decades, support for lesbian and gay equality has gone from being a stance that might risk alienating a celebrity's fans to the opposite, especially for celebrities who seek a younger fan base. You can see that in the outpouring of celebrity support for same-sex marriage, or in the celebrity participation in phenomena such as the "It Gets Better" campaign. (I expect over the coming decade we will start to see a similar thing in the area of transgender politics.) That kind of public embrace by celebrities of the fight for LGBT rights and freedom is a remarkable and relatively new thing.

There's also a simpler and more obvious change. The number of openly gay, lesbian, bisexual, and transgender celebrities has increased greatly over the past decades, and picked up steam in recent years. Sometimes this has involved coming out, which for years has been a signature "personal-is-political" of gay politics, as with folks like Ellen DeGeneres, Ricky Martin, Rosie O'Donnell, Meredith Baxter, Anderson Cooper, Ellen Page, and Matt Bomer. What strikes me is that the coming out of a celebrity closet is no longer big news. Now we have gay celebrity marriages on the pages of *People* magazine, mixed in with heterosexual ones. Maybe more significantly, we see celebrities emerge who have never really been closeted, such as *Glee*'s Kurt Hummel and Alex Newell, Adam Lambert, and Laverne Cox. That's the start of a bigger change. All of this celebrity outness is another way in which some aspects of sexuality and gender politics have been moved forward by popular culture: a politics of integration and assimilation, of the "normalizing" of sexual and gender difference.

With the closet door opening in popular culture, and with hit shows like Glee *and* Modern Family, *is homophobia still a force in Hollywood?*

First, the closet door has been opened but not smashed. And even as homophobia diminishes, heterosexism is still a powerful force in pop cultural industries. I think this has less to do with individual attitudes, which tend to be quite liberal in Hollywood, but with how cultural industries work. As I've emphasized, industry-based pop cultural production is typically a high-investment, high-uncertainty endeavor, and this breeds a decision-making logic that hedges bets, minimizes risks, plays it safe, and looks towards previous successes. It's still hard to convince an executive that it's worth casting an openly gay actor in a leading heterosexual role, risking audience disbelief, rather than an avowedly heterosexual one who does not raise that issue. (Tellingly, casting an avowedly heterosexual actor in a gay role doesn't seem to raise the same issues, but instead is seen as demonstrating his acting chops. That double standard, although a step past the older, still prominent claim that "playing gay" is career suicide, seems to rest plainly on homophobia.) Pop cultural producers only stray from tried-and-true conventions under rare conditions, and the fare produced remains, on the whole, relentlessly heterosexual and heterosexist. This is perhaps clearest in children's and teen programming, which operates still as if all children have one mom and one dad and as if all teenagers are seeking attention from and romance with the "opposite" sex. Despite all the changes I've described, the logic of mass pop cultural production keeps it well within a framework that assumes and reiterates conventional, heteronormative understandings of gender and sexuality.

chapter 45

"She isn't whoring herself out like a lot of other girls we see"

Heteronormative propriety and "authentic" American girlhood on Taylor Swift fan forums

Adriane Brown

On the Taylor Swift fansite *Taylor Connect*, threads such as "The Swiftie Code" establish behavioral norms for Taylor Swift fans (sometimes referred to as "Swifties"), based on fans' readings of her songs and her personal life. For instance, Taylor Changed My Life writes:

> A Swiftie strives to . . .
> Stays true to themselves, and doesn't change for anyone.
> Believes in love, prince charming, and fairytales.

SamSam adds:

> A swifte strives to:
> not be afraid to cry on the
> bathroom floor
> still believe in love and in love
> stories fight for what you believe in

This discussion board thread demonstrates the ways that Taylor Swift's music and persona serve as a kind of model that young girl fans attempt to live up to. On discussion boards, fans assert that Taylor sings about subjects that are relevant not only to teenage girls, but to everyone, such as falling in love, feeling like an outsider and coping with heartbreak. However, while fans assert that Swift is universally relatable, they also position her as a beacon of morality because of her adherence to standards of white heteronormative propriety, and there is little acknowledgement of the ways that these two discourses are contradictory. TaylorChangedMyLife and SamSam identify two themes that run through discussions about "The Swiftie Code": staying true to yourself, and believing in love. Yet, the notion of "being true to oneself" is mediated through heteronormative terms of femininity and sentimentality: "prince charming," "fairy tales," and "cry[ing] on the bathroom floor."

"Propriety" generally denotes conformity to accepted standards of morality; however, it is also implicitly and inextricably tied to femininity. Girls are exhorted to act like "proper young ladies" or "good girls" by covering up all hints of sexuality—keeping their legs together when wearing a dress, refraining from engaging in explicit sex talk in public, and concealing contraceptives in drawers and cutesy containers. While there is increasing acceptance of the once-scandalous notion that young women *have* sex, dialogue about young women's sexual *desire* is still frequently suppressed. White women in particular are characterized as bearers of sexual propriety, both historically and contemporarily. Girls of color are instead conceptualized as inherently tainted, incapable of sexual innocence and thus acceptable targets for white fantasies of sexual violence (Odem 1995). White girls, on the other hand—especially blonde, blue-eyed ones—are upheld as chaste and sexually unattainable.

I also contend that the demand for propriety is inherently heteronormative—that is, built around the assumption that heterosexuality is the normal and desired sexual orientation. While heterosexual romance can easily be represented as chaste—look no further than the plethora of princess films marketed to preschoolers—queerness is often taken to be immediately and irrevocably sexual, unfit for children's eyes and ears (Edelman 2004). Thus, propriety involves walking a tightrope of displaying chaste heterosexual romantic interest but not explicit heterosexual desire.

Celebrity culture provides a particularly useful focal point for analyzing societal discourses around propriety. Celebrities' personal lives become part of their media persona and their appeal to fans, particularly in an era shaped by social media. The celebrity girl represents the embodiment of both girls' and adults' cultural fantasies about who girls are and who they should be, and there is no celebrity who currently fulfills these fantasies more than Taylor Swift. She has won hundreds of awards, including multiple Grammys, Billboard Music Awards, and two Country Music Awards Entertainer of the Year award, a prize typically reserved for artists who have been successful for decades. Although Swift is in her twenties, media and fan rhetoric still explicitly and implicitly reference her girl-ness, labeling her "the girl next door," "an ordinary girl," and "a girl just like me." Even Swift herself insists that she is "a lot of things. Overtly sexy is not one of them" (Access Hollywood 2015). Swift's demure attitude, conservative dress, and valorization of romantic (but not sexual) love situate her as an ideal carrier for societal investments in protecting, upholding, and promoting the propriety of middle class white girls.

This chapter examines the forum sections of two websites devoted to Taylor Swift: *Taylor Connect*, Swift's official website, and *Taylor Swift Web*, a popular fan-produced website. Adolescent girl fans on these sites insist that Taylor Swift is an ordinary girl just like them, and they continually suture her musical and extratextual personas by emphasizing the autobiographical nature of her songs. Swift's supposedly "authentic" image—which is, of course, impossible to separate from capitalist marketing strategies—validates the fantasy that Taylor *is* the subject of her songs in a completely genuine way, that she experiences what "normal" teens do, and that "everyone" can relate to her, regardless of their gender, race, social class, or sexuality. Although Swift is currently an adult woman in her twenties, her music and her media persona frequently "re-girl" her by emphasizing her relative innocence, and her image produces the normative expectation that there is a universal experience of adolescent love and romance. Swift's positioning as an "authentic" American girl subject is wholly tied to her status as a white, middle class, heterosexual, normatively feminine young woman—characteristics that are repeatedly shored up through the lyrical and visual elements of her music and music videos and through fans' insistence that she is a "good girl" whose infallibility makes her a good role model for young girls.

In contrast to artists such as Lady Gaga and Nicki Minaj, who explicitly foreground sexuality both visually and lyrically, Taylor Swift represents a nostalgic longing for a piece of Americana in which women's sexual desires were kept under wraps. Swift's music implicitly and explicitly insists that race and gender no longer matter; yet, it privileges "traditional values" such as monogamy, propriety, and chastity—values which are historically and inextricably tied to whiteness, heterosexuality, and normative femininity (Coontz 2000: 181; Davy 1997: 212; Odem 1995: 3). The idealization of American girlhood that Swift represents constantly and implicitly privileges a vision of "authentic" girlhood that is invested in heterosexual monogamy, romance, and middle-class propriety.

I begin with a discussion of the ways that the invocation of the autobiographical nature of Swift's songs enables a depiction of her as an "authentic, all-American" girl. Next, I turn to a specific analysis of Taylor Swift fans' statements on discussion boards and in instant messenger interviews. Fans frequently assert that they "know" Taylor through her music and media persona and that Taylor's relatable lyrics make them feel like she understands them deeply. The collusion of fans' two main claims about Swift—that she is a girl just like them and that she is an infallible role model—creates a situation in which fans simultaneously confirm Swift's highly idealized image and assert that they can live up to it. The implicit and explicit messages about propriety in Swift's music both constrain fans' understandings of "appropriate" sexual subjectivities and enable them to stigmatize behavior that falls outside of this strict moral code.

Methods

I used a two-part approach to conducting my research: visual and textual analyses of websites and instant messenger interviews. I examined both Taylor Swift's official website, which is produced by her management company, and one unofficial site, which is produced and maintained by fans. *Taylor Connect* is the forum section of taylorswift.com, Swift's official website. In addition to the forums, the website also includes a biographical statement about Taylor, song lyrics and explanations, music videos, concert dates, photo galleries, a Taylor merchandise store, and an online journal supposedly written by Taylor. *Taylor Swift Web* (formerly *Amazingly Talented*) is the most popular fan-created Taylor Swift site. Fans express the perception in several forum threads that this website is more youth-dominated than *Taylor Connect* or other Taylor Swift fansites, with a number of users self-identifying in the 11–15 age range. I solicited instant messenger interviews through forum posts and private messages on both sites. This article focuses on posts by and interviews with users who self-identified as girls between 14 and 18 years old.

In the context of this article, I constitute "fans" as users on Taylor Swift fan sites. Users on these sites are not necessarily representative of Swift's fandom as a whole (for instance, fan ages may skew younger on websites than among her fans more generally). I also note that participatory cultures of fandom, such as these websites, tend to attract more intensely devoted fans than casual ones (Jenkins 1992: 138; Stenger 2006: 26). Thus, this study is not an examination of the entire range of Swift's fans, but rather of a self-selected group of individuals whose devotion to Swift and her music extends beyond listening to albums and attending concerts.

"If you listen to my albums, it's just like reading my diary": Taylor Swift, autobiography, and musical authenticity

While Swift's fans identify other teen pop sensations, such as Selena Gomez, as commodities—overproduced pop pageant princesses whose images and careers are completely controlled by their record companies—they see Taylor Swift as a sweet country girl who stumbled upon international fame and success while writing personal and emotionally significant songs about romance and heartbreak. Swift writes the majority of her songs, and she has explicitly used the pull of the autobiographical narrative to promote her albums. When interviewed about her songs, she has repeatedly emphasized the "realness" of her lyrics. For instance, she said of the love-themed songs on her *Speak Now* album, "They're all made very clear. Every single song is like a roadmap to what that relationship stood for, with little markers that maybe everyone won't know, but there are things that were little nuances of the relationship, little hints. And every single song is like that. Everyone will know" (Willman 2011).

Both fans and music critics typically evaluate writing one's own songs as a positive marker of artistic ability as well as an affirmation of musical truth-telling (Dyer 2002: 152; Mayhew 2004: 151; Whiteley 2000: 45). The lure of the autobiographical lies in the assurance that the affective content of songs is "real" because it is based in experience; thus, fans' attachments to songs are validated because the lyrics were ostensibly crafted not for purposes of mere profit but out of a genuine expression of artistic emotion. For instance, Allison (*Taylor Swift Web*) states that if Taylor's songs were not "real,"

> Then it wouldn't be nearly as special to me. That's one of the main reasons I love her. She gets it what girls specifically are going through.

Thus, many fans strongly identify with Taylor Swift's music because they emotionally connect not just to the lyrics, but ostensibly to Taylor herself. Other interview subjects specifically cited the "real"-ness of Swift's lyrics as the reason that girls relate to her:

Kelly, Taylor Connect: Yes, I do because they are all about real life and real situations.

Caitlin, TaylorSwiftWeb: I suppose so, a lot more for some than others. I definitely don't think Taylor does it intentionally. Since she writes from experience though, it just happens to relate to a LOT of people.

Caitlin suggests that Swift's music is relatable for some girls more so than others, but she asserts that the autobiographical nature of Swift's music makes it inherently relatable to "a LOT of people." Later in the interview, when I probed her about who might not find Swift relatable, she asserted that any girl could, "if they wanted to." Both of these users situate "real" experience as a significant factor—indeed, the determining factor—in Taylor's relatability. Kelly suggests that Swift's music speaks to the experience of being a girl simply because it is "about real life and real situations," drawing a supposedly uncomplicated line between one girl's experiences—Swift's—and *all* girls' experiences. Caitlin, meanwhile, emphasizes the ways that the autobiographical is popularly misunderstood to be without artifice or intent (Scott 1991: 776). She suggests that Swift's songs don't "intentionally" fall in line with normative understandings of girlhood; instead, Swift's songs "just happen to relate to a lot of people" because she writes from her own experiences as a girl. Experience is explicitly juxtaposed to intent—Swift is presumed to simply be writing about her own life, without ever considering whether her songs would be relatable for other people.

I insist, however, that it is essential to consider the ways that "authenticity" is itself commodified. The notion that a musician is relaying her "true self" through her lyrics is one that carries a strong affective pull for fans, and thus carries a great deal of commercial significance. Promoting the "truth" of a singer-songwriter's music often proves to be a lucrative marketing strategy for record companies, as evidenced by the ways that fan excitement exploded over news of "hidden clues" about the subject of Taylor Swift's songs in the liner notes of her *Speak Now* album (a tactic also used for her 2012 album, *Red*).

Moreover, "authenticity" does not always imply progressive or transgressive musical content. Swift publicly presents an image of sexual innocence, wears relatively conservative clothing, and sings about romance in nonsexual ways—but her music has frequently gone beyond that, declaring the dangers of straying from sexual purity—particularly in the three albums released when she was a teenager. Swift's celebrity status suggests that she is the ultimate idealized girl subject, a focused and successful role model for all girls to emulate. However, the "girl next door" image is predicated upon a degree of economic advantage and feminine propriety that most girls cannot achieve. Thus, examining Taylor Swift and her fans provides an important criticism of girl power rhetoric—while Swift is the ultimate can-do girl, her intensely idealized image of fame, femininity, and sweetness reveals that the "all-American girl" is a subject position that is embedded in middle-class consumption, chaste heterosexual desire, and proper white girlhood.

Swift's musical persona relies on narratives of postfeminist ideals of feminine authenticity. McRobbie (2004: 255) suggests that postfeminist discourse consists of a "double-entanglement": the promotion of conservative values and the insistence on a primary ethic of choice. Taylor Swift embodies both components fully, intentionally rejecting a hypersexual image of girlhood and instead performing a more conservative, demure form of femininity implicitly juxtaposed to masculinity. She has cultivated a visual image of sweet wholesomeness by wearing soft dresses and pastel colors—often white—in real life, in images on her website, and in her music videos, bolstering her image of demure white femininity, frequently in opposition to other girls.

The video for her song "Fifteen," for example, features Taylor and her real-life high school best friend, Abigail Anderson (who also plays herself in the video). Soft lighting emphasizes Swift's flowing blonde hair and her pale white skin, and her modest sun-dress marks her as a middle-class "girl next door." Meanwhile, Abigail's heavy makeup and ripped jeans distinctly situate her as a poor girl, a visual marker which Swift lyri-cally connects to promiscuity. Taylor sings that she breaks up with her boyfriend because she "realized some bigger dreams," while "Abigail gave everything she had to a boy who changed his mind." In the context of the song, it's clear that "everything she had" was her virginity—Abigail is marked as a tragedy for having sex with a boy who later broke up with her, and she seemingly has nothing left to offer after the demise of her purity. These visual and lyrical elements emphasize the impossible position that poor white girls and girls of color must occupy: while they are always already marked as sexually irresponsible prior to even engaging in sex, exploring sexual behaviors that are counter to hegemonic conceptions of chaste female sexuality further stigmatizes them as improper (Carter 2007: 19; Odem 1995: 3; Stokes 2007: 51).

Swift is centrally depicted, in both this video and in her public image, as a "proper girl," one who achieves popularity and happiness through avoiding "inappropriate" influences (such as parties or sexually active boys) and through maintaining an image of ultra-feminine innocence. Her image of propriety unquestionably holds distinct racial and class connotations. Propriety involves not only avoiding sexual promiscuity, but also as refraining from talking about sex, expressing sexual desires, using swear words, or even speaking too loudly—qualities which are encouraged in white middle-class girls' upbringings much more so than working-class white girls and girls of color (Brown 1997: 685; Tolman 2005: 35–36). Consequently, while virginal Taylor is the one to recog-nize the limitations of her adolescent relationship, deflowered Abigail is dumped, ostensibly because the boy was no longer interested in her after she had sex with him; consequently, Taylor is empowered to control the conditions of her life while Abigail is not. Thus, it is critical to interrogate the ways that Swift's supposedly "authentic" status is crucial to her popularity and to her status as a potential role model for girls.

"She's like . . . perfect. All-American": Idealizing Taylor Swift's image of proper young womanhood

On the two websites I examined, fans indicate that they look to Taylor and her music as a guide for how to approach romantic relationships, cope with unpopularity, and live according to particular moral codes. They frequently say that they love Swift because she sings about topics of central importance in their own lives. Identification with a celebrity serves an important function for fans, because seeing a celebrity as someone "just like them" enables them to see the celebrity's fame and fortune as validation of their own identity and experiences (Redmond and Holmes 2007: 14). Diana Fuss suggests that "identification is the detour through the other that defines a self" (1995: 2), and in that vein, role models serve as important points of identification. Adolescents—especially girls—are often characterized as flighty and unserious by adults, and the issues that are important to girls are often marginalized (Kearney 2006: 6; McRobbie 1978/2000: 13; Raby 2007: 41). For Taylor Swift fans, Swift's popularity removes the stigma attached to adolescent emotionality and recasts it as a positive attribute.

Fans frequently express strong connections to both Swift and her music. On a *Taylor Connect* discussion board titled "Please stop complaining about songs about boys and love", messofadreamer writes:

> She writes what she feels. Boys are a teenager's life pretty much. There are days where you feel like a princess and there are days where you're heartbroken.

Messofadreamer marks heterosexual romance as centrally important to the experience of adolescent girlhood, defending Swift's frequent use of romantic themes in her music by universalizing the significance of heterosexual relationships. Yet, she is not simply defending Swift as an artist, but also as a representative of girlhood—the thread's title is a plea not only to stop criticizing Taylor, but implicitly also to stop criticizing teenage girls in general for "obsessing" over heterosexual romance. This user situates having a boyfriend, experiencing heartbreak, and feeling like a princess as "a teenager's life pretty much." Adolescent relationships are popularly trivialized as silly incidents with no lasting significance, so users' defenses of Swift also represent a desire that they themselves be recognized as mature subjects. In the same way, Swift's popularity and commercial success validate a fan's sense of self, since public approval of the messages in Swift's music indicates that her perspectives (which mirror fans' own perspectives) are important.

On both *Taylor Swift Web* and *Taylor Connect*, girls unanimously situate Taylor Swift as a paragon of girlhood perfection, worthy of their devotion and admiration. Fans see Swift's fame and fortune as evidence not only of her musical talent but also of her moral rectitude. I asked all of my interview subjects about whether they saw Taylor as a role model. Caitlin (*Taylor Swift Web*) replied as follows:

Caitlin: Okay, yeah, I think Taylor is a perfect role model!
AUTHOR: What makes her a good role model?
Caitlin: She's like . . . perfect. All-American. She isn't involved in drugs or partying, she hasn't taken the wrong road such as Miley Cyrus has, which lost her a lot of fans . . . she's just not involved in anything that would suggest otherwise.

Miley Cyrus frequently emerges on discussion boards as a foil for Taylor Swift. While Taylor is often cited as being "good" or "sweet," Miley Cyrus is used as a cautionary tale of a good girl gone bad. Caitlin confirmed this.

Adriane Brown

AUTHOR:	What do you mean by "the wrong road"?
Caitlin:	[. . .] So "the wrong road" for Miley was basically leaving her younger fans . . . going all sex-appeal and trying to come off as more mature. I don't think it's working too well for her, so I hope Taylor doesn't do that!

Swift's propriety is often established through the use of foils, such as in the song "Better than Revenge." Taylor has confirmed that the song was directed at actress Camilla Belle, who was reported to be the cause of Swift's breakup with Joe Jonas. The chorus asserts that Belle is "better known for the things that she does on the mattress." The line caused some debate on the boards as to whether it was appropriate, especially for younger fans, but users overwhelmingly expressed their appreciation for and identification with the song:

DoubleK, Taylor Connect:	In a way, it's kind of Camilla's fault that she has a reputation for those things. Plus, what she did was just plain cruel, and taylor let her know that. I know what it's like to have your love stolen from you, and if I wrote a song about the girl who ruined my life, on a scale from 1–10 for badness, it would be 20.

It is notable that in both Swift's song and in this fan's comment, the individual at fault is not Swift's boyfriend, but rather the girl who supposedly stole him. Taylor Swift's image as a sexual innocent is thus bolstered by her juxtaposition to a girl who supposedly used her sexuality to hurt Swift—a girl who, it is worth noting, identifies as biracial (Steele 2011). Thus, Swift's image of propriety and goodness are marked through her whiteness as well as her chastity.

Taylor's desexualized image was frequently cited as a reason for her role model status. Universally, fans on the sites asserted that they admired Swift's demure image. I asked Katie (*Taylor Connect*) about Taylor's role model status, and she replied:

Yes. She is. Not to sound like a sound byte here... but she isn't whoring herself out like a lot of other girls we see. She's got an image based around being a good girl and still being fun. I think that's good for girls to look up to.

However, Katie made a distinction between Taylor's public persona and private life:

I think it's kind of naive to suggest that a beautiful very successful superstar like Taylor Swift would be a virgin at 20 years old. With that being said, the fact that she's not capitalizing on her sexuality and I'm pretty positive she won't ever is what makes her a good role model. It's not about her being "perfect" and "pure," it's about her not flaunting it like other young girls.

Katie's comment points to two important components of Swift's image of propriety—"not capitalizing on her sexuality" and "not flaunting it." While Katie does not chastise Swift for potentially having a sex life, she asserts that both talking about her sexual practices and making money from it would make Swift a bad role model who "whor[es] herself out." This carves out a limited place for women and girl musicians, allowing them to sing about chaste heterosexual romance but to never acknowledge desire. It also affirms what Michelle Fine calls "the missing discourse of desire" (1988: 29) a cultural silence on girls' sexual desires which implicitly asserts that girls do not have sex for their own pleasure or enjoyment.

It is also notable that Katie openly identified herself as a lesbian on the site, and she experienced harassment and censorship from other *Taylor Connect* users because of her sexuality. Katie told me about a few incidents:

> I've gotten some people from TC who spammed my formspring a while back with stuff like "you only like Taylor because of your sick perversion!" [. . .] On TC there was a thread about which we preferred, Taylor with her red lipstick or a more natural look and I said I like the red because her lips looked more kissable. That post was flagged as abusive and Jordan hid it. [. . .] I've had issues with the moderators and administrators about it pretty much the whole time I've been a member.

Here, it becomes evident that Katie's expression of desire violated the site's adherence to standards of heteronormative propriety. Katie's comment about Taylor's lips would have been deemed G-rated if it had been posted by a teenage boy, but within heteronormative frameworks, queer desire is always already obscene (Driver 2007). In a different discussion board thread, male members of the site asked other users for advice about girls, and Katie jumped into the conversation to lament her own difficulty in determining how to best approach girls. Most people on the thread ignored her comment, but one user responded to tell Katie that she would "personally feel uncomfortable" if she discovered someone she knew was a lesbian, but that Katie would find someone eventually. While Katie's sexuality is made evident on the site through both her posts and the "LGBT Swiftie" icon that she made for her forum signature, she is only welcome on the site as long as she keeps her desire under wraps. When Katie explicitly brings up her homosexuality, she is met with silence, uncomfortable remarks, and sometimes by homophobic taunts.

However, while Katie has been negatively affected by *Taylor Connect*'s stringent views on sexuality, she does not connect this to the purity that is valorized by Taylor Swift's music, by fans on the site, and by Katie's own interview responses. Katie is herself deeply invested in the kind of heteronormative propriety that other fans see in Taylor Swift's music, and she fully believes that Swift's music is relatable for lesbian girls:

> Yes. I mean, I have had feelings about girls that correlate to her feelings about guys. And although I've not been in her relationships, I can still relate to feelings of love and appreciate those feelings.

Katie suggests that she can incorporate Swift's image of sweet wholesomeness into her own experience and articulation of lesbian relationships; yet, Katie desires to appropriate a piece of heteronormative culture—"Swiftian" propriety and sentimentality—without considering the ways that this strict view on the expression of sexual desire is connected to the ways that she is marginalized within the community because of her sexual identity.

Adriane Brown

The belief among fans that all adolescent girls find Taylor Swift relatable is facilitated by digital spaces. On *Taylor Connect*, harshly criticizing Taylor Swift or talking about her personal life in any form is explicitly banned, so the only voices present on the site are those who admire all of her decisions. Even when comments are not harsh enough to warrant deletion by the site's moderators, detractors are immediately pounced upon by avid Taylor supporters. The restrictions on anti-Taylor content are reflective of a much larger trend of policing on the sites. Both *Taylor Connect* and *TaylorSwiftWeb* have strict swear filters, and *Taylor Connect*'s previous strategy was to translate curse words into cutesy girlish words like "rainbows," "unicorns," "cupcakes," and "kittens"—the latter of which was actually the replacement for the word "sex."

Thus, propriety is not only figured through a ban on explicit discussions of sexuality, but also through a ban on even the mildest of swear words and through the complete discursive denial of the existence of sexual practice. While users commonly assert that "everyone is welcome" and that "every girl can relate to Taylor's music," these statements are embedded in unacknowledged social frameworks that emerge on the site, such as whiteness and heterosexual romance. Idealized American girlhood is purportedly available to everyone, yet the reliance on "good" behavior—engaging in chaste heterosexual romance, and maintaining an image of niceness while denigrating others—limits this subject position to those who embody normative characteristics of femininity and white propriety.

Conclusion

My examination of Taylor Swift fan forums demonstrates that fans simultaneously construct Swift as an ordinary girl and an irreproachable role model. Fans insist that Swift is a girl who struggles with the same issues they do, but they also emphasize the importance of her flawless performance of propriety. This emphasis on perfect demureness presents an intensely restrictive position which girls expect themselves and Swift to occupy, one that leaves little room for desire, boldness, or mistakes. While Swift's third album title insists that girls should *Speak Now*, fans interpret this primarily as a license to speak about desexualized, monogamous romance and to villainize girls who do not live up to this impossibly angelic image.

Certainly, a lack of explicit sexuality in Swift's music should not mark it as inherently antifeminist or more "damaging" to girls than the sexualized lyrics produced by other contemporary artists. However, the ways in which both Swift and her fans explicitly position her against girls who "whore themselves out" sends the clear message that good girls do not have sex and certainly do not profit from sexuality. While Swift herself is under no obligation to make her private sexual desires public, her lyrical innocence is always bolstered through criticisms of those who do speak publicly about sex, and this stakes out a singularly limited view of girls' sexual subjectivities.

Thus, media and fan adulation regarding Swift's propriety has effects that reach far beyond whether the public perceives Swift, in her own words, as "unsexy" (Access Hollywood 2015). When Swift—not Beyoncé, not Nicki Minaj—is continually positioned as a role model for young girls, it elevates white heteronormative propriety as the standard that all girls—not just white heterosexual girls—are supposed to aspire to.

It also marks sexiness as dirty and open declarations of sexual desire as improper, which not only stigmatizes girls who enjoy expressing their sexuality publicly, but also girls of color, who are constantly and non-consensually sexualized by external forces. Expectations of propriety severely constrain who girls are allowed to see as role models, and consequentially, what they envision as their own possible sexual subjectivities. As we continue to see a proliferation of sexual identifications and performances in the media, girls' own possibilities continue to be constricted. Girls deserve more.

References

Access Hollywood. 2015. "Taylor Swift: I'm Not Overtly Sexy & I'm Totally Cool With It." www.accesshollywood.com/taylor-swift-im-not-overtly-sexy-and-im-totally-cool-with-it-exclusive_article_108160 (May 28. Accessed June 1, 2015).

Brown, Lyn Mikel. 1997. "Performing Femininities: Listening to White Working-Class Girls in Rural Maine." *Journal of Social Issues* 53(4): 683–701.

Carter, Julian B. 2007. *The Heart of Whiteness: Normal Sexuality and Race in America, 1888–1940.* Durham, NC: Duke University.

Coontz, Stephanie. 2000. *The Way We Never Were: American Families and the Nostalgia Trap.* New York: Basic Books.

Davy, Kate. 1997. "Outing Whiteness: A Feminist/Lesbian Project." In: M. Hill (ed.) *Whiteness: A Critical Reader.* New York: New York University, pp. 204–225.

Driver, Susan. 2007. *Queer Girls and Popular Culture: Reading, Resisting, and Creating Media.* New York: Peter Lang.

Dyer, Richard. 2002. "In Defence of Disco." In: *Only Entertainment.* London: Routledge, pp. 151–160.

Edelman, Lee. 2004. *No Future: Queer Theory and the Death Drive.* Durham, NC: Duke University.

Fine, Michelle. 1988. "Sexuality, Schooling, and Adolescent Females: The Missing Discourse of Desire." *Harvard Educational Review* 58(1): 29–53.

Fuss, Diana. 1995. *Identification Papers.* New York: Routledge.

Jenkins, Henry. 1992. *Textual Poachers: Television Fans & Participatory Cultures.* New York: Routledge.

Kearney, Mary Celeste. 2006. *Girls Make Media.* New York: Routledge.

Mayhew, Emma. 2004. "Positioning the Producer: Gender Divisions in Creative Labour and Value." In: S. Whiteley, A. Bennett and S. Hawkins (eds.) *Music, Space, and Place: Popular Music and Cultural Identity.* Burlington, VT: Ashgate Publishing Company, pp. 149–162.

McRobbie, Angela. 1978/2000. *Feminism and Youth Culture.* New York: Routledge.

—. 2004. "Post-feminism and Popular Culture." *Feminist Media Studies* 4(3): 255–264.

Odem, Mary. 1995. *Delinquent Daughters: Protecting and Policing Adolescent Female Sexuality in the United States 1885–1920.* Chapel Hill, NC: University of North Carolina.

Raby, Rebecca. 2007. "Across a Great Gulf? Conducting Research with Adolescents." In: A. Best (ed.) *Representing Youth: Methodological Issues in Critical Youth Studies.* New York: New York University Press, pp. 39–59.

Redmond, Sean and Su Holmes. 2007. "Introduction." In: S. Redmond and S. Holmes (eds.) *Stardom and Celebrity: A Reader.* London: Sage, pp. 1–16.

Scott, Joan. 1991. "The Evidence of Experience." *Critical Inquiry* 17(4): 773–797.

Steele, Kay. 2011. "Who is Brazilian Actress Camilla Belle?" *Uinterview.* Available at www.uinterview.com/news/who-is-brazilian-actress-camilla-belle-2641.

Stenger, Josh. 2006. "The Clothes Make the Fan: Fashion and Online Fandom When *Buffy the Vampire Slayer* Goes to Ebay." *Cinema Journal* 45(4): 26–44.

Stokes, Carla. 2007. "'Get On My Level!': How Black American Adolescent Girls Construct Identity and Negotiate Sexuality on the Internet." In: S. Mazzarella (ed.) *Girl Wide Web 2.0: Revisiting Girls, the Internet, and the Construction of Identity*. Toronto: Peter Lang, pp. 45–68.

Tolman, Deborah. 2005. *Dilemmas of Desire: Teenage Girls Talk about Sexuality*. Cambridge, MA: Harvard University Press.

Whiteley, Sheila. 2000. *Women and Popular Music: Sexuality, Identity, and Subjectivity*. New York: Routledge.

Willman, C. 2011. "Taylor Swift Reveals John Mayer Romance on New Album." www.accesshollywood.com/articles/report-taylor-swift-reveals-john-mayer-romance-on-new-album-91712/ (Accessed December 21, 2015).

chapter 46

Gendered dynamics of social media

Sander de Ridder and Sofie Van Bauwel

In September 2014, the *The Gaily Grind* (Garcia 2014) reported on an unfolding drama in San Francisco's drag queen performing community. Facebook, the largest and most well-known social media site, deleted the profiles of hundreds of drag queens who were using their chosen stage names instead of their "real" or official names (names that are stated on official identification documents, such as a driver's license). The drag queen community petitioned against this action by Facebook, claiming that it was discriminatory against transgender and gender-nonconforming individuals. Facebook responded by temporarily reactivating the profiles, allotting a designated amount of time for individuals to change their profile names in order to be in accordance with Facebook's "real name" policy. In response, the drag queen community protested, arguing that they should not be treated like anonymous trolls, but as people who identify by their stage names, which they regard as real names. Eventually, Chris Cox, Chief Product Manager at Facebook, apologized. Facebook promised to reactivate the profiles of people affected and to rethink its policy. Cox explained that they had not intended to offend anyone with the real name policy, though he argued that this policy differentiates Facebook by making it safer than other Internet spaces, where anonymity is the norm.

Facebook's clash with the drag queen community was featured in international news, which demonstrates Facebook's news value, as well as the relevance of social media within gender politics. Social media's gender relevance also becomes evident when considering, for example, the way that societies worry about how girls and young women supposedly contribute to their own sexualization on social media by posting sexy pictures on their profiles (Thiel-Stern 2009).

Social media are digital communication technologies, built on Web 2.0 platforms and applications. (e.g. Facebook, Twitter, Snapchat and Instagram). Web 2.0 is not only a collection of technologies, but a cultural move toward Internet sociality in which the Internet is seen as a space where people can share and interact with content (John 2012). Social media have become deeply embedded in everyday life. They are not neutral platforms and they shape our daily routines. Media such as Facebook have become a meaningful platform for a myriad of social practices, including those that give meanings to the most intimate aspects of our lives, such as dating and our gender and sexual identities (De Ridder and Van Bauwel 2013).

We can learn a number of things from the drag queen example in regard to the gendered dynamics of social media. First, we can learn that in our contemporary culture, social media have become important spaces where people perform *gendered practices and identities*. Social media are a stage for the performance of gendered identities. Second, social media audiences pass time on these platforms to entertain themselves through social voyeurism (boyd 2007). Because people spend a lot of time on social media, it is an important space for *interpreting* the diverse manifestations of gender. A final lesson is that society interprets how people "live" their genders through everyday experiences, including representations of gender in social media.

The argument between Facebook and the drag queen community makes clear that social media are *gendered commercial technologies*. Social media should not be seen as a collection of "neutral" platforms, but rather, they should be seen as having the symbolic power to frame people's identities in particular ways. Software-based platforms offer gendered options to represent identities, and their complex algorithms steer online behavior. Moreover, social media companies develop their marketing strategies and policies based on the way people should "do" online gendered identities "correctly."

We argue in this chapter that the gendered dynamics of social media, the practices and identities, interpretations and technologies, are by no means straightforward. They are dependent on particular socio-technological contexts, the way gender is interpreted, and also on the way a social media platform is designed within particular commercial contexts. While it is often assumed that social media are merely a neutral setting for performing gender, social media are a social and cultural form, which means that software platforms *add particular meanings* to the way people live their genders in relation to the use of social media in everyday life.

The gendered dynamics of social media allow for exciting opportunities for performing gender, yet at the same time, social media gender dynamics are contradictory and messy, and sometimes even abusive. It is clear that it does not make sense to either celebrate the democratic potential of social media, or to exaggerate fears through focusing on gendered risks. Rather, it is more important to understand how social and cultural orders are shaped by understanding how social media work. Social media have a certain logic; they have particular strategies, mechanisms, and economies underlying the platforms and applications they produce (van Dijck and Poell 2013).

Gendered practices and identities on social media

Gendered practices on social media are those practices performed on or related to social media that broadly give meaning to gendered identities. These practices can take many forms, from using the symbolic tools that social media provide – such as the ability to post and send pictures, comment and direct message – to the ability to discuss other people's self-representations. For example, research has shown that young people's pictures on social media are mainly structured by particular gender expressions found in popular media culture such as music videos, advertising and celebrity culture (Tortajada-Giménez, Araüna-Baró and Martínez 2013). Moreover, social media allows users to comment on pictures, which is equally structured around gendered dynamics among youths; girls are thought to typically comment on pictures of "sexy" boys, while boys comment on pictures of "sexy" girls (De Ridder and Van Bauwel 2013).

Social media: empowering or oppressive?

Though social media websites have only been popular since the early 2000s, with Facebook arriving on the market in 2005 (Baym 2010), gendered practices on the Internet have a longer history, dating back to the early 1990s. Guided by the works of Sherry Turkle (1995), *Life On The Screen: Identity in the Age of the Internet* and Sadie Plant (1997), *Zeroes and Ones: Digital Woman and the New Techno Culture*, the Internet was first seen as a "feminist cyber utopia" (van Zoonen 2011). These authors argued that due to the absence of material, biological bodies in cyberspace, the Internet was ideal for experimenting with gender and there was the potential to become liberated from sex and gender binaries of male/female and man/woman (see also Haraway 1991). Turkle introduced the notion of "gender swapping," arguing that the anonymity of online gaming allowed people to potentially switch and experiment with genders and sexual orientations. Plant saw the Internet as a truly feminine space because of women's use of the Internet in empowering ways. For example, Plant argued how women intensively use the Internet to transcend everyday life spaces such as the home by using the global communication networks the Internet provides.

However, in the 2000s, empirical research exposed the Internet as a space in which people do not necessarily experiment and transgress gender norms; rather, it seemed to be an ordinary space that reflected (rather than challenged) gendered social norms and practices of everyday life. It became clear that Internet use could not be separated from its material and domesticated contexts (van Zoonen 2011: 134–135). In other words, gender is still a primary organizing principle in which the material, biological body has significance on social media. For example, the computer and the Internet have a place in the home and are often used for practices that are seen as typically feminine (e.g. looking for cooking recipes online), or masculine (e.g. looking for sport news online).

More recent research on social media suggests that gendered stereotypes and heterosexual norms are not only reproduced, but that gender and sexual ideologies are reinforced online (Magnuson and Dundes 2008; Tortajada-Giménez et al. 2013). For example, when considering the popular social media genre of "selfies," we can see how people make creative and playful reproductions of poses that are typically feminine (e.g. "soft" and "sweet" facial expressions) or masculine (e.g. a "tough" look that gazes directly into the camera lens). A "sexy selfie" can generate a certain status within peer groups. Because of these peer group pressures, gender and

Sander de Ridder and Sofie Van Bauwel

sexual ideologies are reinforced. "Sexy selfies" are therefore very repetitive, highly erotized and stereotyped pictures of mainly heterosexual girls that have become fairly mainstream in youth cultures.

Gender and socio-technical contexts

Gendered practices on social media take on many contradictory and messy forms, depending on their *socio-technological contexts*. Gendered social media practices depend on the media platform or application (app) used, and in turn, specific gender norms greatly differ depending on the media platform. As we can see from Facebook's deletion of "fake" (or stage) name drag queen profiles, gender practices on Facebook need to appear more "authentic," as the site has a more "serious" look and feel to it. In contrast, popular dating applications such as Tinder allow for more flirtatious representations of masculinity and femininity. For example, people often use Tinder to find dates and therefore they communicate with people they do not know. This anonymity often allows them to be more open and playful, while Facebook is aimed at connecting people who you already know from daily offline life (e.g. work, school, family).

Additionally, it is necessary to recognize and respect differences between socio-technological contexts of different social media platforms (e.g. representing the self on Facebook is different than on Tinder) in order to avoid the risk of damaging one's online reputation. Gender identity is signaled in many different ways, but the role of pictures is of primary importance here. By controlling visual aspects such as dress, gaze, and proximity to the camera, gender expression is carefully regulated (Huffaker and Calvert 2005). Young girls in particular are often harshly judged for being "too slutty" or "too public" when representing themselves online. Girls need to continuously negotiate between social status rewards and romantic successes and the gendered risk of being brutally judged (Bailey, Steeves, Burkell and Regan 2013: 108). For example, a social status reward can be won by a girl posting an attractive picture that gets a lot of "likes" and positive comments while at the same time, there are also commentators harshly judging the picture by posting brutal or hateful comments. There are numerous examples of so called "slut pages" on Facebook, where people collect pictures of girls on Facebook who they see as "too slutty."

In Western society, socio-technological contexts have become more complex as social media become mobile, which means that people can simultaneously move between different social contexts and spaces. "Simultaneous presence in a variety of spaces/places allows us to move between frames and perform gender differently in each, with sensitivity to that context" (Humphreys and Vered 2014: 5). Gendered social media practices are thus messy because of the complex socio-technological spaces in which they operate. With the increasing popularity of mobile technologies, the struggle in social media over gendered power dynamics becomes more intense.

An example of a gendered practice in which the socio-technological contexts of social media are characterized by power dynamics is *sexting*. Sexting is "the practice of sending sexually explicit images or text through mobile phones or via internet applications." Because of its mobile character, this form of sexual self-expression can quickly move between different places and thus become a dangerous form of self-exposure.

In contexts where trust is missing, images of naked body parts (mostly of girls) have become "highly valued as commodities." Research has shown that in contemporary youth cultures, boys use cell phones to trade revealing pictures like "currency," which can threaten a girl's sexual reputation (Ringrose, Harvey, Gill and Livingstone 2013: 319).

Interpreting gender on social media

Social media have become a primary source of interpreting how people "do gender" in societies. In response to societal panics on the "risks" posed by young people's gender and sexual practices on social media (Pascoe 2011), academic research has focused primarily on how young people – specifically heterosexual girls – present their gender identities on social media. As social media allow young people to transgress the spatial boundaries of safe spaces such as the home or school, adults fear young people will lose control over their intimacies. These fears range from concerns over the possibility of young people meeting strangers and "predators" (Wolak, Finkelhor, Mitchell and Ybarra 2010) to young girls damaging their sexual reputations.

Relatedly, academics have given a considerable amount of attention to young people's *gendered subjectivities*—how young people become gendered subjects in or in relation to social media. This literature focuses on young people's gendered practices in contexts framed by an ideology of gender inequality and institutionalized heterosexuality (Jackson 2005). The majority of this research concerns the way that young girls' self-representations are subjected to the wider sexualization of culture (Attwood 2009), and how these self-representations operate in a post-feminist context. The post-feminist stance argues that feminism has become obsolete; feminism's social and political goals (such as equality between men and women at work) have been met (McRobbie 2008). Thus, women are now represented (or represent themselves) as enjoying their feminine sexuality while they maintain neo-liberal values such as individualism, choice, empowerment, and consumerism, rather than focusing on political struggles that are still relevant today. Thus, girls' sexual self-representations indicate that the cultural process of sexualization (the objectification of a person or thing as an object of sexual pleasure) has become internalized, meaning that girls sexually objectify themselves (Gill 2007).

Through the use of different methodologies such as online observation and interviewing, the "effects" of sexualization have been observed in a number of studies on girls' self-representations in social media (Dobson 2014; Gómez 2010; Ringrose 2011; Siibak and Hernwall 2011; Sveningsson 2009; Tortajada-Giménez et al. 2013). For example, Canadian scholars interviewed girls about gender stereotypes on Facebook and found that heterosexual girls felt that in order to be socially successful, they needed to be attractive, have a boyfriend, and participate in the party scene. This, girls argued, relates to how femininity is represented in celebrity culture (e.g. just take a look at Kim Kardashian's selfies on the popular smartphone application Instagram) (Bailey et al. 2013: 107). Young people on social media often use popular culture to shape their own self-representations (Willem, Araüna, Crescenzi and Tortajada 2012) such as when looking at pictures of celebrities as examples of how to pose for a selfie. In summary, as these academic studies show, popular culture is essential to interpret

Sander de Ridder and Sofie Van Bauwel

the gendered dynamics in social media. Similarly, gender on social media should be interpreted in relation to dominant heterosexual cultural norms and values (Siibak and Hernwall 2011).

However, not all scholars agree that girls are particularly at risk of internalization of sexualization. First, while the way that young boys construct their genders in relation to social media is understudied, when under observation, it becomes clear that boys also attempt to represent themselves as "sexy" objects, posing in a way that it becomes pleasurable for the viewer (Manago 2013). Second, the notions of "self-objectification" and "internalization" are highly debated in feminist media studies (Duits and van Zoonen 2007). Some scholars question if we should see girls' social media activities as proof of an internalization of sexualization represented in popular media culture. This is essentially a debate about *agency*—the interpretation of actions as deliberate or whether these actions are shaped by societal structures such as neo-liberalism, sexualization and so on (Giddens 1985). For example, girls' self-representations on social media are often problematized because they are taken as proof of an internalized sexualization, while young people themselves see their actions as something that should not be taken so seriously. Young people view social media as a space for fun and for experimenting with idealized selves. They are able to reflect critically on the problematic aspects of sexualization related to social media, which suggests they have a sense of agency (Bailey et al. 2013; Livingstone 2008; Manago, Graham, Greenfield and Salimkhan 2008).

In academic discourse, interpretations of gender on social media have been contradictory. In society, media panics over the way young people behave on social media are ever-present. Social media have brought gendered dynamics in societies onto a stage on which "doing gender" has become very visible, which has led to new representations and interpretations of gender.

Social media as a gendered commercial technology

Social media are often – uncritically – viewed as a "neutral" space in which people have extensive control over their performances and participation. However, social media institutions have symbolic power over people's gendered practices, as evidenced by Facebook's drag queen saga. This symbolic power is situated on many levels, such as the software platform that only allows limited menus for identity representation (e.g. specific choices from which to select a gender identity) and the imposition of certain models of online sociality that are based on authenticity, status, and reputation (van Dijck 2013).

Social media institutions have symbolic power as they co-construct people's gendered practices, contributing to the way that gender becomes meaningful. Social media's market powers rely on building a lucrative and popular platform, which often means that a team of product managers make certain choices about how to organize its sociality. The cultural power of social media thus relies on making marketing choices such as having a fixed organization of identities, rather than reflecting diversity and enabling the political flexibility that is found in everyday life (De Ridder 2013). The example of San Francisco's drag queen community illustrates how Facebook's specific organization of sociality (e.g. the rule that you must have a "real" name) came into conflict with the diverse appropriations by people using the platform. Facebook's marketing strategy to differentiate the website from anonymous online platforms, and the corresponding cultural choice to install a "real name" identity policy, was at the basis of the struggle between the drag queen community and the social media company.

How these gendered inequalities are built into technology is the subject of a feminist approach to Science and Technology Studies (STS) known as *technofeminism* (Wajcman 2010). The argument of this approach is that gender is part of the sociotechnical process when designing a technology. According to Wajcman "the materiality of technology affords or inhibits the doing of particular gender power relations" (p. 150). For example, technofeminist critiques often address how jobs in the technology industry (such as software design) are associated with men. Thus, the organization of work in technology companies – as well as the products they design – are built upon certain ideals of manliness that shape social practices when using the technology (Eriksson-Zetterquist 2007).

Technofeminism's focus is on the *mutual shaping* of gender and technology, which means that "technological innovation is itself shaped by the social circumstances within which it takes place" (Wajcman 2010: 149). The mutual shaping approach is different from a "technologically determinist" approach, which assumes that all changes are caused by technological forces. Mutual shaping argues that technology does *not* directly influence the actions of people using the technology, but rather the negotiation between technology and its uses is continuous and complex. However, technological systems such as software platforms can reinforce certain social and cultural practices that are built into those systems and thus cause identity disputes with users (Van House 2011). For example, although Facebook's real name policy has been disputed, it is still one of the most important features and ways in which the platform differentiates itself from competitors.

Gender as media production on social media

Social media are usually seen as part of *new* and *participatory* media that is radically different from the logic of old mass media (television, film, newspapers). However, we should understand that the workings of mass media and social media are mutually reinforcing (van Dijck and Poell 2013). For example, what people are doing with gender on social media is heavily entangled with how gender is represented in popular media culture, and with the commercial logic of big social media institutions. Therefore, it makes sense to understand gender on social media as a form of media production (Hasinoff 2013). Rethinking gender on social media as a form of media production is a way to understand the practices, identities, interpretations, and technologies of gender not as either democratic or problematic, but as situated contextually within the particular socio-technological, cultural, and commercial contexts of social media.

Making sense of the gendered dynamics of social media as forms of media production is a useful interpretative framework for three reasons. First, this framework can help us understand that when people "do" gender on social media, these self-representations should be seen as highly idealized selves. People produce content that follows the rules of particular digital media genres (e.g. "selfies" as a currently popular genre) to produce attractive content for audiences. Second, this means that this framework can teach us that gender representations on social media are not always a "proof" of how people (and mostly young people) live their genders and intimacies. Social media introduces different social contexts for more playful explorations of gender, which can be very different from how we think about our "core" and "authentic" gendered selves in everyday life. Finally, this interpretative framework should make us aware that these different social contexts are created by large media companies who do not produce neutral platforms and that these socio-technological contexts frame people's gendered identities in particular ways.

References

Attwood, Feona. 2009. "Introduction: The Sexualization of Culture." In F. Attwood (Ed.), *Mainstreaming Sex: The Sexualization of Western Culture* (pp. i–xxiv). London: I.B. Tauris.

Bailey, J., Steeves, V., Burkell, J. and Regan, P. 2013. "Negotiating with Gender Stereotypes on Social Networking Sites: From 'Bicycle Face' to Facebook." *Journal of Communication Inquiry*, 37(2), 91–112. doi: 10.1177/0196859912473777.

Baym, N. 2010. *Personal Connections in the Digital Age*. Cambridge: Polity.

boyd, danah. 2007. "Why Youth (Heart) Social Network Sites: The Role of Networked Publics in Teenage Social Lives." In D. Buckingham (Ed.), *Youth, Identity and Digital Media* (pp. 119–142). Cambridge, MA: The MIT Press.

De Ridder, Sander. 2013. "Are Digital Media Institutions Shaping Youth's Intimate Stories? Strategies and Tactics in the Social Networking Site Netlog." *New Media & Society*. Retrieved from doi: 10.1177/1461444813504273.

De Ridder, Sander and Van Bauwel, Sofie. 2013. "Commenting on Pictures: Teens Negotiating Gender and Sexualities on Social Networking Sites." *Sexualities*, 16(5/6), 565–586. doi: 10.1177/1363460713487369.

Dobson, A. S. 2014. "Performative Shamelessness on Young Women's Social Network Sites: Shielding the Self and Resisting Gender Melancholia." *Feminism & Psychology*, 24(1), 97–114. doi: 10.1177/0959353513510651.

Duits, L. and van Zoonen, L. 2007. "Who's Afraid of Female Agency?: A Rejoinder to Gill." *European Journal of Women's Studies*, 14(2), 161–170. doi: 10.1177/1350506807075820.

Eriksson-Zetterquist, U. (2007). "Editorial: Gender and New Technologies." *Gender, Work & Organization*, 14(4), 305–311. doi: 10.1111/j.1468-0432.2007.00345.x.

Garcia, A. 2014, September 18. "Facebook Warns Drag Queens They Will Delete Every Profile in Two Weeks." *TheGailyGrind*. Retrieved from www.thegailygrind.com/2014/09/18/facebook-warns-drag-queens-will-delete-every-profile-two-weeks/. Accessed July 29, 2015.

Giddens, Anthony. 1985. *The Constitution of Society: Outline of the Theory of Structuration*. Cambridge: Polity Press.

Gill, R. 2007. *Gender and the Media*. Malden: Polity Press.

Gómez, A. G. 2010. "Competing Narratives, Gender and Threaded Identity in Cyberspace." *Journal of Gender Studies*, 19(1), 27–42.

Haraway, Donna. 1991. *Simians, Cyborgs, and Women: The Reinvention of Nature*. London: Routledge.

Hasinoff, A. A. 2013. "Sexting as Media Production: Rethinking Social Media and Sexuality." *New Media & Society*, 15(4), 449–465. doi: 10.1177/1461444812459171.

Huffaker, D. A. and Calvert, S. L. 2005. "Gender, Identity, and Language Use in Teenage Blogs." *Journal of Computer-Mediated Communication*, 10(2). Retrieved from: http://dx.doi.org/10.1111/j.1083-6101.2005.tb00238.x.

Humphreys, S. and Vered, K. O. 2014. "Reflecting on Gender and Digital Networked Media." *Television & New Media*, 15(1), 3–13. doi: 10.1177/1527476413502682.

Jackson, Stevi. 2005. "Sexuality, Heterosexuality and Gender Hierarchy: Getting Our Priorities Straight." In C. Ingraham (Ed.), *Thinking Straight: The Power, the Promise, and the Paradox of Heterosexuality* (pp. 15–38). New York: Routledge.

John, N. A. 2012. "Sharing and Web 2.0: The Emergence of a Keyword." *New Media & Society*, 15(2), 167–182. doi: 10.1177/1461444812450684.

Livingstone, S. 2008. "Taking Risky Opportunities in Youthful Content Creation: Teenagers' Use of Social Networking Sites for Intimacy, Privacy and Self-Expression." *New Media & Society*, 10(3), 393–411. doi: 10.1177/1461444808089415.

Magnuson, M. J. and Dundes, L. 2008. "Gender Differences in "Social Portraits" Reflected in MySpace Profiles." *CyberPsychology & Behavior*, 11(2), 239–241.

Manago, A. M. 2013. "Negotiating a Sexy Masculinity on Social Networking Sites." *Feminism & Psychology*, 23(4), 478–497. doi: 10.1177/0959353513487549.

Manago, A. M., Graham, M. B., Greenfield, P. M. and Salimkhan, G. 2008. "Self-Presentation and Gender on MySpace." *Journal of Applied Developmental Psychology*, 29(6), 446–458.

McRobbie, Angela. 2008. *The Aftermath of Feminism: Gender, Culture and Social Change* London: Sage.

Pascoe, C. J. 2011. "Resource and Risk: Youth Sexuality and New Media Use." *Sexuality Research and Social Policy*, 8(1), 5–17. doi: 10.1007/s13178-011-0042-5.

Plant, Sadie. 1997. *Zeroes and Ones: Digital Woman and the New Techno Culture*. London: Fourth Estate.

Ringrose, J. 2011. "Gendered Risks and Opportunities? Exploring Teen Girls' Digitized Sexual Identities in Postfeminist Media Contexts." *International Journal of Media & Cultural Politics*, 7(2), 121–138. doi: 10.1386/macp.7.2.121_1.

Ringrose, J., Harvey, L., Gill, R. and Livingstone, S. 2013. "Teen Girls, Sexual Double Standards and 'Sexting': Gendered Value in Digital Image Exchange." *Feminist Theory*, 14(3), 305–323. doi: 10.1177/1464700113499853.

Siibak, A. and Hernwall, P. 2011. "'Looking Like My Favourite Barbie' – Online Gender Construction of Tween girls in Estonia and in Sweden." *Studies of Transition States in Societies*, 3(2), 57–68.

Sveningsson, M. E. 2009. "Exploring and Negotiating Femininity: Young Women's Creation of Style in a Swedish Internet Community." *Young*, 17(3), 241–264. doi: 10.1177/110330880901700302.

Thiel-Stern, S. 2009. "Femininity Out of Control on the Internet: A Critical Analysis of Media Representations of Gender, Youth, and MySpace.com in International News Discourses." *Girlhood Studies*, 2(1), 20–39. doi: 10.3167/ghs.2009.020103.

Tortajada-Giménez, I., Araüna-Baró, N. and Martínez, I. J. 2013. "Advertising Stereotypes and Gender Representation in Social Networking Sites." *Comunicar*, 21(41), 177–186.

Turkle, Sherry. 1995. *Life on the Screen: Identity in the Age of the Internet.* London: Weidenfeld.

van Dijck, J. 2013. "'You Have One Identity': Performing the Self on Facebook and LinkedIn." *Media, Culture & Society*, 35(2), 199–215. doi: 10.1177/0163443712468605.

van Dijck, J. and Poell, T. 2013. "Understanding Social Media Logic." *Media and Communication*, 1(1), 2–14.

Van House, N. A. 2011. "Feminist HCI Meets Facebook: Performativity and Social Networking Sites." *Interacting with Computers*, 23(5), 422–429.

van Zoonen, L. 2011. "The Rise and Fall of Online Feminism." In M. Christensen, J. André and C. Christensen (Eds.), *Online Territories. Globalization, Mediated Practice and Social Space* (pp. 132–146). New York: Peter Lang.

Wajcman, J. 2010. "Feminist Theories of Technology." *Cambridge Journal of Economics*, 34(1), 143–152. doi: 10.1093/cje/ben057.

Willem, C., Araüna, N., Crescenzi, L. and Tortajada, I. 2012. "Girls on Fotolog: Reproduction of Gender Stereotypes or Identity Play?" *Interactions: Studies in Communication & Culture*, 2(3), 225–242. doi: 10.1386/iscc.2.3.225_1.

Wolak, J., Finkelhor, D., Mitchell, K. J. and Ybarra, M. L. 2010. "Online 'Predators' and Their Victims." *Psychology of Violence*, 1(1), 13–35. doi: 10.1037/2152-0828.1.s.13.

chapter 47

Internet sex: the seductive "freedom to"[1]

Dennis D. Waskul

The lascivious lure is blunt: hundreds of thousands of "XXX pics," "steaming hot live hardcore sex shows," "the sexiest erotic stories – both text and audio," "hardcore chat 24/7," "adult games" and "the hottest new XXX videos." Although many sites claim "something for everyone," the primary allure is apparently for those who prefer "vixens," "sluts," "nymphos," "whores" and "insatiable girls that bear it all for you" – often of a "cum guzzling" variety who "take it up the ass" from "huge" "throbbing" "cocks" that "stuff" and "pound" "pussy" until they "burst," "explode," and "erupt" a "giant load in her pretty face." "No holes barred." "What are you waiting for?" "Cum inside now." "Free Preview." "FREE." "Instant Access." "Join Now." "No Credit Card Required." Indeed.

According to the motto of Cybererotica – one of the most significant industry leaders in e-commercial pornography – the internet is a place "where fantasy meets reality." However, this particular intersection of fantasy and reality – decidedly androcentric, often misogynistic, aggressive, sometimes violent, and frequently packaged in a carnivalized form of grotesque degradation (see Langman 2004) – is chiefly the product of the hucksters of commercial internet pornography. If the motto of Cybererotica is correct, then this fantasy meets *commercial* internet reality: relatively low start-up costs, the most cost-efficient technology of reproduction to date, a product consumers "access" without distribution expenses, and an instant global market of actual and potential credit card consumers who pay to (click and) play. For these reasons, commercial internet pornography is driven by the market and market competition as much as by consumer demands. Indeed, commercial internet pornography may reveal much more about e-commerce and the internet marketplace than about sexuality (see Perdue 2002).

The situation is quite different when one need not "pay to play" – a form of erotic computer-mediated experience most often called "cybersex." Among those familiar with this sort of activity, cybersex strictly refers to erotic forms of real-time computer-mediated *communication*. Rather than a passive consumption of relatively static pornography, cybersex entails active, interactive, and creative communication with others through typed text, live digital video, sometimes spoken voice (by use of computer microphones), or some combination thereof. Cybersex is typically (but not necessarily) an anonymous experience: participants generally know one another only through a self-chosen screen name (often a name like "BustyBabe," "HungHunk," "SWF4U," or "BiGuy"); while intimate sexual desires are expressed, participants rarely share personal identifying information. Although people may pay a fee – for client software, to a service provider, or an internet "virtual sex worker" (typically a webcam performer) – participants in an authentic cybersex encounter have no ulterior economic motive. In an authentic cybersex encounter, erotic internet communications are strictly for fun and free; motives approximate those of other free-will sexual encounters: desire, expression, intimacy, play, experimentation, arousal, and/or orgasm.

Cybersex is primarily experienced in one of two forms. Cybersex can be a purely textual activity: two or more people connected by a computer network send each other sexually explicit messages that discursively perform an erotic encounter. Chiefly found in internet chat and instant messaging environments, "hot chat" is a written sexual conversation – much like phone sex, only typed instead of spoken – a form of coauthored interactive erotica. Cybersex can also be experienced by use of digital cameras. Using relatively inexpensive "webcams," cybersex participants may not only type to one another but also watch (as they are watched) in live streaming video. Unlike hot chat, webcam cybersex is less about "coauthored interactive erotica" and more about exhibitionism, voyeurism, "I'll show you mine if you show me yours," seeing and being seen nude, masturbating, involving other clandestine sexual pleasures, and even engaging in sex acts with one or more persons "in the flesh" that are shared with one or more persons "in the virtual" (akin, perhaps, to a virtual *ménage à trois*, virtual soft-swinging, or a virtual orgy). The differences between text cybersex and webcam cybersex are not trivial. In the next sections I will briefly detail the distinct nature and expressed motives and virtues of both text and webcam cybersex.

Text cybersex

Text cybersex is a form of discursive role-playing intended to inspire sexual imagination and fantasy. By describing actions and responding to chat partners, participants pretend they are involved in an actual sexual encounter. For this reason, the quality of "hot chat" typically depends on extensive sexual and communicative literacy. In other words, "good" text cybersex depends on the ability to use *words* to evoke vivid, rich, visceral mental images and sequences of events – which is precisely what the participants in my studies of cybersex repeatedly suggested:

> An active imagination and expansive vocabulary help. Using predictable expressions is a little ho-hum. Just saying "I want to suck your dick" is unlikely to arouse many people.

> There are only so many ooohs and mmm hummms you can type.

Text cybersex is purely about "typing dirty", it involves neither touching nor seeing bodies (other than one's own). For this reason, participants are generally free to assume a wide variety of imaginative roles and otherwise playfully toy with alternative vicarious experience. As several text cybersex participants told me:

> Cybersex allows the freedom of sexual expression. Cybersex allows a person to be whoever or whatever they want to be!!

> It's erotic, it turns me on – the mystery of it. Not knowing who is really on the other end is really erotic – you can be anything. I may stretch truth, and live out fantasies . . . it allows you to be with whoever you want – no inhibitions.

> You can do anything you want and you can picture anybody you wish.

> Sometimes I pretend I'm a woman. I've also invented experiences (like 3 somes). . . . Cybersex enables me to play out fantasies . . . it allows you to take your dreams one step closer to reality.

According to many text cybersex participants, these experiences provide a means to learn new sexual techniques, discover or explore new turn-ons, and vicariously experience arousal in ways they would not (or could not) in everyday life. Consequently, text cybersex participants often described the experience as meaningful, highly valued, and full of perceived therapeutic overtures:

> With cybersex I learned stuff I didn't know, like maybe how to do some things better. Everyone should try it!

> Since I've started chatting with people online, I've been walking around in this perpetual state of arousal! It's wonderful! I mean, perpetual, never ending, I'm always thinking about sex, coming up with new ideas, listening to other people's fantasies and expressions and learning things I never knew existed!

> Whether a guy or a girl sends me a private message and wants to talk, it's usually very exciting. I am 32 years old and think I am only now reaching my sexual prime, and I don't know that I'd have discovered certain things about myself without it. I never thought I could be so free with my emotions and fantasies, and it's even spilled over into my real life, I mean now I feel free about talking about my sexuality (bi-sexuality) with other people openly, now that I've discussed it with myself first (which basically is what I'm doing here, talking to a nameless, faceless person, i.e., ME!).

Dennis D. Waskul

I guess the reason I do it is because it is a safe medium by which to explore sexually. To experiment with those aspects of sex that you have not yet explored. To enhance your sex life through the use of new ideas that are learned with a new sexual partner, without risk. It is also a way to be excited sexually without the performance anxiety that is present in face-to-face encounters. It is a way to express yourself sexually in a way you may not feel comfortable doing in a relationship.

Clearly, these cybersex participants view "hot chat" as a context to explore the surfaces and depths of sexual desire, imagination, and fantasy. Because it is purely typed text, these cybersex participants describe the experience as providing unprecedented "freedom of sexual expression," "to be whomever or whatever they want"; a safe medium to explore and experiment with sex. While there are obvious limits to these alleged "freedoms" (see Waskul, Douglass, and Edgley 2000), one cannot deny that in a medium of words (and words alone) people are generally "free" to present themselves as whomever (or whatever) they want – generally "free" to indulge desires and fantasy in a context that is generally "free" of stigma (and other social sanctions) – even if those expressions tend to adhere to relatively conventional sexual and gender scripts. Indeed, it is precisely these freedoms that Cleo Odzer (1997: 43) cites in a frank description of her internet sex life:

> With the freedom to be and do anything, I had sex with three men once. Posing as a man, I had sex with a woman. Posing as a gay man, I had sex with a man. I had sex with a man who was posing as a woman. I learned all about S&M, as the sadist and the masochist. I had all sorts of sex in every new way I could think of.

Webcam cybersex

In contrast, "webcam" cybersex is all about looking at bodies, having one's own body gazed upon, for the explicit purposes of sexual arousal. Consequently, because live streaming video reveals fleshy facts, people are not free "to be whomever or whatever they want." Certain physical characteristics are apparent, for the most part, and all the more so when clothing is removed: gender, race, physique, attractiveness, weight, even a rough approximation of age. Consequently, webcam cybersex may similarly excite sexual imagination and fantasy, but the experience has everything to do with bodies – namely, seeing and being seen as sex objects. As several webcam cybersex participants told me:

> When someone is turned on by watching me, it make me feel that I'm sexier than I truly believe I am . . . it's nice to get compliments on . . . the body . . . I just think it's sexy that people can masturbate and think of me, little ole me.

> Having a few dozen guys tell you how hot you are, etc., really gives you a great outlook on how you see yourself sexually. Positive reinforcement!

> [Webcam cybersex] feels wonderful! Of course, it makes me feel like he desires my body. . . . As you can see, I'm a pretty good size woman. I'm not uncomfortable

about it on here. I feel as desirable as the ladies who are much smaller than me. As a matter of fact, I feel very sexy and seductive on here.

I enjoy most the emotional uplift I get from people telling me I am beautiful. I need to feel that I'm still attractive . . . It's just good to have people tell you you are still attractive.

This is easy to understand – it feels good to be told one is attractive, sexy, and desirable. For these cybersex participants the excitement others receive from seeing them nude is repaid by the comforting knowledge that one's body *is* appealing. As these quotes also illustrate, this is particularly the case for people who feel disenchanted with their body as an object of sexual arousal. Often this disenchantment has everything to do with perceptions of their physical appearances, especially regarding age and weight. As one man explained: "Being 48, it makes me feel attractive when someone compliments me on the body." Another explained, "It feels good when others compliment me. I feel like, even though I'm overweight, I am accepted by them."

Even so, it is misleading to conclude that webcam cybersex is all about aged and overweight people congratulating one another on their continued sexiness. A great number of webcam cybersex participants are highly attractive 20- and 30-year-olds. Yet, they too often share a similar disenchantment, but for different reasons. In fact, these webcam cybersex participants most often relate their disenchantment to marriage and long-term partnerships. For some, the problem is related to the routinization of their normal sexual activities and the desire for a different experience. As one woman told me, "My main reason for being here is to be sociable, hoping to meet that Mr. Right even though I'm married and have a very active sex life at home. The ROUTINE part sucks!" A man told me something very similar: "I've been in a long-term relationship for almost 5 years, and this way I can remain faithful to that while still getting off with hot guys from around the world." However, for most participants I interviewed, the desire for different sexual partners and novel erotic experiences is less important than what webcam cybersex does to re-enchant a sense of their body as an object of sexual arousal.

Murray Davis (1983: 119) once wrote: "[M]arriage seems almost intentionally designed to make sex boring." We may add that long-term sexual relationships also tend to make our bodies boring. In time, being seen nude by one's lover becomes so commonplace that our sexual generators simply run out of gas or otherwise lose their erotic power. Thus, it makes sense. When our own nudity no longer generates appreciative erotic power, a person may come to feel undesirable, unattractive, inadequate, and thoroughly unsexy. For this reason, some participants discover webcam cybersex useful in refueling a connection to their sexual body and rejuvenating their perceptions of the power of that body to generate eroticism:

I've been with my wife for so long now that our bodies aren't as exciting as they once were. Our sex life is ok, but without that special quality I sometimes feel like a piece of furniture around the house. When someone is excited about seeing me in all my nudity I suddenly feel sexually awake again.

Dennis D. Waskul

Hubby is older than I am. He knows nothing of this. I'm not a complainer but he does not have the passion or desire, or at least he doesn't know how to show me. . . . it's hard for him to tap into the part of my brain that triggers stimulation. I'm a very erotic person. The feeling of being naughty is a turn-on too. See, I'm bad, but I love it.

These expressed motives and virtues – of both text cybersex and webcam cybersex – are not particularly surprising. It's hardly shocking to discover that people who engage in cybersex tend to appreciate the experience. However, magnifying the obvious is often worthwhile: people who engage in cybersex tend to find the experience sexually arousing, but they also frequently report other pleasures that have everything to do with exploring, expressing, and cultivating a sexual imagination as well as acquiring new looking-glasses by which they assess themselves as an object and subject of sexual pleasure. Furthermore, exploring these "obvious" dynamics sharply contrasts with much published literature on cybersex, a majority of which seems quite intent on magnifying problems, dangers, and moral issues. Indeed, moral panic regarding cybersex, some of which I will address in the next section, is all too common.

Cybersex and moral panic

There seems no shortage of either "problemizers" or "problematizing" regarding the internet. For example, psychologist Kimberly Young is most known for her questionable assertion that "Internet Addiction Disorder" has reached epidemic proportions in the United States (in 1998 she estimated there were five million "addicts") and that the internet is a "millennial addiction" (1998: 28). Similarly, the subtitle to a book edited by Al Cooper et al. (2000) apparently plagiarizes filmmaker George Lucas: Cooper seeks to expose *The Dark Side of the Force*. However, unlike the movie *Star Wars*, in Cooper's apparent version of the movie fiction "the force" refers to the internet and "the dark side" of sex and pornography. Cooper (Cooper et al. 2000; Cooper 2002) and a growing cadre of associates have sought to provide an empirical foundation for "cybersex compulsivity," its health risks, and the appropriate "treatment." Unlike the run-of-the-mill "internet addict" that so deeply concerned Kimberly Young, these scholars suggest that cybersex – not the internet – is the "drug of choice" (Delmonico et al. 2002: 147, 149). Indeed, a quick review of the published literature on cybersex reveals an obvious bias: a large proportion examines sex on the internet as a form of "sexual addiction," "compulsive" behavior, and otherwise a manifestation of a "hypersexuality" disorder.

The prevalence of these problematizing literatures is curious considering that most researchers report that 1 percent (or less) meet *their own* definitions of internet "sex addicts" or "cybersex compulsives" – far less than the expansive literature on the subject might suggest. In fact, the number is so small that even the most well-known scholars of "cybersex compulsivity" (see Cooper et al. 2000: 19) are forced to admit that "[t]hough the focus of this article is sexually compulsive behavior on the internet, it bears reiterating that one of our major findings was that for the vast majority of respondents, surfing the internet for sexual pursuits did not lead to significant difficulties in their lives." However, apparently unwilling to accept the findings of their own study, Cooper et al. (2000: 20, 24) followed up this statement by claiming that there really *are* more compulsive cybersex addicts who dangerously flirt with the internet because "a significant portion (possibly between 27 and 42%) are likely to be in denial about the true severity of their issues," and that, "[i]n any case, the use of chat rooms for sexual pursuits should be a red flag and something to which clinicians should pay particular attention." Cooper *et al.* (2000: 25) conclude by likening "cybersex compulsivity" to a rampant drug addiction, suggesting that 200,000 Americans are likely to be "addicted" to sex on the internet, which they suggest is "a hidden public health hazard."

I do not deny that some people become compulsive about sex on the internet, but to characterize an empirical one percent as *really* more indicative of a speculative 27–42 percent is at the very least questionable, clearly hasty, perhaps poor science, possibly arrogant, and maybe self-serving. In fact, given the evidence offered, suggesting that sex on the internet might represent a "hidden public health hazard" may even qualify as irresponsible. When scholars are apparently unwilling to accept the findings of their own studies, choosing, instead, to gloss empirical data in lieu of hunches about what they "think" might be more accurate, we should *all* raise an eyebrow of suspicion.

When they are not concerned about the alleged hazards of internet sex to a person's own "health," many scholars are concerned about the perils to a person's relationships with others. This is particularly the case in literature examining what has come to be called "virtual infidelity." While, once again, I do not deny that internet sex can represent problems with "new infidelity" (Glass 2003), nonetheless upon closer examination the problem becomes more complex than is often presumed. For example, in *Cybersex Exposed*, Jennifer Schneider and Robert Weiss (2001) dedicate an entire chapter to "The Cybersex Widow(er)." Schneider and Weiss provide rich ethnographic data on 100 people (97 women and three men) who "felt" they lost their partners to cybersex. Significantly, several people cited by Schneider and Weiss freely acknowledge previous real-life infidelities; as one person said: "My husband has actually cheated on me with a real partner, and it *feels no different!*" (2001: 105; emphasis in original). Although Schneider and Weiss skirt the point, it seems reasonable to presume that a history of violated trust is a significant variable to consider in the tribulations endured by these so-called "cybersex widows." Even more interesting are many accounts from respondents who appear mostly distraught by *masturbation*. Consider, for example, just a few words cited by Schneider and Weiss (2001: 89–90, 93):

> I knew my husband was masturbating all the time, but I thought it was my fault, that I just wasn't attractive enough for him. When I found pornography files on his computer going back five years, everything made sense. . . . I thought I was not good enough because I did not look like the girls in the computer pictures. I thought if I dressed and looked better, it would keep him interested. Eventually, I gave up competing with his masturbating and chose not to have sex with him. His behavior has left me feeling alone, isolated, rejected, and less than a desired woman. Masturbation hangs a sign on the door that says, "You are not needed. I can take care of myself, thank you very much."

Obviously, for these respondents in Schneider and Weiss's study, masturbation within marriage is a "problem." Yet, oddly, Schneider and Weiss gloss the masturbation issue and attribute the trouble to "cybersex." Once again, I do not deny that internet sex can pose difficulties for committed relationships, but clearly there is more to the story than first appears. Pinning these fidelity problems on "cybersex" may be convenient and attention-grabbing – but is it accurate?

I suggest that these problematizing studies are more about morality than social science. Even more, these moral positions are often based on highly questionable assumptions. On one hand, they regularly hinge on questionable determinist views of the effects of media. On the other hand, they are often based on equally questionable essentialist views of sex, sexuality, children, women, men, and the nature of committed relationships (especially marriage). While this is not the place for a full critique of these studies (some of which *do* have merit), I merely suggest a more critical stance on the all-too-easy claims regarding the hazards, dangers, perils, and risks of internet sex. Indeed, as Steven Stern and Alysia Handel (2001: 283, 289) have neatly pointed out, contemporary concerns about sex on the internet are nothing new: "they are part of a recurring pattern in which people worry about the use of new technology for sexual purposes" and "focusing too heavily on these details might distract us from a complete understanding of sexuality on the internet."

Discussion

Like cars and telephones, computer networking technologies bestow a seductive freedom – the "freedom to" (Stoll 1995: 234). In the case of internet sex, the "freedom to" can assume many and multiple forms: the freedom to experiment with the surfaces and depths of one's desires and fantasies; the freedom to present one's self and body alternatively; the freedom to indulge sexual interest with relatively minimal fear of consequence (either physical or social); the freedom to see and be seen as both a sex object and a sex subject to whatever degree one feels comfortable; the freedom momentarily to shed social roles (faithful partner, monogamous spouse, dedicated parent, or whatever); the freedom to play, explore, and discover in ways that one might not (or cannot) in everyday life. One way to characterize these various "freedoms to" is a simple recognition: the internet bestows the freedom to "be" without "being" in a "space" without "place" (see Waskul 2005). On the internet, everybody is any body, and any body is nobody in particular. Likewise, on the internet, everywhere is any where, everyplace is any place, and anywhere is nowhere in particular. Consequently, the internet provides a context, medium, and environment in which people have the "freedom to" slip through the cracks of otherwise mundane everyday life.

It is not surprising that circumstances like these evoke moral condemnation, from many sources (religious, political, legal, social-scientific, and so on). To whatever extent we believe that the whole of a person – sexual or otherwise – is rightly found in an individual's over-socialized roles of society (occupational, family, romantic, etc.), then any "crack" that allows people freely to shed those roles will be deemed a threat to moral and social order. At the very least, as scholars of the social world, it is worth recalling that such a view is the antithesis of many influential theoretical perspectives and conceptual frameworks which detail the nature of human social life (see Waskul 2005). Regardless, internet sex is potentially "sex off the leash" – a form of sexual expression that exists outside of most formal social controls – and that is precisely why it tends to offend some people while also posing a tantalizing draw for others. As Cleo Odzer (1997: 113) rightly points out, "To society, the worst use of sex, of course, is as a means to an end that's not socially sanctioned." The motives and virtues of internet sex certainly represent one such "means to an end that's not socially sanctioned." Perhaps those who adhere closest to Augustinian or Freudian views of sexuality – viewing sex as a potentially dangerous source of both destruction and evil – would agree that unsanctioned sexuality is a timeless peril that requires faithful and vigilant guards. Perhaps others might see sexuality as infinitely more than a person's behaviors, something that includes thoughts, dreams, desires, and fantasies that are not so easily contained by social control – too much of which might result in monstrous expressions. Perhaps others will merely find it all ironic, amusing, and playful. Others still might simply remain fascinated by it all. Indeed, in the final analysis, internet sex is much like many other subjects and experiences – it might well be assessed by how it uniquely moves you.

Note

1   I would like to thank Phillip Vannini and Matthew Bernius for their gracious reviews of early versions of this chapter.

Bibliography

Cooper, Al. (ed.) 2002. *Sex and the internet: A Guidebook for Clinicians*. New York: Brunner–Routledge.

Cooper, Al, David Delmonico, and Ron Burg. 2000. "Cybersex Users, Abusers, and Compulsives: New Findings and Implications." In A. Cooper (ed.), *Cybersex: The Dark Side of the Force*. Philadelphia, PA: Brunner–Routledge.

Davis, Murray. 1983. *Smut: Erotic Reality/Obscene Ideology*. Chicago, IL: University of Chicago Press.

Delmonico, David, Elizabeth Griffin, and Patrick Carnes. 2002. "Treating Online Compulsive Sexual Behavior: When Cybersex is the Drug of Choice." In A. Cooper (ed.), *Sex and the Internet: A Guidebook for Clinicians*. New York: Brunner–Routledge.

Glass, Shirley. 2003. *Not Just Friends*. New York: The Free Press.

Langman, L. 2004. "Grotesque Degradation: Globalization, Carnivalization, and Cyberporn." In D. Waskul (ed.), *Net.SeXXX: Readings on Sex, Pornography, and the Internet*. New York: Peter Lang.

Odzer, Cleo. 1997. *Virtual Spaces: Sex and the Cyber Citizen*. New York: Berkley Books.

Perdue, Lewis. 2002. *EroticaBiz: How Sex Shaped the Internet*. New York: Writers Club Press.

Schneider, Jennifer and Robert Weiss. 2001. *Cybersex Exposed: Simple Fantasy or Obsession?* Center City, MN: Hazelden.

Stern, Steven and Alysia Handel. 2001. "Sexuality and Mass Media: The Historical Context of Psychology's Reaction to Sexuality on the Internet." *Journal of Sex Research* 38 (4): 283–91.

Stoll, Cliff. 1995. *Silicon Snake Oil: Second Thoughts on the Information Highway*. New York: Doubleday.

Waskul, Dennis. 2002. "The Naked Self: Being a Body in Televideo Cybersex." *Symbolic Interaction* 25 (2): 199–227.

—. 2003. *Self-Games and Body-Play: Personhood in Online Chat and Cybersex.* New York: Peter Lang.

—. (ed.) 2004. *Net.SeXXX: Readings on Sex, Pornography, and the Internet.* New York: Peter Lang.

—. 2005. "Ekstasis and the Internet: Liminality and Computer-Mediated Communication." *New Media & Society* 7 (1): 45–61.

Waskul, Dennis, Mark Douglass, and Charles Edgley. 2000. "Cybersex: Outercourse and the Enselfment of the Body." *Symbolic Interaction* 23 (4): 375–97.

Young, Kimberly. 1998. *Caught on the Net: How to Recognize the Signs of Internet Addiction – and a Winning Strategy for Recovery.* New York: John Wiley and Sons.

chapter 48

The political economy of sexual labor

Interview with Elizabeth Bernstein

Elizabeth Bernstein is an Associate Professor of Women's Studies and Sociology at Barnard College. She writes about issues concerning sexual commerce and trafficking. She has written numerous articles and the book *Temporarily Yours: Intimacy, Authenticity and the Commerce of Sex* (2007).

Tell us a little about yourself.

My research occurs at the intersection of the sociology of sexuality and feminist approaches to law and policy. My two books, *Temporarily Yours* (University of Chicago Press, 2007) and *Regulating Sex* (Routledge, 2005), explore the interplay between transformations in political economy, modes of state regulation, and sexual practices and identities in the post-industrial West. My current research examines the coordination of political-economic and religious interests in the development of recent US policies pertaining to the "traffic in women." Throughout all of this work, my agenda has been to illuminate the moral and political convictions that motivate particular sets of social actors and to situate policies pertaining to gender and sexuality within a broader field of social, political, and economic relations.

By training, I am a qualitative sociologist who draws from a combination of participant observation, in-depth interviews, and discursive analysis to ground my theoretical claims. Because my work seeks to connect "micro" with "macro" levels of social transformation, my ethnographic approach is both multi-sited and multi-perspectival. I situate my scholarship within sociological lineages that seek to understand local behaviors and identities in terms of their enabling political-economic and historical conditions. In my writing, I place my own ethnographic research in explicit dialogue with a broad array of empirical and theoretical work on contemporary political economy and cultural transformations, engaging with scholarship from anthropology, history, political theory and law in addition to sociology and interdisciplinary gender and sexuality studies. In contrast to social researchers who aspire to apprehend their data in the absence of any contaminating theoretical apparatus, my own research agenda has developed with an aim to address specific and evolving sets of paradoxes and questions.

Currently, I am a member of the women's studies and sociology departments at Barnard College, Columbia University, where I teach courses on the sociology of gender and sexuality; trafficking, migration, and sexual labor; and contemporary social theory.

For Temporarily Yours, *a research project on contemporary forms of prostitution, you employed a number of methods for researching different aspects of sex work. Could you discuss the different approaches you took and explain why you chose them?*

My primary methodological approach for *Temporarily Yours* was ethnographic – meaning I spent a long time talking to, following around, and "hanging out" with diverse participants in the sex industry. However, the focus of my research evolved a lot over the course of the nearly 10 years that I was working on this book. It actually began as a study of the San Francisco Task Force on Prostitution, which had been formed to look into the possibility of reforming prostitution policy in the city. Initially, I had been intrigued by the abundant media coverage of the Task Force, which suggested that the feminists, prostitutes' rights activists, and neighborhood representatives that formed its core were considering legalizing prostitution (a solution which each of the above groups had historically opposed) and even contemplating such controversial public policy solutions as city-run brothels or municipal licensing. I wondered if and under what guise prostitutes' concerns were being represented in these considerations, who was doing the representing, and which (if any) feminist position would predominate when it came down to the nitty-gritty of policy reform. Most importantly, I was concerned about what the likely impact would be – for sex-workers and other city residents – if the proposed reforms should come to pass.

Most of the prostitutes' rights leaders who held seats on the Task Force told me that they were either currently working as prostitutes or had worked as prostitutes in the past. Yet I was soon to discover that only a few had any experience with street prostitution – the main focus of the Task Force's attention. As I got to know them and the organizations they represented, I came to have a better understanding of the complexity and diversity of local prostitution markets, and the different social realities they entailed. At this point, I decided to expand my project to include participant observation with sex-workers working in diverse ways and at diverse levels, so that I might test empirically my growing suspicion that the dynamics and meanings of prostitution varied systematically across social space. I became particularly interested in the contrast between the self-employed sex workers that I had met in activist groups like COYOTE, and the lived realities of commercial sex work for those who walked the streets.

Like a series of ever-widening concentric circles, my project expanded outward for several years, as I reached for broader and broader contexts to make sense of what I saw. In 1998, I learned that Sweden and the Netherlands were in the process of revising their prostitution policies, and that both countries had assembled task forces similar to the one that I had served on in San Francisco. These two cases were of particular interest to me because Sweden and the Netherlands had both been hailed as "gender utopias" by various groups of feminist activists and the press, yet the two countries were changing their laws in opposite directions: Sweden was implementing a criminalization model, while the Netherlands was legalizing the sex trade. I realized that by looking together at the cases of San Francisco, Amsterdam, and Stockholm, I would be able to compare the lived dynamics of contemporary prostitution under three different legal regimes, in cities that shared a number of common features, including size, economic infrastructure, and reputations for being socially progressive.

Of these different ways of researching the social contexts of sex work that you undertook for Temporarily Yours, *which was the most difficult and why?*

As many ethnographers have noted, the most difficult aspect of social research is "studying up," rather than studying down or horizontally. People with social power – e.g. state agents, middle-class social activists, the police – are the least likely group to be willing to share their opinions or the intimate details of their lives. Even though there were certain things that made my research with policy makers easier to conduct than my research with sex workers (such as the fact that this research generally took place in comfortable indoor settings and during normal business hours), figuring out the state's interests in regulating the sex trade was the hardest nut for me to crack.

My fieldwork with street-based sex workers was actually much easier, and was facilitated by some crucial collaborations. The San Francisco-based prostitutes' rights activist, Carol Leigh, had been doing condom distribution amongst street prostitutes for over a year by the time I met her. She was enthusiastic and welcoming when I asked if I might join her, and we spent the next six months as research and outreach partners. With her 15-year tenure as a prominent local activist, Carol was instrumental in introducing me to a vast network of sex workers who were important informants for this project.

This is not to suggest that my research on the streets did not present me with serious challenges. In his book, *Distinction*, the sociologist Pierre Bourdieu cautions that when researchers attempt to understand social others through a provisional and deliberate engagement with their worlds, the result is likely to be perceptions of these worlds which still derive from the researcher's own habitus[1]. On the streets, there were clearly degrees of social distance that made my provisional entry into this world possible in the first place (such as being white and middle class) and which also allowed me to return home to my own comparatively safe and comfortable surroundings at the end of the night. These social disparities were politically as well as methodologically troubling to me, and led to my growing activist engagement in sex workers' rights issues. They also led to my decision to orient my street-based research around problems that were relevant to the sex workers themselves. When I announced my intention to investigate the police treatment of streetwalkers (which was something that the women on the streets complained about routinely) and indicated that I was prepared to go undercover as a "decoy" and to be taken to jail along with everyone else, the sex workers were very enthusiastic.

What large-scale social changes in the economy have impacted sex work?

There is an abundant literature on the transformations that have taken place within the global economy over the last 30 years. Numerous sociologists have traced the nature and significance of post-industrialism and the emergence and impact of the service economy and the new information technologies, as well as ensuing socio-demographic changes[2]. While sociologists of the family and of culture have extended this project, few commentators have linked postindustrial cultural formations to the changing nature of sexuality.

One of the key arguments of *Temporarily Yours* is that the proliferation of forms of service work, the new global information economy, and "postmodern" families peopled by isolable individuals have produced another profound transformation in the erotic sphere. Both the traditional "procreative" and the modern "companionate" models of sexuality are increasingly being supplemented by a sexual ethic that derives its primary meaning from the depth of physical sensation and from emotionally bounded erotic exchange – what in the book I call *bounded authenticity*. Whereas in the domestic sphere, relational sexuality derived its meaning from its ideological opposition to the marketplace, bounded authenticity bears no antagonism to the sphere of public commerce. It is available for sale and purchase as readily as any other form of commercially packaged leisure activity.

Another important way that contemporary economic transformations and sex work are linked is through the gentrification of post-industrial cities and the decline of streetwalking as a commercial sexual form. From the fall of 1994, when I first began my study, to the early part of 1997, street prostitutes in San Francisco were steadily "pushed" by police sweeps deeper and deeper into the Tenderloin. By 1997, local politicians and police had made a more definitive decision regarding street prostitution in San Francisco: they decided to eliminate it. As in other US and Western European cities, rigorous, combative policing became a frontline strategy for purging sex workers and other marginalized populations (such as the homeless and the mentally ill) from newly desirable downtown real estate. With increased police crackdowns on street-walking, a new array of spatially dispersed sexual services emerged to take its place. In this way, transformations in the forms and functions of urban space were accompanied by changes in the social geography of commercial sex.

Similarly, how has information technology been changing sex work?

Sex workers were among the first and most consistent beneficiaries of the technological innovations that defined the "new economy." The internet has reshaped predominant patterns of sexual commerce in ways that some sex workers have been able to benefit from. At the same time that street-based sex workers have been more severely policed, for many indoor sex workers it has become easier to work without third-party management, to conduct one's business with minimal interference from the criminal justice system, and to reap greater profits by honing one's sales pitch to a more elite and more specialized audience.

By advertising through specialty websites, sex workers can pitch their ads towards clients with an interest in their specific physical characteristics (e.g. fat women, older women, Asian women), or in the precise sexual services for which they can offer expertise (e.g. tantra, sadomasochism, erotic massage). Many such sites are even linked to client websites which feature restaurant-style "reviews" of their services. The erotic review sites that clients frequent are also subdivided by market niche. For example, there are some websites that are geared specifically towards budget shoppers, while other websites contain links to escorts' "blogs," in which the day-to-day musings of the sex worker are intended to serve as a window into her personality. There are also a number of websites such as *Craig's List* where sex workers can advertise if they are interested in working sporadically or informally, and where ads for sex workers appear unobtrusively between the headings for computer help, event planning, and real estate.

How different is sex work from other types of service work that require emotional labor on the part of women?

The sociologist Arlie Hochschild originally devised the term "emotional labor" within the context of her research on airline stewardesses, for whom smiling and the production of cheerfulness are often part of the job. She argued that "this kind of labor calls for a coordination of mind and feeling," and draws on a source of self "that we honor as deep and integral to our individuality" (Hochschild 1983:7). Since Hochschild first devised the term, various scholars have found it to be a useful analytic tool for understanding the kinds of caring work that women are called upon to perform in many different labor sectors, including such arenas as childcare and domestic work, nail salons, bar hostessing, and sex work.

The insecurity and transience of contemporary social life have led some people to divest emotional meaning from their private-sphere relationships, reinvesting it instead in market relations, both as workers and as consumers. Through reliance on such things as psychotherapy, child care, domestic labor, and take-out cuisine, they seek to provide their lives with the necessary "services" – and emotional meaning – that individuals of an earlier era could expect to secure in noncommodified, private-sphere relationships. What Hochschild has termed "women's uneasy love affair with capitalism" is made all the more acute when we consider that many of the flourishing sectors of the late-capitalist service economy, including sex work, are commercialized refinements of services that women have historically provided for free (Hochschild 1997: 221).

You interviewed some male sex workers in your study. Were their experiences different than the women's?

In the post-industrial cities where I conducted my research, male sex workers comprised approximately a third of the overall market. For methodological rather than substantive reasons, my ethnographic research on the streets did not include a sustained focus on male sex workers. The men tended to concentrate on different strolls and did not typically mix with the women that I worked with. Among indoor sex workers, however, gender divisions were less enforced, and my research was able to encompass the experiences of both women and men. Many of the indoor female and male sex workers that I met attended the same activist meetings, advertised in the same venues, and at times even shared clients.

That said, there are also some important differences between the experiences of male and female sex workers that should be highlighted. Socially and politically, male sex workers are less visible than female sex workers, and they are not arrested anywhere near as frequently. Some researchers have also stressed male sex workers' greater propensity to talk about their own experiences of pleasure – as opposed to simply work – in their performance of sexual labor. What I found in my research was that indoor male sex workers often took great pride in offering an experience of bounded authenticity to their clients. When female sex workers offered this, they would call it the "girlfriend experience" in their ads. Many of the male sex workers that I spoke with boasted that the best purveyors of the "girlfriend experience" were actually men. As one sex worker that I interviewed insisted, "You'll hear people talk about 'cold, mechanical, detached.' But to me . . . it's like a sacred, wonderful, beautiful thing to do for other people and to get money for doing that."

Building off the idea of purchasing a "girlfriend experience," there are a number of commentators who say that we are undergoing a "pornification of society" where the boundaries between "normal life" and those of the world portrayed by sex workers are blurring. Does this idea have any resonance for you? If so, what do you think is behind this trend?

It's true that a significant transformation of public culture has occurred, one which is in need of more serious theorizing than the moralizing commentary of the Religious Right (and certain feminists) have offered. Two of the most tangible markers of the new public culture of sexual commerce have included the mainstreaming and ubiquity of pornography and the normalization of commercial sexual products for female consumers (e.g. lingerie, sex toys, and instructional videos). It should also be noted that, despite recent challenges posed by a rising tide of sexual conservatism, the sex workers' rights movement has continued to flourish.

But it is also important to recognize that the normalization of sexual commerce and the policing of the most "deviant" corners of the industry have occurred simultaneously. Notably, all of the developments that I list above occurred during the very same period when public streetwalking was being eliminated from major urban centers and a new global panic around Third World and child prostitutes was gathering steam. In New York City, at the very same moment that streetwalkers and porn stores were being banished by Rudolph Giuliani's infamous zoning ordinances, new members-only erotic events were being mainstreamed for a white, middle-class clientele, who crowded into upscale sex parties by the hundreds. At the same time that Times Square's Harmony Burlesque Theater was shut down, Victoria's Secret was replacing the district's "live nude girls" with mannequins posed as strippers and donning frankly pornographic lingerie. Meanwhile, the ethos of the strip club continued its spread into privatized spaces, as "cardio-striptease" and pole-dancing classes became staple features of the home video market and city gyms.

The simultaneous trends of greater normalization and greater policing are best explained by situating them in terms of broader post-industrial transitions, including the gentrification of urban space, transformations in intimate relations, and changing social norms around gender and sexuality – especially for the affluent middle classes.

There have been a number of scholars who have questioned whether sex work should be legalized and/or regulated. How did your research on sex workers influence your views on this question?

In recent decades, states and municipalities throughout North America, Australia, and Western Europe have sought to contain a burgeoning and diversifying sex trade through a variety of innovative measures – from stepped up enforcement against the perpetrators of "quality of life" crimes to the legalization of brothel keeping to increased client arrests. At the same time, "pro-sex" as well as "anti-prostitution" feminists have argued for an array of competing legal remedies, advocating on behalf of diverse forms of legalization or criminalization.

Few commentators, however, have situated their analyses within the context of post-industrial transformations of sexuality and culture. My comparative research in San Francisco, Amsterdam, and Stockholm (cities which employ three very different legal regimes) demonstrates that the failure to situate sexual commerce within a broader political-economic framework can lead advocates to argue for opposing tactics which, once implemented, might have surprisingly similar effects on the ground. Whether sex work is decriminalized, legalized, or criminalized, the interests of real estate developers, municipal and national politicians, and business owners may overshadow the concerns of feminists and sex workers.

What is arguably most remarkable about the disparate array of legal strategies that Europeans and North Americans have implemented in recent years is how singular they have been in effect: the overarching trend has been toward the elimination of prostitution from city streets, coupled with the state-facilitated (or de facto tolerated) flourishing of the indoor and online sectors of the sex trade. In San Francisco, Amsterdam, and Stockholm, three quite disparate versions of policy reform in the late 1990s resulted in a common series of alterations to the social geography of sexual commerce: the removal of economically disenfranchised and racially marginalized streetwalkers from gentrifying city centers; the de facto tolerance of a small tier of predominantly white and relatively privileged indoor sex workers; and the increased policing of illegal migrant workers, pushing them further underground. While the divergent components of national and local cultures, histories, and regulatory strategies are by no means irrelevant to the configuration of sexual commerce in these cities, the shared realities ushered in by larger patterns of political economy have been more definitive in shaping its predominant forms. In all three cases, the common focus of state interventions has been upon eliminating the visible manifestations of poverty and deviance (both racial and national) from urban spaces, rather than the exchange of sex for money per se.

What are you researching now?

My current research analyzes the social construction of "sex trafficking" in discourse and policy, both within the United States and transnationally. Over the course of the last decade, a good deal of political attention – but scant empirical research – has been dedicated to decrying "the traffic in women" as a dangerous manifestation of global gendered inequalities. Within the United States, the advocacy of evangelical

Christian and secular feminist actors has served to grant the issue of human trafficking unprecedented prominence in both the Bush and the Obama administrations. In my new research, I take as a departure point my earlier research with migrant and domestic sex workers and the diverse social actors that attempt to regulate their movements. As an ethnographer, I have been attending state- and activist-sponsored policy meetings as well as evangelical Christian "pray-ins" in order to investigate the strategies and ambitions of the unlikely coalition of conservative Christians and feminist activists who have pressed this issue. The commitments and activities of these two groups are important to look at because they have produced policy transformations on a scale unparalleled since the White Slavery scare of the Progressive era.

Any final thoughts?

In most debates about the moral and social significance of sex work, commentators' own assumptions regarding the proper relationship between the spheres of sex, intimacy, and commerce are left unstated. Ethical and political evaluations of prostitution often apply an unstated norm by presuming it to consist of a timeless set of practices and meanings. I suggest instead that normative discussions of sexual labor begin with an understanding of the socially and historically specific meanings that affix to commercial sexual transactions and to intimacy and sexuality more generally. Practices of sexual commerce ought to be situated squarely within contemporary economic and cultural currents, rather than regarded as exceptions to be judged apart.

Notes

1   Pierre Bourdieu, *Distinction: A Social Critique of the Judgment of Taste* (Cambridge, MA: Harvard University Press, 1984: 372–73). In Bourdieu's work, the term "habitus" refers to socially specific capacities to think, feel, and act in particular ways. As such, the term connects individual and social levels of experience. For a brief discussion of the term and its usage in Bourdieu's work, see Loïc Wacquant, "Habitus," *International Encyclopedia of Economic Sociology* (New York, NY: Routledge, 2004).
2   See, for example, Daniel Bell, *The Cultural Contradictions of Capitalism* (New York, NY: Basic Books, 1978), David Harvey, *The Condition of Postmodernity* (Cambridge, MA: Blackwell, 1990), Gøsta Esping-Andersen, *The Three Worlds of Welfare Capitalism* (Princeton, NJ: Princeton University Press, 1990), Robin Leidner, *Fast Food, Fast Talk* (Berkeley, CA: University of California Press, 1993), Sherrie Turkle, *Life on the Screen* (New York, NY: Simon & Schuster, 1995), and Manuel Castells, *The Rise of the Network Society: The Information Age: Economy, Society and Culture, Vol. 1* (Minneapolis, MN: Wiley-Blackwell, 2000).

References

Hochschild, Arlie. 1983. *The Managed Heart*. Berkeley: University of California Press. Page 7.
—. 1997. *The Time Bind*. New York: Metropolitan Books. Page 221.

chapter 49

Sex workers

Interview with Wendy Chapkis

Wendy Chapkis is an Associate Professor of Women's Studies and Sociology at the University of Southern Maine. She is editor of two anthologies published by the Transnational Institute in Amsterdam, *Loaded Questions: women in the military* (1979) and *Of Common Cloth: women in the global textile industry* (co-edited with Cynthia Enloe; 1983), and author of two books, *Beauty Secrets: women and the politics of appearance* (South End Press; 1985) and *Live Sex Acts: women performing erotic labor* (Routledge; 1997). Her current research is on medical marijuana use and the "War on Drugs" (*Dying to Get High*; co-authored with Richard Webb, New York University Press, 2008).

How is it that you came to study sex workers?

I don't really see myself as "studying sex workers." That sounds too much like Dian Fossey studying the great apes. I think of myself as studying the practices and meanings of prostitution for women.

Like most women of my generation, I grew up with my mother's understanding that sex was about both pleasure and danger. What defined sex was male pleasure and what haunted sex was the risk to women of rape, pregnancy, and loss of reputation.

I came of age twenty years later than my mother, in the late 1960s and early 1970s. The difference was profound. In a time of free love and women's liberation, the innocence of virginity was far less compelling than carnal knowledge. And in the age of the pill and legal abortion, some of the dangers associated with sex seemed to recede. But while free love might have been packaged as a revolutionary practice, getting paid for it was not. Despite my misgivings about the practice, I was pretty sure that it was an incomplete understanding of exploitation to define it as someone getting paid for what

I was willing to do for free. While men clearly benefited from the institution of prostitution, I wondered who benefited from making criminals of women charging for sex.

How did your sociological and feminist colleagues respond to your research interests?

I started formally studying sex work while in graduate school in the 1980s and early 1990s, at the University of California at Santa Cruz. At least one of my mentors in sociology feared that I was turning away from serious issues (such as global economic inequality) to focus on sex – though of course the two are deeply interconnected. Perhaps he was just concerned that I would make myself unmarketable after first publishing a book about women and beauty standards and then following it up with a dissertation about commercial sex. In general, though, sociology has been pretty receptive to my work. I have experienced somewhat more hostility within feminist circles, including some versions of women's studies.

Why did you choose to study sex work in Amsterdam, the Netherlands?

I have a complex and long-standing connection with the Netherlands. During my undergraduate studies, I enrolled at the University of Amsterdam for a year. Then, after graduation, I returned to the Netherlands for most of a decade (from the mid-1970s to the mid-1980s) to work at the Institute for Policy Studies' international center – the Transnational Institute in Amsterdam. I was both impressed with and infuriated by Dutch culture. On the one hand, it offered a hopeful contrast to the United States of the Reagan years: the Netherlands was a successful social democracy with a deep commitment to both collective responsibility (in the form of a generous welfare state resulting in low rates of poverty) and individual rights (demonstrated through the de facto decriminalization of marijuana use and prostitution). It had a vibrant women's movement. But it also had the lowest rates of female employment in Western Europe. Dutch national identity emphasized "tolerance" but, at the same time, my experience living in the Netherlands as a woman with a moustache was one of unremitting and very public harassment.

When I returned to the United States in 1985 to attend graduate school, I had no sense that the Netherlands would figure prominently in my future research. But as I became reacquainted with sexual politics in the US, I began to draw comparisons between the two settings. America in the 1980s was enmeshed in the so-called "sex wars," with feminists deeply divided over commercial sex. I had just come from a decade in a country with both an active women's movement and a very visible and legal prostitution sector.

As I began developing a research focus for my dissertation, I decided to confront head-on my own ambivalence about prostitution, to begin to examine why commercial sex had become such a central issue in contemporary feminist politics, and to explore whether prohibition of prostitution (which made criminals out of participants) in fact improved the lives of prostitutes in the US. The Netherlands, with its decriminalized prostitution sector, seemed like a perfect counter-example for purposes of comparison.

Can you talk about some of the problems you encountered researching sex workers? For example, was it difficult to gain their trust and did you have to get approval by any government agencies?

Fortunately, neither in the US nor in the Netherlands are government agencies in a position to decide whether sex workers are allowed to speak with researchers. The only state officials I worried about were law enforcement officers in the United States – and then only because I was concerned that the women I interviewed were admitting to engaging in criminal conduct. For that reason, I asked all of my interview subjects whether they wanted to be known by name or to remain anonymous. For safety reasons – that is, to reduce the possibility of police harassment – many of the women I interviewed in the US did ask to be anonymous. Some Dutch sex workers, though far fewer, also requested anonymity; sex work might be legal in the Netherlands but it is still stigmatized.

Trust is, of course, critical in such circumstances. I wouldn't have had any access if the women I wished to interview didn't have some measure of confidence in me as an ally. I worked hard to establish my credentials as a feminist advocate of prostitutes' rights before I began soliciting interviews. In the town in which I lived in California, for example, I organized a political alliance between sex workers and (other) feminist activists to protest against police raids on the local massage parlors. Regardless of our views on prostitution (and they were very mixed within the alliance), we all agreed that closing women's places of employment did nothing to empower them and, in fact, meant that many of them had to resort to working in more isolated and dangerous settings – out of their own homes or on the streets.

Similarly, when I returned to the Netherlands in 1993 to do comparative research, I volunteered with the Dutch prostitutes' rights organization, the Red Thread, as a way to be of service before asking for their time and their experiences.

I can't imagine skipping that step and simply approaching women working the streets, out of their homes, behind the windows, or in the clubs, and asking for an interview, without first having made clear what was at stake for me and offering to be of use. Once I had begun doing interviews, sex workers referred others to me.

I was fully aware that, by establishing access through work with activist organizations, my sample was skewed toward women who were politically involved and who tended to see their involvement in prostitution as work. I attempted to deal with this bias both by being explicit about it in my writing and by making a conscious effort to find women who did not share that sense of commercial sex as potentially empowered work. For example, I contacted the Dutch anti-trafficking organization, the STV, and asked them to provide me with interview data with women who had been victims of forced prostitution. Those interviews were the only ones I did not conduct myself but rather gathered through the organization's own staff; trust and familiarity were clearly critically important for women in situations of forced prostitution.

But it is also important to say that I believe sex workers share their stories with researchers not only because they trust us but also because they see us as useful to them. A common misconception is that sex workers are passive objects used by clients and by scholars for our own pleasures and purposes. In fact, of course, sex workers are also active subjects with their own set of interests. I was well aware that sex workers were using me to help get their stories out, to build sympathy and greater respect for those in prostitution, and – in the United States – to help make the case that their lives were made more difficult and more dangerous by the criminalization of their trade.

What ideas did you have about sex workers before you began your research, and did this change in the course of your research?

My ideas about sex workers have always been complicated and often contradictory. Before I began talking with women in the trade, I imagined some of them to be women with very restricted options motivated by desperation (for money or drugs) and forced by circumstance to surrender control over their bodies to dangerous strangers. I also often imagined some of them to be proudly renegade women who were sexual outlaws, women who made conscious and instrumental use of men's ability and desire to pay for sex, who embraced the stigma of the whore and rejected the social controls meant to discipline women's erotic lives. What I found once I entered the field was that both of these representations are true and that neither is adequate. Women's lives are rarely models of complete victimization or absolute empowerment. Prostitutes are no exception.

How did sex workers understand selling sex? Were they really able to approach their work as "just work"?

This kind of question is impossible to answer. There is no one understanding among sex workers of what it is to sell sex or even what it would mean to say that something was "just work." I believe the question arises in part because of a widespread sense that sex is uniquely difficult to commodify and that the process of doing so necessarily causes unique distress to the worker involved. But it is my sense that it is not the exchange of sex for money that is the cause of most of the difficulty within prostitution; instead it is the poor conditions under which that exchange takes place.

In addition, like many forms of service work, prostitution involves some measure of emotional labor. The challenges of performing emotional labor in other fields have been well described (see Arlie Hochschild's *The Managed Heart*,[1] for example). Some workers are more effective at establishing and maintaining emotional boundaries in those professions than are others. And, because prostitution – like all service work – is interactive, much depends on the behavior of the client. If a client is respectful and demands no more than what has been negotiated, the ability to create and maintain boundaries is enhanced. The intensity of the work also affects how well a worker can maintain a sense of the job as manageable. Working too many hours, seeing too many clients, earning too little money, or being treated with disrespect, all can contribute to worker distress.

But here I must emphasize that it is crucial to recognize that these challenges are not unique to prostitution. Most work shares some of these challenges, especially stigmatized or low-status work, work in the service sector or underground economy, and work that is physically and emotionally demanding. To imagine otherwise undermines our ability to understand prostitution as work and to imagine how to improve the conditions under which it is practiced.

Do you have a sense of how being a sex worker affected their sexual and social relationships outside of work?

I do think that "relationship strain" is an occupational hazard facing many sex workers. A sex worker has to create a clear distinction for herself and her partner between work and intimacy. Even if this is possible for the worker herself, her partner may struggle with it. In addition, the "whore" stigma clearly affects how sex workers are perceived outside of work by those who know what kind of work they do. A sex worker has to deal with both titillation and condemnation.

Could you describe a typical day at work for one of the sex workers you studied?

I find myself resisting this question. It feels both voyeuristic and impossible to fully answer. No single sex worker is representative, no particular form of sex work is "typical." Those differences among sex workers are more characteristic than the details of any one sex worker's day. Among the women I interviewed for *Live Sex Acts*,[2] a typical day was waiting for the phone to ring, talking to some guy, and hoping he shows up (Samantha working out of her home); watching the mirrors that reflect the action on the street to decide if you want to encourage a potential client or instead to turn your back, to apply more lipstick, and to wait until he passes by (Ans working behind the windows in Amsterdam); working the afternoon shift in a place with no windows, chatting up a few clients and realizing you'll have to get them drunk to at least make some money off the bar (Jo doing time in a "really chic" sex club); working the streets all night giving quick blow jobs and discovering you can make more money if you pack a dildo and pretend to be a boy instead of the underage girl you actually are who is trying to get enough money together to leave a sexually abusive home (Sandy discussing being a teenage streetworker); trying to give head in a photogenic fashion under hot lights and really enjoying the challenge of trying to make it all look effortless (Nina on the porn set); scheduling five, or maybe at most ten, clients in a whole week for a lengthy sensuous massage session where the men know that they are entering your temple and must behave respectfully (Vision). There is no typical form of sex work, no typical sex worker.

Are there differences between sex workers in the Netherlands and in the United States?

This question too is difficult to answer. The problem with the question is that there are enormous differences between sex workers within each of those countries; which American sex worker and which Dutch sex worker should we take as the model in order to compare them with each other?

It is more useful to discuss the important differences in national context, in the social and political conditions under which sex work is practiced. The Netherlands has a reasonably intact social welfare system that provides at least basic support for all legal residents of the country, including housing assistance and healthcare.

Drug addiction is understood to be a medical not a moral or criminal problem, and assistance to addicts is available. Dutch women working in prostitution are therefore less likely than their American counterparts to be doing so simply to survive. On the other hand, in many large Dutch cities – such as Amsterdam – many sex workers are not legal residents but rather undocumented immigrants who do not have access to the Dutch social welfare safety net. In addition, many migrant sex workers must earn enough money in the trade not only to support themselves but to send much needed income to family members in their home country.

The most important difference between the practice of prostitution in the Netherlands and in the US is the legal status of the trade: sex work is legal and regulated in the Netherlands while it is prohibited and criminalized in the US (except for several counties in Nevada). In the context of legal prostitution, the police become a potential resource for sex workers rather than an additional risk. When prostitution is legal, sex workers can discuss fully and openly with clients what services are provided (and what are not) and at what price. In the US, sex workers must negotiate in haste in an attempt to avoid police entrapment and arrest.

Once again, however, the advantages of legal prostitution exist only for legal residents of the Netherlands. The many undocumented migrants working in the Dutch sex trade have none of those protections. For them, much like their American counterparts, the police are feared, and deportation, if not arrest, is a constant risk.

Feminists have been divided in their view of women's sex work. Some see it as another form of gender exploitation, while others see it as an issue of women's worker rights. Where do you stand on this debate?

The short answer is that it is both another form of gender exploitation and an issue of workers' rights. It is surely not a coincidence that the vast majority of clients are male while the majority of sex workers are female. Prostitution is yet another social arena in which women perform undervalued service work, work that serves men.

But one of the crucial points here is that prostitution is far from unique in this respect. Women are over-represented throughout the service sector and under-represented in higher-paying occupations. I find it very unhelpful to separate out sex work as if it were uniquely exploitive of women.

In this area of women's work, it is crucial that women be allowed to organize, publicly to demand their rights as workers, to insist on the dignity and respect owed any worker, owed any woman. That is made much, much more difficult when sex work is criminalized and relegated to the underground economy.

And yes, sex work is also about sex. Women and sex are closely linked in our culture – women's sexual status is still defining for many women: virgins, wives, and mothers have a protected status denied to sluts, dykes, and whores. Sex, in other words, is used to separate the good and virtuous from the bad and disposable.

This is a distinction that feminists have been fighting for decades. I believe that it is imperative for the current generation of women's rights activists to recognize that, as long as a woman is prohibited from deciding the terms under which she will engage in sexual activity – whether for pleasure or profit or reproduction – no woman is free. In other words, the struggle of sex workers for legal rights and cultural respect is a shared struggle. We all lose when a whore is a woman who deserves whatever she gets and when a sexually active woman is an object of ridicule unless she is engaged in satisfying her conjugal and reproductive duty.

What do you see as the prospects for a sex worker rights movement in the US?

The movement is well underway. Sex workers in this country have been engaged in collective political action since at least 1973 when COYOTE (the San Francisco-based sex worker self-advocacy organization) was formed. COYOTE and other sex worker rights organizations around the country continue to demand the decriminalization of sex work, improved working conditions, and respect for the men and women performing erotic labor.

In the past decade, at least one group of sex workers in the US successfully unionized and gained collective representation – the exotic dancers at the San Francisco club, the Lusty Lady.[3] The workers not only won union representation in 1996, but in 2003 they bought the business and created a sex worker cooperative. But many forms of sex work are much more difficult to unionize both because most sex work is criminalized in the US and because, even in the legal sectors such as exotic dancing and pornography, workers are most often considered "independent contractors" rather than employees. For this reason, much of contemporary sex worker organizing has been grassroots, informal and educational.

Over the past twenty years, sex workers have begun to add their own voices to those of researchers in writing accounts of the sex trade.[4] In addition, sex workers are writing and publishing magazines directed at those in the trade, including such periodicals as *Danzine*, *Spread*, and *Hook*.

Clearly, sex workers are continuing to come out and, in the process, are making clear that there is no clear and easy distinction between "them" and "us." And it seems to me that Third-Wave feminists seem to be heeding the call to link feminist campaigns for control over our own bodies to the struggles of sex workers for self-determination.

Of course, all of this is happening in the midst of a well-organized anti-sex moral panic in this country, as evidenced by abstinence-only sex "education" in the public schools, the continuing refusal of the FDA [U.S. Food and Drug Administration] to approve over-the-counter sales of the morning-after pill; attacks on abortion rights; new laws prohibiting equal marital rights for same-sex couples; the Bush Administration's policy of denying funding to international family planning, AIDS, and anti-sex-trafficking organizations which support a woman's right to an abortion or which refuse to condemn the practice of prostitution. Clearly sex worker organizing – like all organizing around sexual rights – is facing powerful resistance.

But sex workers, like others engaged in intentionally non-reproductive sex, will not accept state-mandated second-class citizenship. Despite recent right-wing successes in seizing control of the state apparatus, this is not a stable moment for reactionary politics. The right's embrace of violence, repression, and religious intolerance depends too much on fear. Fear is not an emotion that can be mobilized indefinitely. The wheel is turning; a politics that offers more than fear and that acknowledges complexity not moral certainty will return. And I see sex workers among those who are on the front line of a politics of social justice, compassion, and pleasure.

Interview with Wendy Chapkis

Notes

1 Hochschild, Arlie (2003) *The Managed Heart: Commercialization of Human Feeling*, University of California Press.
2 Chapkis, Wendy (1997) *Live Sex Acts: Women Performing Erotic Labor*, Routledge.
3 Query, Julia and Vicky Funari (2000) *Live Nude Girls Unite*. Documentary film distributed by First Run Features.
4 For example, see contributions by sex workers to the following anthologies: Delacoste, Frederique and Priscilla Alexander (eds) (1998) *Sex Work*, Cleis Press; Nagle, Jill (ed.) (1997) *Whores and Other Feminists*, Routledge; Whisnant, Rebecca and Christine Stark (eds) (2005) *Not for Sale*, Spinifex Press. See also autobiographical monographs by sex workers, such as: Burana, Lily (2003) *Strip City*, Miramax Books; Eaves, Elizabeth (2004) *Bare*, Seal Press; Egan, Danielle (2005) *Dancing for Dollars, Paying for Love*, Palgrave Macmillan; Sprinkle, Annie (1998) *Post-Porn Modernist*, Cleis Press; Tea, Michelle (2004) *Rent Girl*, Last Gasp Press.

chapter 50

Intimate labor in the adult film industry

Heather Berg

> *"Porn feels different than it looks"*
> —Nina Hartley®™

Intimate labor, a primer

As can be seen from the quotation above, veteran porn performer Nina Hartley®™ wants to remind us that "porn feels different than it looks" (Hartley 2012). You cannot watch a porn scene and know what happened behind the scenes. Perhaps this should be obvious. Anyone who has held a job knows that products do not tell the story of how they are made. But this seems easy to forget when we are talking about porn—anti and pro porn commentators alike tend to apply the same analyses to finished scenes and the process of producing them (Berg 2014a). What then does porn performance feel like for the workers who do it? What, exactly, does it mean to be a *performer*? Job descriptions in porn specify the particular sex acts a film gig calls for (e.g. "boy–girl" intercourse, oral sex, or "orgy"). But porn involves much more than simply showing up to set, having sex, and collecting a check.

Most jobs are organized this way. The *way* we do the work is more important than the basic tasks associated with it. A restaurant's advertisement for a waitress might list placing orders and delivering food and drink as job tasks, but we know that the work also requires making customers feel comfortable so that they order another round of drinks, tip generously at the end of the night, and return to the restaurant again. This work—the kind a job classified ad will not tell you about—means pretending that one cares how the customer's day was, or whether they are enjoying their meal; not letting one's frustration show when they ask for a fifth free soda refill; or politely deflecting a request for a date rather than exclaiming, "no, don't you see, I'm paid to be nice to you!" These are the tasks implied by "delivering food and drink," and they are more central to the work than the act of carrying beer to a table. Likewise, porn performance is less about the basic physical act of having sex than it is performing genuine interest in one's partner, exaggerating markers of pleasure (cue here the porn moan), and sustaining relationships with directors who may hire one in the future.

Scholars use the term "intimate labors" to describe the ways in which jobs as seemingly different as porn performance and waitressing, call center customer service and childcare, similarly center on "the personal or the daily praxis of intimacy" (Boris and Parreñas 2010: 8). Most jobs call upon some level of interpersonal or emotional labor in workers. Factory workers laboring to appear subservient to management and corporate attorneys courting clients, for instance, do the relational work of performing deference. What makes intimate labor distinct is that intimacy is central to what is bought and sold in these jobs. Intimate labor describes not only emotional labor but also those jobs in which bodily intimacy is constitutive. Selling sperm, for example, does not require directly relating to consumers, but can nonetheless be understood as intimate labor because it trades in an activity that is socially constructed as personal and private (Boris and Parreñas 2010:7).

The personal nature of such jobs makes some people squeamish about calling them "jobs" at all. Such perspectives rely on a "hostile worlds view" which accepts the intimate (or personal) and the market (or public) as discrete and incompatible (Zelizer 2005:20). But intimacy has long been commodified, and wishing this were not so does not help those who do intimate work. In fact, it makes them more vulnerable. In paid and unpaid labor alike, intimate labors in mothering, care work, food service, and sex work, among others, are socially constructed as powered by innate gendered qualities rather than learned skills. In creative industries too, narratives of self-expression ask us to forget that artists are workers (Kleinhans 2011). Across such industries, this perception obscures intimate labor, most extremely when labors such as childcare are so devalued as to not command wages at all (Federici 1975). This mystification impacts not only wages, but also social rights and legal protections, including access to social safety nets and protection from abuse.

Consumers go to restaurants for service, not simply for food, and watch porn to see performance, rather than simply to see other people having sex. As such, employers in these industries derive profit from workers' intimate labor. This is why we call it "labor," and why it matters that we understand porn performance as more than simply having sex that happens to be filmed. Describing porn performance as a form of intimate labor highlights the skill required of porn performers, and can encourage employers, consumers, policy makers, and the public to reject stereotypes of porn and other sex workers as sexual deviants, naive victims, or exhibitionists for whom pay and working conditions are tertiary (Berg 2014b). We can then say that porn performers should have access to the rights often afforded to workers in other industries, including standardized pay, benefits, occupational health protections, and the ability to organize collectively.

Intimate labor in porn work

To say that porn performance is a form of intimate labor is to link it conceptually to other forms of work which market activities that are socially constructed as intimate, not to suggest that all workers in the industry view their labor as particularly intimate. Many explicitly distance themselves from the idea of on-camera sex as intimate. Performers make clear distinctions between "porn sex" and "sex" and refer to their bodies as the "instruments" or "tools" they use to produce scenes. Performers are more likely to speak about having "worked" with one another, for example, rather than having "had sex." They also resist the perception that the emotional and physical strains that can result from their work are unique (or uniquely horrible) because they relate to sexual intimacy. One performer likened the work of gearing up for a scene and finding something attractive in his partner to the emotional work he did in a bookstore job he had previously held. Another protested what she called the "sex negative" and "shaming" way that outsiders view physical strain on porn sets: "What's the big deal?" she asked, "you go to another job you might get sore" (Preston 2013). In these ways, performers construct ideas of intimacy that allow them to sustain careers in sex work and maintain boundaries between their work and personal lives, even as this work involves activities that are popularly associated with the personal.

Porn workers' emotion management strategies vary, but most describe self-conscious performance (in contrast to "being oneself") as something that helps make their work easier and more sustainable. This trend aligns with what sex work scholars in other contexts have documented as the ways in which self-aware performance can reduce job strain. Such scholars have found an indispensable resource in the theory of emotional labor Arlie Hochschild developed in her study of flight attendants (Hochschild 2003 [1983]). In her study of middle-class sex workers in San Francisco, Elizabeth Bernstein found that "bounded authenticity" is both a key emotion management strategy for workers and a central component of the services rendered to clients. "Bounded authenticity" ranges from what Hochschild termed "surface acting" to the work of maintaining real, but time-limited and emotionally and physically circumscribed, intimacy with clients (Bernstein 2007:103). Teela Sanders found that British prostitutes craft workplace sexual identities that simultaneously enhance earnings (by performing femininity in a manner than appeals to customer demand) and emotional health (by encouraging workers to put on a sort of performance that is clearly distinguishable from their non-work selves) (Sanders 2005:322). Likewise, erotic dancers in Susan Dewey's study described emotional labor similar to "surface acting." Diamond, a dancer, noted, "You have to keep smiling and pretending you're having a great time, but the minute you forget its just business, you're really in for it" (Dewey 2011:72). Porn performers' emotion management strategies shift from "deep" to "surface" acting fluidly, changing throughout their careers and even during a given workday. Such flexibility is important in part because porn performers are called upon to perform on at least three levels: performing for the camera, with (and for) co-workers, and for management.

While self-conscious performance and boundaries between life and work are important self-care strategies for porn workers, rigid distinctions between "porn sex" and "real sex" miss the point. These boundaries are fluid for performers, who adjust their approaches to the intimate labor of sex in line with their career trajectories, current relationship status, and the particulars of their jobs at a given time (what a scene requires, who their scene partner is, and etcetera). Intimate labor is a social exercise contingent on coworkers, management, the particular ways in which work is organized, and even one's mood on a given day. As such, sex on a porn set may feel *real* to workers one day and transparently manufactured another. Rigid distinctions between real and porn sex also reinforce the conservative idea that such a thing as real sex exists and can be identified as such, presumably by virtue of its featuring culturally and politically sanctioned sexual activity (Levin Russo 2007).

With these caveats in mind, let us examine how porn workers themselves describe their intimate labor. Here I draw from interviews I have conducted with porn workers as part of a larger study on labor conditions in the industry. Listening to performers reveals how the varieties of intimate work they do both build on each other and sometimes conflict. Chemistry with one's on screen partner, for example, might help to produce intense, realistic scenes. But too much chemistry between partners can also make performers less aware of the camera. Part of the work of porn is making one's partner feel like the only person in a room, while constantly keeping in mind that this is not the case. Performers on set do intimate work not only with one another but also with directors, lighting and camera operators, and production assistants.

"Opening up" for the camera

It need not reinforce the conservative idea of a neat distinction between porn and real sex to say that sex on set is labor-intensive in particular ways. Performers describe what those in the industry call "opening up for the camera" as a key factor in making sex on a set different from sex off one. As performer-director Prince Yashua put it, "We're not fucking at home, we're playing to the camera, everything we have to do is open . . . hold this, arch your back. This is an art form . . . It's only 20% physical; the rest of it is mental" (Yashua 2014). Opening up for the camera requires manipulating one's body such that film crews can capture a variety of angles, including the act of insertion. The positions that make such shots possible tend to be very different and more physically demanding than those performers find most comfortable or pleasurable off-scene. Performers view "opening up for the camera" as part of their jobs, and being able to shoot physically demanding scenes as part of what makes them professionals. As the performer Darling suggests, most performers approach porn as a job rather than a source of sexual pleasure: "This isn't your sex, this is a product we're trying to sell" (Darling 2014).

Performing for the camera requires not only making sex acts visible to the viewer, but also performing sexual pleasure in ways that will be legible to the audience. As such, it means manufacturing both visual and auditory markers of arousal (such as facial expressions, erections, lubrication, and moaning) and, for men and trans-women, reaching orgasm (and visibly ejaculating) at precisely the right time. Ejaculating too quickly (before enough footage has been shot) risks requiring that the scene be re-shot, while taking too long to do so is time consuming and tiring for one's on-screen partner(s) as well as directors and crews. This is a major source of anxiety for men and transwomen performers, from whom both early ejaculation and being unable to maintain an erection for what can be the several hours it takes to film mean "failing a scene" and risking both a day's wage and future job opportunities.

The evidence of pleasure that directors perceive will translate well to film is often different to that which would communicate enjoyment to an off-screen partner. Women performers describe being scolded for becoming flushed after having orgasms on set, for example. Production had to be halted mid-scene so that makeup artists could "fix" the situation. Just as a restaurant manager wants waiters to be friendly, but not so much so that they spend time chatting with customers rather than delivering their food, porn managers want performers to display pleasure, but within the strict boundaries of what they think makes for good production values.

For a wide range of products—from coffee to clothing—"authenticity" is increasingly commodified as a marketing tool (Banet-Weiser 2012). Porn is no different, and genres that promise "authentic" content, including gonzo, much web-only production, and feminist porn, enjoy significant market shares (Tibbals 2014). Performers' subtle and unacknowledged intimate labor is even more centrally part of the product in genres that ask workers not only to perform, but also to act as if they are not performing. Authenticity as a marketing strategy both demands and conceals labor. Critiquing this tendency to mystify the work of performance, queer and feminist porn performer Arabelle Raphael wrote that the language of authenticity "erases the fact that performing is labor and not just 'fun'" (quoted in Q 2014). Echoing Raphael, sex work activist and queer and feminist porn performer Siouxsie Q offered this challenge to queer and feminist producers: "I would like to see more emphasis placed on fair labor practices than on whether or not I have a 'real' orgasm" (Q 2014).

Relating to co-workers and managers

When asked what they looked for in a performer, management cited "professionalism" as a key trait. This meant not only following orders, or having skills such as exceptional sexual stamina, but also being "easy to work with" and "wanting to be there." Being easy to work with means being flexible above all else. If one's scene partner changes, the director asks for a different position or sex act, or the shoot takes longer than expected, "professionals" are expected to go with the flow. It also means seeming authentically to want to be there. Directors actively avoid hiring performers who they perceive to be working out of desperation or need for money. These demands are connected—seeming to want to be there (and not just for money) requires that one act as if staying on set for another few hours is no bother, for example. Workers in most jobs, of course, work because they need money. As with waitresses who are asked to act as if the tip is simply a pleasant surprise at the end of a meal, expecting performers to seem to work not just for the money pushes them to do even more work.

Sometimes managers and scene partners are the same people. As production budgets decrease, it has become more and more common for directors to perform in their own scenes. This requires a different kind of intimate work for all involved. Negotiating pay rates and on-set activity can be complicated for workers who are scheduled to perform in a scene with their boss. Performer-directors, on the other hand, take on distinct and sometimes conflicting roles simultaneously. Tanya Tate, who began as a performer and now directs as well, explained, "you're a one man band, so to speak." After completing such unsexy tasks as coordinating crews, dealing with any no-shows, making sure paper work is done, and checking lighting and sound, performer-directors must "jump behind the camera, be on set, *enjoy everything*. At the same time you're directing the way it's going . . . In the back of your mind, there's still a part that's like, 'is this going well?'" (Tate 2014). Likewise, Alex Linko described the "balancing act between thinking technically and thinking sexually" that informs his work as a performer-director (Linko 2013). Such dual roles are not limited to performers who take on directing positions in an official capacity. Tanya noted that by the time of her first directing gig, she already had years of experience "leading" scenes in which she performed. More experienced performers take on such roles regularly, both because they hope that a well-done scene will enhance their own brand and because they see being helpful in this way as part of what makes them professionals.

Most performers do not restrict their on-screen partners to those they are sexually attracted to, and many described the ability to shoot a convincing scene regardless of sexual chemistry with partners as a key element of their professionalism. Likewise, management expects these skills of performers. Performer-director Lily Cade put it quite plainly:

> We're making a product. I'm not attracted to all my co-stars. They don't know and they shouldn't know that. If you're a good performer, they shouldn't know. Once you show up, even if you're not attracted to [your screen partner], find something you are attracted to and get over yourself.
>
> (Cade 2013: interview)

Porn workers are expected to perform interest not just for the camera but also for their on-screen partners. Appearing aroused on camera is not enough if it is clear to your partner that you would rather not be there. Performers draw energy from one another, and being paired with someone who is unwilling to do the interpersonal work of helping their co-star to feel desirable can make performing for the camera more difficult.

Fostering chemistry with one's partner (but again, not too much!) is itself hard work. It requires a delicate balance of both focusing in on one's scene partner and sustaining a sense of separation from partners as well as the larger context of the scene and sometimes one's own body. Workers have finely honed ways of navigating this process of connection and disconnection. Many describe connections with co-workers as one of the key benefits of porn work. But performers also describe the "emotional hangover" (Raylene 2013) and feelings of alienation from work, colleagues, and sometimes the self, that can result from this intense interpersonal labor. For most performers, relationships with co-workers shift according to the job. In a sentiment echoed by many performers, Chanel Preston explained,

> I just love being on set because you're friends with everyone for the most part; it's like a really weird family. It's easy to be there . . . [But] some shoots are really difficult, [if there is] a lot of negativity or stress on the set for some reason.
>
> (Preston 2013: interview)

Interpersonal connections at work can be a source of pleasure or strain, or both simultaneously.

How workers experience interpersonal connections at work is contingent on a complex social milieu. As in other jobs, relations of power complicate workplace interactions in porn. Racialized and gender nonconforming performers, for example, do interpersonal labor of the sorts I have discussed while also navigating subtle and not-so-subtle aggressions from their peers and management. Transgender performers described being treated as undesirable oddities by others in the cast and crew and encountering transphobic language in scripts and post-production marketing. Performers of color talked about having to film scenes with actors they knew were charging more to work with black co-stars, being hyper-aware of being the only person of color on set, and getting cast for scenes with racist storylines. More subtly but no less insidious, black performers described a general aloofness in some white colleagues. "I feel like people who have yet to meet me are standoffish because I'm black," Ana Foxxx explained. "It wouldn't be hard to say 'Oh, hi, I've seen you like nine times, maybe we should introduce ourselves.' But I get the stare" (Foxxx 2014). Managing such interactions is an intense form of intimate labor.

All performers do intimate labor with those who have economic power over them. This includes their bosses on a given day, but also co-stars who may direct other films or exercise the power to refuse them as partners and thus cause a loss of future work. Workers do relational labor with those who have economic power over them in all jobs. What is distinct (though not unique) about porn work is that class positions change rapidly. Workers in the industry take on multiple roles performing, directing, working on crews, and etcetera. One may be a worker one day and management the next, or both at the same time. Workers do intimate labor on the registers I have described—for the camera, with coworkers, and with management. Their own location in these relations is also shifting.

Conclusion

Have I ruined porn for you? This was not my intent. I have hoped instead to offer a glimpse into how porn performers experience their work, knowing as we do that it "feels different than it looks." As in other jobs—especially those that fit under the banner of "intimate labor"—it is the work we do not see or talk about that makes porn what it is. These are the subtle labors that make porn producers money and that shape the experience of doing porn work. Understanding the intimate labor of porn in this way helps to broaden our understandings of both intimacy and labor, pushing against the boundaries of what we consider work and complicating what counts as intimate.

Bibliography

Banet-Weiser, Sarah. 2012. *Authentic TM: Politics and Ambivalence in a Brand Culture*. New York: New York University Press.
Berg, Heather. 2014a. "Labouring Porn Studies." *Porn Studies* 1(1–2):75–79.

Berg, Heather. 2014b. "Working for Love, Loving for Work: Discourses of Labor in Feminist Sex Work Activism." *Feminist Studies* (40:3):693–721.

Bernstein, Elizabeth. 2007. *Temporarily Yours: Intimacy, Authenticity, and the Commerce of Sex.* Chicago: University of Chicago Press.

Boris, Eileen and Rhacel Salazar Parreñas. 2010. "Introduction." Pp. 1–12 in *Intimate Labors : Cultures, Technologies, and the Politics of Care*, edited by Eileen Boris and Rhacel Salazar Parreñas. Stanford, CA: Stanford Social Sciences.

Cade, Lily. 2013. "Interview by Author. Pasadena, CA."

Darling, Ela. 2014. "Interview by Author. Los Angeles, CA."

Dewey, Susan. 2011. *Neon Wasteland: On Love, Motherhood, and Sex Work in a Rust Belt Town.* Berkeley: University of California Press.

Federici, Silvia. 1975. "Wages Against Housework." In *Revolution at Point Zero: Housework, Reproduction, and Feminist Struggle*. Oakland, CA; Brooklyn, NY; London: PM Press; Common Notions: Autonomedia; Turnaround [distributor].

Foxxx, Ana. 2014. "Interview by Author. Los Angeles, CA."

Habib, Conner. 2014. "Interview by Author. Los Angeles, CA."

Hatley®™, Nina. 2012. "Interview by Author. Los Angeles, CA."

Hochschild, Arlie Russell. 2003 [1983]. *The Managed Heart: Commercialization of Human Feeling.* Berkeley, CA: University of California.

Kleinhans, Chuck. 2011. "'Creative Industries,' Neoliberal Fantasies, and the Cold, Hard Facts of Global Recession: Some Basic Lessons." *Jump Cut: A Review of Contemporary Media* 53. Retrieved (www.ejumpcut.org/currentissue/kleinhans-creatIndus/text.html, accessed Dec 14, 2014).

LaRue, Chi Chi. 2014. "Interview by Author. Los Angeles, CA."

Levin Russo, Julie. 2007. "'The Real Thing': Reframing Queer Pornography for Virtual Spaces." Pp. 239–252 in *C'lickme: A Netporn Studies Reader*, edited by Katrien Jacobs, Marjie Janssen, and Metteo Pasquinelli. Amsterdam: Institute of Network Cultures.

Linko, Alex. 2013. "Interview by Author. Los Angeles, CA."

Preston, Chanel. 2013. "Interview by Author. Los Angeles, CA."

Q, Siouxsie. 2014. "Authentically Yours: Feminist Porn Gets Political | SF Weekly." *SF Weekly.* Retrieved May 6, 2014 (www.sfweekly.com/2014-04-16/culture/whore-next-door-feminist-porn-authenticity/).

Raylene. 2013. "Interview by Author. Reseda, CA."

Sanders, Teela. 2005. "'It's Just Acting': Sex Workers' Strategies for Capitalizing on Sexuality." *Gender, Work and Organization* 12(4):319–42.

Tate, Tanya. 2014. "Interview by Author. Phone."

Tibbals, Chauntelle. 2014. "Gonzo, Trannys, and Teens – Current Trends in US Adult Content Production, Distribution, and Consumption." *Porn Studies* 1(1–2):127–35.

Wylde, Danny. 2014. "Interview by Author. Los Angeles, CA."

Yashua, Prince. 2014. "Interview by Author. Canoga Park, CA."

Zelizer, Viviana. 2005. *The Purchase of Intimacy.* Princeton, NJ: Princeton University Press.

chapter 51

Making politics explicit

Depicting authenticity in women-made pornography

Jill Bakehorn

> *Welcome to my website! I'm Trixie and I refer to myself as a "webwhore" because I run an internet business that is both controversial & sexually intimate. I create & sell autobiographical pornography that is thoughtful, provocative, exciting and REAL. I designed my homemade porn site for people who want more than anonymous pink parts; you want to get off with a real girl next door and know more about her than the diameter of her holes.*
> *(From an amateur woman-run porn site.)*

My research focuses on how women justify and legitimate their participation in a stigmatized profession, how they distinguish their work and products from the mainstream pornography industry, and how they define what they do as activism. I analyze how women strategically use constructions of authenticity to achieve these goals. Because the women do not see themselves as simply selling sex, I argue that talking about their work as "authentic" becomes, in some ways, not only attractive, but necessary.

Authenticity in pornography hinges on creating a product that showcases "real sex," appeals to women, depicts women's genuine pleasure, and features "real orgasms." Because the visual evidence of pleasure can be difficult to portray or "authenticate," other cues to genuineness must be used by focusing on identities, "real people," and "real bodies."

Authenticity has a number of meanings. The Oxford English Dictionary includes words like *original, true, real, consistent, actual, relic, credible, natural, genuine*, and *firsthand*, and it is often defined by what it is not: fake, forgery, copy, or fraud. It is used in numerous social contexts from art work and archaeology to cuisine and tourism and even in discussions of one's "true self." Authenticity is important to our daily lives: for instance, we use the concept to distinguish between cultural products, social groups, and socio-cultural experiences. But sociologists are not interested in determining whether or not something *is* authentic. We are interested in the social process by which groups construct objects, behaviors, and people as authentic; it is not inherent in those objects, behaviors, or people. "Rather, authenticity is a claim that is made by or for someone, thing, or performance" (Peterson 2005: 1086). Claims of authenticity are often moral claims and are not "objective and value-free" (Grazian 2010: 192).

In this chapter, I am exploring the claims and the performances of authenticity and the purpose they serve in the context of women-made pornography. While authenticity has a great deal of appeal in the marketing of women-made pornography, it also can reduce complex human identities and experiences to idealized representations, thus potentially undermining feminist and queer activist goals of diversity.

It is not surprising that many women pornography producers will use the language of "realness." Research has found that it is important for women porn consumers. The little research that has been done on women porn consumers tends to paint a picture of them as conflicted. Ciclitira (2004) found that many women's views of pornography have been impacted by feminist anti-porn messages. Some women felt their involvement with feminism impinges on their ability to enjoy pornography, and some found themselves troubled and feeling guilty: they were aroused by pornography, but had political reservations about the treatment and representations of women in pornography. Ciclitira found some evidence to suggest that as women and lesbians have begun to produce their own erotica and pornography, women consumers begin to feel more "permission to enjoy porn" (295). Similarly, Parvez (2006) found that women porn consumers' arousal was mitigated by concern over the genuineness of the porn actress's pleasure. Women disliked "fake bodies, fake plots, and fake pleasure." Parvez further found that women's references to "fake porn" served as euphemisms for pornography made by and for men. What distinguished "good porn" from "bad porn" centered on women's pleasure: "Good pornography, in other words, is where the female porn actress is *really* enjoying herself. Consequently, bad pornography involves fake pleasure" (617).

Despite differences in aesthetics, filming techniques, and preferences around sex acts, the women pornographers I studied all agree that depicting "real sex" is vital to their work. Real sex means that the pleasure is real and that the orgasms are real; it is a primary way women set their films apart from mainstream porn produced by men and how they attract women consumers. Dorrie, a porn producer and director, emphatically asserted to me, "I'll put it to you this way: all the women in my videos have orgasms." Jaden, a queer-identified actor, told me, "All of the orgasms are real and they should be; it's women getting off for women."

Authenticity is important to women-made pornography because it is an important feature of our modern culture, and because it has always been an integral part of pornography, particularly women-made porn. Claims to authenticity are important for marketing their work, to set it apart from the mainstream. Mainstream porn is framed as fake, inauthentic, not true to life, and not representative of women's desires. Women-made porn promises "real women having real sex."

Authenticity also provides a framework for activism around gender and sexuality. (While my study also addresses issues of race, gender fluidity, and subcultural communities, here I focus only on cisgender women and lesbian identities.) For the women in my study, the creation of alternative woman-centered porn relies upon the ability to depict women's authentic pleasure. Given the difficulties in capturing women's pleasure and orgasm on film, filmmakers need to rely on other measures to ensure authenticity. I discuss three main categories of authenticity used by women in my study: (1) *Constructing authentic identities*; (2) *Constructing real people*; and (3) *Displaying real bodies*.

Constructing authentic identities: identity politics and authenticity

One of the ways that women pornographers set their porn apart from the mainstream (i.e. heterosexual, made by and for men) is to highlight identities. The women in my research use their gender and sexual identities to bolster their claims to authenticity. Membership in these particular groups gives a person the authority to represent that group, making their stance more legitimate.

By women, for women: the gendered identity politics of pleasure

Asserting *gender* identity claims are the most basic: marketing the porn as made by women and for women. The "by women, for women" market has been growing from erotic fiction to include erotica and pornography (Ciclitira 2004; Juffer 1998). I found the "by women, for women" mantra is an important part of marketing for women-run porn companies. Women often take issue with pornography because of who is making it; many women do not believe that men can accurately represent women's sexuality. Ciclitira (2004) found that women are more open to pornography when it is made by women. Many women porn producers situate their work outside of the pornography convention of "by men, for men" and the problems they believe are inherent in this industry: films that degrade women and fail "to portray women's pleasure" (Smyth 1990: 153). They believe that the current landscape of mainstream pornography does not have much to offer women. Alpha, a lesbian filmmaker, claims that most women cannot connect with mainstream pornography made by men: "I would say that the majority of women that I've talked to have said that they don't like to watch any sort of sexy movie because they just don't see themselves in it."

Maxie is an actor who has worked in both the mainstream industry and the women-run industry and began to write and direct her own films. She identifies as feminist and hopes that women-made pornography will lead to more women consumers of porn. She connects this to the empowering of women through their sexuality:

I'm just always down to work with women producers and I think it's really important to get more hot women-produced content out there, that women need to be consumers more of porn. And if there's good high quality erotic material that women feel is approachable and that they can consume, then they will consume it, hopefully . . . So, we really need to get more women feeling comfortable about their bodies. If we're not talking about our bodies, we're not talking about pleasuring ourselves, there's not going to be any reason for us to watch porn.

Thus, if mainstream pornography does not appeal to or cater to women, and mainstream pornography is made primarily by men, then many women in my study believe change needs to come from women.

"Authentic, explicit, sexy lesbians"

Fatale Media was started by Nan Kinney and Debi Sundahl, who "realized that there was no venue for lesbian sexual imagery made by and for lesbians." Starting with a lesbian sex magazine in 1984, *On Our Backs,* they began a production company to produce lesbian pornography the following year. Deborah explained: "At the time, for Nan and I it was very much I think from the gut, from the heart. And our main motivation was to get lesbian erotic imagery out there. Gay men had tons of magazines and videos and lesbians had zero." With the release of their first two films, producers for Fatale claim they had produced the first "sexually explicit footage made by and for lesbians" which featured "real-life lesbian lovers" (fatalemedia.com). Fatale is marketed on its website and promotional materials as providing "authentic, explicit, sexy lesbian videos." Nan explained her motivation for starting the production company:

> Well, first and foremost I want to portray images that the mainstream porn companies aren't portraying. And right next to that is lesbians having lesbian sex. Real lesbians having real lesbian sex. Authentic, explicit, sexy lesbians. I look at what mainstream porn is doing and I just don't want to do the same exact thing. And that's what we mean by alternative. Alternative to what? Alternative to mainstream porn.

When I asked Nan why she emphasizes that her films portray "authentic" lesbian sexuality, she said this had to do with juxtaposing what they produce with the so-called "lesbian" scenes in mainstream pornography. She is referring to a staple of mainstream heterosexual porn, the "girl-girl" scene that many view as heterosexualized because they presumably feature straight women having sex for men viewers. Jenefsky and Miller (1998) argue that this type of scene, which is contained within an otherwise heterosexual context and is overtly marketed to heterosexual men, actually "reinscribe[s] and renaturalize[s] heterosexuality" (375).

Many women market their work in opposition to the "girl-girl" lesbian scenes in mainstream pornography. A review of the film *One Night Stand,* winner of the "Sexiest Dyke Movie" award from the Feminist Porn Awards, includes a caveat about what "real" dyke porn depicts: "I should tell you now. This is not a sanitized, 'girl-girl' version of lesbian sex. This is a lesbian version of lesbian sex . . .You have to like butch women; pierced and tattooed women; trans dyke bois; women in T-shirts and jeans; women with short hair; women with small breasts" (Christina 2009). These complaints about mainstream "girl-girl" scenes are echoed in a study by Morrison and Tallack (2005). They conducted focus groups with women who identified as lesbian and bisexual and elicited their reactions to two films: one marketed to heterosexual men and one for women. The women in the focus groups were highly critical of the heterosexual, "girl–girl" film for a number of reasons: they felt the bodies of the women reflected hegemonic standards for heterosexual women; they did not find the sex between the women to be convincing both in its representation of lesbian sex and women's pleasure; they disliked the robotic nature of the scenes and wanted more intimacy or emotion; and in general felt the film reflected the interests of men.

Others talked about the importance of seeing yourself represented. Sawyer explicitly cites identity politics as an important reason to become involved in pornography:

> Why I became involved in pornography, a lot of it's identity politics. I mean as a queer woman of color like, there's very few places that you see yourself out in the world or like a mirror of yourself. And one of the most, I guess, abundant fields that a queer person can see themselves in is obviously been porn . . . And the majority of those representations are owned by, you know, affluent, white males and they give representation to people who they are not. And so it's like speaking on behalf of someone else . . . And in a way that's what this has become, it's become this like path to say look, there's all these representations of what queers are, what queer women are, what, who these people are and this is one I'm adding myself.

Smyth (1990) agrees that pornography can be important for lesbian visibility. "Lesbian sexuality has been repressed, rendered invisible and impotent by society. By watching porn, we can on some level recognize ourselves, defend our right to express our sexuality and assert our desire" (154).

Constructing real people: autobiography, real-life couples, and amateurs

Authenticity is also constructed by focusing on "real" people. This strategy differs from real identities; rather than focusing on socially salient categories like gender and sexuality, this form of authenticity has to do with people as they "really" are. I found three main ways women represent "real" people in films and on websites: 1) *Providing autobiographical detail*; 2) *Using real-life couples*; and 3) *Featuring "non-professional" sex*.

Autobiographical porn

Women making pornography can construct authenticity through interjecting aspects of their "real lives" into their porn work. They do this by making claims of a "real" performance: this is not acting, it is a representation of real sexuality. Another strategy is to disclose intimate details by providing personal information about one's self to cultivate intimacy. Finally, behind-the-scenes and documentary footage is utilized to convey authenticity.

One way to strive for authenticity is to construct a narrative of people just being themselves during the production. This information cannot be conveyed simply through the pornographic films or photos themselves. Women who want to make these types of authenticity claims often do so in another venue like providing behind-the-scenes footage on DVDs, websites, and by blogging. One actor, Oriana, who performed in a film with her partner of two months, described her scene in an interview for the DVD release:

> For me, the most enjoyable part of the shoot was when the production and camera crew kind of faded to the side and it was just me and her and it didn't really matter what was going on, we were just connecting and being ourselves and enjoying ourselves and occasionally it would come to me, like hey, I'm being filmed, but it didn't really matter it was, that was the most enjoyable part was when the fantasy slipped aside and we were just being real and being ourselves and that was awesome.

Her claims of realness and the backgrounding of the camera crew construct authenticity by claiming that the artifice of the production falls away and we get to see the "real people" behind the performance. Oriana is privileging the kind of sexual experience in pornography that comes from being one's self, claiming that the sex you see in the film is identical to the kind of sex she has at home. She is implying that in mainstream pornography you are not seeing genuine sexual encounters; the performers are just acting.

Because most of the women are actively seeking to create an alternative to the mainstream industry, and because they see themselves as activists, they want to make the women depicted in pornography more than just naked bodies (Mies 2006). Women are presented as whole people, as "real" people. Consumers get more than just nude bodies and sex acts; they learn about the person in non-pornography contexts and allow women to represent themselves. Because consumers get glimpses of who these women really are, they cannot simply be objectified (DeVoss 2002).

Lucy gave an interview for the behind-the-scenes feature of a queer film and ties the film's depictions to her real life: "These types of scenes are definitely reflective of my personal sexuality." This is important to her because as an actor, she does not have a lot of control over the creation, editing, or marketing of the films in which she appears. She told me that what she does have control over is her performance:

> I take it really seriously, my performance . . . One thing that is important to me is to try to be genuine and present with the experience . . . And I do think that porn is really powerful . . . what I think is powerful about pornography is having the diversity of kinds of sexuality represented. So for me that means my own individual sexuality, desire, presentation, that's the best that I can do. I can't represent everybody, but I can be as honest as possible about me and all of the strange, weird, you know, things that I think are sexy. And try to emphasize what's unique about me and my, you know, desires and my abilities to perform.

Even when productions are highly fantasy-driven and scripted, requiring a great deal of characterization on the part of the actors, authenticity can be conveyed through documentaries and behind-the-scenes extras. Filmmakers can talk about/show the real people behind the production, provide information about their personal lives, and reveal any number of things through interviews: the non-professional status of actors, the relationship between two actors, and the motivations behind the production.

When Erica and Madeline made a short pornographic film, they also made a documentary about the making of the film. In the documentary, the audience can learn about the process of finding the actors and filming. This behind-the-scenes aspect is important for women viewers according to Erica:

> I think the reason people can sit through the porn part of [the film] is that they get to know the stars in it. They get to know the people [who] eventually have sex for 5 minutes. And, I don't know, maybe that's the secret of porn that appeals to women . . . I think one of the drawbacks to porn is [it's] so anonymous . . . And so I think the fact that they get to know [the actors], I think makes the porn work for them.

Like most of the women I spoke to, Erica finds anonymous, interchangeable actors, particularly women actors, problematic when it comes to pornography. Using documentaries and behind-the-scenes features allows for a more well-rounded representation of women and gives them a chance to be more than objectified bodies on the screen.

Even while women frame their works as authentic in and of themselves—"we are really lesbians," for instance, or "we feature real-life couples," "we depict real orgasms"—most feature some kind of supplemental material like documentaries, behind-the-scenes glimpses, or interviews to get at another level of authenticity. As I will discuss in the following section, these materials are important for educating audiences on the authenticity they are viewing. Without this material, audiences may be unaware, for example, that the partners they see on film are a couple in real life.

"A really amazing connection": using real couples

Most directors believe that real couples will have chemistry that is palpable to the audience. Jackie, a director of queer porn, acknowledges that even though pornography requires performance, couples can lose themselves in the moment and generate an authentic experience:

> Like I told you before, we have a lot of real-life couples who are, you know, quote unquote amateurs, they've never done this on screen before. So we want to show them how they really are but obviously they're performing 'cause they're in front of a group of people, but a lot of times they'll just lose themselves and be off in their own world . . . we kind of direct them and guide them to be very connected to each other and talk to each other.

Another director, Dallas, makes assertions that her films depict real lesbian sex and these claims are substantiated in interviews with the cast in a behind-the-scenes documentary of a film. Dallas introduces one couple in the film: "Sawyer and Jaden are a couple in real life. They've got just a really amazing connection in life and in like, their sex life, so they bring an incredible amount of energy to the screen." Jaden confirms this in her interview on the DVD: "The scene that Sawyer and I have is really similar to the sex life that we have. We're pretty spontaneous and messy . . . For that short of a scene that was pretty, pretty real. And Sawyer does cum that fast. So, yeah, that was, that was real material." Using real couples is a way to distance themselves from the mainstream where the stereotype of actors having sex dispassionately with dozens of strangers is pervasive.

Non-professional sex: amateur actors and invisible crews

In addition to using real couples, many of the productions use amateur performers, people who are not professional porn actors. These amateurs are often friends and acquaintances of the producers. In addition, producers and directors talk about creating an environment on set that is different than mainstream pornography practices, or what they imagine those practices to be. They focus on letting actors do whatever they want or trying to keep the crew as unobtrusive as possible during shooting.

Many of the producers and directors I spoke with touted the use of real, average people, in contrast with porn stars who are seen as having fake bodies and dialing in their performances. In addition, many filmmakers try to create an unobtrusive filming environment by avoiding the scripting of sex acts, collaborating with actors on their preferences and boundaries, making actors as comfortable as possible, and limiting the starting and stopping of shots. This is often very important because the actors are amateurs who are, perhaps, not used to being naked, vulnerable, and performing sexually in front of others. Directors use these techniques in order to create an environment that is comfortable for their actors. But they also believe that this will lead to "real" sex and genuine pleasure among the actors. For instance, director Barbara DeGenevieve thinks it is important to collaborate with actors as much as possible and to get out of the way when it comes time to film: "I try to involve the actors as much as possible in fact, you know, I think I can count on two hands the number of times that I've actually suggested specific ways for these particular actors to perform."

Overall, depictions of "real" people are an important way to construct authenticity in women-made pornography. Inserting autobiographical detail, using real-life couples, and featuring amateurs are ways to not only set yourself apart from the mainstream industry, but to give agency to the women who are featured in the films. Women who model and act in pornography are able to assert their own identity and subjectivity into an industry that is seen by some as only providing objectified images of women.

Displaying real bodies: embodying realness and making good on authenticity claims

Bodies are important in achieving real sex and embodying authenticity claims about genuine people and identities. First, real bodies are often framed as "natural" bodies, bodies that reflect "real" women. This parallels the importance of using amateurs in pornography. Second, real bodies also means using bodies that read to the producers and audience as authentic and legitimate members of the identity being represented. In this case, identities are encoded into bodies. Thus, not only do the bodies used signal that the sex is authentic, they must embody the identity politics of the filmmakers. In other words, the bodies used in women-made porn must make good on the authenticity claims about real people and real identities.

For the women I studied, bodies are important in their critiques and concerns with mainstream porn. Susan, a producer at an all-women run production company, sums up the stereotype of the porn model:

> [W]hat we've got right now in the world of porn is that image whenever you think of "porn star" you think of the woman who's really scrawny, she's probably pretty white, pretty tan, probably pretty blond and she has augmented breasts. And that is a reality for a lot of the movies out there. That's what porn's been offering to the world. And that's what the world has begun to accept as what they're going to consume as the sexual image.

Regina, co-owner of a large sex toy business, told me why she is not a big fan of pornography:

> And one of the reasons I mean I don't like porn is . . . I really don't like seeing women who just look kind of Barbie-ish, blonds and big boobs and everybody's all skinny and, you know, it just doesn't, I mean it doesn't do it for me in a sexual way and it really turns me off in an intellectual way and so I'm not into it.

Thus, critics of mainstream pornography argue that the industry creates homogenized and normative images of women's bodies.

Natural bodies

A "natural" body is typically described as one that represents "real" or "average" women. In most cases, films with natural bodies feature women without breast implants and women with a diversity of body types that will signal that the people are more real and relatable. One easy way to set alternative porn apart from the mainstream is to not look like the mainstream. Bodies in mainstream pornography are seen as fake: women have fake breasts, fake hair, fake nails, fake tans. Natural bodies help bolster claims to amateur or real women actors. When I asked Christi, who works for a company that strives to make "authentic lesbian" pornography, whether she thought her films were "fighting against certain stereotypes that might be in mainstream pornography," she replied: "Definitely, definitely. I mean women of all different shapes, sizes, colors, for one thing. Women who have their real breasts. And lips. I mean I think that makes a difference." Women pornographers see this perspective as decidedly woman-oriented. A common theme was a belief that audiences, and women in particular, want to see themselves represented, to see "people that look like me." A model for Vegporn, an alternative porn website designed for vegetarians and vegans, discussed how aspects of real bodies normally avoided or air-brushed away are featured on this site, things like "blemishes, scars, wrinkles, cellulite, hairs, fat," telling me that this is one of the features that drew her to the company.

The size of bodies becomes important to some wanting to achieve realness. In our interview, a producer discussed a film that features "voluptuous" women: "We've already shot a women-of-size film. The entire cast and crew and directors and everybody are women, big girls. Not all of them identify as fat, some of them don't.

They just think of themselves as . . . an average size." In a press release, this company promoted itself as creating respectful images and highlighting diverse bodies as well as presenting an alternative to the "male-generated, hetero-focused" adult entertainment industry. Thus the use of diverse and natural bodies is associated with women-focused, women-made porn that is not necessarily heteronormative.

In focusing on diversity, and in particular on non-skinny bodies, filmmakers are not only setting themselves apart from mainstream pornography, but also striving to embody authenticity. Using women who do not resemble mainstream porn stars signals the non-professional status of the women and therefore speaks to the authenticity of their performance. The "Barbie Doll" look of mainstream porn stars, with their "artificial" attributes (breast implants, blonde hair, fake nails), makes their sexual performance suspect. A "natural" looking woman, on the other hand, connects to the claims of "real" people and therefore substantiates claims of real sex.

Real identities: embodying your politics

Closely connected to the use of natural bodies is the use of bodies that "look" like a particular identity. Bodies must make good on identity claims—these bodies should read to producers, and presumably the audience, as authentic and legitimate members of the identity being represented. Any producer can claim, for instance, that they feature real lesbians, but audiences will judge this claim based on the bodies displayed. One of the main critiques I heard of mainstream pornography is that the "girl–girl" scenes in the films do not depict real lesbians. Many argue they know they are not lesbian by the way they look and what they do with their bodies. The "fake" bodies of the women in mainstream porn signal to critics that the pleasure is also fake. The appearance of the woman is connected to her identity and therefore the sexual practices and sexual response are read through this lens. The women do not look lesbian, so the sexual acts and pleasure must not be authentic. Most companies making lesbian pornography promote their films and websites as featuring "real lesbians." For instance, Fatale Media promotes itself on its website and promotional materials as providing "authentic, explicit, sexy lesbian videos."

> I worked as a production assistant on a film that was shadowed by a documentary film crew for a cable television series on lesbian sexuality. The filmmaker says in her interviews (both with me and for this documentary), that she was motivated to make pornography because of the representations of lesbian sexuality in the films sold at the sex toy shop where she worked: "[O]ur dyke porn, lesbian-made porn was very, very slim, you know, it's a lot of big-hair, long nails. They're doing their thing, but you can, like if you're queer, you can look at them and be like, I don't think they're queer. [Laughs.] So after a while I just decided, you know, I have a BFA in film, so I was like, okay, I can do this"
>
> (quoted in Linton, 2007).

In order to set themselves apart from mainstream pornography and correct some of its problematic aspects, the women in my study make claims about the real identities and real people in their films. The bodies of the actors must deliver the goods on claims made about real identities and real people. First, real bodies are often framed as "natural" bodies, bodies that reflect "real" women. This parallels the importance of using real people in pornography. Second, using real bodies also means representing identities. In this case, sexual identities are encoded into bodies. Actors must embody the activist politics and claims made.

Conclusion

Because the women in my study want to distinguish their work from the mainstream porn industry, they strategically use the rhetoric of authenticity to convey to the audience the "truth" of the sexuality depicted: the women and lesbians are real so you can trust that their experiences of pleasure are real. Though it is often presented this way, authenticity is not inherent in an object, person, or performance. Authenticity is a socially constructed fiction, one that constantly changes and evolves depending on particular social, cultural, political, and historical contexts. And claims to authenticity are, at their core, moral claims—they are not objective or value-free. By making claims to authenticity, women are implying that other forms and representations of sexuality are then inauthentic. But in the end, all performances of authenticity are just that, performances. And it takes work to appear authentic.

Authenticity is something that must be accomplished. Lesbians that "look like" lesbians is a particularly contentious issue. There was nearly universal agreement that the women who engaged in lesbian sex in mainstream films were *not really* lesbians; there was less agreement about what a real lesbian does look like. And despite the use of genderqueer and trans bodies, many women undercut their claims to diversity with essentialist ideas about natural bodies or bodies that represent particular identities. Further, while well-intentioned, the championing of a "natural" body can work to privilege cisgendered bodies. What gets to count as a "natural" body: one unaltered by surgery of any kind? What about diet and exercise? It's clear from talking to distributors and porn reviewers that there is a need for greater diversity in representations of queer women's sexuality. The women I studied are committed to creating diverse images. But by connecting bodies so closely to sexuality, they can inadvertently essentialize the connections between gender identity, gender presentation, sexuality, desire, sexual behavior, and sexual response. Claims to authenticity are seen as a necessary strategy to set women-made pornography apart from the mainstream. As the women-made pornography genre continues to grow and proliferate, women may no longer feel the need to make essentializing authenticity claims.

References

Christina, Greta. 2009. "One Night Stand: A Review." *Greta Christina's Blog*. http://gretachristina. typepad.com/greta_christinas_weblog/2009/04/one-night-stand-a-review.html (accessed July 17, 2010).

Ciclitira, Karen. 2004. "Pornography, Women and Feminism: Between Pleasure and Politics." *Sexualities* 7(3): 281–301.

Jill Bakehorn

DeVoss, Danielle. 2002. "Women's Porn Sites – Spaces of Fissure and Eruption or 'I'm a Little Bit of Everything'." *Sexuality & Culture* 6(3): 75–94.

Grazian, David. 2010. "Demystifying Authenticity in the Sociology of Culture." Pp 191–200 in *Handbook of Cultural Sociology* edited by John R. Hall, Laura Grindstaff, and Ming-Cheng Lo. New York: Routledge.

Jenefsky, Cindy and Diane Helene Miller. 1998. "Phallic intrusion: Girl-Girl Sex in Penthouse." *Women's Studies International Forum*. 21(4): 375–385.

Juffer, Jane. 1998. *At Home With Pornography: Women, Sex, and Everyday Life*. New York: New York University Press.

Linton, Katherine. 2007. *Lesbian Sex and Sexuality*. Documentary series broadcast on Here TV.

Mies, Ginny. 2006. "A New Erotica? Alternative Culture and the Porn Industry." *National Sexuality Resource Center*. September 25. http://nsrc.sfsu.edu/article/new_erotica_alternative_culture_and_porn_industry (accessed October 5, 2009).

Morrison, Todd G, and Dani Tallack. 2005. "Lesbian and Bisexual Women's Interpretations of Lesbian and Ersatz Lesbian Pornography." *Sexuality & Culture* 9(2): 3–30.

Parvez, Z. Fareen. 2006. "The Labor of Pleasure: How Perceptions of Emotional Labor Impact Women's Enjoyment of Pornography." *Gender & Society* 20(5): 605–631.

Peterson, Richard. 2005. "In Search of Authenticity." *Journal of Management Studies* 42(5): 1083–1098.

Smyth, Cherry. 1990. "The Pleasure Threshold: Looking at Lesbian Pornography on Film." *Feminist Review* 34: 152–159.

chapter 52

Pleasure for sale

Feminist sex stores

Alison Better

Sex stores can be found in many communities across America. These stores are not standardized or regulated, but have several features in common. Sex stores may sell pornographic media, sex toys and novelties, sexual accessories and devices, and sexually charged humor items. The Supreme Court, through a series of first amendment cases, legalized sex stores in the 1960s. These early sex stores (since the 1960s) catered almost entirely to male clientele and often had pornographic video viewing rooms on the premises. They were designed without windows so customers would not be seen. Such stores often had a reputation for being taboo, dirty, and a menace to the community. As time progressed, sex stores have diversified, both in terms of their atmosphere and their audience. Now, several different sorts of sex stores operate across the country, each catering to different pleasure needs and potentials.

Nonetheless, it is important to note that today several states still criminalize the sale of sex toys. The most restrictive law is in Alabama, where it is not legal to sell sex toys. It is lawful for Alabama residents to own and use toys, provided they were purchased elsewhere. Though several appeals to the 1998 law prohibiting the sale of "any device designed or marketed as useful primarily for the stimulation of human genital organs" have been filed, the Alabama Supreme Court has upheld the state ban in a September 2009 ruling (Chandler and Velasco 2009). However, a loophole exists in the law that toys can also be purchased if they are for "a bona fide medical, scientific, educational, legislative, judicial, or law enforcement purpose" (Brantley 2009). In January 2009, Coweta County, Georgia passed an obscenity ordinance that "prohibits sale or distribution of obscenity," and prohibits anyone from "knowingly" selling, or possessing with the intent to sell, "any device designed or marketed as useful primarily for the stimulation of human genital organs" (Campbell 2009). The state of Mississippi also made the sale of sex toys illegal while allowing citizens to own toys. A Texas ban on promoting or selling sex toys was overturned in 2008. The Texas ruling also overturned any bans on the sale of sex toys in Louisiana and Mississippi as it was heard by the Fifth Circuit Court of Appeals covering those three states. Given this legal context, the following discussion of sex stores does not apply to every US state.

Traditional sex stores

Upon opening an opaque and imposing door and walking into one traditional sex store, I am immediately confronted by a display of sex toys advertised as novelties. Toys intended to provide sexual pleasures are presented on shelves and a selection of lingerie and stockings lined the wall. Many of these packages are covered in graphic images of people using the products, often topless women in suggestive poses giving the camera direct eye contact, luring the viewer through the packaging. On the wall opposite the lingerie stands a large desk raised off the ground with two men working behind it who watch the movements of the customers. The back half of the store is lined with several aisles of shelves filled with pornographic videos with titles like *Big Boobs Power* or *Barely Legal Innocence* 9 that run the length of the floor.

Traditional sex stores can be found in a variety of forms in almost every state in America. They market pornographic films and sexual goods. These stores often have a variety of sex toys and other sexual products. In addition to locally owned adult bookstores and sex shops, there are several large chains of traditional sex stores in America, including Amazing, Romantix, The Lion's Den, and Castle Megastore. Traditional sex shops sell a variety of goods, ranging from gag gifts and novelties like penis-shaped pasta and drinking straws and bachelorette party favors to vibrators to pornographic videos. Such stores are often located on well-traveled main roads or in shopping districts surrounded by other retail shops. They are well-marked and well-lit.

Some traditional stores are more "hardcore." Hardcore sex shops sell the same merchandise as the traditional shops, while fostering a more sexually charged atmosphere. Hardcore shops are a subset of traditional stores where sex acts or sex work may take place on the premises. This usually takes the form of peep booths or video booths and enclosed areas where customers can pleasure themselves while watching a pornographic act (either on video or live) located in a section of the store. Unlike average traditional sex stores, hardcore sex stores are often located in either urban vice districts or in unmarked, windowless buildings outside of city limits.

While traditional sex stores are well-marked and well-lit on the outside, they are often environments shrouded in secrecy and anonymity on the inside. Through my fieldwork in sex stores, I've noticed that patrons do not look at one another and store clerks serve mostly as theft deterrents. Products are arranged on shelves or hooks in rigid plastic packaging, often decorated with pornographic images of a person using the product. These stores can sometimes seem dirty or seedy to patrons; many women I have spoken to as part of a larger study of sex stores have mentioned uncomfortable or frightening experiences including harassment and sexual overtures while shopping at traditional sex stores. This environment is exciting and titillating to some, while it is overwhelming and off-putting to others.

Feminist sex stores: a new type of sex shop

I entered into a brightly lit room through a frosted glass door. A table to my left offered information about events of interest, including an amateur porn night, women's and trans health care, and the local GLBT community newspaper. To my left was a selection of condoms and lubricants, with testers available for each product. Along the back wall were displays of vibrators, many labeled phthalate-free. There was a large selection of silicone vibrators which are easy to clean as well as dual action or "rabbit" vibrators that simultaneously provide clitoral and vaginal stimulation. A sample of each toy was out of its packaging and on a shelf. The electric toys were plugged into an outlet for testing. Further along this wall were anal toys and men's toys, including vacuum pumps and cock rings. Other sections of the store contained dildos and harnesses as well as trinkets and gifts. A nearby table displayed glass dildos and hand-carved wood dildos that look like sculptures. A small room off the main space contained books (both educational and erotic), fetish gear, including whips and gags, and a small selection of pornographic videos for purchase. The clerks were positioned behind a counter that spanned a wall of the store and some walked around asking if they could be of any help as I shopped.

Feminist sex stores began to emerge in response to women's discomfort with traditional sex stores. Since specialized sex retail environments often serve as the only option for the purchase of pleasure goods, traditional sex stores were once the only place to buy sex toys. The first feminist sex shop in America, Eve's Garden, was opened in New York City in 1974. It was quickly followed by Good Vibrations in 1977, a sex shop in San Francisco. Until the early 1990s, these two stores were the only sex stores focusing on feminist ideals and women's sexual pleasure. Since 1991, 23 feminist sex shops emerged in the United States and the current total of feminist sex stores is 26. These stores are in cities both large and small, and occasionally in suburbs just over city limits. Some are small franchises with multiple locations.

Five features are present in all feminist sex shops: (1) Feminist sex shops are committed to understanding the process of their inception and the importance of connections to the past and also to other feminist sex stores; (2) They maintain the importance of safe spaces for women (many stores today are rephrasing this to include people of all genders and sexual orientations); (3) They exist to fill needs in their communities; (4) They promote the importance of healthy and pleasurable sexual lives; (5) To this end, they provide information and education about sexuality.

Feminist sex store creation and cooperation

Feminist sex shops understand that the process of their creation and their history are important. By telling the stories of their creation, current owners share the knowledge with anyone else seeking to bring a safe space for different sexual identities into their community. Current business owners help out aspiring ones as they begin to build new stores around the country. Though store owners do not often interact with one another in person since they live in different cities, it is clear that they identify as part of the same community and are working both together and separately to ensure access to information and products to help all people reach their sexual and pleasure potentials. Many of these stores provide information about their owners, founding, and company history on their websites and in other public information about the store. Though the stores are all independently owned and operated, feminist sex store owners see themselves as part of a larger movement to create a safe space for education and enhancing sexual potentials.

This alignment of political ideals with providing a sex-positive retail environment was also found by Meika Loe, who conducted a case study of a feminist sex store, which she calls Toy Box. Her focus was on the structure of the business and how they balanced political ideals and profits (Loe 1999:706). Through her observations at the store and office, and through interviews with staff and owners, Loe was able to look at changes over time in this feminist business. The store wanted female customers to "come away from visiting the store convinced that sexual pleasure was one's birthright and one's path toward liberation and empowerment" (Loe 1999:713). In addition to selling products, they were selling a pro-sex ideology. In the early 1990s control of the store moved from its owner to its staff, who began making decisions for the business and later became worker-owners in 1992 (Loe 1999:717, 723). The store continues to be successful as it changes over time. Toy Box has transformed its business structure and ownership, yet remained entrenched in feminist values (and changed with them over time).

Safe shopping spaces

For several of the women who opened the feminist sex shops, uncomfortable experiences at traditional sex shops led them to their consciousness-raising "click" moment about the validity of women's sexuality. These feminist pioneers felt that women should have a place to go to explore and learn about their sexuality and to buy well-made sexual aids and other products. Their own open-mindedness about sexuality had brought them into traditional adult stores, but even with their comfort about sexuality, they were intimidated and saw nothing in the stores that catered to their needs. These experiences led each of these women to the same decision: to open a sex store that would cater to women's needs and be a safe place to shop for and explore their desires.

It should be noted that one of the only sociological studies on sex store shopping did not find female consumers to be particularly uncomfortable in that sexualized space. Dana Berkowitz (2006) writes about gender performance in pornographic establishments. This study is based on her fieldwork at the XTC Center (a pseudonym), a traditional sex store open 24 hours a day, seven days a week in the Southeast United States. Berkowitz found an equal number of men and women shopping at the store and looked at their patterns of shopping behavior. She examined four types of shopping configurations, woman alone, man alone, a group of women, and mixed gender. She found that men shopping alone displayed two different types of masculinity, swagger and confidence amongst the "video voyeurs" and weakness and nervousness among the "petrified patrons" (Berkowitz 2006:593–94). Women shopping alone here shopped with confidence, marching over to the section where vibrators were displayed, thoughtfully choosing their purchases, and asking the clerk questions (Berkowitz 2006:596). She found women embraced sexual agency in this setting.

Women in groups tended to act more reserved than women shopping alone, a finding not echoed in my own observations. Berkowitz found the deviant nature of the setting shifted the usual gender norms while patrons were shopping.

In regard to providing safe spaces, in my own research on sex shops, I have found that many women are uncomfortable with the traditional male-focused sex retail establishments and are seeking a safer and more welcoming alternative as they seek to enhance their sexual pleasures.

The shopping experience in adult bookstores is uncomfortable for many women who report feeling watched and find many of the items for sale unappealing. Products in traditional sex shops are oriented to heterosexual men, with naked women appearing on many of the products' packaging. Also, the neighborhoods that housed adult bookstores are sometimes dangerous as these stores were often located in urban vice districts.

The feminist sex shops that women opened differed from traditional adult bookstores in a variety of ways. The storefronts were approachable and located in safer neighborhoods. Stores were painted in soothing light colors and played soft music. Samples of each product were on display on shelves or tables, and customers were invited to see how the products felt. Many sex toys were repackaged to remove pornographic images. Staff members were knowledgeable and approachable and willing to help customers make successful purchases. Many stores wrote up instruction sheets and care information for women to bring home with their purchases so they could safely use and store their new toys.

Filling community needs

Feminist sex shops seek to serve a larger purpose in their surrounding community. Several feminist sex shops have become contemporary outposts for feminist activism and community development. Some of these stores have hosted sexuality discussion groups on topics such as the differences between erotica and pornography, defining sex, and polyamory to raise community consciousness about sexuality. Other stores have held book clubs and knitting groups in their retail spaces. Stores across the country have sponsored educational centers that enhance the community impact of the retail store. Several feminist sex stores have spun off outside educational centers, including the Center for Sex and Culture in San Francisco and the Center for Sexual Pleasure and Health in Rhode Island. These spaces focus on sexuality education and activism.

Sexual health and pleasure

Sexual health is important to all feminist sex shops. One Midwest feminist sex store was created by a sex educator/counselor and a physician. The store sees itself more as a sexuality resource center and provides detailed sex information on both its website and the retail store. Visitors to the store's website or retail locations have the opportunity to ask questions of a medical doctor and co-founder of the store. Information and advice can be found on the website answering questions about all aspects of sexuality, ranging from advice about reproduction, anatomy, and menopause to libido and orgasm. This store sees itself as a place that combines sexual health and pleasure. Several other feminist stores are staffed by sexuality educators and sexual health practitioners.

Another way that concern with sexual health is evident in feminist sex stores is the way they have handled the sales of jelly plastics. In recent years it has become known that certain types of materials used in the making of sex toys can be bad for people's health. Jelly plastics, often used for vibrators and other sex toys, contain toxic phthalates. In addition to leaching toxic gases into the air, this material can cause reproductive harm and is able to be absorbed through skin (Furniss 2006). These materials are also carcinogenic. Furthermore, jelly plastic is harmful as it is porous and not able to be sterilized. This means that bacteria, mold, and fungus can live in a jelly plastic sex toy with no way for the toy to be sanitized.

Feminist sex stores often do not carry any product made with jelly plastic. Although some stores continue to sell them (since customers enjoy their low price), they explain the risks and problems to the consumer and advise them to use a condom with any jelly plastic toy. Stores that are committed to the health and safety of their clients often test products before sale for the presence of phthalates or seek manufacturers who use materials that are phthalate-free. The owner of a Minneapolis sex store founded a consumer advocacy group called Coalition Against Toxic Toys (CATT) to educate the sex toy industry on the harms of some of the products on the market. CATT aims to stop the production of harmful and toxic sex toys. These stores understand sexual health to be a right and refuse to let unsafe, harmful, or toxic products in their stores.

Sexual education

Each feminist sex shop provides workshops and classes on location. Though different courses are taught in each city, these ventures share a common thread. Each class is aimed at continuing to liberate sexuality by both educating participants and working to raise their sexual consciousness. Classes focus on pleasure and confidence in one's sexuality, learning about sex acts, kink, and burlesque, including classes titled "Talk Dirty to Me: The Art of Erotic Talk," "Cheap Sex Workshop," and "Knotty Thoughts: the Eroticism of Rope." Workshops are also offered on flirting, strip-tease, communicating about sex, masturbation, and a variety of sex practices.

Conclusion

Sex-positive feminism seeks to empower women to have agency over their sexuality and sexual pleasure. To this end, the women who founded feminist sex stores embody this new feminism, both in their retail establishments and in their communities. Raising sexual consciousness through feminism, coupled with anger over the lack of resources available for women's sexual gratification in traditional sex stores, led a small group of women to change the landscape of understanding about sexuality and pleasure through the creation of a new site for sexual commerce, feminist sex shops. These shops continue to impact both their customers and their community, opening up dialogue about healthy sexuality and pleasure and making products available to help pursue these ideals.

As feminist sex stores continue to grow, new generations of people of all genders and sexualities find ways to meet their sexual needs and explore the depths of their sexual pleasures through these retail and community spaces. These stores have an impact on their community that surpasses our usual perceptions of retail stores. While most business owners seek entrepreneurship, feminist sex shops go beyond mere commerce and have positioned themselves also as sites of sexual conscious-ness raising, education, and empowerment. Through openness and education, feminist sex stores help contribute to new understandings of pleasure and sexuality in America.

References

Berkowitz, Dana. 2006. "Consuming Eroticism: Gender Performances and Presentations in Pornographic Establishments." *Journal of Contemporary Ethnography* 35: 583–606.

Brantley, Mike. 2009. "Alabama Sex Toy Ban: Court Rejects Challenge." *The Press Register*. http://blog.al.com/live/2009/09/alabama_court_rejects_challeng.html. Accessed March 17, 2010.

Campbell, Sarah Fay. 2009. "Coweta Passes Tighter Obscenity Ordinance." *The Times-Herald*. www.times-herald.com/Local/Coweta-passes-tighter-obscenity-ordinance-646015. Accessed March 21, 2010.

Chandler, Kim and Eric Velasco. 2009. "Alabama Supreme Court Upholds Sex Toy Ban." *The Birmingham News*. www.al.com/news/birminghamnews/metro.ssf?/base/news/12527 43369276790.xml&coll=2. Accessed March 17, 2010.

Furniss, Candace. 2006. "Sex Toys and the Revolution." *Confluence* 12(2). www.stlconfluence. org/article. Accessed March 16, 2010.

Loe, Meika. 1999. "Feminism for Sale: Case Study of a Pro-Sex Feminist Business." *Gender and Society* 13 (6): 705–32.

PART 8

Sexual regulation and inequality

Introduction

When we hear the word "regulation," what probably comes to mind are laws, policies, and rules that government bureaucracies enforce. For example, the US Department of Transportation has explicit regulations governing airline safety. These policies mean that we can only take some items aboard a plane (knives are not allowed), that there are certain things we are not supposed to say on a plane (like making threats), and certain behavior that is not permitted (like smoking in the plane's bathroom). If this is what comes to mind when we think of regulation, then what does *sexual regulation* mean? After all, we don't have security guards watching to make sure we say and do certain things before having a sexual encounter. We don't fill out forms and go through inspections to determine whether or not we can have sex, or have checklists that instruct us about federally approved sexual practices.

Sexual regulation is obviously different from airline safety regulation. However, it's not as different as one might initially assume. There *are* in fact federally approved sexual practices. Likewise, sexual regulation does involve ideas about: safety; what kinds of behaviors are allowed or forbidden; what should and should not be said; and inspection. For example, federal laws and policies concerning everything from health-care to taxes show that there *is* a federally approved sexuality – a straight, married couple where the husband works and the wife stays home to care for children. Or the military policy of "don't ask, don't tell" also demonstrated that homosexuality was federally disapproved of. Moreover, there are also laws that define what is considered sexually "obscene" and therefore what can and cannot be said.

But there is also more to sexual regulation than just government laws, rules, and policies. Other institutions regulate sexuality as well. For example, medical doctors espouse definite ideas of what constitutes "safe" sexual practices. Most religions, including Christianity, have explicit rules about what sexual behavior is permitted and forbidden. And therapists and other mental health professionals regularly perform "inspections" in the form of mental health examinations which delve into an individual's sexual past to determine whether the individual is sexually normal or "pathological" in some way.

Reviewing this list, we can see that sexual regulation differs from airline regulation in three important ways. First, determining how sexuality is regulated involves deeper interpretation and analysis than following a government checklist of forbidden and permitted actions. Second, the "regulators" of sex and sexuality are far more varied than a centralized government bureaucracy; they include other institutions like religion, schools, or health providers, as well as the cultural beliefs into which we are socialized. Third, sexual regulation does not *only* involve formal laws, policies, and rules, but also norms, beliefs, and social practices.

Sexual regulation is about social control – encompassing all the means society has of getting people to conform through every social institution. It encompasses formal laws, rules, and guidelines; for example, laws that govern who can have sex with whom, or who is considered a legitimate citizen with full human rights based on sexual identity. It encompasses the moral guidelines concerning sexual behavior that are espoused by religions like Christianity. And sexual regulation includes ideas of appropriate and inappropriate (or normal and abnormal) behavior that shape and control our sexual beliefs, feelings, and actions. It encompasses the taken-for-granted assumptions we have been socialized to hold about men and masculinity and women and femininity. All of these things tend to socially control in some way – that is, they encourage us to conform. Through following government policies, or the gendered scripts we are taught, the religious beliefs we were raised in, the school environments where we're encouraged to mock others sexually for not fitting in, we are indelibly shaped by sexual regulation.

chapter 53

Sexuality, state, and nation

Jyoti Puri

- Decriminalize homosexuality
- Pakistan does not have any gays
- Brazilian women are hot!
- www.missworld.tv/
- Sex with a girl below 16 years is rape
- Our values are strong, ours is a chaste nation
- Don't ask, don't tell, don't pursue
- She's easy, she's American

Familiar phrases bring us face-to-face with sexuality's inseparability from the state and the nation. We live with such sentiments and policies every day without thinking twice about them. Precisely because the impact of nation and state on sexuality is so routine, it all seems unremarkable. Perhaps the spark of sexual desire set off deep within one's core reinforces the belief that sexuality is personal, private. Nothing could be further from reality; social institutions matter tremendously to issues of sexuality. When pushed to consider which institutions matter, we easily concede the usual suspects – family, media, peer groups, school, and religion. But the above phrases starkly remind us that nations and states are equally important to sexuality, if not more. Think about it: it is easier to ignore parental injunctions about your sexual behavior than what the state sees as sexually legal. This chapter presents a case for how nations and states bear on matters of sexuality and why this is too crucial to ignore.

It is helpful to have definitions of key terms such as nationalism, nation, and state, and that's where I start each of the sections, before going on to draw the connections with sexuality. The chapter is organized into two main parts, one on nationalism and nation and the other on the state. Even though there is overlap between the two concepts and what I have to say about each of them in terms of sexuality, this is an effective way to remind ourselves that the two concepts are not the same. For examples, I focus mostly on India and the USA. The idea is to blend useful examples that may be less familiar to the primary readers of this book with what seems familiar, but the purpose is the same: to question the links between sexuality, nation, and state.

Nationalism and nation

Let's start by defining the tricky thing that is nationalism, and the sibling concept, nation. You may wish to try this as we go, but, when I think of nationalism, coming up with an associated list of things is far easier than a crisp definition: flags, wars, passports, patriotism, and so on. One reason making it harder to abstract a definition is the near impossibility of imagining a world without nations; they seem so . . . what's the word? . . . normal that stating exactly what nationalism is, or what a nation is, is tough. All the more important to pin down the definition. Consider this: nationalism is the belief and practice aimed at creating unified but unique communities (nations) within a sovereign space (states). Said in a different way, nationalism is the belief that a people = nation = state.

Nationalism comes before nation; the *idea* and belief in the (north) American nation came before the Declaration of Independence and the creation of the nation of America, and the United States of America became the sovereign state. More than one nation co-exists in the USA, although unequally – America, Nation of Islam, Cherokee Nation, Queer Nation (now almost defunct), among others. Nationalism is inherently neither good nor bad; rather, it is an abstract idea that unifies us but also separates us from others. We are linked as individuals to a broad collective and, along with others, we become part of a nation that seems uniquely ours. The flip side of each nation as a unique unified entity is to specify how it is different from another. It ought to be difficult to come up with 192 national stereotypes (that's how many nations are recognized by the United Nations), but nevertheless we seem to be able to – the British are stoic, Koreans are hard-working, Americans are loud, Chinese are cheap, Jamaicans are lazy.

Nationalism is a powerful principle, a powerful promise. Power is the ability to make things happen, and nationalism's ability to whip up sentiment and movements, to unify people or divide them, and create policy is awesome. Nationalism has inspired movements of independence (for example, Bangladesh), resistance to oppression (Palestine), a sense of community in times of social crisis (terrorist bombings in Madrid and London), but also genocide (Bosnia), invasion (US in Iraq), war (India–Pakistan), and militarism (South Korea). I don't know of anything more precious to a person than her/his life. And what more sobering measure of nationalism's power is there than the fact that sacrificing one's life or taking the life of another in the name of the nation is considered the highest good?

Nationalism is not merely powerful in the sense of the "power of nationalism"; nationalism is itself a form of power. As a form of power, nationalism is a mechanism of social regulation. Why do I say that? Because we cannot imagine our lives without this social structure; because we are told that it is the highest form of community, over family or religion, to which we owe allegiance; because we are raised within the parameters of national cultural values, and draw from within our sense of self/identity; because we experience kinship with other people whom we have never met, and hatred for people from another nation whom also we have never met, as a result of nationalism; because it works by permeating our desires, not through force, but by making us complicit in policies and ideologies in the name of the nation.

The promise of nationalism is that we are all essentially the same and equal as citizens – a flawed promise, if there ever was one! No nation has been able to ensure genuine equality to its entire people while recognizing differences of race, ethnicity, gender, sexuality, social class, language, religion. It is not a matter of getting it right, of fixing the flaws of nationalism. In fact, the inequalities are not simply incidental but are built into the national social and legal infrastructures; law, military, government, schools, skilled professions in the US, for example, are remarkably skewed in terms of class, gender, and race. And these limitations of nationalism are directly relevant to sexuality.

Nationalism on sex and the nation's sex

Nationalism's greatest impact on matters of sexuality is by defining what is normal and abnormal, what is respectable and what is deviant. The fundamental link between respectable sexuality and nationalism is that ideals or customs of dominant groups are endorsed as national ideals, and are socially and legally enforced. The flip side of this respectable sexuality is what becomes designated as abnormal or deviant. Curiously, heterosexuality frequently corresponds to what is respectable and normal, and deviance to homosexuality.

In India, the norms for adult sexuality are quite unambiguous – it belongs within marriage and is meant to procreate no more than two children. But what lies beneath the marital bed? If this were true, HIV/AIDS would not be affecting young (primarily 15–44 years of age) sexually active persons mostly through heterosexual contact (85.7 percent of transmissions). Whether true or not, for normal sexuality to have influence, abnormal sexuality must also be whipped up. Perhaps no greater misconception exists than the fact that Indian Muslims, the main minority group, are increasing rapidly. This increase is wrongly attributed to rampant male Muslim sexuality and the desire to increase proportions relative to Indian Hindus. The irony is that Hindus vastly outnumber any other religious group in the population, at more than 84 percent, and the threat posed by Indian Muslims and their male sexuality is fabricated but widely believed. Already declining birth rates among Muslims are expected to stabilize at 14 percent of the nation's population. So much for rampant male sexuality (notice the absence of any regard for Muslim women's sexual desires, or their wish for contraceptives).

Women are especially spotlighted when it comes to specifying respectable sexuality. Rape is undoubtedly seen as a form of sexual deviance, but under particular circumstances it can reveal national ideologies about sexual respectability. In May 2005, a young student in New Delhi was kidnapped and sexually assaulted in a moving car by four men. The incident struck a raw nerve in the city that is now called the rape capital of India. English-language newspapers reporting on the assault showed restraint, and in one case even reported on the brave determination of the young woman to put aside her grief and trauma and help the police in nabbing the suspects. But individual persons were less impressed or felt less constrained about expressing their opinions. What dominated their reactions was that this young woman was from northeastern India and that she was walking with a friend at two in the morning. Offensive stereotypes of women from the northeast, labeling them as sexually promiscuous and as unrespectable, were more pronounced in these reactions than the expectation that each person, and all women, have a right not to be touched without their consent. The implications were that this young woman is un-Indian and unrespectable, which doesn't condone the rape but purports to explain how she became the victim of sexual assault. Such can be the tragic and offensive logic when sexuality is part of the domain of nationalism.

If something is to be underlined here, then it is this: the issue is one of who belongs in the national community and who doesn't, and sexuality – normal, respectable – is the litmus test of belonging. The paradoxical catch is that some, by virtue of their religious affiliation, their ethnicity, their gender, their social class, are never going to be seen as sexually respectable and, therefore, as part of the national community. Norms of Indian sexuality, or for that matter North American sexual respectability, are specific to class-, gender-, race-, and sexual-orientation. It is curious to me that college-going women in the US worry about how many sexual partners they can have and under what circumstances (one-night stands, for example) before they need to consider their reputations. Interestingly enough, these are worries shared by some friends in India who are older than the college girls by several years.

Nowhere are the issues of belonging to the national community more precarious than for those who identify as lesbian, gay, bisexual, transgender, or queer. How national communities include or exclude their sexual minorities varies; the recently won right of lesbians and gays to marry, in Spain (2005) and Canada (2005), is about equal citizenship and recognition in the eyes of the nation. More frequently, though, people are excluded either explicitly or through omission on the basis of sexual orientation or because they are transgendered. When was the last time a presidential address in the US made mention of gays and lesbians as an essential and equal part of the national community? This is omission. US President Bush only mentioned them in the context of direct exclusion, by saying that marriage can only exist between a man and a woman.

The disturbing paradox is that, even as lesbians, gays, bisexuals, and transgendered people may be omitted, made invisible in the national community, they are also subject to unusual scrutiny. Another crime committed in New Delhi in 2004 starkly illustrates this point. This time, an upper-class gay man, Pushkin Chandra, and his friend were brutally murdered by two working-class men – as it turned out, over an argument about documenting their sexual activities. The English-language media brought to bear tremendous pressure on the police to solve the crime, but in an outrightly scurrilous manner. Inflammatory articles about "gay lifestyles," their deviant, upper-class, Westernized and, therefore, un-Indian sexual behaviors, littered the newspapers. The police, in their turn, went on a witch hunt within the gay networks of

Jyoti Puri

New Delhi, surveilling gay men, browbeating, threatening, and tracking them. The police officer who supervised the solving of the crime confirmed this in a conversation. Sexuality rights activists rightly questioned the role of the media in whipping up a voyeuristic revulsion against gay men in general and placing them at the edges of the national community. As women's rights activist and educator Pramada Menon poignantly said, "One person's death has brought an entire community into focus. Newspapers are suddenly full of stories about homosexual life – and not in a celebratory way.... A stray incident has been used to stereotype them all and an already marginalized community is being pushed further into the margins."

What I have been doing in this section is noting the obvious ways in which nationalism and sexuality are connected, even though their specific connections will vary by case. I have been also making connections where they may not be so obvious. The idea is that if we start to recognize how nationalism and sexuality are connected, we are more likely to question and undo them. By way of that, here is a summary of the key points made in this section. First, nationalism shapes sexuality by defining what is normal, indeed, respectable. Second, the dominant groups determine the norm of respectable sexuality, which establishes who belongs to the national community. Third, gender, sexual orientation, race, religion, class are among the key social dimensions to determine belonging to national community. Fourth, the nation itself can take on sexual meanings. For example, citizens may associate national identity with exclusively heterosexual citizens. What I am getting at in this point is that, implicitly and sometimes explicitly, nations are seen as heterosexual. This is exactly what happens when the nation is thought of as a community of heterosexuals or when the nation becomes personified as a young desirable woman or as the heroic soldier fighting for family, community, and nation.

State

It is time to underscore a point that is couched in the above discussion, and to segue to the state. We don't think anything of using the concepts of nation and state interchangeably, but any attentive political science student will remind us they are different. The linking together of nation and state, or the equation that a people = nation = state, is itself a modern artifact of nationalism. That's why the terms seem confusing, redundant. The state is a sovereign demarcated territory, and more. It is a set of cultural institutions that generate ideologies (for example: the state is all-powerful), establish administrative policies and procedures (for example: monitoring populations), and enforce them through direct and indirect violence (for example: police and the law). A mouthful of a definition for something that seems awfully boring, no? For all the passion and love the nation inspires, one is hard pressed to find an ode to the state.

So, let's see if we can get to the importance of the state in another way. A student wakes up one morning and goes about her routine. As she gets dressed and heads out of the door, she will not recall that the building she inhabits, her apartment, the kitchen appliances and bathroom fittings, the car that she drives, the university that she attends, are all made possible by fulfilling a long list of state and federal laws. She will not note the police on the streets (for the most part), the post office that she drives by, and the traffic lights at the intersection. She is less likely to forget about the taxes that are withheld from her weekly paycheck or the year's financial aid package. All of this has to do with the presence of the state in our lives, and this is just the start of the list. The tv that she watches, and the communication and broadcast laws, are easier to forget, but it's harder for her to ignore that the content is monitored. The point is that so fundamental a structure is the state in our lives that we see it selectively, and it would have to stop functioning for us to fully appreciate its relevance. This, its semi-invisibility, along with the more obvious institutions such as police, military, law, and government, is what gives the state tremendous power.

State on sex

Sexuality is no exception to the impact of the state in our lives. If one is eligible to have sex, with whom, of what kind, under what circumstances, where, whether sex aids or contraceptives are used, are all matters subject to regulation by the state. And we think sexuality is a personal matter! My point is not that the state is an evil big brother; Hollywood movies have already contributed enough to that myth. That we imagine the state as the evil monster is only a means of working through our anxieties about its impact in our lives. I would rather have us recognize the power of state ideologies, the institutionalization of power in state institutions, and the impact of an intricate administrative machinery. This does not happen in tandem or function smoothly, but can be messy, inconsistent, even contradictory.

Nothing better illustrates the power of the state on issues of sexuality than the mobilization against Section 377 of the Indian Penal Code. The law can be summarized as the "sodomy law," which prohibits "sex against the order of nature." That is really to say, it prohibits anal and oral sex. This poses a problem for heterosexual couples who incorporate a range of sexual techniques. This most certainly poses a problem for gay men and lesbian women, because "sex against the order of nature" is thought to inherently include consenting sex between two adult women or two adult men. Not just anal or oral, but any sex between them could be interpreted as unnatural. Introduced by the British in 1860, this law is not just out of date but it is inconsistent with a cultural past that did not impugn persons with alternative sexualities. Notably, the law is not widely used to prosecute individuals but it contributes to a contemporary culture of violence and intolerance of transgenders, lesbians, gays, and bisexuals in India. It is most typically used by the police, thugs, and opportunists to harass, threaten, blackmail, and extort money and sex. Section 377 of the Indian Penal Code indicates how sexuality is regulated by the state; how it institutionalizes intolerance for some sexualities; how the belonging of lesbians, gays, transgenders and bisexuals in the Indian national community might be unjustly precarious but the state has the power to enforce the injustice through the police, the courts, HIV/AIDS policies, etc. Is it any wonder that there is gathering momentum across India to change Section 377 and to decriminalize homosexuality? Here's hoping.

Earlier, I noted that same-sex sexualities are more systematically targeted; this would include state institutions. Notwithstanding a few nations, gay, lesbian, and bisexual women and men are the objects of regulation by the state through denial. What do I mean by that? In the US, until recently, same-sex couples could not marry outside the state of Massachusetts, or openly serve in the military. This is deeply problematic not just because it limits personal choices. These prohibitions withheld the benefits of citizenship that the state extends to married couples or citizen-soldiers. The other side of this denial is the promotion of heterosexuality by the state. And is it easier to concede the point that gay, lesbian, bisexual, and transgendered people are often denied the privileges enjoyed by heterosexual women and men? Is it harder to concede that heterosexuality is openly or subtly promoted by the state? If so, the reason is that we don't *see* the privileges of heterosexuality. The power of the norm is what makes it disappear from sight: precisely because it is normal, we stop noticing it. Think about the innumerable laws and procedures – inheritance, marriage, birth and adoption, health proxy, death, tax exemptions, parenting, work-related insurance and benefits, home ownership and loans that implicitly say – for heterosexuals only! This is the unequal impact of the state on sexuality.

Sexualizing the state

So far, in this section, the discussion has focused on the state's impact on sexuality. What if we were to turn the lens around? What if we were to look at the state through the lens of sexuality; to sexualize the state, as it were? I think it is an exercise worth doing. For one thing, it would tell us more about how the state promotes and privileges heterosexuality. I am sure you've noticed or heard of the rising tide of Christian right-wing backlash against sexual and gender minorities in the US which began in the 1990s and continues to date. The backlash is unabated but not unchallenged. One such challenge to the right comes from scholar Lisa Duggan (1994), who calls for "disestablishment strategies." This is how Duggan explains disestablishment strategies: to show how the state constantly privileges heterosexuality; and to take the position that the state ought to *stop* its promotion. To make this point, she draws a parallel to why the state ought to remain secular. Think about it: if one of the founding principles of the US state is that it is secular, and not partial to any one religion, then why not have the same approach to sexuality? Why privilege a certain form of sexuality constantly and systematically? The state should divest itself of such heterosexist biases, Duggan rightly declares.

For a second, I think it's important to sexualize the state because it takes us beyond a one-way analysis of the impact of the state on sexuality. We typically see the impact of the state on same-sex sexualities, commercial sex workers, and on other marginalized groups. But, why not analyze the state? Sexualizing the state makes us do the hard work of analyzing how it is thoroughly infused with issues of sexuality. By this, I don't mean just the laws, policies, and ideologies regulating sexuality, heterosexuality, and same-sex sexualities. I mean all of the same that don't appear to be directly about sexuality but whose pre-occupations with issues of sexuality are never far behind (for example, US citizenship laws that are not obviously related to sexuality but, in fact, privilege heterosexuals). This approach moves us away from treating the state as a singular cohesive unit that unrelentingly privileges heterosexuality and marginalizes all else.

This is not meant to be confusing. In this section, I have argued that the state is implicated in privileging and promoting certain sexualities. I have also argued that the state is not cohesive, monolithic, or a singular unit; indeed, it is a messy, inconsistent and contradictory set of institutions. The additional point that I am making here is that it is politically important to see the state as inconsistent, and to identify when and where the state does not privilege heterosexuality (for example: the decriminalization of homosexuality in the US through Lawrence vs Texas, June 2003; the August 2005 ruling by the California Supreme Court that both lesbian parents are to be seen as a child's mothers even after their relationship is over). To take the position that there are no inconsistencies in the state would be to see it as all-powerful (which it is not), would ignore social change (which has occurred), and would identify strategies for further change (in all spheres of life). Put another way, sexualizing the state is necessary for seeing how state power operates, and for challenging it.

Conclusion

It is hard to predict how familiar you are with the concepts of nationalism, nation, and state. It is equally hard to predict to what degree these concepts interest you. I hope this chapter has been successful in its aim to help you see the intertwining of sexuality with nationalism, nation, and state. I also hope that understanding connections of sexuality to these concepts has tweaked or enhanced your interest in issues of nation and state. What I would like to underscore is that nation and state have an impact upon sexuality in ways that affect our personal and collective lives. In the same vein, it is important to recognize the ways in which matters of sexuality are diffused into the nation and the state. It's a matter of recognizing the complex intertwining of sexuality with nation and state, precisely so that we can question how sexuality is regulated by these social structures. If there is one thing I would like you to take away from this chapter, then it is this: we need to challenge how nation and state create inequalities between normal and abnormal sexuality on the backs of women, transgenders, and men, who are socially marginalized because of their sexual orientation, race, gender, social class, or religion.

Bibliography

Duggan, Lisa. 1994. "Queering the State", *Social Text* 39: 1–14.
Hobsbawm, Eric J. 1990. *Nations and Nationalism since 1780: Programme, Myth, and Reality*, Cambridge: Cambridge University Press.

chapter 54

Children's sexual citizenship

Kerry H. Robinson

Many adults view children and young people's agency and citizenship as a challenge to adult power and authority. The idea that *sexual* citizenship has relevance to children and young people's lives is often met with even greater resistance and hostility by some adults and is viewed as inappropriately crossing the adult/child boundary. Sexuality is frequently narrowly perceived as physical sexual acts rather than a process of identity that begins early in children's lives. *Children's sexual citizenship* is about: learning to become ethical gendered and sexual subjects, with an understanding of consent and what it means to respect others in relationships; to respect gender and sexuality diversity that exists in life; having an awareness and understanding of their rights as sexual subjects; to be supported in building confidence and resilience in order to become informed sexual subjects; and fostering children and young people's health and wellbeing. Children and young people's access to ongoing comprehensive sexuality education, both at home and in schools, and throughout their lives, is central to the building of sexual citizenship early in life. However, it is important to understand the impact that the discourse of 'childhood innocence' has on increasing children's and young people's vulnerabilities, in terms of their sexual health and wellbeing, especially through denying them access to this knowledge.

Dominant theoretical perspectives of sexuality, like those of childhood, reflect tensions between biological determinist and social constructionist ways of thinking. Post-structuralist and queer theorists have critiqued fixed biological understandings of sexuality, arguing that sexuality is primarily a fluid, dynamic, and socially constructed aspect of subjectivity (one's self) (Foucault 1978; Butler 1990). Pepper Schwartz and Dominic Cappello (2001) refer to sexuality as being the sum total of our sexual desire, behavior and self-identity. Deborah Britzman (2000: 37) argues: sexuality is 'a human right of free association' and a *force* that is vital to human passion, interest, explorations and disappointments. Children and young people in their own ways share in experiencing this *force* in their lives. It is these views of sexuality that underpin the discussion in this essay. Sexuality is viewed as being experienced and expressed in multiple ways across the life span, which includes the lives of children. Within this perspective, the relationship between sexuality and childhood is a socio-cultural, historical and political construction, representing the values of the dominant cultures of the specific time period (Weeks 1986).

This essay explores the concept of children's sexual citizenship. The discussion focuses on several main areas. First, it examines the socio-cultural construction of the relationship between childhood and sexuality and how the dominant discourse of childhood innocence is central to this relationship. Second, I analyze the concept of sexual citizenship and its relevance to children's lives. Third, I investigate how the discourses of childhood and innocence have been utilized to: regulate children's access to knowledge about sexuality and relationships; to argue that sexual knowledge is irrelevant to children; and deny children's access to sexual citizenship. It is important to point out that the discourses of childhood and childhood innocence are intertwined, working simultaneously to reinforce the power of the knowledge they perpetuate. They are foundational to the power relationships between children and adults, which is socially constructed and variable across different socio-cultural contexts. In other words, the meaning of childhood and the child are socio-culturally defined by *adults*, for adults and determines how a child should behave, what a child should know and how and when they should come to know it (James and Prout 1990; Gittins 1998). Finally, I investigate how the discourses of childhood and innocence are also used to regulate the 'good' adult sexual citizen subject – one who operates within heteronormative and Christian moral frameworks (Bell and Binnie 2000; Berlant 1997; Richardson 1998). Throughout this essay I argue that children's sexual citizenship and access to sexuality education is a social justice and children's rights issue.

Childhood, innocence and sexuality

It is important to understand how childhood is constructed in relation to sexuality in western countries in order to understand children's precarious and difficult association with sexual citizenship. Theorists of child development have argued that childhood is a natural, universal and a biologically inherent period of human development (Piaget [1929] 1973). This biologically universal perspective fixes and homogenizes ideas of what it means to be a child, how children 'develop' (what they are capable of doing, knowing and thinking over time) and experiences of childhood. This perspective also defines the child in opposition to what it means to be an adult. This either/or thinking is linked to commonsense understandings of adults and children that supposedly reflect the 'natural order of things.' However, more recently, social constructionist theorists have critiqued these biologically determined perspectives of childhood for failing to acknowledge the multiple and changing experiences of childhood across history, political contexts, genders, sexuality, social class, ethnic backgrounds and geographical locations, amongst other variables. In social constructionist perspectives of childhood, what it means to be a child is constituted through socio-cultural values, beliefs and practices. For example, Cindi Katz's (2004) research in a Sudanese village points out that children's autonomous participation in everyday life is integral to the socio-cultural, political and economic success of the village community. The transfer of knowledge required by these children to play an active and central role in their communities, including political and economic knowledge, begins in early childhood.

Childhood innocence, especially sexual innocence, is the ultimate signifier of the child and has become the defining boundary between the adult and the child. It defines the child and adult's place in the western world today. In a post-Freudian context, sexuality is primarily viewed as an 'adults-only' domain. Sexuality is generally viewed to begin at puberty and mature in adulthood, correlating with biological understandings of human development, which reinforce biologically determined understandings of childhood. However, there have been a range of competing and contradictory discourses that prevail about children and sexuality. These discourses include: 'children are asexual and innocent'; 'children's sexuality is dangerous to society and needs to be regulated'; 'children's sexuality is normal and critical for the development of creative and vibrant society'; 'sexuality is dangerous to the moral development of the child'; and 'children are vulnerable to abuses and exploitation by adult sexuality and need to be protected' (Robinson 2013).

These discourses reflect the way that sexuality, ironically, has been constituted as both irrelevant to young children's lives and, simultaneously, also as a 'danger' to them. In western cultures today, sexuality is often perceived as something from which children need protection. That is, protection from the abuses and exploitation of adults; from the perceived sexualization of children in the media, especially in advertising; and also from what some adults perceive as children's inability, due to their age, to regulate their sexual behaviours according to the sexual mores of society.

While there's a dominant perception that prevails that sexuality is irrelevant to young children, social practices demonstrate a different narrative – one in which there is an emphasis upon dismissing children's desires and curiosity about sexual knowledge, or keeping them contained, often through myths and misinformation (Robinson and Davies 2010). For example, historically, in some children's institutions, the arms of children's pyjama tops were often sown down to the sides of the top so children could not freely move their arms to touch their genitals. These tops operated like a straight jackets. Children were also often told stories that babies were delivered by storks, or found under cabbage patches, or that they came out of the mother's stomach through the bellybutton (Robinson and Davies 2010).

Research clearly demonstrates young children are actively constructing themselves as gendered and sexual beings and regulating the gender and sexual identities of other children (Blaise 2009; Goldman and Goldman 1982; Jackson 1982; Renold 2005; Robinson 2013; Robinson and Davies 2010). Like adults, children are constantly negotiating the discourses of sexuality available to them. Importantly, young children's conceptions of sexuality are generally framed within heteronormative expressions of gender. Mindy Blaise's research (2009) with a group of young girls and boys aged five and six points out that young children are highly regulated by heteronormative discourses of gender. For example, the perspective that girls have to be sexy and/or pretty to get a boyfriend prevailed amongst the young girls in the group. Emma Renold's (2005) research with primary school-aged children demonstrated that for the boys, having a girlfriend was a signifier for their heterosexuality and a means for evading any potential harassment from peers that might be associated with a questioning of their 'normative' gender and sexuality. Both Renold's and Blaise's research echoes the findings of the research of Robinson (2013) and Robinson and Davies (2010) with children four and five years of age. Children's understandings of relationships, marriage and sexuality were expressed through heteronormative discourses. Children also regulated any transgressions from this practice by other children. For example, mock weddings were often part of children's play, but some were persistent in regulating other children's behaviours if they wished to marry a person of the same sex. Drawing on current heteronormative conventions of marriage in Australia, young children insisted that two boys or two girls could not get married.

The socio-cultural process of constructing children as heterosexual subjects depends heavily upon the perpetuation of heteronormative gender narratives in childhood, like those just discussed. The regulatory practices of both adults and children are integral to this process. In addition, the discourse of child/human development reinforces this process through its assumption and representation of the normative child as being heterosexual. Children's engagement in heteronormative mock weddings, in playing boyfriends and girlfriends, kiss and chase, and so on are generally considered a normal part of boys' and girls' socio-cultural gender development. This process of heterosexualization of gender in childhood is generally rendered invisible as it is seen as a part of children's healthy normal development. We never really question this process of construction of gender; it only becomes problematic when children transgress what is viewed as normal – for example, two boys playing kiss and chase with each other, and/or wishing to marry each other in the mock wedding.

This process of constituting the normative child as heterosexual is essential to laying the foundations of the good (adult) citizen. Good sexual citizens are usually represented as heterosexual and those who adhere to the dominant sexual mores of that society (e.g. being celibate or non-promiscuous if you are single; married and monogamous). Another critical component of this heterosexualization involves controlling what sexual knowledge is available to children. For example, many parents do not feel it is appropriate to talk about same-sex sexuality or sexual fluidity with children. This knowledge is also generally not available to children in school curricula. The discourse of childhood innocence is often used to defend and regulate not allowing children access to this knowledge.

Children's access to knowledge of sexuality is seen as breaching childhood innocence and is often perceived as developmentally inappropriate and harmful (Corteen and Scraton 1997; Jackson 1982). The fears and taboos that prevail about children and sexuality have resulted in increasing limitations concerning children's access to sexual knowledge. This creates anxieties that permeate all aspects of children's early sexual education, including parents' practices of sexuality education at home (Robinson 2013). In recent research (Robinson 2013; Robinson and Davies 2010) conducted with parents of elementary (or primary) school-aged children, some mothers discussed their fears in speaking publicly about how they provided their young children (particularly girls) with comprehensive information about sexuality. They were anxious that they would be judged as bad mothers, especially by other mothers who believed that they were giving their children 'too much' information 'too early' about sexuality.

Some adults believe that older children's access to sexuality education will encourage them to engage in sexual activity prematurely. However, research conducted in countries with more open and liberal approaches to children and young people's comprehensive sexuality education (for example in Holland and Scandinavia) challenge this claim (Levine 2002). While practices limiting access to sexuality knowledge are done in the name of 'protecting children' and protecting childhood 'innocence,' such regulations actually increase children's and young people's vulnerabilities and negatively impact their health and well being. In particular, limiting children's access to sexuality knowledge can undermine children's ability to think quickly, critically and in an informed manner, if put in a potentially abusive situation by an older person. It also leaves children with little options to find information they want and need from sources, including the Internet and peers, that may provide information that is misinformation, based on myths and stereotypes, outdated, or not based on rigorous research. In some developing countries, particularly in regions of Africa, there is a critical need for sexuality education as a means of intervening in the spread of sexually transmitted infections (STIs) HIV and AIDS (Bhana 2010; UNESCO 2009). Knowledge of bodies and sexuality is important to all children and young people for acquiring a sense of control and responsibility about who they are as sexual subjects across the life span.

Limiting children's access to sexual knowledge is a form of censorship. Censorship is often considered the appropriate approach to maintaining childhood 'innocence.' In terms of regulating children and young people's access to sexually explicit advertising, media and popular culture, censorship does little to deal with the issues raised, but as Foucault (1978) points out, it only intensifies the interest and the problem. Censorship also dismisses children's agency in this process. Building children's critical literacy skills and knowledge of the issues is a more strategic way forward.

Sexual citizenship and its relevance to children

Tensions and contestations surround sexual citizenship, yet it does provide an important public space in which to raise critical equity issues pertinent to sexual identities, including those of children and young people. David Bell and Jon Binnie (2000) have argued 'all citizenship is sexual citizenship, in that the foundational tenets of being a citizen are all inflected by sexualities' (2000: 10). In this respect, Brenda Cossman's (2007: 5) definition of citizenship is a useful foundation for understanding sexual citizenship:

> A set of rights and practices denoting membership and belonging in a nation state . . . including not only legal and political practices but also cultural practices and representations . . . also . . . invoking the ways that different subjects are constituted as members of a polity, the ways they are, or are not, granted rights, responsibilities, and representations within the polity, as well as acknowledgement and inclusion through a multiplicity of legal, political, cultural, and social discourses.

Sexual citizenship is therefore not only linked to notions of membership, belonging, participation, responsibilities, equity and rights, as sexual subjects, but also about processes of exclusion from these areas. It is also about different citizens sharing the power across these areas. Within mainstream political and legal foundations of citizenship, the *normal* and *natural* citizen has been inherently heterosexual (Bell and Binnie 2000; Berlant 1997; Cooper 1993; Duggan 1994; Richardson 1998).

Gays, lesbians and people who are transgender experience different citizenship status (Bell and Binnie 2000). Lesbian, gay, bisexual and transgender citizens are pressured to be private, politically un-radical and de-eroticized in order to be seen as acceptable sexual citizens by the State (Binnie and Bell 2000; Weeks 1998). Diana Richardson (1998: 90) points out: '[L]esbians and gay men are granted the right to be tolerated as long as they stay within the boundaries of that tolerance, whose borders are maintained through a heterosexist public/private divide.' Sexual 'others' are often legitimized as good citizens when they are secured and rendered invisible in 'private' contexts, especially within the confines of heteronormative *family* structures.

So how is sexual citizenship relevant to children? The concept of children's rights in western cultures have largely been articulated and considered relevant in the context of the private family home and family relationships rather than in the broader public economic, social and political arenas. Consequently, the privatisation of childhood and parent–child relationships is reinforced, as is parental decision-making on all aspects of children's private and public lives. Children's agency in their lives is limited or non-existent. The heteronormative family has thus been viewed as central to the constitution of the 'good' heteronormative sexual citizen subject. It has also been the institution in which the 'normative' child and children's developing citizenry has been primarily regulated and monitored.

Public debates around children's sexuality education are framed within the dualistic politics of the private/public spheres. There is a long-standing debate over whether sexuality education is a private family matter and the responsibility of parents/guardians, or a public social and community responsibility taken on by schools (Jackson 1982; Robinson and Davies 2008b; Walker and Milton 2006). Frequently, some parents/guardians and teachers deem certain knowledge to be the parents' responsibility to impart to children. Often, this is knowledge considered more politically sensitive and value laden, for example non-heteronormative information, such as same-sex relationships and same-sex families. For younger children, it also includes information about sexual bodies, human reproduction (animals and plant reproduction are often considered more appropriate) and desire, which are perceived as developmentally inappropriate knowledge. Sexuality education in schools reflects a scientific heteronormative narrative framed within Christian monogamous marriage (Davies and Robinson 2010). Within this heteronormative social context, sexual minorities are viewed as deviant and abnormal, and are problematized, marginalized, and silenced (Robinson and Davies 2008b).

Many issues facing children and young people are relevant to sexual citizenship discourse (see Robinson 2012). The following three areas are examples of this relevance. First, the construction of 'childhood innocence' as a sexual commodity fundamental to the exploitation and abuse of children is a major issue relevant to sexual citizenship (Robinson 2013). Through the repression of children's sexuality and the process of equating innocence with children's bodies, childhood and children have become increasingly fetishized and eroticized. The child beauty pageant is an example of the hypersexualization of girls' bodies (Robinson and Davies 2008a). Childhood innocence, along with power, is often the titillation in the sexual abuse of children (Elliott 1992; Kitzinger 1990). Second, another example of a relevant sexual citizenship issue is children and young people as consumers of and key performers in media, advertising and popular culture in which sexuality, including young people's sexuality, is central to the selling of products. The sexualization of children in media and advertising, especially of young girls, sends a strong message to children about what is generally considered representative of powerful and attractive femininity and masculinity. The 'sexy' female becomes part of the heterosexualization of gender in girls and the ways in which many boys come to view girls and women. Third, sexual citizenship is also relevant to children in terms of their experiences of love, family and social relations. Children are building intimate relationships with other children who are special in their lives; involved in family relationships, some of which may be same-sex families; and encountering and engaging in social relationships with a range of people, from different gender and sexuality backgrounds in their every day interactions. Building an understanding of ethical relationships early in children's life across all these contexts is central to sexual citizenship.

The development of children and young people as informed, critically aware, ethical gendered and sexual subjects is essential for sexual citizenship and for citizenship more generally in a society. It is fundamental to young people's health and wellbeing as sexual subjects. For example, some children grow up lesbian, gay, bisexual, queer, and/or transgender, or live in same-sex families. Homophobia, heterosexism, transphobia and the lack of public, legal and institutional support for lesbian, gay, bisexual, queer and transgender identities can impact young people's daily lives, concepts of self, and perceived future choices (Mayo 2006). The levels of self-harm, thoughts of suicide, and drug and alcohol addiction amongst these young people, in comparison to their heterosexual and cisgender peers, is a stark reminder of the significance and relevance of sexual citizenship to young people (Robinson, Bansel, Denson, Ovenden and Davies 2014). This situation highlights the importance of including gender and sexuality diversity in the constitution of national identities and significance of equal access to political, economic, social, educational and legal rights for all citizens. Gay/ Straight Alliances in some schools are an example of young people's engagement in sexual citizenship, working together to counteract homophobia and heterosexism to improve the social and educational experiences of LGBTQ youth.

Conclusion

In this essay I have briefly outlined how dominant discourses of childhood and childhood innocence work simultaneously to position sexuality as problematic and/or irrelevant to children. However, as pointed out in this discussion, sexuality is experienced in multiple and fluid ways and is central to one's identity, including those of children and young people. Sexual citizenship is relevant and important in children's and young people's lives as it is about developing ethical gendered and sexual subjects; understanding the importance of consent and respect in relationships; respecting gender and sexuality diversity; awareness and understanding of one's rights as gendered and sexual citizens; building confidence and resilience in order to become informed sexual subjects; and fostering sexual health and wellbeing. In order to become ethical, agentic, competent sexual citizens, children and young people need access to sexuality knowledge, including ongoing comprehensive sexuality education that is part of their schooling. As such, children's access to sexuality education is a social justice and children's rights issue.

Bibliography

Bell, David and Binnie, Jon. 2000. *The Sexual Citizen: Queer Politics and Beyond*. Cambridge: Polity Press.

Berlant, Lauren. 1997. *The Queen of America Goes to Washington City: Essays on Sex and Citizenship*. Duke University Press: Durham.

Bhana, Deevia. 2010. 'How much do children know about HIV/AIDS?' *Early Childhood Development and Care*, 180(8): 1079–1092.

Blaise, Mindy. 2009. '"What a girl wants, what a girl needs": Responding to sex, gender and sexuality in the early childhood classroom.' *Journal of Research in Childhood Education*, 23(4): 450–60.

Britzman, Deborah. 2000. 'Precarious education.' In S. Talbut and S.R. Steinberg (eds) *Thinking Queer: Sexuality, culture, and education*. New York: Peter Lang Publishing.

Butler, Judith. 1990. *Gender Trouble: Feminism and the subversion of identity*. New York: Routledge.

Cooper, D. 1993. 'An engaged state: Sexuality, governance and the potential for change.' *Journal of Law and Society*, 20: 257–275.

Corteen, Karen and Scraton, Phil. 1997. 'Prolonging "childhood", manufacturing "innocence" and regulating sexuality.' In Scraton, P. (ed.), *'Childhood' in 'Crisis'*. London: University College London Press.

Cossman, Brenda. 2007. *Sexual Citizens: The Legal and Cultural Regulation of Sex and Belonging*. Stanford: Stanford University Press.

Davies, Cristyn. 2008. 'Proliferating panic: Regulating representations of sex and gender during the culture wars.' *Cultural Studies Review*, 14(2): 83–102.

Davies, Cristyn and Robinson, Kerry. H. 2010. 'Hatching babies and stalk deliveries: Risk and regulation in the construction of children's sexual knowledge.' *Contemporary Issues in Early Childhood* 11(3): 249–262.

Duggan, Lisa. 1994. 'Queering the state.' *Social Text*, 39: 1–14.

Elliott, Michele. 1992. 'Images of children in the media: "Soft kiddie porn."' In Itzin, I. (ed.) *Pornography: Women, violence and civil liberties. A radical new view*. New York: Oxford University Press.

Foucault, Michel. 1978. *The History of Sexuality: Vol. 1, an introduction*, trans, Robert Hurley. Harmondsworth: Penguin.

Gittins, Diana, 1998. *The Child in Question*. London: Macmillan.

Goldman, Ronald and Goldman, Juliette. (1982). *Children's Sexual Thinking*. London: Routledge & Kegan Paul.

Jackson, Stevi. 1982. *Childhood and Sexuality*. London: Blackwell Publishers.

James, A. and Prout, A. (eds) (1990). *Constructing and Reconstructing Childhood: Contemporary issues in the sociological study of childhood*. London: The Falmer Press.

Katz, C. 2004. *Growing Up Global: Economic restructuring and children's everyday lives*. Minnesota: University of Minnesota Press.

Kitzinger, Jenny. 1990. 'Who are you kidding? Children, power and the struggle against sexual abuse.' In James, A. and Prout, A. (eds) *Constructing and Reconstructing Childhood: Contemporary issues in the sociological study of childhood*, pp. 157–183. London: The Falmer Press.

Levine, Judith. 2002. *Harmful to Minors. The perils of protecting children from sex*. Minneapolis: University of Minneapolis Press.

Mayo, Chris. 2006. 'Pushing the limits of liberalism: Queerness, children and the future.' *Educational Theory*, 56(4): 469–487.

Piaget, Jean. [1929] 1973. *The Child's Conception of the World*. St Albans: Paladin.

Renold, Emma. 2005. *Girls, Boys, and Junior Sexualities: Exploring children's gender and sexual relations in the primary school*. London: Routledge.

Richardson, Diana. 1998. 'Sexuality and Citizenship,' *Sociology*, 32(1): 83–100.

Robinson, Kerry H. 2008. 'In the name of "childhood innocence". A discursive exploration of the moral panic associated with childhood and sexuality.' *Cultural Studies Review*, 14(2): 113–129.

Robinson, Kerry H. 2012. 'Childhood is a "queer time and space": Alternative imaginings of normative markers of gendered lives.' In Robinson, K. H. and Davies, C. (eds). *Queer and Subjugated Knowledges: Generating subversive imaginaries*, pp. 110–139. Bentham Science.

Robinson, Kerry H. 2013. *Innocence, Knowledge and the Construction of Childhood: The contradictory nature of sexuality and censorship in children's contemporary lives*. London: Routledge.

Robinson, K.H. and Davies, C. 2008a. 'She's kickin' ass, that's what she's doing': deconstructing childhood "innocence" in media representations.' *Australian Feminist Studies*, 23(57): 343–358.

Robinson, Kerry H. and Davies, Cristyn. 2008b. 'Docile bodies and heteronormative moral subjects: Constructing the child and sexual knowledge in schools.' *Sexuality and Culture*, 12(4): 221–239.

Robinson, Kerry H. and Davies, Cristyn. 2010. 'Tomboys and Sissy girls: Exploring girls' power, agency and female relationships in childhood through the memories of women.' *Australian Journal of Early Childhood*, 35(1): 24–31 (Special edition: Childhood and Sexuality).

Robinson, Kerry H., Bansel, Peter, Denson, Nida, Ovenden, Georgia and Davies, Cristyn. 2014. *Growing Up Queer: Issues facing young Australians who are gender variant and sexuality diverse*. Young and Well Cooperative Research Centre, Melbourne.

Schwartz, Pepper and Cappello, Dominic. 2001. *Ten Talks Parents Must Have with their Children about Sex and Character*. Rydalmere: Hodder Headline Australia.

UNESCO. 2009. *International Guidance on Sexuality Education: An evidence-informed approach for schools, teachers and health educators, vol. 1 – Rationale for sexuality education*. Paris: UNESCO.

Walker, Joy and Milton, Jan. 2006. 'Teachers' and Parents' roles in the sexuality education of primary school children: a comparison of experiences from Leeds, UK, and Sydney, Australia.' *Sex Education*, 6(4): 415–428.

Weeks, Jeffrey. 1986. *Sexuality*. London: Routledge.

Weeks, Jeffrey. 1998. 'The sexual citizen.' *Theory, Culture and Society*, 15(3–4): 35–52.

chapter 55

One is not born a bride

How weddings regulate heterosexuality

Chrys Ingraham

All aspects of our social world – natural or otherwise – are given meaning. Culture installs meaning in our lives from the very first moment we enter the social world. Our sexual orientation or sexual identity – or even the notion that there is such a thing – is defined by the symbolic order of that world through the use of verbal as well as non-verbal language and images. Heterosexuality as a *social* category is much more than the fact of one's sexual or affectional attractions. What we think of when we talk about heterosexuality or refer to ourselves as heterosexual is a product of a society's meaning-making processes. In reality, heterosexuality operates as a highly organized social institution that varies across nations, social groups, culture, history, region, religion, ethnicity, nationality, race, lifespan, social class, and ability. In America and elsewhere, the wedding ritual represents a major site for the installation and mainte-nance of the institution of heterosexuality.

The title of this chapter pays homage to French feminist Monique Wittig whose classic and provocative essay "One is Not Born a Woman" examines what she calls the political regime of heterosexuality and its requisite categories of man and woman. She argues that the category of woman and all of the meaning attached to that cate-gory would not exist were it not necessary for the political regime of (patriarchal) heterosexuality. For the purpose of this chapter, the same holds true of the taken-for-granted category of bride. While it may seem obvious to most that one is not born a bride, in reality many women see themselves as following a naturalized path toward heterosexual womanhood.

Chrys Ingraham

But how did this contrived and constructed social practice become naturalized? The task of examining this taken-for-granted social arrangement requires a conceptual framework capable of revealing how heterosexuality has become institutionalized, naturalized, and normalized. Any attempt to examine the institution of heterosexuality requires a theory capable of understanding how this institution with all its social practices such as dating, proms, and Valentine's Day, is often viewed by many of us as natural.

The heterosexual imaginary

French psychoanalyst Jacques Lacan's concept of the "imaginary" is especially useful for this purpose. According to Lacan, the imaginary is the unmediated contact an infant has to its own image and its connection with its mother. Instead of facing a complicated, conflictual, and contradictory world, the infant experiences the illusion of tranquility, plenitude, and fullness. In other words, infants experience a sense of oneness with their primary caretaker. Louis Althusser, the French philosopher, borrowed Lacan's notion of the imaginary for his neo-marxist theory of ideology, defining ideology as "the imaginary relationship of individuals to their real conditions of existence." The "imaginary" here does not mean "false" or "pretend" but, rather, an imagined or illusory relationship between an individual and their social world. Applied to a social theory of heterosexuality the *heterosexual imaginary* is that way of thinking that relies on romantic and sacred notions of heterosexuality in order to create and maintain the illusion of well-being and oneness. This romantic view prevents us from seeing how institutionalized heterosexuality actually works to organize gender while preserving racial, class, and sexual hierarchies. The effect of this illusory depiction of reality is that heterosexuality is taken for granted and unquestioned, while gender is understood as something people are socialized into or learn. The heterosexual imaginary naturalizes male to female social relations, rituals, and organized practices and conceals the operation of heterosexuality in structuring gender across race, class, and sexuality. This way of seeing closes off any critical analysis of heterosexuality as an organizing institution and for the ends it serves (Ingraham 1994, 1999). By leaving heterosexuality unexamined as an institution we do not explore how it is learned, how it may control us and contribute to social inequalities. Through the use of the heterosexual imaginary, we hold up the institution of heterosexuality as fixed in time as though it has always operated the same as it does today. This imaginary presents a view of heterosexuality as "just the way it is" while creating obligatory social practices that reinforce the illusion that, as long as one complies with this naturalized structure, all will be right in the world. This illusion is commonly known as romance. Romancing heterosexuality is creating an illusory heterosexuality for which wedding culture plays a central role.

The lived reality of institutionalized heterosexuality is, however, not typically tranquil or safe. The consequences the heterosexual imaginary produces include, for example, marital rape, domestic violence, pay inequities, racism, gay-bashing, femicide, and sexual harassment. Institutionalized heterosexuality and its organizing ideology – the heterosexual imaginary – establishes those behaviors we ascribe to

men and women – gender – while keeping in place or producing a history of contradictory and unequal social relations. The production of a division of labor that results
in unpaid domestic work, inequalities of pay and opportunity, or the privileging of
married couples in the dissemination of insurance benefits, are examples of this.

Above all, the heterosexual imaginary naturalizes the regulation of sexuality
through the institution of marriage, ritual practices such as weddings, and state
domestic relations laws. These laws, among others, set the terms for taxation, healthcare, and housing benefits on the basis of marital status. Rarely challenged – except by
nineteenth-century marriage reformers and early second-wave feminists – laws and
public- and private-sector policies use marriage as the primary requirement for social
and economic benefits and access rather than distributing resources on some other
basis such as citizenship or ability to breathe, for example. Heterosexuality is much
more than a biological given or whether or not someone is attracted to someone of
another sex. Rules on everything from who pays for the date or wedding rehearsal dinner to who leads while dancing, drives the car, cooks dinner or initiates sex, all serve to
regulate heterosexual practice. What circulates as a given in Western societies is, in
fact, a highly structured arrangement. As is the case with most institutions, people
who participate in these practices must be socialized to do so. In other words, women
were not born with a wedding gown gene or a neo-natal craving for a diamond engagement ring! They were taught to want these things. Women didn't enter the world with
a desire to practice something called dating or a desire to play with a "My Size Bride
Barbie," they were rewarded for desiring these things. Likewise, men did not exit the
womb knowing they would one day buy a date a bunch of flowers or spend two months'
income to buy an engagement ring. These are all products that have been sold to consumers interested in taking part in a culturally established ritual that works to organize
and institutionalize heterosexuality and reward those who participate.

Heteronormativity

A related concept useful for the study of the heterosexual imaginary and of institutionalized heterosexuality is heteronormativity. This is the view that institutionalized
heterosexuality constitutes the standard for legitimate and expected social and sexual relations. Heteronormativity represents one of the main premises underlying the
heterosexual imaginary, again ensuring that the organization of heterosexuality in
everything from gender to weddings to marital status is held up both as a model and
as "normal." Consider, for instance, the ways many surveys or intake questionnaires
ask respondents to check off their marital status as either married, divorced, separated, widowed, single, or, in some cases, never married. Not only are these categories presented as significant indices of social identity, they are offered as the only
options, implying that the organization of identity in relation to marriage is universal
and not in need of explanation. Or try to imagine entering a committed relationship
without benefit of legalized marriage. We find it difficult to think that we can share
commitment with someone without a state-sponsored license. People will frequently
comment that someone is afraid to "make a commitment" if they choose not to
get married even when they have been in a relationship with someone for years!

Chrys Ingraham

Our ability to imagine possibilities or to understand what counts as commitment is itself impaired by heteronormative assumptions. We even find ourselves challenged to consider how to marry without an elaborate white wedding. Gays and lesbians have maintained long-term committed relationships yet find themselves desiring state sanctioning of their union in order to feel legitimate. Heteronormativity works in all of these instances to naturalize the institution of heterosexuality while rendering real people's relationships and commitments irrelevant and illegitimate.

For those who view questions concerning marital status as benign, one need only consider the social and economic consequences for those who do not participate in these arrangements or the cross-cultural variations that are at odds with some of the Anglocentric or Eurocentric assumptions regarding marriage. All people are required to situate themselves in relation to marriage or heterosexuality, including those who *regardless of sexual (or asexual) affiliation* do not consider themselves "single," heterosexual, or who do not participate in normative heterosexuality and its structures.

One is not born a bride, and yet to imagine oneself outside of this category is to live a life outside of the boundaries of normality and social convention. To live outside this contrived and constructed social practice is to live on the margins of society, excluded from the social, legal, and economic rewards and benefits participation brings. To resist membership in the heteronormative social order – as bride or as groom – is to live with the penalties and challenges to all those who resist. It means living a life where you have to defend your sexual loyalties on a daily basis – are you straight or are you gay?

Weddings

To demonstrate the degree to which the heteronormative wedding ritual regulates sexuality we must begin with an investigation into the ways various practices, arrangements, relations, and rituals standardize and conceal the operation of institutionalized heterosexuality. It means to ask how practices such as weddings become naturalized and prevent us from seeing what is at stake, what is kept in place, and what consequences are produced. To employ this approach is to seek out those instances when the illusion of tranquility is created and at what cost. Weddings, like many other rituals of heterosexual celebration such as anniversaries, showers, and Valentine's Day, become synonymous with heterosexuality and provide illusions of reality that conceal the operation of heterosexuality both historically and materially. When used in professional settings, for example, weddings work as a form of ideological control to signal membership in relations of ruling as well as to signify that the couple is normal, moral, productive, family-centered, upstanding citizens and, most importantly, appropriately gendered and sexual.

To study weddings means to interrupt the ways the heterosexual imaginary naturalizes heterosexuality and prevents us from seeing how its organization depends on the production of the belief or ideology that heterosexuality is normative and the same for everyone – that the fairytale romance is universal. It is this assumption that allows for the development and growth in America of a $35 billion-per-year wedding industry. This multibillion dollar industry includes the sale of a diverse range of products, many of which are produced outside of the USA – wedding gowns, diamonds, honeymoon travel and apparel, and household equipment. Ironically, the production of these goods frequently occurs under dismal labor conditions where manufacturers rely on a non-traditional female workforce, indirectly altering cultural norms in relation to heterosexuality and family. In Mexico, Guatemala, and China, for example, the effect has been to shift the job opportunities away from men with the consequence of significant levels of domestic violence and femicide. Sexual regulation in these locations is directly related to the gendered division of labor working to produce goods that support the American heterosexual imaginary. Veiled in the guise of romance and the sacred, these social relations conceal from view the troublesome conditions underlying the production of the white wedding.

When you think of weddings as "only natural," think again! This process of naturalization begins with children. By targeting girls and young women, toy manufacturers have seized on the wedding market and the opportunity to develop future consumers by producing a whole variety of wedding toys, featuring the "classic" white wedding, and sold during Saturday morning children's television shows. Toy companies, generally part of large multinational conglomerates that also own related commodities such as travel or cosmetics, work to secure future markets for all their products through the selling of wedding toys. Mattel, the world's largest toymaker and a major multinational corporation, has offices and facilities in thirty-six countries and sells products in 150 nations. Their major toy brand, accounting for 40 percent of their sales, is the Barbie doll – all 120 different versions of her. Mattel's primary manufacturing facilities are located in China, Indonesia, Italy, Malaysia, and Mexico, employing mostly women of color and at substandard wages. Annually, Mattel makes about 100 million Barbie dolls and earns revenues of $1.9 billion for the California-based company. The average young Chinese female worker whose job it is to assemble Barbie dolls lives in a dormitory, sometimes works with dangerous chemicals, works long hours and earns $1.81 a day. Since 2013, Mattel's profits on Barbie dolls have been declining in relation to their other lines, such as their vampire-based *Monster High* dolls (Anderson, 2013).

The staging of weddings in television shows, weekly reporting on weddings in the press, magazine reports on celebrity weddings, advertising, and popular adult and children's movies with wedding themes or weddings inserted, all work together to teach us how to think about weddings, marriage, heterosexuality, race, gender, and labor. Through the application of the heterosexual imaginary, the media cloak most representations of weddings in signifiers of romance, purity, morality, promise, affluence or accumulation, and whiteness. Many newlyweds today experience their weddings as the stars of a fairy-tale movie in which they are scripted, videotaped, and photographed by paparazzi wedding-goers, not as an event that regulates their sexual lives and identities along with those of the laborers who make their wedding possible.

The contemporary white wedding under multinational capitalism is, in effect, a mass-marketed, homogeneous, assembly-line production with little resemblance to the utopian vision many participants hold. The engine driving the wedding market has mostly to do with the romancing of heterosexuality in the interests of capitalism. The social relations at stake – love, community, commitment, and family – come to be viewed as secondary to the production of the wedding spectacle.

Chrys Ingraham

The heterosexual imaginary circulating throughout the wedding industry masks the ways it secures racial, class, and sexual hierarchies. Women are taught from early childhood to plan for the "happiest day of their lives." (Everything after that day pales by comparison!) Men are taught, by the absence of these socializing mechanisms, that their work is "other" than that. If they are interested in the wedding it is for reasons other than what women have learned. The possibilities children learn to imagine are only as broad as their culture allows. They are socialized to understand the importance of appropriate coupling, what counts as beauty, as appropriate sexuality, what counts as women's work and men's work, and how to become "good" consumers by participating in those heterosexual practices and rituals that stimulate their interests and emotions and reap the most rewards.

One is not born a bride. One learns to comply with the social and cultural messages that flow to and through the wedding ritual. It is the rite of passage for appropriate heterosexual identity and membership. It is everything but natural.

References

Anderson, Mae. 2013. "Barbie sales slide as Mattel profit falls." *USA Today*. Online at www.usatoday.com/story/money/business/2013/07/17/mattel-2q-profit-falls-barbie-sales-slide-again/2523879/. Last accessed April 16, 2016.
Ingraham, Chrys. 1994. "The heterosexual imaginary", *Sociological Theory* 12(2): 203–19.
—. 1999. *White Weddings: Romancing Heterosexuality in Popular Culture*. New York: Routledge.

chapter 56

The marriage contract

Mary Bernstein

Many girls and young women dream of a beautiful white wedding, where they can be queen for the day. For young men, the idea of marriage often marks the transition into adulthood, a time when they become responsible adults rather than immature play-boys. For men, marriage also confirms their heterosexuality, as a middle-aged single man can easily be suspected of being gay. Marriage is seen as a mark of maturity and earns social status for the married couple. However, if we look beyond the lavish wed-dings, we can see that marriage is more than just a white dress, bridesmaids' gowns and lots of gifts. Marriage is a legal contract. Historically, marriage laws have served to regulate sexual behavior and enforce gender roles and notions of racial and national purity. Socially, families that do not meet the romantic notion of the husband, wife, and children, are considered deviant. Politically, marriage is promoted as the solution to reducing crime, eradicating poverty, and expanding health insurance. Advocates of same-sex marriage point out that marriage provides benefits to the couple that can be obtained in no other way.

In this chapter I examine the history of marriage as a legal contract, and its rela-tionship to procreation and gender roles. Then I look at the ways in which marriage is promoted by current public policy as a way to solve a variety of social problems. Finally, I briefly consider the debate over same-sex marriage to understand why so many lesbian and gay couples wanted the right to marry.

Marriage for procreation

The intended purpose of marriage has historically been for procreation, and so the law regulates the sexual lives of married couples and unmarried individuals with that goal in mind. At its most basic level, until 2004, when the state of Massachusetts began to issue marriage licenses to same-sex couples originating from that state, marriages in the USA could only take place between one man and one woman. In fact the law even dictated what sexual acts couples were allowed to perform. The so-called "sodomy" statutes forbade what was once called "the abominable and detestable crime against nature." In practice, this included any oral–genital contact or anal contact between partners, whether married or not (Bernstein 2004). The last of these laws was overturned in 2003 in the US Supreme Court case *Lawrence v. Texas*. Fornication by unmarried adults was also once prohibited in most states in the country. Infertility, or a failure to consummate a marriage, could be used as grounds for divorce. Thus the only lawful sex, historically, was vaginal intercourse by married couples for the purpose of procreation. Those couples unable to procreate could divorce. Marriage laws also prohibit bigamy and polygamy, as well as extra-marital relations, all of which would get in the way of producing legitimate children. Even when these sex laws were not enforced, their existence served as the state's symbolic effort to promote sex for procreation within marriage and to decry any other expressions of sexuality that did not fit into the form of a monogamous married relationship where sex was solely for the purposes of procreation. Thus the law enforces what can be termed "heteronormativity" – that is, sexually monogamous marital relationships geared toward procreation (Bernstein and Reimann 2001).

Historically, procreation as a goal of marriage was an economic necessity. By having children, families could increase their household workforce, which was particularly important, for example, in farming families where the children worked in the fields beside their parents. Peasants would often delay marriage until a pregnancy occurred, in order to verify the woman's fertility. Upper-class men who needed legitimate heirs would divorce their wives for failing to produce children. Of course, at the time, no one considered that it might be the man, rather than the woman, who was infertile. Marriage for love, rather than strictly for procreation, is a relatively new phenomenon, one that has emerged slowly over the past 200 years (Coontz 2005).

Since one of the primary goals of marriage was to produce children (Weitzman and Dixon 1999), government feared that allowing interracial couples to marry would produce children who were "mixed-race," thus "diluting" the white race (*Loving v. Virginia*). Laws against interracial marriage, known as anti-miscegenation laws, served to maintain "racial purity." In the 1960s, Mildred and Richard Loving, an interracial couple, decided to challenge the anti-miscegenation laws. Married in the District of Columbia, the Lovings' marriage was lawfully recognized until they moved to Virginia, where their marriage was considered illegal. The Lovings turned to the Court to pursue their right to marry. The case, *Loving v. Virginia*, eventually made its way to the US Supreme Court. In 1967, the Court ruled in favor of the Lovings and overturned all the remaining laws against miscegenation. In its verdict, the US Supreme Court stated: "The fact that Virginia prohibits only interracial marriages involving white persons demonstrates that the racial classifications must stand on their own justification, as measures designed to maintain White Supremacy" (https://www.law.cornell.edu/supremecourt/text/388/1). Marriage laws also served to maintain national purity in a curious intersection of gender inequality and xenophobia. For example, until the mid-twentieth century, if a woman who was a US citizen married a man who was not a citizen, then she would lose her US citizenship.

In cases where an American man married a foreign woman, however, the man would not lose his citizenship, attesting to women's precarious status as citizens.

Marriage and gender roles

Historically, the marital contract was built on and served to enforce a sexual division of labor. When a man and woman married, any property that she owned became his upon marriage and she was no longer allowed to enter into her own contracts. The wife took the husband's name and, of course, she was not allowed to vote. After all, the man was considered the leader of the family and it was assumed that his political interests reflected the interests of his family, including his wife and children. It was not until the late 1800s, with the passage of the Married Women's Property Act, that married women were allowed to own their own property. It was not until 1920 that women in the US won the right to vote. Despite these changes, the law continued to enforce gendered roles within marriage. For example, as late as the 1960s, husbands, not wives, were allowed to sue for a loss of personal services such as housekeeping and sexual relations. Rape within marriage was not considered a crime by most states until the 1980s because it was considered the wife's duty to have sex with and produce legitimate children and heirs for her husband (Coontz 2005).

Over the past 120 years or so, many of these gendered and racialized aspects of the marital contract have entered the dustbin of history, so that the US marital contract now treats husbands and wives mostly the same. What this means is that the law treats marriage as a partnership and (although this varies by state) upon the dissolution of the marriage, divides property equally. Under conditions of continued gendered inequality, however, this means that in practice divorced women fare much worse financially than divorced men, because their earnings are on average substantially lower than men's earnings.

Although marriage has become increasingly based on love over the past 200 years, rather than being about "acquiring in-laws, jockeying for political and economic advantage" (Coontz 2005), it is still a legal contract. So, in the USA, what laws are covered by the marital contract? More than one thousand federal laws, and hundreds of laws in each state, are covered by the marital contract. These laws rest on assumptions about the emotional bonds between spouses, take for granted that marriage is the best environment for raising children, and presume certain economic relations between partners (Chambers 2001), protecting both the children and the parents.

Because the law assumes close emotional ties between spouses, in the event that one spouse becomes physically incapacitated, the law gives the other spouse the right to make any medical and financial decisions for the partner who is ill (including whether or not to donate the partner's body parts upon their death). If a third party injures a married person, the partner can sue for a loss of "consortium" or companionship. Should a married person die intestate (without a will), the law makes the partner the rightful beneficiary of the inheritance. Upon divorce, the law also regulates child custody, visitation, and child support (Chambers 2001).

The law also makes certain assumptions about the financial relationship between married partners, treating the couple as a single economic unit which helps to promote a gendered division of labor. If only one spouse works, then that spouse pays less tax than she/he would if she/he filed as a single person. However, if the partner also works outside the home, then the couple pays *more* tax than they would pay if they both filed as single people. As a result, some couples choose not to marry because they would rather not pay this extra tax, what some have termed a "marriage penalty." In families where the husband earns substantially more than the wife, the couple may decide that it is economically unwise for the wife to work outside of the home, because her earnings would not offset the extra tax the couple would have to pay (Chambers 2001). Technically, this problem would also arise if the wife earned substantially more than the husband, but in the vast majority of cases the wife's earnings are significantly lower than her husband's. If the couple has children, then it is even more likely that the wife's earnings would not pay for childcare, thus making it economically wiser for the wife to stay home and take care of the children. Thus, under the realities of economic inequality based on sex, tax laws promote a gendered division of labor in the home. Although the law no longer enforces a gendered division of labor in the home, married women continue to spend significantly more time on housework and childcare than their husbands, even when both are employed full time.

Marriage as the solution to social problems

The term "family" carries great emotional and cultural force. Although lawyers, sociologists, and psychologists all mean different things by the term "family," the privatized-nuclear family holds a sacred place in the American psyche and is embedded in most major social and legal institutions. As an ideal type, *The Family* consists of a legally married (biologically male) husband and a (biologically female) wife, approximately two children, and the obligatory dog or cat. Although a wife may work, her primary responsibility remains taking care of the home, husband, and children; while the husband's main task is breadwinning, though he may, on occasion, deign to "help out" around the house. Although clearly not representative of the majority of American families (Bernstein and Reimann 2001), this view of *The Family* is hegemonic, and has been called an "ideological code" (Smith 1999: 159) or a "privileged construct" (Weston 1991: 6). Heteronormative assumptions about appropriate gender roles underpin the hegemonic view of family and are appropriated by policymakers as a way to detract attention from the structural causes of social problems.

Historically, "the traditional family" – or the "modern family" as Stacey (1996) terms it – is a recent and, in light of demographic trends, a rather short-lived phenomenon (Coontz 1992, 2005). Industrialization and urbanization prompted massive changes in family life throughout the nineteenth and twentieth centuries worldwide. The material need for extended families diminished, children lost in economic but gained in emotional value, nuclear families became smaller, and, as the lifespan lengthened and economic dependencies decreased, marriages for life were no longer the reality for an increasing number of couples. As a result, families come in all shapes, sizes, and colors, ranging from "traditional" families to couples without children, single-parent families, step families, and families of choice whose members are not always related by marriage, blood, or law (Stacey 1996; Weston 1991).

Despite the heterogeneity of contemporary family forms, families that deviate from the ideal type of the "modern family" are judged inadequate. For example, immigrant and poor families, and families of color, have drawn criticism from conservatives and liberals alike for their diverse, nonconforming family organizations. Their difference from the ideal of the white, bourgeois, native-born family was and continues to be interpreted as the primary source of each group's social problems, and of society's ills in general (Coontz 1992; Rubin 1994).

Daniel Patrick Moynihan's report (1965), for example, sparked a decades-long debate about the relationship between African-American family structures – extended kinship networks and lower rates of marriage – and the plight of blacks in America. Many commentators attribute poverty within the black community to African-American family structures. In response, other researchers see the low incidence of two-parent married African-American couples as a result of racism and poor economic opportunities (Wilson 1987). In either view, African-American families are compared to white, middle-class families, and seen as deviant. The main difference between conservative and liberal critics lies in whether they blame such families for their "deviation" or attribute these "deviations" to structural factors.

The state not only continues to promote the heterosexual nuclear family as the norm but is pouring billions of dollars into promoting marriage as a way to overcome a variety of social ills. In short, marriage is not only ideologically important, it has become an important goal of public policy and is used as a way to detract attention from structural issues such as those related to poverty or a lack of health insurance.

A failure to marry, rather than the lack of job opportunities, affordable and safe childcare, and educational opportunities, is often said to be the cause of poverty. Promoting marriage, rather than promoting economic self-sufficiency, has become an important part of US welfare policy. In 1996, then-President Clinton signed a bill to abolish Aid to Families with Dependent Children (AFDC), a public assistance program that provided a minimum income for the poor. Laden with assumptions that poor women were sexually promiscuous or irresponsible, as well as a failure to recognize the gendered nature of the labor market, the Personal Responsibility and Work Opportunity Reconciliation Act of 1996, like much of US welfare policy, attempted to encourage marriage as a way to move poor women and their children off the welfare rolls. More recently the Bush administration proposed spending $1.5 billion dollars in programs designed to promote marriage rather than to reduce poverty in other ways. These programs include counseling and courses in conflict resolution. Thus, for many of the poor, marriage is defined and promoted as a primary way to achieve economic independence from the state, rather than looking at the structural causes of poverty. The *New York Times*, for example, stated: "the fiscal lift that occurs when middle-class couples marry and combine resources does not come about in neighborhoods where jobs have long since disappeared and men in particular tend to be unskilled and poorly educated" (*New York Times* 2004). Sociologist Barbara Risman points out the problem with marriage promotion programs. She says: "When people don't get married, including the poorest of people whom these projects are aimed at, it's not because they don't believe in the institution of marriage. They don't have the financial resources to make it work" (quoted in Barrett 2004).

Mary Bernstein

Similarly, marriage is often posed as the solution to a lack of available healthcare. Unlike many Western countries, the United States does not provide universal healthcare for its citizens. In fact, in the United States, millions of working Americans and their children do not have health insurance. Rather than promote universal health insurance, the Bush administration worked to promote marriage as a way to provide health insurance to poor women and children. The idea is that, by marrying, poor women will be able to gain health insurance through their husbands. This policy fails to take into account the fact that millions of working men do not have health insurance to pass on to their wives and children. Poor people in general do not have healthcare, and marriage is no guarantee that they will get health insurance. Criticizing individuals for not being married distracts attention from discussing the lack of affordable health insurance.

Same-sex marriage and the future of marriage

Historically, marriage was inextricably tied to procreation and the enforcement of gender roles, as well as to maintaining notions of race and national purity. While anti-miscegenation laws are no longer in place, and the law no longer dictates that procreation be strictly linked to marriage, public policy condemns those who do not conform. While the law no longer enforces a strict gender hierarchy within marriage, common practice and continued economic inequality between men and women often have the same effect of promoting a gendered division of labor that leaves women in a disadvantaged position. Homemakers are dependent on husbands, and women who work outside the home must work a "second shift" of housework and childcare in addition to their paid work responsibilities (Hochschild 2003).

Given this history of marriage as an institution that privileges certain kinds of relationships at the expense of others, marriage's ties to procreation and maintaining gender roles, lesbians and gay men have debated the wisdom of pursuing same-sex marriage as a goal (Bernstein and Reimann 2001). However, even those lesbians and gay men who feel that they themselves would not get married believe that lesbians and gay men should not be denied access to the right to marry. Same-sex marriage advocates point out that marriage provides social recognition for valued relationships. A wedding provides friends and family an opportunity to congratulate the couple and provide support for their relationship. From a legal standpoint, while any couple (same- or different-sex) can draw up wills, this is an expensive process, and it is impossible to privately contract access to the thousands of federal and hundreds of state laws that are involved in the marriage contract. Furthermore, the legal rights that come with marriage are comprehensive, and are especially important in protecting children. For example, the ability to marry assures that both parents in a same-sex couple have the right to make medical decisions when a child is sick or hurt and protects the rights of both parents and children in the event that parents separate or one parent dies. Others argue that the separation of procreation from heterosexual marriage as witnessed by the current "gayby" boom, and the fact that by definition there is no division of labor based on gender roles for same-sex couples, will transform the institution of marriage. Time will tell how much lesbians and gay men will transform the ever-changing institution of marriage in the United States, as same-sex couples have finally won the right to marry.

References

Barrett, Barbara. 2004. "Does Marriage Need Government's Help?" *Newsobserver.com*. Available online at www.ncsu.edu/news/dailyclips/0104/012004.htm (accessed 21 March 2006).

Bernstein, Mary. 2004. "'Abominable and Detestable': Understanding Homophobia and the Criminalization of Sodomy." In Colin Sumner (ed.), *Companion to Criminology*. Oxford: Blackwell.

Bernstein, Mary and Renate Reimann (eds). 2001. *Queer Families, Queer Politics: Challenging Culture and the State*. New York: Columbia University Press.

Chambers, David L. 2001. "'What If?' The Legal Consequences of Marriage and the Legal Needs of Lesbian and Gay Male Couples." In Mary Bernstein and Renate Reimann (eds), *Queer Families, Queer Politics: Challenging Culture and the State*. New York: Columbia University Press.

Coontz, Stephanie. 1992. *The Way We Never Were: American Families and the Nostalgia Trip*. New York: Basic Books.

—. 2005. *Marriage, a History: From Obedience to Intimacy, or How Love Conquered Marriage*. New York: Viking.

Hochschild, Arlie. 2003. *The Second Shift*. London: Penguin.

Moynihan, Daniel Patrick. 1965. *The Negro Family: The Case for National Action*. Washington, DC: Office of Policy Planning and Research, U.S. Department of Labor.

New York Times. 2004. "Heartless Marriage Plans." *New York Times* 17 January.

Rubin, Lillian. 1994. *Families on the Fault Line: America's Working Class Speaks about the Family, the Economy, Race, and Ethnicity*. New York: HarperCollins.

Smith, Dorothy E. 1999. *Writing the Social: Critique, Theory, and Investigations*. Toronto: University of Toronto Press.

Stacey, Judith. 1996. *In the Name of the Family: Rethinking Family Values in the Postmodern Age*. Boston, MA: Beacon Press.

Weitzman, Lenore J. and Ruth B. Dixon. 1999. "The Transformation of Legal Marriage Through No-Fault Divorce." In Arlene S. Skolnick and Jerome H. Skolnick (eds), *Family in Transition*. New York: Longman.

Weston, Kath. 1991. *Families We Choose: Lesbians, Gays, Kinship*. New York: Columbia University Press.

Wilson, William Julius. 1987. *The Truly Disadvantaged: The Inner City, the Underclass and Public Policy*. Chicago, IL: University of Chicago Press.

chapter 57

Lesbian and gay parents

Situated subjects

Yvette Taylor

Introduction

What is the current status of lesbian and gay parented families? Have such families moved from conditions of invisibility and hostility towards visibility and respect? The answer varies across socio-cultural contexts. There has been a growth of visibility and rights of lesbian and gay families in the United States and Europe, even as there continues to be a strong assertion of traditional "family values." In my view, same-sex marriage has been over-emphasised in the current citizenship debates, as if such rights would end the discrimination that lesbian and gay parented families experience. But also, too much research and politics around lesbian and gay families assumes a middle-class family, which is now able to feel socially included. This assumption ignores the real class differences between families, both in terms of material resources and in terms of subjective evaluations about what are "good" or "proper" families.

If times are changing in light of socio-legal reform, how do inequalities of class endure in lesbian and gay parental experiences? How, for example, does social class influence the way parents negotiate the schooling of their children as well as children's services provided by the community? Are lesbian and gay parents now the "same" as their heterosexual counterparts, or are their experiences marked by profound differences? What difference does class make in understanding lesbian and gay parents as socially situated subjects, who are sexualised, gendered, and racialised in specific ways?

There is now a wide range of research on lesbian and gay parenting. Perhaps the enduring political necessity to present such families in a positive light has resulted in a sidelining of "harsher" stories, where the classed experiences of parenting have been particularly sidelined and where most studies of lesbian motherhood predominantly sample white, middle-class, educated professional women. So although a now growing research field, much current work on lesbian and gay parenting still overlooks the significance of social class. Even where there has been attention to gendered dynamics and constraints, class, as a crucial component of parental choice and experience, has been neglected. Based on US research, Amy Agigian (2004) is somewhat unique in exploring the intersection between sexuality, race and class in practices of lesbian insemination. Yet, there are other routes to lesbian parenting; and class shapes parenting in myriad ordinary ways such as interactions with social and educational providers and with other parents. I intend to use the concept of social class to refer to the disproportionate allocation of material resources as well as involving values or estimations of worth, for example, judgements about "good" and "bad" parenting. Classed ideas and resources frame ways of doing parenting, effecting too the construction of "respectable," legitimate routes into parenting.

Class and sexuality: intersections

In my book, *Lesbian and Gay Parenting: Securing Social and Educational Capital*, I explore intersections between class and sexuality in lesbians' and gay men's experiences of parenting. I examine the initial routes into parenting, the household division of labour, residential preferences, and schooling choice (Taylor 2009). Forty-six lesbian mothers and fourteen gay dads were interviewed across a range of localities in the UK. All of the respondents were white and ranged in age from 18 to 63. Their routes to parenting varied. Most participants (*n* = 36) had children through previous heterosexual relationships, some of these parents resorted to heterosex and now lived open lesbian or gay lives. Respondents who had pursued alternative routes to parenting, such as adoption or assisted insemination, were mostly from middle-class backgrounds. Interviewees were asked to self-identify in class terms, with about half of the interviewees identifying as "middle-class" or "lower middle-class" and half identifying as "working-class." While these were broadly congruent with "objective" positioning (including employment, income, and education), several respondents claimed a "working-class" background, often set against their current "middle-class" status. In exploring the ways that class and sexuality frame possibilities, I argue that middle-class lesbian and gay parents seek to protect their children by securing specific educational and social environments which are tied to classed resources.

Examining lesbian and gay routes into parenthood casts light upon the complications involved in achieving and affirming parental status. Lesbian and gay parents often navigate hostile contexts unknown to their straight counterparts. Discrimination and difficulty can be experienced in attempts to access reproductive technologies, creating inequalities which can also be compounded in everyday parental spaces, such as in school settings or in residential locations. Lesbian and gay parents may experience "family," "school," "community" and "home" in quite different ways from their heterosexual counterparts, where there may not be an easy fit into normalised expectations and ways of being. While lesbian and gay parents' "creative" routes into parenting have been evidenced as innovative (e.g. assisted insemination, surrogacy, adoption), this emphasis perhaps sidelines more normative pathways as well as their challenges (Weston 1991; Stacey 1996; Weeks et al. 2001; Agigian 2004). Challenges still persist in accessing alternative routes to parenthood, including compelled interactions with social and clinical providers, such as social workers and medics, who are responsible for considering planned parenthood. Such providers may themselves endorse quite fixed notions of what it means to be a family, making the "creating" of other types of families quite difficult. Moreover, such practitioners are working within legal and social contexts, which often sanction the heterosexual family as the ideal type. Within this already challenging context, some classed advantages and disadvantages can be highlighted, where sexual status may be seen to intersect with class positioning. The emotional, social and material resources which parents are able to draw upon to consolidate and affirm their sense of family is highly dependent on class status. For example, the *choice* to become parents was often shaped by class and framed by both implicit and explicit classed "costs." For parents choosing a more "do-it-yourself" approach to pregnancy in accessing sperm donors directly, there were often still costs to negotiate, such as the sperm donor's expenses. Other parents accessed designated but expensive clinics, often also feeling vulnerable about their sexual "outness" and the potential hostility this may invoke from health providers. The choice exercised was often not one of easy access or straightforward privilege. Instead it depended on a knowledge of where good clinics were, at times involving consultation within the broader LGBT community, varying too in the time and finances needed to access these. Both middle-class and working-class lesbian and gay parents face struggles in their routes into parenting, ever threatened by, for example, the (un)known status of donors, legal and clinical costs, custody battles and through the general social disapproval as not being deemed "fit for purpose." While interviewees reported disagreements with (ex-)partners, clinicians, social workers and medics, middle-class status could often partially buffer and protect against these.

Gay and lesbian parented families continue to face discrimination and class-specific challenges. One of the ways that middle-class parents resist stigma is to reframe themselves as more responsible and thoughtful than their heterosexual and working-class counterparts. This claim is based on their experiences as "family planners" who carefully choose when and how they wish to be parents (typically by means of expensive reproductive technologies). Working-class gay (and heterosexual) parents, according to this narrative, often become parents accidentally, or without the same level of thought and agency. Many working-class interviewees had children from previous heterosexual relationships and/or did not have the financial resources to seek out expensive reproductive technologies. Indeed, some working-class parents had not "chosen" to parent, but instead spoke of it as "just happening," continuing a likely (mis)reading of them as "thoughtless" and "irresponsible." In this regard, to the extent that researchers mirror middle-class parents' own accounts, for example, value reflexive choice, their studies will devalue or negate working-class experiences, even calling into question the quality and *legitimacy* of their parenting. In my book, I explore how a middle-class culture of parenting may lead some working-class parents to avoid gay parenting groups and other sites where the narrative of choice and responsibility has a strong framing presence.

To demonstrate the way class and sexuality intersect, a couple of examples are useful here. Having become pregnant through assisted insemination, Gemma, a middle-class lesbian, claims an "active choice" where family doesn't easily "just come packaged," positioning herself against that which "just happens" to "het people":

> You make an active choice . . . and the vast majority of het people, it just sort of happens to them. You know, very rarely do they actively make the choice. It's interesting talking to women who go for fertility treatment because they have to make the active choice.

Another middle-class lesbian, Jacqui, also contrasts the responsible choice of parenthood with those who come to parenthood unexpectedly and accidentally. In both Jacqui's and Gemma's accounts it is difficult to reconcile notions of "good planning" alongside other interviewees' experiences, where they would not be recognised via the "choice" invoked:

> I think that if you're going to that much trouble to have a child, it must be really wanted. I think that if it's a question of you going down the pub, you're getting pissed and you get laid and you come home pregnant, that child hasn't really been thought about or chosen, or decided on, or anything. I think that when gay people decide they want to have children they put a lot of thought and a lot of effort into it, so it's not just happening to them, they are making choices and I think that's a good thing.

Lesbian and gay parents' "creative" routes into parenting have been observed as innovative and deliberate, foregrounding a reflexive, choosing subject, politically mobilised against expected attacks on their incapacity to parent. All interviewees had to consider and negotiate their relationship to what are considered the "respectable" routes into parenthood. Crucially, respectability often meant an "attack" on the "poor" parenting of others, where "poor" meant the absence of choice and responsibility. The articulation of the middle-class norm of "choice" (family planning) reinforces very conservative notions of who is and is not capable of parenting – revealing the intersection of class and sexuality.

The relevance of class is clearly observed in parental choices and interventions in their children's education. Lesbian and gay parents often spoke of needing to access a good, tolerant and understanding school, which would be able to welcome and recognise their particular family circumstances. Such "tolerant" schools were frequently located in middle-class areas, while schools in working-class areas were often positioned, in a classed contrast, as "intolerant" and failing. Middle-class parents had more resources to negotiate educational routes, just as they could negotiate pathways to parenting, where working-class parents had little choice over educational provisioning. From accessing the "right" school, to having no choice but the "wrong" school, both class and sexuality are relevant in understanding parental expectations and entitlements. Both are intertwined in the construction of educational need, with middle-class parents often stating that being from a different family meant that their child needed special support and an accepting educational environment. The ability of the school to respond to and welcome Carol's lesbian-parented family is a vital part of their inclusion:

> We went together and made sure that they understood who we were and wanted to gauge what their response to us would be as a family and what they would, how they would handle any issues that arose . . . she [the head teacher] also added that she positively welcomed the idea of us as a family in the school and would be happy to tackle any issues and raise, you know, the issues of lesbian parents with the kids as a part of their development which was great.
>
> (Carol, 53, middle-class)

For Carol, the relationship between school and home is a very important and highly constructed one, with expectations and demands placed on the system and the individuals within it. Carol went with her partner into the school and felt welcomed, knowing that their domestic situation was also mirrored in other pupils' families. Interestingly, this particular composition is also seen as a matter of educational "development" more generally where lesbian and gay parented families are seen to embody diversity. Clearly, parents do not arrive at the school gate from "nowhere" – instead they rely on their knowledge and sense of entitlement, which is also connected to their economic status. There are times when such "entitlements" are not straightforwardly guaranteed, given that parents are still often operating in the context of institutional hostility. Yet working-class parents are faced with a double burden of hostility, unable to relocate and spatialise their claims, in accessing a different educational and residential setting (a "good mix" of balanced, tolerant, cosmopolitan space). It is not that such parents are completely "stuck" in place but rather they are unlikely to be recognised in discourses and research which emphasises an expansive sense of choice and of capacities to relocate as essential to "good parenting."

The desire for "good" parental space, such as schooling and neighbourhood, highlights the ways that negotiation of everyday space is often difficult for lesbian and gay parents across the class spectrum. That said, many middle-class parents articulated a desire for a "good mix" in their immediate localities and neighbourhoods. The sense of a "good mix" was articulated in middle-class parents' choices of places where there would be a "mix" of people in terms of race, class and sexuality as well as a "mix" of facilities and services, from good schools to good restaurants and entertainment venues. This "good mix" could suddenly be compromised by the existence of too many of the "wrong" people: working-class and minority ethnic groups were often seen to compromise the balance of a "good mix," threatening this middle-class idealisation of space. The ability to manage and occupy correctly "mixed" space is a classed process, where a "mixed" terrain, as opposed to a homogeneous middle-class setting – or an excessively working-class setting – was considered beneficial, even necessary, in facilitating a sense of belonging and integration.

Middle-class parents are situating their need for space and for "tolerance," desiring to be in a comfortable and accepting space. Yet in doing so, such sentiments and practices reproduce ideas of "intolerant others," situated elsewhere in other kinds of classed places. Thus it seems that both class and sexuality are relevant factors in considering locational journeys and (dis)locations (Weeks et al. 2001; Weston 1991). Carol, for example, tells of her previous, and preferred, "culturally diverse" (intersecting class and race) area, where her child learned and indeed embodied difference. Her child is seen as able to challenge homophobia and articulate "a strong sense of justice," in an "accepting" and "tolerant" environment:

> Hatton Vale . . . is predominantly Black and Asian and it's a fantastic place to live. It's very culturally diverse and you can get all sorts of exotic foods from your corner shop . . . and people are pretty well accepting and tolerant of each other. Where we lived was a little tree lined street and was pedestrianised and it was lovely, it was a good place for kids to play. When Abby was out playing in the lane she would hear some homophobic abuse . . . and Abby always tackled it she has a very strong sense of justice . . .
>
> (Carol, 53, middle-class)

The well-resourced, active, even politicised child is placed at the centre of her environment, commanding attention and visibility, against a "safe," "blended" background.

Paula's strategies of assessment before "coming out" are understandable, as she does not want to risk telling the wrong people. But what is interesting is the ways the "right people" are easily aligned, in her account, with those in a professional status. These dispositions are decoded at the "good" school gate, where Paula encounters other like-minded parents. The "mix" she references encompasses dispositions ("broad mindedness") read off professional status and other "clues":

> Sandbank was quite a kind of mixed area and you could choose whether you were gonna be friendly with people or not . . . I just try and figure out where their politics are at and how kind of, em, "right on," for want of a better description, people are and it's very hard to say what the clues are. I suppose you just you might start talking about certain . . . I mean, it is fair to say that people involved in social work you tend to be a little bit more broad minded . . . so you kind of think, *Guardian* reader type you know so you make, you make it based on those sorts of clues.
>
> (Paula, 48, middle-class)

Distinctions occur in imagining tolerant, accepting parents ("right on"), also known through and read off employment positions and credentials. Sarah describes living in a "very middle-class area, it's full of social workers and teachers." At the same time that she is aware of its limitations, she still emphasises the good "mix" of the area, with a range of prices and a range of different types of people. Her physical and subjective situation in space changes in relation to those around her, as she expresses being "obviously" on the lower income bracket, while still seeking a garden, an acceptable level of diversity and, crucially, a good school, as linked to residence. Again, this demonstrates the choice and control which middle-class parents can exercise over their immediate environments:

Because we wanted a bigger garden and we lived in a part of Birch Field, again, a very diverse area, but lots of cheaper housing, so it had a lot of lesbians living there, often because we are in a lower income bracket. Lots of large racial mix, sort of African, African Caribbean families there, so we were basically looking for a bigger garden and this is the next price range up and still in this side of the city and near a main road, so easy to get into town and what have you. We also had friends up here who knew the area. We knew that the schools were okay – that's about it really.

(Sarah, 42, middle-class)

The "knowingness" Sarah speaks of goes beyond friendship ties, also including a sense of the tone, composition and accessibility of the area as a whole (Weeks et al. 2001). Interestingly, all lesbians are situated in the same financial situation if not the very same place. Sarah is also aware that her previous area would be perceived as "professional" and "middle-class," although she experiences her own movement within and between areas as quite "confusing" and "contradictory," in terms of assigning class to such locations. Nonetheless, she still recognises the better choices on offer and the material consequences of such relocation:

I find it quite confusing or contradictory . . . I live in an area now where I am sur-rounded by others who are professionals and would be seen as middle-class and previously we lived in an area where, again, it was big classes of working-class area and I'm now moving back into an area which is very much on the edge of there, of that community . . . However, I also very much recognise that living on a lower income and often, therefore, you are living in areas on the outskirts of cities and everything that comes with that, that exclusion from society. It will funda-mentally affect your opportunities in life and your children's opportunities in life and, therefore, those factors then you may start trying to attach those to a model around class, etc. . . . this is very much a mixed area, but it gives us choices.

(Sarah)

Sarah seemingly more readily identifies with locale than class position, but her account then goes on to detail the intersections between class and parenting (im)-possibilities, and the opportunity to "mix" with others, noting varying geographies of choice within this. Importantly, Sarah speaks of having real, material choices – with real material consequences, contrasted with those on the social and geographical "outskirts." With such "good choices" available in the everyday negotiation of space, Sarah is more likely to be also recognised as a "good parent," actively taking parental responsibility and spatialising such claims, even if she also articulates a "confusing" "contradictoriness" in this inhabitation (Byrne 2006; Gillies 2006).

Overall this research seeks to intervene in re-situating the terms of the debate on lesbian and gay parenting, highlights the relevance of the intersectionality of class and sexuality as pertaining to parental (im)mobilities and geographies of choice, where perceptions, experiences and materialities of and in place vary. The "families of choice" literature provides a corrective to "straight and narrow" definitions of families and parenting. Yet it does so often without rigorous attention to the relevance of class, as facilitating and constraining "choice." Broader social and legal changes are also important here, where debates on sexual citizenship move between notions of assimilation/transformation, challenged by attention to the difference that class makes in accessing, claiming and gaining a respectable "ordinary" status. The desire to be the "same" in accessing a range of social spheres – as well as the (im)possibility of being so – may be understood as classed *and* sexualised. In this chapter I've highlighted the limitations and re-circulation of social resources, intersecting with economic capital, where (non-normative) middle-class lesbian and gay parenthood could indeed be troubled but also recuperated in enacting spatial entitlements, choices and movements.

Bibliography

Agigian, A. 2004. *Baby Steps: How Lesbian Alternative Insemination is Changing the World.* Middletown, CT: Wesleyan University Press.

Binnie, J. 2004. *The Globalization of Sexuality.* London: Sage.

Byrne, B. 2006. *White Lives: The Interplay of "Race," Class and Gender in Everyday Life.* London and New York: Routledge.

Gillies, V. 2006. "Working Class Mothers and School Life: Exploring the Role of Emotional Capital." *Gender and Education,* 18(3): 281–93.

Stacey, J. 1996. *In the Name of the Family: Rethinking Family Values in the Postmodern Age.* Boston, MA: Beacon Press.

Taylor, Y. 2007. *Working-Class Lesbian Life: Classed Outsiders.* Basingstoke: Palgrave Macmillan.

—. 2009. *Lesbian and Gay Parenting: Securing Social and Educational Capital.* Basingstoke: Palgrave Macmillan.

Weeks, J., Heaphy, B. and Donovan, C. 2001. *Same Sex Intimacies: Families of Choice and Other life Experiments.* London and New York: Routledge.

Weston, K. 1991. *Families We Choose: Lesbians, Gays, Kinship.* New York: Columbia University Press.

chapter 58

Purity and pollution

Sex as a moral discourse

Nancy L. Fischer

If you read the newspaper or Internet news headlines regularly, you're likely to come across ones that express fear that our culture is becoming morally corrupt. This moral corruption is often linked to sex. The media is a common target as the cause of corruption for exhibiting explicit sexual content. The media is not the only institution that is allegedly corrupting youth through exposure to sex. Educational institutions are also under fire. In many school districts parents have protested sex education that gives students birth control information as part of the curriculum. The opinion of these protesting parents is that exposing students to this knowledge will give students ideas that will lead them down the path to premature sexual relationships and unwanted pregnancies.

All this talk about sexual morality raises some questions: Where have our current ideas about sexual immorality come from? What is morality all about? Who labels others as immoral? Who gets labeled? And who is seen as vulnerable to the dangers of sexual corruption? In this chapter, I will show how what is considered right and wrong, sexually speaking, is not fixed and absolute, but has changed over time. Moreover, I will discuss how past ways of thinking about sexuality have influenced what we think about sexual morality today, and how moral rhetoric often reveals deeper cultural tendencies and meanings.

The arbitrariness of sexual immorality

One thing to keep in mind when thinking about how we talk about sexual immorality is that sexual acts have no meaning in and of themselves; it is only the surrounding culture which gives sexual practices or the people who engage in them particular meanings. Thus, in one sense, we could say that what gets defined as moral or immoral in a culture is arbitrary. Throughout the world, there is no universal agreement as to what constitutes sexually immoral behavior. For example, in the United States, a woman baring her breasts at the beach is considered morally questionable, but not so in France, while in other parts of the world where women are expected to dress modestly, showing one's calves might be considered morally questionable.

Moreover, what gets defined as moral or immoral is arbitrary in a historical sense. Two hundred years ago, any sex act other than missionary position was considered sodomy and sinful. At this time, it was specific sexual acts such as oral sex or masturbation that were considered morally corrupt. Today, sexual immorality is not necessarily evaluated according to specific acts, but instead is often judged according to who engages in that behavior. In American culture, usually only married couples are safe from having their sex acts associated with moral corruption. Even for devout Christians, it seems that any sex act between married people is considered potentially acceptable. For example, the 2003 Colorado Statement on Biblical Sexual Morality states that, "Sexual behavior is only moral within the institution of heterosexual, monogamous marriage." Notice that the emphasis in this statement is on who is practicing the sexual behavior, not on the type of sexual behavior itself. This reflects an important historical shift that took place in the 1800s when Western society became more concerned with conceptualizing deviance in terms of identities rather than acts (Foucault 1990 [1978]). Sexual behavior came to be seen as indicative of some deep truth about the individual's character rather than as a sinful act for which one could repent and be forgiven by one's community. This had enormous implications in that individuals who engaged in immoral acts were no longer considered as displaying a mere aberration in their behavior. They were considered fundamentally different types of people than those who are "normal." In the words of Michel Foucault, "The sodomite had been a temporary aberration; the homosexual was now a species" (Foucault 1990 [1978]: 43). Calling someone a "slut" or a "pervert" reflects this logic; it suggests that sexual immorality is part of the person's character rather than a behavior that arose out of a specific situation.

The implications of these cross-cultural and historical differences in what is considered morally corrupt means that we should be suspicious of any group's claims that a particular type of person or a sexual practice has always been regarded as immoral. Moreover, we should keep in mind that sexual practices considered as being within the confines of acceptable moral behavior today could be construed to be morally corrupt in the future.

What is morality about?

So what is morality all about? Why do people judge others as morally corrupt, particularly in cases between mutually consenting partners? Activist Michael Warner argues that "most people cannot quite rid themselves of the sense that controlling the sex of others ... is where morality begins"; thus, in Warner's viewpoint, sexual morality is about controlling someone else's sex life (Warner 1999: 1). From a sociological point of view, there is some truth to this statement, though morality is also more complex.

Nancy L. Fischer

Sociologists who have studied how individuals and communities defend their moral values have observed that on one level, morality can be about communicating to others that they are not fitting into the shared values of the group. People may use what we call informal social control – gossip, shunning, giving people nasty looks, calling them names – to communicate that they are not following the norms of their social milieu and that they better step in line and conform if they want others' acceptance and friendship. In this sense, sexual morality is indeed about trying to control others' sex lives.

But there is more to morality, even if we stay at this most basic level of thinking about it in terms of small group dynamics and interpersonal relations. Think about the last time you heard an acquaintance refer to someone as "nasty" or "dirty" or as a "slut" or "perv." The speaker is trying to say something about *themselves and their own sexual morality* as much as they are saying something about someone else. The implication of calling someone else immoral is the unsaid statement, "I would never do that!" Social psychologists refer to this type of statement as "downward social comparison" where an individual tries to raise their own self-image and feel better about themselves by putting down someone else. Expressions of morality on an interpersonal level often involve this social psychological dynamic. And in this sense, sexual morality is not just about trying to control someone else's sex life. It is about claiming a morally superior position for oneself through stigmatizing others. This dynamic is often visible when people or groups make claims about morality, whether at the interpersonal level or at the level of the larger society.

Frameworks for conceiving of sexual immorality: purity and pollution

Some who study morality say that how a culture labels moral and immoral behavior reveals deeper cultural patterns. American culture is often described as a dualistic culture in terms of how members are taught to make sense of physical and social reality. Dualistic cultures conceptualize the world through mutually exclusive, opposing values: right and wrong; black and white; male and female; good and bad; sacred and profane. People that are strongly socialized to think in a dualistic manner tend to make judgments in either/or terms: either someone is right or wrong, good or bad, black or white, male or female; there is no in-between. Such people are often uncomfortable with categories that could potentially fall in the middle of the polarities. Discomfort with the in-between means that people feel ill at ease with anything or anyone that falls in the liminal zone – the realm of the in-between – and they would rather categorize something or someone as belonging on one side of the polarity or the other. For example, in the United States, many people are not comfortable with "morally gray issues," with people who claim biracial identity (rather than claiming to be black or white), or with intersexuals (people whose bodies fall somewhere between male or female on a continuum).

Dualistic thinking affects how we think about sexual morality. Sociologist Eviatar Zerubavel (1991) suggests that one reason many Americans seem to find sex morally repugnant is because the bodily fluids associated with sex such as saliva and semen are sticky, a liminal category between solid and liquid. He also argues that many people feel uncomfortable with sex because it is associated with the breakdown of boundaries between two people – literally the opening and merging bodies, and perhaps even a merging of consciousness.

One of the most important dualistic metaphors that cultures use to organize social reality along moral lines is purity and pollution. In her classic work *Purity and Danger*, anthropologist Mary Douglas argues that cultures try to impose order and meaning on a chaotic, meaningless world through classifying some things as "dirty," "polluted," "dangerous" or "taboo" while other things are labeled as "clean," "pure" and "safe."

Things that get placed into the "polluted" side of the equation – such as dirt, mold or bodily fluids – are often metaphorically associated with disease, and thus are thought to contaminate whatever they come into contact with. Things designated as "polluted" are thought to be dirty and dangerous. For example, one is not supposed to eat food that has fallen on the floor because that is where dirt accumulates, which will pollute the food. The expression "One rotten apple spoils the whole barrel" is based on the idea that mold or rot is something that spreads, ruining what it touches. By contrast, that which is categorized as "pure" is thought to be clean. Those who study morality argue that the purity and pollution metaphor serves as an organizing system in a culture. This has implications for how moral arguments are made and what the underlying meanings associated with such moral arguments are. What this means is that when we call someone "nasty" or "dirty" we are invoking the pollution metaphor and all that goes with it. That is, we are implying that someone is potentially dangerous and that they are likely to contaminate others.

It is easy to see how the pollution metaphor operates in the ways that people talk about sexuality. For example, in the late 1800s, white upper-class parents often spoke about their own moral purity in sexual matters. They saw themselves as morally superior to members of the working class, African Americans and new immigrants to the United States. Their illusions of grandeur concerning their own moral purity led the white upper class to become consumed by fears that their own sons and daughters would be sexually corrupted by the "degenerate" lower classes and people from different ethnic backgrounds (Beisel 1989). Rumors and urban legends spread that black servants and other people of low social standing were constantly seeking to expose upper-class children in boarding schools to sexually prurient materials like photos of naked women, people engaged in sex acts, or "purple prose" (writing that contained explicit sexual content).

One need not look back to the 1800s to witness metaphors of pollution and contamination being applied to sex. Consider those who argue marriage equality laws allowing same-sex marriage will damage the institution of heterosexual marriage. This is a clear case where we can see the contamination logic operating. Logically speaking, allowing same-sex couples to marry should not induce heterosexual individuals to suddenly seek same-sex lovers; nor should it cause them to avoid marrying or suddenly break off an existing relationship. However, the pollution metaphor helps make sense of this type of moral corruption argument. It is not rational logic but metaphorical logic of contamination that is operating. Understanding this metaphorical logic of pollution can help us understand why many people do not have a "live and let live" or a "to each his own" attitude when it comes to judging others' sexual morality. In many people's minds, sex and anything associated with sexuality is placed on the pollution side of the pure/polluted dualism. Therefore, sexual immorality becomes rhetorically associated with danger, rot and disease. Because of this metaphorical logic, at some level, people believe that those whose behavior they find distasteful will contaminate and corrupt others.

It is important to keep in mind that these distinctions between what a culture considers pure/polluted or sexually moral/immoral are socially constructed. The metaphorical logic only reflects social reality to the degree that these metaphors become self-fulfilling prophesies. There are no sexual practices that are universally condemned across cultures or throughout history. Even incest – long thought to be the universal taboo – shows variation cross-culturally in terms of which relatives are and are not forbidden for sexual relations. Those practices that a culture defines as impure or morally corrupt tell us more about the society that created the categories than the individuals who are labeled as immoral.

Who labels others as morally corrupt?

The purity/pollution dualism is invoked by cultures in order to draw symbolic boundaries around groups. Symbolic boundaries describe how communities either include or exclude people based upon certain criteria. Moral boundaries are one type of symbolic boundary. People within a community will try to claim that someone doesn't belong because their behaviors supposedly don't match up to the community's moral standards. Moral boundaries mark a group's borders in much the same way countries arbitrarily decide that a river or a line drawn on a map marks a national boundary. Those inside the line are citizens who deserve certain rights and privileges; those on the other side of the line are not. With moral boundaries, people claim that members of their own group (like Christians or upper-class whites) are morally superior, while those outside the group are morally suspect.

Sexuality is a key axis along which groups draw moral boundaries and regulate behavior. For example, in high school, girls in the popular cliques may exclude other girls by calling them a slut, inferring that their sexual morality doesn't measure up. In her book *Slut!*, Leora Tanenbaum found that calling someone a slut had little to do with girls' actual sexual behavior like whether or not they were promiscuous, but the label was used as a weapon in social conflicts between girls. Who labels whom as morally corrupt reflects power relations in the relationships between dominant and subordinate groups. In the example above, Tanenbaum found it was often the more dominant, popular girls doing the name-calling. It is their more powerful position that allows this group of girls to portray others as promiscuous and make the label stick.

Likewise, at the societal level, groups that have more power are able to label others as sexually immoral in ways where the stereotype is likely to persist. The labeling of subordinate groups (such as the lower class, different ethnic and racial groups, GLBT individuals) as sexually immoral has been used to justify personal insults, systematic discrimination and even violence against members of a subordinate group. Unfortunately, there are numerous examples of this in U.S. history. In the example above where white upper-class Americans made claims about their own moral superiority, they did so by labeling black servants, immigrants and working-class people as sources of moral corruption.

Claims of immorality often reflect societal tensions between the upper and lower classes, the native-born and the foreign born, and between black and white (Beisel 1989). History is rife with examples of whites making claims that black people are sexually immoral in order to rationalize violence and racial oppression. During slavery, white slave owners justified raping black slave women by claiming that they were promiscuous and thus were "asking for it." Similarly, after the Civil War, the lynching of black men by white mobs was almost always justified by whites claiming that black men were "hypersexual" and that they were driven to rape white women. Whites were not just maintaining a moral boundary, but were using charges of sexual immorality to maintain a racial boundary as well.

If we look at who labels whom as morally corrupt today, power relations between dominant and subordinate groups are frequently apparent. Majority populations or members of culturally dominant groups have the power to suppress minorities through sexual scapegoating. African American men and women are still targets for being labeled as sexually immoral. For example, this can be seen in white middle-class criticisms of black hip hop artists for having sexually explicit lyrics. Likewise, the sexual double-standard where women who have sex with numerous partners are considered sluts while men are considered players shows the power relations between these two groups. In this sense, drawing lines between who is considered sexually pure and impure is not a simple matter of a culture going through some natural process of determining its own particular norms and sorting out who follows the rules and who breaks them, but is one more way that dominant groups demonstrate their power against minorities.

Who gets corrupted?

According to our culture's dualistic logic, in order to become polluted, one must first be pure; corruptibility only makes sense in relation to innocence. Which groups of people can be portrayed as symbols of sexual purity? Who can be socially constructed as innocent in a society? Sexual innocence is not symbolically available to everyone in society. For example, adult men are almost never thought of as sexually innocent.

There has been some change in who historically has been constructed as innocent. Victorian upper-class white women were once symbols of moral purity. In Victorian society, there were dichotomized public and private spheres for upper-class men and women which carried moral implications. The public sphere was the place where competition and the desire to get the upper hand meant that "anything goes" in terms of moral behavior. Bourgeois men braved this dangerous public world and those they thought were its seedy constituents – working-class men and foreigners. Many an upper-class man used this notion of a sullied, prurient, seedy public sphere to excuse their own immoralities as they sought sexual relationships with working-class women and men (D'Emilio and Freedman 1998). Meanwhile, upper-class wives were safely tucked away in the private sphere of blissful domesticity, nurturing and watching over their children. They were supposed to be the moral pillars of Victorian society. This

Nancy L. Fischer

meant that they were responsible for controlling sexual relations within marital relationships, making sure that conjugal relations were more about procreation than recreation (Smith-Rosenberg 1978). Sex between married partners was to be viewed by wives as a necessary evil or part of one's "wifely duties," and was not necessarily something to be enjoyed. This lack of sexual desire helped define mothers as innocent and made them the pinnacles of morality in Victorian society. But, not all women in Victorian times could be constructed as innocent. The working-class woman who had to work for living – either in the factory or on the street – was at the bottom of the moral hierarchy and was often characterized as a "fallen woman."

However women – not even Victorian mothers – could not remain the symbols of moral purity in the twentieth century. Women began to recognize the constraints of this virgin/whore stereotype, seeing how it limited their roles to caring for children and ensured their financial dependence upon men. It also left them out of the important political decisions of the day. Women began to protest by demanding the vote. Additionally, many women argued for new ways of organizing society on a sexual basis. Women played strong roles in movements for birth control and were vocal advocates for free-love societies (communities that believed in sexual relationships without marriage) (D'Emilio and Freedman 1998). In the wake of these sexualized protests, women could not remain the symbols of moral purity in American society.

According to Estelle Freedman (1987), children took women's place as symbols of moral purity. At one time, children were thought to be inherently evil; they were born into sin, and the devil must be beaten out of them. The phrase "Spare the rod and spoil the child" reflects this ethos. But by the turn of the twentieth century they were instead constructed as innocent and free from sin until they became enveloped in the adult world of moral corruption. In the realm of sexuality, children were considered blank slates, unaware of adult desires and lust. In the late 1800s, fears arose about children becoming the victims of adult sexual corruption. Sexual knowledge was thought to morally ruin children. For example, here are Postmaster General Anthony Comstock's thoughts in 1877 on what effect exposure to sexual imagery would have on the minds of innocent upper-class boys:

> The boy's mind becomes a sink of corruption and he is a loathing unto himself. In his better moments he wrestles and cries out against this foe, but all in vain . . . Despair takes possession of his soul as he finds himself losing strength of will – becoming nervous and infirm; he suffers unutterable agony during the hours of the night, and awakes only to carry a burdened heart through all the day.
>
> (Quoted in Beisel 1989: 110)

Not surprisingly, the dominant ideology became one where people believed that children must be protected from sexual knowledge and experiences at all costs. This belief that can be traced to the late 1800s has remained with us today.

Today, most adults equate sexual innocence with the assumption that children should be ignorant of all sexual matters. To that end, they actively try to shield them from sexual knowledge in terms of talking about sex or allowing them to see sexual imagery. One the most notable ways we can observe that kids are shielded from sexual knowledge today is in the push for abstinence-only sex education in schools. Abstinence-only sex education avoids discussion of birth control options or ways for teens to have safe sex and instead recommends that the only way to prevent unwanted pregnancies and sexually transmitted infections is to avoid all sexual contact. Politicians and parents who promote abstinence-only education claim that comprehensive sexual education programming that includes instruction on birth control will put ideas into children's heads and lead them to sex and unwanted pregnancies. However, the price of shielding children from more comprehensive sexual education programming seems to be more sexual violence and coercion in teen relationships, higher rates of sexually transmitted illnesses and more teen pregnancies than our European counterparts who incorporate sexual education throughout the entire school curriculum and begin talking with kids about sex when they are young (Levine 2002).

Conclusion

If we consider current discourse about sexual corruption in newspaper headlines, in politicians' speeches or in battles of words between activists, it seems apparent that in the United States, most people do not have a libertarian view when it comes to sexual morality. A libertarian view could be described as having a "live and let live" attitude, where other people's sexuality is not a concern as long as they are not harming others. In this essay, I have provided some historical and cultural context that helps explain why this is the case. Sexual morality is a loaded issue in our culture in the sense that we can unpack deeper cultural meanings and long historical trends that influence how people understand sexuality. Whenever we talk about how people express themselves sexually, we invoke deeper cultural meanings about purity and pollution, innocence and guilt, acts and identities, and power relations between dominant and subordinate groups.

References

Beisel, Nicola. 1989. "Constructing a Shifting Moral Boundary: Literature and Obscenity in Nineteenth-Century America" in *Cultivating Differences: Symbolic Boundaries and the Making of Inequality*, M. Lamont & M. Fournier, eds. Chicago, IL: University of Chicago Press.

D'Emilio, John and Estelle Freedman. 1998. *Intimate Matters*. Chicago, IL: University of Chicago Press.

Douglas, Mary. 1966. *Purity and Danger*. London: Routledge & Kegan Paul.

Foucault, Michel. 1990 [1978]. *The History of Sexuality: Volume I*. New York: Random House.

Freedman, Estelle. 1987. "Uncontrolled Desires: The Response to the Sexual Psychopath, 1920–1960." *Journal of American History* 74: 83–106.

Levine, Judith. 2002. *Harmful to Minors*. Minneapolis, MN: University of Minnesota Press.

Smith-Rosenberg, Carroll. 1978. "Sex as Symbol in Victorian Purity." *American Journal of Sociology*. 84: s212–47.

Tanenbaum, Leora. 2000. *Slut! Growing Up Female With a Bad Reputation*. New York: Harper.

Warner, Michael. 1999. *The Trouble with Normal*. Cambridge, MA: Harvard University Press.

Zerubavel, Eviatar. 1991. *The Fine Line: Making Distinctions in Everyday Life*. Chicago, IL: University of Chicago Press.

Nancy L. Fischer

chapter 59

Christianity and the regulation of sexuality in the United States

Joshua Grove

Despite predictions that religion would fade as societies modernized, this has not happened. Religion, especially Christianity, continues to play a major role in Americans' lives – their personal and public lives. This chapter discusses the roles that various Christian denominations play in defining and regulating sexuality. I will discuss how Christianity has been a key social force in shaping sexual attitudes and influencing social policy and laws. In this sense, Christian churches are caught up in the politics of sexuality in America. I will illustrate this by discussing the relationship between the church and homosexuality. Finally, prospects for change are considered.

What is conventional Christianity?

By conventional Christianity, I include the Christian denominations with the largest member affiliation rates in the country. This includes the following families of churches in order of national size: Roman Catholic; Baptist (Southern and National Conventions); Pentecostal (Churches/Assemblies of God); United Methodist; Lutheran (Evangelical Lutheran Church in America and Missouri Synod); Presbyterian Church USA; US Episcopal Church; and the United Church of Christ. Although this is not an exhaustive list, most Christian denominations are similar in their responses to questions of sexuality and conduct. Furthermore, I will contrast the policies of these conventional churches with other religious groups, such as Unitarian Universalism and Reform Judaism.

Regulating sexuality

It should come as no surprise that Christianity has had a significant influence on how we define and *feel* about sex. Perhaps more importantly, Christianity also condemns and at times punishes sexual behavior deemed deviant or inappropriate. In conjunction with other social institutions such as the economy and government, religion creates sexual hierarchies. At the top of this hierarchy is heterosexuality. Not all heterosexual types, however, maintain this position of power.

Religious doctrines and moral teachings are key factors in enforcing the *normative status of heterosexuality*. This means that only heterosexuality is considered in line with Christian values. Only heterosexuality is natural and moral. But it is not just heterosexuality that is viewed as sacred. Good Christians must conform to a particular set of behavioral norms, such as marriage, monogamy, and creating and raising a family. Within much of conventional Christianity, individuals who deviate from these sexual norms become outsiders or less than fully respected Christians. This has made the inclusion of gays and lesbians a very difficult undertaking, as it clashes with the heterosexual ideal.

Within Roman Catholicism, heterosexual marriage is celebrated as a *sacrament*. A sacrament is a religious rite or ritual celebrating a sacramental occasion, such as a wedding, baptism, or communion. In short, sacraments represent the belief in God's grace and in Jesus Christ. Sacraments are the foundation of Christian theology and practice. Conventional Christian denominations teach that sex is to be restricted to marriage, and argue that this is only open to heterosexual couples. And although marriage may not be an official sacrament in every Christian denomination, it continues to be one of the most celebrated institutions in all of Christendom.

Members of the Christian Right and Moral Majority have been arguing for decades against the gay and lesbian movement, declaring that homosexuality is destroying the nation and the family. In fact, in 2005 popular evangelical Rev. Louis P. Sheldon released a book entitled *The Agenda: The Homosexual Plan to Change America*. "The homosexual agenda is an attack on everything our Founding Fathers hoped to give us. But I am convinced that we can witness a tremendous victory, and with God's help, we shall overcome." Overcome what? The author and his supporters believe that homosexuality is a choice and the gay and lesbian community is trying to convert heterosexuals into homosexuals. These groups of Christians fear that homosexuality will lead to the ultimate decline of family values, which really means the decline of a specific and narrow idea of family – heterosexual, married with children, wife as mother and father as breadwinner. It is clear that same-sex marriage is not likely to be supported by conservative Christianity at any time soon.

Aside from not being able to marry, gay and lesbian couples of conventional Christian denominations are forbidden from having their unions blessed. In addition, gay and lesbian persons are not able to become clergy. The single exception to this rule is the United Church of Christ, which ordained its first openly gay member, the Rev. William Johnson, in 1972. In the summer of 2005, the Evangelical Lutheran Church in America Church-Wide General Assembly voted to uphold their policy excluding gays and lesbians, but only by a narrow margin. The policy also states that "any church policy that seems to approve of such behavior is a betrayal of the authority of Scripture and an ignoring of the natural order." The natural order here, of course, is normative heterosexuality, where sexuality is *assumed* to be inherently a function of biology, meant for monogamous marriage and childrearing.

These exclusionary policies have implications for heterosexual clergy as well, specifically those who are sympathetic to the gay and lesbian movement. In 1999, the Rev. Greg Dell, a United Methodist minister in Chicago, was convicted of breaking church law when he blessed the union of a same-sex couple. He was punished by being suspended from the ministry until he promised his Bishop in a letter that he would not "officiate at another such union, as long as the rule against them remained." In late 2003, members of the US Episcopal Church experienced the first election of an openly gay bishop, Rev. Gene Robinson. Voting members faced a great deal of social pressure to line up for or against him. Indeed, many heterosexual pastors who supported the election of Robinson met with mixed reactions when they returned to their home dioceses. By promoting the image of a sexually inclusive church, proponents of gay and lesbian religious participation risk some of the same consequences as gays and lesbians themselves.

To be sure, the way clergy behave is crucial to the growth of congregations. However, the sexual views of the clergy also influence the beliefs and behavior of the members in their faith communities. In other words, if the pastor doesn't support same-sex marriage, why should we? Disagreements about questions of sexual morality often turn faithful adherents toward other religious alternatives, or, turn them away from organized religious practice altogether. Never before in American history has spirituality and religion been more diverse, with a growing number of people describing themselves as spiritual and *not* religious. Since religion is often in competition with other social institutions to attract members, they must be mindful of shifts in public attitudes.

Prospects for change

Why have many congregations and churches begun to welcome the gay and lesbian community into their folds? Changes in public opinion and laws greatly affect the ways in which conventional churches respond to questions of sexuality. It seems clear that, in the last decade or so, the attitudes of Americans towards gays and lesbians have changed considerably. Jeni Loftus (2001) analyzed personal opinion data from 1973 through 1998 to track America's growing acceptance of gay and lesbian persons. She found that Americans are much more tolerant and inclusive than even fifteen years ago. In 1973, just over 70 percent of those surveyed believed homosexuality was "always wrong." By 1998, this number dropped to 56 percent. Along these same lines, in 1987 only 13 percent reported homosexuality was "not wrong at all." In 1998, this number increased to over 30 percent. It is interesting to see how these numbers change over time as the visibility of gays and lesbians continues to increase.

Since the late 1960s, the rise in the visibility of the gay and lesbian community has been unprecedented. More gays and lesbians are out of the closet and openly celebrating their relationships, fighting for the right to marry. There are gay and lesbian small-business owners, corporate managers, lawyers, doctors, teachers, and yes, elementary school teachers. Gays and lesbians are even in Congress, their voices represented by gay and lesbian public servants such as Congressmen Barney Frank, Jim Kolbe, and Tammy Baldwin. As I see it, this increased social visibility of the national gay and lesbian movement has been fundamental to its success.

Changes in public attitudes toward the gay and lesbian community often translate into positive court decisions and government legislation. This, of course, does not happen without the considerable political influence and labor of gay and lesbian lobbying groups. Consider the recent decision of the Massachusetts State Supreme Court that led the state to recognize same-sex marriage as of April 2005. This was the first state in the union to allow same-sex marriage, following the same legal precedents as Canada (2005), Belgium (2003), the Netherlands (2001), Spain (2005), and the UK (2005). Finally, in June 2015 in the Obergefell vs. Hodges decision, the U.S. Supreme Court legalized same-sex marriage.

While this progress is important, gays and lesbians still face serious opposition. The most powerful of these groups is the conservative branch of Christianity. Make no mistake, religious ideals and principles often find their way into politics and government. In 1996, President Clinton signed into law the Defense of Marriage Act (DOMA), defining marriage as a legal relationship between a *man* and a *woman*. At the time, this gave states the right to decide for themselves how to deal with same-sex marriage. Imagine if each state were to regulate heterosexual marriage and not recognize the union between your mother and father, your best friend and his/her spouse, or perhaps your own marriage.

Should states be permitted to make those decisions on your behalf? Many politicians not only believe this, they had proposed the Federal Marriage Amendment (FMA), which would amend the United States Constitution. In effect, the FMA would define marriage, *on the national level*, as the union between a man and a woman. This would overturn any state decision supporting same-sex marriage. This, of course, stems partly from the religious convictions of politicians, as well as the Republican base, which is highly influenced by the Christian Right. Thus, although it is crucial to celebrate the victories of the gay and lesbian movement toward full inclusion, it is also necessary to be aware of the losses and possible obstacles to these political goals. This demonstrates how, even in secular components of society, religion still maintains significant influence.

Change within the American church

A sign of dramatic change in the status of gays in America is that there are many religious faiths, including some conventional Christian denominations, which fully include gays and lesbians in their ministries, as both clergy and laity. Gay and lesbian clergy currently serve in churches, hospitals, university campuses, and counseling centers across the country in *most* religious traditions, regardless of policies and doctrines. Some of these pastors still live in the closet because their passion for the ministry overrides their need to be free from its sexual regulation. Other pastors work with congregations that are accepting of lesbians and gay men, even when threatened by the administrative hierarchies of their denominations.

To be sure, change is happening everywhere within conventional Christian denominations. The United Church of Christ (UCC) ordains gay and lesbian persons and has done so for over thirty years. In 1985, the UCC General Synod adopted the resolution known as "Open and Affirming," which publicly declared that those of all sexual orientations are welcome to the life and ministry of the church. This was meant to encourage local congregations to adopt an open and affirming statement, letting the gay and lesbian community know that they are welcome. In addition, the United Church of Christ has a specific branch of ministry known as Lesbian, Gay, Bisexual and Transgender Ministries. This has been quite successful.

However, not all attempts made by the United Church of Christ to promote inclusion have been accepted with open arms. For example, when the UCC launched a multi-million-dollar campaign in 2005 to promote inclusivity, television networks NBC and CBS refused to air their commercials, arguing that they were too controversial. Specifically, the commercial began with two bouncers protecting the entrance to a church and deciding which people are "good enough" to attend services. Then, on the television screen, you read: "Jesus didn't turn people away. Neither do we." A voiceover then announces the United Church of Christ's commitment to Jesus's extravagant welcome: "No matter who you are, or where you are on life's journey, you are welcome here." The ad can be viewed online at www.stillspeaking.com/resources/indexvis.html (accessed 21 March 2006). Fortunately, networks including ABC Family, Discovery, History, Travel, and TV Land aired the commercial.

This progression of the United Church of Christ is important because, since 1998, it has been in "full communion" with the Evangelical Lutheran Church in America, Presbyterian Church USA, the Reformed Church, and the Disciples of Christ. This involves an agreement in the ways in which Gospel messages are preached, as well as sharing communion and growing together in word, ministry, and Christian teachings. In fact, in the Lutheran, Presbyterian, and Reform Church, margins of victory for those opposed to gay and lesbian inclusion have become smaller and smaller over the past decade. The Evangelical Lutheran Church in America, Presbyterian Church USA, United Methodist, and US Episcopal Church each have national programs ministering specifically to the gay and lesbian community.

One example is Lutherans Concerned/North America, which is a private organization supporting the inclusion of gay and lesbian persons into the Lutheran Church, and into Christianity in general. In 1984, they initiated a program entitled "Reconciling in Christ," which is similar in nature to the United Church of Christ's "Open and Affirming" statements. If a Lutheran congregation decides officially to open their doors to the gay and lesbian community, they do so through an official statement known as "Reconciling in Christ." The same is true for Presbyterians, where the accepting congregations are known as "More Light Churches." For Episcopalians these churches are known as "Oasis Churches," and in United Methodism they are called "Reconciling Congregations."

It is also possible that these changes in attitudes and church-wide discussions on sexuality stem from religious faiths outside of conventional Christianity. Founded in 1968 by the Rev. Troy Perry, the Metropolitan Community Church became the world's first church established primarily for ministry to the gay and lesbian community. With almost 300 congregations spread across twenty-two countries, the Metropolitan Community Church has a long history of celebrating positive images of gay and lesbian Christians and fighting for social equality.

Unitarian Universalism has consistently supported the full inclusion of gays and lesbians, not only in church policy, but also in secular, governmental politics. In 1987, the Unitarian Universalist Association (UUA) General Assembly voted overwhelmingly to initiate the "Welcoming Congregation" program to educate its members about the inclusion of gay, lesbian, bisexual, and transgender persons. In fact, Unitarianism has acknowledged the role of the church in the oppression of sexual minorities and vowed to challenge this form of injustice. In 1973, the UUA created the Office of Bisexual, Gay, Lesbian, and Transgender Concerns. The main purpose of this office is to promote education across Unitarian churches and foster ecumenical cooperation among different religious faiths. Today, Unitarian Universalism is growing in membership and is a supportive, encouraging environment for *any* person who is interested in a spiritual community and social advocacy.

The support of gay and lesbian persons can also be seen in Reform Judaism. In 1996, the Central Conference of American Rabbis, serving almost 2 million Reform Jews, condemned government attempts to ban gay marriage. Moreover, in 2000 they officially gave rabbis the right to preside over civil ceremonies blessing same-sex unions. To be certain, Reform Judaism does not view this issue as being about gay rights or women's rights. Rather, this is about *human* rights, and they urge people to view it in the same way.

Conclusions

I hope that this chapter raises questions in your mind about how religion regulates sexuality in the United States. How would you feel if you were told the love you had for your partner was cursed by God? Would you believe it to be true, dedicate yourself to celibacy and not question the authority of that which condemns you? In part, this has been the reaction of many gay and lesbian Christians throughout the world, and throughout history. Unfortunately, it has been the core teaching of sexuality in most conventional Christian denominations, which have only recently opened the doors of discussion about sexual morality outside of heterosexual marriage. It may take some time before significant progress has been achieved. Patience, as they say, is indeed a virtue.

Many men and women have spent a great deal of their lives believing that they would be damned to hell and social marginalization if they expressed a gay or lesbian sexual identity. We can only hope that, as time passes and more people are educated, homophobia will fade into the past. I urge you to challenge any individual, group, or institution that condemns a person simply for being gay or lesbian. Indeed, you may find that you have to challenge your own perceptions of morality and sexuality. Some take for granted the privileged status of heterosexuality; empathy and compassion are achieved only when you step outside of yourself.

Bibliography

Publications

Black, Dan, Gates, Gary, Sanders, Seth, and Taylor, Lowell. 2000. "Demographics of the gay and lesbian population in the United States: Evidence from available systematic data sources." *Demography* 37(2): 139–55.

Loftus, Jeni. 2001. "America's liberalization in attitudes toward homosexuality, 1973 to 1998." *American Sociological Review* 66(5): 762–82.

Oswald, R. F. 2002. "Resilience within the family networks of lesbians and gay men: Intentionality and redefinition." *Journal of Marriage and Family* 64(2): 374–83.

Patterson, Charlotte. 2000. "Family relationships of lesbians and gay men." *Journal of Marriage and Family* 62(4): 1052–69.

Seidman, Steven. 2002. *Beyond the closet: The transformation of gay and lesbian life.* New York: Routledge.

Sheldon, Louis P. 2005. *The agenda: The homosexual plan to change America.* Available at https://archive.org/details/TheAgenda-TheHomosexualPlanToChangeAmerica.

Stacey, Judith and Biblarz, Timothy J. 2001. "(How) does the sexual orientation of parents matter?" *American Sociological Review* 66(2): 159–84.

Weston, Kath. 1991. *Families we choose: Lesbians, gays, kinship.* New York: Columbia University Press.

Websites for further information

www.catholic.org [Roman Catholic Church]
www.elca.org [Evangelical Lutheran Church in America]
www.hrc.org [Human Rights Campaign]
www.mcc.org [Metropolitan Community Church]
www.pcusa.org [Presbyterian Church USA]
www.rj.org [Reform Judaism]
www.stillspeaking.com [United Church of Christ Advertisement for GLBT Inclusion]
www.thomas.loc.gov [U.S. Library of Congress]
www.ucc.org [United Church of Christ]
www.umc.org [United Methodist Church]
www.uua.org [Unitarian Universalism Association]
www.vatican.va [Vatican: The Holy See]
www.whitehouse.gov [U.S. White House]
http://en.wikipedia.org/wiki/Category:LGBT_civil_rights [Encyclopedia of GLBT civil rights]

chapter 60

Healing (disorderly) desire

Medical-therapeutic regulation of sexuality[1]

P. J. McGann

Sex matters – to individuals, to be sure, but also to social groups. Consequently all societies define and enforce norms of how to "do it," with whom, when, where, how often, and why. Yet how such sexual norms are enforced, indeed which acts are even considered to *be* sex ("it"), varies tremendously. In some cases sexual regulation is informal, as when girls or women admonish one another to control their sexual appetites lest one gain a "reputation." In others, regulation is more formal, as when a female prostitute is arrested and sentenced for her sexual misconduct. Of course, the legal system is not the only institution that formally regulates acceptable and unacceptable sexual practices. Religion also helps construct and enforce ideals of normal sex, defining some acts as sinful, others as righteous. In both cases, the moral language of sin and crime renders the social control aspects of legal and religious sexual regulation apparent.

But what of therapeutic approaches, as when a girl viewed as having "too much" sex is referred to juvenile court for "correction" of her incorrigibility? Is not intervention then for the girl's own good? Might it, for example, derail her developing delinquency, perhaps even prevent her subsequent involvement in prostitution? And what of the prostitute herself? What if rather than sending her to jail we instead direct her to therapy – based on the belief that a woman who sells her sexuality to others must, *obviously*, be sick? Do these therapeutic approaches also count as sexual regulation?

Here it is helpful to speak of social control, a broad concept that refers to any acts or practices that encourage conformity to and/or discourage deviations from norms (Conrad and Schneider 1992). From this perspective a medical-therapeutic response to violations of sexual rules *is* a form of sexual social control. However, in contrast to the transparently moral language of law and religion – good/bad, righteous/sinful, right/wrong – therapeutic regulation of sex relies on more opaque dichotomies of health and illness, normality and abnormality. Although such terms may camouflage the moral evaluation being made, the result is the same; whether the means are legal, religious, or therapeutic, a negative social judgment is made and a sexual hierarchy is produced (Rubin 1993). A dichotomy of good versus bad sexual practices, good versus bad "sexual citizens" (Seidman 2002), is thus created and enforced:

> Individuals whose behavior stands high in this hierarchy are rewarded with certi-fied mental health, respectability, legality, social and physical mobility, institu-tional support, and material benefits. As sexual behaviors or occupations fall lower on the scale, the individuals who practice them are subjected to a presump-tion of mental illness, disreputability, criminality, restricted social and physical mobility, loss of institutional support, and economic sanctions.
>
> (Rubin 1993: 12)

Medical-therapeutic approaches – medicine, psychiatry, psychology, social work, and juvenile justice – are part of a web of practices that help define and enforce a society's sexual hierarchy and sexual norms. The "helping" ethos of therapeutic approaches, however, disguises their regulatory dynamics and effects. An illness diagnosis pro-vides a seemingly positive rationale for restricting or changing sexual behaviors found to be disturbing; intervention is, after all, *for our own good*. Even so, what is considered a sexual disorder may have disciplinary consequences. Whether or not a sexual activ-ity is "really" a dysfunction or even causes distress for those diagnosed, individual sexual choices deemed non-typical are curtailed, and sexual culture is restricted in the name of health.

Some consider such matters the proper province of politics rather than medicine. Cloaked in the garb of sexual health, therapeutic intervention seemingly depoliticizes judgments of sexual normality and abnormality. This sleight of hand renders medical-therapeutic regulation of sex an insidious form of social control, a way to induce con-formity to sexual norms while seeming not to do so. What's more, an individual need not be under the direct care of a helping professional to suffer the repressive conse-quences of therapeutic sexual regulation. Medical images of normal sexuality filter out of therapeutic settings into other institutions and everyday life. There they inform com-monsense notions of sexual abnormality, illness, and perversion. Expert medical knowledge also helps legitimate the criminalization of non-standard sexual practices (Rubin 1993). These understandings simultaneously construct what we think of as sexually normal, healthy, and proper. In this way, sexual disorders reflect – and help reproduce – a society's sexual norms. Intended or not, medical-therapeutic approaches to sex enforce sexual ideals.

This chapter explores some of the politics of "healing" disorderly desire. Using three contemporary sexual difficulties – erectile dysfunction, gender identity disorder, and sexual addiction/compulsion – I show how medical-therapeutic approaches shape and direct sexual expression. Some forms of regulation are directly repressive; they limit or deny sexual options construed as unnatural, abnormal, or unhealthy. Other forms of medical-therapeutic regulation are more subtle; their "normalizing" dynamics work by producing cultural ideals of natural and healthy sexuality. The ostensibly objective medical model of sex is especially important in this regard. It provides both the taken-for-granted understanding of what "sex" is (and is for) and the reference point from which sexual abnormality and sexual disorders are defined. As we shall see, this intertwining of the individual and cultural levels, and of repressive and normalizing forms of power, is a central dynamic in medical-therapeutic sexual regulation. Moreover, given that some individuals who "have" sexual disorders suffer neither distress nor impairment, it seems that diagnostic categories are not purely scientific entities, but social constructs that reflect social and political dynamics and concerns.

Medicalized sex and medical social control

When something is "medicalized" it is conceptually placed in a medical framework. The "problem" is then understood using medical language, typically as a disorder, dysfunction, disease, or syndrome, and is approached or solved via medical means (Conrad and Schneider 1992). A "sex offender," for example, might be sentenced to rehabilitative therapy rather than prison, or a man concerned about his homosexual desire might consult a psychiatrist rather than a priest. Although such medical-therapeutic regulation may be less punitive than criminal or religious sexual intervention, medicalizing sex produces positive and negative results.

On the plus side, defining sexual difficulties as medical problems may make it easier for people to talk more openly about sex and thus seek information and advice. Accordingly a medical approach to sex may enhance individual sexual pleasure. Yet medicalization also raises the possibility of "medical social control" (Conrad and Schneider 1992) – in this case, the use of medical means to increase conformity to sexual norms and/or to decrease sexual deviance. Prescription drugs, talk therapy, behavioral modification, negative or aversive conditioning, and/or confinement in a juvenile or mental health facility, can be enlisted to ensure adherence to sexual norms. Even without such direct medical intervention, viewing sex with a "medical gaze" often leads to a limited, biologically reductionist understanding. Stripped from its social context, sexual *difference* may become sexual *pathology*.

Medical social control sometimes has a slippery, elusive character. When individuals consult therapeutic professionals regarding sexual matters, they typically anticipate alleviation of sexual distress rather than restriction of sexual freedom. For their part psychiatrists, doctors, therapists, and social workers may neither intend nor understand their therapeutic practice as tools of sexual repression. Despite this mismatch of intent and effect, therapeutic intervention has regulatory consequences. The "promiscuous" girl can be held against her will in a mental or juvenile justice institution. The man who desires multiple sex partners might be forced to remain monogamous and to refrain from masturbation lest his sexual "addiction" overtake him.

Sexology and its legacies

Although some of our categories of sexual disease are new, medicine and sex have long been entangled in North America and Europe. Sexology, the science of sex, originated in mid-nineteenth-century Europe when physicians such as Magnus Hirschfeld, Richard von Krafft-Ebing, and Havelock Ellis turned their attention to sexual behavior. At the time Europe was caught up in a cultural mood of scientific rationality, evolutionism, and fantasies of white racial superiority. These currents inspired detailed scientific description of sexual diversity, and the delineation of sexual practices into normal and abnormal types. The latter were dubbed "perversions" and seen as sickness rather than sin. With the emergence of sexology, formal regulation of sexuality shifted from predominantly religious to secular modes of social control. Regulation of deviant sexuality thus became the province of medical authority (Foucault 1990 [1978]).

Commonsense understandings of categories of disease view them as morally neutral descriptions of states of un-health. Yet even cursory consideration of the malleability of sexological categories shows that sexual disorders reflect more than just the accumulated sexual knowledge of the time. Forms of sexual behavior once considered abnormal and diseased are now "known" to be a normal part of sexual health. Some sexual illnesses reflect the normative standards of more powerful groups at the expense of those with differing sexual tastes and less power. And some sexual disorders seem more like reflections of prevailing cultural currents rather than actual sexual dysfunctions.

Masturbation, for example, was once the disease of "Onanism" (Conrad and Schneider 1992). A dangerous illness on its own, "self-abuse" was also a sort of gateway disease – a disorder that could so weaken the afflicted that he might fall prey to other perverse "infections" such as homosexuality or sadism. Now, though, masturbation is considered a "natural" (even if private) part of healthy sexuality; in fact, masturbation is prescribed as a therapeutic treatment for some sexual disorders, such as "premature ejaculation" (ejaculation that occurs before coitus) or "anorgasmia" (inability to orgasm). Healthy and normal sexual practices may also become disordered or unsavory over time. Visits to female prostitutes, for example, were once part of the prescribed treatment for male (but not female) "lovesickness." Massage of female external genitalia by a doctor or midwife was once the preferred treatment for "hysteria" (Maines 1999). However, in most locales today the former is illegal and the latter might be considered sexual misconduct or abuse. The female "psychopathic hypersexual" illustrates how disease categories reflect cultural concerns. Female sexual psychopaths "suffered" from an excessive amount of sexual desire at a time when it was "known" that girls and women were naturally modest and chaste, or at least sexually passive. Interestingly, the hypersexual female diagnosis emerged at the end of the Victorian era – a time of changing gender relations and rising anxiety over the increasing independence and agency of women. The psychopathic hypersexual diagnosis reflects these concerns and codifies the violation of normative gender standards as disease. Finally, the declassification of homosexuality as a mental disorder in response to social and political developments outside psychiatry is the example *par excellence* that disease categories rest on more than scientific facts (Conrad and Schneider 1992). One wonders: if historical categories of sexual disease are so obviously shaped by non-scientific factors, might the same be true of contemporary constructions of normal and abnormal, healthy and diseased sex?

The medical model of sex

Although many concepts from classic sexology are no longer accepted, there are continuities between nineteenth- and twenty-first-century medical approaches to sex. The thrust to describe and delineate the diversity of sexual practices and types persists. So, too, does the "medical model" of sex. This view posits sex as an innate, natural essence or drive contained in and released from the body. Bodies, in turn, are understood as machine-like composites of parts. When the parts are in proper working order, bodies are able to achieve their functional purposes. Sexual organs become engorged as blood and other bodily fluids accumulate in anticipation of sexual activity. These changes, as well as sexual drives, patterns of sexual behavior, and even sexual types (bi, homo, hetero), are understood as universal properties of individuals independent of society. Cultural variation in sexual practice is seen as relatively superficial; changes in surface social details do not alter the deeper biological reality of sex (Tieffer 1995). Because reproduction is considered the natural function of sex, the medical model depicts heterosexuality as natural and neutral, not in need of explanation or scrutiny – unless, that is, something goes awry with the hydraulic sexual machine. Thus, nineteenth-century sexology and modern sexual science have mostly observed, described, and catalogued deviations from or problems with sex oriented toward reproduction.

The contemporary Human Sexual Response Cycle (HSRC) is the iconic embodiment of this approach. First conceived by Masters and Johnson in the 1960s, the HSRC describes a presumably universal pattern of physiological changes that occur during "sex": excitement, plateau, orgasm, and resolution. In the "excitement" stage, for example, penises become engorged with blood and vaginas lubricate in preparation for "sex." Most medical-therapeutic professionals concerned with sexual disorders now rely on a three-stage derivative model of desire, arousal, and orgasm. Despite its supposed scientific neutrality – the HSRC model was based on seemingly disinterested laboratory observation of heterosexual genital intercourse – the HSRC has been critiqued as heteronormative and androcentric, and for reifying a limited understanding of "sex" as the cultural sexual ideal (Tieffer 1995).

Although the array of potentially normal human sexual activity is vast, HSRC constructs only a narrow range of acts relating to coitus (penile–vaginal intercourse) as constituting "sex." Other forms of sexual activity are relegated to "foreplay" – preparatory, albeit pleasurable, preparations for the "real thing." Forms of sexual activity that do not culminate in coitus are viewed as perverse substitutions for, or distractions from, the real thing (Tieffer 1995). Oral sex followed by heterosexual coitus may be normal foreplay, for example, whereas oral sex in the absence of coitus is considered abnormal or dysfunctional. The HSRC thus constructs both what *should* and *should not* be done during normal sex. In so doing the HSRC helps constitute "sex" itself.

What, for example, comes to mind when one person says to another, "We had sex"? Despite the nearly endless possibilities (given the number of bodies and body parts that may or may not be involved, variations in sequence, pace, position, sexual aids or toys, and the like) the meaning of "We had sex" is typically unproblematic in everyday life. In fact, a common response might be a titillated "Really! How many times?" The answer to this question is also typically unproblematic, given that we know both what "sex" is and what "counts" as a time. Now, though, let's make it explicit that the two people who "had sex" are of the same sex. Did the meaning of "having sex" change in your mind? What counts as a "time" now? Will your answer change if our partners are male, female, or transgendered? What if we add a third or fourth participant? Is the sex that was had still the *normal* kind? Or does it now appear abnormal, maybe even *sick*, despite being consensual and mutually pleasurable?

The HSRC is also critiqued as androcentric (male-centered), given that the orgasm in question is the man's. Clinically, male ejaculation/orgasm marks the transition to the "resolution" stage. As such, male orgasm is the basis of counting how many "times" sex occurs, or even if sex is "had" at all. Moreover, although the HSRC codifies "foreplay" as an official part of sex, there is no category of "afterplay" – such as sexual activity focused on female orgasm after the man ejaculates. Even adding this concept, though, leaves coitus intact as the defining sexual moment. The (heterosexual) male's orgasmic experience thus defines "sex," whereas female orgasm is not considered. Indeed, female orgasmic pleasure is not a necessary part of real sex. Female orgasm does not count, at least not from the perspective of the supposedly universal and natural HSRC – unless, that is, the counting concerns "abnormal" female sex response. Since at least 70 percent of women do not achieve orgasm from penile–vaginal penetration alone, the HSRC focus on coitus and male ejaculation as the goal and purpose of "sex" renders most women sexually unhealthy, defective, disordered, or dysfunctional (Tieffer 1995). Despite these shortcomings, sexual activities that diverge from the HSRC are defined as abnormal, pathological, deviant, unnatural, dysfunctional, and disordered.

Sexual disorder in DSM

"DSM" is short for *Diagnostic and Statistical Manual of Mental Disorder*. Published by the American Psychiatric Association, DSM is a professionally approved listing of diagnostic categories and criteria. It is the central text for those working in the mental and sexual health fields in the USA, and the key to second-party reimbursement for medical-therapeutic services. DSM has undergone five revisions since its initial publication in 1952. A roman numeral in the title denotes placement in the revision sequence: DSM-II in 1968, DSM-III in 1980, DSM-III-R in 1987, DSM-IV in 1994, DSM-IV-TR in 2000 and the DSM-V in 2013. Categories of disease are refined and re-conceptualized over the course of these editions. Sometimes this results in a disorder being relocated within DSM's typological system, as when homosexuality shifted from psychopathic personality disturbance (DSM-I) to type of sexual deviance (DSM-II); sometimes it leads to the complete removal of a disorder, as when homosexuality was left out of DSM-III.

The most recent DSM lists three major classifications of Sexual Disorder: Paraphilias, Sexual Dysfunctions, and Gender Identity Disorders. "Paraphilias" include exhibitionism, fetishism, frotteurism, pedophilia, sexual masochism, sexual sadism, transvestic fetishism, and voyeurism. (Many of these types were the original "perversions" described by nineteenth-century sexology.) "Sexual Dysfunctions" concern impairments or disturbances related to coitus. Three subtypes directly mirror the derivative HSRC model: disorders of desire, disorders of arousal, and disorders of orgasm. The fourth subtype, pain during coitus, also reflects the centrality of coitus in constructing the sexual dysfunctions. The last major classification of sexual disorder in DSM is "Gender Identity Disorders." With subtypes for adults and children, these disorders represent deviations from "normal" gender embodiment.

DSM facilitates communication among an array of sexual helping professionals with diverse training, specialization, and institutional placements and practices. Using DSM categories, individuals as varied as a social worker with one year of postgraduate academic training, a psychiatrist with over ten years of medical and clinical training, or a college intern working in a residential juvenile treatment program, can communicate with one another. This is helpful, to be sure. But the shared language of DSM may also make the sexual disorders seem less politically contested and more objectively real than they really are. This may, in turn, make it more difficult for practitioners to recognize the biases built into DSM diagnostic categories. Far from being neutral classifications, the major DSM categories of sexual disorder encode normative assumptions of sexuality. Paraphilias delineate that which we should *not* do sexually; sexual dysfunctions reflect incapacities in what we *should* do; and gender identity disorders concern how we should appear and who we should *be* while doing it.

One way to avoid uncritically replicating these biases is to rename the major types of sexual disorder based on their ideological effects rather than naming the types based on their relationship to coitus. "Sexual dysfunctions," for example, seems a neutral and comprehensive term; in reality it is a specific reference to *hetero*sexual dysfunctions of penile–vaginal intercourse. Consider instead "disorders of prowess" – disorders based on one's compromised ability to engage in coitus. We could similarly disrupt the heteronormativity of HSRC and speak of "disorders of appetite" – disorders of too much or too little desire to engage in coitus, and/or having desires that do not include or that extend beyond coitus. Finally, "gender violations" seems an apt tag for forms of gender expression and embodiment that violate the traditional gender styles underpinning normative heterosexuality. Having linguistically interrupted diagnostic business as usual, I now turn to some specific disorders and consider how each reflects and reproduces dominant North American sexual norms and the sexual hierarchy built on them.

Sexual disorders and the maintenance of ideal sexuality

Some people do experience distress in relation to sexual matters. Treatment of sexual disorders may alleviate such distress and thereby enhance sexual pleasure. This does not mean, however, that medical-therapeutic intervention does not also produce negative consequences or operate in repressive fashion. Moreover, since some of the DSM's sexual disorders are not necessarily *dysfunctions* but violations of dominant sexual norms, therapeutic intervention may enforce conformity to the dominant sexual ideal. Sexual codes, though, are political, ethical, moral, and existential matters – not medical ones. While bringing one's sexual practices into line with prevailing sexual norms may alleviate individual distress, it also obscures the social, cultural, and ideological sources of sexual difficulties.

The Western sexual ideal has become less oriented to procreation and more pleasure-based over time. This new "relational" sexual code (Levine and Troiden 1988) understands sexual activity as creating, expressing, and enhancing a couple's intimacy, and mutual sexual pleasure is accordingly thought of as a normal part of healthy sex. This does not mean, of course, that anything goes. Ideally sexual pleasure occurs within an on-going committed monogamous relationship between two conventionally gendered people of "opposite" sexes (Rubin 1993). In some locales homosexuality may be approaching this sexual ideal – provided, that is, the same-sex couple and their relationship is otherwise normal: the partners are committed to one another, their sex is an expression of love and caring, and they are, like heterosexuals, either masculine men or feminine women (Seidman 2002). Ideal sex occurs in private, is genitally centered (as per the HSRC construction of coitus as "sex"), and is caring rather than aggressive or violent (Rubin 1993). Individuals who engage in such normal sex are good sexual citizens, while those who engage in non-normative sex are thought of as bad. The latter are perceived as immoral, abnormal, unhealthy, diseased, perverted and socially dangerous (Seidman 2002).

Erectile Dysfunction: a prowess disorder

At first glance it may be hard to grasp how improving a man's erection may be a form of sexual regulation and repression. Certainly treatment of Erectile Dysfunction (ED) holds the promise of increased sexual pleasure! It also, however, channels pleasure toward particular sexual acts and body parts in a manner that reflects and reinforces the limited HSRC construction of coitus as the be-all and end-all of "sex." The focus on erections also helps reproduce traditional masculinity and associated stereotypes of "natural" male and female sexuality.

Previously known as the psychological and interpersonal disorder of "impotence," ED is now understood as a physiological impairment of arousal. ED has recently risen to prominence alongside the increased visibility of drug-based treatments; indeed, the discovery of a pharmacological treatment is intertwined with the discovery that impotence is "really" a hydraulic and mechanical disorder. In this, the "Viagra age" (Loe 2004) is emblematic of the biological reductionism that often results when sex is medicalized. The individualized focus removes sexual problems from their interpersonal, social, and cultural contexts. ED thus seems a purely medical rather than a political matter.

The proliferation of penile fixes – Viagra, Cialis, Levitra, and the like – has made it possible for many men to achieve the full, long-lasting erections they desire. The penile fix has also raised expectations and created new norms of male sexual performance. In the Viagra Age it is easy enough to rebuild him, make him bigger, harder, and get him that way faster regardless of his age, fatigue, or emotional state. With the little blue pill and some physical stimulation a real man can get the job done, whether or not his heart is in it. That the perfect penis is now but a swallow away reinforces the cultural understanding of male sexuality as machine-like, uncomplicated, straightforward, and readily available. This reinforces the commonsense view that men are "about" sex whereas women are "about" relationships, while constructing female sexuality as complicated and mysterious (Loe 2004). These contrasting images of male and female sexuality reflect the notion that men and women are "opposite" sexes. This gendered assumption in turn bolsters the seeming neutrality of heterosexuality as complementary opposites that "naturally" attract the other. In this way ED reflects and reinforces heteronormative cultural ideals of sexuality *and* gender.

The ED treatment focus on producing erections "sufficient" for penetration also disciplines the sexuality of individual men. For starters, it directs attention to preparing the man for "sex"– understood, of course, as coitus. While this constructs sex in an image of male orgasm, it also constrains the realm of pleasurable and culturally valuable sexual activity. The phallic focus comes at the expense of the man's other body parts and their pleasures, and construes other sexual activities, including other types of intercourse (anal or oral), as less than the real thing. The phallic focus even deflects attention from the wider possibilities of pleasure linked to other penile states (the soft penis, for example, or movements between soft and hard). Preoccupation with the size and "quality" of erections also reinforces a sexual "work ethic" that emphasizes active male performance rather than sexual enjoyment and/or receptivity. The man's sexuality is thus restricted and restrained, his potential pleasures lessened. Pharmaceutical ads disseminate these messages widely in their depictions of ED treatments as being for caring, committed heterosexual couples rather than, say, homosexual couples, single men, men who masturbate or use pornography, or men who engage in multiple-partner sex (Loe 2004).

Gender Identity Disorder: a gender violation

The gendered nature of ED and its treatment suggests the close coupling of traditional gender and normative sexuality. As Seidman (2002) points out, good sexual citizens are gender-normal citizens: their gender identities and expressions fit traditional gender images and understandings. Thus, normal sex occurs between individuals whose gender styles and gender identities are seen as appropriate for their sex category – men are masculine and see themselves as male; women are feminine and see themselves as female. The gender identity disorders reflect and reinforce these essentialist understandings of the "natural" relationship between sex category, gender identity, and gender embodiment, by pathologizing alternative configurations of sex and gender (McGann 1999). Non-normative ways of doing gender – a feminine man, for example – and atypical gender identities – such as a female-bodied person who identifies as male – are examples of clinical "gender dysphoria." Whether or not their ego functioning is impaired, they experience distress related to their condition, or other psychopathology exists, gender dysphoric individuals, including children, may be diagnosed with and treated for Gender Identity Disorder (GID). Although

P. J. McGann

a GID diagnosis can have the positive result of facilitating access to medical technologies of bodily transformation, it does so by constructing gender difference as disease. GID thus also provides a rationale for medical social control of gender difference – an especially troubling possibility for gender-different children.

When GID first appeared in 1980, it included two types of diagnostic criteria. One concerned impairments in cognitive functioning centered on sexual anatomy, such as a boy thinking his penis ugly or wishing he did not have a penis, or a girl insisting that she could one day grow a penis. The other diagnostic criteria were thought to indicate the child's desire to "be" the other sex. In actuality, however, these criteria focused on cultural violations of gendered appearance or activity norms – boys who look and "act like" girls, for example. Although a child need not demonstrate distress regarding the condition – in fact, DSM notes that most children deny distress – a child had to demonstrate *both* the cognitive functioning and cultural criteria to be diagnosed. That is, a child could not be diagnosed with GID on the basis of cultural gender role violations alone. This two-tiered diagnostic requirement has weakened over subsequent DSM editions. Since 1994 (DSM-IV) it has been possible to diagnose a child as gender disordered based *only* on cultural criteria – that is, based only on the child's violations of social standards of traditional masculinity and femininity in the absence of demonstrated impairment of cognitive function. Thus, a girl with short hair, whose friends are boys, and who refuses to wear dresses, may now "have" GID. In effect, the diagnostic net has widened; a tomboy considered normal under DSM-III-R became abnormal in DSM-IV.

Interestingly, this expansion of GID has occurred alongside the removal of homosexuality from DSM-III and the increasing "normalization" of homosexuality in everyday life (Seidman 2002). None the less, organizations such as Focus on the Family publicize and support therapeutic treatment of gender-different children in order to stave off their future homosexuality. Because children can be and are diagnosed and treated solely for gendered appearance and role violations, GID enforces our cultural gender dichotomy and our understanding of heterosexuality as the natural attraction of gendered opposites (McGann 1999).

One need not be gender-dysphoric oneself to suffer GID's disciplinary effects. As noted earlier, medical judgments of health and illness influence everyday life understandings. In this case the construction of atypical gender as illness discourages gender openness and fluidity for all. GID also regulates sexual expression directly by limiting normal sex to that which occurs between traditionally gendered people; cross-dressing sex play by individuals who are otherwise gender-normal, for example, is "known" to be abnormal or perverse. The sexuality of gender-atypical but non-dysphoric people is also distorted by GID. The wholly normative heterosexual desire of a "tomboyish" woman may be invisible to her potential partner, for example. Alternatively, her erotic draw to males may be dismissed as unbelievable or insincere since she is, *obviously*, a lesbian, based on her appearance (McGann 1999).

Sexual Addiction/Compulsion: a disorder of appetite

At times the terms "sexual addiction" and "sexual compulsion" are used interchangeably; at times they refer to different disorders. Neither is currently listed as an official mental disorder in the DSM. None the less, patients are treated for sexual addiction/ compulsion, books and articles are published on the disorder, practitioners are trained in its treatment modalities, therapeutic institutions specialize in it, and tv documentaries such as Discovery Health's *Sex Mania!* present it as a valid diagnostic category. Sexual addiction/compulsion is thought to be similar to other chemical or behavioral dependencies, such as those on alcohol or food. In practice, the diagnosis can refer to nearly any sexual behavior deemed "excessive" in the therapist's or clinician's professional judgment. In this, sexual addiction is a near-perfect obverse of the prevailing sexual ideal, the dark shadow of the good sexual citizen. As with GID, many individuals diagnosed with sex addiction deny that their disorder causes them distress or harm, and helping professionals often have to work long and hard to convince their "patients" that they are in fact "sick." For this reason sexual addiction aptly illustrates how disease categories crystallize political differences regarding sexual norms. It also shows how disease categories reflect the social currents and concerns of their origin.

Sexual addiction was "unthinkable" in the relatively sexually permissive, sex positive 1970s (Levine and Troiden 1988). At the time sex was seen in a more recreational, pleasure-based light and therapeutic concern consequently focused on "Inhibited Sexual Disorder" (Irvine 2005). But in the 1980s and the early days of the AIDS epidemic, fears of sexual chaos came to the fore and therapeutic attention turned instead to excessive – thus dangerous – sexual desire. As the dominant sexual ideal shifted from a recreational to a relational code, forms of sexual expression that had been normalized in the 1970s were pathologized as addictive and compulsive (Levine and Troiden 1988).

Gay men were at first thought to be especially prone to sex addiction. Indeed, the gay press worried that the diagnosis was a medical form of homophobia, a way to pathologize behavior construed as deviant by the hetero majority, but that was normative within some gay communities (Levine and Troiden 1988). While gay male acceptance of anonymous and/or public sex may have initially swelled the sex addict rank, heterosexuals also "suffer" from the disorder. Straight women who deviate from relationally oriented monogamous sex may be considered addicts, for example. A broad range of sexual activity outside of coital monogamy is considered indicative of addiction/compulsion, including multiple partners (at the same time or as successive couplings), "frequent" masturbation, the use of pornography, "recreational" sex (sex solely for pleasure), anonymous or public sex. Sex addiction also manifests within the otherwise sexually normal hetero couple, as when one partner desires coitus more frequently, and/or wants to engage in activities in addition to or instead of coitus. In these cases a therapist may tip the balance in favor of the more traditional partner by elevating one personal preference as "normal" while deeming the other compulsive or addictive. Here, use of the term "lust" rather than "desire" in the sex addiction literature reveals a moral evaluation masquerading as neutral medical description. Other morally charged "retro-purity" terms are also common in the sexual addiction literature, such as promiscuity, nymphomania, and womanizing (Irvine 2005).

Although the activities presumed indicative of sexual addiction or compulsion may be atypical, they are not inherently pathological. It seems, then, that medical ideology has retained the theme of morality but has done so in seemingly apolitical terms. The sex addict diagnosis codifies prevailing erotic values as health (Levine and Troiden 1988). This move privileges a certain style of sexual expression while marginalizing others. Indeed, the sex addict diagnostic guidelines read like a description of a dangerous sexual citizen. The construction of sexual activities not oriented toward coitus, polyamorous relationships, and non-relational, pleasure-based sex as illness ends political debate on these matters before it begins.

Sexual disorders or disorderly sex?

Medicalized sex is not necessarily the enemy of pleasure. As Rachel Maines (1999: 3) documents regarding the preferred treatment of hysteria: "Massage to orgasm of female patients was a staple of medical practice among some (but certainly not all) Western physicians from the time of Hippocrates until the 1920s." This example is titillating, of course. It is also instructive: it points to the necessity of separating the therapeutic professional's *intent* from the potentially repressive *effects* of therapeutic intervention, and to the importance of viewing both in the context of cultural understandings of sex and eroticism. The clinical phenomenon of "hysterical paroxysm" certainly looks now to be orgasm. But in a cultural moment that understood vaginal penetration as necessary for "sex" to occur it was seen instead as the climax of illness. Just as the physician treating the hysterical patient did not necessarily intend to incite his patient's pleasure, contemporary helping professionals may not intend to restrict the sexual freedom of their patient-clients.

Medical-therapeutic sexual regulation works at the cultural level via a normalizing dynamic that constructs a limited range of sexual activity as healthy, natural, normal sex. Medical-therapeutic regulation also works repressively directly on individuals, limiting their sexual choices and/or serving as justification for coercive "therapeutic" responses to non-normative sexual variation. Both dynamics and more are apparent in the sexual disorders just discussed. Erectile dysfunction illustrates the strait-jacket that is the medical model of sex. It also shows the chameleon-like nature of medical social control; therapeutic response to a sexual problem can simultaneously enhance and reduce pleasure. GID demonstrates how medical constructions of "normality" at the cultural level intertwine with the individual level; the enforcement of normal gender on individuals reinforces the cultural concepts of gender that the naturalness of heterosexuality is built on. Together, ED and GID show that one need not be diagnosed to have one's sexuality regulated by medical-therapeutic approaches. Finally, much like the female hypersexual diagnosis, sexual addiction/compulsion demonstrates the political danger that arises when illness categories embody prevailing erotic ideals. At such times sexual disorder can be wielded as a "baton" to force erotically unconventional individuals to adhere to sexual norms (Levine and Troiden 1988). Perhaps then, rather than speaking of sexual *disorders* – a term that suggests objective disease and dysfunction – we could more accurately speak of *disorderly* sex: sex that is socially disruptive, sex that disturbs the dominant cultural sexual ideal.

As individuals attempt to negotiate or realize increased sexual freedom, by seeking, for example, to engage in consensual but non-normative sexual acts, to form atypical sexual partnerships, or to increase their sexual activity outside of prevailing cultural standards of frequency or duration, we would do well to keep in mind something we might call "Oliver's predicament." Oliver Twist's simple request – "Please, sir, may I have some *more*?" – is an illustrative instance of appetite exceeding the capacity (or *willingness*?) of those in charge to satisfy desire. Like Oliver, individuals often stand vulnerable and alone, looking upward meekly into the face of more powerful persons or social forces such as widespread public support for a cultural sexual ideal (for example, monogamy) and/or for medical diagnosis as abnormal (for example, sex addict) of those who violate such ideals. In comparison to credentialed medical-therapeutic "experts," individual "perverts" lack credibility to speak on their own behalf – to argue, for example, that while their choices may be different that does not make them "sick." And even if allowed to so speak, experts who know better may deem the simple request for "more" to be evidence of the pervert's pathology. Moreover, culturally defined sexual ideals regarding valid forms of sexual activity and relationship are institutionally supported (defining marriage as the union of two rather than three persons, for example); such institutionalization confers legitimacy, value, and power such that questioning or challenging the norm seems to threaten disorder.

Medical diagnoses may be preferable when other definitional options include depravity (you sinner! you freak!) or personal moral failing (how *could* you?). But medical neutrality is false neutrality given the negative social judgment that is illness (Irvine 2005; Conrad and Schneider 1992). The helping ethos and humanitarian ideal of medicine may obfuscate but does not negate the reality that therapeutic intervention in sexual matters has disciplinary effects. Disease categories are forms of power that enshrine and enforce prevailing sexual standards in the name of sexual health. Disorders of desire are thus as much about the *social* body as they are about the corporeal one. Medical-therapeutic discourse, though, disguises the ways in which the personal has always been political when it comes to sex.

Note

1   This work was supported in part by NIMH Grant T32MH19996, and benefited from many stimulating discussions with Kim Greenwell.

References

Conrad, Peter, and Joseph Schneider. 1992. *Deviance and Medicalization: From Badness to Sickness*. Philadelphia, PA: Temple University Press.

Foucault, Michel. 1990 [1978]. *The History of Sexuality*. New York: Vintage.

Irvine, Janice. 2005. *Disorders of Desire* (2nd edn). Philadelphia, PA: Temple University Press.

Levine, Martin P. and Richard R. Troiden. 1988. "The myth of sexual compulsivity." *Journal of Sex Research* 25, 3: 347–63.

Loe, Meika. 2004. *The Rise of Viagra: How the Little Blue Pill Changed Sex in America*. New York: NYU Press.

Maines, Rachel P. 1999. *The Technology of Orgasm: "Hysteria," the Vibrator, and Women's Sexual Satisfaction*. Baltimore, MD: Johns Hopkins University Press.

McGann, P. J. 1999. "Skirting the gender normal divide: a tomboy life story." In Mary Romero and Abigail J. Stewart (eds), *Women's Untold Stories: Breaking Silence, Talking Back, Voicing Complexity*. New York: Routledge.

Rubin, Gayle S. 1993. "Thinking sex." In Henry Abelove, Michele Aina Barale, and David M. Halperin (eds), *The Lesbian and Gay Studies Reader*. New York: Routledge.

Seidman, Steven. 2002. *Beyond the Closet: The Transformation of Gay and Lesbian Life*. New York: Routledge.

Tieffer, Leonore. 1995. *Sex is Not a Natural Act and Other Essays*. Oxford: Westview Press.

chapter 61

Sex and power

Kristen Barber

Many of us do not question the popular ideology that views sex as natural. Yet, for the purpose of this chapter, I ask that the reader temporarily put aside the assumption of sex as natural and view sex rather as a social construct in order to explore sex as it relates to social power. In this chapter, I discuss the way some feminists have thought about the link between gender, sexuality, and power.

Heterosexuality and power

In the 1980s, Andrea Dworkin and Catherine MacKinnon argued that hetero-sex is a mechanism by which men dominate women. MacKinnon (1989) argues that, in order to understand the subordination of women in the United States, one *must* analyze the practice of heterosexuality. Dworkin and MacKinnon assert that, in America and elsewhere, sex is about male dominance and female subordination. In *Intercourse* (1987), Dworkin asks whether sex is a loving, intimate act between two mutually consenting people, or if it is the display of male social, political, psychological, and economic dominance over women.

Dworkin and MacKinnon argue that the expression of masculine traits such as aggression, power, and violence during sex shapes the meaning of sexuality for both men and women. In America, men define what sex is, and they have defined it in terms of men's dominance and women's submission. Dworkin and MacKinnon claim that women then come to understand their role within hetero-sex as passive and accommodating. Dworkin claims that women are expected to say "yes" to sex because they are expected to be compliant and to fulfill the man's "implicit right" to get laid regardless of the woman's desires. She suggests that women learn to view sex in a way that reflects men's desires and wishes.

There are, however, feminist critics. Pat Califia (1994) agrees that we live in a society where power and privilege lie within the hands of men. She also feels that patriarchy controls women and limits their freedom. However, she does not believe that heterosexual sex is only about power and women's lack of it. This perspective reinforces an image of women solely as victims. Califia argues that under conditions of male dominance women's sexuality is limited. Women may have less freedom to explore, discover, and play with their own desires and pleasures, but they are not completely powerless.

Instead of viewing sex as dangerous for women, as just another area where men control them, Califia affirms sex as necessary for women's sexual liberation. She argues that women need to explore their own desires and sexualities and fully embrace sexual variety, so long as it is between adults and consensual.

In this regard, Califia defends sadomasochistic sex, which involves eroticizing power in a consensual sexual exchange. For Dworkin, women who participate in masochism are traitors, self-haters, who are socialized into wanting to be helpless and assaulted. Califia argues that sadomasochism is usually understood, among those involved, as an intimate act between two mutually consenting people who come together to experience intense sexual pleasure. "Vanilla people send flowers, poetry, or candy, or they exchange rings. An S/M person does all that and may also lick boots, wear a locked collar, or build her loved one a rack in the basement" (Califia 1994: 177).

Califia argues that sadomasochism is not about dominance, but rather about using power for sexual pleasure. She says that this is because the relationship between the individual who plays the dominant role and the one who plays the submissive role is freely chosen by the individuals depending on their erotic preferences. The roles are negotiated and the power is understood as play, enacted through role playing. "Hardly instruments of the sexual repression of women, fetish costumes [including leather, rubber, and spiked heels] can provide women who wear them with sexual pleasure and power" (Califia 1994: 176).

Pornography: gender domination or sexual liberation?

Pornography has also spurred much debate among feminists. Some feminists reject pornography because they feel that it is an expression of men's power over women; other feminists find in porn a potential avenue by which women may learn to be more sexually open and assertive.

Dworkin (1981) criticizes pornography because she believes it teaches men and women "gender appropriate" sex which reinforces women's oppression. She claims that male power is the chief theme throughout pornography. She defines pornographic sex as women being humiliated, beaten, hung, having objects shoved up their vaginas, killed; all of which are supposed to illicit sexual arousal from the male consumer. Dworkin asserts that the force depicted in pornography is real because it is used against women. She argues that men form their understanding of sexuality and of women through their consumption of pornography. Pornography may depict a woman smiling as she is being raped. Thus, as feminist Susan Cole (1995) points out, men learn that women have uncontrollable sexual urges and enjoy being dominated and humiliated.

Critics of Dworkin do not deny that some porn is hateful toward women. However, they argue that much pornography offers images that encourage women to explore and enhance their sexuality and erotic freedom. Another feminist, Drucilla Cornell (2000), agrees that women need both to view images of sexually active women and to explore their bodies and desires. She suggests that pornography has the potential to prompt women to play with sex and can create an image of a healthy, unconstrained female sexuality.

Cornell refers to the pornography-producer Candida Royalle as creating a form of feminism that encourages women to explore their sexuality. Royalle (2000), traditional porn actress turned feminist porn-producer, produces films that are not sexist and are meant to be enjoyed by women and couples alike. She aims to create pornography that is enriching. Royalle claims that anti-porn feminists tend to associate good sex for women with romantic or vanilla sex. She argues that this keeps women from exploring and expressing their sense of sexual and sensual power. Royalle argues against the assumption that women want delicate sex. Instead, she contends that her pornography creates a safe place for women to play with power and erotic variety. She says that women have power if they are able and encouraged to control their own fantasies, even if their fantasies are of rape and being dominated.

Royalle is critical of much pornography to the extent that it is defined by genital sex and cum shots. Rather, she expands pornography for women to encompass the entire body as an erogenous zone. She encourages women and couples to sexually explore their entire bodies, expanding their understanding of what is sexy.

Califia criticizes some feminists for being prudish and uptight about sex. She is especially critical of anti-porn activists such as Women Against Violence in Pornography and Media (WAVPM) who have tried to censor pornography. Censoring sexual material, Califia argues, hurts women and all sexual minorities such as lesbians. By censoring sexual material, it will become more difficult to talk about issues such as birth control, safe sex, and pregnancy. Further, censorship laws will make it possible to remove educational materials that encourage women to get in touch with their bodies, selves, and desires. In short, Califia believes that stigmatizing pornography reinforces the ambivalent and negative feelings many women already have about sex.

Rape and state-sponsored sexual terrorism

While hetero-sex and pornography may be morally and politically debatable because they involve both power and consent, sexual violence such as rape stands in stark contrast. Even further removed is rape as state-sponsored sexual terrorism. Unlike an individual man having sex or consuming pornography, soldiers are not acting as individuals. Rather, they are agents of the state who participate in sex acts that are not consensual, but coerced and violent.

R. W. Connell (1995) suggests that sexual violence is part of what it means to be a "real" man in Western society. Men are believed to be uncontrollably aggressive and sexual. Society therefore has a tendency to understand rape as a natural consequence of men's uncontrollable sexual desires and natural tendency toward violence.

In any event, many sociologists have shown that men, as the dominant gender, use violence as a means to obtain and sustain power over women, and sometimes over other men. Men also sustain their dominance by using sex to intimidate women.

This can include anything from catcalls on the street to rape. Given the social privilege of masculinity, such sexual abusers feel that it is their right to exercise power over women, because they are "authorized by an ideology of supremacy" (Connell 1995: 83).

In *Race, Ethnicity, and Sexuality: Intimate Intersections, Forbidden Frontiers* (2003), Joane Nagel explores rape as an important aspect of war. She argues that sexual assault is a means of obtaining power and a way to humiliate and victimize the enemy. The use of sex as power is especially prominent during wars between ethnic groups. Military men often use sex in order to exercise power over men of an opposing ethnicity. For example, in the former Yugoslavia in the 1990s, the Serbs exercised power over Croatian and Bosnian men by having them castrated.

However, it is women who are typically the focus of sexual violence during wars of ethnic conflicts. Militaries often set up camps that they fill with local enemy women whom they refer to as "comfort" women. These women are at the disposal of the soldiers as sexual servants. During war, women are involuntarily rounded up and given to soldiers as rewards. They become sex slaves. Nagel states that the sexual worth of the women is based on their class and ethnicity. For example, the Japanese, during World War Two, forced 200,000 women into camps. Most of these women were of the lower class. The Korean and other Asian women were given to low-ranking soldiers. The Japanese and European women (often Dutch), however, were reserved for the high-ranking Japanese officers.

Nagel points out that, in times of war, it is not power over the *woman* that is the ultimate goal of rape. Rather, ethnically different enemy women are raped and sexually assaulted in order for *men* to exercise power and dominance over one another. She argues that, ultimately, the raping of the enemy's women is used to intimidate, humiliate, and dominate the enemy men.

Rape as a war tactic can further be understood as psychologically degrading the enemy. Since women often stand as a symbol of nationality (take the Statue of Liberty, for example), Nagel posits that sexually assaulting a woman pollutes not only her and her family, but also her entire nation.

> The logic of rape in war is always the same: rapes are committed by both sides for the familiar time-honored reasons . . . to terrorize and humiliate the enemy, and as a means of creating solidarity and protection through mutual guilt among small groups of soldiers.
>
> (Nagel 2003: 153)

Nagel goes on to say that raping the enemy women also serves as a technique of ethnic cleansing. For example, Serbian men raped Croatian women in order to impregnate them so that the women would give birth to Serbian babies. Often these women were gang-raped. In order to ensure that these women would not have an abortion, the Serbian military set up concentration camps in which they would imprison women until they gave birth to the next generation of Serbs.

I want to underscore a key point here. Some governments breed and train their soldiers to be sexually violent and aggressive. The widespread social belief that men are aggressive, especially sexually aggressive, justifies and conceals the role of the government in promoting sexual violence. In fact, the government is in effect teaching soldiers that they should, as a matter of national loyalty, sexually violate enemy women.

References

Califia, Pat. 1994. *Public Sex: The Culture of Radical Sex.* San Francisco, CA: Cleis Press.

Cole, Susan G. 1995. *Power Surge: Sex Violence & Pornography.* Toronto: Second Story Press.

Connell, R. W. 1995. *Masculinities.* Berkeley: University of California Press.

Cornell, Drucilla. 2000. "Pornography's Temptation." In D. Cornell (ed.), *Feminism and Pornography.* New York: Oxford University Press.

Dworkin, Andrea. 1981. *Pornography: Men Possessing Women.* London: The Women's Press.

Dworkin, Andrea. 1987. *Intercourse.* New York: Free Press Paperbacks.

MacKinnon, Catherine A. 1989. *Toward a Feminist Theory of the State.* Harvard, MA: Harvard University Press.

Nagel, Joane. 2003. *Race, Ethnicity, and Sexuality: Intimate Intersections, Forbidden Frontiers.* New York: Oxford University Press.

Royalle, Candida. 2000. "Porn in the USA." In D. Cornell (ed.), *Feminism and Pornography.* New York: Oxford University Press.

Kristen Barber

PART 9

Sexual politics

Introduction

We live in a world where, at least in most countries, heterosexuality is the norm. In many nations, heterosexuality is not simply a sexual preference of the majority of people – it is an institutional force that organizes social life.

In a world where a narrow version of heterosexuality is institutionalized as the norm, individuals – nonheterosexual and heterosexual – sometimes become the target of social efforts to stigmatize and even criminalize their behavior or identity. A wide variety of social institutions – the law, the criminal justice system, education, the mass media, and so on – might be enlisted to control and punish specific sexualities. When this happens, individuals might organize to contest these forms of social discrimination or oppression. Sexual politics is about social conflict about which sexual desires, acts, identities, and relationships should be socially supported and which should be socially punished and repressed.

By far the best examples of sexual politics come from the lesbian and gay community. Since the 1950s, lesbian and gay people have been organized against the social institutions that have criminalized them and made them into second-class citizens in America and elsewhere. Gays and lesbians have fought discrimination in the workplace and housing. They have fought to have their sexuality de-criminalized. They have organized against homophobic depictions in the mass media. Especially during the 1980s and 1990s, gay people fought against homophobic laws and social policies that stigmatized and endangered gay people with AIDS. By far the most heated political challenges gays and lesbians have faced recently is on the front of marriage. Gays and lesbians have challenged marriage laws that exclude their relationships. They have also fought to challenge the limited definition of what constitutes a family. All of these battles – against the criminal justice system, marriage and family, the media, and public opinion – are examples of sexual politics.

Of course gays and lesbians are not the only people to have organized around sexual political issues. Although AIDS politics grew largely out of the gay community, many other people (especially people of color, and people in the developing world) are now organized to resist the discrimination people with AIDS face from pharmaceutical companies and world governments. Many people have protested against the way certain sexual images and ideas are censored by the government and mass media. Ida Craddock was a woman who was arrested for publishing sex education manuals in the early twentieth century. She and others protested against laws which the government used to define obscenity. Prostitutes and sex workers in recent years have organized to demand the legalization of prostitution, as well as social benefits like healthcare. These are all examples of sexual politics, too.

What about mainstream, ordinary, average heterosexuals – do they have sexual politics? The answer is yes, especially in America. In response to what they view as a permissive sexual culture, conservative heterosexuals have organized politically against divorce and homosexuality. As America and other places become more accepting of a wider variety of sexual expressions and lifestyles, defenders of a narrow, "traditional" version of heterosexuality have become increasingly outraged and vocal. The covenant marriage movement is one example. In a covenant marriage, heterosexuals promise not only to marry each other, but to abide by much more rigid rules should they decide to divorce. Heterosexuals have also organized to exclude gays from the right to marry. They have attempted to change sex education curricula, arguing that an "abstinence only" education promotes moral, healthy sexual behavior amongst youngsters. Most of these struggles have been articulated as a defense of "the traditional family" and "family values."

In this part of the book, we present a wide variety of examples of sexual politics – liberal, conservative, gay, straight, and otherwise. You'll learn about the various marriage battles, sex education, AIDS politics, the politics of sex workers and gender/sexual conflicts in America. You'll be treated to a really interesting discussion of the differences between gay and lesbian politics in the Netherlands and the US. There is also a fascinating interview about the politics of sex education with a leading scholar in the field. In all of these essays, you will see that sexual politics is simultaneously personal, cultural, and institutional.

chapter 62

The evolution of same-sex marriage politics in the U.S.

Kathleen E. Hull

The story of same-sex marriage in the United States has been one of bitter conflict followed by astonishingly rapid legal and cultural change. A little over a decade ago, the question of legal recognition for same-sex couples was an effective wedge issue in state and national politics, most prominently in the 2004 election. In that year, President George W. Bush used his State of the Union address to call for a federal constitutional amendment banning same-sex marriage. San Francisco Mayor Gavin Newsom responded by issuing marriage licenses from San Francisco City Hall, and 11 states approved state constitutional bans on same-sex marriage in the November general election, bringing the total number of states with constitutional or statutory prohibitions on same-sex marriage to 41. By contrast, only one state – Massachusetts – granted recognition to same-sex marriages (starting in May 2004), with a few other states recognizing marriage-like statuses such as civil unions and domestic partnerships. Poll after poll showed clear majority opposition to legal same-sex marriage. The federal Defense of Marriage Act (DOMA), denying federal recognition to same-sex marriages and affirming the rights of individual states to refuse to recognize same-sex marriages formed in other states, had been on the books since 1996.

Today the picture looks quite different. The U.S. Supreme Court's landmark ruling in *Obergefell v. Hodges* in June 2015 declared state-level bans on same-sex marriage unconstitutional, making marriage licenses available to same-sex couples nationwide. The *Obergefell* decision followed two Supreme Court rulings in 2013 that had repealed the section of DOMA denying federal recognition to same-sex marriages

(*United States v. Windsor*) and upheld the court-ordered recognition of same-sex marriage in California (*Hollingsworth v. Perry*). In the wake of those 2013 rulings, many states had seen their marriage bans ruled unconstitutional by state or federal courts, leading to same-sex marriage recognition in traditionally conservative states like Oklahoma, Utah, Wyoming, and Idaho. Other states had enacted same-sex marriage recognition legislatively, and by 2014 national polls consistently showed majority support for legal same-sex marriage.

How could such a momentous shift in laws and attitudes have occurred in such a short timeframe on such a controversial issue? Certainly the historical precedents are few. Consider, for example, the country's long, slow progress toward legal equality for women and racial minorities. A century elapsed between the end of slavery and the dismantling of legal racial segregation, as reflected in Jim Crow laws. For many decades after women secured the right to vote, they faced continuing legal disadvantage and discrimination. Or consider a hot-button social issue like abortion. Despite a 1973 Supreme Court ruling establishing women's right to obtain abortions under specified circumstances, more than four decades later Americans remain deeply divided on the issue, and many states continue to pass laws intended to severely curtail women's access to abortion services.

One of the enduring questions about social change is whether legal changes merely reflect changes in underlying social beliefs and practices, or whether laws sometimes stimulate changed viewpoints and behaviors. This is always a complicated question, and in reality most change probably occurs as an evolving interplay between laws and attitudes. But in the case of same-sex marriage in the American context, a strong case can be made that legal change has followed changes in attitudes, rather than the other way around. Although it is true that most Americans opposed legal same-sex marriage back in 2004, when Massachusetts became the first state to recognize it, it is also arguable that public attitudes shifted more quickly than the law in the decade that followed. Indeed, the shift in public opinion on this issue has been so rapid that it merits closer scrutiny. But before we look at the growing support for same-sex marriage, it is worth pausing to review why this has been such a challenging issue for many straight people, and also why many lesbian, gay, bisexual and transgender (LGBT) people have themselves questioned the desirability of marriage and the priority attached to the same-sex marriage issue by the LGBT rights movement.

Opposition to same-sex marriage: strange bedfellows

By now most Americans have been exposed to many of the conservative arguments against same-sex marriage. In broad terms, these arguments focus on the impact of same-sex marriage on the institution of (opposite-sex) marriage, and on the consequences for children. Some opponents contend that same-sex marriage violates the very definition of marriage, as dictated by nature, tradition, or religion. Some arguments against same-sex marriage boil down to the assertion that homosexuality itself is unnatural or immoral, although other opponents have asserted that they are not anti-gay but marriage is an inherently heterosexual institution, and thus for same-sex couples to seek inclusion is a claim to "special rights." A related argument has pointed to majority opposition to legal same-sex marriage, noting that in a democratic system the majority's will should prevail (although this line of argument is now problematic as majority sentiment swings in the other direction, at least at the national level). Finally, some opponents argue that same-sex marriage recognition harms children, in two ways: by making opposite-sex marriage less desirable and stable (and therefore increasing the risk that children of heterosexual couples will grow up without two married parents), and by encouraging same-sex couples to become parents, which is presumed to have negative impacts on their children. Over time, there has been a shift away from arguments that are primarily based on the immorality or unnatural-ness of homosexuality and same-sex marriage, and toward arguments focused on the impacts on children. This shift probably resulted from opponents' realistic assess-ment of which arguments were potentially most persuasive to those judges and unde-cided voters who wanted to distance themselves from charges of anti-gay bigotry.

Social science expertise has been most visible in same-sex marriage debates on this very question of the impacts on children. Both sides in legal cases have called social scientists as expert witnesses, or bolstered their cases with amicus curiae (friend of the court) briefs from social scientists, to make evidence-based arguments about child impacts. Opponents have referenced a substantial body of research sug-gesting that children raised by two married biological parents do better on a range of outcomes than kids raised in other family structures. However, almost all of this research draws comparisons with family structures such as single parents and step-families rather than with families headed by same-sex couples. A number of profes-sional organizations submitted amicus briefs for the recent Supreme Court marriage cases summarizing the limited research on children raised by same-sex couples or gay/lesbian parents; such studies consistently find a lack of evidence that children are harmed or disadvantaged by same-sex or gay/lesbian parenting. For one good exam-ple, see the brief filed by the American Sociological Association in the *Obergefell* case (American Sociological Association 2015).

The conservative arguments against same-sex marriage have been highly visible in public debates and media coverage on same-sex marriage, but many Americans have had less exposure to LGBT voices opposing same-sex marriage. Yet these voices exist, and the so-called intra-community debate among LGBT activists and commen-tators has raged for decades. LGBT critiques of same-sex marriage – as a cultural ideal or political goal – have their roots in the gay liberationist, lesbian-feminist, and queer movements (Bernstein and Taylor 2013). Gay liberationism, which emerged in the late 1960s but was eclipsed by the gay rights framework by the mid-1970s, was a radical political perspective emphasizing the importance of sexual freedom and chal-lenging dominant cultural norms concerning gender and sexuality. For gay liberation-ists, marriage represented a stifling, straight institution characterized by sexual control and rigid roles, the antithesis of liberationist thinking on sexuality and rela-tionships. In roughly the same time period, lesbian-feminist voices within sec-ond-wave feminism decried marriage as an inherently patriarchal and oppressive institution; they saw marriage as central to women's ongoing subordination and thus an institution that should be abolished rather than expanded to include same-sex couples. More recently, queer activists and scholars have reiterated many of the core liberationist and feminist critiques, rejecting the goal of same-sex marriage as assimilationist and normalizing. Queer critics have also argued that legal same-sex marriage will create new forms of inequality among LGBT people, rewarding those who most closely approximate heteronormative models of relationship, and will privatize and depoliticize queer identities and communities.

However, it is not clear how much traction the critiques of marriage articulated by prominent LGBT activists and scholars have had among ordinary, non-activist LGBT Americans. A recent random-sample survey of LGBT adults found that 93 percent thought that same-sex couples should be allowed to marry (with 74 percent "strongly" favoring it) and 58 percent thought that marriage should be the top priority for the LGBT rights movement (Pew Research Center 2013a). In the Minnesota Close Relationships Study, an interview-based study of 105 LGBT respondents in the Minneapolis-St. Paul metro area, my co-author and I found nearly universal support for legal same-sex marriage, and a majority of our respondents identified marriage and family issues as a top priority for the LGBT rights movement (Hull and Ortyl 2013). Transgender respondents and queer-identified respondents were somewhat less likely to support the movement's work on same-sex marriage, but there were no clear differences in our sample by race/ethnicity or social class. But I have also found that support for legal recognition of same-sex marriage does not necessarily signal broadly pro-marriage views or a personal aspiration to get married (Hull 2014a). Many of the respondents in the Minnesota study favored legal same-sex marriage as a matter of principle, but had more ambiguous feelings about the institution of marriage or its suitability for same-sex couples. So LGBT critiques of marriage rooted in gay liberationist, feminist and queer perspectives may have fostered more critical or questioning views of marriage in the LGBT population, even if these critiques have not undermined support for the political goal of legal recognition.

Conservative and feminist/queer opponents of same-sex marriage certainly make strange bedfellows. Whereas conservative arguments against same-sex marriage have mostly been rooted in a reverence for the institution of (opposite-sex) marriage and a desire to shield it from the corrupting influence of same-sex relationships, the feminist and queer opponents of same-sex marriage ground their arguments in a negative view of marriage as an outmoded social institution that fosters inequality, conformity and sexual repression. Despite these differences, these critics of same-sex marriage do appear to share the destiny of irrelevance as same-sex marriage takes root as the law of the land and finds growing acceptance among the American population.

Public attitudes: from opposition to acceptance

American public opinion has shifted swiftly and dramatically toward support for same-sex marriage over the last two decades. The Gallup organization has been surveying American attitudes on same-sex marriage since 1996, the year Congress passed the Defense of Marriage Act. Figure 62.1 presents the trends in response to a question about whether "marriages between same-sex couples should or should not be recognized by the law as valid, with the same rights as traditional marriages" (McCarthy 2014). Back in 1996, more than two-thirds of Americans believed such marriages

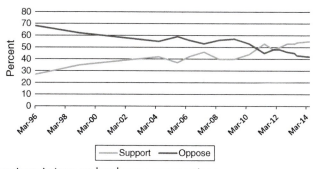

Figure 62.1 Americans' views on legal same-sex marriage.
Source: Gallup.

should not be valid, with just over a quarter supporting their recognition. The gap between opposition and support narrowed over time, with support for legal same-sex marriage climbing above 50 percent for the first time in spring 2011. After falling slightly in late 2011, the percentage of Americans supporting same-sex marriage has held at 50 percent or higher in Gallup polling since May 2012 (see Figure 62.1). Of course, these national data do mask regional variations. For example, in a May 2014 poll, two-thirds of Americans living in the East region supported same-sex marriage, compared to less than half in the South (McCarthy 2014).

I have argued that several factors have contributed to the growth in support for same-sex marriage (Hull 2014b). One is what social scientists call a cohort effect. As older people with particular worldviews die out of the U.S. population, they are replaced by younger cohorts of adults with different viewpoints on issues. In the case of same-sex marriage, older Americans have typically expressed greater opposition compared to younger people, so the cohort effect over time leads to gradual increases in support for legal same-sex marriage. A recent study examined the reasons underlying these generational differences in views on same-sex marriage (Hart-Brinson 2014). This study notes that Americans born before 1964 came of age in an era when homosexuality was viewed as a mental illness or a deviant lifestyle. These stigmatizing understandings of gayness probably stuck in the minds of many older Americans, even if they were more liberal on other issues. By contrast, the youngest American adults, those born since 1978, came of age in a time when homosexuality was viewed as a collective identity, akin to race or gender. With a less negative lens for viewing homosexuality, younger people developed more accepting attitudes about same-sex marriage. Of course, not everyone in the same age cohort holds the same views, on marriage or any other issue, so this cohort effect refers to broad trends in beliefs across generations.

Cohort effects usually happen quite gradually, and indeed the cohort effect alone is not sufficient to account for the kind of rapid attitude change captured in Figure 62.1. Recent survey findings from the Pew Research Center indicate that people *within* age cohorts are also changing their minds on the marriage issue. Historical data show support for same-sex marriage rising within every age cohort over the last decade, and more than a quarter of Americans who now support same-sex marriage told Pew their views on the issue have changed (Pew Research Center 2013b). These individuals cited a variety of factors that caused them to rethink the issue, including knowing someone who is gay or lesbian, thinking about the issue more, getting older, becoming more open, or seeing same-sex marriage as an inevitability. I have argued that at least two other factors are probably in play: the growing cultural visibility of homosexuality and same-sex relationships, and the spreading reality of legal same-sex marriage in the U.S. and abroad.

There has been a remarkable increase in the visibility of LGBT people, and same-sex relationships, in American popular culture. Today many tv shows and movies feature LGBT characters or serious same-sex relationships, and this cultural inclusion no longer inspires the kind of backlash it once did. (Back in 1997, when comedian Ellen DeGeneres came out, both as herself and as the lead character on her tv sitcom, her decision to do so was bold enough to land her on the cover of *TIME* magazine, and several tv stations refused to air the coming-out episode of her show.) Gay-themed movies and shows are no longer seen as remarkable, and some of the most prominent (and profitable) entertainers of recent years have been outspoken advocates for LGBT rights. This kind of cultural visibility chips away at some Americans' ignorance and discomfort regarding LGBT people and same-sex relationships. Likewise, many Americans probably noticed that the advent of legal same-sex marriage in multiple U.S. states, as well as countries around the world, did not produce the dire consequences predicted by its most vociferous opponents. The simple reality of legal same-sex marriage in more and more jurisdictions had a desensitizing effect over time; the idea of two men or two women getting married became less strange, and therefore less frightening.

Looking ahead: will same-sex couples change marriage, or vice versa?

The 2015 *Obergefell* ruling probably settled the legal question of same-sex marriage for good, but the future of marriage as a social institution is difficult to predict. Some observers expect the inclusion of same-sex relationships to forever alter the institution of marriage. Social conservatives predict same-sex marriage will make marriage less desirable for opposite-sex couples, with negative impacts on marriage rates and thus on children denied the opportunity to be raised by married parents. Conservatives also argue that same-sex couples will fundamentally alter the cultural norms of marriage, for example by practicing sexual non-monogamy within marriage, further weakening the institution. Queer critics, by contrast, fear that co-optation of same-sex couples into marriage will actually strengthen marriage and make it more difficult to dismantle an institution that privileges some forms of relationship over others. On the positive side, some supporters of same-sex marriage predict it will lead to more egalitarian relationships for all married people, as same-sex couples model relationships freed from constricting gender roles and inequalities.

But perhaps the arrow of change will point mostly in the opposite direction, with the institution of marriage changing same-sex couples more than they change it. Queer critics warn that same-sex marriage will lead to the assimilation and de-politicization of conforming same-sex couples. Some wonder whether the highly gendered nature of marriage as a cultural form will cause same-sex couples to gravitate to stereotypical roles and thus less egalitarian relationships. And some conservatives, including prominent gay conservatives like Andrew Sullivan and Jonathan Rauch, hope that marriage will encourage gay men in particular to abandon practices of sexual promiscuity in favor of a settled life of stable, long-term relationships.

Whether any of these specific predictions prove accurate, it seems safe to assume that legal same-sex marriage will have both practical and symbolic benefits for same-sex couples who choose to marry, increasing their economic and emotional security, their legal control over their affairs, and their legitimacy in the eyes of some family and friends as well as the broader society. Indeed, some of the early studies of same-sex couples who have gotten legally married in the U.S. and Canada find the spouses reporting these sorts of impacts (Green 2013; Kimport 2014; Lannutti 2011; Richman 2014). It is not hard to imagine that such benefits might also translate into more stable and satisfying relationships for many of these couples in the long run.

The issue of same-sex marriage has played out in the context of broader changes in American marriage. Social scientists are beginning to talk about a "retreat from marriage" in the U.S., characterized by lower marriage rates, the decoupling of marriage and child-bearing, and a cultural shift from viewing marriage as a taken-for-granted aspect of adulthood to one lifestyle option among many. Marriage trends are contributing to increasing inequality in several ways. College-educated people are still marrying at high rates, and their marriages are relatively stable, but people with lower levels of education and income (who are also disproportionately people of color) are increasingly bypassing marriage, viewing it as a luxury good that is beyond their financial reach or as an outdated institution with little to offer. In addition, marital homogamy has been rising, meaning that people are more likely to choose spouses from similar social backgrounds. Fewer marriages crossing class lines also contributes to rising inequality. We appear to be moving toward a two-tier system, in which people of higher socioeconomic status continue to avail themselves of the material and symbolic benefits of marriage while people lower on the socioeconomic ladder increasingly view marriage as optional, unattainable, or irrelevant. When future historians of American marriage look back at the early decades of the 21st century, they may view these trends, rather than the arrival of same-sex marriage, as the most sociologically significant changes in the institution of marriage.

References

American Sociological Association. 2015. "Brief of *Amicus Curiae* American Sociological Association in Support of Petitioners." Retrieved September 4, 2015 (www.asanet.org/documents/ASA/pdfs/ASA_March_2015_Supreme_Court_Marriage_Equality_Amicus_Brief.pdf).

Bernstein, Mary and Verta Taylor. 2013. "Marital Discord: Understanding the Contested Place of Marriage in the Lesbian and Gay Movement." In *The Marrying Kind? Debating Same-Sex Marriage within the Lesbian and Gay Movement*, edited by Mary Bernstein and Verta Taylor. Minneapolis: University of Minnesota Press.

Green, Adam Isaiah. 2013. "Debating Same-Sex Marriage: Lesbian and Gay Spouses Speak to the Literature." In *The Marrying Kind? Debating Same-Sex Marriage within the Lesbian and Gay Movement*, edited by Mary Bernstein and Verta Taylor. Minneapolis: University of Minnesota Press.

Hart-Brinson, Peter. 2014. "Discourse of Generations: The Influence of Cohort, Period and Ideology in Americans' Talk about Same-Sex Marriage." *American Journal of Cultural Sociology* 2(2): 221–252.

Hollingsworth v. Perry, 570 U. S. —. (2013). Available at: https://supreme.justia.com/cases/federal/us/570/12–144/ Accessed April 4, 2015.

Hull, Kathleen E. 2014a. "Same-Sex Marriage: Principle vs. Practice." Presented at the annual meeting of the Law and Society Association, May 29, Minneapolis, MN.

—. 2014b. "Same-Sex, Different Attitudes." Retrieved December 19, 2014 (http://thesocietypages.org/papers/same-sex-different-attitudes).

Hull, Kathleen E. and Timothy A. Ortyl. 2013. "Same-Sex Marriage and Constituent Perceptions of the LGBT Rights Movement." In *The Marrying Kind? Debating Same-Sex Marriage within the Lesbian and Gay Movement*, edited by Mary Bernstein and Verta Taylor. Minneapolis: University of Minnesota Press.

Kimport, Katrina. 2014. *Queering Marriage: Challenging Family Formation in the United States.* New Brunswick: Rutgers University Press.

Lannutti, Pamela J. 2011. "Security, Recognition, and Misgivings: Exploring Older Same-Sex Couples' Experiences of Legally Recognized Same-Sex Marriage." *Journal of Social and Personal Relationships* 28(1): 64–82.

McCarthy, Justin. 2014. "Same-Sex Marriage Support Reaches New High at 55%." Retrieved January 1, 2015 (www.gallup.com/poll/169640/sex-marriage-support-reaches-new-high.aspx).

Obergefell v. Hodges, 576 U.S. —. (2015). Available at: http://www.supremecourt.gov/opinions/14pdf/14-556_3204.pdf. Accessed Sept 4, 2015.

Pew Research Center. 2013a. *A Survey of LGBT Americans: Attitudes, Experiences and Values in Changing Times.* Washington, D.C.: Pew Research Center. Retrieved January 2, 2015 (www.pewsocialtrends.org/2013/06/13/a-survey-of-lgbt-americans/).

—. 2013b. *Growing Support for Gay Marriage: Changed Minds and Changing Demographics.* Washington, D.C.: Pew Research Center. Retrieved January 2, 2015 (www.people-press.org/2013/03/20/growing-support-for-gay-marriage-changed-minds-and-changing-demographics/).

Richman, Kimberly D. 2014. *License to Wed: What Legal Marriage Means to Same-Sex Couples.* New York and London: New York University Press.

United States v. Windsor, 570 U. S. —. (2013). Availale at http://www.supremecourt.gov/opinions/12pdf/12-307_6j37.pdf. Accessed April 4, 2015.

chapter 63

Gay men and lesbians in the Netherlands

Gert Hekma and Jan Willem Duyvendak

Since the 1970s the Netherlands can be regarded as one of the most liberal countries with regard to sexual politics. It transformed from a country that was strongly religious and conservative in sexual morals to one that is highly secular and liberal in affairs of sexual morality. Around 1970, the Dutch changed from positions that rejected divorce, pornography, prostitution, homosexuality, contraception, teenage sexuality to more liberal views on all these topics. The change of climate was followed by a change in laws. Divorce was made easier, pornography and prostitution were decriminalized and contraception was made generally available. The criminal law, containing different ages of consent for homosexual and heterosexual sex (21 versus 16 years), was changed; both were set at 16. Contraceptives were made available to all postpubescent women in the 1970s and became part of medical care provisions.

Amsterdam has known a vibrant gay culture since the 1950s and its Red Light District has become a major tourist attraction. In 1973, gays and lesbians were allowed to serve in the army. Marriage was opened for same-sex couples in 2001, the Netherlands being the first country to do so. Prostitution became legal in 2000. However, street prostitution is strictly controlled in the towns where it is permitted, and many city councils have forbidden it. The existing bordellos are regulated for reasons of safety, health, policing and taxing. Cities cannot outlaw them, as prostitution is regarded as normal labor.

Why exactly these changes took place in the Netherlands during the sixties and seventies is not entirely clear, but they have had such a tremendous impact. The liberal sexual culture of the Dutch is partly a result of a political culture that is based on the idea of the separation of state and church. Sexual affairs are viewed as the private business of Dutch citizens and should not be regulated by the state. The Dutch inherited this secular model of political culture from the French.

The sexual revolution of the 1960s had a powerful impact on the Netherlands. In part, this relates to a broad change that occurred in the Netherlands, the so called depillarization of society. Until the 1960s, the Netherlands had a type of social organization in which all citizens were members of a distinct community or "pillar" – Roman Catholic, Protestant or Humanist. These "pillars" were encompassing for the individual. For example, each had its own schools, church, media, political representatives, and culture. This community-based social order collapsed in the sixties as a result of increased social and spatial mobility, individualism, creeping secularism, and the rise of a national media. The two social groups (pillars) that had been most in favor of a strict sexual morality, the Catholics and the orthodox Reformed Calvinists, were influenced by psychiatrists and social workers to reconsider their sexual beliefs and values. In the course of the sixties, these religious orthodox groups relaxed their ideas of sexual morality. This change of opinion among the more orthodox groups made it easier for the majority of the population to support a liberal sexual morality.

Of course, the sixties also witnessed the rise of the youth, student and feminist movements that supported sexual choice and variation. The relative strength of the sexual reform movements, and the lack of resistance by religious and political authorities, resulted in a rather easy transition to a liberal sexual culture. Parallel to this development, Dutch society became highly secular (nowadays 50% of the population are non-believers) while the religious pillars and parties lost their predominant position. A fundamental value change occurred, resulting in the fact that since the 1980s the Dutch are among the most "post-materialist," liberal people of the world. There is a new, moral majority of a clear progressive signature.

The rise of a gay and lesbian movement

In 1969, psychiatrist Wijnand Sengers declared that homosexuality was not a pathological problem, but that homosexuals nevertheless could have psychological problems just like heterosexuals. His research concluded that he could not find one convincing case of a homosexual whose sexual orientation had been changed to heterosexual. It would be better to help homosexuals to adapt to their preferences and social situation, which included referring them to gay organizations. He was not the first to declare that homosexuality was not a disease, but this time his profession accepted this position. He set out to help homosexuals.

At the same time, priests and clergymen set out to tell the public that the homosexual should be accepted. There was still a discussion whether homosexuals should live a chaste life, but the general feeling among clergy was that they should be accepted. In 1971, the parliament decided to get rid of the only existing criminal law targeting homosexuals. Until the sixties homosexuality was generally considered to be a sin, crime, and disease and now, within 10 years, it was none of these things. This was a radical change.

These changes led to discussions in the gay and lesbian movement about their social and political goals. Generally, the movement favored the aim of social integration and acceptance. However, the Federation of Student Working Groups on Homosexuality and later the lesbian groups, Purple September and Lesbian Nation, and the

Gert Hekma and Jan Willem Duyvendak

male group Red Faggots, criticized integration as the chief goal of the movement. These more radical groups advocated that society be changed allowing for greater visibility and acceptance of sexual and gender variation. The issue of whether gays and lesbians should seek assimilation or social change remains a point of debate to this day. The heterosexual population may have embraced gays and lesbians in their roles as sons and daughters, and as comedians on television but, radicals argue, isn't Holland still overwhelmingly heterosexual?

Actually, a homosexual movement in Holland began as early as 1946, but it really took off in the sixties. Initially, the major organization was the Culture and Recreation Center, which, in 1964, became the Dutch Society for Homophiles COC and in 1971 Dutch Society for Integration of Homosexuality COC. It became a serious cultural and political force that attracted general attention. In 1967, the Schorer Foundation was established to provide psychological care for homosexuals. Before the AIDS crisis in the 1980s, the movement had already succeeded in becoming a part of society and the government. Gay and lesbian groups were established in political parties, trade unions, universities, the army and the police, medical care, and the churches. And, with the AIDS crisis, and its rippling effects throughout society, the government, medical authorities and representatives of the gay movement met and set up a committee that would prepare medical care, prevention activities and counseling. Gays and lesbians were becoming part of the government. Soon, the first openly gay politicians were elected and the agenda of gay rights was now on the agenda of the state.

Since the early eighties, the annual gay parade has moved from Amsterdam to other towns, following the logic that such a demonstration of gay and lesbian visibility was more important for people in the provinces. When it was held in 1982 in Amersfoort, centrally located on the Dutch Bible Belt, local youth attacked gays and lesbians and unprecedented violence broke out. It created uproar in Dutch media and politics and led to the enactment of gay and lesbian anti-discrimination policies on a local and national level. Soon there passed an Equal Rights Law (1993) that extended equal legal, social security, housing, pension, legacy, and asylum rights to gays and lesbians.

In many respects, AIDS proved a turning point. Cooperation between the gay and lesbian movement and local and national authorities took place. This cooperation followed the Dutch model of bringing representatives of "minority" groups or communities into the government with the aim of eliminating discrimination or establishing tolerance and equality. In this case, gays and lesbians were appointed to take responsibility for political decisions regarding AIDS and gay/lesbian rights. The system worked generally well, but raised dissenting voices. Nonetheless, openly gay men and lesbians were represented in various political bodies. Eleven of the 150 Dutch MPs (member of parliament) in 2000 were openly gay or lesbian. The question remains though what this type of political representation means for establishing real equality and acceptance.

Since the early 1980s a strong subculture – more for gays than for lesbians – developed: gay and lesbian sport clubs got for instance a strong stimulus from the Gay Games that were held in Amsterdam in 1998. In general, it was non-political groups that flourished, such as organizations for hikers, traditional dancers, lovers of old timers, book clubbers, and so on.

Same-sex marriage

When the issue of homosexuality and marriage first hit the Dutch media in 1968, it was estimated that about 90,000 homosexuals were in straight marriages. Although doctors had often advised homosexuals to marry to get rid of their homosexual desires, this strategy was seen as wrong from the late 1960s on. Marriage would not change sexual orientation and married homosexuals made their partners, children and themselves unhappy.

Through AIDS and the urgent medical problems it created, gay men had learned the importance of legal recognition for issues such as housing, social security, hospital visits, pensions, and inheritance. Although some social institutions and businesses offered something like domestic partnership benefits, these benefits did not include national rights and benefits. After several years of steady social and political pressure, "registered partnerships" were established for both same-sex and other-sex couples in 1997. Giving full marital rights was a step too far for the liberal-socialist government at that time. But three years later its successor administration decided to open up marriage for same-sex couples and give them the same rights as other-sex couples. The first marriages of gays and lesbians were celebrated in Amsterdam on April 1, 2001. The large majority of the population now supports gay marriage, and even the Christian Democratic Party, which initially opposed the law, now accepts it and has even an openly gay married man as MP.

The question of identity and politics today

When it comes to identity, most gays and lesbians in the Netherlands prefer to keep it low key. They will often say, "my homosexuality is just one part of my personality." However, the attention in the media to critical pronouncements by imams on homosexuality, and a growing awareness of antigay violence, especially among recent immigrant communities, makes it clear that homosexual emancipation is an ongoing project: legal change has not guaranteed social change. Some gays and lesbians will now be open and visible, while others decide to stay in the closet out of fear of consequences, for example, teachers.

The absence of strong sexual identities parallels the lack of spatially concentrated gay and lesbian communities. The bigger towns in the Netherlands have their "gay districts," mainly places where bars are located. These locations, however, are always used for other public functions as well. The Amsterdam leather district, for example, is in the Red Light District where English hooligans, tourists and the people who come for the world of prostitution sometimes mix uneasily with the leather men. Although many gay men live in the inner cities, they have not created "ghettos." This is difficult because housing associations and urban authorities distribute most housing in cities. Most Dutch gays and lesbians also have little inclination to live in exclusively gay or lesbian neighborhoods. The same holds true for social life. Partly as a result of Dutch tolerance, gay men and lesbians often choose to live in places that are gay-friendly. Also in the Netherlands gays and lesbians tend to migrate from places where they face intolerance and discrimination to places that are more gay-friendly. This lessens the

Gert Hekma and Jan Willem Duyvendak

necessity for them to create their own organizations. The main field of special socializing, apart from the world of bars, has become sport. Even in this sphere, most sports organizations will proudly declare that they welcome straight people.

Also, gays and lesbians are under pressure from straight people and the media not to create separate organizations because "we are so tolerant that you don't need them." This is the common line when gays and lesbians organize their own institutions and events, for example with the Gay Games in 1998. Since the decline of the time when the Dutch were organized into distinct communities (pillars), liberal and progressive Dutch have been critical of attempts to create separate communities by Muslims, ethnic minorities or homosexuals.

With the opening up of marriage for same-sex couples there are no provisions in civil or criminal law that discriminate against homosexuals. The legal fight for gay rights is effectively at an end. As a result, most Dutch citizens believe that homosexual emancipation is finished. They argue that there is no longer any need for a movement. But these legal changes have proved no guarantee for social acceptance of gays and lesbians. Several reports made clear that teachers have become less willing to come out of the closet and that gay men have to face verbal and physical abuse in certain urban neighborhoods, especially those with a high percentage of ethnic minorities. The self-congratulatory complacency that has become a landmark in Dutch discussions on homosexual emancipation appears to be unrealistic. Homosexuality is still a problem. Authorities such as school boards or policemen continue to refuse to defend gay and lesbian rights. Since the Gay Games, many straight and some gay people say that gays and lesbians should not be so open so as not to offend others. And, some people say, that given the availability of bars and discos and marital options for gays and lesbians, they don't need to flaunt their sexual expressions in public.

A chief source of conflict around homosexuality concerns the Muslim community. Keep in mind that about 10% of the Dutch population are recent immigrants. The major groups are Surinamese, Turks and Moroccans. Almost all of these immigrants are Muslim. Within the Muslim religious community homosexuality is condemned. The first ethnic party with a political program, the Arab-European League, has identified three main targets: prostitution, homosexuality and alcohol. Not only has the Muslim community challenged the Dutch culture of tolerance but it has made being gay very hard for Muslim individuals. Recently, they have established their own bars in Amsterdam. Gay Muslims also established a successful foundation "Yoesuf," which provides information on Islam and homosexuality, organizes workshops and offers social support.

Sexual attitudes now

The Dutch are highly ambivalent about the gains of the sexual revolution. They are citizens of the country that most profited from it, but often people complain that "we have gone too far" or "perhaps we should return to the morality of the fifties when Holland was a safe and pleasant country." Gay cruising areas have become controversial and as the public demands their closure, some city governments comply. Women who are "promiscuous" are still labeled "sluts." Erotic postcards, that staple of the

Amsterdam tourist industry, had to be removed from visible places on the streets after complaints of some tourists. At the same time, women prostitutes who are visible in Red Light Districts are spared criticism. The reputation of Amsterdam as a gay or sex capital is somewhat in decline. Tourist Information Boards are reluctant to provide the relevant information although half of the visitors to Amsterdam come for the Red Light District or gay venues. Notwithstanding all changes that have occurred in the field of moral politics, the Dutch continue to feel unease and ambivalence when it comes to the day-to-day concerns of sexuality.

Bibliography

Jan Willem Duyvendak, "The Depoliticization of the Dutch Identity, or Why Dutch Gays Aren't Queer", in: Steven Seidman (ed.), *Queer Theory/Sociology*, Cambridge, MA and Oxford, 1996, pp. 421–438.

—. "Identity Politics in France and the Netherlands: The Case of Gay and Lesbian Liberation", in: Mark Blasius (ed.), *Sexual Identities – Queer Politics*, Princeton, NJ and Oxford, 2001, pp. 56–72.

Gert Hekma, "Imams and Homosexuality. A Post-gay Debate in the Netherlands", in: *Sexualities* 5:2 (2002), pp. 269–280.

—. "How Libertine is the Netherlands? Exploring Contemporary Dutch Sexual Cultures", in: Elizabeth Bernstein and Laurie Schaffner (eds), *Regulating Sex: The Politics of Intimacy and Identity*, New York, 2005, pp. 209–224.

Judith Schuyf and André Krouwel, "The Dutch Lesbian and Gay Movement. The Politics of Accommodation", in: Barry D. Adam, Jan Willem Duyvendak and André Krouwel (eds), *The Global Emergence of Gay and Lesbian Politics*, Philadelphia, PA, 1999, pp. 158–183.

Steven Seidman, *Difference Troubles. Queering social theory and sexual politics*, Cambridge, 1997, Ch. 12.

van Naerssen, A.X. (ed.), *Gay Life in Dutch Society*, New York, 1987.

chapter 64

Queering the sexual and racial politics of urban revitalization

Donovan Lessard

If we look at the results of national surveys measuring societal acceptance of gays and lesbians, we get a rosy picture of increasing tolerance. For example, 48% of Americans in 2012 supported gay marriage, as opposed to 11% in 1988 (Smith and Son 2013). A 2013 poll even found that 52% of Republicans and conservative independents between ages 18 and 49 support same-sex marriage (Cohen 2013). Additionally, visibility and representations of gays and lesbians in US media have steadily increased from "almost no gay characters" before 1970 (Fisher et al. 2007) to 64 LGBT characters on scripted prime time television (Gay and Lesbian Alliance Against Defamation 2014). Gay marriage is now legal in the US. It appears that we have arrived in an unprecedented era of tolerance for gays and lesbians.

But is this the reality for all LGBTQ people? Are some LGBTQ groups accepted more than others, valued more? Which LGBTQ groups are less likely to be accepted? And how does that acceptance/intolerance manifest itself in urban space? Taking a spatial, intersectional approach complicates this notion of a queer golden age—a productive complication, in my opinion.

Sexuality, space, and intersectionality

Sexual identity does not exist in a spatial vacuum. This becomes especially evident when we look at the historical importance of how the establishment of gay neighborhoods in cities throughout North America created economic and political bases for gay identities and communities (Levine 1979; D'Emilio 1998; Knopp 1987; Castells 1983). Numerous gay and queer scholars and novelists have written about the role of "sites of male-centered sexual opportunity"—gay bars, parks, truck stops, bathhouses, and bookstores—in the formation of gay collective identity in the mid-20th century (Higgins 1999; Leap 1999; Chauncey 1994; White 1982). During the same period, lesbians also claimed space in urban centers through running and operating bookstores, coffee shops, and bars that created networks that enabled the development of a political identity, created a sense of community, and challenged heterosexism (Enke 2007).

Space is also important because it is where the actual operation of hierarchies and power relations take place. As opposed to an approach that is just focused on specific identities (gay/lesbian, Black, white, etc.) queer and feminist theorists who take a place-based approach to studying social movements and identity are able to see the operation of multiple identities and power relations and how they interact with each other on the ground and change over time; this is one of the strengths of a place-based approach. This is what is meant by an *intersectional analysis*—an analysis that considers the interplay of multiple identities, forms of power, and oppression, including race, ethnicity, sexuality, gender, and ability. This intersectional perspective is especially important when we begin to think about the current state of GLBTQ acceptance in communities around the United States.

Urban revitalization and GLBTQ communities

Following white flight from urban centers in the 1950s and 1960s, to deindustrialization in the 1970s and 1980s, and the recent foreclosure crisis, city planners, tourist agencies and real estate developers are strategizing ways to "revitalize" inner cities around the United States. Curiously, gays and lesbians are increasingly looked to as a niche market of "urban pioneers" who "turns neighborhoods around" (Murphy 2010; Manalansan 2005; Chasin 2001). "Urban pioneers" is a term used to describe the middle-class people who initially move into a working-class or poor neighborhood. Historically, these are people with middle-class cultural capital (high education attainment and middle-class origins) but lower income than their wealthier middle-class peers. Artists and students are two social groups that have historically been "urban pioneers." Another is middle-class, often white, gay people. For instance, Richard Florida, a well-known writer on the topic of urban revitalization and the "creative class," theorizes that higher proportions of gay couples and artists in a given area raise housing prices and regional income (Florida and Mellander 2007). Indeed, many researchers and theorists on urban revitalization have argued that gay populations are often "urban pioneers" who raise housing prices in poor neighborhoods (Castells 1983; Zukin 1995; Smith 1996).

But this begs several questions: *which* groups of gay people become valued citizens courted by developers as an expanding niche market and are hailed by urbanists as "adventurous creatives" who may bolster neighborhood housing values? In contrast, which gays and queers become labeled violent deviants thought to be jeopardizing neighborhood safety and well-being?

Donovan Lessard

In the summers of 2010 and 2011 I performed seven months of ethnographic research. I interviewed 35 GLBTQ activists, organizers, and frequenters of various queer spaces in Minneapolis, Minnesota. In this chapter, I argue that the gay people that urban studies scholars, city planners, developers, and many lay people hail as "urban pioneers" become visible as "gay" because of their class status and race. This is supported by my ethnography of Athena, a majority white queer art space in a neighborhood targeted for "urban revitalization." I then present the story of Minnemen, a majority GLBTQ youth of color space across town in a different neighborhood, a neighborhood experiencing urban blight. I describe how the poor and working-class GBLTQ youth of color of Minnemen experience disproportionate policing. In this way, they are unfairly rendered as indicators of "urban blight"; their claims to space vigorously opposed by local media, neighbors and police. It should be noted that both of Athena and Minnemen spaces are attempting to form underground, unlicensed spaces for the people who frequent them. Both are incredibly meaningful for those who frequent them. However, their differing class and racial make-up and differing neighborhoods lead to very different perceptions of their value to their neighborhoods by neighbors, media, police, and the city.

Reluctant queer arts "urban pioneers"

In the summers of 2010 and 2011 I helped organize, conduct, and clean up after events at a queer community arts center in Minneapolis called Athena. Athena is located on the second floor of an apartment building on Chicago Avenue, a busy thoroughfare two miles south of downtown Minneapolis that serves as the boundary between the Central and Powderhorn Park neighborhoods. At the time of this research, Athena did not have a mission, a board of directors, or any type of licensing with the city—it was a technically illegal, underground space. The rent for the space was generated through several art studio spaces used by artists during the day and through a wide breadth of events programming at night—ranging from foods swaps (which were shut down by the Food and Drug Administration shortly after this research was concluded), life-drawing classes, a feminist film series, and a particularly wild performance art and dance night called Divine. In interviews, many patrons emphasized the benefits that Athena's space had brought them, as a place for meeting other radical queers, creating a base of support in the face of increasing HIV infection rates, and dealing with gay bashings, among other things. The organizers of the space meet on a monthly basis and understand it to be an affinity space for queer community groups needing a place to meet and hold events. While there is a degree of diversity of age, race, and class amongst attendees of events, a common topic of conversation and concern was the overwhelming whiteness of Athena. The majority of those I interviewed from Athena were white, in their early 20s or 30s, and had attended at least some college.

Athena became located where it is largely because of the timing of their search for space, available money, and its central location. In 2010, when the organizers signed the lease on the space, the neighborhood was still relatively affordable for renters, with a median rental unit rate of US$844 a month. However, average housing values in the neighborhood have almost doubled, from US$118,150 in 2000 to US$203,543 in 2011. This rapid increase in housing values occurred in the latter part of the decade, following the conversion of a formerly empty catalogue distribution center into a mixed-income development with low-income rental housing, 50 shops, restaurants, and bars. Next to the converted factory a new transit hub has been put in, which allows for bus access to nearly every part of the city and many suburbs. New organic restaurants and coffee shops are opening at both the north and south ends of the neighborhood. Despite a poverty rate that still hovers around the 40% mark, the neighborhood is undergoing noticeable change as students, artists, and young professionals increasingly see the neighborhood as a place to live and socialize.

These changes are the actualization of a "Framework Plan" for "neighborhood revitalization" drafted in 2007 by neighborhood associations, the business council and adopted by the City Council in 2008 (Community Design Group 2007). The Plan calls for the repurposing of existing buildings for mixed-income housing, artist live-work studios, re-zoning for new development, reducing visible indicators of "blight" through strict enforcement of zoning and land use regulations, as well as increasing police presence and changing "perceptions of lack of safety in the project area."

Although the goal of these changes is to revitalize the neighborhood, it may also work in tandem with the beginning of the gentrification of the neighborhood. Gentrification is not a uniform process and varies according to the city and neighborhood it takes place within, but it typically includes middle- or upper-middle class people moving into formerly poor or working class neighborhoods, housing development corporations knocking down, rebuilding, and/or renovating the housing stock, and increasing housing values that can displace the poor or working-class residents of the neighborhood. The new organic coffee shops and restaurants and bicycle lanes in the neighborhood work as symbolic markers for the changes occurring in the neighborhood.

These changes are not lost on the organizers of Athena, and they strive to be a community institution that does not contribute to the changes in the neighborhood. However, that is challenging. For instance, Connor, a white queer man organizer in his late 30s at Athena, told me that at an early open house for the space a white woman "who positioned herself as a recent arrival" to the neighborhood walked up to him and told him "thank you for helping get the gangs out of the neighborhood." Connor says that he told her,

> You know, we're actually trying to keep a low profile, and we don't really necessarily want to change the composition of anything. Our goal is just to try to make the space work without having an intervention in the way that anyone else lives their life in the neighborhood.

He then said, "But of course that isn't possible."

This does not mean that the queers running the art space do not try, however. The organizers at Athena were very aware of the impact they *could* have on the neighborhood. For instance, Brian, a queer man in his early 30s, told me, "The people across the street . . . they're Latino and there are quite a few people living there. We don't want to have these blaring loud parties keeping them up—maybe they're undocumented and can't call the police." Early in the summer of 2010 someone donated air conditioning units to the space. At first glance, it seemed that this was for the benefit of the patrons of the space. However, Tim, a bearded, white queer man in his late 20s, told me that the A/C units were there to keep the windows shut so that the neighbors would not be bothered and the police would not come. Similarly, when a party in the summer of 2011 filled the space far over capacity, with people outside on the sidewalk, drinking and smoking cigarettes and talking loudly around midnight, the organizers of the event decided to shut it down and asked everyone to leave.

These vignettes illustrate how the queers of Athena are aware of and seek to avoid abusing their privilege or playing into the "urban pioneers" narrative that newly arriving, higher socioeconomic status residents (such as the one who thanked Connor for moving to the neighborhood), the police, and developers may ascribe to them. Despite their intentions, several structures of power interpret them as "urban pioneers" who are helping to "revitalize" the neighborhood.

Constructing Black queer space as a violent threat to neighborhood safety

Located about three miles east of Athena in a different neighborhood is the Minnemen space, an unlicensed, underground warehouse space that draws a mostly queer youth of color crowd. I first heard about Minnemen when I attended a "ball culture" primer event at a non-profit office building next door to Athena that hosts several non-profit organizations that serve trans people of color. Ball culture is a primarily youth of color subculture and balls usually consist of drag performers competing in several categories. I first saw Michael, an energetic Black gay man in his early 30s who runs the Minnemen space, speaking at a rally in defense of CeCe McDonald (a Black Minneapolis trans woman who defended herself against a white supremacist attacker, killing him in the process, and faced several years of prison). Michael began the space for the stated purpose of promoting "HIV and safe sex awareness in our GLBT community" and aiming to bring together "people of all colors, men and women between the ages of 15 to adult." Jillian, the head of a non-profit organization providing services to trans youth of color, told me that Minnemen is, "a good place to meet folks and just be making sure that flyers are being passed out, and folks know what else is happening in the community." The events typically include DJs, dancing and performing dancers and sometimes run into the early hours of the morning. The Minnemen space has become an important space of sociability for queer youth of color in Minneapolis, many of whom are homeless or have tentative housing situations and cannot afford to go to gay bars or clubs in downtown.

In the summer of 2011 Minnemen came under fire from neighbors, the police, and the city. In a sensationalistic article about Minnemen in *The Star Tribune* in September of 2011, the author wrote that a recent party was, "an alcohol-fueled orgy with male strippers." The article emphasizes the violence of the space, with McKinney (2011) writing that in six months prior to the article, "29 police calls were made to the building for loud music, fights and weapons." A (white) neighborhood resident is quoted as saying, "The neighborhood has been trying to stop them for six months now." A local city council member assures that, "city staff is pursuing every possible angle to deal with this illegal business."

Key to understanding the crackdown on Minnemen is an attention to the larger demographic and economic forces that are changing the neighborhood, dynamics that are quite different from the neighborhood that houses Athena. Census and American Community Survey data show that the neighborhood's median household income fell from US$40,390 (in 2010 inflation adjusted dollars) to US$37,382 from 2000 to 2010. Furthermore, whereas the neighborhood was only composed of 6% African Americans in 2000, in 2010 the neighborhood was 16% African Americans, with double and triple the percentages of Native Americans and Asians moving to the neighborhood by 2010, respectively. The disparities in poverty rates by race are stark: while 20% of whites in the neighborhood live below the poverty line, more than 60% of African Americans in the neighborhood are living below the poverty level. A wave of poor and working-class African Americans, perhaps displaced from other neighborhoods, had recently moved into this majority white working-to-middle class neighborhood. Minnemen, and the increasing visibility of Black and Brown bodies—especially at night—appears to be a lightning rod for anxieties that the predominantly white residents have about changes in their neighborhood. This has resulted in increased neighborhood and police surveillance, with the effect of criminalizing queer youth of color.

Race, sexuality, and urban revitalization

While Athena organizers actively try to avoid participating in potentially gentrifying the neighborhood (thus aiding developers or the police), they nonetheless benefit from their majority status of whiteness and their arts orientation. In the view of the police, other neighborhood residents, and the City government, their queerness, sexuality, and edgy performances can be folded into a freedom-of-the-arts and arts-as-urban-revival narratives that shield them from the types of repercussions that Minnemen faced. Similarly, even though they may not agree with being lumped in with actors and processes gentrifying the neighborhood, they sometimes are: this is especially evident from the response of the new arrival who thanked Connor for "helping to get the gangs out of the neighborhood."

Athena is contending with a history of white, middle- and upper-class gay people both actively and passively participating in gentrification and aiding police in purging poor people of color from neighborhoods—taming the supposed wild, forgotten inner-city for the manifest destiny of development, commerce, and "renewal." For instance, white gay activists actively participated in "neighborhood safety patrols" in New York and San Francisco in the 1970s and 1980s that originally began with the good intentions of protecting gay people from being bashed, but this quickly dovetailed with state and private developer interests to target poor people of color as threats to "public safety" in need of being "cleaned up" (Hanhardt 2013). Additionally, Manalansan (2005) documents how homeless queer youth of color in New York City have been systematically targeted for removal from the Christopher Street Pier, historically a "gay" haven, after high-end condominiums were built in the early 2000s. Interestingly, the piers were marketed heavily to gay and lesbian professionals.

Many of the same things that the media accused Minnemen of—overt sexual behavior, loudness, weapons—I had seen occur at Athena. I had seen creative performances that included nudity and an informed, queer vulgarity that was of a quality that could be at art museum events, art shows and theater festivals. I had observed people drinking illegally, loudly yelling at each other outside. I knew people that carried pepper spray, batons, or other self-defense weapons because they had been attacked before and needed to be able to defend themselves if it happened again. During the time of this research, the only police censure that Athena received was a warning issued to the landlord for posting a flyer for an event that advertised cheap alcohol.

Through a philosophical commitment and several practical measures to respect neighbors, Athena limited their exposure to neighbors and the police. However, this could only be done so much. There were times when over 50 people were on the sidewalk drinking, shouting, and smoking cigarettes and police drove by but did not stop. The same actions by Athena's mostly white patrons and Minneman's mostly Black and Latino patrons are viewed quite differently by police and neighbors. It seems likely that the race and class of these queer neighborhood organizations and how they interact with the demographic characteristics of the neighborhood shape the interpretation through larger narratives of neighborhood change (whether revitalization or decline).

Indeed, Athena is contending with a common urban ideology that represents "gay people" as middle- or upper middle-class, white people. These gay folk are the "urban pioneers" who supposedly help restore blighted neighborhoods. This urban ideology holds that blighted neighborhoods become rundown as a result of the irresponsibility of the poor people of color who lived there. It crucially ignores the many federal, state, and local policies that segregated people of color into specific urban neighborhoods and encouraged white flight into the suburbs after World War II, the practices of banks refusing to give housing loans to people of color in majority white neighborhoods throughout the 20th century (commonly referred to as "red lining"), and a century of failed public housing policies that concentrated Black poverty in inner cities.

Conclusions

City officials and police have a vested interest in claiming victory in the "renewal" of the inner-city, reductions in crime and increased perceptions of safety. The comparison of the situations of Athena and of Minnemen shows how neighborhood-level processes of urban revitalization and attendant demographic changes, along with city planning and policing objectives, lead to differential perceptions of the value of queerness to a neighborhood.

This case study also reveals the power of a space-based, intersectional lens in disentangling the complicated ways that race and class shape interpretations of sexuality and the differential experiences of GLBTQ groups, based on their race and class. The simplistic argument that "gays" raise housing values and propel gentrification relies on an extremely narrow, racialized and class-specific definition of "gays." Problematically, this narrow definition whitewashes gay identity with a middle-class sheen and renders GLBTQ people of color, working-class, and poor people—those more likely to be *displaced* by later phases of gentrification rather than propelling it—invisible. This exacerbates the already existing race and class divides between GLBTQ people and makes it even harder for these divides to be crossed, much less bridged.

Queer space matters. It matters because it gives GLBTQ people a place to be creative, to create art, to create new ways of doing gender and sexuality, to challenge heteronormativity, and to create friendships and families and share resources. I would venture to argue that queer space is even more important to social groups with less resources, such as the Black, young, working-class, poor, and homeless patrons of Minnemen. This is because they cannot afford access to many gay clubs and bars and they may be aggressively carded or kicked out of bars and clubs for using the "wrong" bathroom if they are trans. Even Athena is in a tenuous place: they are threatened by being priced out of their location as the value of the housing stock in their neighborhood rises. Through an intersectional lens, then, the common narrative that gay people raise housing values and propel gentrification (Florida and Mellander 2007) can be flipped. As gentrification renders many formerly affordable neighborhoods unaffordable and racialized policing heightens to sanitize these areas for middle-class consumption, the structural conditions for queer space evaporate. And the world becomes just that much less queer.

Bibliography

Castells, Manuel. 1983. "Cultural Identity, Sexual Liberation and Urban Structure: The Gay Community in San Francisco." In *The City and the Grassroots: A Cross-Cultural Theory of Urban Social Movements*, pp. 138–170. London: Edward Arnold.

Chasin, Alexandra. 2001. *Selling Out: The Gay and Lesbian Movement Goes to Market*. New York: Palgrave.

Chauncey, George. 1994. *Gay New York*. New York: Basic Books.

Cohen, Jon. "Gay Marriage Support Hits New High in Post-ABC Poll." *The Washington Post*. 18 March 2013. Available at: www.washingtonpost.com/news/the-fix/wp/2013/03/18/gay-marriage-support-hits-new-high-in-post-abc-poll/. Accessed April 2, 2013.

Community Design Group, LLC. 2007. The 38th Street and Chicago Avenue Small Area/Corridor Framework Plan. Available at: www.ci.minneapolis.mn.us/www/groups/public/@cped/documents/webcontent/convert_274471.pdf. Accessed May 27, 2013.

D'Emilio, John. 1998. "Capitalism and Gay Identity." In *The Lesbian and Gay Studies Reader*, eds H. Abelon, M. A. Borak and D. Halperin, pp. 467–476. New York: Routledge.

Enke, Anne. 2007. *Finding the Movement: Sexuality, Contested Space, and Feminist Activism*. Durham: Duke University Press.

Fisher, D. A., Hill, D. L., Grube, J. W. and Gruber, E. L. 2007. "Gay, Lesbian, and Bisexual Content on Television: A Quantitative Analysis Across Two Seasons." *Journal of Homosexuality* 52(3–4): 167–188. doi: 10.1300/J082v52n03_08.

Florida, Richard and Mellander, Charlotte. 2007. "There Goes the Neighborhood: How and Why Bohemians, Artists, and Gays Effect Regional Housing Values." Available at: http://creativeclass.typepad.com/thecreativityexchange/files/Florida_Mellander_Housing_Values_1.pdf. Accessed December 10, 2015.

Gay and Lesbian Alliance Against Defamation. 2014. "2014: Where are we on TV?" Washington: DC. Available at: www.glaad.org/files/GLAAD-2014-WWAT.pdf. Accessed January 4, 2015.

Hanhardt, Christina. 2013. *Safe Space: Gay Neighborhood History and the Politics of Violence.* Durham: Duke University Press.

Higgins, Ross. 1999. "Baths, Bushes, and Belonging: Public Sex and Gay Community in Pre-Stonewall Montreal." In *Public Sex/Gay Space*, ed. William Leap, pp. 240–268. New York City: Columbia University Press.

Knopp, L. 1987. "Social Theory, Social Movements, and Public Policy: Recent Accomplishments of the Gay and Lesbian Movements in Minneapolis, MN." *International Journal of Urban and Rural Research*, 11(2): 243–261.

Leap, William. 1999. "Introduction." In *Public Sex/Gay Space*, ed. William Leap, pp. 1–22. New York City: Columbia University Press.

Levine, M. P. 1979. "Gay Ghetto." In *Social Perspectives in Lesbian and Gay Studies: A Reader*, eds Peter M. Nardi and Beth E. Schneider, pp. 194–206. London: Routledge.

Manalansan, Martin. 2005. "Race, Violence, and Neoliberal Spatial Politics in the Global City," *Social Text* 23(3–4 84–85): 141–155.

McKinney, Matt. 2011. "That's Not Me: Man at Center of City Investigation Says He's Unfairly Targeted." *Star Tribune*, Sept. 28, 2011. Available at: www.startribune.com/man-accused-of-running-wild-minneapolis-club-says-he-s-unfairly-targeted/130710943/. Accessed April 16, 2016.

Murphy, Kevin P. 2010. "Gay Was Good: Progress, Homonormativity, and Oral History." In *Queer Twin Cities*, eds. Twin Cities GLBT History Project, pp. 305–318. Minneapolis, MN: University of Minnesota Press.

Smith, Neil. 1996. *The New Urban Frontier: Gentrification and the Revanchist City.* London: Routledge.

Smith, Tom and Son, Jaseok. 2013. *Trends in Attitudes Toward Sexual Morality.* Chicago: NORC.

White, Edmund. 1982. *A Boy's Own Story.* New York: Random House.

Wyatt, Edward. 2013. "Most of U.S. is Wired, But Millions Aren't Plugged In." *The New York Times.* August 18, 2013. Available at: www.nytimes.com/2013/08/19/technology/a-push-to-connect-millions-who-live-offline-to-the-internet.html?pagewanted=all&_r=0. Accessed December 10, 2015.

Zukin, Sharon. 1995. *The Cultures of Cities.* Cambridge, MA and Oxford: Blackwell Publishers.

chapter 65

Transgender biopolitics in the U.S.

Regulating gender through a heteronormative lens

Jody Ahlm

Think about the last time you filled out a government form, maybe your college applications, your college applications, your financial aid forms, or a driver's license application. Likely you had to answer whether you were female or male (or woman or man, depending on the form). Did you question whether your gender was relevant to what you were applying for? For example, under current law in the U.S. both men and women are eligible to vote, but in some places the voter registration card asks for your gender. We take for granted that gender matters because gender, and the idea that there are two complimentary genders, is everywhere.

Gender essentialism, the idea that men and women have natural characteristics that are inherent in their biology, dominates thinking about gender, sex, and bodies. Inherent in this type of thinking is the idea that bodies come in two types, male or female. Scientists have shown this to be false (Fausto-Sterling 1993, 2000; Kessler 1990). The combination of chromosomes, hormones, and anatomy in human bodies is more diverse than this. Intersexuals are people who have a combination of these sex features that does not fall neatly into the categories of male or female.

Until very recently, it was common practice for doctors to operate on infants with ambiguous genitals, in order to make a body that fits neatly into the category male or female. If the clitoris/penis was less than an inch long, doctors would surgically construct a "normal" vagina. The logic behind this was based on the belief that to be a man, you must have a penis and, furthermore, in order to count as a penis, it must be capable of penetration. Often, the gender on a birth certificate is left blank until doctors decide what type of surgery, if any, should be done. The importance given to genitals in the determination of whether to operate on an infant is part of a general emphasis on genitalia in determining the gender of a person. Heteronormativity, the belief that heterosexuality is normal and the structuring of social life around an assumption that everyone is heterosexual, guides the determination of whether to operate on intersex babies.

The gender binary not only assumes that bodies come in only two shapes, it also assumes that gender is stable and never changes. In fact, many people do not identify with the gender they were assigned at birth. Trans* is an umbrella term used to refer to people who do not identify with the gender they were assigned at birth. The asterisk is a convention borrowed from Internet and database search engines, where it indicates any word that shares the same root word. Thus, "trans*" is used to indicate a broad range of identities that are at least loosely related by their rejection of a biologically based binary gender identity. This includes individuals who identify as transgender, transwoman (a woman who was assigned male at birth), transman (a man who was assigned female at birth), MTF (male to female), FTM (female to male), transsexual, genderqueer and many individuals who do not identify specifically as any of these terms. Many trans* people talk about feeling as if they were "born in the wrong body," but not all trans* people feel this way about themselves.

"Transitioning," or moving from living as one gender to living as another, can include many different psychological and physiological changes. Common procedures today include hormone therapy to increase the presence of secondary sex characteristics. For example, many transmen take testosterone regularly, allowing them to grow facial hair, increase muscle mass, and masculinize the figure of their body and face by redistributing fat and muscle. Many transmen also have reconstructive chest surgery that removes breast tissue and creates a masculine looking chest. Some have hysterectomies. Many transwomen take a combination of hormones that feminizes their body shape. Many also have electrolysis or other hair removal procedures to get rid of or minimize facial and body hair. Transmen and transwomen may also have genital reconstructive surgery, and transwomen may have their Adam's apple surgically removed. All of these medical treatments and surgeries are very expensive and rarely covered by insurance in the U.S.

For trans* individuals, gender markers—the official gender on government and other documents—become a complicated matter. If your birth certificate says "male" but you identify as female, what box do you check? Laws and government policies dictate whether or not the gender marker on your birth certificate can be changed, and the rules for this vary across the federal, state, and local level, often creating a conflicting set of documents. People may have a birth certificate that says "male" and a driver's license that says "female." Central to all of these rules is what medical procedures are required to consider a person officially the "other" gender.

Like the practices concerning intersex babies, the common medical procedures for trans* individuals have historically been structured by heteronormativity. Though this is changing some (as are the procedures for intersex babies), heteronormativity continues to guide regulations governing whether someone can have their gender markers changed. Gender markers, though most people take them for granted, play a big role in our lives. Conflicting gender markers can mean being denied access to homeless shelters and domestic violence shelters, and denied benefits such as food stamps and Medicaid.

Gender markers that do not match a person's embodied gender create dangerous situations in sex-segregated institutions such as prisons, where trans* individuals are often put in horrible conditions of solitary confinement to avoid conflicts with transphobic and homophobic prisoners, or "outed" as transgender and intentionally put in situations where their safety is at risk. Access to domestic violence shelters and homeless shelters can be a matter of life or death, but these facilities are almost always sex-segregated, and trans* individuals are routinely turned away because their appearance does not match their gender markers, or they have conflicting gender markers.

Trans* people are, "basically unfathomable to the administrative systems that govern the distribution of life chances: housing, education, health care, identity documentation and records, employment, and public facilities, to name just a few" (Spade 2011: 11). Gender matters in all of our dealings with the State—the name for the social institution that encompasses laws, courts, administrative policies, law enforcement, and the many agencies that make up the government. There are clear consequences to this for people who do not fit into one of the two available gender boxes, but how did gender become so important to our relationship with the State? In other words, why does gender show up on almost every official form we fill out? Why do governments keep track of the gender of each person?

Trans* biopolitics

To answer these questions, we can turn to philosopher Michel Foucault's ([1978] 1990, 2010) concept, *biopolitics*. Foucault developed the concept of biopolitics to explain how modern governments regulate their populations. In the Middle Ages, European monarchs controlled populations through the monarch's "right of death." Their power was in the ability to inflict death on their subjects. Violent public executions were used to remind people that it was the sovereign's right to decide when (and how) someone died.

This shifted, with the emergence of the nation-state as the primary form of government. Now, governments exert power through the "power over life." In other words, preserving and improving life is both the purpose of government and how it exercises its power. Even when a government goes to war or executes someone, it does so in the name of the health and lives of its population. Wars are fought in the name of preserving life, and executions are carried out in the name of public safety. The main concern of government is managing life, even when it metes out death.

The State's investment in issues of gender and sexuality is a core element of biopolitics. Foucault argued that sexuality, because it is related to the reproduction of life, is central to power in the modern nation-state. If power is exercised through preserving and improving life, life must be defined and measured. The transition to biopolitics, to the "power over life," was possible in part because of the development of modern statistical methods and increasingly efficient methods of keeping records and information. This allowed modern governments to control populations by track-ing and regulating reproduction and sexuality.

A great example of this is the Census. Beginning in 1790 and conducted every ten years, the U.S. Census attempts to count every person living in its borders, house by house. Census questions have varied, representing changes over time in socially constructed categories such as race, but the Census has always tracked reproduction by keeping records of the relationships of members of each household. Until 2010, when adopted children were first counted as family members, only marriage and birth ties were recognized as familial. The Census is one way that the State keeps track of not only the genders, but also the family relationships of every person. The definition of family has historically relied on the State's interest in the family as a reproductive unit. The Census does more than count people; it keeps track of the reproduction of life.

In the U.S., the family is a standard unit of government policy at all levels. Given that the State controls the distribution of resources, it matters a great deal how fam-ily is defined. For example, Social Security benefits extend to the spouse of the per-son receiving the benefits, when someone dies, any money or assets that go to the spouse and legal children are taxed at a lower rate than money given to non-family members, and social welfare programs such as Temporary Aid to Needy Families (TANF) and the Women, Infants and Children Program (WIC) have eligibility require-ments based on definitions of family that vary, by state, from biological ties only to including legal guardians and official foster parents as family. Thus, one way the government regulates sexuality is by attaching "proper" family structure to the distri-bution of resources.

The definition of family is changing. Same-sex marriage is now legal in the U.S. This makes the many resources and benefits of being defined as family extend to same-sex couples that get legally married. However, if the government did not track the gender of every person the very idea of same-sex marriage would not matter. The current biopolitical regulation of sexuality is dependent on knowing the gender of each person in the population. Even as definitions of family change, recognition by the government and access to resources continue to be restricted by the requirement that everyone fit into one of two gender boxes.

Gender non-conformity: from criminal act to medical disorder

How the State deals with people who do not fit into either gender box has changed over time, but heteronormativity has been a consistent factor. Laws against cross-dressing—males wearing women's clothing and "passing" as women or females wearing male clothes and "passing" as men—existed since early colonial times (Feinberg 1997; Stryker 2008). The criminalization of cross-gender identifica-tion was connected to the regulation of heterosexuality and the control of women's sexuality (Brier and Parsons 2012). The mid- to late 19th century saw a large migration of people from rural areas to the cities of the North and Midwest U.S. Migration often meant a weakening of traditional family and community ties, and a degree of anonymity in city life. For the first time, large numbers of unmarried women were living outside of their parents' homes. This created a panic over the autonomy and sexuality of women and the perceived decline of the stability of the heterosexual, patriarchal family. Arrests for cross-dressing often involved a female dressing and living as a man and either living as the husband of a woman or courting a woman. The anxiety about cross-dressing was an anxiety about the stability of heterosexuality as the dominant relationship structuring family life.

The fear of cross-dressers was part of a broader fear of women's autonomy, and of homosexuality. The State policed what it considered to be the natural connection between biological sex at birth and gender, and simultaneously regulated the limits of heterosexuality. Heterosexual relationships were determined based on the biological sex of the couple, not their gender presentation or gender identity. Determinations of criminality were accomplished through either connecting the person to past documents, such as prior names, birth certificates, kin, etc., or the determination of a doctor. Even when gender non-conformity was primarily policed by the State, medical authority was often used to support or refute claims. The accused person was required to undergo an examination by a doctor to determine their "real" sex (Brier and Parsons 2012).

It was only with the ascendency of science and medicine in the 20th century, particularly after WWII, that deviance was increasingly medicalized (Conrad 1980). Behaviors that were previously considered criminal were brought under the authority of medical professionals to diagnose and treat. Medicalization is the process whereby something socially deviant comes to be defined in medical terms, generally by being assigned a diagnosis, and is assumed to be solved through medical intervention. In the period from the mid-1960s to the late-1970s, a small handful of "gender clinics," located at elite medical schools, controlled access to transgender related treatments and procedures.

During this time, a panel of doctors and medical professionals created the Harry Benjamin Standards of Care for diagnosing and treating "gender identity disorder (GID)," (Meyerowitz 2004; Stryker 2008). Transgender individuals wishing to access medically administered body modifications, such as hormone therapy and surgeries, had to meet specific requirements for GID as laid out in the Diagnostic Statistical Manual (DSM). In order to be diagnosed with GID, and thereby gain access to medical services, patients had to show a life history of identifying with the "opposite" gender, such as the toys they played with as a child, the clothes they preferred to wear as a child, the gender of their childhood friends, and childhood fantasies of having different genitalia.

They also had to exhibit a desire to be heterosexual. Often times, "sex reassignment" surgeries were seen as a way of correcting homosexuality. An individual assigned male at birth, sexually attracted to men, and with evidence of life long feminine behaviors was deemed a good candidate for surgery and hormone treatment. The goal was to create a heterosexual female. The success of genital surgery was measured by whether the newly constructed vagina could be penetrated with a penis during heterosexual intercourse.

Under pressure from trans* activists, including Louis Sullivan, an influential gay transman in the San Francisco bay area, the heterosexual requirement was dropped from the Standards of Care in 1994 (Meyerowitz 2004; Stryker 2008). Sullivan himself did not live to see this change, as he died of AIDS in 1991, but the community he created and the visibility he brought to the diverse sexualities of trans* people had lasting effects. Identifying as heterosexual and describing a life long attraction to the gender "opposite" to their own gender identity was no longer necessary for being diagnosed with GID, making trans* related medical treatments available regardless of sexual identity.

This was a major improvement in the lives of many trans* people who had previously been denied medical services because of a stated, or perceived, non-heterosexual identity. Today, many medical facilities have dropped most of the Harry Benjamin Standards, though conforming to the narrative of childhood cross-gender identification and life long distress over gender identity continues to informally affect diagnosis and eligibility. In addition, lack of financial resources, health insurance, and non-coverage by most insurance plans continue to be a barrier to medical services for many trans* people.

Trans* people and the law today

What about the State? Despite the changes in medical regulations that have increased access to medical services for non-heterosexual trans* individuals, trans* people pursuing legal document changes face numerous obstacles. Though medical institutions have stopped requiring that trans* people be heterosexual, the legal system assumes all trans* people are heterosexual and defines sexual intercourse based on how (and if) one's body is able to perform heterosexual intercourse.

Currently, only six states, New York, Rhode Island, Vermont, California, Oregon, and Washington, will issue a new birth certificate without proof of "sex reassignment surgery," meaning the surgical construction of genitals that meet normative standards of male or female. Twenty-five states will issue a new birth certificate if the person provides proof of sex reassignment surgery, generally a letter or testimony from the doctor completing the surgery. Sixteen states will issue an amended birth certificate upon proof of surgery, but amended birth certificates are still connected to the individual's previous name and gender marker. Three states, Ohio, Tennessee, and Idaho, will neither issue a new birth certificate nor an amended birth certificate (transgenderlawcenter.org 2015).

Laws regarding changes to the gender marker on state IDs or drivers' licenses also vary by state and require verification by a doctor or therapist, though completion of sex reassignment surgery is often not required. A letter from a psychologist or therapist testifying that the person is being treated for Gender Dysphoria is sufficient in most states. If a person's state ID and birth certificate do not match, a U.S. citizen can still get a passport by submitting a letter from a doctor verifying that they are "in the process of gender transition" (transequality.org 2015).

Sometimes, trans* individuals must look to the courts to determine whether they qualify for a name change or legal gender change, often in cases where administrative policies do not allow them to change the gender marker on either their birth certificate or state ID. Sociologist Tey Meadow (2010: 821) analyzed 38 cases, between 1966 and 2007. Meadow noticed a difference between status cases – those cases that involve establishing legal status as a spouse or parent – and identity cases – those cases consisting of a request to reclassify the petitioner's legal gender status and/or legal name. Meadow found that, "status cases overall employ far less permeable gender schema than identity cases." In other words, judges were more willing to agree to a trans* person's desire to have their gender marker changed if it did not change their legal relationship to another person or persons involved in the case. "In this way, gender shifts from a property of individuals to a relational construct, and law becomes less an arbiter of fact than a regulatory mechanism producing specific relationship formations," (823). For example, a transman lost his case based on a judge's belief that sex with his wife was not real heterosexual sex because it involved a prosthetic penis. The ability to have "real" heterosexual intercourse was the determining factor for the legitimacy of the marriage. Another case was decided against a transwoman because, despite successful surgery to construct female genitalia, she did not have a uterus and ovaries and, therefore, could not procreate. In this way, heteronormativity continues to structure the State's view of gender.

Even as laws change to be inclusive of same-sex couples, gender remains a ubiquitous classification system, and gender and sexuality remain central to the biopolitics of the modern State and the distribution of resources. Civil unions and same-sex marriages have actually increased the presence of the State in the lives of non-heterosexuals, tracking and regulating their relationships in ways it previously did not. Allowing same-sex couples to marry does not change the fact that marriage continues to be the determination of what constitutes family, and this determination affects access to many benefits. Additionally, the legalization of same-sex marriage does not change the difficulty trans* people have accessing sex-segregated resources such as domestic violence shelters or gender-specific social welfare programs, nor does it protect them from trans-phobic violence. Same-sex marriage may benefit some trans* individuals, but it does not address the most prevalent, and most life threatening inequalities and injustices trans* people face. Looking at the role the State plays in regulating the sexuality of trans* people reveals much about how the State regulates all people, but it also points to the limits of the marriage equality movement for eliminating inequality.

Conclusion

Laws restricting individuals from changing their gender marker rest on assumptions about the naturalness of gender. Looking closely at these laws allows us to see the importance of heteronormativity to our understandings of gender. Trans* individuals are called upon to "prove" their gender identity by demonstrating that their bodies have been medically treated to match our cultural assumptions about what men and women's bodies should look like. Most often, it is genitalia that are the determining factor in whether a person is legally considered a man or woman. The obsession with genitalia in our gender classification system is rooted in the centrality of heterosexuality to our understandings of women, men, and their natural relationship to one another.

Jody Ahlm

Laws about gender marker changes are part of a larger biopolitics. The State concerns itself with the gender and sexuality of its population because it is through managing life, and the reproduction of life, that the State maintains its power. The concept of biopolitics shows us that the State exercises power by improving and extending the lives of some, while neglecting others. Individuals who do not fit the State's definitions of man or woman are denied access to even the most basic benefits. These gender definitions continue to rely on heteronormative ideas about what it means to be a man or woman.

Bibliography

American Psychiatric Association. 2013. *Diagnostic and Statistical Manual of Mental Disorders: DSM-V*. 5th edition. Washington, DC: American Psychiatric Association.

Brier, Jennifer and Anne Parsons. 2012. "Gender Crossroads: Representations of Gender Transgressions in Chicago's Press, 1850–1920." In *Out in Chicago: LGBT History at the Crossroads*, edited by Jill Austin and Jennifer Brier. pp. 23–40. Chicago: Chicago Historical Society.

Conrad, Peter. 1980. *Deviance and Medicalization: From Badness to Sickness*. Philadelphia: Temple University Press.

Fausto-Sterling, Anne. 1993. "The Five Sexes: Why Male and Female are Not Enough." *Sciences* 33(2): 20–24.

—. 2000. *Sexing the Body: Gender Politics and the Construction of Sexuality*. New York: Basic Books.

Feinberg, Leslie. 1997. *Transgender Warriors: Making History from Joan of Arc to Dennis Rodman*. Boston: Beacon Press.

Foucault, Michel. [1978] 1990. *The History of Sexuality, Vol. 1: An Introduction*. New York: Vintage.

Foucault, Michel. 2010. *The Birth of Biopolitics: Lectures at the Collège de France, 1978–1979*. New York: Picador.

Kessler, Suzanne J. 1990. "The Medical Construction of Gender: Case Management of Intersexed Infants." *Signs: Journal of Women in Culture and Society* 16: 3–27.

Meadow, Tey. 2010. "'A Rose is a Rose': On Producing Legal Gender Classifications." *Gender & Society* 24 (6): 814–837.

Meyerowitz, Joanne. 2004. *How Sex Changed: A History of Transsexuality in the United States*: Cambridge, MA: Harvard University Press.

Sears, Clare. 2005. "'A Tremendous Sensation': Cross-Dressing in the 19th century San Fransisco Press." P. 328 in *News and Sexuality: Media Portraits of Diversity*, edited by Laura Castañeda and Shannon B. Campbell. Thousand Oaks: SAGE Publications, Inc.

Spade, Dean. 2011. *Normal Life: Administrative Violence, Critical Trans Politics and the Limits of Law*. New York: South End Press.

Stryker, Susan. 2008. *Transgender History*. Berkeley: Seal Press.

Trans Equality.Org 2015. Accessed January 16, 2015 (http://transequality.org/Resources/passports_2014.pdf).

Transgender Law Center. 2015. Accessed January 16, 2015 (www.transgenderlawcenter.org).

chapter 66

Politics of sex education

Interview with Janice M. Irvine

Janice M. Irvine is Professor of Sociology at the University of Massachusetts. She is the Director of the Five College Women's Studies Research Center. She is the author of *Talk About Sex: The Battles over Sex Education in the United States* and *Disorders of Desire: Sex and Gender in Modern American Sexology*.

In your first book you wrote a historical analysis of twentieth-century sexology, and recently you published a book on the history of sex education controversies. Is there a theme that ties together this research?

As a sociologist, I approach sexuality as a domain that is profoundly social rather than thinking of it as a purely biological and instinctive part of life. In my research, I have tended to study different types of sexual discourse, by which I mean the specific webs of meaning that shape how we think, talk, and feel about sexuality. In my first book, *Disorders of Desire: Sex and Gender in Modern American Sexology*, I examined the history of sex research in the twentieth century. The book explores how sexology – the scientific study of sexuality – invented medical categories, languages, and norms regarding sexuality and gender, and at the same time played a role in turning sex into a marketable commodity in the form of advice and therapy.

I have always been interested in relations of power and the production of sexual knowledge. This led me to study the controversies over sexuality education in the United States. Since the 1960s, we have been fighting over what forms of sexual knowledge we will impart to our young people in the public school system. Basically these are political battles, because they involve disagreements about what types of sexualities are valued and therefore teachable and what forms of sexuality are so devalued that we cannot speak about them. Sex education is an important sexual discourse because it influences how young people become social and sexual actors.

Another theme that links these two books is the stigma that both sex researchers and sex educators have historically endured. Even today, sexology can be rendered suspicious and sex researchers themselves can be stigmatized with little difficulty. Sexology remains marginal or even ignored in the academy. Sex research has been consistently unfunded, under-funded, or de-funded after attacks by legislators, conservative groups, or the media. Sex educators have been under attack as well. The stigmatization of anyone who works in the area of sexuality is one indication of the deep cultural anxieties about sex in the United States.

How long has sex education been part of the curriculum in public schools?

The first calls for school sex education came in the early twentieth century from moral reformers interested in what was then called "sex hygiene." These included groups as different as suffragists, clergy, temperance workers, and physicians, all of whom wanted to eliminate venereal disease. As early as 1919, mainstream organizations such as the US Public Health Service endorsed formal sex education programs, believing that the schools would be the most effective sites for instruction of young people. In the first half of the twentieth century, many schools implemented sex education programs, such as in Chicago, Washington, DC, and Toms River, New Jersey. Still, many educators were uneasy about discussion of sexual health in the classroom, and sex education's progress was slow and sometimes controversial.

In 1964, a small group of professionals, led by Mary Calderone, a staid Quaker physician who had been the medical director of Planned Parenthood Federation of America, founded the Sex Information and Education Council of the United States (SIECUS). Calderone spearheaded a crusade to normalize the topic of sexuality by emphasizing the public health dimension rather than the morality of it. She sought to include sex education in curricula from kindergarten through graduate training, in particular medical schools. Even today, SIECUS remains the most visible organization calling for comprehensive sexuality education.

What kind of sex education do we find in public schools now?

Generally there are two types of programs taught in public schools today: comprehensive sexuality education, and what is variously known as abstinence-only or abstinence-only-until-marriage education.

SIECUS pioneered a model for comprehensive sexuality education in which young people would receive, from kindergarten through high school, age-appropriate information on a range of topics such as human reproduction, anatomy, physiology, and sexually transmitted infections, as well as issues such as masturbation, contraception, and abortion. Comprehensive sexuality education offers young people the opportunity to discuss sexual values and attitudes in the classroom. Advocates of comprehensive sex education endorse what they consider to be the health benefits of frank sexual discussion in the classroom. They believe that silence has fostered ignorance, shame, and social problems like teenage pregnancy. Supporters of comprehensive sexuality education view sexuality as positive and healthy, and they typically support gender equality and acceptance of sexual diversity. Comprehensive sexuality education stresses abstinence for youth, and it also provides information on topics such as contraception and abortion.

Advocates of abstinence-only education believe that the best approach to sexual health is to teach young people to abstain from all sexual behavior until they are married. All sexual behavior, in their opinion, should be confined to marriage. Controlling or eliminating sexual discussion best allows for the protection of young people and preservation of sexual morality. Discussion about topics such as contraception, in their view, has led to high levels of adolescent sexual activity, teenage pregnancy, and sexually transmitted diseases. They believe, therefore, that if we talk to young people about sexuality it should be controlled so as not to lead to destructive and immoral thoughts and behavior. They generally favor restrictions on other forms of sexual expression, such as masturbation or homosexuality, and they often oppose feminism and the gay rights movement.

Is there any research comparing the effectiveness of comprehensive sexuality education compared to abstinence-only curricula? Basically, which programs work?

The question of effectiveness is a very important one, especially since the United States government been generously funding abstinence-only programs since 1982. In fact, this level of funding drastically increased under the administration of George W. Bush. Abstinence-only sex education received $170 million in fiscal year 2005, more than double the funding it received in fiscal year 2001.

Unfortunately, despite all this federal funding, there is mounting evidence that these programs simply do not work. In 1996, when the welfare reform law was enacted which funds so many of these programs, an independent review concluded that there were no solid data to demonstrate the effectiveness of abstinence-only curricula. Evaluations of three prominent abstinence-only curricula – Sex Respect, Teen-Aid, and Values and Choices – did not support advocates' claims that the programs delayed sexual initiation among young people.

An independent research institute, Mathematica Policy Research Inc., has been conducting evaluation research on abstinence-only programs funded through the 1996 law. An interim report issued in June 2005 shows that, while young people who have attended these programs report positive attitudes about abstinence, the programs have little or no impact otherwise. They did not affect youth's intentions to abstain and had no impact on important decision-making factors such as self-esteem and open communication with parents. In addition, a report issued by Democrat Congressman Henry Waxman evaluated the content of the abstinence-only programs funded by the federal government. It found that over 80 percent of such curricula contained false, misleading, or distorted information about reproductive health.

On the other hand, there is some evidence that comprehensive sexuality education is effective on a number of levels. Independent researcher Douglas Kirby found that several curricula are effective in preventing teen pregnancy. Significantly, he found that curricula that teach about contraception and safer sex do not hasten the onset, or increase the frequency of, sex among young people, as many critics of comprehensive programs allege. Also, a study commissioned by the Joint United Programme on

HIV/AIDS (UNAIDS) found that a number of good comprehensive programs are successful in delaying the onset of sexual behavior, reducing the number of partners, or reducing unplanned pregnancy and rates of sexually transmitted diseases.

Which approach to sex education in the schools do most people in the US support?

Repeatedly, most people tell pollsters they broadly support comprehensive sex education. Public opinion polls since the 1960s have consistently shown widespread support for sex education. A 2000 poll sponsored by the Kaiser Family Foundation indicated that, by a large majority, parents want their children to have *more* classroom hours of sex education that covers more "sensitive topics" than such programs currently do. A 1998 national poll found that 87 percent of Americans supported sexuality education in the public schools and a poll commissioned by SIECUS and Advocates for Youth found that 89 percent believe that, along with abstinence, young people should also have information about contraception and STD prevention.

So what do most public schools teach? Comprehensive or abstinence-only programs?

As I show in my book, *Talk About Sex: The Battles Over Sex Education in the United States*, the scope of sex education is narrow in the public schools. Although most public schools offer some form of sex education, very few students receive the type of comprehensive sexuality education advocated by SIECUS. Some students might have a semester-long course, while some hear only one or two sessions from an outside group like Planned Parenthood. Most students undergo a few class periods of instruction sometime between the seventh and twelfth grades. However, since the growth of abstinence-only education, many students only hear abstinence messages in those few classes they might have received. While in 1988 only 2 percent of teachers taught abstinence as the *sole* means of pregnancy and disease prevention, 23 percent did so in 1999. A poll of schools in September 2003 indicated a sharp increase to 30 percent among instructors who taught abstinence only and did not provide information about condoms and other contraceptives.

A study of public schools revealed that, among all districts in the US, 10 percent had a comprehensive sexuality education policy, 34 percent promoted abstinence as the preferred option for teenagers but allowed for discussion of contraception, and 23 percent required the sole promotion of abstinence. Thirty-three percent of districts had no policy on sexuality education. The abstinence-only-until-marriage districts either completely prohibited any instruction in contraception or required that teachers only emphasize its failures. The researchers concluded that of all US students who attended a public school including grades six and higher, only 9 percent were in districts with a comprehensive sexuality education policy.

Why is comprehensive sex education shrinking, given popular support for it?

Sex education has been a central issue in the culture wars that have flared in the United States since the 1970s. Since the 1960s, religious conservatives have viewed sex education as a powerful vehicle by which to agitate parents, recruit constituents, raise money, and ultimately consolidate political power through election to school boards and other political positions. Social conservatives believe that, like abortion, sexuality in the media, and gay rights, comprehensive sexuality is dangerous and immoral. Conservative national organizations and political movements have been actively involved with shaping sexual values in this country, and they have taken on sex education as one of their most important political issues. Therefore, by the end of the twentieth century, more than 700 communities had experienced intense controversies over sex education in their local schools. Often cast as spontaneous eruptions of grassroots outrage, sex education conflicts actually constitute one flank of this self-described initiative by national religious right groups. Moreover, these conservative groups were able to dominate the public conversation about sex education.

What does it mean that conservatives dominate the public conversation about sex education? How have they been able to do this?

Conservative national religious organizations, for example Concerned Women for America, and Focus on the Family, captured the terms of debate about sex education through the strategic use of emotionally powerful rhetoric used both nationally and locally at school board sessions and town meetings. Provocative and stigmatizing sexual rhetoric has played an important role in igniting community battles. One common tactic has been the use of highly charged sexual language in community debates. This includes, for example, calling a curriculum a "sodomy curriculum" or describing it as "pornographic." They also use provocative language to stigmatize sex educators themselves, calling them perverts or pedophiles.

Conservatives have also distorted and misrepresented comprehensive programs, for example claiming that if students learn about condom use or birth control they will go out and have sex. Studies indicate otherwise, but that does not stop conservatives from making the claim.

Finally, conservative critics employ what I call depravity narratives, which are tales about sexual groups or issues that rely on distortion, hyperbole, or outright fabrication. Many depravity narratives spread during controversies in the late 1960s. One recounted that a sex education teacher had had intercourse in front of the class as a pedagogical strategy. Other tales circulated to the effect that children were being encouraged to fondle each other, sexual intercourse would be taught in kindergarten, schools would install coed bathrooms with no partitions between stalls, and youth were being told about bestiality with donkeys and sheep. Depravity narratives are designed to shock people and to exploit popular anxieties about the destructive power of unleashed sexuality.

All of these strategies have been incredibly effective because of America's culture of sexual fear and shame. Regardless of whether these allegations about comprehensive sex education were actually believed, by either the activists themselves or their audience, they could mobilize sexual fears for political purposes. Stigmatizing accusations are difficult to refute, and they cast suspicion upon local programs and sex educators themselves. Highly charged sexual language and graphic symbols could scare and outrage people, turning a local debate into a civic brawl.

Interview with Janice M. Irvine

Has there been organized support for comprehensive sexuality education?

Comprehensive sexuality education is supported by a wide range of religious and public health agencies. Over 140 national organizations comprise the National Coalition to Support Sexuality Education. These include the American Medical Association, the American Public Health Association, the American Academy of Pediatrics, and the United Church Board for Homeland Ministries. They are committed to medically-accurate, age-appropriate comprehensive sexuality education. In addition, a new wing of advocacy emerged in the late 1990s. Prompted by the funding of abstinence-only programs in the 1996 welfare law, the National Coalition Against Censorship, along with other free-speech activists, took up sex education as a First Amendment issue. In broad public education campaigns, NCAC argued that federal funding of abstinence-only education represented censorship, in that it is state restriction on what teachers can or cannot teach about sex.

You have written a great deal about the intense emotions involved in sex education debates. What do you mean by this, and why are emotions important?

Early in my research, I saw how discussions about sexuality education became highly impassioned public arguments across the US. Community meetings erupted in shouting matches and even physical violence. I heard neighbors scream at each other and saw angry shoving outside of public meeting halls. School board members told me about receiving hate mail and death threats. Town meetings went from sleepy affairs to late-night shouting matches involving hundreds of residents. After a sex education foe collapsed from an anxiety attack while addressing an especially rancorous meeting, the tense minutes in the hushed school auditorium as he was carried out rank among the most dramatic in my research career.

Whereas early on I had thought volatile emotions were inconsequential compared to the rational terms of political debate, gradually I understood that the furious public displays of feeling were significant and required analysis and theorization. I began to recognize community battles as the outcome of political strategy such as the highly charged rhetoric I described earlier.

Emotions are significant for several reasons during local sex education conflicts. On the simplest level, they heat up the climate and draw attention to the issue. Intense emotions can mobilize followers, at least in the short term. Media coverage often intensifies when town meetings explode. In turn, headlines and articles that emphasize these outbursts of feeling not only sell newspapers but they coach citizens in the emotional expectations of town meetings. Even more important was the emotional climate of danger and shame that was reinforced by the rhetoric used during these conflicts, even if an audience was skeptical of some of the more outrageous claims. The intense feelings displayed in sex education controversies can teach us that emotion is not simply an instinctive reaction that is beyond the reach of social influences but that emotions have their own social and cultural logic. In turn, this means they are important in the political arena. In the end, I discovered that emotions are central in sex education politics, which seems to bring me full circle to my interests in power and knowledge.

chapter 67

The pro-family movement

Tina Fetner

We often think about our sexuality as very private and personal. However true this might be, sexuality is also social in a number of ways. One of the clearest examples of the social aspect of sexuality is the recent "culture war" in the United States, which is largely a struggle over what the social rules governing sexuality should be. Should comprehensive sex education be provided to students through public education? Should same-sex couples be allowed to marry under the law? Should pregnant women have the right to decide whether they get an abortion? What about girls who are under 18 years old? These issues about sexuality certainly have a profound impact on people's personal lives. The policy battles over these issues, however, are taking place in the public sphere, fought by activists and politicians.

Much of this activism is in response to the many changes in the social norms governing sexuality in the United States over the last thirty years or so. The fight for women's equality, the "sexual revolution," and the growth of lesbian and gay communities are a few of these important changes, but they are not the only ones. For example, cultural changes marked by an expansion of the consumer sphere means that advertising for consumer products reaches every nook and cranny of our daily lives. The use of sexually suggestive images in advertising has provoked many to declare that we live in a "sex saturated" environment.

In response to these and other changes, a social movement has emerged to lobby for the return of stricter norms governing sexuality. This social movement has been known by a number of names, such as the Moral Majority, the Religious Right, the New Christian Right, and the Pro-Family Movement. Though the pro-family movement gained public notoriety in the 1990s, it actually began in the 1970s and has been active ever since. This social movement has been particularly successful at integrating its issues into the agenda of the Republican party, and so it has become a very powerful social movement in the United States today. This chapter will trace the history of this social movement and discuss the implications for a number of social policies governing sexuality.

What is the pro-family movement?

The pro-family movement is a group of social movement organizations that share both a wide-ranging conservative political agenda and a (primarily evangelical) Christian identity. For the pro-family movement, these two are closely tied together, in that their religious perspective informs their political goals, such as legalizing prayer in school and criminalizing abortion. Though the movement claims to be concerned with building strong families, their policy goals reach far beyond the institution of the family. For example, pro-family activists advocate ending medical research that uses stem cells, stopping legalized gambling, and eliminating some topics from being discussed in schools.

While the pro-family movement is a self-identified Christian movement, it is important to remember that not all Christians, nor all evangelical Christians, are pro-family activists. Many evangelical Christians have diverse opinions on each of the issues supported by the pro-family movement, and even people who join the movement might feel strongly about one of the movement's issues, but disagree with the movement's stance on other issues. In any social movement, there is much more diversity among members than we might see at first glance. Pro-family leaders add to the confusion by frequently making statements that imply that all Christians agree with their political goals. By making claims about "the Christian perspective" on one policy or another, pro-family activists try to make it sound like millions of Christian Americans agree with them, even though this is often not the case.

History of the pro-family movement

How did the pro-family movement come to be? Why is it so much stronger in the United States than in other, similar countries? The answer lies in the unique history of evangelical Christianity in the United States, out of which this movement was born. Ironically, the roots of what makes this social movement so powerful lie in evangelical Christians' historical belief that politics had no place in the life of good Christians. I will explain.

Through much of the middle of the twentieth century, Christian evangelicals were dedicated to withdrawal, not only from politics, but also from what they perceived to be immoral secular influences. From the 1930s through the 1960s, evangelical Christians were dedicated to building alternative social networks, religious and educational institutions as a shield from the cultural influences of the outside world. Many Christian evangelicals thought that popular music was a particularly evil influence on children, as was the sexual content of magazines, films, and television.

Public schools presented material which contradicted biblical literalism, evangelical Christians' faith that the bible is the true word of God rather than a metaphorical representation of God's message. Because of this particularly evangelical Christian understanding of the bible, parts of the curriculum were contentious, even before the days of sex education. For example, the teaching of evolution in science classes contradicts a literal reading of the bible, which says that God built the world in six days. In response, evangelical Christians retreated from the secular world, built private, independent schools, libraries, and other institutions that supported their own values and ideology.

They developed networks among churches, as well as bible institutes, summer camps and other religious retreats, television and radio networks, videos and a host of other Christian children's books, bible study pamphlets, and so on. These Christian institutions and media turned out to be very popular, and soon evangelical Christian organizations had amassed incredible financial resources and membership numbers, and had created wide informational networks and an ideological consistency among their members that would turn out to serve political ends very well. Of course, none of this was intentional during the era of retreat from secular politics, but all of that changed in the 1970s, when one group of evangelical Christians decided to stop retreating and start changing the secular world through political activism. These evangelical Christian church networks, schools, radio stations, television shows, and publishing houses, and the distinctly Christian values and identity they created, became the backbone of the pro-family movement.

The development of the pro-family movement

Two important grassroots movements preceded the pro-family movement and influenced it greatly. The first was the fight against the Equal Rights Amendment of the early 1970s, led by Phyllis Schlafly, which was responsible for defeating the legislation that would have added this language to the US constitution: "Equality of rights under the law shall not be denied or abridged by the United States or by any state on account of sex." Schlafly's multi-state crusade was among the first examples of grassroots activism for conservative social causes, and her organization, the Eagle Forum, is still one of the leading pro-family groups in the United States. The second important movement is Anita Bryant's fight against gay rights in the late 1970s. American sweetheart and former beauty queen Anita Bryant led a series of grassroots efforts across the country to repeal local legislation protecting gay men and lesbians from discrimination. In her 1977 autobiography, *The Anita Bryant Story*, Bryant says, "homosexuals cannot reproduce – so they must recruit. And to freshen their ranks, they must recruit the youth of America."

Both of these movements were successful in their legislative goals, and they set an example to some conservative Christian leaders that politics and evangelism can go together. Jerry Falwell was reluctant at first to enter politics, because he worried that his followers would reject his active participation in the secular world. But Bryant's work demonstrated that conservative Christian evangelicals supported secular activism, and he founded the Moral Majority in 1979, with a plan to integrate an evangelical Christian agenda into mainstream party politics. Falwell's success in building a national movement led to the emergence of other organizations that built coalitions with Republican party insiders to create what the media called the New Christian Right. This brand of Christian activism was quite successful in integrating conservative social policy concerns into the platform of the Republican party at both national and state levels over the course of the 1980s. The Moral Majority's voter registration drives signed up both unsatisfied Christian Democrats and nonvoters to the Republican party.

In the 1990s, the relationship between conservative Christian activists and the Republican party became even stronger, despite the objections of more moderate Republicans. Some pundits in the 1990s predicted that the Republican party's turn toward a socially conservative agenda would create a crisis in the party, which has a long history of opposition to government intrusion into personal matters. This, however, did not come to be, as the pro-family movement's influence on the Republican party continued to grow throughout the 1990s and into the current century, culminating in the election of President George W. Bush, a born-again Christian who supported the platform of the pro-family movement.

What began in the 1970s as a group of conservative Christian political outsiders writing letters and carrying picket signs has turned into a powerful political force with great influence in the legislative and executive branches of the federal government, as well as many state and local governments across the nation. The various organizations in the movement took up multiple issues and packaged them into one "pro-family" agenda. Critics complain that this pleasant-sounding tag hides an agenda to undermine the separation of church and state in the United States. In fact, many pro-family leaders have been quoted stating explicitly their desire to create a system of "Christian governance" for America. Today, they continue to exert great influence on many laws and policies governing sexuality.

Pro-family activism and sexuality

Many items on the pro-family agenda have to do with restricting sexuality and reversing some of the changes in sexual norms that have occurred over the past several decades. Pro-family activists fight for policies that limit the sexual freedoms of individuals and censor sexual information, especially from young people. Below, I outline a number of the pro-family movement's priorities regarding sexuality.

Sexuality in television, music and film

Pro-family activists are concerned with the amount of sexually suggestive material in the media these days. They take a variety of paths to try to limit the sexuality published through television, music, and film. First, they advocate boycotts of particular shows and songs that they find offensive. They publish guides for parents to limit sexually suggestive materials their kids view and listen to. They also pressure businesses to refuse to sell music or DVDs that are offensive, and they encourage their supporters to patronize the stores that adopt such policies.

In addition to the sexually suggestive material available for general consumption through television, radio, and the film industry, the pro-family movement is also concerned with sexually explicit material, or pornography. Some pro-family activism has shut down local adult film stores, created local zoning laws that limit where these stores can be opened. These days, however, sexually explicit material is no longer relegated to the back rooms of video stores and the dark, seedy parts of town; it is easily accessed in people's homes over the internet. The pro-family movement is working to censor internet pornography through federal legislation. These anti-pornography measures have broad public support that goes well beyond the pro-family movement itself.

Sex education in public schools

One of the biggest battles the pro-family movement continues to fight is for limits on information on sexuality in public schools. In the beginning of this fight, the pro-family movement made direct arguments for censorship of this information. As time went on, pro-family activists became more politically savvy, arguing *for* what they call "abstinence-only" sex education, rather than *against* sex education in general. However, abstinence-only sex education is more about keeping scientifically accurate information from students than providing them with sex education. For example, abstinence-only educators can only talk about pre-marital sex in terms of the problems it causes. Critics of abstinence-only curricula contend that some programs even go so far as to include inaccurate information, such as the myth that condoms have holes in them bigger than the HIV virus, in order to scare young people away from having sex.

Abstinence-only sex education was one of the pro-family movement's biggest policy victories. In 1996, special funding for abstinence-only education was established by the federal government, meaning that resource-starved public schools had an incentive to provide this sort of sex education curriculum, rather than more comprehensive and accurate education. From 1996 to 2010, the U. S. federal government only provided funding for abstinence-only sexual education in public schools. In 2010, President Barack Obama ended federal funding for abstinence-only sexual education, and instead directed funding to comprehensive sexual education programming for public schools.

Civil rights for lesbians and gay men

The fight against civil rights for lesbians and gay men has been a longstanding plank in the pro-family movement's platform. Currently, this fight is taking the form of opposition to laws that recognize marriage between two people of the same sex. However, this is not the only anti-gay position of the pro-family movement. The movement also opposes extending anti-discrimination legislation to include lesbians and gay men, not to mention bisexuals and transgender people. That is, pro-family activists want the law to allow landlords to be able to refuse housing to people who are gay or lesbian, and to allow businesses to fire people just for being gay, and allow restaurants, hotels, and other service providers to have the legal right to refuse to serve lesbians and gay men.

Tina Fetner

The pro-family movement also has attempted to block kids from forming Gay–Straight Alliance groups in their high schools. These groups are extracurricular social clubs that provide a safe space for kids to talk about sexuality, and often have a diverse mix of straight, gay, lesbian, bisexual, or "questioning" youth (those who are unsure of their sexual identities), as well as kids who don't follow traditional gender norms. Though a federal law dictates that public high schools cannot discriminate against extracurricular groups based on the content of their discussions, the pro-family movement has supported those high schools that have tried to shut these groups down.

Abortion

Abortion is a very contentious issue in America, with people holding very strong feelings for or against making this procedure available to pregnant women. The pro-family movement is squarely positioned on the "pro-life" side of this debate, and works diligently to restrict women's access to abortion. This battle occurs in a number of venues, including the "front lines" of medical clinics that provide abortions or abortion counseling. Picketers protest outside these clinics, and often try to convince women who enter the clinics to change their minds about getting an abortion.

Another front in this battle is legislative, and although the US Supreme Court has determined that women have a constitutional right to choose to terminate their pregnancies, the pro-life and pro-family movements have urged legislators to curtail that right whenever possible. They have successfully limited the number of women who have access to abortion by implementing parental consent and parental notification laws that require pregnant women under the age of 18 to obtain signatures from their parents before they can obtain an abortion.

The impact of the pro-family movement

The success of the pro-family movement on some issues, and their ongoing battles on other issues, have an impact upon different groups in different ways. Below, I look at the pro-family agenda through a few different lenses.

Youth

From the pro-family perspective, keeping information about sex away from young people is tantamount to protecting children from harm. But there is little acknowledgement by pro-family activists that youth, those years between sexual maturity and legal adulthood, is an age category that is distinct from childhood. Thus, the pro-family agenda does not distinguish small children in grade school from high school seniors.

Many pro-family policies are targeted at youth. Some, like abstinence-only sex education, make it more difficult for young people to get accurate information about condoms and other birth control, rape crisis assistance, and options such as emergency contraception, or the "morning after pill," which prevents pregnancy when taken soon after sexual intercourse. The pro-family movement has successfully lobbied five states to adopt policies that prevent teachers from discussing homosexuality in the classroom, and dozens of others to require parental permission before youth can participate in such a discussion.

Other policies have direct impact upon young people's bodies and physical well-being. Parental consent requirements for abortion procedures put young women's choices in the hands of their parents. And the pro-family movement's opposition to anti-bullying laws mean that schools will be less safe for lesbian, gay, bisexual, and transgender kids.

Women

Restricting access to abortion is one pro-family policy that directly impacts on women's lives. The pro-family agenda includes reversing the 1973 Supreme Court decision, *Roe v. Wade*, which determined that abortion is a constitutional right. Pro-family activists are hopeful that new judicial appointments to the Supreme Court will set the stage for a legal challenge to this historic ruling.

Other pro-family policies have a disproportionate impact on women, such as restrictions on the distribution of emergency contraception and legal protections for pharmacists who refuse to fill prescriptions for birth control pills. Other policies that restrict women's sexuality include bans on the vibrators and other sex toys that many women use to achieve orgasm. The pro-family movement would also like to change marriage laws to make it more difficult to get a divorce, which will be the most harmful to women who are victims of domestic violence.

Women outside of the United States are also affected by pro-family policies. The pro-family movement's successful implementation of the "Mexico City Policy" (commonly known as the "global gag rule") in US foreign policy means that federal funds will not go to any foreign aid organization that provides abortions, refers women to abortion providers, or even discusses abortion as an option with pregnant women. Other pro-family-supported foreign aid policies, such as de-emphasizing condom use in HIV-prevention efforts in Africa, will cost both women and men their lives.

Lesbian, gay, bisexual, and transgender people

Lesbian, gay, bisexual, and transgender people are major targets of the pro-family movement, which claims that lesbian and gay people are a threat to the family. Pro-family activists actively opposed same-sex marriage and succeeded in writing laws that prevented lesbian and gay couples from marrying until same-sex marriage was legalized in 2015.

Marriage is not the only anti-gay item on the pro-family agenda. As I have mentioned, the pro-family movement also opposes anti-discrimination protections for lesbian, gay, and trans-gender people. They also want to exclude sexual identity from states' hate crimes laws, and they work to prevent lesbian, gay, bisexual, and transgender people from adopting children or becoming foster parents.

Sexual politics as social movement politics

Each social policy, whether it is at the level of the federal government or the local school board, has a direct impact on the way that individuals experience and can express their sexuality. Even though sex is very personal and intimate, it is also very social at the same time, because many different aspects of our sexual lives are governed by laws, policies, and more informal social norms. Even something as simple as how and where we can talk about sex is influenced greatly by social policies and norms.

The conservative pro-family movement has recently had a strong influence on this public debate about sexuality. By insisting that very restrictive policies govern sexuality and that the conservative social norms guide sexual behavior, they take a position directly opposite the liberal agenda set in the sexual revolution of the late 1960s, which calls for a "live and let live" approach to social norms, and argues for reductions in governmental restrictions on people's sexuality. In the United States, we have become increasingly polarized between two ends of the political spectrum when it comes to sexuality.

In other countries, which have less social movement activity on these issues, policy debates about sexuality tend toward compromise. As a result, more moderate policy outcomes are common, and we see a slow but steady liberalization of sexual policies in Canada, Australia, and much of Europe. In the United States, as a direct result of the pro-family movement, there is more controversy and less compromise on issues of sexual politics. So, the US is not following the same pattern as other nations. In fact, there is not much of a pattern at all, but more of a patchwork of court decisions, legislation, and executive orders that sometimes favor the pro-family movement, and at other times do not. The final outcome of the "culture war" in the United States remains to be seen, but the strength of both the pro-family movement and their political opponents seems to be increasing over time. This means that more Americans are taking up one side of these issues or the other, and as time goes on, the chances that we will reach a middle ground on sexual policy in the United States is shrinking.

chapter 68

Iran's sexual revolution

Pardis Mahdavi

On November 4, 2009, thousands of young Iranians poured onto the streets of Tehran to protest the fraudulent election of Mahmoud Ahmadinejad in June of the same year. As much as for what it commemorated, this day was important for what it demonstrated – namely that a social movement had become political. November 4, 2009, was the 30th anniversary of the hostage-taking in the US Embassy in Iran, often referred to as the Iranian Hostage Crisis. The 1979 taking of American hostages in Tehran sent a strong signal to all of Euro-America. Through their actions, members of the Iranian Revolution were saying that "This is a new Iran," and that they would not be under the thumb of the United States or Western powers or the Shah, Iran's monarch. Revolutionaries claimed the Shah was leading Iran down a path of decadence, "westoxication" (or *gharbzadegi* as it was called), that meant the country was straying from core ideals and values. During the Iranian Revolution, the Shah was overthrown and Iran underwent a regime change.

In November 2009, the scene on the streets of Tehran resembled the mass demonstrations that had led to the Iranian Revolution 30 years previously. Young people, disenchanted and frustrated with a regime that does not embody their hopes and dreams for Iran, took to the streets, coalescing behind a leader and movement referred to as the *Sabze*, or Green Movement. The process (set in motion after the fraudulent election of President Ahmadinejad on June 12) is part of a social movement that has been building amongst various groups of Iranians within the country, most prominently spurred by Iran's sexual revolution, multiple women's movements (religious and secular), and civil and political reform movements.

A sexual revolution, which has been taking place in Iran since the late 1990s, has coalesced with other movements (women's rights, minority rights, etc.) and has developed into the political movement known as the Green (*Sabze*) Movement. This movement was, until recently, without a leader and a definite agenda. Groups found their leader in the presidential candidate Mir Hossein Moussavi, who was (according to opposition leaders) denied his rightful place as the president of Iran by a corrupt regime. The Green Movement is about more than Moussavi. This movement is about Iranians communicating through their actions to the global public that they are not happy, that they want a change in their political system, and that they want to reclaim their full rights as citizens.

In this paper I chronicle the trajectory of what began as a sexual revolution and social movement among certain groups of middle- and upper-class young Iranians in Tehran, and then move from sexual politics to the civil rights movement we are witnessing in Iran today. I focus on the transformation of a sexual movement into a political movement in post-revolutionary Iran. I will first situate the current Iranian social movement in relation to other sexual and civil rights movements across the globe.

Sexual revolutions and social movements in Euro-America

This is not the first time the world has seen an association between sex, civil rights and social revolution. Sex, drugs, and rock-n-roll were key components to the countercultural sexual revolution in the United States and Europe in the 1960s and 1970s. The sexual revolution that took place in the United States in the 1960s (and similar versions of social movements taking place in parts of Europe around the same time), set the stage for larger social movements that culminated in changes in attitudes towards social justice, equality, and the self.

In the United States, the 1960s were marked by shifting views on sexuality, gender relations and social recreation. The US sexual revolution was about more than changing views of sexuality and intimacies; it was about a search for authenticity, claiming autonomy and resisting authority (Allyn 2001; Escoffier 2003). During this time, youth experimented with sexual relations outside of traditional familial arrangements and heteronormativity. A series of interconnected movements emerged that included the struggle for civil rights, women's rights, minority rights, the rights of the disabled, and lesbian and gay liberation. These movements were often connected to broader justice issues such as anti-poverty, low-income housing, unionization and so on.

The prevailing attitude underlying this sexual revolution and its accompanying social movements (often captured under the umbrella phrase "counterculture"), was a profound distrust of authority, and a resistance to "the establishment," or the government. This distrust was fueled by a series of events including President Eisenhower's 1960 deception over the U-2 incident, the botched Bay of Pigs invasion in 1961, skepticism towards the investigation into the assassination of President Kennedy in 1963, the resistance to the Vietnam War, and a number of clashes between activists/protesters and the police. Activists in the counterculture movement began pointing at the shortcomings of the US government and questioning law enforcement (this was a time when words like "pigs" and "fuzz" entered the vernacular to refer to policemen).

Though opposition movements were not a new occurrence in the history of the United States, the counterculture movement had a series of defining characteristics which set it apart from its predecessors. First, and perhaps most importantly, was that this movement seemed to be driven by young people. Many of today's "baby boomers" were leaders of these social movements, and students were at the heart of the counterculture on university campuses. The baby boomers were seeking to break free from the repression of the 1950s, and sought to transform notions of social justice, tolerance and equality. Furthermore, resistance to authority through civil disobedience was a centerpiece of activism. Finally, its culture of experimentation extended from the body and gender roles to dress and drugs. The societal shifts set in motion in the 1960s are still being felt to this day.

In Eastern Europe, countercultural movements spread rapidly as a series of collective reactions to the harsh authoritarian regimes of the Soviet bloc. The Hungarian Revolution of 1956 was perhaps the first instance of a civil rights social movement in Eastern Europe; it was met with a harsh crackdown by the Soviet government. This was followed in 1968 by Czechoslovakia's "Prague Spring" which laid the groundwork for the Velvet Revolution that took place in Czechoslovakia in the late 1980s.

In Western Europe, countercultural movements spread rapidly to major European centers such as Amsterdam, Berlin, London and Paris. The German student movements of the 1960s and the French general strikes of 1968 were manifestations of the counterculture. In Britain, the emergence of the "New Left" was a movement of leftist activists that first centered on labor unions and then expanded into a broader movement seeking social justice, tolerance and equality for different populations. The UK, like the United States, was also home to counter cultural influences, giving birth to pop groups like The Beatles and Pink Floyd and to many types of countercultural style movements such as the Mods, the Rockers, the Teddy Boys and the Punks (Hebdige 1981).

These social movements were about challenging established views on politics, gender, the body, and the self; they were also broad movements for social justice and cultural change. They relied on activism on the streets, but also on cultural productions such as music, and the "body politics." Civil disobedience and opposition to "the establishment" were manifested through dress, music, and lifestyle experimentation as well as public protests. These various aspects of the counterculture combined in the United States and parts of Europe to push for major socio-political change.

Iran's sexual revolution

During the summer of 2000 I went to Tehran to write about the daily lives of young people. When I arrived, the phrase constantly on the minds and lips of the youth with whom I spoke was "sexual revolution," a phrase that would keep me coming back to Iran for the next seven years. The phrase "sexual revolution" or *enqelab-i-jensi* (in Persian) was one that ordinary Iranians used. Young people and their parents would talk about a change in the discourse around sexuality and especially heterosexuality and heterosocial relations. These changes were referred to as *their* sexual revolution. By "sexual revolution" they often meant a change in the ways communities of young people think, act, and talk about sex. This sexual revolution was just one part of a larger movement that my interviewees referred to as a sociocultural revolution, or *enqelab-i-farhangi*. This social movement encompassed behaviors such as pushing the envelope on Islamic dress, sexual behaviors, heterosocializing, the creation of an underground rock-n-roll scene, driving around in cars playing loud illegal music, partying, drinking, dancing and so on. Basically, the sociocultural revolution involved young people doing what they aren't supposed to do under current clerics' interpretations of Islamic law.

The Islamic Republic of Iran (IRI) is governed by Islamic law (or the *Shari'a*). The many meanings of *Shari'a* are complex and vary depending on who is interpreting the laws and how. In this chapter, I refer to Islamic law as it has been interpreted by members of the clerical regime in power in Iran since the Revolution, though I acknowledge that this is just one set of interpretations of Islamic law. This version of Shari'a law contains strict rules on comportment, leisure, sociality and sexuality. Shari'a mandates, among other things, that women and men should interact minimally before marriage. For example, this means that an unmarried young man and woman seen in the company of one another without a chaperone could technically be arrested and punished since young men and women are not to spend time alone with one another. Opposite-sex young people should limit their interactions to conversations at school, in groups, or in the presence of family members. Furthermore, this version of Shari'a mandates that women should be covered in "proper" Islamic dress (ideally a cloak from head to toe, hiding any bodily shape). Islamic law, as interpreted by the Iranian "morality police," also mandates a somber comportment and devotion to higher powers as the main source of pleasure and recreation. In 2006, President Ahmadinejad rolled out a new "Morality Plan" that sought to re-enforce his vision of Islamically approved behavior and comportment. It is important to note that what may seem to those of us in the West to be superficial or casual behaviors (such as wearing make-up, attending underground parties or gatherings, and driving around in cars playing music deemed illegal by members of the regime) is understood as potentially risky political behavior in Iran.

Under this interpretation, everything in Iran becomes political and politicized. It has politicized Islamic dress, certain types of music, and even certain websites. Examples include internet bans on sites such as Facebook, Orkut, or Friendster, and the banning of many popular Iranian bloggers, underground rock musicians, and film makers. Those who violate its rules are harassed, punished, or sometimes forced to leave the country. Many young people in Iran have become inspired to engage in political activism through their involvement in these social movements.

This movement began (as have other sexual revolutions in other parts of the world at various points in history) among the middle and upper middle class in Tehran – the most urban center – and then moved to other socioeconomic groups in other parts of the country. What began as a small movement seeking to shift attitudes about morality, comportment and sexuality in Tehran quickly broadened to a larger focus on the body, sociality, and comportment in opposition to what many young people view as a repressive regime. Young people, in an attempt to subvert the fabric of morality woven by the Islamic regime in power in postrevolutionary Iran, are using their bodies and social behaviors including sexual activity, recreational drug use, and the creation of an "underground" music scene (sex, drugs and rock-n-roll) to challenge the regime (Mahdavi 2009).

A movement led by youth

The sexual revolution is led by educated, restless youth and is changing sexual and social discourses, redefining pleasure and recreation, and leading some young people to become involved in the larger movement pushing for general social change. Today, 70 percent of Iran's population is under the age of 30. Literally *children of the revolution*, many of these young people were born during or right after the 1978–79 Iranian Revolution which led to the Islamic Republic of Iran. Urban young adults who comprise almost two-thirds of Iran's population are highly mobile, highly educated (84 percent of young Tehranis are currently enrolled at university or are university graduates, with 65 percent of these graduates being women) and underemployed (there is a 35 percent unemployment rate amongst this age group). Many are also highly dissatisfied with the current regime, and use their social behaviors to resist what they view as a repressive government.

Having fun and carving out spaces for recreation have been politicized by Islamists in power (Bayat 2007) who seek to regulate social activities and cleanse the public sphere of "morally questionable" behavior. Behaviors deemed "morally questionable" differ based on interpretation, but can range from small things like wearing excessive make-up or bright colors, to public displays of affection, to drug use and sex work.

"Me wearing lipstick," noted Mahnaz, a 20-year-old beautician, "is more than just looking good, it's about pissing off them, the morality police, and about me getting satisfaction." Another young man talked about the meaning of resistance to him: "Look, this regime, the one in power, they are all about taking away fun," explained Ali Reza, a 22-year-old student from Tehran University. "They are so focused on what we do, they made fun political, so we use our fun, we use our day-to-day looks, fashions, and fun times to tell them we don't care what they think. This is us resisting," he added. Another young woman commented on the regime's focus on make-up and expressed her confusion. She lamented:

> What I'm trying to understand is, why can't I do *namaz* (prayer) wearing nail polish or make-up? Why do I have to wipe those things off for doing *namaz*? Why can't I present myself to God the way I want to? The way I present myself to my friends? I have so many questions, the regime is full of contradictions, and then they wonder why we don't want to follow.

Her boyfriend Saasha, a 21-year-old religious studies major, took her sentiments one step further.

> They sit for hours and tell us, when you want to enter into the bathroom, enter with the right foot. If you sit on the floor, cross this foot over this one. Ay, *Khoda* [God]! We are really out of it, this regime is really out of it. This is what they want to teach us. They want to focus on going to the bathroom, and when and where to have sex. There are more important things like dealing with our huge unemployment or traffic problems, but they have chosen these things to focus on, so this is how we fight back, by focusing our attentions on social, sexual and cultural relations [*ravabet*]."

Many of the young people I spoke with said that they had decided to often engage in "extreme" behaviors to challenge the Islamic regime. Notes Ashghar, a young jewelry salesman residing in the northern part of Tehran:

> The regime complains about the youth and our cultural revolution. But it's their own fault that the young people have become like this. They breed this version of Islam. They tell us *this* is our culture, Islam. It has been beaten into us, and we don't like it, so us young people, we reject everything that has to do with religion or their version of culture. Why do we want to move to be more Western? They hate the West; by default we love it!

Young people emphasized that they were exploring their sexuality, engaging in a sexual revolution that they see as a movement for social change, and they are trying to renegotiate intimacy, citizenship, and a sense of self in ways that challenge the current regime.

Inspired by the women's movements and reform movements (movements pushing for a reform of principles of Islamic law) the sexual revolution started to take hold as a social movement and led some young people to begin to move from sexuality activism to a larger push for social justice and equality. Azar, a 23-year-old student at Azad University in Tehran, explains:

> For me, well it started out about looking good, having fun, and dating. But then I saw the politics behind what we were doing. I saw that it meant something, that it was threatening. I began to see things differently. I began to view my actions as my rights, and that's how I got involved in pushing for social change.

Azar's comments echo at least a dozen other interviewees who told of a similar trajectory. In the aftermath of the fraudulent election of Ahmadinejad in June 2009, these movements began to coalesce in the Sabze Movement.

Civil disobedience in the Sabze Movement

"The personal is political" was the phrase that echoed across the United States during nationwide civil rights protests. Just as civil disobedience was the primary strategy in the counterculture of the United States and Europe four decades ago, so too is this the strategy employed by members of the Green Movement in Iran today. Though met by violent responses from the regime's Revolutionary Guard and police, the activists of the Green Movement continue to pursue peaceful means of resistance. They have employed creative strategies such as the currency campaign. This involved marking various money bills with slogans criticizing the hypocrisy of the regime and calling for social justice. For example, Rial and Toman (Iranian currency) bills marked with slogans from the opposition movement (such as a one-dollar/toman bill bearing the slogan "Where Is My Vote?") have increased exponentially, with each slogan a call to others to engrave their large bills with slogans demanding freedom of speech and a return of individual autonomy. The government attempted to take these bills out of circulation but found that there were so many of them that it would lead to a financial collapse if it were to do so.

This movement is perhaps one of the largest and most profound examples of civil disobedience the region has seen in decades. The protests led by the Green Movement involve activists walking, sometimes silently, other times chanting "God is great," a slogan used during the Iranian Revolution to oust the Shah. This slogan has been reclaimed by the opposition to signal that God is now on the side of the opposition and that the actions of the regime violate the ideals of Islam. The Green Movement also distributes images and videos that show members of the Revolutionary Guard and police using violence against peaceful protesters. During the bloodiest clashes between the opposition and Revolutionary Guards that took place on December 27, 2009, video clips showed police harassing, shooting, and even using their cars to run over the protesters. By contrast, the protesters were shown trying to stop the violence. One prominent clip showed a scene where protesters outnumber policemen. Instead of violently clashing with the police, the protesters had formed a human wall, backing the police into a corner so that they could not use violence on other activists. Another clip featured a woman who threw herself on top of a policeman in order to prevent him from hitting her and her co-protesters. She was not trying to hurt the man, but rather using her body as a shield to stop him from hurting others.

Gender in the Sabze Movement

Similar to the counterculture of the US and Europe, activism around issues of sexuality and gender have played a major role in shaping the contours of the Green Movement. Many of the protests are led by women and involve men and women protesting side by side, thereby challenging norms requiring gender segregation. Furthermore, many of the public leaders and icons of the Sabze Movement have been women. For example Zahra Rahnavard, wife of the opposition leader and presidential hopeful Hossein Moussavi, was an important part of his campaign; she was often seen standing by her husband, holding his hand at times, and has been a key political figure during and after the campaign. There is also the martyred figure of Neda Agha-Soltan, the young woman gunned down during the early weeks of the protests in June. Her face and story have become a call to action for the Green Movement.

More importantly, there has been the use of the *hijab* (head covering for women) by men, a public demonstration of gender-bending that serves as a call for equality by the activists. This campaign began during and after the arrest of one of the opposition activists, a student leader by the name of Majid Tavakoli, who was arrested after a speech that was highly critical of the regime in early December of 2009. Following his arrest, the authorities published photographs of Tavakoli wearing the *hijab* as he tried to flee the police. The police published these photographs to shame him as one of the public figures of the Green Movement by portraying him as unmanly and cowardly. This strategy backfired on the regime, however, when the pictures became a symbol of a grassroots movement with hundreds of men posting online photographs of themselves in *hijab*, with captions reading "We are all Majid." In the protests that have followed, many men have been seen wearing head coverings in a public statement against the regime.

The hypocrisy of the regime has also been highlighted by evidence of the rape and torture of political prisoners. In particular, the use of rape has been pointed to as evidence that the regime has lost touch with Islamic values. The fraudulence of the mass trials, combined with the heavy use of violence by members of the Revolutionary Guard, have contributed to a large-scale delegitimization of the regime and what it purportedly stands for.

Looking ahead

What started as a sexual revolution and a series of small-scale social movements has become a large-scale civil disobedience movement. What seemed to some outside observers as young people falling prey to the pitfalls of "sex, drugs, and rock-n-roll" has evolved into a social and political movement that is now challenging the Iranian Islamic regime. As was the case with countercultural movements in the United States and Europe, social movements can often combine to become forces of broad societal change. Today, the sexual revolution, combined with the women's movement and minority rights movements, has led to a far reaching civil rights movement, the likes of which the country has never before seen, and which will certainly change the future of Iran.

References

Allyn, David. 2001. *Make Love, Not War: The Sexual Revolution: An Unfettered History*. Boston, MA: Little, Brown.
Bayat, Asif. 2007. "Islamism and the Politics of Fun." *Public Culture*, 19(3): 433–60.
Escoffier, Jeffrey (ed.). 2003. *Sexual Revolution*. Philadelphia, PA: Running Press.
Hebdige, Dick. 1981. *Subculture: The Meaning of Style*. 2nd ed. New York: Routledge.
Mahdavi, P. 2009. "Who Will Catch Me if I Fall?" in A. Gheissari (ed.), *Contemporary Iran: Economy, Society, Politics*. Oxford: Oxford University Press.

chapter 69

War and the politics of sexual violence

Margarita Palacios and Silvia Posocco

When one hears the words "sexual violence," one normally thinks about domestic sexual abuse (from one family member to another one), sexual harassment in the work place, sexual abuse of children, and different sorts of sexual assault, including rape. In regular peace time, these are indeed the most frequent sexual crimes that take place in our society. There is, however, a second context of sexual violence. Sadly, there are numerous examples of warfare situations where not only soldiers, but civilians, have been the target of violence. Sexual violence during war takes place either through sexual slavery (i.e. the establishment of brothels for the military), gang rape of women right after a military conquest or victory, and through different forms of sexual torture of war prisoners. Some of the most striking examples of this type of sexual violence during the twentieth century include the sexual enslavement of Korean women by the Japanese army (between 1910 and 1944) and the mass rape of women during the partition of the Punjab region between India and Pakistan in 1947. Most recent examples include the rape camps established by the Serbs in the middle of Europe in the early 1990s to the mass rape of Bosnian-Muslim women, and the mass rape, sexual torture and killing of Tutsi women by Hutu militia during the Rwandan genocide in 1994.

There is yet another fairly current example of sexual violence in the context of warfare. Although not comparable with the previous ones – neither in terms of direct state intervention in its planning and execution, nor in terms of sheer number and death rates – the case of sexual torture of prisoners by US military personnel in Abu Ghraib Prison in Iraq, shook the world when pictures of naked prisoners simulating sexual acts were made public through the media.

Although there are evident differences between civilian sexual violence and warfare-related sexual violence, it is still possible to establish a line of continuity between them. Indeed, feminist research has attempted to move beyond this division between what could be called "private" versus "public" sexual violence. Feminists have argued that both types of sexual violence are indeed political insofar as they respond to prevailing social constructions of femininity and masculinity, and to the unequal relation of power between the genders. This perspective opposes "essentialist" ideas about genders and sexuality, and particularly challenges the notion of sexual violence as being the expression of otherwise irrepressible male sexual desire. From our cultural perspective, we argue that gender relations have to be understood as connected to other aspects of our identity, such as our nationality, class, ethnicity and race. Furthermore, gender and sexual dynamics are intimately linked to processes of nation-state formation and to the exercise of state power, in particular, the way the state regulates our bodies and intimate lives.

In order to develop this argument, we have divided this chapter in three parts. In the first part we present our analytical framework where we discuss a range of approaches to the understanding of sexual violence. In the second section we analyze the case of two war-torn societies, namely the former Yugoslavia and Rwanda, where mass rape aimed at ethnic cleansing took place. In the third and last section, we discuss the images of sexualized torture in the contemporary War on Terror and aim to relate these images to contemporary expressions of sexual violence. We finish with a short reflection about what can be called "structural violence" – a set of larger processes of economic exploitation, social marginality, and political exclusion – and how it can shed light on the understanding of the current mass killings of women particularly in Ciudad Juárez, Mexico.

Building an analytical framework

In public discourse, sexual violence is often portrayed in "essentialist" gendered terms; men are always portrayed as perpetrators and women as victims. From this perspective, sexual violence is understood as the expression of a masculine predisposition towards sexual aggression and violence. There are several problems associated with this sort of approach. First, in a paradoxical way this framing provides both a justification for the occurrence of sexual violence (suggesting its inevitability), and a "double victimization" of the targets of sexual violence, as victims of rape are often blamed for the violence they have suffered. Second, we object to the view that always understands women as victims and men as perpetrators. On the one hand this gender stereotype jeopardizes the possibility of male victims of sexual torture to come out to the public and to seek help and justice for what has happened to them. The concealment of violence against men reduces public awareness of sexual violence as a common war strategy. On the other hand, a women-only victim approach ignores the available research which shows how race impacts gender and sexual dynamics, including violence. As we will see, countering essentialism in the analysis of sexual violence therefore means not only understanding relations between men and women, but also relations between masculinized and feminized positions and how these may be marked by histories of racism, irrespective of the gender or ethnic identification of the persons involved.

One of the most compelling illustrations of this latter dynamic is the analysis of the "myth of the Black rapist." In the American South, for example, this myth played out in the wave of lynchings of Black men that would routinely follow episodes of the sexual assault of White women; the myth provided a justification for lynchings. More recently, the "myth of the Black rapist" has resulted in the automatic treatment of men of color as suspects and the indiscriminate use of rape charges, punitive procedures, and carceral regimes against them. In this context it has been argued that even today the politics of rape accusations against Black men cannot be disconnected from an analysis of the history of slavery and its legacy, and the way it has helped to create a public discourse as well as specific legal procedures which continue to foster forms of social exclusion and criminalization.

Moreover, anti-sexual violence initiatives focusing exclusively on male violence against women miss the way violence has profoundly different consequences for differently racialized and gendered subjects. Rather than leading to relevant forms of activist mobilization or examples of benign state protection for the vulnerable, state intervention may result in the unjust criminalization of gendered and racialized populations – men of color, in this specific instance – and the proliferation and consolidation of racist discourses. As stated previously, a non-essentialist analysis of sexual violence requires opening up the categories of men and women into notions of feminine and masculine positions. Only then is it possible to see how women are not exempted from, but may be deeply implicated in, such masculine logics and their effects.

The third problematic aspect of a view of sexual violence based on male-biological instincts is its inability to link sexual violence with broader political aspects of our identity, such as those related to our ethnicity or nationality. According to our view, in order to understand sexual violence one needs to consider the broader political context, in particular the role of the state. From this perspective, sexual violence functions as a sort of "identity technology," which aims to consolidate or annihilate certain specific (gendered/sexual/racial/national) identities. In other words, sexual violence can be viewed as an intervention in the world which *produces* identities and social relations. As we demonstrate in the case studies that follow, sexual violence can be used as a social technology through which notions of nation, ethnic identity and belonging are fabricated, or indeed, destroyed. The connection between sexual violence and projects of nation-building is in part due to the way the body of women, as in the figure of the archetypal mother and reproducer, is often made to stand for the nation in a range of contexts. Women represent the future, in both cultural and biological terms. Culturally, because women are seen as embodying the main values of the community and as the bearers of the identity and honor of the group. Biologically speaking, women represent the future because it is assumed that through reproduction a certain "pure genetic pool" is passed from generation to generation. Men, on the contrary (and through masculine-militaristic ideologies), are often presented as the guardians and saviors of those identity boundaries. As we will see in the case studies that follow, one of the main ideas behind nationalist ideologies has to do with the "myth of origin," which means that one can only join the collectivity if born into it. Sexual violence in this context is often the result of attempts at "purifying" the nation from perceived threats or forms of cultural pollution.

Margarita Palacios and Silvia Posocco

Bosnia, Rwanda, and Abu Ghraib Prison

As stated above, sexual violence, and particularly rape, is often connected to myths about an irrepressible male sexual drive. However, sexual violence cannot be explained simply as a result of a pre-social sexual instinct; rather it is related to racial and complex gender-social processes. As a form of power, sexual violence either contributes to the reinforcement of existing power relations (between different members of a community or between different communities), or it aims to re-establish structures of power that are being challenged. Now, although rape is an instrument of violence which attempts to degrade, dehumanize and humiliate the victim, it would be misleading to assume there is nothing "sexual" about it. Indeed, one of the most complex issues to understand is precisely the interplay of power and sexual desire, or more specifically, the way power operates through the sexualization of racialized bodies.

Let's look at the following three case studies of Bosnia, Rwanda, and Abu Ghraib Prison in Iraq.

Bosnia

The demise of the Soviet Union was followed by declarations of independence by Slovenia and Croatia during 1991, and a year later was followed by the declaration of independence by Bosnia-Herzegovina, which led to a civil war between Serbs, Croats and Muslims. This war lasted several years and resulted in more than 100,000 deaths, the displacement of millions, and the rape of thousands of women and girls. In year 2000, 16 women survivors of the war in Bosnia testified in the "Foca Rape Trial" before the International Criminal Tribunal for the former Yugoslavia in what was the first international trial focusing on rape as war crime. Its verdict was that sexual enslavement and rape are crimes against humanity. In Bosnia, as well as in Rwanda, the aim of mass rape was to destroy a particular culture or ethnic group, and both cases were described by the court as experiences of "rape as genocide or ethnic cleansing."

As it has now been documented, Serbian attempts at building a "Greater Serbia" faced, among other challenges, low birth rates which led to government and the Serbian Orthodox Church policies that encouraged Serbian women to be "faithful to the nation" and become mothers. The Serbian low birth rate was lower than that of other ethnic groups (such as Albanians, Muslims and Romanians), and this trend was perceived as a threat to the purity of the Serbian nation. Thus, in the context of the war between the Croats and the Muslims of Bosnia-Herzegovina the idea of women as having a duty to produce more children became a policy of forced impregnation or forced maternity of Bosnian-Muslim women.

Although sexual violence occurred at different moments and with different purposes (as part of lootings and intimidation in order to terrorize the local residents; as forms of sexual torture of male and female prisoners; and as sexual slavery), the most striking form of sexual violence was aimed at reproducing the Serbian people and the consequent elimination of the Bosnian-Muslim community. The Serbs established mass-rape camps in public places such as hospitals, schools, hotels, etc., where women were raped repeatedly in order to increase the Serb population. Women who became pregnant received special attention and were denied the right to abort. Considering the fact that those children would grow up not with Serbian but Bosnian families, it is interesting to note here that this policy of forced impregnation assumed that the identity of those children would still be Serbian and not Muslim. This assumption shows how not only the "biological contribution" of the mother is denied, but also the cultural upbringing of those children.

Since female purity is a central value within Muslim culture, it has been argued that rape was also intended to "pollute" women, to debase them and in doing so destroy the basic pillars upon which Muslim families and communities were built. Indeed much debate has arisen regarding the double victimization of these women who, after rape, became outcasts in their own communities.

Rwanda

In the case of Rwanda, it has been argued that land disputes and economic hardship due to the civil war that started in 1990 helped radicalize Hutu militias and allowed them to recruit large number of unemployed boys and young men in order to fight the Tutsi. Certainly, the economic hardship suffered by the Hutu while Tutsi elites enjoyed a privileged social position during the era of Belgian colonial power bred ethnic resentment. In fact, tensions between the two ethnic groups go back to the period of Rwandan independence. After independence in 1961, the Hutu rose to power and pursued a social revolution which attempted to free the country from both colonialists and Tutsi (indeed, Tutsi went into exile during the 1950s and 1960s).

Within this already very tense social context, the murder of two consecutive Hutu presidents (1993 and 1994) by Tutsi rebels triggered the violence that in three months killed 75 percent of Tutsi people. Some 800,000 Tutsi died and an estimate of 250,000 to 500,000 women and girls were raped. Since Tutsi and Hutu lived side by side (as family, friends, neighbors), these killings were not only political but very personal. Hutu were forced to show loyalty, and if one was Tutsi one was often killed along with one's family, friends and neighbors.

As in the case of Bosnia, ethnic cleansing had a clear gender component. Although Tutsi men were blamed for social problems such as unemployment, anti-Tutsi propaganda was very much directed against women. The negative and threatening features of their alleged "promiscuity," arrogance and "sexual adventures" with foreigners helped to position them at the "outer" boundary of the Hutu nation.

Once violence started, men and boys were the first ones to be killed. Women, however, before being killed, were the target of atrocious sexual violence and torture. There were mass rapes, their breasts were cut off, their pubic hair burnt, and their genitals cut wide open with spikes and machetes. These brutal acts of violence against women show the way women's bodies come to symbolize a nation and their mutilation serves to intimidate and debase the enemy.

Abu Ghraib

In 2004, photographs of Iraqi prisoners being subjected to a range of sexualized acts at the hands of United States military personnel were made public and circulated among news media globally. The images portray the explicit sexual abuse of prisoners. In one image, for example, a young woman, the US soldier Lynndie England, holds a distressed prisoner on a leash against the background of the Abu Ghraib detention facility which is located near the Iraqi capital, Baghdad. In another image, Iraqi prisoners are made to pile up on top of each other simulating sodomy, as two US soldiers, Lynndie England and Charles Graner, smile and give the camera the thumbs up (Figure 69.1).

When these photos were first published, the images provoked outrage and anger. They seemed to expose practices of abuse and torture which contradicted the official American rhetoric which portrayed the military invasion of Iraq and the War on Terror as liberating. As these photos provoked a public outcry, the official response from the American military and government was to isolate the case, call it an exception, and prosecute the individuals responsible for the crime. From our perspective, we question whether this practice was an exception. We also wonder what sort of conditions allowed for this kind of abuse of power? And we ask: What racialized and sexualized image of the Muslim subject is conveyed in these practices?

As both an offensive weapon and an instrument of torture, these dehumanizing images implying male Muslims engaging in sodomy have a double effect. First, they project the Muslim subject as both sexually deviant and potentially homosexual. From the Islamophobic *and* homophobic perspective that informs the perpetrators' actions – which considers the Muslim subject as inherently sexually conservative and socially illiberal – this appears as a cruel irony particularly tailored to offend the prisoners. The role of women as agents of torture brings yet a second symbolic layer worth analyzing here: it is *precisely* women who, in the gendered logic of the torturers, can inflict particular harm, as they can further feminize, emasculate, and therefore humiliate, the anonymous male Muslim subjects. This is an example of the dynamics which we have described previously as the feminization of the victim of sexual violence and the masculinizing of the perpetrator – regardless of the gender identification of the persons involved.

(a)

(b)

Figure 69.1 Torture at Abu Ghraib.

In the context of Abu Ghraib, sexual violence clearly functions as an "identity technology" which *produces* racialized, sexually deviant Muslim bodies alongside neo-colonial White female masculinity specifically deployed to humiliate the enemy. Sexual torture therefore functions through the racial prejudice, cultural stereotyping, gendered and homophobic imaginary of the perpetrators, the US military.

Structural violence during peace time

The cases discussed above suggest that sexual violence is often a deliberate weapon of war and have confronted us with the complex dynamic of the social construction of the enemy target. As we have shown, sexual violence during warfare functions as a form of technology which produces or annihilates certain types of gendered/sexualized/racialized identities. Although difficult to grasp, we have also attempted to stress the ambiguous relation between aggression and desire, or between violence and sexuality.

In this last section we would like to introduce the notion of structural violence. This idea speaks to the way violence is connected to broader social processes of economic exploitation, social marginality, and political exclusion. Also, structural violence is related to the way that certain bodies are deemed dispensable, not only during war, but also in peace times.

For example, the murders of women in the US–Mexican border region – notably in the Mexican town of Ciudad Juárez, in the border state of Chihuahua – have struck a chord in both popular and academic discourse. The systematic occurrence of hundreds of violent murders since the early 1990s has been deemed a *feminicidio*, that is, a form of systematic gender violence against women. The neologism *feminicidio*, or "femicide," reflects feminist activists' deliberate effort to highlight the importance of gender in violence, including genocide. This case also underscores a key point: sexual violence extends well beyond the domain of war and conflict. As other scholars have documented, in a global economy there are certain populations, often women or poor laborers and migrants, who are construed as sources of exploitable and disposable labor. The labor regime of border regions in towns such as Juárez, in the context of a neo-liberal model of capitalism, determines whose lives are viable and whose lives are wholly dispensable. The rationale for the brutal sexually motivated murders of women in Juárez, therefore, is clearly sustained by this specific extractive industrial model but also by the wider symbolic frameworks which construct women as disposable. The "disposability" of the women working in the Juárez factories extends from the factory (where they constitute a flexible resource which can be done away with and easily replaced depending on market demands), to the street and into the home – all spaces where they can be assaulted and murdered with impunity.

The notion of structural violence also stresses the fact that violence is a dimension of social life, and as such, it is best studied and approached not as an aberration or anomaly of violent "individuals," but rather as something which occurs in routine social processes. In summary, several issues emerged in this chapter. The first one refers to the coupling of power and sexuality. Questions that emerge here, for example, are about "bio-power" or how our identities (bodies, desires and subjectivities) are linked to the operations of state power, and through which processes these bodies

Margarita Palacios and Silvia Posocco

come to embody either the "honor of the nation" or an enemy. A second theme refers to the social consequences of sexual violence: how do societies rebuild themselves after episodes of sexual violence? How do victims of sexual violence reintegrate into their communities? As we have seen, this has been a difficult experience not only for the raped women but also for their children born with the stigma of war.

Finally, the notion of structural violence has also confronted us with questions of justice. As discussed above, new developments in the law have allowed us to recognize sexual violence as constitutive of warfare, and have provided new frameworks for understanding the possibilities for justice and reparation. However, as the examples discussed above also suggest, legal instruments are themselves the crystallization of cultural and historical processes. As such, they are often the expression of specific exclusionary and punitive logics – as illustrated in the analysis of the "myth of the black rapist" – and therefore they fall short in the realization of justice. The understanding of sexual violence as structural – and not exceptional – allows us therefore to acknowledge the most fundamental and problematic space of difference between the *socially situated law* and the always deferred *and yet to come in the realm of ethics*. It is this space of difference that sustains our critical approach to the study of sexual violence.

Bibliography

Davis, Angela. 1983. *Women, Race and Class*. London: Women's Press.
Puar, Jasbir K. 2007. *Terrorist Assemblages: Homonationalism in Queer Times*. Durham, NC and London: Duke University Press.
Yuval-Davis, Nira. 1997. *Gender and Nation*. London: Sage Publications.

PART 10

Global and transnational sexualities

Introduction

When commentators use the term "globalization," they are often referring to the idea that the world seems as though it is getting smaller. There are a number of ways in which the world is, at least figuratively speaking, getting smaller. For example, air travel (and fairly broad economic access to being able to use it) has made flying the distance between Washington, D.C. and London roughly the same as getting in a car and driving from Washington to Boston. Moreover, e-mail, Skype, and constantly updated websites mean that the world is getting smaller in terms of the time it takes information to travel – one goes on a trip to Japan and posts photos via Facebook before one's friends back home have even gotten out of bed for the day. Thus, two key aspects of globalization involve space and time compression – technologies make vast distances seem shorter and shape our expectations to send and receive information almost instantaneously.

Globalization as a concept also encompasses changes in the world's economic system that have accelerated since the 1980s. Japan, North America, the United Kingdom and Europe have largely shifted manufacturing jobs to other regions such as Southeast Asia or Latin America. These economic powers now have post-industrial economies that primarily employ workers in the service sector – jobs in retail, cleaning services, secretarial work, financial planning, health services, security services, food services, etc. This means that workers are on one of two economic tiers – upper-tier jobs that require higher education, pay reasonably well and provide benefits, while the lower-tier jobs feature part-time (or temporary) minimum-wage jobs with no benefits. The world economic system is tiered as well, with workers from poorer countries providing the cheap labor for the manufacture of consumer goods or the cheap labor of the hotel, restaurant and other service industries that cater to tourists.

Globalization is linked to the concept "transnational," which means extending beyond the boundaries of the nation. Transnational carries the connotation of movement across borders. To the degree that the world has become smaller through globalization, a higher proportion of people's lives are now transnational in some way than 30 years ago, meaning that they travel across borders to work, play, and live, and they have responsibilities to more than one nation.

Globalization and the transnational movement of people affect sexuality in a number of ways. As media/internet sources more widely circulate particular versions of Western heterosexual ideals, globalization has a homogenizing influence on cultural ideals such as the norms of masculinity or standards of beauty and what it means to be sexually desirable. Sometimes it is partially for sexual reasons that people move transnationally – tourists seeking adventure, others immigrating because they believe they will find more sexual freedom and acceptance in a new country. Or, sexual labor may be the means by which (primarily) women are able to finance transnational movement. Sexual labor may also be a means for migrating women to support themselves in a new country or supplement the low wages associated with post-industrial service work. Additionally, sexual stereotypes of "foreigners" have been a consistent part of the immigrant and migrant worker experiences, where they may be interpreted as more sexually promiscuous or sexually prude than the native population. These stereotypes greatly impact the experiences of transnationals.

It's difficult to predict where globalization and transnational movement will ultimately lead. While globalization is associated with having a homogenizing influence on sexual norms, there are also those who actively resist homogenization; this can happen in quite opposite ways. One type of response to globalization has been moral leaders who have created sexual revisionist national histories that claim that sexual openness to things like same-sex intimacy is merely part of Western cultural imperialism. Another type of response has been for sexual subcultures within countries to reject rigid sexual and gender binaries and rethink sex and gendered norms and practices in more diverse, boundary-breaking ways.

chapter 70

Mexican immigrants, heterosexual sex and loving relationships in the United States

Interview with Gloria González-López

Gloria González-López is a sociologist at the university of Texas at Austin. She conducts ethnographic research and in-depth interviews in her books *Erotic Journeys: Mexican Immigrants and their Sex Lives* (2005) and *Family Secrets: Stones of Incest and Sexual Voilence in Mexico* (2015).

First, tell us about yourself.

I was born and educated through my undergraduate years in Monterrey, Mexico before I migrated to the United States in the mid-1980s. I eventually mastered my (still accented) English and have lived for almost 25 years in Texas and California. Prior to becoming a researcher, I was trained as a couple and family therapist in Los Angeles, and I have worked with Latin American immigrant families and women at community-based agencies located in Houston and Los Angeles. I received a Ph.D. in sociology from the University of Southern California in 2000. I have conducted sexuality research with Mexican and Mexican immigrant populations, and I currently teach graduate and undergraduate courses on sexuality, gender and society, and qualitative methods and sexuality research at the University of Texas at Austin. I am the author of *Erotic Journeys: Mexican Immigrants and Their Sex Lives* (University of California Press, 2005) and co-editor of an anthology titled *Bridging: How Gloria Anzaldúa's Life and Work Transformed Our*

Own (2011). I am currently conducting sociological research on the sexual, romantic, and life experiences of adult women and men with histories of incestuous relationships and who currently live in four of the largest urbanized areas in Mexico.

In the book Erotic Journeys, *you study gender and sexuality from a relational perspective. Could you explain what it means to study gender and sexuality this way?*

By relational I mean at least two specific things. First, theoretically, "relational" means that I have a special interest in learning about and closely examining individuals' sex lives not in isolation but within the context of their relationships with other human beings including but not limited to partners, families, friends, and other personal relationships within specific situations. As a sociologist, I think that sexual expression is best understood in the context of relationships with others, that is, relational sexuality, rather than individual sexuality.

And second, methodologically speaking, "relational" means that I am studying the sex lives of my informants within the context of the two-way professional relationship that emerges during the research process; that is, the relationship I develop with them and the relationship they develop with me. For example, I gather my data by establishing a relationship with another human being who is willing to open up, share, and explore in depth her/his sex life through a relationship with me which involves dialogue, deep listening, and storytelling within a context of mutually respectful and honest interaction, while making sure that other ethical issues and concerns are taken into account including but not limited to confidentiality, anonymity, and a sense of safety, in the broadest sense of the word.

Women's virginity can have multiple meanings in different cultures. You coined the term "capital femenino" to refer to virginity as a type of social endowment. Could you explain this, as well as the different meanings of virginity that you found in your research?

First, I would like to share why virginity has been a social enigma for me for a long time and in some way the driving force sustaining my sexuality research project with Mexican immigrant women. In 1997 I started to conduct interviews with the immigrant women who eventually gave life to my book *Erotic Journeys*. As a researcher and as a Mexican woman, I was driven by my special interest and curiosity in understanding virginity within the context of Mexican society and culture.

My curiosity had its roots in the 1970s, back in the Northeast region of Mexico. I must have been 13 years old or so and I recall being terribly shy with regard to sexually related matters. I remember experiencing both curiosity and fear when I heard about a physician who advertised her services (mainly on tv and in newspapers) of "repairing women's virginity" in her small town which was located close to my hometown of Monterrey. I remember not being able to understand an interview with this woman physician, who was identified as "controversial." I also recall listening to people who would jokingly talk about "the buses loaded with women" who would go to her small town to supposedly have their virginity repaired. As a shy adolescent, I witnessed these dialogues in silence. Back then I did not even know what the word "virginity" meant, but I kept thinking about why people would be constructing narratives of scandal around these topics.

As I grew older, I kept remembering the controversial doctor who had been performing hymen reconstruction on bodies of women (women who could have been my sister or a close friend). Twenty years later, and as I was ready to defend my doctoral dissertation examining the sex lives of immigrant women, I looked for this woman physician. I was fortunate to find her. I talked to her about my project and requested an interview, which I later conducted in her small town in 1998.

"When and why did you start repairing a woman's virginity?" was among many of the questions that I asked during our conversation. She explained to me that back in the late 1960s she used to work as a doctor in small towns in the region and one day a group of mothers came to her crying. She learned that these mothers were in pain because their daughters had been raped. But besides the act of violence exercised against a young daughter's body, their main concern was that their daughters would not be able to find a good man who would eventually accepted them "as is" (that is, non-virgins) and would be willing to marry them. In other words, these mothers were deeply concerned about their daughters being rejected by a future boyfriend and potential husband because they were no longer virgins. The doctor thought that repairing a woman's virginity through hymen reconstruction (while making sure the vagina would bleed after being re-ruptured) would be a way to protect women from this kind of potential rejection from a man. Since the late 1960s to the day I interviewed this doctor in 1998, she had been conducting hymen reconstruction on countless women, usually free of cost or for a modest fee or donation, according to the financial situation of the woman. She explained to me that this service has never been for profit but as a way to protect women from sexism.

Although we could engage in a debate and argue that this doctor could be in fact reinforcing sexism by validating a woman's need to prove her virginity to a man, the contradictions, tensions and paradoxes that emerged in my head during the interview helped me understand what I was only beginning to understand through my research with Mexican immigrant women. So as I was analyzing the long in-depth interviews my 40 women informants so generously offered to me, I was about to learn an important sociological lesson with regard to women, virginity and gender inequality in Mexico: a woman who is a virgin (and presumably has an intact hymen symbolizing moral integrity) can actually exchange her virginity (i.e. virginal vagina) for the possibility of having a financially stable life via marriage. As I discovered this and engaged in previous published research on sexuality and sociological theory, the idea of *capital femenino* became the ideal concept to capture and examine the ways in which virginity may acquire a higher or lower "value" depending on very specific socioeconomic contexts and circumstances shaping the economic opportunities for women educated in a patriarchal society.

While my interview with this doctor helped me tremendously to understand what my informants were telling me through these in-depth interviews I conducted in Los Angeles, I was also becoming aware of the many socially constructed meanings that virginity may acquire within some patriarchal cultures. From the women and men that I interviewed, I learned that virginity may represent, symbolize, and/or mean many things including (but not limited to) decency, moral integrity, moral responsibility, and respect for oneself and for the family (especially the parents). For some women and men, virginity may symbolize a "little treasure," a "gold medal," or "a gift." Beyond the white dress, which may symbolize many things besides the "purity of the bride," blood stains on the honeymoon bed sheet may become proof and a reason to celebrate the virginity of a newly wed woman, or blood stains on a modest piece of cloth that a newly married woman might have used to clean herself after the sex act may become a memento to keep in a special place as she reminds herself and her husband of the moral integrity she possessed when they married.

While both women and men may construct the multiple meanings of virginity through countless expressions and in specific contexts and circumstances, we should remember that these meanings are vulnerable to future social constructions as both Mexican society and Mexican-American and other US-Latino immigrant communities reinvent their sexual moralities and social realities, in an increasingly connected and wired world, which goes hand-in-hand with the consequences of globalization.

A central point of Erotic Journeys *is about how Mexican immigrants' sexual lives are transformed by the experience of migration. Could you explain some of the ways their sexual lives changed after migration?*

As I conducted my fieldwork, these immigrant women and men taught me that their sex lives are fluid, unstable processes; they are always in flux, evolving. I learned that it would be practically impossible to establish a rigid "before-and-after" migration examination of their sex lives. After coming to this country and settling within their receiving communities (in Los Angeles in this particular case), these informants reinvented their sex lives in very specific ways and within very specific migration- and settlement-related contexts, situations, and circumstances.

First, immigrant women and men migrate to this country with a set of pre-established ideologies and practices, which upon migration and settlement are unpacked and revisited. I learned, for instance, that mothers who teach a new generation of Mexican-American girls may renegotiate the ways in which they educate their daughters with regard to sexuality. With regard to virginity, for instance, I learned that some mothers perceived the United States as a country where men "do not care about virginity" and therefore a daughter who has premarital sex might not be at risk of being stigmatized for not being a virgin at marriage. Interestingly, from this perspective, women still depend on their perceptions of men's opinions about women and sexuality. In other words, on either side of the border, gender inequality is redefined by women's perceptions of what men expect of them as women. In this regard, some of the men who were fathers raising daughters told me that virginity was no longer "a tradition." Instead, a new concern for them was to make sure a daughter would not get pregnant and drop out of high school and thus decrease her chances of going to college. For them, the dream-come-true of a daughter attending college would not only make them feel honored as parents (who might not have had these opportunities while growing up), but would also compensate for their hard work as immigrants now raising a new generation of Mexican-American children.

Second, I learned that a sense of anonymity and geographical relocation and physical distance from parents and other family authorities may give some young immigrant women an opportunity to reclaim their sex lives, especially now that they are not under the close moral surveillance of a parent or authority figure. For example, I interviewed a woman who told me that after she migrated she finally had the opportunity to have sex for the first time and eventually established a cohabitation relationship with a man. Being far away from her parents allowed her to have sex and "to live with a man" without being married, something unthinkable had she stayed in her small town in Jalisco. However, distance did not necessarily soften the emotions associated with being "morally disobedient" as a woman. For example, this same woman told me that she still felt shame and guilt for behaving in that way, even without her parents knowing about her sexual behavior.

Third, I also learned that immigrants migrate to the United States with a socially constructed image of the United States. However, upon settlement in these marginalized inner-city barrios, they feel a deep sense of disillusionment. The United States is not the country they have constructed in their fantasies before migrating. Drug and gang activity, poverty, racism, a fast-paced life, segregation, the presence of homeless people, their everyday struggles to attain employment and survive, among other dimensions of their social realities, transformed the "American dream" into an "immigrant nightmare" for informants who settled into marginalized sectors of the country. The United States became a sexually dangerous place and a morally decadent nation characterized by lack of moral restraint, or *libertinaje*, an expression used by these informants as they described this country.

Fourth, women and men develop social networks with others who live within their immigrant communities. Conversations (formal and informal, individual or collective) evolved upon settlement and these interactions between immigrants may become a source of information for them (most notably women in this study) as they explore potential answers to their sex-related concerns, for example, with regard to HIV/AIDS, sex education of children, and sexual and romantic relationships with their partners, among other themes.

And fifth, men who work as day laborers (or *jornaleros* as they are known in some Mexican immigrant communities) may be exposed to sexual harassment from a potential (white, male, presumably "gay") employer as they look for work in the busy corners of the city of Los Angeles. This finding actually made me redefine my earlier radical approaches to gender studies and taught me an important sociological lesson: men who might have enjoyed some patriarchal privileges before migrating may experience the vulnerability of these same privileges as their lives are now shaped by complex race and class relations (among other factors) which place them in positions of disadvantage in the new social contexts shaping their everyday lives and survival journeys.

Building on that, how is the experience of immigration different for Mexican women who come to the United States versus Mexican men in regards to sex?

For the women and men that I interviewed, patriarchy might have been challenged as part of the immigration and settlement processes within some of the complexities I identified above, but patriarchy did not disappear. For example, the women I interviewed, more frequently than the men, reported "sexual gains" as part of the immigration journey. I would like to outline these gains for the women (as I discuss in page 218 in *Erotic Journeys*): (a) Paid employment and control over their paycheck may help women redefine their relationships with their heterosexual partners and in turn develop some kind of sexual autonomy and/or empowerment as women; (b) women may experience "woman-to-woman networking" (for example, social interactions with other immigrant women) as having a positive impact on the quality of their sex lives; (c) none of the women that I interviewed reported any kind of involvement in commercial sex (which may become extremely dangerous and exploitative for Mexican immigrant women); (d) none of the women reported exposure to drug, alcohol or gang activity and none of them had been homeless (for some of the men it was the opposite); (e) geographical distance from parents resulted in a weaker family control which allowed some of the women in the study to experience their sex lives with an enhanced sense of freedom.

In my interviews, it was not unusual to learn that some men may perceive that Mexican women "change" after they migrate (e.g. becoming assertive as a woman and calling 911 in the event of domestic violence) as men themselves are deciphering racial, class, citizenship status uncertainties, and linguistic challenges, among other forms of discrimination. These complexities invite us to look at how both women and men decipher patriarchy in both nations, especially within a changing Mexican society and in increasingly complex Latino barrios in the United States.

You found that your interviewees sometimes brought up machista or machismo during their interviews. What does machismo mean, or rather, how might it have multiple meanings?

Machismo has become a popular concept in Mexican society to refer to in order to explain different expressions of gender inequality. For example, it is not uncommon to hear people who would say that *machismo* is responsible for violence against women. In other words, *machismo* has become some kind of cultural translation or equivalent for sexism. Accordingly, my informants would use the concept of *machismo* to explain different forms of sexism in our interviews. Other concepts related to *machismo* include *machista* (which could be translated as "sexist"), or *macho*, which is also used to identify as "sexist man." The concept of *macho*, however, may have many nuanced meanings that may not necessarily have a negative connotation. For example, "being a macho" for men who belong to a particular generation may mean being a man who is a good, hard-working father. It may also have a special connotation associated with pride of being a man, or manhood. However, in my study, none of my informants used, and/or associated the concept of "macho" with any kind of positive connotation.

One recurring theme in Erotic Journeys *is that there are often differences in the sexual beliefs, practices and experiences of individuals who grew up in rural areas versus those who grew up in urban areas. In what ways do rural and urban sexualities differ?*

This is a good question because Mexico is becoming an increasingly urbanized. However, the women and men I interviewed who were from rural areas were born and raised in locations that were still far from being urbanized. So based on these in-depth interviews, I learned that for women educated in rural areas – where exposure to education and paid employment opportunities was limited or non-existent – virginity was highly valued. As *capital femenino*, virginity became a form of social endowment these women could exchange for marriage opportunities and a stable financial future. As part of this process, women and men may construct specific ideologies that may associate a desirable moral integrity with lack of premarital sexual activity in a woman, and women who do not comply with these moral expectations may become stigmatized and rejected. In this way, socioeconomics and ideologies seem to go hand-in-hand as some specific expressions of (desirable and undesirable) womanhood (i.e. being a woman or "femininity") are established. It is important to mention that this is relational; that is, it happens in the context of relationships with men and their families.

Moreover, I learned that in rural towns, some ideologies promote the sexual initiation of young men with a sex worker as part of a ritual initiation into manhood. These experiences were coercive and emotionally challenging for the men I interviewed. Interestingly, although these rural ideologies and practices with regard to sexuality may selectively affect both women and men, they are fluid and nuanced and not necessarily uniform for all those raised in rural contexts.

At the same time, being raised in urban contexts does not automatically mean that women and men will become "more progressive" in terms of sexual morality. Some of the women and men from Mexico City explained that they have been exposed to some versions of these ideologies and practices. Interestingly, I learned that more exposure to paid employment and education along with ideals of "modernity" may offer alternative, fluid, discourse-changing beliefs and practices in regard to sexuality and sexual morality. The presence of women's groups advocating for gender equality and the presence of activists advocating gay and lesbian rights are examples of the social forces that go hand-in-hand with the fluid and changing ideologies and practices with regard to sexuality that may allow for a possibility to embrace more gender equality and respect and acceptance within and beyond heterosexual relationships.

Many of your interviewees were Catholic. To what degree did you see Catholicism shaping sexuality?

This is a great question. As a woman who was raised in the Catholic faith, I was especially curious and interested in this aspect of my informants' sex lives. As I asked them questions about sexual morality, the church, and their own sex lives, the most important lesson that I learned was the following: the values and ideologies traditionally promoted by the church with regard to sexuality and relationships were neither the only direct cause nor the most influential social force controlling the sexual desires, behaviors, or beliefs of my informants. I also learned that when Catholic morality became an important force of social control in their sex lives, this was identified as influential more frequently *a posteriori* rather than *a priori*. What do I mean by this? After engaging in the sex act, for example, a woman may experience religious guilt and shame *after* the fact, but not necessarily *before* she had sex. I also learned that although the church has historically established in *theory* these moral ideologies and values with regard to sexuality in Mexico, it is the family as a social institution that puts these beliefs into *practice*. For example, this is exemplified by women who said that they did not have premarital sex because they were afraid of god but because they were afraid of an unexpected pregnancy and the risk of their parents forcing them to marry a partner who was not desirable as a husband. I remember the illustrative case of a woman who told me that her fear arose while engaging in premarital sex with her boyfriend: "No, I was not afraid of god, I was afraid of my mother!"

In my research I also learned that the Catholic faith had a more influential role on the sex lives of women and less significant (or limited) influence on the sex lives of men. In a book chapter called "Confesiones de mujer: The Catholic church and sacred morality in the sex lives of Mexican immigrant women," in *Sexual Inequalities and Social Justice* (Teunis and Herdt 2007), I talk about the complex ways women reconcile their Catholic faith, practices, and behaviors closely related to their sex lives, especially with regard to contraceptive use, condom use, and abortion, among other related issues.

Sexual story-telling frequently contains themes of pleasure and danger. Were there typical ways that you saw these themes in the sexual stories immigrants told you?

Yes, definitely. The point of intersection between both danger and pleasure was revealed to me: engaging in something "prohibited" increased the meaning of something being perceived as "forbidden" and thus the sensation of excitement and anticipation would increase. Some of my informant women, for example, told me that even though sex was "prohibited" and they would have to conceal a relationship with a boyfriend, the "dangerous" situation in itself became a source of "pleasure." Engaging in romantic and sexualized activities thus became a process that is both pleasurable and dangerous. For example, I learned that men may go out to bars in increasingly vibrant and visible social spaces, and they may drink and engage in unprotected sex with people they do not know, which may similarly expose them to the same dynamics involving pleasure and danger. Although this is not necessarily exclusive to immigrants (this may happen in any town on earth and with "local" people), it is relevant in the context of immigration because of the larger social contexts and structures shaping their lives. For example, for men living in conditions of crowded housing where emotional isolation, poverty, and alcohol and drug use (among other factors) are part of the immigration experience, these exciting sexualized interactions may unleash conditions of vulnerability to sexually transmitted diseases, HIV/AIDS in particular.

You conducted three-hour in-depth interviews with Mexican immigrant women and men about their sexual lives. What are the challenges and rewards of employing in-depth interviews in sexuality research?

I have experienced more rewards than challenges while conducting sexuality research with Mexican women and men. I think the biggest reward is that it is always both an honor and a privilege (as a human being and a researcher) to have the opportunity to engage in such a deep and meaningful personal dialogue with another human being who is willing to share so much – so generously and so unconditionally – about the most intimate aspects of his or her personal life, sex in this case.

Second, each in-depth interview becomes a lesson for me as a researcher: I am always reminded of how little I know about sexuality and society. For example, conducting in-depth interviews on sexuality has allowed me to explore the ways in which

I can stretch out, the ways in which I can continuously grow and develop intellectually and professionally, methodologically and theoretically. Each individual dialogue with a research participant keeps me humble as a scholar who is curious about understanding the intimate interconnections between sexuality, society and culture. An in-depth interview allows me to give my hand (metaphorically speaking) to another human being and invite her/him to teach me about the many complexities and nuances of sexuality within the context of social and cultural forces.

Third, in-depth interviews allow me to identify and learn more about the tensions, contradictions, and paradoxes with regard to how a human being may recall, interpret, and articulate their sex life as part of their own personal growth and development. In that regard, it is always invaluable to see how people may develop some kind of awareness as they immerse themselves in their own personal histories and stories. It is always a gift to be interviewing someone who may experience an "aha!" moment during the interview, someone who may learn more about their own personal and family life through the interview process. The interview may help provide answers to questions that they might have never asked themselves. It is always a reward for me as a researcher to recognize the ways in which our interview could be potentially and immediately beneficial for the informant.

And finally, one of the biggest rewards of conducting in-depth interviews is that this kind of methodology allows me to capture people's actual voices. I find this process to be very political and potentially self-empowering for an interviewee in the sense that this methodology allows people to articulate their own life histories and stories.

Some of the challenges that I have experienced include the following. First, I have learned that being alert and self-monitoring during the interview process may become an emotionally and intellectually exhausting process. This has become evident when I am driven to go on, but then the interview may become longer and equally exhausting for an informant. I learned about this in the beginning of my career and am now more aware of this situation; I think it is happening less and less.

Second, in-depth interviews involve dialogue that becomes very personal and intimate, which brings a sense of trust that may stimulate curiosity in an informant, who may in turn want to interview the researcher. When I conducted the interviews for my book *Erotic Journeys*, I was frequently asked about my own personal life during or after the interview. When this was the case, I always explained the methodological rigor I needed to follow but accepted that I would answer any question after the interview was completed. However, I realized by the end of the interview, an informant was ready to be done and she/he was not interested in asking any questions and/or had completely forgotten about it. Relatedly, I always had a list of professionals in various fields in case an informant had a question, or when histories of abuse were revealed during the interview and there was the need to refer them to a professional.

These are the rewards and challenges that come to mind at this moment and especially as I think of the research project that resulted in the book *Erotic Journeys*.

Do you have any concluding thoughts on immigration and sexuality?

In my study I felt like I was barely touching the surface of the sex lives of my informants, especially with regard to heterosexual relationships. I think there is an urgent need to do more sociological research on the sex lives of women and men in non-heterosexual relationship arrangements, especially for Mexican immigrant women who are in these romantic arrangements and who are practically invisible in the social science literature on gender and sexuality.

Bibliography

González-López, Gloria. 2007. "Confesiones de mujer." In *Sexual Inequalities and Social Justice*, ed. Niels F. Teunis and Gilbert Herdt, pp. 148–73. Berkeley: University of California Press.

—. 2005. *Erotic Journeys: Mexican Immigrants and their Sex Lives*. Berkeley: University of California Press.

Teunis, Niels F. and Gilbert Herdt (Eds). 2007. *Sexual Inequalities and Social Justice*. Berkeley: University of California Press.

chapter 71

Uganda's Anti-Homosexuality Bill

Reflections from a transnational frame

Marcia Oliver

What does it mean to think about sexuality transnationally, or within a transnational frame? The concept "transnational" refers to the movement of people, ideas, practices, institutions, and capital across national borders. Transnational movement affects sexuality in diverse and often unpredictable ways, like the global circulation of Western (particularly Western European and North American) cultural ideals of normative heterosexuality (e.g., standards of beauty) or lesbian and gay identities via mass media technologies; the movement of people across borders in search of sexual ventures or freedom from persecution; or people who engage in sexual labor as a means to support themselves and their families after migrating to a new country.

The movement of information and people across borders also plays a major role in facilitating transnational activism and solidarities around issues of global justice, such as campaigns to end war and torture, neoliberal development, violence against women, or homophobic policies and regimes. Yet, not all forms of transnational activism set out to challenge global economic and socio-cultural inequalities or support the human rights claims of marginalized or non-normative populations. For instance, transnational activism can also include conservative or right wing movements – many of which are concerned with defending and (re)installing "traditional" institutions and values across the globe, especially concerning gender (e.g., women's roles in society and rights to bodily autonomy) and sexuality (e.g., gay and lesbian sexualities). Take for example the growing activism in recent years that supports greater criminalization of homosexual behavior and harsher penalties for gay people. This is perhaps most evident by the horrific acts of violence committed by the Islamic State against gay men or the recent wave of anti-gay legislation that has been passed (or reinstated) in different parts of the world, including Russia, Iran, India, and a number of sub-Saharan African countries (e.g., Uganda, Nigeria, and Gambia).

A transnational frame enriches our analyses of sexuality and sexual politics by focusing on the specific sites where transnational flows of ideas, resources, and people are happening to better understand how global and domestic factors – institutional, cultural, economic, political, religious – intersect to produce, reinforce, reconfigure, and often times challenge sexual injustice and violence in particular contexts.

This chapter focuses on the emergence of recent anti-gay legislation in Uganda, a country in the Great Lakes Region in East Africa. It reflects on some of the assumptions informing global reactions to Uganda's Anti-Homosexuality Bill, which has been widely criticized by scholars and human rights activists for perpetuating ahistorical and deeply problematic accounts of "African" sexuality. What kinds of accounts about "African" sexuality do we hear from both opponents and supporters of the legislation? On the one hand, Western critics of the legislation have often engaged in racist and imperialist campaigns that equate "African" countries with unbridled homophobia and violence, while "Western" countries represent "modern" sexual liberation and freedom. Accompanying this racialized discourse is the paternalistic assumption that "African" sexual minorities are passive "victims" in need of Western protection and liberation. For example, in a recent BBC documentary, *The World's Worst Place to be Gay?*, Scott Mills names Uganda as the world's most dangerous place to be gay, which (like other Western commentaries) tends to reduce homophobia to an ahistorical and monolithic account of "African" morality or culture. The colonial origins of homophobic laws and violence are ignored (more on this point below), as are the more recent interventions of U.S. evangelicals in supporting and promulgating anti-gay sentiments in Africa. These accounts also erase the continued violence and exclusionary practices that lesbian, gay, and transgendered people face in the Western world (see Mogul et al. 2011); the many voices that support LGBTI rights and equality in Africa; and the significant gains that have been made in the struggle to recognize sexual minority rights across the continent (see Ward 2013), such as the legalization of same-sex marriage in South Africa (2007) and the numerous African countries that have signed statements in support of gay and lesbian rights in the UN General Assembly (2008) and Human Rights Council (2011).

On the other hand, there are those who have shown support for the legislation within Uganda and from other African nations by denouncing homosexuality as "unAfrican" and an immoral imposition from the West. In making such claims, religious and political elites employ a fictive and essentialist understanding of "African" culture that erases the colonial roots of Christianity (and the colonial re-making of African sexualities as "naturally" heterosexual and reproductive) and the sexual pluralism and diversity that comprise African cultures (as elsewhere in the world). In other words, it is not homosexuality that was imported to Africa, but rather the institutionalization of legalized homophobia through colonial laws that define homosexuality as a crime "against the order of nature" (Penal Code Act 1950). This chapter aims to provide readers with a more situated and critical reading of Uganda's Anti-Homosexuality

Bill that accounts for both the transnational and domestic dynamics that have fueled its emergence, its formulation and key provisions, and support by many of the country's conservative religious and political leaders.

Uganda's Anti-Homosexuality Bill: mapping its emergence, demise, and return

Post-colonial Uganda is part of the Great Lakes Region in East Africa, bordered by Sudan in the North, Kenya in the East, Tanzania and Rwanda in the South and the Democratic Republic of Congo in the West. With a population of roughly 37 million, the vast majority of Ugandans are Christian, identifying primarily with one of the "two traditional pillars of Ugandan Christian life": the Anglican Church of Uganda or the Roman Catholic Church (Ward 2015: 128). These two pillars of Christian life are themselves a product of Uganda's colonial history – marked by the arrival of French (Catholic) and British (Protestant) missionaries in the late nineteenth century. With Britain formally declared the protectorate and authority of Uganda in 1894, the Anglican Church of Uganda became the informal established church of the colonial state, despite Catholicism's greater popularity with the rural masses. By the time Uganda gained independence in 1962, Christianity was deeply embedded within Ugandan society.

Colonial rule was principally concerned with breaking down old forms of life and creating the conditions that would bring new forms of life into being that would ensure civilization, security and trade. Many of Uganda's pre-colonial customs and laws were altered by colonial and missionary interventions, subjecting personal and social relationships to greater restrictions and surveillance. Those aspects of Ugandan culture that were perceived as "immoral" or against the laws of "nature" were targeted by colonial authorities who implemented a range of "civilizing" practices that were often informed by Christian and Victorian sensibilities about gender, sexuality, and morality. For instance, colonial laws based on Judeo-Christian values were enacted to encourage Ugandans to adopt the bourgeois (white) patriarchal family as the site for sexual expression and procreation (such as increasing bridewealth rates to impede customary marriages and encourage Christian ones). Integral to these "civilizing" projects were depictions of "African" bodies and sexualities as distinct from the West as primitive, deviant, excessive and ruled by desire (Tamale 2011). Imagining "African" sexualities as rooted in "nature" led to the absurd conclusion that African sexualities could not be anything but heterosexual and reproductive (Lewis 2011). This narrow representation of African sexualities informs the establishment of colonial sodomy laws that criminalize homosexuality (e.g., Uganda's Penal Code), as well as the recent social and political campaigns to intensify anti-gay legislation in the country (e.g., Anti-Homosexuality Act 2014).

In 2009, ruling-party Member of Parliament (MP) David Bahati introduced Uganda's Anti-Homosexuality Bill "to protect the cherished culture of the people of Uganda" and to "strengthen the nation's capacity to deal with emerging internal and external threats to the traditional heterosexual family," such as "sexual rights activists seeking to impose their values of sexual promiscuity on the people of Uganda" (Bill No. 18. 2009).

In February 2014, President Yoweri Museveni signed an amended version of the Bill into law. Although same-sex activity has long been prohibited under colonial law, the Anti-Homosexuality Act (AHA) sought to further criminalize same-sex sexuality to include "attempted" homosexuality, the "promotion" of homosexuality, "conspiracy to commit" homosexuality, and "aiding and abetting" homosexuality. It also imposed mandatory testing for HIV and life imprisonment for certain acts classified as "aggravated homosexuality," such as when the offender is HIV-positive.

International and national responses to the legislation were divided, with support voiced mainly by other African nations considering similar legislation and some of Uganda's (mostly Pentecostal) religious leaders and political elites (many of whom have connections with conservative evangelical actors and organizations in the United States). The Bill initiated extensive criticism both within and outside Uganda, ranging from LGBTI communities to progressive religious leaders (like retired Ugandan Bishop Christopher Ssenyonjo), from human rights activists to public health and HIV/AIDS experts, and from academics to state leaders and Western donors (including the U.S. and Britain). One of the most significant initiatives to emerge in response to the legislation – which led to the Anti-Homosexuality Act's (AHA) annulment in August 2014 – was a petition launched in the Constitutional Court of Uganda by a coalition of gay, lesbian, and transgender activists, academics, members of parliament, journalists and human rights organizations. Just months after the law was passed, the Constitutional Court of Uganda ruled in favor of the petition and struck down the legislation on the grounds that it was passed without parliamentary quorum. Although the court's decision represents a significant win by human rights advocates, it is noteworthy that the judicial reasoning was based on a procedural technicality, not on a normative or moral rejection of the substantive content of the Bill (such as opposing the AHA on the grounds that it violates Ugandans' constitutionally guaranteed rights to privacy, freedom from discrimination and cruel and degrading treatment, to dignity, and freedom of expression, thought, and assembly). At the time of this writing a revised version of the anti-gay legislation has been drafted (though not yet tabled in Parliament), despite President Museveni's recent warnings that the country's economic security and trade relations with key donors would be severely undermined should parliamentary members pursue additional anti-gay legislation (Vision Reporter 2014).

To some critics this revised Bill, entitled "The Prohibition of Promotion of Unnatural Sexual Practices Bill, 2014," is even more repressive and far-reaching than the country's previous Anti-Homosexuality Act. As its title suggests, the revised Bill reveals a much more concerted effort to prohibit the promotion of "unnatural" sexual practices, defined as "a sexual act between persons of the same sex, or with or between transsexual persons, a sexual act with an animal, and anal sex, within the meaning of section 145 of the Penal Code Act" (Draft Legislation 2014: 2). From a social constructionist perspective, the very language of "unnatural" sexual practices reflects a naturalistic view of sexuality, which functions to normalize reproductive heterosexuality as the only socially acceptable form of sexuality. All non-heterosexual forms of sexuality are rendered "unnatural" and, in this instance, criminal. Like the previous Anti-Homosexuality Act, anyone convicted of promoting "unnatural" sexual activities is liable to imprisonment for seven years, where promotion is understood broadly to mean "recruiting, encouraging, soliciting, or inciting a person to engage in unnatural sexual practices by providing premises, distributing textual or visual material or any other means to interest a person in unnatural sexual practices" (Draft Legislation 2014: 2). The revised Bill makes it a criminal offence for any person to lease or sublease premises for the purpose of engaging in "unnatural" sexual activities, raising fears among lesbian, gay, and transgender communities that if the Bill is passed they will face even greater violence and state persecution, including homelessness. Frank Mugisha, a gay-rights activist in Uganda, warns of the far-reaching consequences that the "promotion" aspect of the Bill will have on all Ugandans, including landlords who rent to LGBTI Ugandans, international aid and non-governmental organizations that provide services or advocate for LGBTI people, hotels that provide space for LGBTI meetings, journalists, academics, or LGBTI activists that disseminate information about homosexuality, and personal or organizational Twitter or Facebook accounts that contain LGBTI-related material (Johnston 2014).

Mugisha's concerns have not gone unwarranted. During a recent fieldwork trip in Uganda (August 2014), my colleagues and I witnessed first hand the chilling and harmful effects that the Anti-Homosexuality Act has on democratic governance, freedom of expression, and the lives of marginalized populations. Just weeks after President Museveni signed the Bill into law, the government began restricting the activities of one of the country's largest human rights organizations, the Refugee Law Project (RLP), under allegations that it "promotes" homosexuality under the guise of its human rights work. More specifically, the organization was denied access to refugee settlements throughout the country and was prohibited to work with refugee clients at its Kampala headquarters. Although the RLP has been particularly active in opposing the anti-gay law and organizing a coalition of civil society organizations to contest it (known as the Civil Society Coalition on Human Rights and Constitutional Law), the vast majority of its work focuses on providing legal assistance, mental health and psychosocial support, and conducting research and policy advocacy on issues that affect the more than 380,000 refugees and asylum seekers in the country (such as peace-building and transitional justice initiatives). As of summer 2015, the Refugee Law Project had resumed its work with refugees and asylum seekers after a 10-month suspension.

Homosexuality, Western conservatives, and political power in Uganda

The Anti-Homosexuality Act was not the first time that debates over homosexuality entered public discourse in Uganda; there has been a dramatic increase in public talk about homosexuality since the late 1990s (Hassett 2007; Tamale 2007). Nor was the legislation simply the product of Uganda's conservative political and religious leaders. As I have argued elsewhere (Oliver 2013), the wording and timing of the Anti-Homosexuality legislation were themselves influenced by both transnational and domestic factors. Of particular significance is the influence of the U.S. Christian Right (hereafter CR) in supporting anti-gay sentiments in Africa and, in particular, the crafting of the Anti-Homosexuality Act in Uganda. Although the CR has been tremendously successful in shaping gender and sexuality-related policies and laws in the U.S. for decades, the gay rights movement has made significant headway in shifting public attitudes toward greater tolerance and acceptance of gay and lesbian rights and marriage equality (especially among younger generations), culminating in the recent U.S. Supreme Court ruling (2015) that declared a fundamental right to marriage for same-sex couples. With its influence waning at home, the CR has turned its attention outward to the global realm, and more specifically to Africa, to spread its "pro-family" agenda. In 2005, the BBC's Focus on Africa reported: "Africa is being colonized and Christianized all over again. The colonizers this time are American, not Europeans, and the brand of belief they are bringing to Africa is Evangelical Christianity" (cited in Huliaras 2008). Although there is nothing "natural" about the Christian Right's vision of the family, it informs a worldwide alliance of conservative religious faiths committed to defending a particular vision of the family as "inscribed in nature and defined by heterosexual marriage whose primary purpose is procreation" (Buss 2004: 57).

The CR's global influence can be seen in U.S. foreign policies on HIV/AIDS prevention (especially the emphasis on abstinence and fidelity programs) and family planning; the elaborate communications network of CR broadcasting across sub-Saharan Africa (e.g., the Christian Broadcasting Network and the Trinity Broadcasting Network); its increased presence and activism within the United Nations over issues of gender, sexuality, and women's rights; as well as the dramatic increase in the number of Western conservative organizations working (and financing projects) in Africa since the 1990s. An important factor in this development is the recent controversies over homosexuality within the worldwide Anglican Communion, which has provided fertile ground for CR actors to join forces with conservative Episcopalians and allies in the global South to defend biblical orthodoxy on matters of human sexuality.

With global Christianity now concentrated in the global South (with over 30 million of its 80 million worldwide membership residing in Africa, notably in Nigeria, Uganda and Kenya) (Kaoma 2009), African bishops have become a powerful force in Anglican Communion politics. In the lead up to the 1998 Lambeth Conference (a large meeting that takes place every 10 years of bishops of the Anglican Communion to discuss key issues of the day), U.S. conservatives sought alliances with church leaders in the global South to oppose the more tolerant and liberal positions on sexuality supported by some Western Anglican provinces (Hassett 2007). Western efforts to build alliances with Southern Anglicans paid off: at the 1998 Lambeth Conference, African bishops were integral to passing a resolution that declared homosexuality to be "incompatible with Scripture" and recommended against the blessing of same-sex unions and the ordination of homosexuals as bishops. Moreover, following the U.S. Episcopal Church's decision in 2003 to ordain Gene Robinson (an openly gay man) as Bishop of the Diocese of New Hampshire, several Southern provinces severed ties with the Episcopal Church, rejected funding from the more liberal Western churches (Duin 2005), and offered their churches to U.S. conservatives who have broken ties with the Episcopal Church U.S.A. As Daly (2001) notes, the Church of Uganda is a significant player in the U.S. conservative Episcopal movement's growing international network: it is the second largest Anglican Church in the worldwide Communion (with roughly 8 million members or 30% of the country's population) and has become a popular "spiritual home" for many Western conservatives (see also Hassett 2007).

Marcia Oliver

The transnational linkages between U.S. and Ugandan conservative evangelicals have been well documented (Kaoma 2009; Sharlet 2008; Hassett 2007), with some of the most vocal religious and politically engaged anti-gay Ugandan activists having connections with CR actors and organizations (such as the secretive CR group known as the Family, or the Fellowship, California mega-church Pastor Rick Warren, and Lou Engle from The Call). As Reverend Kopya Kaoma's (2009) research reveals, it is many of the same U.S. evangelical organizations supporting anti-gay sentiments in Africa that have long been active in domestic anti-gay politics in the U.S. For him, and other human rights activists, the rise in homophobia throughout Africa is directly linked to the global anti-gay activism and alliance building of U.S. Christian conservatives. Just months before the Anti-Homosexuality Bill was introduced in Parliament, the Family Life Network (a fundamentalist Christian NGO in Uganda) organized a seminar that featured three prominent U.S. conservative Christians who spoke about the "truth" of homosexuality and the "dark and hidden" global agenda of homosexuality. Scott Lively from California's Abiding Truth Ministries was one of the speakers at the Kampala-based seminar. Speaking to religious leaders, parliamentarians, police officers, teachers, and concerned parents, he reiterated a number of claims that are well established in CR anti-gay discourse and literature: homosexuality as an irrefutable sin condemned by God; homosexuality as distinct from race (as a chosen, rather than innate, behavior) and undeserving of human rights; homosexuality as predatory (especially towards children); and the existence of a global gay agenda that promotes homosexuality and aims to destroy the moral foundations of society and human civilization itself (see Oliver 2013).

The direct influence of CR strategies and literature on Uganda's recent anti-gay campaigns is clearly apparent in a follow up meeting that was held just days after the anti-gay seminar, where the organizer (Stephen Langa of Uganda's Family Life Network) described Richard Cohen as one of "the most authoritative writers who has written on the subject [of homosexuality]" (Langa 2009). For those of you who may not be familiar with Richard Cohen, this is particularly alarming not only because in 2002 he was expelled from the American Counseling Association for ethics violations, but also because his text, "Coming Out Straight" (2000), cites the widely discredited research of Dr. Paul Cameron (director of the Family Research Institute, Colorado Springs) that claims homosexuals are more likely to abuse children. This outrageous assertion was a centerpiece of Langa's performance, exemplified by his claim that "what we're dealing with here is not a joke . . . they don't care about you. They want your children!" (Langa 2009), as was a dramatic narration of a passage from Michael Swift's (1987) "Gay Revolutionary," which is a staple in numerous CR publications (Herman 1997). Despite the text's explicit satirical nature, conservative anti-gay campaigns often use it as "evidence" of a powerful global gay movement that promotes homosexuality and aims to recruit the world into its "immoral" ways.

In some sense, there is nothing particularly unique about the anti-gay rhetoric that was affirmed at these meetings in Kampala: Christian Right actors have been formulating their anti-gay positions in the U.S. for decades and, as part of their efforts to build a transnational conservative Christian alliance, have increasingly distributed CR anti-gay literature and built alliances throughout Africa and elsewhere in the world (such as Kenya, Nigeria, Zimbabwe, and Russia) (see Federman 2014; Baptiste 2014).

Similar anti-gay sentiments are well established in the Ugandan press and circulated by Ugandan conservative religious and political leaders (see Oliver 2013). For instance, years before Scott Lively told his Kampala audience that gay rights are not human rights because unlike race, "there is no definitive study that has ever proved that homosexuality is innate" (2009), Pastor Martin Ssempa wrote in a letter to Human Rights Watch (a U.S.-based organization):

> I can certainly understand why organizations like yours [Human Rights Watch] want people to think that homosexuality is fixed, like race, and cannot be changed, because you know that would make people more sympathetic to your "sexual rights" agenda which conflicts with the strong family values of Uganda.
>
> (Ssempa 2007)

Within this letter, Ssempa not only denies LGBT rights by reiterating the CR positioning of homosexuality and race as distinct and mutually exclusive categories, he also equates Human Rights Watch with the encroaching "global gay agenda" that promotes homosexuality and threatens to destroy Ugandan culture and "traditional" family values. For Ssempa, and other conservative anti-gay activists, heterosexuality is "natural" and exists outside power relations, which (as critical sexuality and gender scholars note) ignores the multiple power relations that produce and regulate sexuality in socially desirable, albeit narrow, ways according to hetero-patriarchal and reproductive norms.

While it is apparent that many Ugandan anti-gay positions – including the wording of the Anti-Homosexuality Act – are profoundly shaped by CR strategies and discourse, these positions are not determined by the CR. Rather, conservative evangelicals in Uganda make claims to "African" culture and national sovereignty to denounce homosexuality as "un-African" and a neo-colonial imposition from the West. For instance, President Museveni has commended the Church for "resisting homosexuality, a decadent culture being passed on by the Western nations"; Archbishop Orombi has publically claimed that "homosexuality is against our culture;" and James Buturo, the former Ethics and Integrity Minster, has asserted that "we shall not allow those people from the West to define our identity and destiny" (see Oliver 2013: 98). Statements such as these rely on a particular conception of "African" culture, as historically fixed, homogenous, and fundamentally different from the West. The claims to African culture made by conservative religious and political leaders are particularly powerful; they speak to and manipulate very real social anxieties that many Ugandans experience everyday in relation to family and the nation, especially concerning the power of money to influence "corruptive" and "immoral" behavior (Sadgrove et al. 2012). This is particularly significant in a context of global neoliberalism, which has produced deeper inequalities and greater socio-economic difficulties for the vast majority of Ugandans.

Human rights activists draw on a number of strategies to counter the conservative claim that homosexuality is "un-African" or "against African culture," like pointing to the colonial roots of Christianity and, it follows, the institutionalization of the monogamous heterosexual family itself. Sexual pluralism long comprised African cultures and traditions. As historical and anthropological research shows, there is ample evidence of sexual and familial diversity in pre- and post-colonial Africa (Nyanzi 2013),

Marcia Oliver

including the expression of same-sex intimacies, which have acquired many different social meanings over time and in different contexts ranging from sin to special powers to the noblest form of love, as well as a way to establish hierarchy or exercise political resistance through history (Hoad 2007; Tamale 2014).

Other critics have shown how the "resurrection of official gay-bashing" (Olopade 2012) distracts the Ugandan public from the government's neglect of socio-economic issues and official abuses of authority (abuses that, for the most part, have been met with silence by both Western donors and conservative Christians). Sylvia Tamale, for instance, argues that anti-gay rhetoric serves as a "political tool" for conservative leaders to maintain power and divert attention away from more pressing socio-economic and political problems. In her words:

> Instead of blaming political mismanagement and corruption for high unemployment, the high cost of living, and poor health facilities, the population is encouraged to focus, inter alia, on red herrings such as "the vice of homosexuality" and "the evil of prostitution" which are fished out of the sea of morality particularly when electoral accountability is looming.
>
> (Tamale 2013: 39)

The Anti-Homosexuality Bill was introduced to Parliament just 16 months before Uganda's presidential elections. With debates over sexual morality taking the center stage in the international and national imagery, other pressing social, economic and political issues were marginalized and displaced from mainstream public discourse, such as the illiberal and authoritarian practices of Museveni's regime. For example, human rights activists in Uganda have widely criticized Museveni's grip on political power (since 1986), his use of violent tactics to crush political dissent (such as the recent Walk-to-Work campaign led by opposition leader Kizza Besigye) and restrictions on civil liberties (including freedom of assembly, media, and association), government corruption and reckless state expenditures on fighter jets and political campaigning and events – while millions of Ugandans face high unemployment, poor wages and working conditions, rising inflation, excessive living costs, and poor social welfare services.

I began this essay with a question: what does it mean to think about sexuality transnationally? In turning our focus to Uganda, we've learned that the rise in anti-gay sentiments and the emergence of the Anti-Homosexuality Act cannot be viewed in a vacuum, but must be seen in relation to a series of transnational and domestic factors. Of particular significance is the colonial re-shaping of African sexualities and the enactment of legal codes that criminalized homosexuality, the power and influence of Western Christian conservatives in supporting (and arguably inciting) the rise in anti-gay sentiments in Africa, and the instrumentalization of sexuality by diverse political and religious actors to support self-serving agendas. For conservative religious leaders both within and outside Uganda, anti-gay campaigns may serve to bolster their public standing and social relevance in global Christian politics; for Uganda's political elite, anti-gay rhetoric may help to sustain one's hold on political power and detract attention away from socio-economic and political misconduct; and for Western donors, anti-gay legislation may provide the necessary justification to impose aid conditionalities on African governments and nongovernmental organizations. One of the most significant (albeit unintended) effects of transnational anti-gay activism in Uganda (and elsewhere in Africa) has been the vibrant activism of LGBTI groups and human rights allies across the continent. Not only have they exposed the repressive and unconstitutional effects of anti-gay legislation on the lives of sexual minorities (and Africans more broadly) but, to close with the words of Sylvia Tamale, have made "the question of sexuality an intrinsic part of the democratic struggle on the continent, and not peripheral to it" (Tamale 2013: 42).

Acknowledgements

The author extends her gratitude to the many people in Uganda who gave their time and insights to her research over the years. She acknowledges the Uganda National Council for Science and Technology for granting her permission to conduct this research and the financial support from the Centre for International Governance Innovation, Waterloo, Canada (P.I. Dr. Suzan Ilcan, University of Waterloo). The author also thanks members of the Canadian Network for Critical Sociology (especially Elisabeth Rondinelli) and the editors of this collection for their helpful comments and suggestions.

Bibliography

Baptiste, Nathalie (2014). It's not just Uganda: Behind the Christian Right's onslaught in Africa. *The Nation*, 4 April 2014. URL: www.thenation.com/blog/179191/its-not-just-uganda-behind-christian-rights-onslaught-africa.

Bill No. 18 (2009). The Anti-Homosexuality Bill, Uganda. October.

Buss, D. (2004). The Christian Right, globalization, and the "natural family." In M.A. Tétreault & R. Denemark (Eds.), *Gods, Guns & Globalization: Religious radicalism and international political economy* (pp. 57–78). Boulder: Lynne Rienner Publishers, Inc.

Daly, L. (2001). A church at risk: The Episcopal "Renewal Movement." *IDS Insights*, 2(2), 1–2. URL: www.idsonline.org/publications.html.

Draft Legislation (2014). *The Prohibition of Promotion of Unnatural Sexual Practices, Bill, 2014.* 29 October 2014.

Duin, Julia (2005). African bishops reject aid. *The Washington Times*, 7 June 2005. URL: www.washingtontimes.com/news/2005/jun/07/20050607-115436-7061r/?page=all

Federman, Adam (2014). How U.S. Evangelicals fueled the rise of Russia's "pro-family" Right. *The Nation*, 27 January 2014. URL: www.thenation.com/article/177823/how-us-evangelicals-fueled-rise-russias-pro-family-right.

Hassett, M. (2007). *Anglican Communion in Crisis: How Episcopal dissidents and their African allies are reshaping Anglicanism.* Princeton: Princeton University Press.

Herman, D. (1997). *The Antigay Agenda: Orthodox vision and the Christian Right.* Chicago and London: The University of Chicago Press.

Hoad, N. (2007). *African Intimacies: Race, homosexuality and globalization.* Minneapolis: University of Minnesota Press.

Huliaras, A. (2008). The evangelical roots of U.S. Africa policy. *Survival*, 50(6), 161–182.

Human Rights Watch (2011). *UN Human Rights Council: A stunning development against violence.* URL: www.hrw.org/news/2011/03/22/un-human-rights-council-stunning-development-against-violence.

Johnston, Chris (2014). Uganda drafts new anti-gay laws. *The Guardian*, 8 November 2014. URL: www.theguardian.com/world/2014/nov/08/uganda-drafts-anti-gay-laws-prison-promotion-homosexuality.

Kaoma, K. (2009). *Globalizing the Culture Wars: U.S. conservatives, African churches, and homophobia*. Somerville: Political Research Associates.

Langa, S. (2009). Follow up meeting on the homosexuals' agenda, 15 March 2009. Kampala. URL: www.boxturtlebulletin.com/2009/03/28/10171.

Lewis, Desiree (2011). Representing African sexualities. In S. Tamale (Ed), *African sexualities: A reader*.(p. 45). Cape Town: Pambazuka Press.

Lively, S. (2009). Seminar on exposing the homosexuals' agenda, 5 March 2009. Kampala. URL: http://wn.com/Scott_Lively.

Mogul, Joey, Ritchie, Andrea, & Whitlock, Kay (2011). *Queer (In)Justice: The criminalization of LGBT people in the United States*. Boston: Beacon Press.

NCAVP [National Coalition of Anti-Violence Programs] (2014). 2013 Report on LGBTQ and HIV-Affected Hate Violence. URL: http://avp.org/resources/reports/term/summary.

Nyanzi, Stella. 2013. Dismantling reified African culture through localised homosexualities in Uganda. *Culture, Health & Sexuality: An International Journal of Research, Intervention and Care* 15(8): 952–967.

Oliver, Marcia (2013). Transnational sex politics, Conservative Christianity, and antigay activism in Uganda. *Studies in Social Justice*, 7(1): 83–105.

Olopade, D. (2012). Gay bashing, a government diversion. *International Herald Tribune*, 22 February. URL: http://latitude.blogs.nytimes.com/2012/02/22/gay-bashing-in-uganda-is-a-diversion-from-government-malfeasance/

Sadgrove, J., Vanderbeck, R., Andersson, J., Valentine, G. & Ward, K. (2012). Morality plays and money matters: Towards a situated understanding of the politics of homosexuality in Uganda. *Journal of Modern African Studies*, 50(1): 103–129.

Sharlet, J. (2008). *The Family: The secret fundamentalist at the heart of American power*. New York: Harper Collins.

Ssempa, M. (2007). Homosexuality is against our culture. *New Vision*. URL: http://www.newvision.co.ug/new_vision/news/1219820/homosexuality_culture.

Tamale, Sylvia (2007). *Homosexuality: Perspectives from Uganda*. Kampala, Uganda: Sexual Minorities Uganda (SMUG).

Tamale, S. (2011). Introduction. In S. Tamale (Ed.), *African Sexualities: A reader* (pp. 1–7). Cape Town: Pambazuka Press.

Tamale, Sylvia (2013). Confronting the politics of non-conforming sexualities in Africa. *African Studies Review*, 56(2): 31–45.

Tamale, Sylvia (2014). Exploring the contours of African sexualities: Religion, law and power. *African Human Rights Law Journal*, 14(1): 150–177.

Vision Reporter (2014). Museveni calls for fresh debate on homosexuality. *New Vision*, 3 October 2014. URL: www.newvision.co.ug/news/660387-museveni-calls-for-fresh-debate-on-homo-sexuality.html.

Ward, Kevin (2013). Religious institutions and actors and religious attitudes to homosexual rights: South Africa and Uganda. In C. Lennox & M. Waites (Eds.), *Human Rights, Sexual Orientation and Gender Identity in The Commonwealth: Struggles for Decriminalization and Change* (pp. 409–427). London, UK: Institute of Commonwealth Studies.

Ward, Kevin (2015). The role of the Anglican and Catholic Churches in Uganda in public discourse on homosexuality and ethics. *Journal of Eastern African Studies*, 9(1): 127–144.

chapter 72

Foreign-*f* females

Debating women's transnational sexualities in China

James Farrer

A "normal perspective" on "foreign-*f(uck)* females"

On October 19, 2012, the overseas edition of the *People's Daily* – the official voice of the Chinese Communist Party – published a column asking readers to take a "normal perspective on the foreign-*f* females" (*wai f nu*) (Zi 2012). First, we might ask, what is a "foreign-*f* female" and, second, what would be a "normal perspective"? For the term itself, the most common explanation is a "Chinese female who '*fucks*' foreigners" with the English "f" referring to "fuck." Others suggest, perhaps euphemistically, that the term means "foreign fly females" (*wai fei nu*), or women who want to "fly away" from China (see Douban 2012). All the discussions focus upon a Chinese woman who is sexually or romantically involved with a foreign, usually white western, man. And, even though there is an equivalent term – "*wai-f nan*" for men – the controversy centered on heterosexual Chinese cis women and their foreign lovers. Most of this debate takes place in Chinese on Chinese language websites.

The idea of a "normal perspective" is, of course, a contested one, and unpacking this politics of the normal is a primary goal of this chapter. I discuss Chinese media representations of international relationships, including the "foreign-*f* females," in order to trace out what I label a discourse of "ethnonational heteronormativity," meaning sexual norms ascribed to Han Chinese cultural traditions. (Non-Han, ethnic minorities inside of China, are excluded from this discourse, hence the term *ethnonational*.) In the Chinese context, ethnonational heteronormativity involves expectations that a Chinese woman should definitely marry, that she should naturally prefer an ethnically Chinese man, and that she should behave virtuously until marriage. I then use ethnographic research I conducted in Shanghai to show how some women in Shanghai actually talk about their transnational sexual experiences in ways that violate the expectations of ethnonational heteronormativity.

Patterns of transnational intimacy in the People's Republic of China (PRC)

Cross-border marriage is increasing since China opened up to more interactions with the outside world in the "opening and reform" era announced in 1978. Nonetheless, given China's 1.6 billion population, cross-border marriage is a small-scale phenomenon, even when one includes all marriages of PRC nationals to Hong Kong, Taiwanese, overseas Chinese and foreign nationals. In 1979, less than 8,500 couples registered a Chinese-foreign marriage in mainland China, only 300 of which involved a foreign national. Cross-border marriages peaked at 79,000 couples in 2001 (26,000 with a foreign national), but decreased by 2010 to just over 49,000 couples (23,000 with a foreign national). Marriages to foreign nationals have remained relatively steady over the most recent decade, but still only account for roughly 0.2% of all marriages in China in recent years. It should also be noted that many of these "international" marriages actually include a "foreign" spouse who is ethnically Chinese, including many former citizens of the PRC (Jeffreys and Pan 2013).

So, given the small numbers involved, why is the phenomenon of Chinese women dating and marrying foreigners even an issue? One reason is the skewed gender ratio of these marriages. For decades, far more women have married "out" of China, than Chinese men have married non-PRC women. The percentages of marriages involving a PRC male (and non-PRC female) has slowly risen from around 3 percent of the total in 1979 to around 22.7 percent in 2010, yet the skewed gender ratio remains (Jeffreys and Pan 2013). My ethnographic research in Shanghai suggests that the international dating scene still favors couples in which a Chinese woman is partnered with a foreign man. Many foreign white women living in Shanghai complained that western men preferred Chinese women, while white men described a relatively easy time finding Chinese women (See Farrer 2008, 2010; Farrer and Dale 2013). Given these gendered racial preferences, a type of statistically rare but still highly visible transnational relationship between Chinese women and white men became the focus of discussions about "foreign-f females."

Border policing: female virtue, nationalist masculinity, and compulsory marriage

The anonymous online comments on the "foreign-f females" phenomenon often targeted Chinese women studying abroad, criticizing them for sexual promiscuity with white men, for "looking down on China," or for pursuing a chance to emigrate (see Douban 2012; Zi 2012). Such criticisms seemed aimed at policing the sexuality of a growing population of Chinese women studying and living in the West. According to these views, Chinese women, even when abroad, should not violate traditional moral principles by sleeping around, nor betray China by preferring foreign lovers, nor make unreasonable demands from potential partners who are Chinese men.

This moral panic over mobile women "lacking in feminine virtue" has much in common with Japanese media criticisms of the overseas sexual adventures of Japanese women in the 1980s. During this "bubble era" of high Japanese economic growth in which single, educated Japanese women were traveling abroad and studying in great numbers for the first time, Japanese tabloid journalists labeled them "yellow cabs" (employing a term reportedly used in the USA) to describe Japanese women as easy to "pick up," like a taxi cab. In Japan, the derogatory term was reemployed less to expose the racist attitudes of some American men than to criticize these Japanese women for promiscuity with foreigners (Kelsky 1996).

Discussions in the censored China state-run media tend to take a less blatantly accusatory tone towards mobile Chinese women than anonymous internet postings. However, these messages also involve equally clear forms of sexual boundary policing. One longer article in the online *Chinese News* points out two general attitudes towards "foreign-*f* females" in the USA. The first is that these women are "worshiping the West and admiring the foreign" (*chongyangmeiwai*), while looking down upon Chinese men. Consequently, Chinese men living abroad have a hard time getting married. The other attitude, the author states, is more neutral, arguing that the reasons for women's attraction to particular men were personal and not racial, and women's choices should not be considered as the cause for overseas Chinese men's marital difficulties (Liu 2012). In this view, reflecting long-term state policies favoring romantic choice in marriage, women who married for love were virtuous, while those who did so for more pragmatic reasons were not.

Even the statements of self-proclaimed defenders of "foreign-*f* women" may serve to police the boundaries of proper Chinese women's sexuality. "My husband is an American," wrote one woman, "so I guess I am one of those foreign-*f* women everyone is writing about" (Brocci 2009). She goes on to write that everyone is criticizing foreign-f women for "sexual promiscuity, seeing a green card, looking down on Chinese, worshipping white people," and failing to personally take care of aging parents. In her case she writes:

> Many people think "foreign-*f* females" are promiscuous, and there must be a reason for why they think that. But that is not fair. It is like saying all black people are thieves . . . My husband and I were classmates. We knew each other two years, and like most Chinese girls, I maintained my purity right up to the time I married. My husband is not a promiscuous person. He and I have never been to a bar, and we have never [been] to a crazy party. Sometimes we two have a glass of red wine at home, and even that feels like a secret pleasure that "break[s] the rules."

She then points out that her parents paid for her studies, that she did not seek to marry a foreigner, that she was not in need of a husband's support for a visa, and that she plans to buy an apartment nearby so her parents can visit her as often as they want (Brocci 2009).

This self-defense in terms of traditional Chinese feminine virtue draws a moral line between "most Chinese girls" (including the writer) and women who are promiscuous, venal, or unfilial. Framed through these comparisons, the personal choices of more hedonistic (and less affluent) women remain morally questionable.

While women are the chief targets of these discourses, men's sexuality is also policed, beginning with Chinese women's foreign partners. One of the incidents which precipitated the "foreign-f female" discussion involved an anonymous white blogger who posted an on-line diary bragging of his numerous affairs with Chinese women (Chinabounder 2007). In response, an angry Shanghai-based Chinese academic man called for on-line mass action by "Chinese men with beating hearts" to "chase out this garbage foreigner" (lajilaowai) (Zhang 2006). Quoting from a 2007 book by the same Chinese academic (Zhang 2007), blogger Agostic posted in 2009, "Most foreigners actually come to China because (1) they can't make it at home and (2) they want to get Chinese girls." He explains that such men are known in the USA as "white trash" (Agostic 2009).

The stereotype of the foreign man who comes to China because he is unable to find financial and romantic success at home is increasingly common in China, especially after the global financial crisis of 2008. He is dismissed as an "English teacher" with no qualifications other than a white face. In actual practice the Chinese national government in 2012 tightened visa regulations to make it difficult for those without a university degree and years of relevant work experience to obtain a visa to work in China. Most westerners in China can thus be classified as skilled migrants, students or dependents (see Farrer 2014). The "white trash" moniker, however, seemed to be a useful way to label the increasing numbers of young westerners in Chinese cities as marginal men undeserving of Chinese women's sexual and romantic attention.

Chinese men themselves were also targets in these discussions. While acknowledging that Chinese men are victims of racist stereotypes in the USA, author Zi Mu, argues that men should "look to themselves for solutions," discard their old-fashioned ideas, and consider non-Chinese women as romantic partners. Moreover, she writes, most overseas Chinese men are science and engineering students and do not have very high "emotional intelligence" and lack the ability to communicate well with women. More nationalist voices call on Chinese men to "raise up their heads," and take more pride in themselves and China, standing up to the foreign men inside China (Agostic 2009; Zhang 2006, 2007). In these discussions, Chinese masculinity is tied specifically to a sexual competition with foreign men.

The background of ethnonational heteronormativity

The online conversations surrounding the "foreign-f female" are shaped by a set of assumptions that I label ethnonational heteronormativity. A basic assumption is that moral and cultural differences between Chinese and "foreigners" are profound, and that intercultural intimacies can be seen as a political issue. A Chinese women's feminine virtue is defined through her Chineseness, and a Chinese men's masculinity is based on his degree of national pride and China's status in the world. This ethnonationalism is paired with marital heteronormativity, a notion that sexual desires and activities should be contained within a pathway to heterosexual marriage. While premarital sex in the PRC is no longer culturally prohibited, it is mostly condoned in romantic relationships with a clear goal of marriage (see Farrer 2002, 2006). This folding of ethnonationalism into heteronormativity prescribes a "natural" romantic relationship between Chinese young men and women, while problematizing relationships with foreigners or any sexual adventures that deviate from the marriage-oriented path.

The pattern of ethnonational heteronormativity is not a recent invention. We can see it emerging in the late 19th and early 20th centuries as Chinese students began traveling abroad. In an atmosphere of a national crisis surrounding foreign imperialism in China, there was a sense that marriage to foreigners entailed a loss to China. In these years most of these relationships involved Chinese men and foreign women, since Chinese women had few opportunities for study abroad. In response, both the late Qing government in 1910 and the Republic of China government in 1918 established rules that foreign students should not be allowed to marry foreigners (Qin Bo 2014). During the 1950s, Chinese students studying in the Soviet Union were strongly discouraged from dating and marrying Russians (McGuire 2010: 367). Such attitudes were not limited to study-abroad students. Even university students within China were discouraged, or even prohibited, from dating foreign students in the 1980s and even into the early 1990s.

Throughout the 1980s and well into the 1990s, Chinese media portrayals of international romance were cautionary. Foreign husbands were labeled "airplane tickets" or "passports." Chinese magazine articles in the 1980s and 1990s emphasized: the mercenary motives Chinese women had for marrying foreigners; problems dealing with parental opposition to international marriage; adjustment problems Chinese wives faced abroad; and the dangers of illegal agencies promoting international marriage for emigration purposes (Farrer 2010). In popular cultural works such as *My Wife from America* (Tang Yin 1995), Chinese women's strategies of emigration through international marriage were interpreted as a sign of a crisis of Chinese masculinity.

In the commercialized media culture of 1990s China, a counter discourse emerged that portrayed western men as desirable yet exotic partners for Chinese women. The 1990s saw a small boom in personal accounts of international romance with titles such as *My Berliner Lover, Your Golden Hair, My Black Eyes, My Hawaiian Love Affair* and *I went to Germany and Became a Bride* painting a more positive and romantic image of the Chinese women's motives for dating foreign men (Farrer 2010). Reaching a broader audience, the award-wining Shanghai Broadcasting program "OK Xintiandi" (1999–2005) described the rewards of international married life in the city. A survey of residents in Beijing, Shanghai, and Guangzhou found generally positive attitudes toward international marriage. Thirty-eight percent of Shanghai respondents knew someone in an international marriage, while one third of the single respondents expressed a willingness to marry a foreigner themselves if the right person emerged (*Beijing Youth Daily* 2003). In general, however, even these stories of international relationships weighed heavily in favor of marital heteronormativity, and an emphasis on courtship leading up to marriage. The exoticizing nature of these portrayals also played up the gaps between Chinese and foreigners – often staged as amusing cultural misunderstandings between spouses – thereby reinforcing the idea of a cultural chasm between China and the West.

Not all representations of foreign–Chinese romance followed this official eth-nonationalist and heteronormative pattern. Young novelist Zhou Weihui's accounts of her illicit sexual affairs with western men in Shanghai, *Shanghai Baby*, became a Chinese and international bestseller (Wei Hui 1999). However, her novel also became a lighting rod for criticisms of Chinese women's sexual adventures with foreigners. In a sense, Wei Hui was the "foreign-*f* female" of her generation.

Voices of PRC women: challenging ethnonational heteronormativity

Unlike the representations of women in the official discourses above, young women I spoke with in Shanghai about their interracial sexual practices often openly chal-lenged the assumptions of ethnonational heteronormativity. Some challenged the idea that cross-border relationships involved a fundamental cultural gap between Chinese and Westerners or that sex always should happen in the context of courtship leading to marriage. Others explored sexual relations with other women, including foreigners. The following accounts are based on ethnographic research I conducted in Shanghai from 1994 until 2014. Quotes are from interviews conducted by myself or by research assistants between 2000 and 2014. Most interviews were conducted in Chinese, and the westernized pseudonyms of informants reflect their self-naming preferences. For more detailed reports on this research see Farrer 2008, 2010, 2013, Farrer and Field 2015.

Becoming cosmopolitan

Most informants considered themselves "Chinese" but many challenged the concep-tion that their Chineseness was an unchanging aspect of their identity or determined their relationships with men. Some women explicitly used international love stories as a way to live as a "cosmopolitan woman" with both Chinese and Western cultural traits (Farrer 2013). They described intercultural relationships as a space for cosmo-politan self-development, free from Chinese norms of sexuality, marriage and other expectations of female deportment. Others described their pre-existing investment in a cosmopolitan identity as a reason for why they came into contact with foreign men. Jane (27, from Shanghai) remembered her admiration of the foreign lifestyle she had encountered at a high school exchange event in Shanghai:

> I think I have a natural like for foreigners. Maybe I shouldn't say it like that, but like it's just that *I'm so free when I'm being with them. I can laugh aloud. I don't need to be a lady. I can wear something which I cannot wear in the Mainland.* And I think that sense of freedom influenced me a lot.
>
> (2008 interview, words in italics were in English.)

In stark contrast to the standard notion of deep communication gaps, one of the reasons several women stated for dating foreigners and making foreign friends was *ease* of communication. They contrasted the directness of communication with

Westerners with their experience of Chinese social communication as ambiguous and treacherous. As Linda (22, Shanghai) said:

> I don't really have a preference for people from any place, but I really like making friends with foreigners. They are easy to communicate with. I don't mean in terms of talking, but foreigners are not as hypocritical, or superficially polite. Especially now, in this society, this kind of messy social relationship is so common with Chinese, presenting one thing to your face, and another behind your back. With foreigners you don't have to constantly strategize. Relatively speaking its more real.
>
> (2008 interview)

Throughout these accounts of developing a cosmopolitan identity, the relevant distinction is less one of race or nationality, than a distinction between transnational "foreign" and local Chinese ways. Local (Chinese) men were described as unable to accept or affirm women's cosmopolitan side, while foreign (mobile western) men were. For some informants, international romance was their point of entry into this role as cosmopolitan women. For others, it was an extension of an identity they had already assumed through work, hobbies, and especially through language study. This construction of the cosmopolitan self may be partly realized and partly aspirational, a mix of what one hopes to be and what one already is. Moreover, we should also be clear that not all actual intercultural relationships matched these expectations for self-development (Farrer 2013).

Challenging compulsory marriage

Many informants complained of marriage pressures from parents and larger Chinese society. These include pressures to marry before age thirty, to a socially appropriate man with higher educational and economic achievements. Such marriage pressures fall especially heavily on highly educated, successful, and geographically mobile women. After years pursuing higher education and careers, many feared being labeled "left-over women" (To 2015). Some urban women who felt they were already too old for Chinese men (usually over 30) saw foreign men as an alternative marriage market (i.e. as less concerned about a woman's age and past sexual experiences). Others saw foreign men as a way of pushing away concerns of marriage. For some, international dating began out of a sense of play and curiosity, without future commitments. Irma (34, Shanghai) describes her first sexual relationship with a French man:

> This was my first foreign man I went out with, so I never even thought about that sort of thing [the future], and I wasn't sure about what he was thinking. I just thought we could get together, without a *serious* type of *relationship*.
>
> (2008 interview)

As this case illustrates, a foreign man could be a means to avoid marriage pressures. Mandy describes how she ended up dating a married German man and thereby exiting an emotionally unsatisfactory relationship with a Chinese boyfriend bent on a quick marriage:

After being with him, I found out that despite the language barriers, despite the fact that my English was not good, I found out we were happy talking with each, really happy. We could really talk, even with my broken English. So I started thinking about it. I couldn't talk like that with that Beijing guy, even though we spoke the same language. Why couldn't we? So I started thinking, even though this was just an affair, it made me realize I was not happy, and I was bored. So I broke up with the Beijing guy. The main reason was that I couldn't talk to him.

(2008 interview)

These stories should not be taken to mean that women were not interested in marriage with foreign (or Chinese) men. However, they show that women employed intercultural relationships outside the normative framework of courtship and compulsory marriage.

Becoming sexual

Other women more explicitly used foreign lovers to explore sexual interests that went beyond the romantic. Wendy, who I met in 2002, described her experiences with foreign men as a coming-of-age story (see Farrer 2010). In her last year of college in 2001, she met her first foreign boyfriend by accident in a shopping mall. After he returned to the US, she began frequenting Shanghai's international bars with a group of Shanghainese girlfriends, forming friendships with English-speaking foreigners (men and women), developing shared interests such as the US tv series *Sex and the City*. For the most part they dated only western men, sometimes engaging in casual sex, including experiments with polyamory, or open relationships. Like many women I interviewed, she initially found these various sexual experiences disorienting, sometimes pleasurable, sometimes not, and a complete break with her preexisting moral categories (including the ideal of premarital virginity). In a conversation five years later, in 2007, she said with an air of both wistfulness and pride, "I guess I am a completely different person now."

Wendy described how she also tried dating Chinese men after breaking up with her second foreign boyfriend, but found their attitude toward sexuality off-putting: "They expect you to act like a virgin, and wait for like two months to have sex. With a foreign guy you know you are going to do it, and it just happens. It's more natural." Over the years she formed a complex social identity around her foreign cultural experiences, both sexual and social. Her English became nearly native, which she used to her advantage to build a successful consulting business. For four years, she lived with a Canadian man nearly 30 years older, continuing practices such as "threesomes" with him and other men. She also had a secret and purely sexual affair with one of these men. Uneasy about the idea of marriage with a much older man, she broke up with him in 2010. She still saw marriage as a goal. Going back to dating a "local" Chinese man and living a conventional Shanghainese lifestyle were impossible to imagine, she said.

By 2014, Shanghai women did not automatically associate foreign men with sexual freedom and Chinese men with conservative attitudes. Moreover, an individual's preferences could change. In 2014, Wendy was still unmarried, but dating a Chinese-American man, and in a more conventional monogamous sexual relationship. However, her story shows how some women in China's "reform era" used transnational relationships as a way of pursuing their own sexuality outside the expectations of marriage, while challenging orthodox Chinese expectations of feminine virtue.

Challenging heteronormativity

The cosmopolitan experience of transnational sexuality in Shanghai was not limited to private or coupled experiences, but could involve immersion into a much larger community in which ethnically mixed company was the norm. This could include, for example, the established communities of intermarried couples in Shanghai (see Farrer 2008). Another type of cosmopolitan sexual community could be found in the city's growing number of gay and lesbian bars. Shanghai's gay bars could be the place for finding partners as well as for establishing a cosmopolitan identity as a gay man or lesbian (Farrer and Field 2015, 201–202).

In a 2012 interview, one 28-year-old Shanghainese lesbian named Xue Tao described her experiences in the Pink Home club, a gay bar which opened in 2006, that served as a congenial spot for lesbians and gay men, including foreign gays and lesbians. The club hosted events of the Shanghai LGBT group that were attended by both men and women. When asked about her most memorable clubbing experience, Xue Tao described a night several years earlier when a foreign dominatrix named Iris performed at the club:

> That day Stacey [the woman manager of Pink Home] gave Iris a room to change clothes. We were both in that hotel room together, and I think that day I had a problem in my love life, and was talking to Iris, and she just picked up her whip and starting hitting me! Iris was an American girl, and our relationship was really good … We knew each other and met at Pink Home. Because I knew she was going to perform that day, I was especially happy … She likes SM; I also like it. I like to be on the passive side, so when she took that whip and hit me, it felt really great (*shuang*).
>
> (2011 interview)

The cosmopolitan gay and lesbian clubbing scene in Shanghai thus supported public and private sexual expressions that violated the heteronormative expectations of the larger Chinese public sexual culture.

Ethnonational dreams and personal dreams

Labels such as the "foreign-*f* female" are flexible in their uses. As described above, the term can invoke Chinese national pride to police women's sexuality. Equally, it can involve using sexual stigma to police political boundaries, to dissuade mobile men and women from straying away from the Chinese nation. Although the Chinese state generally disavows both racism and sexism, state media have had a very important influence on establishing and supporting the ethnonationalist ideology within which stigmatizing discourses like the "foreign-*f* female" function. The Communist Party slogan "Chinese Dream," with its goal of "ethnonational regeneration" (*minzu fuxing*), is the most recent expression of nationalist ideology centered on an ideal of shared Chinese ethnicity. However, we should not confuse these political visions with the lives of ordinary women pursuing their own varied and personal dreams.

The point of the individual stories above is not to characterize all transnational or interracial relationships as inherently transgressive or liberating. Indeed they may also be spaces in which gendered and ethnic inequalities are reproduced (see Nemoto in this book). Nor do I claim that all *intra*ethnic relationships between Chinese reproduce a heteronormative patriarchal norm. However, my retelling of women's stories is indeed meant to challenge a dominant ethnonationalist narrative in which Chinese women's cross-border and interethnic relationships are seen as inherently problematic. They are also meant to show how some women may use these relationships to construct a cosmopolitan sense of self, to avoid or delay marriage, to challenge ideas of female virtue, or challenge the norm of heterosexuality altogether.

Bibliography

Agostic. 2009. Laowai weishenma yao gao wai *f* nu? (Why do foreigners want to fool around with foreign-*f* females?) posted Aug. 26 on http://blog.sina.com.cn/s/blog_4a0a2bb20100egvg. html (accessed Jan. 15, 2015).

Beijing Youth Daily. 2003. Sanfenzhiyi weihun beifangzhe yuanzhao laowai (One-third of unmarried respondents are willing to marry a foreigner) Dec. 10, available on http:// eladies.sina.com.cn/2003-12-10/83857.html (accessed Nov. 6, 2007).

Brocci. 2009. Wo yinggai jiushi dajia shuode wai-f nu ba (I guess I am what everyone is calling a foreign-*f* female) posted Aug. 18 on http://bbs.taisha.org/thread-1318435-1-1.html (accessed Jan. 15, 2015).

Chinabounder. 2007. Sex and Shanghai: Western scoundrel in Shanghai tells all, available on http://chinabounder.blogspot.com/ (accessed November 6, 2007).

Douban. 2012. Ou zhenshi gulouguawende!!! You shei zhidao wai-*F* shi shenma !!! (I'm really ignorant and uneducated!!! Who here knows what is a foreign-F!!!), available on www. douban.com/group/topic/31913781/ (accessed Jan. 15, 2015).

Farrer, James. 2002. *Opening Up: Youth Sex Culture and Market Reform in Shanghai.* Chicago: University of Chicago Press.

—. 2006. "Sexual Citizenship and the Politics of Sexual Storytelling among Chinese Youth" in Elaine Jeffreys ed. *Sex and Sexuality in China*, pp. 102–123. London: Routledge.

—. 2008. "From 'Passports' to 'Joint Ventures': Intermarriage between Chinese Nationals and Western Expatriates Residing in Shanghai" *Asian Studies Review.* 32(1): 7–29.

—. 2010. "A Foreign Adventurer's Paradise? Interracial Sexuality and Alien Sexual Capital" *Sexualities.* 13(1):69–95.

—. 2013. "Good Stories: Chinese Women's International Love Stories as Collective Sexual Story Making" *Sexualities.* 16 (1/2): 12–29.

—. 2014. "China Wants You: The Social Construction of Skilled Labor in Three Transnational Fields" *Asian Pacific Migration Journal.* 23(4): 397–420.

Farrer, James, and Dale, Sonja. 2013. "Sexless in Shanghai: Gender Mobility Strategies in a Transnational Sexual Field in Adam Isiah Green ed. *Sexual Fields: Towards a Sociology of Collective Sexual Life*, pp. 143–170. Chicago: University of Chicago Press.

Farrer, James, and Andrew David Field. 2015. *Shanghai Nightscapes: A Nocturnal Biography of a Global City.* Chicago: University of Chicago Press.

Jeffreys, Elaine, and Wang Pan. 2013. "The Rise of Chinese-Foreign Marriage in Mainland China, 1979–2010" *China Information*. 27(3): 347–369.

Kelsky, Karen. 1996. "Flirting with the Foreign: Interracial Sex in Japan's International Age" in Rob Wilson and Wimal Dissanaya eds. *Global/Local: Cultural Production and the Transnational Imaginary*, pp. 173–92. Durham NC: Duke University Press.

Liu Mei. 2012. Mei huaren nuzi jia laowai yin wangluo reyi: chongyang meiwai OR jiyuan qiaohe (American Chinese women marrying foreigners prompts a hot discussion on the internet: is this worshipping the West or love's destiny?) *China News*. Oct. 17, available on www.chinanews.com/hr/2012/10-17/4253691.shtml (accessed Jan. 15, 2015).

McGuire, Elizabeth. 2010. "Between Revolutions: Chinese Students in Soviet Institutes, 1948-1966" in Thomas P. Bernstein and Hua-Yi Li eds. *China Learns from the Soviet Union*, pp. 359–390. Lanham: Lexington Books.

Qin Bo. 2014. "The History and Context of Chinese Western Intercultural Marriage in Modern and Contemporary China (From 1840 to the 21st Century)" *Rozenberg Quarterly* (April), available on http://rozenbergquarterly.com/the-history-and-context-of-chinese-western-intercultural-marriage-in-modern-and-contemporary-china-from-1840-to-the-21st-century/ (accessed Jan. 15, 2015).

Tang Ying. 1995. *Meiguo laide qizi (Wife from America)*. Shanghai: Shanghaiyuandong Press.

To, Sandy. 2015. *China's Leftover Women: Late Marriage among Professional Women and its Consequences*. New York: Routledge.

Wei Hui. 1999. *Shanghai Baobei. (Shanghai Baby)*. Shenyang: Chunfengwenyi Press.

Zhang Jiehai. 2006. Wangluo zhuizhu liumang waijiao xingdong (Calling for an online movement to expel the hooligan foreigner) Posted Aug. 8 on http://blog.sina.com.cn/s/blog_49187b2001000x4n8.html (accessed Nov. 6, 2007, available as of Jan. 15, 2015 in English translation on the blog EastSouthWestNorth at http://zonaeuropa.com/20060828_1.htm).

—. 2007. *Wo fen nu (I am angry)*. Shanghai: East China Normal University Press.

—. 2009. *Zhonguo nanren diaocha (The Investigation on Chinese Men)*. Nanjing: Jiangsu Literature and Art Publishing House.

Zi Mo. 2012. Yi zhengchang xinkou kandai "wai F" nu (Looking at "foreign-*f*" women from a normal perspective) *People's Daily Net International Edition*, Oct. 19, available on http://paper.people.com.cn/rmrbhwb/html/2012-10/19/content_1128085.htm (accessed Jan. 15, 2015).

chapter 73

Condoms in the global economy

Peter Chua

Many of us think of condoms in terms of personal use. We may think about condoms as preventing disease and pregnancy, especially in the age of AIDS and high rates of teenage pregnancy. We may also think of condoms in terms of how they will affect our sexual experience. Will using condoms reduce pleasure? Will condoms interfere with the romance of sex?

Many sociologists and social researchers also study condom use. They have focused on condom use among different groups. In particular, researchers have been interested in condom use among groups at risk, such as young women and gay men. Researchers have also sought to understand the social factors that prevent condom use. For example, there are studies of the role of education and public information in rates of condom use among different groups. Much of this research is intended to be used by public and private agencies, often public health agencies, to minimize unwanted pregnancies and disease.

Studies of condom use have also been central to organizations that promote antipoverty programs. Since the 1970s, national and global organizations have linked overpopulation with increased poverty and have called for state-led population reduction programs. By 2000, many First World governments, international NGOs, and for-profit corporations have provided experts and financial resources to many Third World governments. These organizations promote programs encouraging condom use and modern birth control options – ranging from "natural" methods to contraceptive and permanent surgical procedures.

Whatever their successes, birth control campaigns and programs have also functioned to control women's sexuality by shaping how they think about and approach sexuality (see Russell, Sobo, and Thompson 2000). For example, Third World feminists argue that modern contraceptives have actually limited Third World women's auton-omy (see Briggs 2002; Kluasen 2004). Many poor women of color in the Third World such as indigenous Peruvian women experience family planning as coercive and not helpful. Instead of gaining greater personal and household autonomy, these women have understood birth control policies as government attempts to affect their sexual thinking and family planning practices. Government programs have intimidated them through contraceptive use campaigns in the media that *promote one type of family (small, heterosexual)* and stigmatize other family arrangements. Moreover, medical pro-cedures such as unsafe abortions and sterilizations have been imposed without their consent, and often having unhealthy consequences.

While the study of condom use is important, the study of condoms as commod-ities has been neglected. Condoms are a commodity or a good produced by corpora-tions for profit. In this chapter, I want to look at this hidden side of condoms – the economic, global production of condoms as commodities.

Capitalism and condoms

The story of condoms begins in the late nineteenth century. With the greater availabil-ity of latex extracted from Third World rubber plantations in the 1880s and the devel-opment of mechanical assembly lines, the making of male condoms became industrialized. It was only until World War II that condoms were mass-produced, ini-tially for soldiers and later for post-war middle-class consumers in many First World areas. With population control programs starting in the late 1950s and HIV preven-tion in the late 1980s, condom manufacturing grew rapidly to meet demands from governments, target groups, and new consumers.

For example, during the 1980s and 1990s, the southern Christian city of Dothan, Alabama, was the global condom-making capital. The area had two of the largest condom corporations: Ansell – makers of the Lifestyles brand – and London Interna-tional Group – makers of the Durex brand. In these and other condom factories, the corporations made assembly-line employees work with chemically unsafe materials. They relied on improved machineries to produce more condoms and to check their quality, while intensifying and speeding up the employees' work without increasing wages. In these ways, the assembly-line employees worked harder and earned the same pay, while more condoms were mass produced and the corporations obtained greater profits.

Work tasks in the Dothan plants were highly segregated along racial and gender lines. Such segregation often makes sexual harassment and intimidation possible. For instance, white men and white women held top executive and management posi-tions. Working-class white men typically operated dipping machines that extrude latex or synthetic condoms. They received extensive technical training to operate these huge machines. Black men operated machines that mixed chemicals and other mate-rials. They received lower wages and less training opportunities, which limited their chance to operate extruding machines. Many working-class white women and women of color were concentrated in quality-testing positions. As low-skilled, less-desired, and lower-pay positions than machine operators, quality-testing required employees to pay detailed attention and to conduct testing accurately and fast. The lowest pay was reserved for hand packers, who were typically working-class women of color.

The drive for greater profits reduced labor costs. Eventually, sporadic global competition caused condom-producing corporations to close factory plants (as they did in Dothan and many parts of western Europe) and shift operations to new plants in Thailand, India, and other Third World areas.

Leading condom manufacturers have relied on contracts from governments for business, growth opportunities, and global distribution. For instance, the United States through its Agency for International Development (USAID) provided 10.4 billion US-made condoms as part of international development projects in 114 countries from 1969 to 2000. It gave out these condoms at no or subsidized costs for population assistance, reproductive health, and HIV/AIDS projects. As a result, US corporations and project contractors such as Macro International and John Snow Inc. benefited financially at the economic expense of poor and marginalized people. While the US government provided millions of dollars to reduce fertility and increase HIV/AIDS prevention in the Third World, most of the money actually stayed within the US, employing thousands of US residents over the years. In contrast, poor Third World people who were expected to gain a large share of the US development money and to have their lives improve dramatically simply got US-produced health media messages and US-made condoms.

My research shows that condom distribution as part of First World aid to Third World countries actually makes them more economically dependent on the First World and free-market solutions (Chua 2001, 2003). The continual dependency on condoms made in the First World, and on First World reproductive health experts, hampers many local Third World solutions aimed at reducing poverty. As such, many First World countries benefit from these trade, economic, and political arrangements, increasing inequalities between the First and Third Worlds.

Further, the marketing of condoms and other contraceptives in Third World nations is accompanied by certain ideas about gender and lifestyle. In particular, First World corporations and governments and agencies promote an ideology that associates "Western" lifestyles and values with progress and freedom. In other words, it is not just condoms that are marketed but modern Western ideals of personal and social life.

Governments and corporations – by themselves – are not able to create new condom markets. They have had to rely on global project contractors, national health and welfare organizations, and local groups to promote condoms aggressively in the media and targeted outlets, and to change local understandings of health, sexuality, and gender relations. Reduced visibility of state–corporate programs seeking to change the sexual behavior of "risk" groups would then occur when health and women's organizations (such as the global Family Health International and a Senegalese group, Agency for the Development of Social Marketing) aggressively promote a free market economy.

While often seen as small and local, these groups extend the interests of governments and condom-producing companies. Consequently, they restructure and infuse free-market solutions such as the privatization and commercialization of public health promotion. These solutions amplify local inequalities by unevenly allotting large amounts of financial support, training, and material resources, including the public distribution of condoms.

While the promotional materials produced by these organizations perpetuate static and idealistic images of family, class, and gendered sexuality, they evoke particular desires and identities among their targeted groups. In rural India, US-funded Population Services International (PSI) has promoted the popular *Masti* brand of condoms – *masti* meaning pleasure in Hindi. Executive Director for PSI-India Cindy Squires informed me during our interview that PSI redesigned the brand to promote the "new positive image of Indian men," which is connoted by a black silhouette stallion logo. PSI wanted something more subtle than the earlier *Masti* branding of a "classic macho man who takes charge," than other condom brands with more family-caring or erotically suggestive images. In particular, PSI wanted to make rural men – the brand's market niche – identify less as traditionally macho (as characterized by PSI) and to exude low-key sexual energy as the new ideal gender and sexual identity.

Still, some individuals and groups produce more unconventional readings of these condom images, materials, and promotions, generating racial, gender, sexual, regional, and economic identities in ways that are often unexpected. Take for instance the promotion of the US-sponsored TRUST Premiere condom brand during a car show in the Philippines sponsored by DKT International. While generating greater public awareness and media attention about condoms, the swimsuit winner of the car-show beauty pageant Liezl Pecson highlighted the gender contradictions of the event. She said: "This [to be pageant contestants] is one way of showing what we can do as women. . . . Beauty is not enough. We need a thinking mind and a compassionate heart to be able to exceed society's common notion that women are second class to men, and even to their cars." While DKT International expected to use cars and the objectification of young Filipinas to promote condoms to urban poor Filipino men and, in the long run empower women, Pecson made a point to acknowledge the contestants' sexualized experiences at the same time attempting to address gender subordination in her remarks.

Protesting condom use

Supporters of condom use continue to face challenges from at least two dissimilar positions. The first involves social morality. Often, social and religious conservatives take this position, arguing that condoms encourage immoral sexual activities. Some contend that condoms act as a barrier to the procreation of children in nuclear families. Thus, they argue condoms undermine the naturally ordained idea of a heterosexual family structure.

This position is most frequently directed at unmarried men and women (particularly the young), as it asserts that condoms encourage heterosexual sexual promiscuity by having sex outside marriage and with multiple partners. The position suggests young people would practice sexual abstinence if government programs and others would not make condoms available. Hence, condoms should be prohibited.

Many – including contenders of Neo-Malthusianism and the Modernist position – fault social moralists for their support of heterosexism and women's inequality, and their opposition to diverse and consenting sexualities.

In contrast, the second position protesting against condom use places stronger emphasis on social justice globally. This position highlights that social justice and social equity lessen when corporations and governments advocate condom use. It shows how the ongoing political and economic interests of corporations and governments have led to the lessening of free clinics, free condom distribution, and public campaigns on reproductive health and HIV/AIDS prevention in the Third World.

While Third World public health withers from privatization, corporations and non-profit agencies supported by First World governments increasingly strengthen private-sector infrastructures and make them responsible for providing reproductive health services and promoting healthy practices. The few who manage these infrastructures gain monetarily through long-term government contracts, and also through the excessive fees they charge their clients (who are often poor women). The higher fees for reproductive health services and contraceptives reflect greater commercialization of government programs, thereby reducing the proportion who can afford to get these services and commodities.

Even while privatization and commercialization of public health programs restrict poorer groups from participation, corporations and governments remain highly interested in scientifically studying and regulating the sexual attitudes and behavior of poor and other "risk" groups. The corporations and governments support this social scientific research on sexuality that intrudes in women's sexual lives with the goal of making them conform to expected norms about how they should think and act sexually. This treats women as malleable objects for research. Consequently, greater privatization, commercialization, and scientific surveillance widen the economic gap and power imbalances among various social groups, further disadvantaging women, the poor, and people of color.

Protest has emerged from the Third World, principally from groups who have different ideas about personal and community health. For instance, dissident healthcare groups in the Philippines criticize their government for encouraging private enterprise "at the expense of the Filipino people." Or, the Council for Health and Development, which serves rural Third World populations, argues that condoms and similar First World modern products are luxuries, often inaccessible to the rural poor. In general, Third World critics contend that the privatizing and commercializing of reproductive healthcare may actually limit access to contraceptives, increase corporate and expert control over people's lives, and reduce women's participation in healthcare decision-making.

Bibliography

Briggs, Laura. 2002. *Reproducing Empire: Race, Sex, Science, and U.S. Imperialism in Puerto Rico.* Berkeley: University of California Press.

Chua, Peter. 2001. "Condom Matters and Social Inequalities: Inquiries into Condom Production, Exchange, and Advocacy Practices." PhD dissertation, Department of Sociology, University of California, Santa Barbara, CA.

—. 2003. "Condoms and Pedagogy: Changing Global Knowledge Practices", in Kum Kum Bhavnani, John Foran, and Priya Kurian (eds). *Feminist Futures: Re-Imagining Women, Culture, and Development.* London: Zed Books.

Ginsburg, Faye D. and Rayna Rapp. 1995. *Conceiving the New World Order: The Global Politics of Reproduction*. Berkeley: University of California Press.

Hartmann, Betsy. 1995. *Reproductive Rights and Wrongs*, revised edn. Boston, MA: South End Press.

Kluasen, Susanne M. 2004. *Race, Maternity, and the Politics of Birth Control in South Africa*. Basingstoke: Palgrave.

Russell, Andrew, Elisa J. Sobo, and Mary S. Thompson (eds). 2000. *Contraception across Cultures: Technologies, Choices, Constraints*. London: Berg.

Peter Chua

chapter 74

Sexual tourism

Interview with Julia O'Connell Davidson

Julia O'Connell Davidson is Professor of Sociology at the University of Nottingham. She has spent more than a decade researching sex commerce in the affluent and developing world, and has written extensively on prostitution, child prostitution, sexual tourism, and "trafficking." Her most recent book is *Children in the Global Sex Trade* (2005, Cambridge: Polity), and she is currently involved in research on migrant domestic and sex workers in Britain and Spain.

What do you mean by sexual tourism?

In the 1970s, the governments of both Thailand and the Philippines began to pursue economic policies that placed tourism at the center of their plans for economic development. Both countries already had large-scale sex industries that were put in place to serve United States military personnel. By the 1980s, a visible segment of the tourism markets in Thailand and the Philippines consisted of men from the affluent, economically developed world (Western Europe, North America, Australia and Japan) who were attracted by the cheap commercial sexual opportunities available in these much poorer countries. In tourist-sending countries, there was a proliferation of small companies that offered "sex tours" as well as guide books that promoted travel to consume commercial sexual services. Destinations like Bangkok in Thailand and Manila in the Philippines were marketed as a sexual "paradise" for single men.

From the late 1970s through the mid-1990s the term "sexual tourism" was largely used to refer to this form of tourism to Southeast Asia, a form of tourism that relied upon and reproduced racist and sexist fantasies, as well as economic and political inequalities. However, it is now widely recognized that other regions also attract tourists in search of plentiful and affordable sexual opportunities with exoticized Others (Latin America and the Caribbean, Africa, and the Indian subcontinent), and that sexual tourism is not always linked to a large-scale, formally organized sex industry.

The further we move from the stereotypical view of "sexual tourists" as men who take organized sex tours to Southeast Asia, the more difficult it becomes to draw a clear boundary between "sexual tourism" and other forms of tourism, because tourism and sex are so often entwined. There have historically been strong associations between travel and sex, and today, in the age of mass tourism, sex is widely understood to be part of the tourist experience. Whether with their own spouse or partner, with other tourists, or with sex workers, many people expect to have more sex whilst on vacation.

How widespread is sexual tourism? Are there certain countries that are centers of sexual tourism, and why is it tolerated in these countries?

It is impossible to say how widespread sexual tourism is. Even when you can get good data on the sex sector in any given country or region, it's very difficult to determine what proportion of the sector owes its existence to tourism, as opposed to local demand, or demand from domestic or foreign military. Also, even when reliable data on tourism is available, it's hard to say what percentage of tourists engage in sexual-economic exchanges with locals. Additionally, the world of sexual tourism is fluid and changing. For instance, Thailand's popularity amongst men who travel with the purpose of buying sex dwindled fast in the 1990s, while Cambodia and Vietnam started to attract more of this type of sexual tourist; in the mid-1990s, Varadero was *the* hot sexual tourism resort in Cuba, but by the turn of the century it was losing this reputation, and sexual tourists were advising each other to go to other parts of Cuba in search of cheap sex. And because the development of sexual tourism is linked to broader political and economic factors (in particular the pursuit of neo-liberal economic policies in poor and developing countries), new sites continually emerge. Prague in the Czech Republic was not on the "sexual tourism" map in the 1980s, but by the mid-1990s it had gained a reputation as a city where tourists can readily buy sex; also since the mid-1990s, sites of sexual tourism serving demand from domestic tourists have been emerging in China in towns along the borders with Vietnam and Myanmar.

Why is sexual tourism tolerated? Economics is an important part of the answer. Often governments will turn a blind eye to a sex trade that is intimately linked to a flourishing tourist industry. In the 1980s and early 1990s, some governments viewed a close relationship between prostitution and tourism as inevitable. But today, after extensive campaigning against sexual tourism by various groups and a great deal of negative publicity for countries deemed to have a problem with sexual tourism, there are few government officials in any country who would still openly condone direct links between tourism and prostitution. But here's where the more general association between tourism and sex becomes a serious problem for developing nations that rely on tourism as their main foreign-exchange-earning industry.

These countries are now under pressure to suppress sexual tourism, but as they have been marketed in affluent tourist-sending countries as "sensual" and "exotic," and tourists often want sex, as much as sun, sea and sand, and as local and migrant people in tourist areas earn so little from other forms of work in the tourist industry, this is a tall order. To effectively prevent all forms of tourist sexual exchange from taking place would not only be extremely costly but would also require such draconian actions on the part of the authorities that it would almost certainly have a negative impact on the overall tourist trade. Thus, most governments in developing countries where sexual tourism takes place approach the problem with one eye open, the other eye shut. There are sporadic police clampdowns on the most visible forms of prostitution in specific resorts or towns (often at the end of the tourist high season, or following bad publicity about sexual tourism in that location), but then the authorities allow its re-emergence in another resort or town.

Is there sexual tourism in Great Britain and the United States? Does sexual tourism in these nations differ from that in poorer nations?

I think we can safely say that neither Britain nor the United States has ever been explicitly marketed as a dream destination for amorous heterosexual male tourists in search of gorgeous, willing women. But then we can also safely say that some tourists – both international and domestic tourists – buy commercial sexual services whilst vacationing in Britain and the United States, and for some, the consumption of commercial sex may be an integral part of the planned "tourist experience." For example, tourists are amongst those who use Nevada's thirty-five licensed brothels, and given the fact that Nevada is the only state in the US in which brothels can be legally operated, it seems probable that some tourists travel there specifically in order to consume both the spectacle of the "Wild West" brothel and the services of a sex worker.

Soho in London also attracts British and overseas visitors who wish to consume the spectacle of its red-light area, and there are heterosexual male tourists whose itinerary for a trip to London includes a visit to one of Soho's famous "walk-up" brothels. Some gay travelers, especially men, are attracted to destinations in Britain (London, Brighton, and Manchester in particular) and in the US (New York, Los Angeles, San Francisco, Miami Beach, to name a few) that have strong associations with gay history and/or identity and that also offer extensive opportunities for both commercial and non-commercial sexual experience. Male sex workers and sex club managers in such cities report that tourists (domestic travelers as well as visitors from Europe, Japan, Australia and elsewhere) represent a significant portion of demand for commercial sexual services.

But having said this, neither Britain nor the United States experiences the large-scale, highly focused forms of sexual tourism that are found in cities and resorts in economically developing countries. One obvious reason for this is that it would cost a great deal more to stay in London or Las Vegas for two weeks and pay for commercial sexual services every day than it would to do the same thing in Hanoi or Recife. Another important difference between sites of sexual tourism in developing and affluent countries is that, in poorer countries, tourism is often associated with what has been termed "open-ended prostitution." Rather than entering into brief cash-for-sex exchanges, sex workers will often provide anything from two hours to two weeks of full access to their persons, performing non-sexual labor for the tourist (shopping, tidying, washing, translation, and so on) as well as sexual labor. Also, in tourist destinations in poorer countries, there are individuals who do not identify as "sex workers," but who seek sexual relationships with tourists either in the hope of receiving gifts that will supplement their very low income, or because they wish to migrate to a richer country and hope to find a sponsor or marriage partner who will facilitate their migration.

This means that tourists can have sex with local or migrant people without necessarily thinking of themselves as paying for it. For example, a tourist might pick up a woman in an ordinary tourist bar, wine and dine her, take her back to his hotel for a night of passion, and when in the morning she asks for $15 for her taxi fare home, he can give her the money, and perhaps a little extra (because he knows these people are poor and he's a generous guy), without seeing this as payment for sexual services. It follows that sexual tourism in poorer countries can appeal to a much wider range of people – to those who are happy to contract for the sexual services of someone they know to be a sex worker, and also to those men and women who would not dream of having sex with someone they considered "a prostitute." The same opportunities for self-delusion are not available in Britain and the US, partly because sex workers who are willing to spend twenty-four hours with a client simulating a romantic adventure charge a great deal more, and partly because the tourist cannot draw on exoticizing racisms to shore up his or her fantasies of mutuality with regard to individuals who are so obviously much poorer and more vulnerable. An ordinary, middle-aged, white American woman on vacation in London is unlikely to start flirting with a homeless black teenage boy sitting on the pavements begging for spare change, then invite him out for dinner and back to her hotel for sex – his poverty would be too obvious for her to read his sexual acquiescence as motivated by anything other than material need, and his place in the social order too familiar for her to eroticize him as an "exotic" Other. But in Jamaica, many ordinary middle-aged white women from Europe and the US are perfectly willing to embark on "holiday romances" with impoverished local men and boys who flirt with them on the beach.

Can you tell us something about the people who are involved in selling and buying sex?

This is a difficult question to answer because, whether you're talking about affluent countries or developing countries, the sex sector is extremely diverse and also stratified in terms of earnings, working conditions, and the motivations of workers. So you get many different people selling sex – male, female, and transsexual, old and young, straight and gay, people from ethnic or racial majority and minority groups. You also get some highly educated and socially privileged people selling sex, and although many people trade sex because they're forced into it either by economic desperation or other factors, in both affluent and poor countries there are some people who elect to sell sex for more positive reasons. But I think it would be true to say that, for most people in developing nations, the decision to enter into sexual-economic exchanges with tourists is linked to material need and the absence of other opportunities for earnings or attaining personal goals such as migration or starting a business.

In most of the countries where sexual tourism is widespread, governments have had little choice but to enter into a variety of International Monetary Fund agreements and World Bank structural adjustment loans, sector adjustment loans and program loans over the past three decades, and the policy packages associated with these loans have had a devastating impact on the poor. Structural adjustment processes are widely reported to have undermined traditional forms of subsistence economies, led to high levels of unemployment, redirected subsidies away from social spending and basic commodities towards debt servicing, encouraged massive currency depreciations, and driven down wages of those in work. This helps to explain the rapid growth of the informal economic sector in the countries affected, as ordinary people desperately seek ways in which to earn a living, or supplement impossibly low-waged employment. For those who live in, or have migrated to, tourist areas, prostitution and other forms of sexual-economic exchange often have much greater earning potential than other forms of informal tourist-related economic activity, such as hair-braiding or selling fruit, sweets or souvenirs. And for those people who manage to find employment in hotels or tourist bars or restaurants, sexual relationships with tourists can be a way to supplement wages that are inadequate to live on.

The tourists who enter into sexual-economic exchanges with locals and migrants are also a diverse group. They can be men or women, straight or gay, seventeen or seventy years old, middle-class professionals or working-class budget tourists, single or married, and from any ethnic or racial group. They also vary in terms of their sexual practices and attitudes towards sexual life, because, as I've said, sexual-economic relationships in tourist areas in poorer countries can be organized in ways that tourists from affluent countries don't recognize as "prostitution," which means that even people (both straight and gay) who strongly disapprove of, or are sexually turned off by the idea of, commercial sex can get involved in sexual tourism.

Having said this, there is a distinct and sizeable subgroup of what I would describe as "hard core" sexual tourists. These are people for whom the desire for particular kinds of sexual experience (generally those which are expensive, scarce, or risky at home, such as sex with multiples of prostitute women or men, and/or with children, or transsexuals) is a chief part of the motivation to travel. Some hard-core sex tourists find the pleasures associated with a particular destination so great that they eventually decide to settle permanently in their chosen "sexual paradise." Such expatriates (or "sexpatriates") often play an active role in promoting sex tourism and organizing tourist-related prostitution in a given destination. Predominantly male, white, and heterosexual, the worldview of this type of sexual tourist is often aggressively racist, sexist, and homophobic.

What is the role of children in the sex tourism industry?

The United Nations' Convention on the Rights of the Child defines children as persons under the age of eighteen. A sizeable minority of those who enter into sexual-economic transactions with tourists in developing countries are children. Most are aged between fifteen and eighteen, though there are younger ones as well. Although these younger children are but a tiny fraction of the people involved in the general phenomenon of sexual tourism, they have been significant for the development of sexual tourism in some places. In particular, there are resorts or towns in a number of countries that do attract pedophile tourists and others with a focused interest in sex with children. Young children's presence in the tourist-related sex trade has also been the focus of intense interest and concern from non-governmental organizations (NGOs), journalists, and national and international policymakers, to the extent that many people now have the mistaken impression that sites of sexual tourism are largely peopled by pedophiles, small children, and their pimps.

Campaigns against child prostitution in general, and "child sex tourism" in particular, have assumed that there is a firm line of demarcation between adult and child prostitution. However, this does not reflect the realities of sex commerce. Those aged above and below eighteen typically work alongside each other, in the same conditions, serving the same clients. With the exception of a limited number of cases in which a small "niche market," catering to demand from pedophile tourists, has emerged, the role of children in sexual tourism is pretty much identical to the role played by their adult counterparts.

How does a child become involved in international sex tourism and sex trade?

Children who become involved in the sex trade are usually members of impoverished communities, and/or groups that are socially, economically, and politically disadvantaged on grounds of race, ethnicity, or caste, or groups that are forgotten, feared or despised by the wider community (homeless, gay, slum-dwellers, drug users). Poverty (alongside racism and other forms of discrimination and the social devaluation of women and girls) very often also plays a key role in the phenomenon of forced, debt-bonded, or indentured child prostitution, for children are vulnerable to this type of exploitation, when they and/or their parents or other adult carers do not enjoy basic economic and social rights.

Can you tell us something about the adults who participate in child prostitution?

"Pedophile tourism" is a reality, and numerous cases have been documented in which Western and Japanese men travel as tourists, or take up permanent or temporary residence in poor and developing countries in order to gain sexual access to local children. The countries targeted include Sri Lanka, Cambodia, Thailand, the Philippines, the Dominican Republic, Costa Rica, and Brazil. These men know that it is easier, cheaper and safer to obtain sexual access to a child in poor and developing countries than it is back home. Also, racism plays an important part, as does the illusion of sexual and emotional mutuality that is more easily sustained when relationships are not explicitly constructed as "prostitution." Many pedophiles claim they want affectionate, non-coercive, and reciprocal sexual relationships with children. In poor countries, tourists' relatively much greater economic power allows them to draw children into more open-ended and longer-term sexually abusive relationships, within which the economic basis of the relationship can be disguised as sympathetic "help" (food, clothes, school fees) or indulgence of childish fancies (toys, excursions). The adult can more easily tell himself that he is genuinely loved and wanted by the children who visit him and acquiesce to sex.

Still, pedophiles are a minority amongst sexual tourists. The majority of children trading sex are aged between fifteen and eighteen. They are often too physically mature to be of interest to pedophiles. In most societies, older teenagers' participation in sexual and economic life is considered in a different light from that of younger children. The age of sexual consent is set below eighteen in many countries, and a great deal of sexual and esthetic value is placed on youth, so that a 16- or 17-year-old is not necessarily perceived as childlike or sexually immature.

Sexual tourists generally rely on popular ideas about childhood and sexuality, and their own personal sexual preferences and moral values, to make choices between potential sexual partners of different ages. So, while some tourists may be at pains to avoid younger sexual partners, others do not care very much whether the local person they pick up is fifteen or twenty, providing they fancy the way the partner looks. I have interviewed many sexual tourists (aged anywhere between seventeen and seventy) who like "fit" young sexual partners – they are not necessarily seeking out someone under the age of eighteen, but how are they to tell the exact age of the locals who proposition them, especially given that many are drunk by the time they "pull"?

What are international agencies and national governments doing to combat sexual tourism and especially child prostitution? What success have they had?

The national governments of countries that send large numbers of tourists to the developing world appear to be doing absolutely nothing to combat sexual tourism. They have, however, responded to a campaign against "child sex tourism" – a campaign largely orchestrated by one NGO, End Child Prostitution, Pornography and Trafficking in Children for Sexual Purposes (ECPAT). A key objective of ECPAT's campaign has been to shift the perception that sex with children in poorer countries is a low-risk crime by encouraging laws and policies in both receiving and sending countries that will make the prosecution of foreigners who commit sexual offences against children abroad easier and more likely. ECPAT lobbied hard and with a good deal of success for tourist-sending countries to introduce extraterritorial criminal laws that would allow states to prosecute their nationals for sexual crimes perpetrated against children in other countries. By 1998, twenty countries had introduced extraterritorial laws pertaining to child sex offences committed abroad, but in many of these countries no court cases had yet been initiated. Germany, the country where most cases had been pursued, had only prosecuted thirty-seven people under these laws, and only six of these cases led to conviction. Campaigners also lobbied for action against those who organized "child sex tours," again with some success. The Australian government enacted legislation in 1994 designed to strengthen action against tour operators who promoted "child sex tourism," and Britain introduced a similar law in 1996. But again, there have been few prosecutions under such laws.

In 1996, a World Congress Against the Commercial Sexual Exploitation of Children was held in Stockholm, and the governments of 122 nations signed the Congress Declaration and agreed to implement an Agenda for Action focusing on national and international cooperation with regard to policing "child sex tourism," and measures for prevention, protection, and the recovery and reintegration of children affected. Some national governments in developing countries have subsequently introduced changes to laws that bring their legislation on child prostitution into line with Article 34 of the Convention of the Rights of the Child (which states that all those under the age of eighteen should be provided with protection against all forms of sexual exploitation and abuse); some have worked more closely with children's rights NGOs in relation to prevention and recovery and reintegration issues; a few have run or supported campaigns to inform tourists that sex with minors will not be tolerated in their country. However, for obvious reasons it is very difficult for governments of poorer countries to implement the kind of measures that would be necessary to provide children with meaningful economic alternatives to sex work, and, without this, everything else looks very much like window-dressing.

I am increasingly cynical about campaigns against "child sex tourism." First, although NGOs involved in campaigns against "child sex tourism" have been keen to work with the tourist industry to combat the problem, because they focus attention on the minority of "deviant" tourists who travel in pursuit of sex with young children, they actually ask very little of that industry. Hugely profitable multinational corporations are applauded for assisting with the distribution of baggage tags emblazoned with the logo "No to child sex tourism!", for agreeing to monitor accredited members of travel agents' associations to ensure they are not advertising "child sex tours," for being willing to show in-flight videos telling people that it is illegal and wrong to have sex with 6-year-olds. But the industry is not being similarly pressured to address questions about the derisory wages paid to hotel workers, or to think about how this might connect to the phenomenon of sexual tourism, including that involving children. Nor have campaigns focused public attention on the social and environmental costs of tourism as an industry, or the fact that profits from tourism are largely repatriated to affluent tourist-sending countries and so will never "trickle down" to those who pick up tourists' litter, clean their toilets, make their beds, serve their food, and fulfill their sexual fantasies.

Second, campaigns against "child sex tourism" have emphasized that this is an international problem because those who exploit children cross national borders to do so, and this has encouraged a tendency to imagine that all we need are stronger laws and stricter law enforcement to "smoke out and hunt down" the bad guys. But "child sex tourism" is also an international problem in the sense that it is directly linked to the neo-liberal policies forced on developing countries by the IMF and the World Bank, policies that have encouraged economic dependence on tourism whilst simultaneously slashing public expenditure on services such as health and education, increasing unemployment, and reducing the already low living standards of the poor. In other words, these policies have created a situation in which large numbers of people willing and able to pay for sexual services are brought together with large numbers of people – adult and child – for whom selling sex is the best or only means of subsisting. For this reason, I would argue that sexual tourism is a problem of global justice, as much or more than of criminal justice, a point that often gets lost in campaigns against "child sex tourism."

Third, those who campaign against "child sex tourism" insist that children should not be stigmatized for their involvement in the commercial sex trade. But they generally remain silent about the stigmatization and criminalization of adult women in prostitution for fear of alienating potential allies, especially religious and other morally conservative thinkers. Similarly, although homophobia is often a factor precipitating teenage boys' entry into the sex trade, campaigners against "child sex tourism" have seldom sought to develop links with those who campaign for lesbian and gay rights. I don't believe it is possible to leave intact profoundly conservative gender and sexual ideologies that allow for the routine and systematic violation of the human rights of sex workers and homosexuals, and yet secure some kind of "stay of execution" for those aged under eighteen. It's therefore no surprise to find that governments of poorer countries have often responded to campaigns against "child sex tourism" by engaging in extremely brutal clampdowns on female sex workers in tourist areas, and that the numbers of women and teenagers who have ended up deported, or behind bars, or in "re-education," "rehabilitation," or whatever euphemism is preferred, as a result of international concern about "child sex tourism" far outstrips the number of Western pedophiles or "sex tour" operators who have been similarly treated.

chapter 75

Migrant sex work and trafficking

Sorting them out

Laura Agustín

When trafficking is mentioned in the media these days it's usually linked seamlessly with sexual abuse, exploitation, pimps, slavery and ruined lives. Although some hold that we live in a postfeminist world, everyone seems predisposed to assume the worst about women who sell sex – especially how helpless and sexually vulnerable they are, just because they were born female. My research over the past 15 years has broken the many suppositions behind such clichés into manageable pieces, not to say everything is hunky-dory but to get closer to the actual problems rather than the sensationalist, sexist fantasies. The fact that the problems have little to do with sex itself is illustrated in the following description.

A few years ago I met five women in Thailand and Australia, at the request of local NGOs who wanted a Spanish-speaker to visit them. In Sydney I was introduced to the owner of a legal brothel and two of her workers; in Bangkok I visited two undocumented migrants in a detention centre. The women came from Peru, Colombia and Venezuela and were mostly middle-class, although one had little formal education. But their travel stories were diverse.

The brothel owner was a permanent resident in Australia. Her migrant workers had come on visas to study English that gave them the right to work, but they had been required to pay for the entire eight-month course in advance and were in debt. The madam treated them well but kept them close, living in her house and travelling with her to the brothel.

One of the women in the detention centre had been caught with a fraudulent visa at Tokyo airport and deported back to her last stop, Bangkok. Originally invited to join her sister in Japan, she spent a year jail before being sent to the detention centre. The other detainee had been caught during a robbery carried out by her travelling companions in Bangkok (one stop on their travels around Southeast Asia). She spent three years in jail before being sent to the centre (and, by the way, all her papers were false, including a change of nationality). Both women were in the centre because they had no money to pay their plane fare home, and, so far, no one was offering to pay it for them, since both were complicit in the plans for their nonlegal travel and work – disqualifying them as victims of trafficking.

The two recently arrived migrants in Sydney seemed to accept doing sex work, but they didn't have much choice of jobs, given the cost of the language course and their inability to speak English. The migrant to Japan said she believed she had not been destined to sell sex even though her sister had, but she felt guilty because her own family had been involved in getting her false papers. The woman caught in the robbery had sold sex informally during her travels, and seemed satisfied she'd be able to make money that way. The numerous people involved in these arrangements were said to be Pakistani, Turkish and Mexican.

Complex, ambiguous stories like these are often described and denounced as sex trafficking. Much of the outcry revolves around an abstract point – whether prostitution can ever be seen as a "real" job. This question is less relevant to undocumented migrants who have no visas allowing them to work in *any* legal job. Travels that involve selling sex are often talked of as though they were inherently different from all other kinds of travel to work, mostly because migration in general is little understood. In this chapter I'll examine generalisations that erase individual experiences and lead to non-productive debates. I'll look at ideas about migration, job markets, the informal economy, the sex industry, trafficking – and the idea of good sex itself.

Why do people leave home?

> You work, work, work and then they don't pay you, because there's no money . . . I worked in an ashtray factory, and when there was no money to pay me they said "take ashtrays," 100 ashtrays. So? Can you eat ashtrays?
> (Ukrainian woman in Spain: Agustín 2005)

> There wasn't any work and I wanted to be independent. I have a big family, but I didn't get along with them. I wanted to be on my own. I saw the neighbours who are doing okay, who have money because there's someone in Italy.
> (Nigerian woman in Italy: Danna 2004)

Both these migrants were selling sex when researchers spoke to them. Scholars explaining why people move to another country to work cite many causes: international structural conditions and globalisation of markets; national immigration policies; the feminisation of poverty; wage differentials between countries. They talk about loss of land, recruitment by foreign employers, the desire to join family abroad, flight from violence, persecution and natural disasters. Any single person may have multiple reasons to consider migrating, but no single condition guarantees that he or she *will* migrate. None of the theories accounts for the desires and aspirations that poorer people feel, just as richer ones do (to see the world, to get ahead, to escape limited lives), or for personality traits that make a migration seem plausible to some people and not to others (willingness to take risks, ability to tolerate uncertainty).

Working in informal economies

Legal jobs (in what's known as the formal sector) are regulated and tracked in government accounting. Legal migrant workers possess a work permit and visa; if they work in the informal economy, where no permits can be had, they are not working legally. This fact does not discourage many people from travelling or migrating, however, since they know that jobs in informal economies are plentiful all over the world. That is, they know that if they get across the border, someone will hire them, because there are jobs open. That migration policies don't mention these flourishing markets is confusing, since many of the jobs available are fairly ordinary, if non-prestigious, and can serve to bring in incomes significant to migrants and enhancing social life: manual labour on construction sites, farm labour, live-in domestic service and caring for children and the elderly in private homes, factory labour, restaurant kitchen employment, cleaning, home piecework and a wide variety of jobs in the sex industry. To take advantage of such jobs, migrants must first arrive.

Legal status is limited to entering as a tourist, student or temporary business traveller with the appropriate visa, or to enter with a job offer and formal working papers in hand. Obtaining a tourist visa can be next to impossible for citizens of many countries, or may require years of waiting because of country quotas. Or the potential tourist/migrant may be able to get a visa but not have the money to buy tickets and survive while looking for work. The imbalance between jobs available to migrants and visas offered to them creates a niche for those able to provide services to undocumented migrants. Many who want to travel search actively for help getting around the rules at home, while others search for them, to sell them trips and jobs. These vendors in the informal economy are known by a variety of names, from businessmen and travel agents to coyotes on the Mexican border and snakeheads in China. They are often relatives or friends, and they may be tourist acquaintances met during vacations who bring friends over to visit or work. Marriage may be part of the deal. Intermediaries may play a minimal part in the migration project or offer a package which links them closely to migrants every step of the way.

Without access to a charge account or formal bank loan, the would-be migrant probably goes into debt to pay for services that may include the provision of passports, visas, changes of identity, work permits and other documents, as well as advice on how to dress and handle interviews with immigration officials or police, the loan of money to show upon entrance with a tourist visa, pick-up service at the airport, land transport to another country or to pre-arranged lodgings, and names of potential employers. These services are not difficult to find in countries where out-travel has become common, and, in certain countries, formal-sector travel agents offer them under the table. Furthermore, for unauthorised migrants, no matter what job they get, under-the-table services continue to be needed after borders are crossed.

Migrating involves a series of risky judgements and decisions. Each step of the way, migrants must weigh information they're given against what they have heard from returned migrants, friends and family living abroad and news reports. Whether migrants buy a full package from a single entrepreneur or make a succession of smaller decisions, only one link in the chain needs to be weak for things to go wrong. Moreover, people who are over-eager to travel may do little research to test information given to them and connive in situations that later make them vulnerable. The relationships are further complicated when intermediaries are migrants themselves. Institutions in countries of origin, including embassies and consulates granting visas, know that people are migrating quasi-legally or illegally. These countries have come to rely on money sent back by migrants. It is no wonder that migrants fail to view themselves as really "illegal," much less criminal. Intermediaries, many friends and families of migrants, are also not all criminal exploiters. Such networks have always existed, but only with heightened attention to the sex industry has this varied group been attacked en masse as unequivocally violent and cruel. Travel that results in selling sex is often positioned, in the mass media and amongst social crusaders, as different from all others.

Travelling to work in the sex industry

Selling sex may make travel possible, providing the money to buy tickets. It may be the way people from the countryside or small towns can begin to make a living in cities while they look for other jobs. Or it may be the most lucrative job available once people have arrived at their destination. All kinds of vendors, including domestic and sexual, follow soldiers on campaigns, pilgrims and seasonal and itinerant workers such as miners, seamen and farm workers. Mobility has been associated with selling sex throughout history; some Europeans migrating to the Americas and Australia sold sex to finance their voyages in the eighteenth and nineteenth centuries. These migrations were sometimes called "white slavery," to distinguish the migrants from formerly enslaved Africans. Avidly covered by the press, the idea that white women were forcibly prostituted created an international movement dedicated to its eradication. Research has shown that many or most of these women migrants (like today), simply saw a chance for new lives in other lands and were willing, at least temporarily, to sell sex to get a chance at them. Between the last upsurge of trafficking discourse and now, *the way* people migrated was not considered of great interest – in dramatic contrast to the present. Now the slavery idea is back in full force.

The sex industry, largely unregulated and outside official government accounting, operates through informal networks; to gain access, newcomers must meet an insider. The haphazard nature of this information economy is illustrated by a Ukrainian woman's story:

> Once I was talking with a friend and she asked if I wanted to go to Spain. I knew why, so I said: "Ah, do you want to . . . ?" and I don't know where she met this guy, he got the papers for us, made the passport, everything, the money and we left . . .

This guy went to look for work, where are the best places to work, where there are men . . . He talked first with the boss . . . said he was looking for work for us.

(Agustín 2001)

Many who work in the sex industry knew that their jobs abroad would have a sexual dimension, but they probably did not understand how they would feel or what working conditions would be. The commercial sex they knew about at home may have little in common with the options they have now: standing almost nude in a window or by the side of a highway for many hours, or doing hand jobs in a massage parlour all day, with little other social contact with clients. When part of the migration package included signing a contract without understanding what it meant, the value of foreign money or the language in which the contract was written, problems can obviously become severe. But, even when migrants say that they were deceived, it's not the sex work per se they want to get out of; often they would like to remain in the industry, but in less exploitative conditions.

A friend proposed that I come, she knew a girl who could bring me . . . You sign a note for seven million pesos [€4,207] and they tell you that you can pay it back working for a month. You know what you're going to be doing. Anyone who says she didn't know, it's a lie, a married lady with children, how can she not know what she's going to be doing here? When you arrive, you crash, because the work is bad and it's a lie that the debt can be paid in a month. You talk with the other girls and see that the debt is more than it cost the girl to bring you. [But] I want to pay her, because she takes a risk, too, to bring you over . . .

(Oso 2003)

Paying off debts in the shortest amount of time is nearly every migrant's primary goal, so the focus is on the future, not on past abuses. While the most tragic situations so often cited by the media and nongovernmental organisations come to light precisely because the police have become involved, reporters and activists seeking victims do not meet migrants who have *not* sought help, and some of them don't want to be found and rescued. In many cases, family or friends have collaborated in deceiving or misleading migrants. Sometimes, recently arrived and disoriented migrants feel psychologically dependent on intermediaries, who then can exercise too much control or influence. In the worst cases, migrants are threatened and held against their will, their personal documents are withheld and they are forced to have and sell sex.

As soon as I was brought to Turin I understood that I had ended up in a blind alley: I found myself with a madam who ordered me onto the sidewalk and wanted 50 million [lire] [€25,800]. It was a real nightmare, I cried all the tears I had.

(Kennedy and Nicotri 1999)

Every girl that worked for Cindy knew which day she was going to be there and that she had to give her the money or deposit it in her account. Later Cindy would stay a while in each place where she had left girls . . . at the same time she was maintaining control over what happened to them.

(Likiniano 2003)

Laura Agustín

These kinds of situations have prompted not only appropriate concern but also a moral panic that drastically generalises *all* cases as dire and excludes more complicated stories like those at the beginning of this chapter. The words *force* and *exploitation* are bundled into a monolith that sweeps away individual migrants' degrees of knowledge, will and desire. Some women, for example, *feel forced* who could physically escape; others start out doing domestic work but *feel obligated* to sell sex because of the differential in pay, in order to send more money home or pay off debts faster.

The difficulty is that the fundamental terms of the argument attempt to pin down enigmatic issues of will, consent, understanding and choice – the extent to which people travelling with false papers understood the possible consequences of using them, whether they felt love for someone facilitating their journey, whether they knew what a contract meant, how their parents' participation in a deal affected their judgement, if they realised the consequences of being in debt. Such epistemological questions are often unfathomable when involving people secure in their homes, but they become even more so when those involved have left their homes behind to face cultural disorientation on a grand scale through migration. It is also patronising to assume people don't understand that all projects to change one's life involve risks. Women selling sex in Nairobi were asked if they realised it could be dangerous, to which they replied that they were not selling sex in order to live safely but to earn money and be independent (Pheterson 1996).

The purpose of showing the many forms a migration can take is not to deny that some forms are dangerous and unfair but rather to avoid homogenising hundreds of thousands of women's experiences and reducing all to a single supposedly universal truth. It is, of course, harder to deal with multiple, confusing levels of innocence and guilt, criminality and victimhood. But if we try to do that, we find that sex itself is not the centre of most stories.

The sex in sex work

> I don't understand what is bad about selling love for money ... With this job I have made it possible for all my brothers to study and I have supported my mother, so I am proud of being a prostitute.
>
> (Nigerian woman in Italy: Kennedy and Nicotri 1999)

Is it hard to believe that some people prefer selling sex rather than washing dishes, babysitting, or picking fruit? Consider that migrants, who come in all sizes, shapes and colours, and from infinitely varying backgrounds, need to be flexible and adaptable to succeed. They often do not know beforehand how they will be living, and they may not know the language. They may fear the police and feel enormous pressure to pay back debts. Their past work experience and diplomas, whether white-collar or blue, are usually worthless. Migrant schoolteachers, engineers, nurses, hairdressers and a range of others find only low-status, low-paying jobs open to them. Many of them, from everywhere on the social spectrum and of every gender identity, prefer to work at least temporarily in the sex industry, in one or another of a variety of jobs.

Bars, restaurants, cabarets, private clubs, brothels, discotheques, saunas, massage parlours, sex shops, peep shows, hotel rooms, homes, bookshops, strip and lap-dance venues, dungeons, webcam sites, beauty parlours, clubhouses, cinemas, public toilets, phone lines, shipboard festivities, as well as modelling, swinging, stag and fetish parties: sex is sold practically everywhere. Where these businesses operate without licences, undocumented workers with nothing to lose can easily be employed: this is a paradox of prohibition. Already working illegally, migrants may consider these jobs no riskier than others and even advantageous.

> One day I met a friend of mine while I was walking in the town centre . . . I learned that she was a prostitute so her children could live in a decent way. This work has the advantage of financial ease and freedom to work schedules that allow spending more time with the children.
>
> (French woman of Algerian parents in France: Cabiria 2002)

On the other hand, selling sex is definitely not for everybody, and some migrants will take on worse-paid or riskier jobs to avoid it: many live-in maids in the first case, "mules" transporting drugs inside their bodies in the second.

What is it that outrages people about women who sell sex? Why are some sexual jobs considered worse than others? Why do some people think better-educated women with more job opportunities *can* choose to sell sex while poorer women cannot? What's going on when people in privileged countries set out to rescue women in the Third World from the sex industry?

The idea of good, and equal, sex

In this day and age, many people believe that sex should express love and that "good sex" must be loving. It is assumed that feelings of love intensify pleasure and that the resulting passion is meaningful and should lead to long-term, emotionally committed relationships. Departing from this supposition, other kinds of sexual relations appear to be inferior: anonymous, public, promiscuous, uncommitted, non-monogamous and commercial.

In the case of commercial sex – all the many varieties – convention would have it that the presence of money means a sexual relationship cannot be good because the parties are not equal. But what does *equal* mean here? One idea holds that sexual intimacy and money must be kept separate, because the person with money has the power to command and control what the other does. But that's not how people talk about buyers of other intimate services like psychotherapy, or services involving physical contact like chiropractics, acupuncture, manicure or therapeutic massage. Does anyone think these professionals' clients have all the control? The reply says that using the body isn't the problem per se but that when sexual organs are involved, everything is different, because sex is key to our innermost selves and when we have sex without love we alienate our deep personal identities. This makes sense to you or it doesn't, but cannot be proved. On such grounds all sexual jobs are decreed soulless, mechanical and damaging activities *when the person providing the sex is a woman*: this idea

Laura Agustín

forms part of a larger theory about violence against women that sees women as particularly sexually vulnerable to men who are prone to violence and invasion and who will, given the opportunity of paying for sex, behave violently or demeaningly. This set of ideas about women's sexual vulnerability must be situated in time and culture: not that long ago, vaginas were imagined to be dangerous and devouring and prostitutes to be aggressive, violent women who mugged and robbed potential customers.

The demand that sexual relationships be equal plays a central role in framing migrant sex workers as victims of trafficking. If it's assumed that women from other cultures, because they are economically poorer, are backward, passive, vulnerable objects existing only to be exploited by men with money, then all sexual exchanges between them can be condemned as inequitable. This only works, however, if no other conditions are taken into account: the possibility of strong, controlling sex workers and unassertive clients; migrants' hard-headed determination to get ahead; many people's ability to separate their sexual experiences into meaningful and non-meaningful or into work and play; many workers' affectionate or conventional relationships with clients.

Everyone does not feel the same way about sex: that's the pure and simple of it. Everyone does not think sex is utterly different from all other human activity, or feel their personal identity is linked to it, or think that enjoyable sex must always lead to monogamy or means they are in love. Or that money changes or ruins sex. The suspicion that non-loving, noncommitted-partner sex is amoral is recurring at the same time that forms of commercial sex are proliferating. So although we tell a powerful story about sex and love belonging together, we also understand that people want other kinds of sex, and, in fact that present-day searches for personal identity often encourage sexual experimentation. Only the sketchiest data can be gathered when businesses operate outside the law, as sex businesses do in many societies, so we cannot revert to a body of facts that tell us how much exploitation and unhappiness exist relative to how much empowerment and wellbeing. We hear about people who buy and sell sex from our friends, acquaintances, the media, and sometimes through reporting on migration – which is where sex trafficking comes in.

To understand why headlines and social commentators scream that all migrant women who sell sex are victims of trafficking, we need to go back to the still hegemonic idea that the proper place for sex is at home between committed lovers and family. This idea is particularly applied, for not the best of reasons, to people from poorer and non-Western cultures, so that it's imagined that people uprooted from there are particularly sad cases, with women who sell sex abroad imagined to be saddest of all. That notion requires us to reduce migrants to pawns on a global economic chessboard where they have no will or agency at all. Even those who concede that poorer migrants may want to leave home and even prefer to sell sex often insist that they are not *really* choosing anything because capitalism's structural conditions make them into victims by definition. Add that analysis to an emotional antipathy to selling sex and you see why headlines scream.

Positioning most of the world's women as pathetic sexual victims does serve to make their rescuers feel important, and there's no doubt that some people are helped and saved by campaigners. But the neocolonialism required to ignore what so many migrants say about themselves – their experiences, feelings, desires – is a backward step for women's movements that originally hoped to de-link women and sex as an inevitable couplet. It fails to respect different cultures and imposes values *currently* considered the best, rather than looking at the personal or local.

Many migrants reject being defined as sexually vulnerable and in need of rescue and protection.

> When you work a lot in one place then you . . . you get tired of the clients . . . Even though it will be the same, you imagine another place with other people, and then you come to life inside . . . I go to another country, another city. Lately I live between Mallorca and Barcelona . . . In summer I always go to Mallorca to spend a little time with my son.
>
> (Latin American woman in Spain: Cuanter 1998)

> Sometimes I enjoy working; I can travel and see beautiful places. I can go to nice restaurants. I enjoy that the Turkish men view us as desirable.
>
> (Ukrainian woman in Turkey: Gülçür and İlkkaracan 2002)

Granting migrating individuals the capacity to make decisions does not mean denying the vast structural changes that push and pull them. On the other hand, it does not mean making them over-responsible for situations largely not of their own making, as global, national and local conditions, as well as luck, intervene in individuals' decisions. As far as the sex goes, it takes too many forms, in a huge proliferation of venues and cultural contexts, for any generalisation to be made (Agustín 2007). If you are interested in complexity and challenge, this subject area is for you!

References

Agustín, Laura. 2007. *Sex at the Margins: Migration, labour markets and the rescue industry.* London: Zed Books.

—. 2005. "Migrants in the mistress's house: Other voices in the 'trafficking' debate." *Social Politics: International Studies in Gender, State and Society*, 12(1): 99.

—. 2001. "Mujeres inmigrantes ocupadas en servicios sexuales." In *Mujer, inmigración y trabajo*, ed. Colectivo Ioé, 647–716. Madrid: IMSERSO.

Cabiria. 2002, 2004. *Rapport de synthèse.* Lyon, France: Le Dragon Lune.

Cuanter. 1998. "Las notas características de la prostitución y su acceso a los Servicios Sociales." Madrid: Instituto de la Mujer.

Danna, Daniela. 2004. *Donne di Mondo: Commercio del sesso e controllo statale.* Milan: Eleuthera.

Gülçür, Leyla and İlkkaracan, Pinar. 2002. "The 'Natasha' experience: Migrant sex workers from the former Soviet Union and Eastern Europe in Turkey." *Women's Studies International Forum*, 25(4): 411–21.

Kennedy, Iyamu and Nicotri, Pino. 1999. *Lucciole Nere. Le prostitute nigeriane si raccontano.* Milan: Kaos.

Likiniano. 2003. *Tráfico y Prostitución: Experiencias de mujeres africanas.* Bilbao, Spain: Likiniano Elkartea.

Oso, Laura. 2003. "Estrategias migratorias de las mujeres ecuatorianas y colombianas en situación irregular." *Mugak*, 23: 25–37.

Pheterson, Gail. 1996. *The Prostitution Prism.* Amsterdam: Amsterdam University Press.

chapter 76

The public and hidden sexualities of Filipina women in Lebanon

Hayeon Lee

There are about 200,000 migrant women domestic workers – the majority from Sri Lanka, Ethiopia and the Philippines – in Lebanon, which has a population of about 4 million. Although the Philippine government officially banned citizens from coming to Lebanon following the July War in 2006, an estimated 40,000 Filipinos, mostly female domestic workers, still live and work in Lebanon. Since 1975, migrant women have gradually replaced Lebanese and other Arab women from poor backgrounds, who once made up the dominant domestic labor force (Jureidini 2009). In recent years, the human rights situation of domestic workers has been of public interest due to widespread media coverage of the abuse of these women, as this appears to have led to several suicides. However, the mechanisms of power behind these abuses are often overlooked, as are the complex ways in which Filipina women negotiate within these power structures in order to shape their lives in Lebanon.

Based on 37 interviews with Filipina women, 14 in-depth interviews with Lebanese employers, two interviews with recruitment agencies, and participant-observation mostly carried out in Beirut in 2007, this essay explores the sexuality of Filipina women. (All names have been changed for privacy.) The perceived sexuality of Filipina women – along with all the negative stereotypes – is often used as a means to control these women. Yet, I will argue that Filipina women do not surrender their sexual agency; they actively negotiate the challenges of living in an alien and sometimes hostile social environment, and this includes their sexuality.

Binit (girl) and sharmuta (whore)

The most common advice given to all madames[1] in Lebanon is to not let the live-in maid outside of the house alone. One recruiting agent named Ahmad always tells his customers, "Don't let her [the live-in maid] out by herself." He explains,

> My daughter [who is in her early teens], where she go out? She go to the school, she come back home, and if she goes out, she goes out with me or her mother. She's young. I don't let her go out alone. The housemaid, she comes to Lebanon. They are coming to work. She goes out with madame everyday . . . You go to Hamra? You see the man? All the man in Beirut take girl. Go sleep with her. Give her money . . . and she come back. She come back good, [or] she come back pregnant. Or make love for one, two, three [men] for money . . . But the girl, she didn't know this man. Where he comes from, is he working or not. He sleep with her . . . He don't have AIDS or syphilis, you don't know . . . I prefer to don't let her out because I know the girl [who goes] out. They are free visa. They don't have license.

Ahmad makes several points. First, he likens the live-in maid to his own young daughter. It is not surprising that many Lebanese refer to the migrant domestic worker as a *binit* – or girl, with an undertone of virginity – sometimes even for women well into their forties. Since the keeping of a daughter's chastity is seen as crucial to upholding family honor in a patriarchal society like Lebanon's, the live-in maid, who works and lives at the employer's home and literally carries the employer's name on her residence card and work permit, is under the same rules as the daughter. However, when daughters are married, they receive recognition as adult women. As for the maid, she might never be treated as an adult – even when she arrives in Lebanon married and with children. As a naïve and gullible *binit*, the Filipina woman who comes back to her madame's house without AIDS or syphilis the first time she goes out is considered lucky; employers think, however, that it is only a matter of time that she will come back pregnant or diseased.

Sometimes, the fact that a *binit* is working in the private home without kin protection in a foreign country is translated as her being sexually available for male members of that home. While most interviewees have only heard of cases of rape, there were some who experienced sexual harassment. For example, the male employer of Lorna, a Filipina woman in her thirties, would from time to time hug her from behind, peek into her room while she was napping in minimal clothing, and make sexual comments. One time, when no one else was home, Lorna was terrified and ran to her room when her male employer showed up naked in front of her. Another time, he said that if she let him touch her breasts, he would pay her. "I don't need your money! Keep your money," Lorna shouted. Leonilda, a Filipina woman in her twenties, switched employers after first arriving in Lebanon, when the male employer of the family kept harassing her. "Sometimes he was taking a shower, but he will call you to give him something, like that. It's insult for you, *yanni* [I mean]. Especially me, I don't have a husband! [Laughs]. That's why I said, *la'* [no], I don't want," she said.

Second, Beirut is portrayed as full of dangerous men and temptations. This perception is strengthened by the widespread harassment Filipina women receive on the streets, more so than Lebanese women, who are also often treated as sexual objects. Many madames add that it is unsafe for the live-in maid to go out alone. They believe there are many bad men and women, who are often viewed as a *sharmuta*, or whore, and who are waiting to corrupt innocent live-in maids. For example, Nisrine, a Lebanese madame in her thirties, does not want the live-in maid to meet others "for her own sake and for ours . . . because I have a special relationship with her. I really like to keep it like this. [If I allow her to go out,] I will lose her I think." In addition, she believes Lebanon is unsafe for the maid:

> Talk[ing] to strangers is very dangerous here in Lebanon. Security, *ma fi* [there isn't any]. One time, she was going to throw garbage very near, and after, I didn't let her. There was no electricity in the evening after ten o'clock, and then, some-one stopped the car and he say, "Come, come." She was very scared, and I told her, "You will not go, especially when there is no light on the road. Me or [my husband] will throw the garbage."

Third, there is no acknowledgement that domestic workers' sexual desires are natu-ral. It is assumed that she is only here to work and it is common practice to bar her from socializing outside unless supervised, especially in the first few years of employ-ment. For example, although Cynthia, a Lebanese woman in her thirties working for an international organization, is conscientious in terms of the Filipina live-in maid's treatment and workload, she does not allow the maid to have a day-off outside the house. She tells any Filipina live-in maid who works in her home, "The minute you decide that this is not your priority – working and making money for your family – and your priority is finding somebody, you tell me, you [must] leave."

It is convenient and economic for recruitment agencies to discourage madames to allow live-in maids to have a day-off outside the house: There is a three-month guarantee period for the customers, and if anything goes wrong, it is the agency that pays. And many madames, who pay up to US$2,700 to hire a woman from the Philippines to work in their home, are not willing to risk losing their "investment" after hearing stories of Filipina women sleeping with men, getting pregnant, running away, and bringing disease to their home. Furthermore, the *kafala* (sponsorship) system, along with domestic work-ers' exclusion from the labor law, ties workers to their Lebanese employer, creating a legal dependency of the former on the latter. Such an arrangement delegates near-absolute power to the employer to dictate her relationship with the live-in maid (Longva 1997: 91–94). The negative sexual stereotypes of Filipina women often legitimize this control.

The stereotypes of Filipina women (and other migrant domestic workers) as naïve girls or whores are further reinforced by gossip, rumors, advice from family and friends, and horror stories. As James Scott points out, rumors tend not to only reflect a real event but speak to the desires and fears of those who spread it (1990:145). They are used to justify and regulate the behaviors of those who are subject to them. Madames themselves have commented on how, often times, conversations at tea parties, chil-dren's birthday parties, and other casual gatherings among women are devoted to problems stemming from their relationship with the live-in maid. Advice is exchanged, assessments given, and stereotypes confirmed. Cynthia justifies her refusal to give a day-off outside to the live-in maid, explaining, "I hear so many stories . . . The dirty kind about girls running away, girls meeting Egyptian workers, girls meeting Syrian workers on Sundays. . . . I don't want to get involved in that."

Even if one hates gossiping about the maid – as most of my Lebanese interviewees asserted – the norms set by such gossip and the warnings from recruitment agencies make up the same gauge Lebanese employers use to assess their own level of generosity toward the live-in maid. For example, Muhammad, an employer in his forties, believes his family is exceptional for letting the Filipina live-in maid keep her own passport, which he gave back to her after obtaining her residence permit. Such cases are rare. One study estimates that 91 percent of Lebanese employers believe it is their right to hold the maid's passport and legal papers (Caritas 2005). And after the first few weeks, Muhammad always gives the newly arrived live-in maid a day-off and allows her to go outside of the home. This is also not common. He says that many people warned him that this is not a good idea, but Muhammad says his family is "crazy." But what Muhammad has come to see as a difference of *values*, is, according to international human rights standards, one of *rights*, since it is a worker's right to keep her passport and to exercise her freedom of movement. In other words, employers who go against "harsh" norms regarding the maid, but are actually respecting the maid's basic human rights, may feel especially generous in relation to other Lebanese employers. And if something goes "wrong," everybody knows who to blame: the generous madame or mister.

Hence, the pretext of Filipina women's uncontrollable sexuality is used to justify exercising tight control over these women and refusing their freedom of movement. Such control often breeds isolation and loneliness, which could be related to the high suicide rate among this demographic.

Racial hierarchy

There is a clear division in terms of how Filipina women are viewed compared to Ethiopian or Sri Lankan women in Lebanon. According to Lena, who previously hired a Sri Lankan, two Ethiopians, and currently employs a live-in Filipina, the best maid to hire is the Filipina: "If you want an idiot, take a Sri Lankan . . . But from the moment you take a Filipina, you say to yourself, look, there's a certain respect of the person and the right of the person." Maha, a Lebanese madame in her forties, said the following about Sri Lankan and Ethiopian live-in maids: "I don't like them at all . . . They have bad character . . . They are very stubborn, the Ethiopians . . . They have a special character. I don't like them. Even the Sri Lankans, I don't like. They're really idiots. The best are the Filipinas."

Racial stereotypes and a hierarchy of foreign live-in maids and domestic workers, who dominate the domestic service sector, permeate Lebanese society. While many madames believe that it depends on the individual, rather than their nationality, many also believe that Filipina women are probably smarter, more educated, and more professional than, for example, Ethiopian, Sri Lankan or Bangladeshi women.

In addition, Cynthia, a Lebanese madame, says Filipina women are more "presentable," reflecting the Lebanese preference for the fairer (and thus more attractive) appearance of Filipina women. "There are people who prefer a white girl . . . and the children aren't afraid of them," says Ahmad, the previously mentioned owner of a recruitment agency in Beirut. And because Filipina women are known as the most expensive, Nepalis, who only demand $100 per month as salary, have become popular in recent years. "Nepalis are pretty and white like Filipinas. When everyone is taking

$100 salary, no one will want Filipinas if they take $200," says Muhammad. (In fact, this is how Muhammad justifies lowering the Filipina women's salary to $150 upon arrival to Lebanon, when most of these women believe they will be receiving $200. The arbitrary lowering of salary for live-in maids of all nationalities upon arrival is common-place among recruitment agencies.) Ibrahim, another recruiting agent, thinks it is absurd that some madames look for white and "good-looking" girls. "It's racism . . . when you ask about color," he says. "The [customer is] stupid because when she asks . . . 'good-looking,' . . . Something strange, because she has husband, she has boys staying at home," he says. He has heard of many things that happen within the homes to these so-called "good-looking" domestic workers. According to one researcher, "So the sexual relations with the domestic maid can be viewed . . . as a threat to the honour and integrity of the family and . . . as providing assistance in the validations of one's heterosexual masculinity" (Jureidini 2006:142).

The view that Filipina women are "whiter" and more beautiful has also influenced their perception of their own sexuality. Many Filipina women are aware that, unlike their Sri Lankan or Ethiopian counterparts, Lebanese see them as more beautiful. Mercedita, a Filipina domestic worker, says, "Make-up, not even just powder, was *mamnu'* [forbidden]. Madames are too jealous, because they know Filipina, when they put make-up, some Filipina beautiful, you know? Not the same as Sri Lanka, Ethiopia. They are [also] beautiful . . . but black . . . Some [Lebanese] don't like. Not the same [as] Filipina, they are clean," says Mercedita. Muhammad, a Lebanese employer, con-firms a tendency to sexualize Filipinos. "In Lebanon, they say they [Filipinas] are [sex-ually] easy." Jessica says some men in Lebanon prefer Filipina women over other nationalities. She says, "Egyptians like Filipinas, because they say Filipinas . . . are *clean*, they smell *good*, like that. *Loving*, like that."

Nevertheless, Filipina women are seen as secondary choices as spouses or even girlfriends, and Lebanese men who fall in love with Filipina women are stigmatized and seen as "losers," who could not make a Lebanese woman fall in love with them. In a dramatic case, Beatrice, who had been together with her Lebanese boyfriend for more than five years, was forced to tip-toe around her boyfriend's house in the dark, lest his mother see Beatrice's shadow from the balcony, which is across from the boyfriend's balcony. This was because the mother of Beatrice's boyfriend, who had met with Beatrice on several occasions, had implored him to stop seeing her, and he promised to do so. She says, "It's humiliating. They are very superficial and act nice in front of you, but inside, they think Filipinas are all just maids." So while Filipina women might be seen as superior to maids of other nationalities, this superiority is only among maids, who occupy a socially inferior status. In other words, Filipina women are simply viewed as a better fit for domestic service and sexual adventures, compared to domestic workers of other nationalities.

From an invisible to a public self

Filipina women are often seen by Lebanese as naïve, sexually desirable, and promis-cuous. To what extent are these perceptions correct? While Filipina women are hyper-sexualized and exoticized within Lebanese society, and this image is used to legitimize the tight control madames have over the live-in Filipina maids, the same image gives Filipina women space to explore and enjoy their sexuality. This space is also due to Filipina women's specific living and working conditions in Beirut, especially for those who have a day-off or have left their employers to work as illegal freelancers.

Marissa believes she has changed in terms of how she views her own sexuality after she came to Lebanon. She had never been one to frequent night clubs, but here, she goes to clubs from time to time with her Filipina friends. When asked about what she thinks of how Filipina women dress here, especially on their day-off (usually Sunday), she says, "Sexy clothes . . . Big earrings . . . Of course in your own country, you cannot . . . We're just adapting the culture of the Lebanese now. They'll think you're *sharmuta* [whore] in the Philippines." While Lebanese point to Filipina women as *sharmuta*, Marissa believes it is Lebanese society's standards of sexuality that affect Filipina women. Pointing to her medium-size hoop earrings, she adds, "I never wore big earrings like this in the Philippines. This is already big for me. But now I have a bigger one."

Twenty-nine-year-old Gladys has four children in the Philippines, and when I met her on a Sunday she was wearing extremely tight clothes, along with long, bleached, flowing hair and blue contact lenses. At the time, she was dating four boys. When I asked how she could see all of them when she only has Sundays off, she said, "I have time . . . Two hours of [each of] them. [We both laugh.] I have one Egyptian, I have one Syrian, I have one Armenian, and I have one Lebanese." I ask who she thinks is the best. "The Syrian. What do you mean 'best?' In the bed?" We laugh again, and I clarify, "In everything." She answers again, "Syrian." Ironically, Gladys's designation of her boyfriend solely by their nationality mimics the simplification and stereotyping of migrant domestic workers by color and nationality.

I met Lara, a Filipina in her late forties who has been working in Lebanon for over 10 years, on a Sunday afternoon on a public bus in Beirut. At the time, Lara was showing her friend graphic photos of herself with her boyfriend, either French-kissing or in other sexual poses. Everyone in the bus was observing these ostentatious acts. Lara, who sat next to the aisle, was not showing her pictures in the middle of her seat toward her friend, but toward the aisle so that even I, who was sitting two seats behind them, could see the pictures. It felt as if she was trying to show off her young, cute Kurdish boyfriend in his mid-twenties (Lara was 47 years old at the time), boasting of her sensuality and sexual "achievements" before the Lebanese on the bus.

Curious, I spoke to Lara; she invited me to go to two birthday parties and then clubbing at Jazira – the most popular among several nightclubs in Beirut that specifically cater for Filipina women on Sunday afternoons. In the conversation before the birthday parties, Lara told me she has five children and that they have all grown up. For this reason, her children understand that their mother wants to be "happy" and don't mind that she parties with her young boyfriend in Lebanon. One of her friends, Nerissa, however, made fun of Lara for the way she dances. And despite all the claims Lara made to me regarding how much she loves partying and how there is no need for communication with her boyfriend except "I love you" and "I miss you," Lara seemed somewhat out-of-place at Jazira. After supporting her children for so long as the mother, she was clearly in the process of experimenting with her sexuality. She enjoys the attention she gets from men, telling me that she hopes her boyfriend is not at the club because she would like to dance with other men.

Lara crafts her relatively new sexuality specifically in the context of her acceptable absence from the Philippines, where she would be under the tighter control of her family. The fact that Filipina women are stereotypically seen as attractive – in the racial hierarchy of domestic workers – and sexually available has given Lara the chance to date someone 20 or more years younger than herself. Lara's sexual expression reinforces the stereotype of Filipina women as promiscuous, since she is married with children. But her investment in this self allows her to be "happy," as she puts it, on one of the seven days when she is not taking care of two children, cleaning a huge home, and serving the Lebanese family that employs her. Furthermore, Lara demonstrates how Filipina women use the stereotype directed against them as a resource for cultivating a "sexual self." This is a self which is not available to them back home and is an alternative to the self as the invisible maid.

To continue with the day I spent with Lara, we met the first birthday girl Nerissa at a tiny flat near Bourj Hammoud that belongs to a mutual friend. When we arrived, Nerissa was cooking for 15 people, almost naked in her pink tank top and underwear, with blasting music that could be heard a hundred meters away. Neighbors were peeking out of their windows to see what was happening. Because the kitchen had no ventilation, Nerissa was sweating and her eyeliner was dripping, but her long hair remained down, while she took a break from time to time, coming out to the living room to dance with her friends.

Nerissa is sexy and glamorous, and prides herself on how most Lebanese think that she is in her twenties by her hair, make-up, and the way she dresses, although she is in her forties. When we all went to Jazira, she quickly disappeared to dance with her several boyfriends. The second time I saw her at Jazira, I interviewed her. Like many other Filipina women, Nerissa has been working in Lebanon for the past 11 years to support her children and husband, who barely makes any money. She says she spends only $50 a month on herself and sends the rest to her family in the Philippines. She is professional at the workplace. Nerissa says that she is an excellent cook, but her "glamorous self" is equally important to her. She cultivates this sexual self and shows off, even if it's only for herself. When the madame is not home, she says she dresses the way she would when she goes clubbing and dances to the music while she cleans. At one point, her madame told Nerissa not to put on make-up when she is working. "Ma fi [no] make-up please," she told Nerissa. But the children and the male employer do not mind. According to some Filipina interviewees, Lebanese madames often see the Filipina woman in their home as a sexual threat.

Nerissa, like Lara, invests in her sexy, glamorous self in the specific context of being a Filipina woman in Lebanon. Perhaps the expectation and constraint of having to be the invisible and asexual maid makes this self even more important for Nerissa in Lebanon than in the Philippines. This is because the self as glamorous woman gives her a way to diversify her identity, rather than being stuck with that of a Filipina maid. And by investing in the sexy, glamorous self, at least once a week, Nerissa is the protagonist and attention-getter of everyone around her.

"Life outside" and "going with the flow"

For Marissa, who is in her early thirties and married in the Philippines, having a boyfriend in Beirut was not just an option, but a necessity. She says,

> I'm not proud what's happening here. I am happily married! Everybody will kill me
> . . . But it's common outside and you go with the flow [i.e. having a boyfriend]. It's
> the life outside . . . You need somebody to help you . . . because [the boyfriends]
> are the ones supporting you for the food, clothes, the house, and your money is
> for the Philippines only.

In a sense, Filipina women implicitly exchange sexual favors or romance for some form of financial security from local or migrant men. Mercedita, like Marissa, who ran away from her employer and works two waitressing jobs at a five-star hotel in Beirut, has a Lebanese boyfriend. He pays for her rent, buys her clothes, and pays for her cell phone. "He tells me, 'Mercedita, save your money so that we can make your [legal] papers,' because I don't have papers," she says.

Marissa worked for two years as a nanny for a rich Lebanese family before she was tempted and "brainwashed," as she puts it, into believing that there is a better life "outside." Although Marissa was tightly controlled, often yelled at by her madame, and felt emotionally and verbally abused, she regrets her decision to leave her madame three years ago. She met her current boyfriend through her Filipina friend's Lebanese fiancé, and has been living with him for most of the time since she left her employer's home. She has a strong bond with her boyfriend. He "learned to love me," and is, she says, committed to her.

The constant stress and fear of living illegally in Beirut is exacerbated by Marissa's concern that someone back home will find out about her extramarital relationship. "I don't want to fight with other Filipina friends. I don't want . . . them [to] . . . tell my family that I'm living with a Lebanese man." And as there is much gossip, Marissa is always careful.

Marissa has a group of friends who are also Filipina freelancers (usually illegal), who get together regularly at someone's house to enjoy a generous Philippine feast, often joined by Egyptian, Kurdish, Lebanese, or Syrian boyfriends. Despite the fact that many of these women were married with children back home, it was rather uncommon to see a Filipina freelancer without a boyfriend at these gatherings. If a woman is single, her Filipina friends will try to find a boyfriend for her.

Even when a Filipina woman is a live-in maid, if she has a regular day-off and is permitted to leave the house, she will likely have a boyfriend. Out of the 25 Filipina I interviewed, whether working as freelancers or as live-in maids who have Sunday off, more than half had a boyfriend. Furthermore, nearly half of these women were married back home. Indeed, certain Filipina women act as matchmakers. For example, Nida, a woman in her thirties working for a retired and divorced man, is separated from her husband but has two sons. After two years, she was allowed to go out alone on Sundays. Nida found herself in the midst of a community of Filipina women who pressured her to date. In fact, Nida related that one time a man, who her Filipina friends nagged her to go out with, called her employer's home during the day. Luckily,

Nida answered the phone, but she was furious that her employer's private number was given without her permission. Nida distanced herself from this circle of women and now confides with only a few Filipina friends.

In many cases, it is mutual attraction and loneliness that drives many Filipina women to date and have boyfriends, typically with migrant men, who are also working in the country alone. When I commented at a Filipina friend's house party that many Filipina boyfriends seem to be migrant laborers, Leonilda explained that they are all like family because "we are all strangers in Lebanon."

Although Leonilda is sometimes embarrassed by the explicit sexual displays of Filipina women in Beirut's nightclubs, she is not critical. Commenting on the fact that many married Filipina women sleep with local men, she says:

> As they say, we are going to face the modern world. When you taste it, you always want it. [Laughs]. In the Philippines, it's different. [Women are not promiscuous]. But sexual life, it changes . . . Here, you are independent. You are alone . . . You don't have family. You have to start on your own . . . If you have a problem, if somebody helps you . . . they expect something from you . . .

Janet came to Lebanon in order to forget her last lover in the Philippines, who was married. She did not want to break apart the family. At the time of the interview, she was in a relationship with a married Egyptian man. She met him through the boyfriend of her sister, who was also working in Lebanon. She observed that many married Filipina women have boyfriends, because they want to be happy. They want "companionship" since many women work from Monday to Saturday; on Sunday, they want to be happy. "I am confused. I make [a] relationship . . . Am I happy because he is with me or [because he] loves [me] or what?"

The good woman and the whore

Several Filipina women I spoke with, particularly those who were religious and conservative, believe that the bad reputation Filipina women have in Lebanon is deserved because many of them seem to exhibit stereotypical behavior. These women believe that the only way to improve the image of the Filipina is to be a chaste, trustworthy person or avoid sex altogether. "We are here to work, not to have fun," some say. While most Filipina live-in maids believe that it is their right to have fun on Sundays, many believe that it is the responsibility of each Filipina to avoid giving Filipina women a bad name in Lebanon. For example, Pia is a domestic worker turned professional beautician who married a Lebanese. She laments how some Filipina women seem obsessed with gaining men's attention and end up with more than one boyfriend. While single Filipina women have a right to have a serious relationship, she thinks it is wrong for them to have many boyfriends and especially when they are married back in the Philippines. "I hate Filipinas who are *sharmuta*. They ruin the reputation of all Filipinas in Lebanon," she says.

Women like Pia are trying, in effect, to claim a status as "honorable" women by differentiating themselves from others who are *sharmuta*. It is also a form of censorship or social control when Filipina women who sleep around are stigmatized. But Filipina women like Pia often overlook the fact that the same kind of behavior by Lebanese women, and even more so for that of men, is not necessarily stigmatized. And the symbolic gain of "honorable" women is at the expense of reinforcing a stereotype that legitimizes the control of Filipina women's bodies and persons. Moreover, the focus on Filipina women's promiscuity drives the discussion far away from the real issue, which is that it is difficult for Filipina women to have a personal life outside of "work" and that they are not allowed to bring their partners and families to Lebanon. Even recent legislation enacted by the Ministry of Labor in January 2009 to improve the situation of domestic workers in Lebanon requires that all foreign maids work for three years without family reunification and still does not guarantee a weekly day-off outside the house.

Conclusion

The perceived sexuality of Filipina women in Lebanon is double-sided: on the one hand, the Filipina live-in maid is seen as an asexual *binit* (girl) who must be protected in order to guard the family honor; on the other hand, she is seen as a threatening *sharmuta* (whore). The *binit* can become a *sharmuta* at any moment and bring chaos to the home if the madame's control over the live-in Filipina maid is lessened and the latter gets corrupted by the outside world. For this reason, many Lebanese madames are reluctant to let Filipina maids outside of the home alone. In many cases, a domestic worker's sexual desires are assumed unnatural and inappropriate. The negative stereotypes associated with Filipina women's sexuality are spread through warnings and stories told by recruitment agencies, and rumors. Filipina women, compared to their Ethiopian and Sri Lankan counterparts, are seen as fairer, sexually more attractive, and promiscuous. These images of Filipina women legitimate employers' tight control of their bodies and persons.

For Filipina women, their assumed sexual promiscuity and attractiveness sometimes give them opportunities for exploring and experimenting with their own sexuality. For those who are allowed a day-off outside the house or who freelance illegally, some might start dressing and acting in a sexually assertive manner. They might go clubbing, have much younger boyfriends, or have multiple sexual partners. Among Filipina women, there is both acceptance and ambivalence towards their sexual conduct. Some resent them for perpetuating the bad reputation that Filipina women have acquired in Lebanon.

Ironically, then, while negative sexual stereotypes might legitimate control over Filipina women in Lebanon, these same stereotypes might also permit these women to exercise more choice in how they express their sexuality.

Note

1   This is the most common way people refer to female Lebanese employers, so the word "madame" will be used interchangeably with "employer" hereafter.

Bibliography

Caritas. 2005. "Summary of the Caritas Survey, 'Female Migrant Domestic Workers in Lebanon.'" In *Report of the Awareness Raising Workshop on the Situation of Women Migrant Domestic Workers in Lebanon*. Beirut: Caritas, June.

Jureidini, Ray. 2009. "In the Shadows of Family Life: Toward a History of Domestic Service in Lebanon." *Journal of Middle East Women's Studies*, 5(3): 74–101.

—. 2006. "Sexuality and the Servant: An Exploration of Arab Images of the Sexuality of Domestic Maids in the Household." In Samir Khalaf and John Gagnon (Eds), *Sexuality in the Arab World*, pp. 130–51. London: Saqi Books.

Kondo, Dorinne K. 1990. *Crafting Selves: Power, Gender, and Discourses of Identity in a Japanese Workplace*. Chicago, IL: University of Chicago Press.

Longva, Anh Nga. 1997. *Walls Built on Sand: Migration, Exclusion, and Society in Kuwait*. Boulder, CO: Westview Press.

Scott, James. 1990. "Voice under Domination: The Arts of Political Disguise." In *Domination and the Arts of Resistance: Hidden Transcripts*, pp. 136–82. New Haven, CT: Yale University Press.

Index

Page numbers in **bold** refer to figures, page numbers in *italic* refer to tables.

relational perspective 616; and sex 34–5; and sex at birth 40; and sexuality 113–4, 159; social construction of xiii–xiv, 9; social expectations 117–9; socio-technical contexts 415–6; state definition 581; and technology 418; and violence 610–1

gender categories, limitations 7

gender conforming 129

gender difference 289–90

gender discrimination 228

gender dynamics 2, 16–7

gender dysphoria 539

gender equality 292–3

gender essentialism 574

gender exploitation 445

gender expression 21

gender flexibility 193

gender identity 2, 7, 16–7, 22–3, 40, 126–7; acceptance 131–2; category crisis 127; children 487–8; non-binary 127; norms 230; partners of transgender people 284; policing 145; and sex at birth 33; and sexual fluidity 203; social designation 113; and social media 413, 415; transgender 126, 575; and women-made pornography 458–9

Gender Identity Disorder 538–9, 541, 578–9

gender markers 575–6, 579–80, 580–1

gender non-conformity: Arab World 154–8; criminalization 577–9

gender norms 22–3

gender oppression 27

gender order xiv

gender patterning 114

gender performance 23, 152–9, 218; in sex stores 471–2; and social media 413

gender politics 17–8

gender relations, later-life sexualities 310

gender roles 230, 289, 289–90, 502–3

gender swapping 414

gendered behaviors 34

gendered commercial technologies 413

gendered practices: on the Internet 414–5; on social media 413–4, 415–6

gendered subjectivities 416–7

gender-neutral pronouns 195

genderqueer 195, 196

generational divide 2

genetic revolution, the 49, 67

genetic technologies 66

genitalia, one-sex model 70

George, Matthew 275

Georgia 468

Germany 598, 659

Gerschick, Thomas J. 90

Giddens, Anthony 196, 205, 269, 291–2, 294, 340

Gillespie-Sells, Kath 90

girls, adolescent 402; authenticity 403–5; being true to oneself 401; experience of 404; proper 405; propriety 401, 402, 405, 405–9; and romance 406; and sexual desire 401; sexual desire 408, 409–10; sexual harassment 144; sexuality 136–41; sexualization 416–7; and Taylor Swift 400–10; virginity 405

Girls Gone Wild franchise 140

Giroux, Henry 296

Giuliani, Rudolph 437

globalization 167, 295, 613–4

Golfus, Billy 92–3

Gómez, Antonio 372

Gomez, Selena 403

gonads 116

González, Alfredo M. 359–60

González-López, Gloria 7, 615–24

Gorzalka, Boris 183

Graner, Charles 609, **609**

gray-asexual 182

Grazian, David 457

Greece, Ancient 264

Green (Sabze) Movement 597, 601–3

Green, Adam Isaiah 277

Guatemala 498

Gülçür, Leyla 670

Gutiérrez, Jennicet 130

Halberstam, Judith 286, 288

Hale, C. Jacob 286

Handel, Alysia 429

Hanhardt, Christina 570

Hans, James 376

Harry Benjamin Standards of Care 578–9

Hartley, Nina 448

healthcare: access 174; and marriage 505

hegemonic masculinity, rejection of 152–9

Herdt, Gilbert 209–10

heteroflexibility 241–2

heteronormative publics 188

heteronormativity 496–7, 501, 575–6, 644

heterosexism 27

heterosexual imaginary, the 495–6, 497–9

heterosexual kiss, the 254–5

heterosexual womanhood 494–5

heterosexuality 23, 229, 240–9; ambiguity 237–8; children 488; and Christianity 524; compulsive 148–50, 150; feminism and 16–7; homophobic 231–5; institutionalized 241, 248, 495–6, 549; intimate relations 289–94; male privilege 236, 544–5; non-homophobic 235–9; as norm xiv; power relations 544–5;

privilege 248, 484, 529; sexology and 13; and sexual citizenship 488, 489; sexual politics 550; sexual regulation 496; as a social category 494; social construction of 230–1; social institution of 494; state promotion of 483; understanding 241–2; and wedding ritual 497–9; women's sexual narratives of 242–8

Hey, Valerie 368–9

hijab, the 602

Hill-Collins, Patricia 2, 24–31, 127, 295, 356

Hirschfeld, Magnus 12, 47, 533

Hitchcock, Tim 76

Hite, Shere 82, 97, 98, 100

Hite Report on Female Sexuality 72, 82

HIV/AIDS 48, 66, 107, 210, 479, 482, 585, 649

Hochschild, Arlie 436, 443, 450

Hodson, Gordon 187

homophobia 118, 231–5, 239; adolescent boys 143–51; Arab World 158; decreasing 252–3, 257; fag discourse 145, 145–8; harassment 147–8; and masculinity 147, 252–3; in popular culture 398–9; Uganda 625–34

homosexual identity 2, 44, 46–8

homosexuality 34; academic risk 45; acting out 383; aggravated 628; antigay rhetoric 631–2; changes in public attitudes toward 525–6; changes in the meaning 48; in China 644; Christianity and 384, 524–5, 526–9; coming out of 382–4; criminalization 1, 61, 118, 482, 549, 625–34; decriminalization 484, 561; discrimination against xiv; don't ask, don't tell 475; DSM definition 535–6; emergence of modern 20–1; gay and lesbian studies 20–1; gay celibate Christians 386–7, 388; as gender inversion 46; history of 45–6, 230–1; in India 480–1, 482; invention of 46–8; joking 147; Latin model 210; and marriage 48; in the Netherlands 559–64; normalization 227–8, 397, 539; one-time rule 252; in popular culture 394, 395, 557; and pro-family movement 592–3; pro-family movement policy 594; sexual addiction 540; social categorization 46; social organization of 1; social perspective on 2; social status 48–9; societal acceptance 565; state regulation 482–3; stereotypes 396–7; treatments 62, 63, 251; in Uganda 625–34; visibility 229, 230, 232, 233, 237, 238, 396, 526, 557, 563; Weeks on 45–6

homosexualization 253

honor killings 163, 165

hooks, bell 127

Hoover, Carl Joseph Walker 145

hormone blockers 126

hormone replacement therapies (HRT) 62–3, 63

hormones 64

Horner, Evalie 218

hostile environment harassment 315

House (TV series) 181, 182, 189

How to Get Away with Murder (TV series) 29

human rights 528

Human Sexual Response Cycle (HSRC) 534–5

Humphreys, S. 415

Hungary 598

hymen reconstruction 616–7

hyperfemininity 298, 300

hyper-heterosexuality 26

hypermasculinity 155, 297, 360

hypoactive sexual desire disorder 186

hysteria 533, 541

idealized representations 457

identity; acceptance 131–2; and asexuality 182–3; and authenticity 458–60; authority-based model 223–4; and bisexuality 210–1; and context 204; continuum of 126; ethnic model 209; formation 23, 375; gay celibate Christians 386–7, 388; homosexual 2, 44, 46–8; labeling 19; and medicine 61, 67; non-heterosexual 152–9; and partners of transgender people 283–6; queer 40; and race 236–7; reconsideration of 284; religious 384, 385–6, 386–7, 387; sex 40; and sexual desire 180; and sexual fluidity 215–24; and sexual violence 606, 610; shifting 201–2; social xiv, 1; straight 229–39; transgender 124–35; validation 406. *see also* gender identity; sexual identity

identity politics 29–30, 249, 458–9

Illouz, Eva 263–71

imperial feminism 161

imperialism 161

incest 518–9

inclusive masculinity 253

India 479–80, 480–1, 482, 626, 650

Individualism 266–7

industrialization 340, 503

inequality 479; and condom distribution 649; gender 38–9; and intimacy 292–3, 294; lesbian and gay parental experiences 508–9; trans categories 38–9

infertility 65–6

infidelity 330–1; virtual 428–9

information technology, and sex work 435–6

inhibited sexual desire 186

Inhibited Sexual Disorder 540

Inis Beag 98

race relations 297
racial purity 13, 296
racial stereotypes 297–8
racism 2, 13, 25, 26, 26–7, 64–5, 210, 295, 299, 302, 356
Rahnavard, Zahra 602
Rant, James, QC 339
rape 316, 479–80, 546–8, 607–8, 672
Rapp, Rayna 66
Rauch, Jonathan 558
Reeve, Christopher 88
Reform Judaism 528
Refugee Law Project (RLP) 629
Reinisch, June M. 76
Reiss, Ira 19
relational perspective 616
relationship strain, sex workers 444
relationships, adolescent 406
religion 60; ex-ex-gays 384–6, 387–8; ex-gay Christians 382–4; frustration with 385; gay celibate Christians 386–7, 388; LGBTQ-friendly 386; and sexual identity 381–8; sexual regulation 475–6, 483, 523–9; and sexuality 621–2
Renold, Emma 487–8
reproduction xiv, 63–4, 65–6
reproductive decision making: abortion 174–6; context 170–7; contraception 172–4; family planning futures 174–6
reproductive desires 177
reproductive technologies 65–6
research methods 7, 432–3; access 442–3; anonymity 442; case studies 13; ethnographic 7, 433–4; fieldwork 434; interviews 7, 622–3; sex work 433–4; sex workers 442–3; studying up 434; surveys 51–5; trust 442
Revolutionary Association of the Women of Afghanistan (RAWA) 161–2
Rhimes, Shonda 28
Rich, Adrienne 16–7, 150, 329
Richardson, Diana 490
Ridge, D.T. 107
Risman, Barbara 504
Rivera, Sylvia 129–30, 135
Rivers, Ian 255
Robinson, Brandon Andrew 355
Robinson, Kerry. H. 487, 488
role models 131
romantic closeness 183
romantic love 263–71; and capitalism 265–6, 270, 271; changes in the meaning 269; and class 270; culture of 266–7; and dating 268–9, 270–1; experience of 270; and feminism 269; and marriage 264, 270, 271;

and monogamy 327; neuro-psychology 264; origins of concept 264; and psychologism 269; social construction 263–5; utopianism 267–8
romantic relationships 181
Ross, Michael 371
Rothblatt, Martine 126
Rowbotham, Sheila 44
Royalle, Candida 546
Rubin, Gayle S. 17–8, 187, 539
Russell, Stephen 218
Russia 626
Rutter, Virginia 253
Rwandan genocide 604, 608

sadism 337, 338
sadomasochism 337–45, 545; aftercare 342–3; behaviors 339; communities 339, 340–2; consensual 338, 339–40, 342–5; contracts 343–4; legal status 339–40; media coverage 340; motifs 342; negotiation 342, 343; neo-tribes 341–2, 345; participants' voices 338; pathologization 338, 342; population, 341; prevalence 347; safe, sane, and consensual 342–5; safewords 342; sub-cultures 340–2. see also BDSM (Bondage, Domination, Sadism and Masochism)
safe sex 51, 67
Said, Edward 161, 162
Saima Love-Marriage Case 163, 163–5
same-gender sexuality, social organization 1
same-sex desire 208; fear of 146
same-sex interactions, men 250–8
same-sex marriage 30–1, 48, 240–1, 327, 480, 500–1, 505–6, 507, 518, 580; biopolitics 577; Christianity and 524–5, 526; cohort effects 556–7; impacts 557–8; impacts on children 553; LGBT opposition 553–4; in the Netherlands 562; *Obergefell* decision 526, 551–2, 553, 557; opposition to 552–4; politics of 551–7; pro-family movement policy 594; public opinion 554–6, **555**; societal acceptance 565
same-sex sexual coercion 319
San Francisco Task Force on Prostitution 433
Sanders, Stephanie A. 76
Sanders, Teela 450
Sartre, Jean Paul 375
Sawyer, Diane 124, 130–2
Scherrer, Kristin 189
Schilt, Kristen 38–9
Schlafly, Phyllis 590
Schneider, Jennifer 428–9
school shootings 145
Schwartz, Pepper 253, 485

movement 615–24, 625–6; urban 620–1; and urban revitalization 570; as verb 374–5; in the Viagra era 81–6; Victorian era 261; women xiii–xiv, 17, 76

sexuality education 485, 488–9, 490, 492, 583–4, 584–5

sexualization, adolescent girls 416–7

sexually transmitted diseases 59, 66–7, 75, 174, 279

Shakespeare, Tom 90, 95

shariah law 162–3, 164–5, 166, 599

Sheldon, Rev. Louis P. 524

Shusterman, Richard 364–5

Siegler, Mark 51

sildenafil citrate 78

Simon, William 19, 46, 50, 52, 98–9, 107, 108, 112, 272

singlehood, 328

slavery 520, 606, 665

Smid, John 382

Smith, Kristen 220

Smith-Rosenberg, Carroll 20, 46

Smyth, Cherry 460

Snapchat 412

social apps 279

social construction: asexuallity 7; of categories 8–9; of childhood 486, 486–7; conceptualiz-ing 5–6; definition 5–6; earlobe scenario 3–5, 6–7, 8, 10; evaluation 7–8; fact-making process 6; foundations 6; of heterosexuality 230–1; and realness 8–10; reconstructing 10; and research methods 7; resources 7; romantic love 263–5; of sexual identity 179–80; of sexuality xiii–xiv, 1–2, 3–11, 33, 43–50; truth claims 6

social constructionism 45, 49–50, 79

social constructs 5

social control 21–2, 476, 478–9, 531, 532–3, 679–80

social forces, and sexual behavior xiv

social identity xiv, 1

social justice 24, 31, 651

social life, the body in 88–90

social media: and authenticity 419; definition 412–3; gender dynamics 412–9; and gender identity 413, 415; gender interpretation 416–7; and gender performance 413; gender production 418–9; gendered inequalities 418; gendered options 413; gendered practices on 413–4, 415–6; logic 413; peer group pressures 414–5; platforms 415; and popular culture 416–7; and sexualization 416–7; sexy selfies 414–5; social status reward 415; symbolic power 417–8

social network theory 52

social norms xv, 414

social roles 113

social space 274

socialization 277–8, 496

sociology 19–20

socio-technical contexts, gender 415–6

sodomy xiv, 107–8

sodomy statutes 501

South Africa 626

space: black queer 569–70; compression 613; and sexual identity 565–6

Spade, Dean 576

Spain 480, 526

Spelvin, Georgina 109

spiritual love 230

Spivak, Gayatri 161

Ssempa, Martin 632

Stacey, Judith 503

state, the: biopolitics 576–7; definition 481; and gender 581; importance of 481–2; power 581; promotion of heterosexuality 483; sexual regulation 477–8, 481–4; and sexuality 482–3; Sexualizing 483–4

status categories 34

Stein, Arlene 225–8

sterilization 173

Stern, Steven 429

Stone, Sandy 127

straight-acting 129, 357

Strassberg, Donald S. 251

strip clubs 437

structural violence 610–1

Stryker, Susan 127

Sullivan, Andrew 558

Sullivan, Louis 578–9

Sundahl, Debi 459

surveys 51–5

Sweden 433–4

Swift, Michael 631

Swift, Taylor 400–10, 405–9; authenticity 403–5; 'Better than Revenge' 407; desexualized image 407; "Fifteen" 405; musical persona 405; *Speak Now* album 404, 409

Symonds, John Addingtom 44

Taliban, the 161–2

talk shows 396

Tallack, Dani 459–60

Tamale, Sylvia 633

Tanenbaum, Leora 519

Tang Yin 640

Tantric sex websites 372, 374, 375–7

Tantrism 102, 373

Virginia 501–2
virginity 405, 616–8, 618, 620–1, 643
virtual infidelity 428–9
von Krafft-Ebing, Richard 12

Wajcman, J. 418
Walkowitz, Judith 46
war, sexual violence 547–8, 604–11, **609**
Ward, articulation. 375
Ward, Jane 287, 354
Ward, Kevin 627
Warner, Michael 516
Waskul, Dennis 372, 374, 375, 429
Web 2.0 412–3
webcam cybersex 425–7
Weber, Max 269, 314, 321
wedding industry 497–9
wedding ritual 494, 497–9
Weeks, Jeffrey 2, 19, 43–50, 61, 77; *Coming Out,
    Sex, Politics and Society* 44, 45, 45–6; *Sexuality
    and its Discontents* 44; *Socialism and the New
    Life* 44
Weinzierl, R . 341
Weir, Johnny 117
Weiss, Margot 277–8
Weiss, Robert 428–9
Welsh, Irvine 105
Westbrook, Laurel 2, 38–9
White, Edmund 44
whiteness 296, 301
Whittier, D.K. 272
wikisexuality 371–8, 376; articulation 374–5, 376;
    definition 371; editable 372; as performance
    375–7, 378; process 373–4; research methods
    372–3; sex-play 375–7
Wilchins, Riki 146
Wilde, Oscar 47
Williams, Andy 145
Williams, Cristan 37
Williams, Linda 109–10
Willman, C. 403
Wilson, Elizabeth 350
Wittig, Monique 494
women: and abortion 175, 176; activism 521;
    Afghan 161–2; African American 2, 24–5; as
    agents of torture **609**, 609; anti-promiscuity
    discourses 330; Asian American 297–8,
    299–301, 302; autobiographical pornography
    460–2; Chinese 636–45; contraception 173;
cosmopolitanism 641–2; defining traits 113;
with disabilities 93–4; divorced 502; domination 544–5; dress codes 166–7, 599, 602; ejaculation 102–3; emotional labor 270, 436;
empowerment 458–9, 471, 473; extra-marital
sex 330–1; feminine traits 290; first sex 171;
friendship networks 225; gender flexibility 193;
heterosexual sexual narratives 242–8;
heterosexual womanhood 494–5; independence 324; and Islam 160–9, 599; male
domination 17; and migration 618–20; Muslim
160–9; nonmonogamous practices 332;
objectification 110; older 58, 81–6; oral sex
53–4; physical and sexual abuse 94; porn
consumers 457, 458; pornography 456–66;
pro-family movement impact on 594;
psychopathic hypersexual 533; role of 16, 230;
senior 84–6, 304–5, 305, 307, 310; sexual addiction 540; sexual body 58; sexual coercion
strategies 318; sexual desire 186, 402; sexual
dysfunction 55; sexual fantasies 243, 244, 246,
248; sexual flexibility 252; sexual fluidity 192–4,
195–205, 227, 240–9, 245–6; as sexual
initiators 84; sexual innocence 520–1; sexual
liberation 17, 545; sexual orientation 242, 245;
sexual partners 54; sexual pleasure 2, 76;
sexual regulation 163–9; sexual respectability
479–80; sexual status 445; sexual vulnerability
669, 670; sexuality xiii–xiv, 17, 76; social role
xiii–xiv; straight 233–5, 237–9, 240–9; tolerance
for intimacy between 20; and Viagra 78–9,
81–6; views of pornography 457; virginity
616–8, 618, 620–1; voting rights 502–3
World Congress Against the Commercial Sexual
    Exploitation of Children 659
world economic system 613–4

Yashua, Prince 451
ÿlkkaracan, Pinar 670
Yoshino, Kenji 212
Young, Kimberly 427
YouTube 143–4
Yule, Morag 183

Zerubavel, Eviatar 517–8
Zhang Jiehai 639
Zhou Weihui 641
Zi Mu 636–7, 639
zina (or illegitimate sex) laws 163, 165–6, 168